CADOGAN

Turkey

Cadogan Guides
West End House, 11 Hills Place,
London W1R 1AG, UK
becky.kendall@morrispub.co.uk

Distributed in North America by
The Globe Pequot Press
246 Goose Lane, PO Box 480, Guilford
Connecticut 06437–0480

First published 1986
Updated 2000 by Alex Lay
Copyright © Dana Facaros and Michael Pauls
1986, 1988, 1993, 2000
Illustrations © Suzan Kentli

Book and cover design by Animage
Cover photographs by Alex Lay (*front and inside back*)
and The Travel Library—John R. Jones (*back*)
Maps © Cadogan Guides, drawn by Map Creation Ltd

Editorial Director: Vicki Ingle
Series Editor: Linda McQueen

Editor: Kate Paice
Specialist Reader: David Pollard
Indexing: Isobel McLean
Production: Rupert Wheeler Book Production Services

A catalogue record for this book is available from the British Library
ISBN 1–86011–078–9

Printed and bound in Italy by LEGOPRINT

Please Note

The author and publishers have made every effort to ensure the accuracy of the information in the
book at the time of going to press. However, they cannot accept any responsibility for any loss,
injury or inconvenience resulting from the use of information contained in this guide.

About the Authors

Dana Facaros and Michael Pauls are professional travel writers. They have occupied an assortment of homes in various states of dilapidation across Europe and now live in a cottage in southwest Ireland. In Turkey they were, in their own words, 'fortunate to have had experiences as diverse as participating in a dervish ceremony and being invited in for tea by Cappadocian troglodytes squatting in the remains of a 2,000-year-old underground city'. They have written over 30 books for Cadogan Guides.

About the Updater

Having already supplied cover photos for guidebooks in the Cadogan series, **Alex Lay** jumped at the chance to update *Turkey*. His normal work making TV documentaries was put on hold in his bid to become a döner connoisseur. He says: 'Turkey's effect on me was best summed up by a resident of Kaş, who told me over *rakı* one evening: "People come as tourists and leave as friends".'

Acknowledgements

Dana and Michael would like to thank Hasan Kocatürk, Assistant General Director of Information and Promotion of the Ministry of Culture and Tourism; Kamil Muren, Director of their National Tourist Office in New York; and Köksal Başaran of the Tourist Ministry for their kind assistance and insights into 'the whole bird'. We also owe a considerable debt of gratitude to the many provincial and local tourist offices throughout Turkey, and especially to Fuat Özdoğru of Diyarbakır, Zeki Selçuk of Van, and Leyla Ilova of the city tourist office in Bursa. Also special thanks to the Turkish Tourism Office in London for their kind assistance at the last minute.

Alex would like to thank Mr Savaş Küce and Hülya Soylu at the Turkish Tourist Office in London; Döne Mattock of Turkish Airlines; Melih Fereli, Bruno Leclercq, Uğur Mantur and Mustafa Naci Aksop in İstanbul; Cemal Gül in Marmaris; Ali Nerse in İzmir, and Hakan Göktürk for loan of the trusty *şahin*; Mustafa Aydın at the tourist office in Kaş as well as Philip, Tevfik, Ufuk and Evy for taking Turkish hospitality to new heights; Fatih and Emmy Sertel in Antalya; Süha Ersöz for generously sharing his contacts and company in Ürgüp; Derya Yüceel and Metin Göksan in Nevşehir; Kaili Kidner and Lars-Eric Möre in Göreme and Ruth at Indigo Carpets for the carpet educational; the Özkan family from Antakya; Reşit Akgüneş in Diyarbakır for introducing me to the dubious pleasures of the *kibe-mumbar*; veteran Turkophile Geoffrey Smith-Wyatt; Remzi Bozbay in Van; Necmi Demir in Artvin; and finally to Catherine, not only for her help with updating, but for bright days along the Black Sea and beyond.

Thank you to Kate in London, for performing wonders in keeping me in line and pulling the whole book together, and to Linda for making that initial call.

The publishers send thanks to David Pollard, who checked the Turkish grammar and spelling, and to Isobel McLean for her sterling work on a tricky job and a tight deadline...as always.

Contents

Maps

Once again Turkey is popular. As other fleshpots of Mediterranean tourism burst at the seams with tour buses, jewellery shops and hyperactive teenagers, this ancient land offers a new frontier. Lovely resorts and low prices make Turkey attractive to every vacationer, but there is more to it than broad beaches and a touch of the exotic conjured up in a puff of smoke from a traditional water pipe.

Introduction

Turkey has more classical ruins than Greece, and more Islamic monuments than Arabia. Its attractions range from the huge, exaggerated decapitated stone kings of Mount Nemrut, to the exquisite and refined tilework in the imperial mosques of İstanbul. You can ski in an Alpine-style winter resort or bathe in the Mediterranean sea in November; watch the dervishes whirl in December and greased wrestlers tussle in the spring. You can take in the renowned biblical sites, from the Harran of Abraham to the Ephesus of St Paul, or go on a gourmet tour, sampling ingenious dishes first prepared for the Ottoman sultans.

In our travels from the Aegean coast to the Armenian border, we have met every sort of traveller—carefree young backpackers and chic sophisticates, beachcombers and folklore scholars, Canadians, Iranians, and people from every country in between. Some are regular visitors to Turkey, and almost all of the first-timers say they'll be back as soon as they can. Don't be surprised if you find yourself among them. Whatever you have heard about Turkey, behind the enigmatic face it turns to the outside world there is a land and a people whose unaffected charm and surprising hospitality will make your travels easy and pleasant.

You'll probably bring home souvenirs—everyone who sets foot inside a Turkish bazaar does—and the low prices may make you stay longer than you intended. The best part of Turkey, though, is free—landscapes untouched by industry, goatherds and their charges wandering through the olive groves and ruined temples, women gossiping around the neighbourhood well in İstanbul, banana-shaped dwellings carved from the rocks of Cappadocia, an amiable mystic demonstrating the 99 names of God inscribed on the human palm, hundreds of giggling, well-scrubbed schoolchildren in their black smocks snaking single file through a museum at a breathless pace, only pausing to ask you in earnest English, 'Is Turkey beautiful?'. It is indeed.

Guide to the Guide

Slicing up a 1,000-mile-long rectangle into digestible bits is necessarily a complex job; we think we have done it in a convenient way. For starters, there's incomparable **İstanbul**, the main attraction for most visitors to Turkey. After that, there is a brief foray into **Thrace**, the three per cent of Turkey on the European continent, which includes Edirne and the battlefields of Gallipoli as well as Bursa with its magnificent mosques.

Turkey's coasts, separated from the interior by difficult mountains, are a world unto themselves, and we have grouped them together, beginning with the **Aegean coast**, with its famous resorts and Greek ruins, as well as ancient Troy and modern İzmir. The **southern coast** divides neatly into four distinct regions: lovely Lycia, with its spectacular coastline; the flat Pamphylian coast, jam-packed with ancient ruined cities; the pine-scented, largely undiscovered Cilician coast; and finally the Hatay, the hinterlands of ancient Antioch, bordering on Syria. The cooler, less touristed **Black Sea coast**, where tea and cherries grow, is considered next, from İstanbul to Trabzon and beyond to the Georgian border.

We have quartered Anatolia, the interior: first the **northwest**, with the archaeological sites of the Phrygians and Hittites, Ankara, Turkey's thoroughly up-to-date capital, and the pretty Yeşilırmak valley. The **southwest** offers the little-visited lake district around Eğirdir, Konya, the city of the whirling dervishes, and the well-known natural wonderland of Cappadocia. In the **northeast**, wide open spaces are the rule, and lots of snow in winter; the star attractions are the ruined city of Ani and Mount Ararat. And finally the **southeast**, hot and dry and formidably exotic, with fascinating cities like Şanlıurfa and Diyarbakır, the bizarre mountaintop shrine of Nemrut Dağ, and the most memorable scenery of all, around Lake Van.

Travel

By Air

From the UK

British Airways, 156 Regent St, London W1R 6LB, ✆ 0345 222111, and THY (Turkish Airlines), 125 Pall Mall, London SW1Y 5EA, ✆ 020 7766 9300, *turkishairlines.uk @btinternet.com*, both have daily **scheduled flights** to İstanbul from London Heathrow. THY fly to İstanbul four times a week direct from Manchester. The lowest official fares start at £170 return and can be double that in high season, July and August. Discounted tickets for scheduled flights are available from bucket shops. İstanbul Airlines, c/o President Holidays, 92 Park Lane, Croydon, Surrey, CR0 1JF, ✆ 020 8688 7555, has flights from Heathrow, Stansted and Manchester to İstanbul; fares from £159 to £279, including tax.

You don't have to go via İstanbul for destinations on the coast. İstanbul Airlines fly to northern Cyprus; Cyprus Turkish Airlines, 11–12 Pall Mall, London SW1Y 5JG, ✆ 020 7930 4851, offer direct flights to İzmir and Antalya, with fares varying from £220 to £310 (including tax) according to season; flights leave from Heathrow on Mondays and Saturdays and from Stansted daily in summer, four times a week in winter.

There is not much advantage in **charter flights** either in price or convenience, but it's worth perusing the travel pages of the Saturday and Sunday papers, or trawling Teletext or the Internet in search of a bargain. During May–October Onur Air, 23 Princes St, London, W1R 7RG, ✆ 020 7499 9992, offers seats on charter flights to İzmir from Glasgow and Newcastle, and to Dalaman from these two airports plus Birmingham, Bristol, Cardiff, East Midlands, Gatwick, Humberside, Luton, Manchester and Teeside. Flights to Bodrum leave from East Midlands, Edinburgh, Gatwick, Humberside, Manchester, Newcastle and Teeside. Fares range from £180 to £235, including tax.

Thomson Holidays, ✆ 0990 502555, offers good-value flights from late May–October to Dalaman, Antalya and Bodrum from Gatwick, Manchester and a variety of regional airports. Fares range from £245 to £309. Much cheaper fares are available, but be careful from whom you buy your ticket. It's not worth taking a cheap charter flight to Greece for the purpose of visiting Turkey. Greek border officials zealously scrutinize passports on departure and even if only a single night's stay in Turkey is revealed (day trips are OK), the price of the return flight can be increased to that of the scheduled flight.

From the USA and Canada

THY, 437 Madison Avenue, New York, NY 10022, ✆ 212 339 9650, flies non-stop daily from New York (JFK) to İstanbul. Prices start from around $600 return in low season, although cheaper promotional fares are sometimes offered. There are no other direct flights but several European airlines, for example British Airways, American, Delta, TWA and KLM, have daily flights from the States with onward connections to İstanbul. It is less expensive to fly to London on Virgin, and take a cheap flight to Turkey from there. As yet, there are no direct flights between Canada and Turkey. A connecting flight is the only option, with an airline such as Alitalia or THY from Toronto, Vancouver or Montreal.

From Europe

THY and the relevant national carriers fly to İstanbul daily from most European capitals. Flights from Germany are the most frequent due to the high concentration of Turks working there; daily services operate from Munich, Frankfurt and Berlin. Some smaller carriers also operate from Germany with bargain fares, as from London. From southern Europe, Olympic Airways and THY connect Athens with İstanbul at a cost of around £140 including tax.

Airline Offices in İstanbul

British Airways: Cumhuriyet Caddesi 10, Taksim, ✆ 0212 234 1300.
Cyprus Turkish Airlines (KTHY): Mecidiyeköy, ✆ 0212 267 0973.
İstanbul Airlines: Tur İstanbul, opposite Taksim Park on Cumhuriyet Caddesi, Ceylan Apt No.27, 2nd Floor, ✆ 0212 256 5670.
KLM: Abdi İpekçi Caddesi 8, Nişantaşı, ✆ 0212 230 0311.
Lufthansa: Esentepe, ✆ 0212 288 1050.
Olympic Airways: Cumhuriyet Caddesi 203, Elmadağ, ✆ 0212 246 5081.
THY: Atatürk Airport, Yeşilköy, ✆ 0212 663 6363; Aksaray, ✆ 0212 514 0022; Taksim, ✆ 0212 252 1106.

THY's city terminal for İstanbul's Yeşilköy airport is at the Meşrutiyet Caddesi office in Şişhane (Beyoğlu). *See* 'İstanbul', pp.84–8, for getting in and out of the city).

By Sea

Turkish Maritime Lines runs a year-round weekly **car ferry** from Venice to İzmir, leaving Venice every Sat at 9pm to arrive in İzmir the following Tues at noon. In summer there are also four ferries a week from Brindisi to Çeşme. Prices in summer range from £125/$205 for a Pullman seat to £320/$530 for a luxury cabin; £125/$205 extra for a car. Students get a 15% discount on TML fares. Med Link Lines leave Brindisi Tues, Wed and Sat in summer, for Çeşme via Patras. Another summer service is the Stern Line, on Sat from Bari to Çeşme.

Car ferries also operate from Haifa, Alexandria, Cyprus and Odessa, and, year round, between the Greek islands and their nearest Turkish port. Crossings are daily in summer but can drop to only one or two a week in winter; boats cross between Rhodes and Marmaris, Mytilini (Lesbos) and Ayvalık, Kos and Bodrum, Samos and Kuşadası, and Chios and Çeşme (the last two have some room for cars). Both Greeks and Turks levy capricious 'port taxes' on these short runs, which are all very overpriced as it is.

The London agent for Turkish Maritime Lines is Alternative Holidays Ltd, 146 Kingsland High St, London E8 2NS, ✆ 020 7241 2687, *res@alternativeholidays.co.uk*. In İstanbul, the TML office is on Rıhtım Caddesi, Karaköy, ✆ 0212 249 9222, and in İzmir it is at the harbour in Alsancak, ✆ 0232 421 1484.

By Rail

From the UK and Northern Europe

Although the direct rail routes from London to İstanbul no longer operate, it is still possible to travel from London to İstanbul by train, via Hungary, Romania and Bulgaria, although this involves changing trains at Paris, Vienna and Budapest or Belgrade—a three-day trip, and about £100/$165 more expensive than the cheapest air fares. For more information on available routes, and for reservations, contact **Rail Europe**, 179 Piccadilly, London W1, ✆ 08705 848848. A transit visa will probably be needed to cross Romania (check at the time of travel, ✆ 020 7937 9667), and Bulgaria (check on ✆ 020 7584 9400).

Even with the discounts that are on offer to pensioners, children and those under 26, going by rail is still more expensive than flying. However, both one-way and return tickets are valid for two months and you can break the journey and restart it at any of several points within that time; the train offers a good opportunity to see a little of Europe en route to Asia.

From Greece

A train leaves Athens daily for İstanbul via Thessaloniki. The journey time will be an excruciating 36 hours taking into account the likely long delays at the border. There are no first-class seats. Fly, sail or take the bus instead.

InterRail and Eurail

Anyone travelling **InterRail** (£259 full price, discounts available for under-26s), which offers unlimited travel on all European railways for one month, can use his ticket to travel to and within Turkey. However, since rail travel in Turkey is so slow and so cheap, it's far better to use up the month's travel on the more expensive lines in northern Europe before heading south. The InterRail ticket is available to all EU citizens who have been resident for six months in the country in which they purchase their ticket. It can be bought from any British Rail main line station or from some travel agents. North Americans can travel to and within Turkey on a **Eurail** ticket, but like InterRail, it is not really cost- or time-effective.

By Bus

This is no longer the cheapest way to get to Turkey, as it was in the 1970s and '80s, and there is no longer any direct service from London. Still, with some effort and planning true masochists may enjoy the pleasure of bumping across Europe's highways on the three-day slog to İstanbul, with changes in Paris, Munich or Budapest and perhaps elsewhere. For further information and to reserve the initial parts of the journey, contact **Eurolines**, ✆ 020 7730 8235, or any National Express booking agent.

A bus runs daily between Athens and İstanbul, taking about 24 hours and costing around $40. It won't be pleasant but it will be better than doing the same journey by rail. Travel agents in the Plaka and Omonia Square areas of Athens sell tickets. Occasionally the Greeks are wont to hassle people at the border stop, but recent travellers report no problems.

By Car

From London, it's a good four-day 1,900-mile (3,000km) drive to İstanbul. The quickest route—through Ostend, Munich, Salzburg, Ljubljana, Belgrade and Sofia—cannot be recommended, because of the instability of former Yugoslavia. Possible alternatives are to detour to the east, via Hungary, Romania and Bulgaria, or to drive to Venice and take the ferry (*see* above). A transit visa may be needed to cross Hungary (call ✆ 020 7235 2664), Romania (✆ 020 7937 9667), or Bulgaria (✆ 020 7584 9400): check at the time of travel.

Motorists have a choice of four points of entry from Europe: İpsala and Kastanea-Pazarkule on the Greek border, or Kapikule and Aziziye on the Bulgarian frontier. To bring your car into Turkey you'll need an **international driver's licence** and **insurance** that covers both European and Asian Turkey; the AA Five-Star policy is specifically designed for motorists abroad and can be adapted to cover this. Otherwise, a Turkish policy may be purchased at the border. The vehicle is noted on your passport and must be taken with you when you leave, or else be placed in the care of customs until you return to Turkey. A *Carnet de Passage* is required for a stay of longer than three months. Motorists must carry a fire extinguisher, a first-aid kit and two warning triangles.

The driver's best friend in Turkey is the **Turkish Automobile Club** (Türkiye Turing ve Otomobil Kurumu or **TTOK**) which gives information on all aspects of driving in Turkey, as well as a repair service (free if you belong to a home auto club) and excellent maps; for TTOK addresses in Turkey, *see* below.

Entry Formalities

Visas

Citizens of many western nations require a visa for Turkey. They are no trouble to obtain and can be purchased upon entry. Visas for British visitors cost £10; for the Irish it's only £5. US citizens, however, have to fork out a whopping $45, and Australians $20. Nationals of Austria, Belgium, the Netherlands, Portugal, Spain, Hungary, Poland and Italy have to buy visas; citizens of most other countries, including New Zealand, do not.

Those intending to travel on to either Armenia or Georgia from Turkey should contact the relevant embassy in their home country before leaving, as border formalities concerning these countries are in a state of flux. If there is no embassy, speak to the Russians. Iranian visas must be purchased before leaving home, a lengthy process that can take up to three months. They are impossible to obtain at the border. You can't get a visa at the Syrian border either, although you can get one quite quickly at home. You may be able to purchase a visa at the Syrian Embassy in Ankara, depending on your nationality (less chance if you're British or American) and on the mood of the official at the time. Remember that for the Syrians, as with so many people of the Middle East, 'no' may mean 'not unless you can convince me otherwise'. The border with Iraq is, at present, closed.

Customs

Turkish customs officials generally don't look in the luggage of tourists entering the country. You are allowed to bring in 400 cigarettes, 5 litres of wine or spirits and 1.5kg of coffee, something you may want to consider if you can't live without it. Most places serve only Turkish coffee, thick, black and in Lilliputian cups. Customs controls are very tight on leaving the country. Keep receipts of any large purchases and *see* Antiques', p.16.

currency

Limitless amounts of foreign currency may be brought into Turkey but no more than $5,000-worth of Turkish lira (TL) may cross the border, going in or coming out. Up to $5,000-worth of foreign currency may be bought from Turkish banks. **Currency exchange receipts** should always be retained: they help prove to customs the cost of large purchases, and are also needed to reconvert any extra TL into foreign currency before you leave. On your last few days in Turkey, keep close track of the amount of TL you have; it's expensive to convert it back to any other currency, and you'll find it's almost impossible to get rid of back home.

Main Tour Operators and Special Interest Holidays

Over 100 companies offer holidays and travel to Turkey; make sure the one you choose has an ATOL licence and/or is a member of ABTA or AITO. The Turkish Tourist Office (1st Floor, 170–73 Piccadilly, London, ✆ 020 7629 7771, ✆ 020 7491 0773, *tto@turkish tourism.demon.uk*) can send you a useful list of companies and destinations offered. Mainstream operators with large programmes, and flights from a variety of UK regional airports, include **Cosmos**, ✆ 020 8464 3444, **Intra Travel**, ✆ 020 7619 6700; **Metak Holidays**, ✆ 020 7935 6961; **Mosaic Holidays**, ✆ 020 8574 4000; **President Holidays**, ✆ 020 8688 7555; **Sunquest**, ✆ 020 7499 9992; **Thomson Holidays**, ✆ 0990 502555.

Tour operators are becoming quite sophisticated concerning holidays in Turkey. Seven days yachting, seven days *terra firma* holidays are growing in popularity, as is fly-drive, unheard of in Turkey only a few years ago. Also, together with the standard, attractively priced two-week-plus beach package, several alternative, more off-beat options are available.

Before Sunset Travels (culture tours of İstanbul, trekking tours), Zambak Sokak, Beyoğlu, İstanbul, ✆ 0212 293 0438

Fotograf Evi (nature tours all over Turkey for photography enthusiasts), Zambak Sokak, Beyoğlu, İstanbul, ✆ 0212 251 0566

in the UK

Crestar Yacht Charters (luxury yachts), Colette Court, 125 Sloane St, London SW1X 9AU, ✆ 020 7730 9962

Exodus Travels (adventure, trekking), 9 Weir Road, London SW12 0LT, ✆ 020 8675 5550

Holt's Battlefield Tours (Gallipoli peninsula), 15 Market St, Sandwich, Kent CT13 9DA, ✆ 01304 612248

Mastersun (religious tours), Thames House, 63–67 Kingston Road, New Malden, Surrey, KT3 3PB, ✆ 020 8942 9442, *holidays@mastersun.co.uk.*

Naturetrek (birds and flowers of eastern Anatolia), Cheriton Mill, Cheriton, nr Alresford, Hants, SO24 0NG, ✆ 01962 733 051

Prospect Music and Art (art and archaeology), 36 Manchester St, London, W1M 5PE, ✆ 020 7486 5704, *enquiries@prospecttours.com*

Sherpa Expeditions (trekking and mountaineering), 131a Heston Road, Hounslow, Middlesex TW5 0RD, ✆ 020 8577 2717

Simply Turkey (trekking, flowers, yachting, painting, cuisine), Chiswick Gate, 598–608 Chiswick High Road, London W4 5RT, ✆ 020 8747 1011

Tapestry Holidays (archaeology, art, hot-air ballooning), 24 Chiswick High Road, Chiswick, London, W4 1TE, ✆ 020 8235 7777, *justin@tapestryholidays.com*

Worldwide Christian (Seven Churches of Asia), 36 Coldharbour Road, Bristol, BS6 7NA, ✆ 0117 973 1840, *info@hadlertours.co.uk*

Adriatic Travel (adventure and religious), 777 West 9th St, San Pedro, CA 90731, ✆ (310) 548 1446, ✉ (310) 831 8382, *www.adriaticl.com*

Apollo Tours (historical/archaeology, custom tours), 1701 Lake Ave, Glenview, IL 60025, ✆ (800) 228 4367, ✉ (847) 724 3277, *www.apollotours.com*

Blue Heart Tours (historical and religious), PO Box 16930, Alexandria, VA 22310, ✆ (703) 329 6400, ✉ (703) 329 6777, *www.BlueHeart.com*

Blue Odyssey (sailing and adventure), 485 Prince St, Oakland, CA 94610, ✆ (510) 763 5797, ✉ (763) 763 0334, *jale@inow.com*

Destination Turkey (yachting, adventure and religious tours), 3581 S. Uravon St, Aurora, CO 80013, ✆ (800) 653 3249, ✉ (303) 766 2792, *www.KeyTours.com*

Elder Treks (sailing and historic tours), 597 Markham St, Toronto, Ontario M6G 2L7, ✆ (416) 588 5000, ✉ (416) 588 9839, *www.eldertreks.com*

Elite (history, adventure, yachting, religion), 3 Kelly Ct, Stormville, NY 12582, ✆ (914) 227 6042, ✉ (914) 226 3456, *www.elitetour.com*

Homeric Tours Inc. (archaelogical sites, history), 55 East 59th St, New York NY 10022, ✆ (212) 753 1100, ✉ (212) 753 0319, *www.homerictours.com*

R&H Voyages Inc. (yachting), 1100 East Broadway #304, Glendale, CA 91205, ✆ (800) 457 2476, ✉ (818) 507 9636, *www.rhvoyages.com*

Skylink Travel, 1730 K St NW, Suite 101, Washington DC 20006, ✆ (202) 822 8018, ✉ (202) 775 8046, *skylad@msn.com*

Treasures of Turkiye Inc. (set and custom tours), 17120 15th Ave NE, Ste 205, Seattle WA 98155, ✆ (800) 572 0526, ✉ (206) 368 9096, *www.treasuresofturkey.com*

Trek Holidays (trekking), 8412-109 St, Edmonton, Alberta, T6G 1E2, ✆ (403) 439 9118, ✉ (403) 433 5494, *www.trek.ca*

Valef Yachts (yachting), 7254 Fir Rd, PO Box 385, Ambler PA 19002, ✆ (800) 223 3845, ✉ (215) 641 1746, *www.valefyachts.com*

Getting Around

By Air

The air network is relatively undeveloped. You can easily get from İstanbul to İzmir, Antalya or Ankara. Besides these, there are less frequent services from İstanbul to Dalaman Airport (between Fethiye and Marmaris), Adana (the nearest airport to the eastern Cilician coast) and Bodrum, as well as to Denizli in summer. Most connections will be by the old standby THY, the national airline. But deregulation in recent years has opened the airways to smaller lines: İstanbul Airlines, besides its flights to Britain (*see* above), makes connections from İstanbul to İzmir, Antalya, Dalaman, Bodrum, Adana, Erzurum, Trabzon and Van.

The airlines change schedules and prices from season to season and year to year. In general, the longest internal flights cost around £75/$120 for a single ticket, without discount. Fares are generally slightly higher on THY than on their competitors. Children between 2 and 12 get a 50% discount on THY flights, and infants of 2 years and under 90%.

Flights to Dalaman are less frequent in winter. İstanbul–İzmir and İstanbul–Antalya flights run daily at least, even in winter. THY runs a daily service to Konya in summer, weekly in winter. No matter what flight, it is best to book your ticket a few days in advance as seats can be in great demand. On any flight, make sure you're at the airport **two hours in advance**. Security at Turkish airports is admirably tight, or annoyingly tight, depending on your point of view. Passengers are frisked and their baggage X-rayed when they enter the airport terminal and—remember this—you will subsequently be asked to **identify your luggage** on the tarmac before it is loaded; watch out for this while you're getting on the plane. All unidentified luggage is destroyed.

İstanbul's **domestic** terminal is about half a mile from the **international** terminal; a bus service connects the two. Some domestic flights, however, do leave from the international terminal. For details on İstanbul's airports, and getting in and out of the others, see the 'Getting Around' sections for each town.

By Sea

Turkish Maritime Lines, which not so long ago operated a substantial schedule of long-distance ferries and cruises around the Aegean, is now sadly reduced to an İstanbul–İzmir run (another goes to Trabzon via other main towns on the Black Sea). The İzmir line runs weekly all year, leaving İstanbul at 3pm Fri, arriving at İzmir at 9am the following day, and leaving İzmir for the return leg at 2pm Sun to arrive in İstanbul at 9am Mon. Between May and October, every two or three weeks, a ferry leaves İstanbul for a 10-day **cruise** stopping at İzmir, Kuşadası, Bodrum, Marmaris, Kaş and Antalya. Dates and times are not specified until a couple of weeks before sailing. These large, slightly dilapidated floating hotels are very popular, and you should make reservations, especially for a cabin, in advance. Their main address is in İstanbul, Rıhtım Caddesi, Karaköy, (by the Galata Bridge) © 0212 249 9222; in London contact Alternative Holidays Ltd, 146 Kingsland High St, London, E8 2NS, © 020 7241 2687, *res@alternativeholidays.co.uk.*

Turkish Maritime Lines has frequent **car ferries** over the Dardenelles and Bosphorus, as well as metropolitan ferries around İstanbul (*see* p.87), and ferries to the Marmara Islands and their nearest port, Bandırma, and to Gökçeada and Bozcaada in the Aegean. They also run the ferries to the Turkish Republic of Northern Cyprus, from Taşucu to Girne (Kyrenia) with hydrofoils and car ferries several times weekly, and less regularly from Mersin to Gazimağusa (Famagusta; © 0392 366 5786); in summer there are also services from Alanya to Girne. Note that if your passport carries the stamp of the Turkish Republic of Northern Cyprus, you will be barred from entering Greece (officials at the border will stamp the visa on a separate sheet of paper for you).

By Rail

Turkish State railways (TCDD) has a rail network 5,127 miles long. However, for the most part the trains are old and slow; buses are much faster, much more convenient, and almost always cost less. Lack of speed is the big drawback. Turkey built its railway network a century ago on the cheap; there are few bridges and tunnels, and tracks meander all over the countryside instead of taking the most direct route. You're sure to see parts of Turkey out of your window that no tourist ever visits. If you have the time and money, however, it's fun to take the train, especially overnight, where you can get an inexpensive *küşet* (couchette). For a change from riding buses, a comfortable, air-conditioned first-class seat is nice; compared to anything in the world besides a Turkish bus, the fare is still a great bargain. A reduction of up to a third is available on return tickets; students get 10% off in addition.

In İstanbul, the starting point for routes to Europe and the west is Sırkeci Station, ℗ 0212 527 0051; all trains to Anatolia depart from Haydarpaşa Station on the Asian side, ℗ 0216 336 0475. Highly popular are the night express trains between Ankara and İstanbul (the *Yataklı Ekspres* and the *Fatih Ekspres*) and the Ankara–İzmir express, all with sleeping cars. The country's 'old faithful', however, is the *Doğu Ekspresi*, which leaves Haydarpaşa daily at 11.55pm to wheeze its way for nearly two days across Anatolia to Kars, calling in at İzmit, Bilecik, Eskişehir, Ankara, Kayseri, Sivas, Erzincan and Erzurum. Note that there are no trains at all on the southern coast: the mountains foiled the engineers completely, and they never got further than Aydın. You can get to little Eğirdir on the lakes by train, but not to the major city of Antalya. In the provinces the train always seems to come in the dead of night— and even if it's the only train in 24 hours, there may well be eight timetables posted, all utterly incomprehensible. The TCDD publishes an annual schedule, the *Yolu Rehberi*, which is more helpful than anything you'll see in the stations. The nation's rail network is also marked on the Tourist Map of Turkey, available from any Turkish Tourism Office.

By Bus

Forget the trains; you are most likely going to spend a fair piece of your holiday riding the humble but praiseworthy Turkish bus, with white-shirted businessmen and penniless army recruits, housewives and laughing children, students and scholars. The Turkish bus is a great democratic institution, and one of the most pleasant ways of getting around ever invented, an essential part of the Turkish experience. The coach companies are privately owned, highly efficient and incredibly cheap. Fares are usually proportionate to time: as a guideline, each hour on the bus costs around $2. All buses are Mercedes-Benz and quite comfortable.

You can buy tickets in advance from bus company offices in the city centres, but between cities this is hardly ever necessary. All you do is show up and, before you know it, a bus agent will have you on a vehicle to your destination; occasionally you'll have to wait an hour or two, but half the time someone will put you on a bus to your destination within fifteen minutes. There's a carnival atmosphere in the average **otogar**, or bus garage, nowhere more so than in İstanbul, where a hundred or so line employees scour the new, ultramodern terminal for potential passengers, shouting out the names of destinations and hauling away passive Danish backpackers who never suspected they were on their way to Erzurum.

It's worth shopping around in the station ticket hall. Another company may have an earlier, faster or more direct bus; it is permissible to look for it while the first agent to have found you is already carrying your bag. Prices are supposedly controlled, but some companies may offer a slightly better deal. Since almost all of the otogars are on the outskirts of towns, some of the bigger companies have **shuttle** buses (*servis arabası*) in and out of the centre; remember to ask if you buy your ticket in advance. Usually, you'll have to take a city bus, taxi or dolmuş to and from the otogar, which is no problem. Some are close enough to walk to from the centre with a bag or two; details for each town are in the 'Getting Around' sections.

Some of the companies are growing quite large and monopolistic in their areas, which may reflect itself in better service, swank double-decker buses, tea and biscuits and old Burt Lancaster westerns on the bus TV; *İstanbul Seyahat*, *Varan*, Bursa's *Uludağ* and *Edirne Birlik* are all dependable lines. Others, especially the ubiquitous *Pamukkale*, have a habit of treating their passengers like cattle; this one should always be avoided if you have another convenient choice. Further east, the smaller *Kent* and *Akdeniz* always give a good ride. Almost every bus station (and train station) has an *emanet*, a **left-luggage** facility. These are very convenient, but always remember to find out when they close.

One problem on the buses is that the **windows** don't open. On hot days, try to get a seat directly behind a roof vent; also, look at the map while you're waiting, to see which side will be away from the sun. A few small companies, as a point of honour, seat foreigners in the front. On steep mountainous routes, this is a dubious privilege: one can only do as the signs over the driver's seat advise, and 'Trust in Allah'. **Stops** for tea and snacks are frequent, usually lasting about 20 minutes, and on long journeys there will be a stop for lunch or dinner in a roadside inn, where meals will inevitably be simple and very cheap. Most buses carry cold bottled water, free on request from the conductor. They also have another of the sweet courtesies that surprise first-time visitors to Turkey: every hour or so, the conductor will appear with a bottle of lemon cologne to splash into your cupped hands. Rub the cologne over your face, neck and arms: it will both refresh you and mitigate the more malodorous effects of a bus crowded with 52 sweaty passengers on a roasting day.

By Car

Apart from in İstanbul, where traffic is a law unto itself, driving can be the best way to see the country, especially its many archaeological sites. Many of these cannot be reached by any public transportation. And there are always unspoiled beauty spots along the coast or up in the mountains only a half-hour away from you—if only there were a way to get to them.

Most of the main routes along the coasts have been finished, improved and widened, and traffic is still usually light. Almost all signs have been converted to conform with the international highway code, and towns are clearly signposted (blue), as are most archaeological sites (yellow). Petrol is a little cheaper than in most of Europe, and the Tourist Office's free map is very helpful, updated regularly to show all new stretches of asphalt.

Law enforcement on the roads is in the shaky hands of the ***Trafik Polis***, a force nearly indistinguishable from the regular police except for special markings on their black-and-white cars. They either clear up traffic jams or create them in the cities, and molest bus and truck drivers at rural intersections to make sure papers are in order and the weight limits observed. They may stop you too, and give your car the once-over, looking for mechanical faults. They do not seem to be much of a nuisance to tourists. Some of their behaviour can be alarming, though—they may zoom up behind you in heavy *trafik* and screech something incomprehensible over their loudspeakers, which may mean *pull over*, but is actually more likely to mean *hurry up!* It's your guess. Occasionally, in İstanbul, they will block a busy street and send everyone up the side streets, or even dead-end alleys; apparently the plan is to prevent big blockages down the road by breaking them up into smaller ones everywhere else.

Be careful: Turkey's **accident** rate is disproportionately high. Night driving is best avoided, simply because you can't see many of the hazards, such as sharp winding roads, cattle and sheep crossings, drag-racing tractors, slow buses or oil trucks careering to petrol stations that close at 10pm. Getting involved in an accident can be a major problem. Find someone to call the *Trafik Polis*, and wait at the scene to make a police report (no matter how long it takes). Do not move the vehicles. You may be taken for a breath test; if it's a serious accident there will be a court hearing, which can be the same day, to determine the cause.

According to the highway code, **passing** is on the left, but in practice you will be overtaken on either side (or both at the same time). The busiest stretches are on the motorway between Edirne and İstanbul, from İstanbul to Ankara, and on the highway east of Adana. Auto club repair trucks are available to those in need. The **speed limit**, unless otherwise marked, is 90kph in the country and 50kph in villages and towns. **Traffic lights** are scarce even in İstanbul and are rarely heeded; **street signs** anywhere are also rare. The basic principle of driving, as in most other Mediterranean countries, is that wherever a car *can* go, sooner or later it will; Turkish Fiats seem to be specially adapted for driving up and down stairways, and creating third and fourth lanes on two-lane roads.

Signs conform to the international standard, and there are only a few cases where you're likely to be confused:

dur	stop	tek istikamet	one way
yavaş	slow	**şehir merkezi**	city centre
dikkat	caution	**yasak bölge,**	forbidden area,
tehlike	danger	**askeri bölge,**	military area,
girilmez	no entry		(no photographs)

In the cities, especially İstanbul, **parking** can be a real headache (*Park Yapılmaz* means 'No Parking'). If Turks are parking on the pavements, they probably have special permits to do so. If your car has foreign plates, you may park anywhere as the police won't ticket you. They may, however, haul your beast away, something that is increasingly common in cities and even in some resorts, such as Bodrum, where parking problems are as bad as in cities. Fines are not high, but the inconvenience can be considerable. The *Trafik Polis* often do drivers the courtesy of announcing a sweep, cruising down the avenue with a siren that sounds like an eagle with haemorrhoids, bellowing the tag numbers of illegally parked cars over a loud-speaker, a warning before they haul them away. If you hear any such noise (outside electoral campaign periods, when sound trucks are everywhere) go out and check.

If you have a **breakdown** or need a repair, every town has a street or quarter on the outskirts called the *oto sanayi*, given over to mechanics, each specializing in a certain type of repair. In İstanbul, the closest to the centre is in the Dolapdere neighbourhood in the centre of Beyoğlu; in other cities, there are little car-repair compounds that hardly ever close on the outskirts. **Spare parts** are likely to be your chief problem (though not for most Renault or Fiat cars, which have Turkish-made counterparts), especially outside the big cities. Bring a kit with you if you can. Turkish mechanics, however, are very experienced: if they can't fix the problem, they can probably get your car going so that you can get to the next big city.

Most of the **filling stations** are along the main highways: you'll find BP, Mobil and Shell and the Turkish company, *Petrol Ofisi*, at the sign of the wolf, and *Türkpetrol* at the sign of the tipped cap. The price of **petrol** varies from one place to another, depending on how far the fuel has to be transported. Unleaded fuel is available at most stations.

car hire

Credit cards can be used for car rental in the major centres. Plastic money should not be relied upon in the outlying provinces, and in general the further east you go, the more decrepit your Renault or Fiat-Murat will be. Local car hire companies can charge as little as half as much as the big international firms, but usually charge extra if you need to drop the car off at another point. The large firms usually don't charge for this. Unfortunately, for whatever reason, hiring a car is the only prohibitively expensive thing you can do in Turkey; rates are currently as high as in any European country.

It's best to arrange your car rental in advance, either through your travel agent, or direct with companies like Avis, UK ✆ 0870 6060100, US ✆ 0516 222 3000; or Hertz, UK ✆ 020 8679 1777, US ✆ 0405 755 4400. Your valid UK or EU driver's licence is acceptable.

The Türkiye Turing ve Otomobil Kurumu

The TTOK is one of the nation's most remarkable institutions. They do the things an Auto Club is supposed to do—help with breakdowns, insurance and such—but even if you aren't driving you will cross their path many times. Under its longtime director Çelik Gülersoy, a legend in his own time, the TTOK became the country's major force in promoting tourism, and also in historical preservation. Especially in İstanbul, you will be enjoying the lovely parks and drinking in the cafés they have refurbished. They have even started hotels in some of the wooden Ottoman houses they restored, around the Aya Sofia and Kariye especially. Most of the park benches and street signs you'll see are their work too.

The TTOK has mobile repair units along many of the main highways. They have reciprocal agreements with the British AA and RAC (whom you should contact before you go if you're a member and mean to drive), though not the American AAA. They have **offices** in many towns across Turkey, including:

Ankara: Maraşal Fevzi Çakmak Caddesi, No.31/8, Beşevler, ✆ 0312 222 8723
Antalya: Milli Egemenlik Caddesi, Dallar Yıldız Çarşisi 9, ✆ 0242 247 0699
Antakya: Cilve Gözü, ✆ 0326 432 3005
Gaziantep: A. Fuat Cebesoy Bulvarı, Orkide Apt 24/A, ✆ 0342 325 1610
İstanbul: 1 Oto Sanayi Sitesi Yanı, Levent, ✆ 0212 282 8140
İzmir: Atatürk Bulvarı 370a, Alsancak, ✆ 0232 421 3514
Samsun: Liman İşletmeleri Müdürlüğü, ✆ 0362 445 0676
Taşucu: Abdi İpekçi Caddesi 27b, ✆ 0324 741 4463
Trabzon: Devlet Caddesi, Tünel Çıkışı, No.2/2, ✆ 0462 321 7156
Mersin: Mücahitler Caddesi 10, ✆ 0324 232 0492

and at the following border posts: **Kapıkule** (Bulgarian, ✆ 0284 238 2404), **Gürbulak** (Iranian, near Doğubayazıt, ✆ 0472 321 2036, and **İpsala** (Greek, ✆ 0284 616 1574).

By Taxi

The Turkish driver can coax movement out of a car that would remain dead to any other driver. He can also drive a car containing singularly few of the more generally accepted essentials, such as windscreen, mudguards, brakes. As long as the engine can turn over, a Turkish driver will somehow manage to take his car across open country and to the tops of mountains.

H.V. Morton, *In the Steps of St Paul*

Morton wrote this back in 1936, but some day, out in the wilds looking for an obscure ruin, you may find it's still true. Taxis are ubiquitous and by European standards very cheap. Almost everywhere, they are equipped with meters, and within towns there's no nonsense about them—no bargaining, no surprise, and only rarely a surcharge (for airport runs, night driving, when the meter says *gece*, night-time, rather than the usual *gündüz*, daytime, etc.). Turkish taxi drivers are usually honest, but don't be surprised if it costs more to ride in a vintage '55 Chevy, where such things still exist, than a new car; this is because the former consume more petrol. Almost always (except in İstanbul and İzmir, where folks have taken on big-city manners) taxis provide another object lesson in the amiable differences of Turkish life. If you care to, sit in front—you aren't a *paşa* being chauffeured, but a companion, at least for the duration of the trip. Often, the driver will offer you a cigarette (if you don't offer him one first). And—wonderful to relate—when you reach your destination this gentleman may well *refuse* a tip. Of course, if you're on your way to the bus station, he may offer to drive you to wherever you're bound instead. He'll bargain the rate ferociously even if he knows you have no intention of taking a taxi to Erzurum; it passes the time.

If you haven't a car, taxis are the only alternative for seeing many of the outlying archaeological sites; in many places, the drivers do it regularly and have set prices, for a half or a whole day or for individual excursions. To cut costs, you can often share the taxi fare with other travellers. In many places the tourist office will arrange a trip for you.

By Dolmuş or Minibus

Dolmuş ('stuffed') **taxis** run in and between cities and towns. You can tell them by the little sign in the corner of the windscreen stating the destination. You just wait for a suitable one, and pile in. You can get off wherever you like along the route. Once the car would probably have been a shiny old American bathtub with tons of chrome, left behind in their thousands by the US military in the 1950s. Today, the dolmuş is more likely to be a purpose-built minibus (*dolmuş* and *minibus* are used interchangeably in this book, as they commonly are by the Turks). Your fellow passengers—a woman with a giant potted geranium, a man with a chicken on his lap—will welcome you aboard in the grand old spirit of dolmuş conviviality. Using them is an excellent way to meet the locals and they are very cheap.

In cities: Regular city buses are gradually replacing dolmuş lines, but there are still some around. The red dolmuş stop signs are rare, but anywhere on the main streets of a town you can wait and flag one down; usually though, it is more convenient to go to one of the dolmuş terminals (in the centre of most cities; İstanbul has many), and find one that goes near your destination. They're very cheap, and the driver will make change while he's waiting for a green light; no need to hurry to pay as you go in. (Dolmuşes just like Turkey's were very popular in US cities eighty years ago. They were called *jitneys* then, from a Yiddish slang word for a nickel, the usual fare; bus lines used their influence with city governments to force them out of business after 1920.) City dolmuşes are very, very cheap, but you almost always need a ticket before you board. These are sold at the main stops, at little stands.

Between towns: On long-distance routes, you get a proper bus; for towns close together, or between a provincial capital and outlying villages, there'll be a dolmuş or minibus. In some places, they leave from a central minibus otogar; in others, they start from the main otogar, or at least make a stop there. In some small towns there's no terminus at all, but only a stop along the main street (see the 'Getting Around' sections). In practice these work just like the city dolmuşes; all you have to do is find one for your destination and you're gone. They usually run very frequently, and you'll be using them all the time to get around.

Orientation
Turkish cities

Most Turkish cities are compact and easy to explore on foot. Many larger cities, such as Bursa, have grown up on a linear plan, with all the main points of interest spread out along one or two main routes, served by dolmuşes. You'll know you're in the centre of town if you can see the Atatürk monument. One major problem in towns of all sizes is the lack of street signs, but almost every local tourist office can provide you with a map. City tourist offices almost always provide acceptable maps; those for İstanbul and İzmir are as good as any you pay for. For maps of the country as a whole, do not expect to find anything with the detail available in maps of western European countries; nothing like the Ordnance Survey or US Geodetic Survey is on offer. The familiar 'Tourist Map' of all Turkey, given out by any tourist office, is surprisingly accurate and helpful within its limits. Commercial maps are no better; their road networks particularly will usually be far out of date.

Addresses can be a minor nightmare. İzmir is the worst town, with its bizarre habit of numbering streets randomly, up to four digits—imagine trying to ask someone the way to the corner of 1348 and 655 Streets in Turkish. Antalya and other cities do this too. Often an address includes the city district, or *mahalle* (abbreviated *mah.*), with the street name after it. Often, too, instead of or in addition to a district name there will be the name of a main street; so if your hotel is at Gazi Mah. Atatürk Cad. Zeytın Sokak, you're looking for a side street called Zeytın, just off Atatürk Caddesi, in the Gazi neighbourhood. *Caddesi* means avenue; *Sokak*, street, *Bulvar*, boulevard, *Meydan*, square. In smaller towns, you'll find yourself looking up addresses like *Hasan Postaci Evi*—'by the house of Hasan the postman'.

historical sites

Most sites are near villages, and can be visited without recourse to a taxi, by taking a minibus from your base to the village and walking (a place that was convenient for a town in 500 BC is often just as convenient in 2000 AD—they're rarely more than a mile or two apart). However, **be sure you have transport back**. If it's a very small village, the minibus that brought you will often not return until noon the next day, and there may not be anything resembling food or lodging. If you do get stuck, hitching a ride back is your best bet. Buses will almost always stop for you anywhere along the road, if there's room.

Practical A–Z

Antiquities

Trying to smuggle antiquities out of Turkey could result in your getting home much later than planned, with a stripey tan gained through the bars of some wretched Turkish jail. Unfortunately, there is no clear legal definition as to what is an antique and what is not. Use common sense: if you are contemplating a large purchase that may be antique, such as a carpet, ask the dealer to draw up a document stating that the item is not antique, and giving the purchase price. If he will not do this, you have a problem: seek advice from either the nearest tourist office or the curator of the local museum (*see also* Shopping, p.34).

Climate

Turkey is large enough for each region to have its own meteorological tendencies. The south Aegean and Mediterranean coastlines get the best of the weather, with a bathing season that extends from early April to mid-October. It rains in winter but is rarely desperately miserable—unlike in İstanbul, the Marmara and Thrace, where in Nov–Feb you can expect snow and long, gloomy spells. The Black Sea is the wettest and most humid region, where only in July and August can the weather safely be forecast as warm and dry. Central Anatolia and Cappadocia can be bitingly cold in winter, but not as cold as in northeastern Anatolia, where the mercury will dip to well below freezing for months on end. Southeastern Anatolia is the driest region; here Turkey touches the Middle East and in summer the sun is malevolently hot, so that even stepping out of the shade can make you feel burnt to a cinder.

	Jan 15		Apr 15		Jul 15		Oct 15	
	°C	°F	°C	°F	°C	°F	°C	°F
İstanbul	5	41	12.2	54	22.8	73	16.1	61
İzmir	8.9	48	16.1	61	27.8	82	16.1	61
Antalya	11.1	52	16.1	61	27.8	82	20	68
Ankara	7.2	45	12.2	54	22.8	73	16.1	61
Trabzon	0	32	11.1	52	22.8	73	13.3	56
Erzurum	−8.9	16	5	41	18.9	66	8.9	48

average daily temperatures

When to Go

For a few days' sightseeing in İstanbul, any time is a good time, although you should take a thick coat and waterproof shoes in winter. To see the Turkish countryside at its most colourful and flower-filled, go in April or May. Those intent on the archaeological sites on the Aegean and Mediterranean shores would do well to avoid July and August, when the sun can be uncomfortably intense. For a guarantee of near-perfect weather, however, these are the months in which to go, especially if you intend to visit the Black Sea. In May, June and September it will still be deliciously warm on the coasts and also less crowded. Eastern Anatolia should only be visited between the months of June and September, even though that is when the south of the region is at its most tinderbox hot. At other times of the year, many towns are either impassable or unreachable due to snow or landslides.

Disabled Travellers

Turkey is not the easiest of countries for the disabled traveller. There's no easy way onto a bus, or around an archaeological site, and pavements are usually in an atrocious condition, full of holes and with kerbs knee-high in places (İstanbul, especially, has bottomless abysses in its pavements, with no rails). Worse, the Turkish tourist industry seems to have no concept of the needs of the disabled. Yet this is not to say that a holiday in Turkey is impossible. Turks are waking up to this poor state of affairs and recently the tourist office has begun to publish hotel lists that include information on which hotels have facilities for the disabled. It's not much but at least it's a start. They do not publish lists of tour operators that provide facilities for the disabled in their holiday packages; however, local and national organizations for the disabled should be able to help out here.

Drugs

You may have thought *Midnight Express* a fine film, or you may have dismissed it as racist trash, but its basic message was spot on: don't do drugs in Turkey. Even a conviction for possession will almost certainly result in a prison sentence. How long depends on the amount in question; for a few grammes, expect at least six months, for anything over 2kg, 15 years and upwards. If you are offered drugs—unlikely but possible, especially if you're young, scruffy and long-haired—don't even think about accepting.

Earthquakes

As the ruins of countless ancient cities destroyed by earthquakes indicate, Turkey has a long history of seismic activity. The earthquakes of 1999, causing thousands of deaths and traumatizing the entire country, came as a violent reminder that Turkey lies on a tectonic plate boundary. Many of the buildings to collapse were shoddily constructed apartment blocks in the *gecekondu* districts; an incensed public is demanding tighter building regulations for new buildings. Experts are divided over whether the devastating earthquakes of 1999 will be followed by further violent seismic activity in the near future. Some Turks keep a torch and a small supply of food and drink by their bedside just in case; you may want to do the same. If you find yourself indoors during an earthquake, head for a doorway or supporting pillar; failing that, small rooms such as bathrooms or walk-in cupboards usually offer greater protection than large rooms. Desks or tables can protect you from falling debris.

Embassies and Consulates

Adana

US Consulate: Atatürk Bulvarı, Vali Yolu, ✆ 0322 454 2145

Ankara

Australian Embassy: Nenehatun Caddesi 83, Gaziosmanpaşa, ✆ 0312 446 1180
British Embassy: Şehit Ersan Caddesi 46/A, Çankaya, ✆ 0312 468 6230
Canadian Embassy: Nenehatun Caddesi 81, Gaziosmanpaşa, ✆ 0312 436 1275
US Embassy: Atatürk Bulvarı 110, Kavaklıdere, ✆ 0312 468 6110

Antalya

British Consulate (honorary): Kızılsaray Mah., Dolapdere Caddesi, Pırıltı Sitesi,
© 0242 247 7000

Bodrum

British Consulate (honorary): Atatürk Caddesi, Adliye Sokak 12/C, © 0252 316 4992

İstanbul

Australian Consulate: Tepecik Yolu 58, Etiler, © 0212 257 7050
British Consulate: Meşrutiyet Caddesi 34, Tepebaşı, © 0212 252 6436
Canadian Consulate (honorary): Büyükdere Caddesi 107, Gayrettepe, © 0212 272 5174
US Consulate: Meşrutiyet Caddesi 104, Tepebaşı, © 0212 251 3602

İzmir

British Consulate: Mahmut Bozkert Caddesi 49, Alsancak, © 0232 463 5151
US Consulate: Kazım Dirik Caddesi, Atabey İş Merkezi 13/8, Pasaport,
© 0232 441 2203

Festivals

The two major national festivals in Turkey follow Ramazan (*see* p.34), and thus the time changes from year to year. The first, **Şeker Bayramı** or Ramazan feast, lasts for 3½ days and comes directly after the month-long fast. Shops are stocked with sweets for the children; the general mood is light and carefree. More important is the 4½-day **Kurban Bayramı** or Feast of the Holy Sacrifice, about a month after Ramazan. It is a time of visiting, giving gifts to children, and feasting. Traditionally, a sheep or lamb is bought and sacrificed on the day the festivities culminate, in imitation of Abraham's sacrifice of Ishmael, who takes the place of Isaac in the Mohammedan version. Both are bad times to travel; buses, trains, and aeroplanes are crowded with people going to visit relatives.

Other annual festivities are listed below. If you're in the vicinity, it would be a shame to miss one; the Turks will probably go out of their way to treat you as a special guest. Indeed, the summer festivals in the major tourist centres along the coast are put on to entertain visitors with displays of folklore, music, and dancing.

Calendar of Events

January

First week   Sarayköy camel fights, **Denizli**, **Aydın** (Sultanhısar) and **Selçuk**

February

6   Camel wrestling, Yenipazar, **Aydın**
Second week   Camel wrestling, Nazilli, **Aydın**

March

13–18   Anniversary of the 1915 Sea Victory, **Çanakkale**

April

14–16	Tulip Festival, **İstanbul**
19–23	Traditional *Mesir* Festival, **Manisa**
Last 2 weeks	International Film Festival, **İstanbul**
29–30	Sultan Hisar Nyssa Arts Festival, **Aydın**

May

First week	International Ephesus Festival, **Selçuk**
	Spring festivities, **İznik** and **Bursa**
	Kirkağaç Pine Festivities, **Manisa**
6–10	Yunus Emre Culture and Arts Week, **Eskişehir**
Second week	Regatta, **Marmaris**
Mid-month	Music and Folklore Festival, **Silifke**
	Tulip Festival, Sincan, **Ankara**
19 May–3 June	**İstanbul** Theatre Festival
20–23 May	Black Sea Aksu Festival, **Giresun**
Last week	**Marmaris** Festival
	Pergamon Festival, **Bergama**
	Mesir Festival, **Manisa**
	Şuhut Karadıllı Wrestling Festival, near **Afyon**

June

First week	Nasrettin Hoca Festivities, **Eskişehir**
	Strawberry Festival, **Bartin**
1–10	International Bandırma Bird Paradise Festival, **Balıkesır**
Second week	International Mediterranean Festival, **İzmir**
11	**Isparta** Cherry Festival
	Kırkpınar Festival and Greased Wrestling, **Edirne**
Second week	Enez Fish Festival, **Thrace**
	Golden Hazelnut Festival, **Ordu**
	Keles Kocayayla Festivities, **Bursa**
	Kafkasör Culture and Art Festival, near **Artvin**
	Tea and Tourism Festival, **Rize**
16–24	International Hittite Festival, **Çorum**
Third week	**Tekirdağ** Cherry Festival
Mid-June–mid-July	International **İstanbul** Music and Arts Festival
	Aspendos Opera and Ballet Festival;
	International **Bursa** Festival;
	International **İzmir** Festival

July

First week	Yarımca Sports and Folklore Festival, near **İzmit**
	Uluborlu Greased Wrestling

	Sea Festival and International Song Contest, **Çeşme**
	İhlara Tourism and Culture Festival, **Aksaray**
	İskenderun Culture and Tourism Festival, Hatay
Second week	Golden Karagöz (Black Eyes) Folk Dance Competition, **Bursa**
	Nasreddin Hoca Festival, **Akşehir**
	Traditional Circumcision Feast, **Kütahya**
Mid-month	Şarkıkaraağaç Halvah Festivities, **Isparta**
Third week	Dereli Yayla (Plateau) Kümbet Festival, **Giresun**
	Antakya Tourism, Culture and Art Festival
Last week	**Datça** Knidos Festival
	Dereçıne Black Cherry Festival, near **Afyon**
	Sultandağı Black Cherry Festival, near **Afyon**
	Avanos Handicrafts and Tourism Festival
	Abana Sea Festival, **Kastamonu**

August

First week	Veli Baba Memorial Day, **Isparta**
Second week	Babaeski Agriculture Festival, near **Kırklareli**
10–18	**Çanakkale** Troy Festival
August 15	Assumption of the Virgin, **Selçuk**
16–18	Hacı Bektaş Remembrance Day and Ceremonies, **Nevşehir**
End Aug	**Burdur** İnsuyu Festival
–mid-Sept	**İzmir** International Fair

September

First week	Elmalı Yeşilyayla Wrestling Matches, near **Antalya**
	Taşköprü Garlic and Hemp Cultural Festival, **Kastamonu**
	Grape Harvest Festival, **Manisa**
10–12	Söğüt Ertuğrul Gazi Commemoration Ceremonies, **Bilecik**
Mid-month	Cappadocia Wine Harvest Festival, in **Ürgüp** and **Göreme**
	Ayvalık Tourism Festival
Third week	Çal Wine Harvest Festival, near **Denizli**
20–22	**Kızılcahamam** Soğuksu Festival
Weekends	**Mahmudiye** Horse Races

October

First week	**Seben** Apple Festival
	Antalya Film Festival
	'Golden Orange' Film Competition, **Antalya**
Second week	**Kırşehir** Ahı Evran Crafts and Folklore Festival

December

All month	St Nicholas festival, **Demre**, near Antalya
10–17	Mevlâna Remembrance Day and Ceremonies, **Konya**

People unfamiliar with Turkey are always pleasantly surprised when they discover Turkish cooking. The Turks themselves are fond of saying that there are three great cuisines in the world—Chinese, French and Turkish. Whether or not you agree, eating is one of the main pleasures of visiting Turkey; there is a wide variety of dishes, the freshest ingredients are common, and, on the whole, the diet of the Turk is a healthy one, based on fresh fruits and vegetables, grilled fish and meat, with many kinds of salad and yoghurt dishes.

Have a close look at any Turkish market. Without too many of the chemical tricks used in Western countries, the Turks manage to grow fruits and vegetables that not only taste better than you get at home, but are much more colourful: tomatoes redder and more luscious than anywhere, and aubergines perfect in form and of a heartbreaking shade of violet (not to mention some exotica like the little purplish carrots of a type that originated in Afghanistan, the ancestors of all the carrots in the world). Western Anatolia has the perfect climate, and some of the most fertile land in the world. Give credit also to the Anatolian farmer, one of the most careful and loving tillers of the soil you'll ever see. Wherever nature permits, he turns his difficult land into little gardens, planted in meticulously straight patterns with never a weed in sight.

Turkey is one of the few nations to be self-sufficient in agriculture. From tea along the Black Sea coast to bananas along the Mediterranean, everything a Turk could desire grows well somewhere in the country—everything except coffee, and they've been diligently working on that for years (so far without success). **Fruit** is abundant and wonderful, especially the cherries, strawberries and peaches from around Bursa. The Turks have been exporting fruit for centuries, and even today in Egypt a lemon is called *adaliya*, after Antalya on the southern coast. Pistachios, almonds, chestnuts, and hazelnuts are often used, plain or in a number of exotic dishes; dried fruits and jams are excellent and plentiful.

Cheeses are also very good, made from the milk of cows, sheep, or goats. Popular varieties found throughout Turkey include *tulum* (made in a skin), *beyaz* (soft, white, salted), *mihaliç* (rich, unsalted, made from sheep's milk) and *kaşar* (hard).

Eating Out

By Western European or American standards, prices are very low; if you're on a limited budget, you can eat well for a couple of dollars a night. The **language section** (p.542–7) has a list of foods and pronunciation.

Although Turkish establishments call themselves either *lokanta* or *restoran*, the difference isn't clear-cut (like that between an Italian *trattoria* and *ristorante*): some fancy places affect the name of lokanta, while some very simple places proudly call themselves a *restoran*. In practice, there are two main types of eating place in Turkey.

The **more expensive type** (usually called a *restoran*) has glass cases full of mezes, with fish and various meat dishes cooked to order, wine and beer available, and probably at least one English- or German-speaking member of staff; here the price of a dinner will be from $6 up. A typical menu will offer hot or cold mezes (*hors d'œuvres*, of which Turks often eat several instead of a main course) and soups (*çorbalar*) for starters. **Cold mezes** (*soğuk mezeler*) will commonly include stuffed vine leaves, 'Russian salad' in mayonnaise, various kinds of beans in sauces, mushrooms, and cooked aubergine salad. Of **hot mezes** (*sıcak mezeler*), the one you'll see most often is *börekler*, stuffed with cheese or meat, but here is the chance for a good cook to be creative (and these can really run up the bill if you aren't careful). Seafood restaurants often have prawns or other shellfish. Almost always, you can pick out what looks good from the cooler or have the waiter bring you a mixed plate with a little of everything, which is the best way to do it. As for **soup**, Turks think about it all the time, and argue constantly about different ways of making it. There are innumerable varieties, but you aren't likely to find them in restaurants. Here the most common is *mercimek çorbası*, red lentil soup served with a squeeze of lemon—nothing could be simpler or more satisfying.

For the main course, there'll be the ubiquitous kebabs (*see* below) or a mixed grill of various kinds of kebab served on *pide*, along with steaks (*bonfile* or a cheaper *biftek*), barbecued chicken, grilled meatballs (*köfte*), roast lamb or grilled lamb chops (*pirzola*). Another popular dish is *saç kavurma*, a stir-fry of lamb and vegetables, often done at your table. If it's seafood, some consultation with the waiter is in order. You should get a chance to pick out your fish; always ask the price beforehand, since fish is the only really expensive food in Turkey. Wine, at a healthy mark-up, can be had, as well as beer and other booze. Along with the main course comes normal bread and/or *pide* bread. The bread is delicious and plentiful: while we look at bread as an accompaniment to meals, Turks look at their meals as something to go with their bread. There may also be chips or pilaf if you want, and almost always a typical Turkish salad of tomatoes, cucumber, onion, peppers (often these will be hot peppers) and parsley, occasionally with olives, lettuce, rocket and other ingredients. After this comes dessert (hardly ever as elaborate as what you can get in pastry shops), and a coffee or glass of tea. In many restaurants you can top off your meal with a fruit platter of plums, medlars, cherries, strawberries, and every Turk's favourite, *karpuz* (watermelon).

At the **less expensive type**, usually called a lokanta, ready-cooked dishes are displayed on a steam table, and you point at what looks good: there will usually be a nice choice of stewed chicken and lamb dishes, plenty of beans and *patlıcan* (aubergine) cooked in various ways, stuffed peppers or tomatoes, rice pilaf and bulgur (cracked wheat, a favourite out in the east). Portions are usually small, so don't be shy about choosing several. Many of these places do kebabs too, as well as salads and sometimes barbecued chicken. Such places, where working Turks dine, are breathtakingly cheap, especially those with self-service (*kafeterya*), but they almost never offer wine or beer. Places serving *ocakbaşı*—a kind of Eastern barbecue, where you sit around a charcoal grill and the chef cooks your food—are also very good value.

As well as the lokanta and restoran, there are several types of restaurants that specialize in particular dishes. **Kebab salons** are popular: *kebap* can really mean almost any kind of grilled, roasted or barbecued meat in small pieces, from favourites like *şiş kebap* and *döner kebap* (a herbed lamb roll that cooks slowly as it rotates, served in slivers with sauce, often as a sandwich on pitta bread) to specialities like *kağıt kebap* (lamb and vegetables cooked in foil), *taş kebap* (stewed lamb, sometimes with vegetables), *çöp kebap* (literally rubbish kebab, small pieces of lamb or beef on wooden spits cooked over charcoal), *fırın kebap* (a roast lamb dish popular in Konya and on the southern coast), or *İskender kebap* (a mixed platter with a tomato-based sauce and drenched in melted butter). This is the speciality of Bursa; a good one can be divine, while a bad one will lurch about in your stomach for hours. *Piliç kebap* is a new fad, white chicken meat done up in a roll and shaved off like a lamb döner (it's a little dry without the right sauce). Look out for places that advertise 'Gaziantep style' or have names like 'Kahramanmaraş' or 'Şanlıurfa'—these three cities out in the southeast are all famous for their kebabs, and cooks from there have spread all over Turkey. Adana has a reputation too, and *Adana kebap* is a special treat for anyone who likes it hot.

Pide salons are the Turkish approximation of pizza parlours; *pide* is a delicious flat bread, served with various toppings. *Lahmacun pide* has ground meat, tomatoes and onions, the delight of the Anatolian peasants. *Ramazan pide*, eaten during the holy month of fasting in lieu of bread, is plain with sesame seeds. Perhaps the best is the Black Sea variety (*Karadeniz peynirlısı*) with cheese, sausage, and so on. **İşkembeci** have only tripe, sweetbreads, brains, etc. The Turks claim tripe soup is the best cure for a hangover, which in part accounts for the popularity of the *İşkembeci*. **Börekçi** specialize in *börekler*, flaky pastries filled with cheese and herbs, or meat. **Muhallebici** concentrate on milk puddings, yoghurts, sweets and chicken soup. Many **meyhaneler** (bars) also do food, either just simple snacks or chips, or perhaps kebabs in the evening.

On the coasts, near highways and around beaches, look out for small **outdoor seafood restaurants**, usually a house with a few tables and no sign. Here the owner goes out with his boat before dawn, and what he catches will be in the refrigerator for you to choose. Another kind of 'informal' restaurant (they don't really exist, you see, and consequently pay no taxes) can be found at picnic spots or any other place in the country where people from towns come for an outing. Someone comes and sets up a grill and tables, and there you are— instant restaurant. Some of these can be amazingly elaborate, with mezes, salads, chips and desserts. Both these kinds of places are fun and very inexpensive, and the food can be a real treat, but you'll only find them by accident, or by asking around.

Some tips on restaurants: every **tourist resort** has lots of them, usually around the harbour. Most of these are open summer only, and scrape by with temporary staff. You'll do better trying to find one that stays open year-round. **Hotel restaurants**—as in most countries—are also usually better left alone. Asking a local where to dine is a good idea, but not so much taxi drivers or hotel staff, who all have cousins with a restaurant around the corner. If you're in a provincial, non-touristy town and can't find a decent restaurant, head for the **town park**; if there's only one place in town, that's where it will be.

Wherever you eat, the service will be somewhere between very good and wonderful. Service is usually included, but it's good form to leave a tip, 10% or so, on the table. The bill is ***hesap***.

Snacks

Pastry shops and some restaurants specialize in sweets, some with evocative names like *Hanım Göbeği* (Lady's Navel) and *Dilber Dudağı* (Beautiful Woman's Lips), both served in syrup as is the better-known baklava and shredded *kadayıf*. Turkish pastry chefs produce a number of excellent cakes (often with chestnuts and hazelnuts), a wide variety of *helva*, good ice cream (*dondurma*) and of course Turkish delight (*lokum*), jellied squares flavoured with rose or mastic, coated with powdered sugar.

Street food, no matter where you go, will be as varied and pleasing as the restaurants. Every street corner seems to have its *büfe*, a small stand that makes sandwiches or plates of döner, köfte or other kebabs; many have a few tables in the shade for you to sit down. Vendors on the street sell sandwiches, *lahmacun pide*, *börek*, mussels and other things (watch out for the carts where something that looks like a very long roast is being barbecued—it's really wound-up *kokoreç*, sheep's gut; in fact it's not too bad). Any of these will do you for a light lunch (or breakfast), and any time of day you will also have your choice of a dizzying array of snacks. Vendors will sell you a *simit* (a bread ring covered with sesame seeds), peeled cucumbers, fruit in season, fruit juice (sometimes from elaborate, jingling brass dispensers borne on the back), pumpkin seeds, chick peas, dried fruit and nuts.

Kahramanmaraş out east is an inferno in summer but every Turk knows it as the capital of **ice cream** (*dondurma*). So when you see a fellow out on the street dressed in a sort of Hollywood-Arabian Nights costume, manipulating what seems to be a gigantic wad of bubble gum with two sticks, he's making Kahramanmaraş-style home-made ice cream (which is pretty much the way your grandma probably made it, only with more exotic flavours). For another summer treat, look for kiosks with coolers of **vişne**—fresh black cherry juice, which is tart and utterly delicious and makes being out in the sun worthwhile (at least when it hasn't been sitting in the cooler too long).

Drink

Turkish **wine** is quite good and inexpensive (except in restaurants). It is produced all over the country, especially in Thrace, Cappadocia and scattered parts of western Anatolia. Two good varieties are *Buzbağ*, a red (*kırmızı*) from out east around Elazığ, and *Turasan*, a Cappadocian white (*beyaz*). The most popular labels in restaurants are Kavaklıdere and Villa Doluca, which come in both red and white. Twenty-five years ago, Turkey was the world's sixth-largest wine producer, but wine has been in steady retreat with competition from beer, the most popular drink in Turkey. Everywhere, you'll find *Efes Pilsen*, made by the state alcohol and tobacco monopoly TEKEL, under licence from Pilsener Urquell. It isn't bad, but you may prefer a good imported beer; most likely this will be Tuborg.

Rakı, the favourite strong drink (50% proof), is distilled from raisins and flavoured with aniseed; it's the same as Greek *ouzo*, really, and always cut with water. You'll often see a group of Turkish men in a cafe or restaurant with a few bottles on the table, arguing for hours—the secret to doing this properly, as every Turk knows, is a long drawn-out meal or a constant supply of snacks to go with it. The *rakı* you'll see most often is the corrosive *Yeni Rakı*. *Külüp* is much smoother (Turkish folklore says the two tipplers on the label are Atatürk and İsmet İnönü), and *Altınbaş* the best of all. All three are made by the state monopoly, as are most of the spirits on offer; imports are much more expensive. In most places, alcohol can be purchased only at TEKEL outlets; there's one in the centre of any town.

Soft drinks are mediocre, though in the generally beerless lokantas and kebab stands you're going to see Coca Cola and a decent orange soda called *Yedıgün*. Fizzy bottled mineral water (ask for *soda* or *gazlı su*) is readily available, and good for you, as the red crescent on the label testifies. Fresh or bottled fruit juices may be found at snack stands (*büfe*) in all but the smallest villages. The white, milk-like drink you see everywhere is *ayran*, yoghurt and water whipped together. Turkish **coffee**—very sweet (*şekerli*), with a little sugar (*az şekerli*) or without sugar (*şekersiz*)—is good and thick, and sold in restaurants and city cafés.

Tea, however, is far more common. It is grown on the Black Sea coast and sold by the state monopoly, and all Turks can afford it. As a guest, you will constantly be offered tea (or even apple tea)—as soon as you arrive almost anywhere, someone will appear with a tray and several glasses. Ubiquitous as tea is, however, the old-fashioned tea houses are increasingly hard to find, with their beautiful gleaming samovars and *nargileler.* But in towns you will never be more than a short walk away from a *çay bahçesi* (tea garden). Every park and square has one or several, and in the town centres there will usually be a whole collection of them, packed in the evening when the Turks make their promenade.

Geography

Turkey is more or less a rectangle, 400 miles wide (north to south) and almost 1,000 miles long (east to west), at once in Europe and Asia and the Middle East. The variety of its topography tends to surprising and dramatic extremes; Turkey is a country of verdant forests and of vast, empty plains, of rivers and lakes and scorched desert wastes. Wherever you go, you are never far from mountains; 89 have peaks that climb to 10,000ft and above, and both the Mediterranean and Black Sea coasts are bordered by tall ranges. The great Anatolian plateau is an extension of the Himalaya-Alpine range that rises gradually as you head east to culminate at majestic Mount Ararat (Ağrı Dağ), 16,786ft high. The Taurus mountains stretching along the southern coast are the largest chain in the country, sweeping upwards in an arch towards Malatya where they become the Anti-Taurus mountains, the roof of Turkey.

With so many heights, Turkey cannot help but be a land of lakes; the most famous is soapy Lake Van, far out in the east, but there is an entire district of big lakes around Isparta in the southwest, an interesting corner of Turkey not yet much bothered with tourism. There are rivers too, many flowing down from the Anti-Taurus mountains; the Tigris (*Dicle*), the Euphrates (*Fırat*), the Halys (*Kızılırmak*) and the Yeşilırmak. Another river famous in antiquity, the Maeander (*Menderes*), flows from the Taurus mountains to the Aegean, its annual floods creating the country's most fertile valley.

Geography has a lot to teach us about Anatolia's history. The west has big rivers that flow all year, the Menderes, Gediz, Sakarya and Göksu among others, but none of them are big enough to be navigable. The coasts are also ringed with mountains. Because of these two factors, Anatolia's coasts have always had different destinies from the interior—as in ancient times, when the coast was populated by Greeks, facing an interior under Persian rule; the two had little to do with each other. Greeks continued to populate much of the coasts until 1923. Until the modern Turkish republic, there has never been a state with an inland capital that also controlled the coasts; even the Hittites couldn't manage it.

Health

No **inoculations** are required for Turkey. However, a tetanus booster and a typhoid jab are wise precautions for travellers heading east of Ankara. A gamma globulin vaccination will protect against hepatitis A and is advisable if you intend to travel in eastern Turkey, which is less developed than the rest of the country. If you plan to visit the Cilician plains east of Mersin, or any place in southeastern Turkey for any length of time, you should consult a doctor about taking **malaria** tablets. While on this subject, we can't help mentioning the **mosquitoes** (*sivrisinek*). Especially on the Aegean and southern coasts, these are lusty, magnificent beasts; they take long drinks. Mosquito coils, available anywhere, are a sound investment; nothing else seems to work.

Rabies does exist in Turkey, as in most countries, although cases are extremely rare. Nevertheless, you should avoid any contact with any animal. If this worries you (and it should no more than if you were going to, say, France or Germany), ask your doctor about immunization shots. If camping rough, particularly amongst rocks, be aware that Turkey has several species of **poisonous snakes and scorpions**.

Tap water is not always safe to drink, especially in summer, when a combination of the high temperatures and the water sitting in pipes for prolonged periods provides an ideal breeding ground for potentially harmful bacteria. Bottled water, however, is inexpensive, and you may want to stick to it rather than have the discomfort of new bacteria in your system.

Most towns have at least one **doctor** that speaks English; in the tourist areas they advertise their bilingual proficiency on the doors of their surgeries. The quality of care is usually good, although as a rule it is better in private hospitals than the state-run hospitals and clinics. Amongst some doctors there is a worrying, ill-informed paranoia about AIDS. For minor problems—if you can make yourself understood—consult a **chemist** (a hospital is a *hastane*, a pharmacy, an *eczane*). Every town has a night pharmacy, or *nöbetçi*, open by turns; most pharmacies have the schedule posted in their window. The Turks themselves are quite fond of herbal remedies, and in the towns you will see special shops for these.

In **emergencies**, call ✆ 112 for an ambulance, and ✆ 110 for the fire service.

Medical Insurance

Turkey has no reciprocal health agreement with any Western country and you must pay for all treatment received. Costs are lower than in Europe and the United States but even so can still be expensive. The best medical insurance policy is one that will fly you home in an emergency. Any tour operator or travel agent will be able to suggest one suitable for your needs. Be sure to read the small print concerning 'activities' before you sign (scuba diving, for example, may be viewed as a 'dangerous activity' by some companies and thus exclude you from protection). Some policies require you to pay on the spot and then to reclaim the cost (in which case you must keep all bills and documentation), while others simply require that the doctor or hospital concerned send the bill directly to the insurance company. The latter is preferable. Policy premiums begin at around £25 a week and usually include cover against theft and loss as well as health problems.

Tummy Bugs

'And how was your stomach?', people will ask on your return from Turkey. Chances are you'll be able to say it was fine. Problems with food poisoning in Turkey are vastly exaggerated and in many restaurants, particularly in the west of the country, standards of hygiene in food preparation are the same as you would expect in Europe. If you are worried though, the things to watch out for are raw, unpeeled fruits and vegetables, restaurants with steam tables where things have been sitting around, the tap water, and certain kinds of street foods (mussels, for one obvious example) in hot weather.

If afflicted with diarrhoea or food poisoning, rest yourself and your digestive system for a day or so, sticking to water and dry bread. It's better to let your body fight the infection first, strengthening your own immunity, before taking codeine or anti-diarrhoea tablets. If you resort to tablets and the symptoms persist after 36–48 hours, see a doctor. Diarrhoea dehydrates the body very fast and can leave you feverish; if suffering, it is important to drink lots of (bottled) water, even if that doesn't seem like a very good idea at the time.

Foreign Hospitals

İstanbul
Italian Hospital (*İtalyan Hastanesi*), Tophane Defterdar Yokuşu 37, ℡ 0212 249 9751
German Hospital (*Alman Hastanesi*), Sıraselviler Caddesi 119, Taksim, ℡ 0212 293 2150
International Hospital, Çınar Oteli Yanı 82, Yeşilköy, ℡ 0212 663 3000
Admiral Bristol Hospital (American), Güzelbahçe Sokak, Nişantaşı, ℡ 0212 231 4050
The American and German Hospitals have emergency services.

İzmir
American Hospital (*Amerikan Hastanesi*), 1375 Sokak, ℡ 0232 484 5360

Gaziantep
American Hospital (*Amerikan Hastanesi*), Yüksek Sokak 3A, Tepebaşı, ℡ 0342 220 0211

Internet

Turkey is rapidly wiring up for the web. Internet cafes can be found in most towns of any size, particularly in tourist areas. Try to use internet cafés with emergency power back-up in case the mains supply fails, which happens surprisingly frequently in Turkey's overburdened towns and cities. Some hotels accept reservations by email. As you'll notice when you first let your fingers loose on a Turkish keyboard, the Turkish ı and i are two separate keys and can cause confusion, since the ı key is usually located where the i key should be, but shows up on emails as a y. At least it makes for quaynt reading to your friends back home. AOL and Compuserve members can connect and log into their accounts by dialling İstanbul, Ankara, Antalya and İzmir numbers. Good websites to log on to when planning a trip include the Turkish government site at *www.turkey.org* and Turkey's only English-language daily newspaper at *www.turkishdailynews.com*.

Maps

The free map distributed by the Turkish Tourism Office is quite good and up to date; for minor roads, the Auto Club (TTOK) map is good. Beware the Turkish habit of putting all provincial capitals in large type; sometimes these have only a few thousand inhabitants (like Bilecik), while an insignificant-looking dot may have a population of 100,000 (like Tarsus). Maps sold in your home country are often out of date or inaccurate; none of the ones we have seen is really worth buying.

Please note: there are no definitive **spellings** of the names of Turkish towns, and you will find different versions in almost any source. We have used the *Ana Yazım Kılavuzu* (Master Spelling Manual, produced under the auspices of the Old Turkish Language Foundation) as a source wherever possible to achieve consistency. Also, Turkish towns and streets undergo frequent changes of name and in some cases (Adapazarı/Sakarya, Eski Foca/Foca) two or more versions may be in use. We have attempted to make this clear in the text.

Media

Turks love reading newspapers, and they are big business, with most of the large dailies being distributed nationally. As in Britain, the press has two levels. *Cumhuriyet*, a highbrow daily with a small readership, is the most respected paper. *Hurriyet*, *Milliyet* and *Sabah* are three more of the better dailies; they bring politics out into the open and scramble for circulation as best they can. Below these comes a vast array of colour-printed mass-circulation rags such as *Tan* and *Bulvar*, focusing on scandal, football and pin-ups; not tabloids though, but full size. For the tourist, there's the *Turkish Daily News*, in English, printed in Ankara, an invaluable source of education on Turkish life and politics—though the lessons are often unintentional, from the cryptic, roundabout and very Turkish way this paper goes about discussing difficult subjects. There's nothing cryptic about its belligerent attitude towards the State Security Courts, the repressive body, constitutionally beyond political control, that has been locking up journalists and intellectuals in growing numbers. This attitude is naturally shared by all the responsible press. Right now there is a war being waged over freedom of the press in Turkey, one that is of the utmost importance for the future of the nation.

The *Turkish Daily News* is available in the big cities and resorts and occasionally turns up elsewhere. Foreign papers and magazines will only be found in İstanbul and the popular resorts, and they may be several days old. Usually you'll be able to find one or two British dailies and the *Herald Tribune*.

If you have a **radio**, the Third Programme of the state-run *TRT* (Turkish Radio and Television) gives very limited news in English, French and German at 9 and 12, and 2, 5, 7 and 10pm, in various places on the FM band (try 88.4, 94 or 99MHz). Turkish radio can be entertaining, with a mixture of Turkish and Western classical music, good home-grown jazz, and wild music-hall entertainments that are funny even if you can't make out a word. In all, there is more good music on Turkish radio than most of its European counterparts, though Western ear candy and Turkish pop are making increasing inroads.

Television, until recently limited to the state-run channels of the TRT, is currently undergoing a revolution. Private channels began broadcasting from over the borders via satellite dish in the late 1980s and are now operating in Turkey itself. Mostly, they show garish, Italian-style variety spectaculars, obscure old Turkish and Western films, game shows, football and such, though tune in late and you may hear a concert of Turkish classical music. More important, though, is the role their news programmes are assuming in discussing political affairs, even those previously taboo, such as the Kurdish question. The new stations are all run by newspapers, or by the biggest Turkish holding companies, and they may not always be entirely professional or well-intentioned, but simply by being there they are bringing new openness to a society that is long overdue for it.

Money

Fifteen years ago, it was 2,000 liras to the pound, and tourists joked about using 10 lira notes as toilet paper in bus station bogs. Five years ago, your pound got you 100,000 liras, and 1,000 lira notes were in jeopardy. At writing, it's a vertiginous 800,000 lira to the pound, or 500,000 to the dollar, and Allah only knows what the going rate will be when you read this. Before you go you had better learn to count at least up to 250,000 in Turkish, because that's how much a döner costs. Your cheap hotel room will be at least 2.5 million. The numbers are in the language section on p.540; study this well, because you're going to need it a dozen times a day. Many Turks have given up trying to make sense of their chronically evaporating currency, and it has become quite common everywhere to hear prices quoted in dollars or Deutschmarks. All the prices in this book are given in **dollars** for this reason.

At present, currency ranges from the impressive 5 million lira note to the rapidly disappearing 5,000 lira coin. The Turks do not like coins, and you'll find yourself carrying huge wads of small notes for change. They don't like bills of large denominations either, because they are a struggle to change. Learn the colour and design of the current banknotes as soon as you can; there are over a dozen varieties of obsolete ones, now legally worthless, and in places frequented by tourists somebody might try to fob one off on you.

Changing money will be a major source of entertainment. We remember a laughing bank teller, showing us the current rate on a telex, and then showing us the time printed in the corner—it was changing every hour, like Germany in the 1920s. When the telexes from the Central Bank break down, which is often, no money can be exchanged at all. Rates and commissions differ from bank to bank, and from day to day. Most banks will have rates posted outside; often the little numbers have fallen off the boards since they were last changed, several years ago—but this is less important than the rate of commission, which you should always find out before handing over any money. Akbank and T.C. Ziraat Bankası will usually give you a fair shake. Many banks across Turkey are equipped with ATMs, some of which accept foreign cards (especially Visa), particularly in areas where tourism is big business, but don't count on finding one when you need it. Many bank offices will give you some cash against a major card; as anywhere, though, fees can be high and this is best left as a last resort. Banks also run exchanges at airports and many border crossings, and you'll get as good a rate there as in their main offices.

Major international **credit cards** are still only honoured in major towns and tourist centres, but bring them along anyhow, as they can be very handy for getting cash in a pinch, for airline flights and for car rentals.

Cash, travellers' cheques and Eurocheques are easily changed in any bank, and sometimes in main post offices too. If you're carrying cash—fat wads of dollars like every Turkish businessman does—you'll want to change it in a *döviz*, private exchanges that have only recently been made legal. These invariably have up-to-the-minute rates displayed on illuminated, computer-controlled screens, and these rates will always be slightly better than any bank. Most of these accept any convertible currency, but very few of them, unfortunately, take travellers' cheques or any other kind of funny paper. Ask at any *döviz* in a large town and they can probably send you to one that does.

Having money sent from abroad to a bank can be very complicated: start the process at least two weeks before you need the money. Bring as much Western currency into the country as you can; dollars or Deutschmarks are best, although sterling is easily changed too. You can use it in most cases to pay for your hotel, or for any large purchase; the Turks prefer it, though they won't give you much of a discount for it (*see also* Entry Formalities, p.x). **Banking hours** in Turkey are 8.30–12 and 1.30–5, Monday–Friday.

Museums

Most museums in Turkey date from the early years of the Republic. To Atatürk, recreating an interest and pride in Turkey's great civilizations of the past was an important part of nation-building, and his government fostered the creation of archaeological collections and the restoration of old buildings throughout the country. Today, besides the great museums of İstanbul and Ankara, almost every town of any size has its own. Don't assume they aren't worth visiting; even the most obscure often have surprises even for the jaded culture tourist. Almost all are government-owned. Hours vary slightly, but most are closed for an hour or so at noon, and almost all are closed on Mondays.

Note that almost all the ruins and castles of Turkey, in fact all the outdoor sites of any archaeological or antiquarian interest, are maintained by the government as 'open-air museums' to which the same closing times apply. There may or may not be an admission charge, and the person on duty or caretaker may or may not feel like collecting it. Very few of the smaller sites are enclosed in any way, so if you can reach them (most of the ruined ancient cities are far from public transport; those that are accessible will be noted in the text), don't worry about 'opening hours'. Someone may be around to sell a ticket or give a guided tour, but you'll be pretty much on your own. If there's a gate, there will also be an easy way around it.

Packing

Those who intend to visit Turkey in the height of summer should pack a few items to guard against the sun's more malevolent effects: a **hat**, for example, which should always be worn. A large (at least one-litre) **water bottle** is essential, particularly if you plan to do some hiking. **Sunscreen** should be at least factor 15 and preferably factor 24.

A **torch** can be useful for exploring dark nooks and crannies (and for when your cheap hotel suffers a power cut), and a **sink plug** is also worth packing. **Fast film** can be difficult to get hold of (although you can buy ASA100 almost anywhere), as can **pipe tobacco**. **Toilet paper** is not supplied in cheap hotels or public lavatories, so unless you're prepared to use your left hand, bring some. Women may want to pack a **headscarf** and a **long skirt** for visiting mosques and for travelling in Turkey's more conservative regions. **Hard cash** (sterling, dollars or Deutschmarks) can be easily changed at hotels or with shopkeepers, and it's handy to have a few notes to cater for emergencies that occur when the banks are closed.

Electricity is 220 volts. Some outlets have two prongs, some three, so if you need to get yourself plugged in, come with **adapters** and **converters**.

Finally, if you're travelling alone, a small **transistor radio** can make for an amiable companion; take one along or get a locally made one in a Turkish radio shop for next to nothing (including licence fee). The BBC World Service, the Voice of America and English-language programmes from Greece, Egypt and Cyprus can all be picked up on medium wave; Turkish radio plays lots of excellent music, from *sanat müziği* to jazz; other programmes border on the insane. Down in the southern reaches of Turkey, all sorts of weird and wonderful programmes come crackling through, from 'Gardeners' Question Time' beamed to Iraq, to lovely traditional Irish music, broadcast to entertain the Irish soldiers in the UN force on Cyprus, to the 'Voice of Peace', Israel's pirate radio station, 'coming to you from somewhere in the Mediterranean...'

Photography

Turkey is wonderland for photographers, with some reservations. Look out for military or prohibited zones; the government can be touchy about them and they aren't always obvious. All the land around the ancient Phrygian site of Gordion is one, for example, and all harbours. At some important sites, such as Aphrodisias, and many museums, cameras are prohibited at the request of the archaeologists. These busy scientists will make you wait until their monographs are in print before you take photographs. Finally, don't make a nuisance of yourself by waving your camera at picturesque country people in traditional clothes; most Turks don't mind at all, but you may find some good Muslims who find the depicting of the human form offensive.

Police

Turkey is certainly a well-policed country, and cops come in all shapes and sizes. The **regular police** wear blue uniforms with golf caps, designed to make them look less threatening. It hasn't really worked, but foreigners will usually find them courteous and helpful. Related to these are the **Trafik Polisi** (*see* p.10), who are assigned traffic duties. In towns, there is a special branch of the police that oversees trade and business matters, the **zabıta**. They control weights and measures in the markets, watch over the bus and dolmuş services, and investigate complaints from consumers about all sorts of things. İstanbul and Bursa have their own **tourist police**, which may be very useful if you have trouble; they always have someone around who speaks English or some other Western language.

In remote country districts (mostly out in the east), the peace is kept by the **jandarma**, part of the armed forces, much like the famous Mexican *federales*; dressed in green fatigues and sometimes carrying rifles. Finally, there are the **military police**, in full army gear with a red stripe on the helmet with the letters ASİZ. They were much in evidence during the troubles of the 1970s; now they stand around post offices waiting for AWOL soldiers.

Crime in Turkey is still rare, except perhaps for pickpocketing in the larger cities, especially in the marketplaces. There are almost no robberies.

Post Offices

These are easy to find: look out for their yellow PTT signs. Larger ones have telephones (*see* below) and *poste restante* (general delivery) services. To make sure letters reach the central post office, have them addressed care of Poste Restante/*Merkez Postanesi*, followed by the name of the town. For telephone services *only*, large central post offices in the major cities are sometimes open 24 hours a day, or as late as 11.30pm. For postal business, most will close at 5 or 6pm.

The Turkish post does work, though it can be slow. Don't count on getting anything to or from Britain in less than a week, even by air mail (two weeks, sometimes). There isn't any real express post, and the only way to do it faster is the *acele* service; there is a special window for this at most post offices, but it is fantastically expensive (about $30 for a mere letter), and even here speed is not guaranteed. Sending packages can be time-consuming, since there are plenty of regulations and red tape. Postal rates are not much cheaper than in Europe or the US, and you might as well carry the thing home with you if there's room in your bag.

Public and Religious Holidays

Banks and post offices are closed during the festival of *Kurban Bayramı* (*see* below) and on the following official holidays:

1 January: New Year's Day

23 April: National Independence and Children's Day

19 May: Atatürk Commemoration and Youth and Sports Day

30 August: Victory Day (victory over the Greeks, that is, in 1922)

29 October: Republic Day (anniversary of the declaration of the Republic)

There are plenty of other holidays, but the only ones likely to interfere with your travelling or shopping are the two important religious holidays, **Şeker Bayramı** ('sugar festival') a 3½-day period at the end of Ramazan, and **Kurban Bayramı**, which lasts 4½ days, in commemoration of Abraham's sacrifice. Trains, buses and resort hotels (in resorts frequented by Turks) will be crowded, and banks and shops will mostly be closed. Both of these holidays are determined by the Islamic lunar calendar, so their dates slide backwards about 11 days each year. Ramazan in 2000 begins on 28 November—the best time for it, in winter when the days are short—*Şeker Bayramı* on 15 December 2000, and *Kurban Bayramı* on 5 March 2001.

Whenever it falls, Ramazan should cause the non-Muslim traveller in Turkey little inconvenience. In resorts and big cities, you might not even notice it, and elsewhere you'll be able to find restaurants open for lunch (though they may put curtains over the windows in conservative areas; in these places, such as Konya, you should be discreet about eating or smoking in public). By Islamic tradition, travellers are exempt from fasting anyhow. You might also consider keeping the holiday; it is a peculiar sensation, a kind of sense of community, knowing that almost everyone around you is doing the same. You'll find yourself sitting in the restaurant in the evening with a big crowd of hungry Turks, waiting for the cannon to boom from the local castle to mark sunset—or more likely, watching the television to see their town's name appear at the bottom of the screen. Dinner appears in an instant, and always tastes wonderfully good.

Customs men in most countries are on to this. 'And what did *you* buy in Turkey?', they ask. There are so many pretty things, and prices are so low, that everyone goes home with something, aided in their choice by a merchant whose spiel will equal that of even the most high-powered time-share sales executive. The real masters of patter are to be found in the Covered Bazaar, İstanbul, where, after a few hours' strolling, you could be forgiven for wondering if the city's name is merely a derivation of 'instant bull'. Almost all purchases in Turkey incur a steep **value-added tax** (KDV). Find out first if it's included in the price (*KDV dahil*) if you're doing any bargaining.

Carpets

Turkish carpets are famous the world over and Turkish carpet merchants think you're only there to see them. They'll entice you into their shop, bring lots of tea and unfurl with a flourish dozens of wonderful creations, from carpets hand-woven in silk to machine-made **kilims**, thin, colourful cotton rugs that serve the Turks as coverings for floors, walls, beds or furniture. Remember, however, that a carpet is not a cheap buy—prices start at around £90/$150. If you've a notion to purchase one, it's worth talking to your local rug dealer before you go, or scouring the libraries, to get some idea of what to look out for. Turks know a great deal about carpets (it's a degree course in many Turkish universities), but for the very basics, read on.

Turkish carpets can be either hand- or machine-made. Hand-made are better: not only will they last much longer (for several generations, if cared for), but they have a greater nostalgic value; knowing that your carpet was hand-woven in an outlying Anatolian (or more likely Afghan or Turkmenistani) village is infinitely more pleasurable than knowing it came off a factory production line in downtown İstanbul. The difficulty, of course, is telling the difference. Look at the knots: if they are irregularly spaced (and thus better binding), the carpet is probably handmade; if the knots are neat, even and tidy, the chances are it came off a machine. The carpet must be of either silk or wool; anything else, such as cotton, will not last beyond a few years. To discover whether the wool used in the carpet was hand- or machine-spun, ask the dealer to snip a length off one of the tassles and burn it: hand-spun wool will flare and exude a strong odour, machine-spun wool will not. In actuality, how the wool was spun makes little difference to the quality of the carpet, but following this ritual may fool the dealer into thinking that you know a little more than you do.

The quality of the dye used to colour the yarn should also be ascertained. Most carpets these days are chemically dyed, and while most are OK, inferior dyes will run and smudge when wet. To check, rub a damp white cloth over the carpet; if colour comes off onto the cloth, imagine the effect of a pot of tea spilt onto it. Investigate the carpet's origins: which outlying village of which town it is from, what the design signifies, whether that design is exclusive to that village, and so on. If the dealer can't tell you, there's something fishy about him. Besides, it's nice to know.

Although the traders there will do their best to convince you otherwise, İstanbul is not the place to buy a new carpet, and neither are the main coastal resorts. The quality of the carpets will still be good, but prices will almost certainly be higher. This is not because the dealer is trying to rip you off (not necessarily, anyhow), but because he will have had to buy in his carpets from wholesalers in the carpet-making regions, around towns such as Ayvacık, Kayseri and Konya. Try to buy your carpet in a 'carpet town' and cut out the middle man.

Always insist on, and keep, an official receipt—customs men sometimes like to see proof of purchase—and never, but never, purchase an antique carpet unless you have no intention of taking it out of the country. If you are caught trying to smuggle an antique carpet out of Turkey (*see* 'Antiquities', p.16), you will almost certainly be jailed. If you are unsure of the age of a particular carpet, consult the curator of the local museum. If he or she then declares it not to be antique (60 years or less should be OK), ask for an official letter confirming this before handing over your money.

Jewellery

Jewellers are everywhere, particularly in İstanbul's Covered Bazaar where whole streets and *bedestenler* are devoted to their wares. The gold is normally of fair quality but be careful about buying silver, unless you know what you're doing. Fakes abound. In general, Turkish jewellery tends towards the heavy and showy, but in recent years the jewellers have learned to adapt a little to the tastes of visitors.

Leather

After carpets, leather is the next big buy, and here again, time spent shopping around is time well spent. Jackets, in particular, can be of very variable quality. Have a look at the stitching, especially on the inner lining, and at the buttons: if buttons are shoddily sewn on, it doesn't say much for how the rest of the jacket was put together. Leather jackets are cheaper in Turkey than elsewhere in Europe, although not substantially so; for anything of decent quality, expect to pay at least $100. Handbags, holdalls and briefcases are also popular buys (check the stitching; it's a good sign if the flaps have been turned twice and double-stitched).

Other Buys

Ceramic plates and **tiles** range from tourist trinkets to works of a very high quality; many are beautifully hand-painted in traditional designs from the 17th and 18th centuries. The widest choice is in İstanbul, where prices range from $6–$650, but you can get a much better deal in their town of origin, Kütahya, the ceramics centre of Turkey, where almost every street is lined with workshops and showrooms. Similar work, though on the whole not as good, is done in İznik, the town that was once synonymous with fine ceramics.

On a more practical basis, **clothes** are very good and very cheap; a trip to Turkey may be your opportunity to outfit your children for the next ten years. It isn't just cheap stuff anymore, though. In İstanbul's modern districts and malls, you will be introduced to the world of Turkish haute couture—sharp designer fashions at very attractive prices (*see* the shopping section in 'İstanbul', p.142). Many well-known Western European and American concerns, such as Levi's and Benetton, have much of their clothing made in Turkey, and it is available here for much less than you'll see it at home. The speciality of Bursa is **linens and embroideries**, on display everywhere in that city's Covered Bazaar. These are one of

Turkey's real shopping joys, everything from simple towels and cloths to spectacular embroidered silk bedclothes. The backstreets of Anatolian bazaars are full of surprises. Ask a tailor to make you up a pair of *şalvar*, the traditional baggy trousers for men or women: he'll do it in an afternoon for about $8, and you'll be a fashion sensation back home.

Copper is also a popular purchase; the best and the cheapest is found out east, in places like the bazaar of Urfa, where you can buy direct from the manufacturer, in a street full of old men and their much put-upon apprentices who beat out designs on trays and plates with careful precision. They've been there for centuries. In the west you'll see them occasionally at big markets. Antique **metalwork** of all kinds is popular, as in the flea markets of İstanbul; just make sure that what you're buying is not a genuine antique that may not be taken out of the country. Traditional **musical instruments**, from a simple *ney* to a hand-made, medieval-style lute, can be tremendous bargains; *see* the shopping section in 'İstanbul', p.145.

Pipe-smokers may want to invest in a **meerschaum** pipe. They can be found across the country but all originate in Eskişehir; the best are beautifully carved with a wealth of intricate detail. Water pipes, daggers, belly-dance costumes, mother-of-pearl inlaid hamam slippers, Karagöz puppets and other such oriental paraphernalia can be bought in all major towns, and in plenty of smaller villages near the tourist centres.

Shopping Protocol

Bargaining (*pazarlık*) is an accepted form of doing business for large purchases and is, except in Western-style shops, entirely expected. 'Tell me what you will pay,' shopkeepers urge. Bargaining is not a game, however, and merchants will be extremely displeased if you waste their time haggling over an item of small price, or one you have no intention of buying. It's a good idea not to disclose immediately the item you're interested in, but to enquire about it last when the merchant is giving up hope of making a sale. As a bargaining guideline, offer a price of about half to two-thirds of what the dealer asks, and go on from there (if you're knowledgeable at all about the wares, offer two-thirds of what you think it's worth). You cannot drop your price to below that of your first offer. If you plan to buy a number of items, get your best price for just one first, and then ask if there might possibly be a discount for buying in quantity.

If you allow yourself to be guided into a shop by a friendly chap with a 'brother/cousin/ friend who sells carpets/jewellery/leather', and then buy something from that shop, you will have paid over the odds. Charming though that chap may be, he will expect a cut of the profit that the shopkeeper makes on your purchase. The shopkeeper will add the cost of the commission to the 'best price' he will offer you.

Don't be intimidated by *pazarlık*. Our Western, fixed-price way of doing things is a triumph of banality over humanity from the Turkish point of view, an aberration that could only have been invented in a society where people basically dislike and mistrust each other. You may look at the glass of tea you are offered as a trick, something that makes you feel obliged to buy. Or you may see it as an elementary courtesy, which it is. You may consider bargaining as a grim battle of wits, in which someone is going to get handled, while the other party is making a sinful extra penny he doesn't really deserve. But how is it any different from the sort of deals Western businessmen make with each other every day? Many Westerners fear paying over the odds, but as a Turkish shopkeeper pointed out to us, just by putting price tags on their goods, shops in the West can get away with charging more than ten times cost price for an item. The point of bargaining is to allow two people to come to an agreement that both will be happy with. No shopkeeper will sell his goods for cost price (a fact that many customers forget in the heat of bargaining) but if business is slow he may let you walk away with a real bargain.

Buying something in the bazaar of a big tourist colony such as Bodrum, though, you may often find the procedure somewhat lacking in grace. Many merchants have become a bit jaded by too many tourists that are either easy marks, or at the opposite extreme are full of suspicions and none too polite. It is also true that the situation encourages some merchants (and their commission minions) to be so persistent that they make nuisances of themselves. To these, just say goodbye.

As shopkeepers are quick to remind you, 'looking is free'. And if just looking is what you intend, say so clearly at the beginning; most shopkeepers, if they have the time, won't mind showing off their wares and teaching you a little something about them. A promise to consider, and perhaps return later on, is something no honest merchant could object to. Never, ever, buy something you don't want, or for a price you aren't happy with. Why should you? Also, don't be put off if whatever you happen to say, about the weather or whatever, he constantly steers the conversation back to those carpets. In most cases, he isn't really being pushy. Many merchants, if they know English at all, have a deceptively good commercial vocabulary in it but are hard pressed to say much on any other subject. It isn't an easy part of their job—they may have to do the same in German, French and Arabic too, and some of the more enterprising ones are polishing up their Japanese.

Bargaining can be pleasant enough if you know what you want, know what you care to spend for it, and go about in a cool and courteous manner (and it's usually over in a minute, unless you're as good a talker as the shopkeeper, and mean to be really hard). Use Turkey as a chance to match wits with the experts; it's good practice for the next time you buy a car.

Smoking

Sublime tobacco! which from east to west
Cheers the tar's labour or the Turkman's rest

Byron, *The Island*

More than almost anything, Turks love to smoke, and they do so at all times of the day and night, on buses, in hospitals, in gas works, anywhere you can think of. Where smoking is forbidden, the ban is generally adhered to—on some local buses and in ferry lounges; shocking though it may seem, the TCDD (Turkish State Railways) and a few of the bigger inter-city bus lines have even introduced non-smoking sections. Otherwise, expect to be shrouded in a grey fog almost everywhere you go. There is very little you can do about this, particularly on the long-distance buses where the situation is worsened by the Turks' dread of draughts, which makes them close all fresh-air vents on anything but the hottest of days; the smoke will be less dense at the front of the bus.

If you want to smoke like a Turk, the proper way to do it is with a *nargile*, or hookah, the glass contraption that the English used to call a 'hubble-bubble'. They seem to be making a comeback, and you'll find plenty of humble *kıraathaneler* (old-fashioned working mens' coffee houses) and boulevard cafés where you can have one brought over, along with a sinister-looking wad of rough-cut *tömbeki* tobacco that smells like a camel's bum even before it's lit. You'll catch Turkey's only legal buzz, and watching you try to keep it going will entertain the locals royally. In between cafés, you'll have to settle for cigarettes. Western imports are prohibitively taxed, but Turkish smokes are better anyhow, with excellent tobacco from the lovely green valley of the Yeşilırmak, near the Black Sea. *Samsun*, as the name implies, are strongest and best, deliciously aromatic like the finest cigars; then *Tokat*, somewhat milder, and finally *Maltepe*, which are closest to Western tastes.

Sports and Activities

Water Sports

Water sports are widely available in the resorts along the south Aegean and Mediterranean coasts. **Yachting** (*see* below) is extremely popular and opportunities for **windsurfing** and **snorkelling** abound. For **scuba divers**, there are schools in Çeşme, Kuşadası, Bodrum, Kaş and several of the other more obvious resorts; rates are relatively cheap when compared to, say, Greece. Sea pollution is only a problem near the main shipping harbours, around İstanbul, İzmir, Mersin, İskenderun and several of the ports on the Black Sea coast. In July and August the Aegean coast is often plagued by the *meltemi* wind, making rough seas.

Yachting

Chartering a yacht or sailing your own along the Turkish coast has been popular for decades. Prices for the former are still quite reasonable when compared to other Mediterranean countries: the Tourist Office has lists of agents and charterers with whom you can reserve a boat (bare or with crew) in advance; outside July and August you can usually get a boat on the spot in the major resorts—Antalya, Marmaris, Bodrum or Kuşadası. One of the most memorable ways of spending a holiday in Turkey is to float along the delightful pine-forested coast, in and out of a hundred picturesque coves dotted with the remains of ancient cities, dining every evening off the day's catch.

Sailing along the southwest coast between Kuşadası and Antalya is known as a **Blue Cruise**. Where you go is up to you, but opting for the full cruise takes you to the following: Kuşadası, Didyma, Güllük, Bodrum, Gökova Bay, Knidos, Datça, Turunç, Marmaris, Dalyan, Fethiye, Kalkan, Kaş, Üçağiz, Demre, Finike, Phaselis and Antalya. You may want to stop off at a few of the Greek Aegean islands en route; nearest to this length of coastline are Samos, Patmos, Lipsi, Kalymnos, Kos, Nissiros, Symi, Rhodes and Kastellorizo. Basic information on some of these is supplied in the text; for more, refer to Cadogan's *Greek Islands* guide.

Since a full Blue Cruise would take at least one month, most prospective sailors have to opt for a shorter voyage that can be fitted within the given length of their charter. As a guideline, in one week you could travel from Kuşadası to Bodrum, from Bodrum around Gökova Bay and back again, or from Bodrum to Marmaris. Two weeks could take you from Kuşadası to Marmaris (via a few Greek islands), or from Marmaris to Antalya.

For companions, you can either get your own group together (between 7 and 12 persons) or take a 'cabin charter', whereby specific berths are set aside for individual passengers. The boats themselves are likely to be *guletler*, pine-built with a rounded aft and a pointed fore, with double berths (bunk beds) measuring 2 metres long by 2 metres wide. Luxury yachts can also be chartered, from a company such as Crestar Yacht Charters Ltd, Colette Court, 125 Sloane Street, London SW1X 9AU, © 020 7730 9962.

The cost will be between £35/$58 and £55/$90 per day, per person, not including food, depending upon the season, the size of the boat and the facilities on offer. April, May, September and October are the cheaper months. The tourist office publishes an annual list of tour operators offering yachting holidays; alternatively, you can talk to owners of the boats that crowd every resort harbour and probably make a better deal if the time is right.

If you have your own yacht, official **ports of entry** are Çanakkale, Bandırma, İstanbul, Akçay, Ayvalık, Dikili, İzmir, Çeşme, Kuşadası, Güllük, Bodrum, Datça, Marmaris, Fethiye, Kaş, Fınıke, Kemer, Antalya, Alanya, Anamur, Taşucu, Mersin, İskenderun, Samsun, Silifke, Trabzon, Adana, Didyma, Derince, Tekirdağ, Zonguldak and Ordu. On arriving in Turkey the captain must fill out a transit log. If you leave Turkish waters for seven days or less, you can leave the transit log with port authorities and reuse it on your return. Foreign yachts may remain in Turkey for up to two years for maintenance and winter berthing.

Mountains, Rafts and Caves

Mountain climbing is another fair-weather sport; due to the dangers involved, it is strictly controlled. Foreign mountaineering groups need special permission before setting off; apply to the Ministry of Foreign Affairs in Ankara. Those wishing to climb the steepest peaks—those only for experienced mountaineers—should contact the tourist office, who can supply names of travel agencies who will arrange all documentation, guides, provisions and so on.

Several other activities, well developed elsewhere, are just being discovered in Turkey. **White-water rafting** enthusiasts have sent out rave reviews about the Barhal river near Yusufeli in the north-east, as well as the River Göksu on the southern coast. The tourist office can help out with information on excursions to Turkey's numerous and often dazzling **caves**. The greatest collection of these is found in the mountains north of Antalya.

Skiing

Skiing, cheaper than elsewhere in Europe, is growing in popularity in Turkey. The best-known and most developed resort is **Uludağ**, located in a national park near Bursa with 25 runs of varying difficulty and a view of the Sea of Marmara. The season here lasts from November to March, although those not enamoured by the patter of tiny skis should avoid Uludağ in late January/early February when the pistes become packed with Turkish school-children. At other times the slopes should be blissfully uncluttered.

The **resorts** with the best snow and most challenging runs are in eastern Turkey, notably at Palandöken near Erzurum, where the 2,200–3,170m-high slopes are emptier and the snow more consistently powdery than elsewhere. Just north of Antalya, in the Beydağı mountains at Saklıkent, in the months of March and April you can ski in the morning and swim in the Mediterranean in the afternoon.

Fishing and Hunting

Fishing for sport requires no licence; **hunters**, however, can only go out in organized groups sponsored by a travel agent. Wild boar hunts in the autumn are organized in Muğla province (Marmaris), in the Taurus mountains and on Mount İda, near Akçay. Write to the Union of Travel Agencies, Atatürk Bulvarı 107/71, Ankara, for a list of sponsors.

National Sports and Recreation

If you're in the right place at the right time (*see* 'Festivals'), you may be able to see three of the Turks' home-grown sports. Although football (*see* p.70) has more of a following, **wrestling** is still considered the national sport, and contests take place throughout the summer. Edirne is the greased wrestling capital of Turkey and hosts the most famous tournament. **Camel wrestling** (*Deve Güreşi*) pits camel against camel in a slow, clumsy-elegant ritual in which one beast eventually establishes dominance; they are separated before doing each other any harm. This is most common along the Aegean coast in December and January, especially in Selçuk. To see **Cirit** ('javelins'), a rather dangerous but exhilarating sport featuring galloping horsemen hurling blunted wooden javelins at each other, you'll usually have to head out east to Erzurum where it's still popular. There are exhibitions in Konya in September.

Less strenuous activities include lounging around a **spa** (there are famous ones in Bursa, Yalova and Gönen, all easily accessible by sea from İstanbul; also at Ilica near Çeşme, Pamukkale and Hüdayı, in Afyon province), playing *tavla* (backgammon) in the coffee houses and, of course, taking a Turkish bath or hamam.

Almost every town has a **hamam**, either with separate facilities for men and women, or open to men and women on alternate days. The Turkish bath is a direct descendant of the Roman bath, adopted by the Byzantines and then the Ottomans; it is a wonderfully sensuous ritual, especially if you have a chance to luxuriate in one of the historic hamams in İstanbul: the 16th-century Çemberlitaş Hamamı, Vezirhan Caddesi 8, near the Burnt Column; the 17th-century Çağaloğlu Hamamı, on Yerebatan Caddesi near the Aya Sofya; the 16th-century Galatasaray Hamamı, at Turnacıbaşı Sokak 24 in Beyoğlu; or the 19th-century Pangaltı Hamamı, on Dolapdere Caddesi 224 in Pangaltı. In Edirne, there's the beautiful 16th-century Sokullu Mehmet Paşa Hamamı.

The *halvet* is the hot room where you perspire; the *göbektaşı* is the hot stone slab on which the bath attendant rubs you down. This they tend to do with great enthusiasm, either with a glove that removes dead skin or even by walking across your back; if it hurts, you can always call out '*yavaş, yavaş*' ('slowly, slowly'). Be sure to tip the bath attendant when you leave.

Telephones

Turkey's telephone service is modernizing rapidly. The entire system is in the process of being rebuilt, and every area has changed over to uniform, three-digit area codes and seven-digit numbers—any old numbers you have won't be good. **Phone cards** (*telekart*) are becoming very common in the west of Turkey and are particularly useful for short long-distance and international calls, saving you the trouble of constantly nourishing the phone with handfuls of *jetonlar* (tokens). The cards come in units of 30, 60, 100, 120 and 180. A 100-unit card should give you an international call long enough to have somebody at home ring you back at the phone box. You'll still see some phones operated by *jetonlar*, but these are being phased out. You can buy both cards and tokens at any post office.

Making long-distance calls from your hotel is as bad an idea as in any other country; hotels always take a substantial mark-up. The other practical way to do it is from any town's central post office, where there is usually a separate room for telephone services. Give the man your number and sit down and wait. Some offices have metered booths, though at others, they'll simply hand you a telephone over the counter when your call goes through, and you can talk to your sweetie back home from the middle of a crowd of amused Turks. You cannot tell the price of the call from the meter, but expect it to be nearly as much as long-distance rates anywhere in Europe (and some postal employees are not above adding a bit on if you're a foreigner). For a long-distance call within Turkey, dial the provincial area code (add the zero prefix before the three-digit code), and the number. For international calls, dial 00, then the country code (Britain 44, US and Canada 1, Ireland 353, Australia 61), then the area code (omitting any 0s before British city codes) and the number.

Useful Telephone Numbers

Police:	✆ 155
Ambulance:	✆ 112
Fire Service:	✆ 110
Directory Enquiries:	✆ 118

Terrorists

With the arrest of the PKK leader Abdullah Öcalan in 1999 (*see* 'History', p.64), the threat of terrorism which kept many tourists away from Turkey in the 1990s has diminished (perhaps only temporarily—if you are unsure of the political situation in Turkey, contact the relevant government office for advice before leaving your home country). Whilst in court, Öcalan publicly admitted that the PKK campaign of violence which he led through the 1980s and '90s had been 'a mistake'. More than a dozen PKK officials turned themselves in to the Turkish authorities to prove their leader was serious about peace. From his prison cell, Öcalan declared a ceasefire and ordered his fighters to leave Turkey. Since then, the number of clashes between the security forces and the Kurds in the southeast has dropped significantly. Whether this uneasy peace will continue or not depends to a large extent on whether Öcalan lives or dies: he has been sentenced to death, and his fate now depends on the vagaries of domestic and international politics. Be aware of the situation; should trouble flare up again, think very carefully before going to the eastern parts of the country

Time

Throughout most of the year Turkey is 2 hours ahead of Greenwich Mean Time and 7 hours ahead of Eastern Standard Time (New York), 10 ahead of California. At times this may vary by an hour either way, depending on when daylight saving hours are introduced.

Toilets

Conveniences in varying states of decomposition will be found in petrol stations, bus depots, etc.—just ask for the *tuvalet* or WC (pronounced 'veh-veh-jeh'); attendants collect a nominal fee. French-style holes in the floor await you in many of the cheaper hotels, but never in the government-listed establishments. The use of toilet paper is not a universally accepted custom (that's what the little taps are for); seasoned travellers carry their own. Turkish loos that flush with enthusiasm are rare. Please put toilet paper in the little bins provided; if no bin is provided, it is more hygienic to start a small pile of paper in a corner than to cause a blockage in the plumbing.

Tourist Offices Abroad

Australia: Room 17, Level 3, 428 George St, Sydney NSW 2000, ✆ (61-2) 92 23 30 55, ✇ (61-2) 92 23 32 04, *turkish@ozemail.com.au*

Canada: Constitution Square, 360 Albert St, Suite 801, Ottawa, Ontario K1R 7X7, ✆ (1-613) 230 86 54, ✇ (1-613) 230 36 83, *toturcan@magi.com*

UK: First Floor, 170–173 Piccadilly, London W1V 9DD, ✆ 020 7629 7771, ✇ 020 7491 0773, *tto@turkishtourism.demon.co.uk*

USA: 821 United Nations Plaza, New York, NY 10017, ✆ (212) 687 2194, ✇ (212) 599 7568, *tourny@idt.net*

or: 1717 Massachusetts Ave NW, Suite 306, Washington DC, 20036, ✆ (202) 429 9844, ✇ (202) 429 5649, *TOURISMDC@soho.ios.com*

The Turkish People

Othello didn't like the Turks very much:

> *In Aleppo once*
> *Where a malignant and a turbaned Turk*
> *Beat a Venetian and traduced the state*
> *I took by the throat the circumcised dog*
> *And smote him thus.*

History has been unkind to the Turkish people, especially history written from a European point of view. To writers and commentators of the past they were slothful, lazy, dirty, backward and devious, yet to be fair to those bigoted scribes, most Ottoman sultans did run their country in a manner that did little to dispel such prejudices. Of course, all of the adjectives above are utter nonsense; in fact, it's hard to meet a people nicer than the Turks.

The word for guest in Turkish is *misafir*, and to the Turks it is almost sacred. Wherever you go, you'll be offered a glass of tea; for many people, Turkish hospitality is almost overwhelming. Yet one never has the feeling that it derives from a sense of religious obligation, rather from a warm and spontaneous friendliness and concern for their fellow man. Coupled with this, especially in the small villages, is a keen curiosity about the foreigner. In eastern Anatolia the good farmer may just stop and stare at you; it's a bit unnerving but he means no harm. Anyone who knows a few phrases of English, especially the school children, will want to try them out on you ('Is Turkey beautiful? Yes?'). The country women are shyer. If they're in a group (you'll see them coming and going from the fields in large trailers pulled by jaunty tractors), they may smile. Otherwise, they probably won't address you, unless you're a woman on your own. Then they open up and are even more friendly than the men. Turks dote on children and if you take them with you, they'll spoil them horribly. *'Maşallah, maşallah!'* they'll say, patting them on the head and giving them more sweets and fruit than they could eat in a year. *'Maşallah'* means 'May God preserve [him or her from evil]'; children are too precious to receive any direct compliments that might incur divine jealousy.

As well as warmth and hospitality, the other central characteristic of the Turks is their intense nationalism and pride. This is the heritage of the Great Atatürk. When Turkey was still referred to as 'The Sick Man of Europe', he boosted his countrymen's morale with slogans that you still see everywhere, even inscribed on hillsides in giant white letters: *'NE MUTLU TÜRKÜM DİYENE'* ('How lucky for a man to call himself a Turk!') and *'DİYENE BİZ BİZE BENZERİZ'* ('We resemble ourselves'). Speak disparagingly of Turkey at your own risk; although you'll find plenty of sympathy on many subjects, from telephones to traffic conditions in İstanbul. Atatürk himself is the one really taboo subject, unless you want to pay his memory a compliment. It's also bad form to say 'Constantinople' instead of İstanbul, or to imply that Turkey is not a member of the Western community. Turks are easily insulted.

While travelling with **children** in Turkey poses no special problem (except that disposable nappies and baby foods are hard to come by in many places, and many children dislike the milk served in the cafés), a **woman** travelling on her own, or with a girlfriend, may have to contend with stares, personal questions and some typical Mediterranean male annoyances. The Turks, especially off the well-travelled tourist routes, are simply not used to seeing women on their own. Don't be afraid to use the word *'ayıp!'* ('shame') loudly if harassment reaches uncomfortable levels; this may elicit the help of passers-by. Face-slapping is stupid and potentially very dangerous. But don't be afraid to go. It is rare for a man to try to force you into something you don't want. Turks may make the women sit in the back of the mosque, but they have a respect for their rights and dignity that could be an example to many men elsewhere. They are also quite **modest and conservative** socially; wearing your bikini in the village, topless sunbathing and becoming noisy and drunk are provocative. Have respect for their ways and you should find that respect reciprocated.

Where to Stay

The mid-1990s were the time of the great tourism bust in Turkey: the crest of a speculative wave of hotel-building arrived at the same time as a drop-off of visitors from continental Europe, frightened off by a pitiful few PKK bombing attacks, heavily reported in the news. Then, just as tourists started returning en masse in the late 1990s, two more stories hit the international news: the arrest and subsequent sentencing to death of the PKK leader Abdullah Öcalan (the sentence is still being hotly debated by politicians and lawmakers and hangs in the balance at the time of writing); and the devastating earthquake of August 1999. As a result, both *pansiyonlar* and hotels were often running at one-third capacity in the height of the season, and harried desk clerks and proprietors were sending their relations out on the pavement looking for somebody, anybody, to fill their rooms at any price. This situation will correct itself over the next few years, but for the time being accommodation in Turkey continues to be a tremendous bargain, and usually easy to find.

Hotels and Pensions

Four- and five-star hotels will supply all that their counterparts do elsewhere in the world. The staff will speak excellent English, and there will be restaurants and bars, usually a disco and often a hamam. Expect a pool (except in city centres) and equipment for water sports on offer. Rooms should have a balcony, and usually satellite TV and air-conditioning; minibars are also common, though with the usual criminal mark-up for drinks. Some of the *luxury* and *expensive* hotels are housed within converted Ottoman mansions or caravanserais (nearly all of these are in this book), though most are very modern and surprisingly sharp-looking, well-designed and well-equipped; the best are as good as those of anywhere in Europe. If you can afford to splurge, these can be great bargains just now, especially out of the high season. Rates are often negotiable (try a little *pazarlık* over the phone). You will often be able to enjoy the comfort and facilities of a top-flight resort hotel for $70–90, and, at the right time, maybe as low as $45.

Two- and three-star hotels will also be what you would expect, although in the tourist areas they can be hastily flung together and consequently very functional and soulless, the kind of places built specifically for package tours. In the **one-star** category, you may struggle to find a member of staff who speaks English, although the rooms will be very clean and often have private showers and toilets.

The **staff** in Turkish hotels, like the Turks in general, are extremely friendly and helpful. They may not shine shoes (this being the exclusive province of the *boyacı*, shoeshine boys or men, who may be found almost everywhere with their artistically embellished brass boxes), but are willing to handle almost any other difficulty that may arise: giving directions, finding taxis, making reservations and handling laundry (*çamaşır*). If you get a room that is dirty, or the lock or lights don't work, don't hesitate to complain or demand another one.

Breakfast, on offer in all hotels with stars and many of the *pansiyonlar*, is usually a simple Mediterranean affair with rolls and jam or honey, cheese, olives and tea or coffee, though in fancier establishments it will often be an elaborate buffet. Before you check into one of the two- to four-star places in resorts that mainly cater to package tours, remember that many of them require at least half-board. Hotel restaurants, even in Turkey, the land of wonderful cuisine, are, in general, overpriced and dull, although we've found several exceptions.

Turkey's *pansiyonlar* and unclassified hotels are a mixed bag: some have en suite rooms and telephones and would not disgrace a two-star hotel; others are miserable flea-pits, especially in the outlying regions, where you should check the sheets (which the staff are sometimes prone to straighten rather than change).

The sort of *pansiyon* you are most likely to encounter in the coastal resorts will usually be quite pleasant: a modern concrete building which your hosts may have all to themselves, or share with other apartments. The rooms are generally bright and airy, and there may be a roof terrace for breakfast (part of the deal in some, but not all establishments; you'll almost always have a choice of whether to take it or not). Most of them also have heating; you'll notice a lack of blankets, though if you ask for some they will be supplied. Unless the hotel has 'continuous hot water', take your shower early in the morning or in the evening when the hot water's turned on. In smaller hotels and *pansiyons* you may have to ask for it to be turned on at the desk.

A double room in a simple *pansiyon* can go from $10–24. Some areas, such as Bodrum and Marmaris, are a bit more expensive than others, but you will find a choice at both extremes of the price range wherever you go. The highest prices in all hotel categories are in Ankara and İstanbul, and there do not expect always to get what you pay for.

There may well be a younger member of the family in your *pansiyon* who speaks some English—but you will already have met him, at the bus station. You don't have to work to find a *pansiyon* in any Turkish town where tourists come; they'll find you. When you're getting off the bus, or even walking down the street carrying a bag, someone will probably materialize from a doorway and start on about the lovely place run by his mom or brother or cousin, where the hot water is ever so dependable. Surprisingly, if you can't find a room in one of the places mentioned in this book, you'll find that just giving in and following him gives you the same odds as hunting up a place yourself. Times are hard and competition is fierce, and if a hotel has to go out looking for trade, it does not necessarily mean their establishment is a dive. It's just as likely that the family that runs the *pansiyon* is working hard to succeed, and will give you the same attention during your stay.

Some **tips** for playing this game. Find out whether the tout is a family member or just someone on commission; a little casual chat will usually tell you a lot about the person you're dealing with. Ask the price straight off; don't wait until you get to the place; then, if you care to, tell them you're looking for some place a third cheaper. Get clear answers about the place's location, facilities, etc. If there are lots of touts around, look helpless and talk to them all, then enjoy watching them bid the price down amongst themselves.

Rock-bottom Accommodation

Even today, it is possible to find a room in non-touristy areas of western Turkey for as little as $3–5 if you look hard. Hotels and *pansiyonlar* at the very bottom of the scale provide little more than a bed and plastic slippers; you have to supply your own towel, soap and toilet paper. Like almost all of the *pansiyonlar*, these unclassified hotels are regulated, not by the Tourism Ministry, but by the municipal authorities (*belediye*), who fix their prices and will listen to any complaints; the chances of being ripped off are very slight. Some are grungy and depressing, others quite tolerable; many proprietors of cheap hotels in outlandish places go to great lengths to provide pleasant accommodation. These places see mostly Turks—migrant workers, TIR drivers and such—who turn in early and snore loudly. Usually, you will find them in provincial towns and villages, inland where few tourists go.

Holiday Villages, Hotel Chains and Ski Resorts

At the opposite end of the scale are the four Club Méditerranée holiday villages (at Kuşadası, Yeni Foça, Kaş and Kemer) and big international chain hotels in Ankara, İstanbul, İzmir and Antalya (Hilton, Sheraton, Ramada, etc.). There are several Turkish chains, almost all along the west coast and Antalya region: Turban (which also operates several yacht marinas and camp sites—get their latest booklet from the Tourism Office); Tusan (mainly motels on the outskirts of the most popular towns); Etap (in Ankara and İstanbul—usually expensive); the luxury Dedeman chain of hotels; and Merit, with sites in many Turkish cities. Chain hotels are never good bargains—they get too many businessmen on expense accounts—and there will always be comparable places nearby with much more character. It must be said though, that in Turkish cities the chain hotels are *the* social centres for the city's elite, with the most lavish (and by far the most expensive) restaurants, gyms and sports facilites (usually open to the public) and night clubs.

Mainly on the coasts, there are several Turkish holiday villages (*tatil köyü*) that are quite nice and very good for families; in listings they are rated TK1 or TK2—but you'll probably always get a better price on these as part of a package deal arranged at home. In Turkey's rapidly growing winter sport centres, there are a number of alpine-style chalets classified as *Oberj* (*auberge*), listed as O.

Prices

We wish we could tell you! Unfortunately, it is utterly impossible to give more than a rough estimate of prices for any establishment. The main reason for this, of course, is Turkey's chronic inflation, and the regular currency devaluations that go with it. But beyond that, in the true homeland of *pazarlık* (bargaining), there is simply no such thing as a fixed price. We ask hotelkeepers their prices, and we know perfectly well that some of them are quoting them too high, hoping that they might get it from our readers, while others give a price too low, hoping to attract some business. All hotels are supposed to post their prices near the desk; a few actually do. It's standard procedure to walk in, scrutinize the price list and then ask the man at the desk the real price of a room ('*Son fiyatı ne kadar?*'). At the time of writing, places in all categories are often happy to get less than half of their officially listed price, especially in the off-season. All this can be confusing for people who like things just so, but it helps make Turkey the best bargain in the Mediterranean today. As people realize this, they'll be coming in increasing numbers—and the prices will start going up. Note that at some establishments, usually in the higher categories, there is an additional service charge and tax, up to 18% of the total bill.

Note also that **all the prices for individual hotels in this book are for double rooms**. And these will be the highest price you can expect to pay, except perhaps in July or August in a place that's really crowded. Listed below are the *average* high season prices for double rooms in each category:

★★★★★	$110–140
★★★★	$80
★★★	$40–50
★★	$35
★	$25
unlisted hotels, *pansiyonlar*	$10–24

Note that there are other ratings: **S** means a special licence, often a historic building (or at least an old one) that has been remodelled, as in İstanbul's Sultanahmet or Antalya's old town; prices for these can be the same as a one- or a four-star hotel. A motel, **M**, is usually on a highway, and charges the same as the higher-class *pansiyonlar*. Holiday villages are **HV1** and **HV2**, roughly corresponding to two- and three-star hotels (though some can be a lot more). And **O** is an *oberj* (auberge, or inn). All categories, as you see, cover a wide range. Of the extremes, the higher are usually in Ankara and İstanbul, the lower in the eastern provincial cities. You may take the middle of these ranges as typical of prices.

Because of the myriad classification systems and the variations in price between hotels with similar ratings, we have divided this book's hotel listings up by price as follows:

luxury	**$150 or more**
expensive	**$70–150**
moderate	**$40–70**
inexpensive	**$20–40**
cheap	**less than $20**

Youth Hostels

Youth hostels are rare. In İstanbul there are several unofficial ones along with the official ones, for which you need either an International Youth Hostel Federation Card or an International Student Travel Conference (ISTC) card. Most are likely to be open only in season. With budget accommodation as cheap as it is in Turkey, they are not worth going out of your way to find, especially as some are a good way out of town.

Camping

As with the hotels, there has been a boom in the opening of campsites in recent years, and if you're travelling this way there will be no problem finding one around any of the coastal resort towns. There are even campsites in İstanbul, near the airport. Don't think of camping here as a way to save money. Prices are complex: separate charges for each person, tent, trailer and so on, but at the average site the total ends up pretty much the same as staying in a *pansiyon*.

A detailed brochure (*Turkey: Camping*), listing over a hundred of the larger, better-equipped places in Turkey, is available at any local tourist office. These often have tent rentals, as well as electricity hook-ups and running water. Most of the bigger campgrounds have restaurants or snack bars, and some cooking facilities, which is fortunate since camping gas bottles and refills are very hard to find. Some of them even have swimming pools. Beyond these, unofficial camp sites are everywhere, although their quality can be very erratic; some are easily as good as the official sites, others offer you little more than a square of grass. Many *pansiyonlar* outside the towns have set up rudimentary campsites.

History

Pontus Euxinus
(Black Sea)

Sinop

Trebizond
(Trabzon)

Rhizus
(Rize)

Kars

Amasia
(Amasya)

Pontus

Ani

R. Iris (Yeşilırmak)

Tokat

Theodosiopolis
(Erzurum)

Mt. Ararat

Sebasteia
(Sivas)

Armenians

Manzikert
AD 1071

PERSIAN ROYAL ROAD

VIA REGALIS

R. Tigris

Ahlat

Tushpa (Van)

Hittites

Lake Van

Sardurihinli

Kultepe
Caesarea
(Kayseri)

Akhtamar

Çavuştepe

Melitene
(Malatya)

Harput

Dacianos

Urartians

Mt. Nemrut

Amida
(Diyarbakır)

R. Tigris (Dicle)

Samosate

Edessa (Urfa)

R. Euphrates (Fırat)

Tarsus

Karatepe

Harran

To Nineveh

Issus 333BC

Carchemish

Carrhae 53BC

Antioch
(Antakya)

N

Seleucia Pieria
(Samandag)

200km

100 miles

Galatia

Boundaries

Pre-Greek sites

Ancient Sites

49

The Turks, in their tourist literature and in the archaeological exhibitions they send round to the world's museums, like to bill their country as the 'Land of Civilizations'. Turkey's present inhabitants are relative latecomers, and the 7,000 years of history before their arrival witnessed an incredible pageant of peoples and cultures. If we learned in school that early history belonged almost entirely to Egypt and the Fertile Crescent, it is only because chance led the archaeologists there first. The mountains and plains of Anatolia can now also stake their claim as one of the birthplaces of civilization.

Ancient History to 2500 BC

Discoveries in the Karain Cave and other sites around Antalya have taken Turkey's history back as far as Neanderthal man, but the really exciting event has been the recent excavation of an accomplished and artistic culture 9,000 years old, at **Çatal Höyük** near Konya, a peaceful, matriarchal town that lived on agriculture and the obsidian trade. It grew into a city of some 32 acres, the oldest truly urban culture ever discovered. Its chubby goddesses and bull-horn shrines, along with the rest of its remarkable artworks, are in the Ankara Museum. The latest levels of the excavations show evidence of fire and strife, and we can take Çatal Höyük's end, *c.* 5500 BC, as the beginning of the first dark age. The Neolithic cultures that replaced it, as at **Mersin** and **Hacılar**, were not nearly as sophisticated.

2500 BC–1180 BC: The Bronze Age

After its great beginnings Anatolian civilization entered a period of little interest, falling behind Egypt and Mesopotamia. Revival came with the **Hattian culture**, another recent discovery, about which little is yet known. The Hatti people flourished in central Anatolia *c.* 2500–2000 BC, caused their neighbours little trouble, and created some of the finest works of art of their age. At this time, a separate Bronze Age culture began to develop around **Troy**, more closely related to the peoples of the Aegean than to those of Anatolia.

Around 2000 BC, a new nation arrived from the Balkans, the **Hittites**, a warrior aristocracy (as the later Turks were to be) who imposed themselves on the Hatti and founded a great capital at Hattuşaş, east of Ankara. They introduced writing to Asia Minor by learning the Assyrian cuneiform and later developing their own hieroglyphics to fit their Indo-European tongue. They also gave Anatolia its first empire, a Bronze Age superpower that contended with Egypt for the mastery of the Middle East after King Mursilis I captured Aleppo and Babylon *c.* 1590 BC. Throughout this era, Hittite control over the coastal areas was tenuous at best. Their records show constant problems with the Kingdom of Arzawa, in the southwest of the peninsula, the 'Lukka Lands' (Lycia) and a people called the **Ahhiyawa** (probably the Mycenaean Greeks, the *Achaeans* of Homer). Besides Greece proper, the Ahhiyawans ruled a bit of the Anatolian coast, with a capital there called Millewanda, probably Miletus.

About 1180, just as the Hittites had reached the peak of their political and artistic accomplishment, their empire came to a sudden end at the hands of unknown invaders from the west (possibly the Phrygians). The slender evidence available suggests a period of warfare, migrations and famines all through the 12th century. A mixed multitude, called the '**Sea**

Peoples' in Egyptian records, seem to have ranged over Anatolia and the Levant, briefly threatening even Egypt; the Achaeans were one of the nations listed among them (the other tribes later spread across the Mediterranean, including the Sicels of Sicily, the Sards, the Etruscans, the Phrygians and the Philistines). This period of catastrophes, which also witnessed the fall of Troy, sent Asia Minor into another dark age.

1180–546 BC: New Nations in Anatolia

Political and cultural unity in Anatolia died with the fall of the Hittites, and for centuries to come the region was divided among a number of new peoples, many of whom had migrated into the region only after the Hittite collapse.

Urartians

During the Hittite empire, a confederation of two peoples, forming the 'Hurri-Mitanni state', lived precariously as a buffer between the Hittites and Assyria. Successors to the Hurrians, a related people, the Urartians appeared in the region around Lake Van in the 12th century BC. They called themselves the Biainili, but as the Urartians (the name by which they are known in the Assyrian chronicles) they gave their name to Mount Ararat. An Urartian state gradually coalesced, reaching its greatest extent under King Sarduri II, c. 750 BC, extending from the Black Sea to the Caspian. The Assyrian King Tiglath-Pileser III soon cut them down to size, however, and the Scythians finished them off in 609 BC. Urartian stone reliefs and metal-work, recently recovered in a number of sites around Lake Van, at its best equals anything produced in that age.

Late Hittite Kingdoms

These survived all over southeastern Anatolia, usually as Assyrian dependencies such as Malatya, Maraş and Carchemish. Kizzuwadna, roughly all of what would later be called Cilicia, was throughout the period ruled by relatives of the Hittite Kings. Though politically powerless, they carried on the traditions of Hittite art, in the occasionally grand but often peculiar sculpture that takes the pride of place in so many museums in Anatolia.

Phrygians

This people, talented in music and art, took the place of the Hittites in much of west central Anatolia; their real name was the *Mushki*, or Moschians. A little empire, ruled by kings alternately named Midas and Gordius, flourished until about 695 BC, when it was wrecked by an invasion of Cimmerians. The Lydians picked up the pieces in 650, and replaced Phrygia as the dominant power. The Phrygian capital was Gordium, west of Ankara. After the conquest, a Phrygian state lived on in the hills south of Eskişehir. A pastoral people, the Phrygians exported wool to the Greeks and diverted themselves with their orgiastic cult of Cybele and their music. They claimed to have invented the pan-pipes; Marsyas, the mythological flautist who had the bad judgement to enter a contest against Apollo, was a Phrygian.

Greeks

Recent finds around İzmir suggest that Greeks began expanding into Anatolia's coasts as early as the 11th century. The colonization was not a unified movement, but undertaken individually by Greek cities, and colonies long retained the tribal characters of their founders: the **Aeolians**, who probably came first, in the north, around Troy and Assos; **Ionians** in the centre; and the latecomers, the **Dorians**, in the south. **Pamphylia**, the 'land of all tribes' on the southern coast, may also have been colonized early.

The cities of Asia Minor never worried much about political unity. The self-sufficient city state was the model, and the greatest of these was **Miletus**, which by the 8th century was probably the leading commercial and sea power of the Aegean. After *c.* 700 BC, the Greek city-states found themselves blocked by the power of Lydia, and unable to expand their territories further inland. Instead, they moved into sparsely-populated coastal areas further north. Miletus took the lead, founding Abydus (Çanakkale) and other towns on the Marmara and Black Sea, while the Megarans founded a number of colonies including Byzantium.

Lydians

The wealthy and commercially minded Lydians lived to the east of İzmir, but in their heyday in the 6th century BC they controlled an empire that included a vast area of western Anatolia. Under kings like the famous Croesus, the Lydians were a contented, blissfully decadent people who exported perfumes and other luxury goods around the Mediterranean. Ancient writers credit them with the invention of money. Before 546 BC, when the Persians under Cyrus put a brutally sudden end to Lydia as an independent power, its kings held sway over all the Greek coastal cities, though they were content merely to collect tribute from them.

Carians

One of the more obscure nations, the Carians, or Lelegians were related to the Lydians and originally occupied the area from Miletus to Lake Köyceğiz; they are mentioned in Homer as allies of the Trojans. Though the Carians may once have been an important sea power, the Greeks pushed them from the coast at an early date. The interior (roughly between modern Aydın and Muğla) remained Carian throughout antiquity, though subject to ever-increasing Greek cultural influence. Their modest cities formed a confederacy on the Greek model.

Lycians

On the southwest coast of Anatolia, the Lycians, like the Phrygians and Lydians, were a native people speaking an Indo-European language who were later Hellenized by the Greeks. Their origins are lost in time, though opinion in antiquity had them coming from Minoan Crete and founding Miletus before migrating to the southern coast. Although they were mentioned by Homer, their relative inaccessibility and reputation for fierceness kept them out of the mainstream of history; their most remarkable accomplishments were the lovely rock tombs they carved into cliffs all over Turkey's southwestern coasts.

None of these states was destined to last long. The aggressive and brutal Assyrian Empire (860–612 BC) kept Anatolia in constant turmoil. Even worse, tribes of mounted warriors from across the Caucasian mountains were constantly marauding through Anatolia. The **Cimmerians** learned cavalry tactics from the Scythians; in the 7th century BC, they occupied most of the eastern half of Anatolia. The **Medes** (*c.* 620–549 BC), who founded the first great Persian empire, destroyed the Assyrians and the Cimmerians, and succeeded to both their domains.

546 BC–334 BC: Greeks and Persians

The Achaemenid kings of Persia, who replaced the Medes in 549 BC, created a world empire for themselves within two generations. After Cyrus' conquest of Lydia had given them undisputed control of the whole of Anatolia, the Persians sent their general Harpagus on a campaign through Ionia to enforce the submission of the Greek cities. Satraps, or governors, were appointed over the various provinces, and although Persian rule was on the whole just, unoppressive and enlightened, the Greeks, accustomed to governing themselves, found it hard to take. An **Ionian revolt** in 499, supported by Athens, was brutally crushed by the Persians, and resulted in the burning of Miletus. Persian military power was now embroiled with Greece at the height of its classical age, and a confrontation was inevitable.

Under King Xerxes, the Persians invaded Greece in 490 and were defeated at Marathon. The second attempt, ten years later, again resulted in defeats at the battles of Salamis and Plataea. In the aftermath, the Greek cities liberated themselves and joined the Athenian-led alliance called the Delian Confederacy. Athenian ambition and arrogance, however, led to this league of equals gradually becoming more of an Athenian empire—the cause of the long and bloody **Peloponnesian War**, in which Athens and her allies were finally defeated by the Spartans (404). Even though the Asian cities had generally managed to avoid the fighting, their fate was no longer theirs to decide. The exhausted Spartans could not maintain control, and by the King's Peace of 387 they reverted to Persian rule.

From the beginning, these cities were more than mere colonies. An integral part of the Greek world, they contributed perhaps more than their share to the culture of Greece's golden age, despite usually being under foreign rule. Homer, who lived in the 8th or early 7th century, was probably born at Smyrna. In the 6th century, the Ionian cities, notably Miletus, produced the first Western philosophers: Thales, Anaximander, Xenophanes and Heraclitus. Art and architecture also flourished. The first temples were only built in the 8th century, but by the 6th century Ephesus and Samos were contending with the equally wealthy Greek cities of Sicily to build the biggest temples in the world.

334–150 BC: Alexander and the Hellenistic World

The Persian army, meanwhile, had not been keeping up with battle tactics. The Greek hoplite, or armoured infantryman, was the ultimate weapon of the day, and it only needed one Greek state to afford enough of them to really make a splash. Thanks to a chance find of gold, that state was Macedonia, and Philip of Macedon recruited his forces with the announced purpose of a crusade against the Persians. After his assassination, the job was left to his son **Alexander the Great**. With 40,000 men, he crossed the Hellespont in the spring of 334 BC, and almost immediately defeated a large Persian army. Within a year, Alexander had conquered all Anatolia, opening up the way to turning the Persian Empire into his own.

Soon after Alexander's untimely death in 323, his generals carved up the newly-created empire for themselves. Anatolia fell to Antigonus, but his attempts at reunifying the empire led the others to combine against him, and his cause died at the Battle of Ipsus in 301 BC. Another general, Lysimachus, seized Anatolia, and was in turn beaten by Selucus in 280 BC; the **Seleucid Kingdom** the latter founded stretched from the Aegean to India, and was to last over a century. Meanwhile, Cappadocia had become a virtually independent kingdom, and another former general, Philetarus, who had grabbed Alexander's treasure after his death, used the booty to found the city state of **Pergamon**, which grew in power and influence for another century and came to control much of western Anatolia by *c.* 150 BC.

Meanwhile, Anatolia was becoming thoroughly Hellenized. Trade and commerce boomed; vast and wealthy new cities appeared, such as Pergamon and Antioch, while older ones, particularly Smyrna and Ephesus, grew to metropolitan size. Greece proper was beginning its long economic decline, partly thanks to the emigration to Asia sponsored by the Seleucids and other rulers, and Anatolia's new wealth and power gradually made it the centre of the Greek world. Most of the ruins you will see in Turkey date from this time, if not from the centuries of Roman rule; Anatolia had another 800 years of calm and prosperity ahead of it.

One unusual event of the time was the invasion in 275 BC of the **Galatians**, Celts really, who installed themselves right in the centre of the peninsula. Though eventually defeated by the Pergamenes, the Celts stayed, and their red-haired and freckled descendants can still be seen on the streets of Ankara and in many other Turkish towns today.

150 BC–300 AD: Under Roman Rule

Roman control came gradually and irresistibly, a province at a time. With Pergamon and Rhodes as close allies, the Romans carefully watched their influence grow through the 3rd century, while they were busy with their struggle to the death against Carthage. An ambitious Seleucid king, Antiochus III (223–187 BC) conquered Syria and Palestine and forged an alliance with Macedon against Rome. The legions marched in and bloodied them both. By AD 146, Greece was under direct Roman rule, and the Seleucid kingdom a mere fragment. In 133 the last king of Pergamon saw the writing on the wall and willed his kingdom to Rome.

Outside their Pergamene windfall, the Romans never ruled much of Anatolia directly; there were client kings, as in Armenia and Cappadocia, and many of the Greek cities maintained control over their internal affairs, and the right to mint their own coins. The Romans were happy to soak the wealthy cities with taxes that were as high as the cities could bear, plus occasionally pillaging art treasures. A trip east with the legions, with its promise of loot and fame, was the perfect stepping-stone to power in Rome. Sulla used his victory over the last independent Anatolian state, the Pontic Kingdom of Mithradates, to become dictator of Rome in 82 BC, and a decade later, Pompey's successful campaign against the Cilician pirates allowed him to become Sulla's successor. After that, Anatolia was disturbed only by the civil wars after Julius Caesar's assassination in 44 BC. Brutus passed through, grabbing all the men and money he could, and sacking cities that resisted. After him came Antony, demanding ten years' taxes in one, and dallying with Cleopatra at Alanya and Tarsus.

After all this, Anatolia deserved a rest, and the new Empire founded by Augustus laid the foundations for over two centuries of peace and prosperity, in which the region reached its peak of wealth and ease, climaxing perhaps, in the reign of Hadrian (117 BC–AD 38), a Grecophile and great benefactor of the cities. Commerce and the arts flourished, and cities like Ephesus, Smyrna (İzmir) and Antioch (Antakya) each counted over 500,000 inhabitants. Throughout this time, the opulence of life and loss of independence and responsibility was working a slow change on the Greeks. It can be seen in the art of the Imperial centuries, wilder, more emotional and intense, and above all in the growing obsession with religion and the 'salvation of the soul'. The old mystery cults of the Anatolian goddesses, especially Cybele, attained new popularity, while newcomers like Mithraism, a Persian import, gained many adepts. In the cities were large and prosperous Jewish communities established after the diaspora; their religion too found many converts. More importantly though, these communities provided the basis for the surprisingly rapid spread of Christianity. St Paul began his travels around Anatolia, as recorded in the *Acts of the Apostles*, in 43 AD.

AD 300–1071: The Byzantine Empire

The **founding of Constantinople** in the 4th century AD, and the division of the empire into halves seemed to confirm Asia Minor in its central role. As the West receded into anarchy, successful Eastern emperors like Theodosius the Great (379–95), Justinian (527–65) and Heraclius (610–41) effected the transition of the state into the theocratically Christian, Greek-speaking Byzantine Empire, while keeping Avars, Alans, Persians and Slavs at bay.

Unfortunately, the diseases that had sapped the strength of the old Empire were built into the new one from its birth: a gigantic bureaucratic state, with crushing taxes to support itself along with the army and the bloated Imperial court. Christianity, while providing a new basis of unity, wiped out what remained of free thought and learning. Meanwhile an already great gap between rich and poor continued to increase. For most of Anatolia, this period witnessed a gradual but irreversible decline, as Byzantine misgovernment slowly strangled the economies of the cities and the great landowners pushed the majority of the country people into serfdom. Remember what you learned in school about the Dark Ages, and then consider that most parts of western Europe managed better under barbarian rule and constant war than Asia Minor did under the successors of the Roman Empire. Beginning in the 7th century, mutually destructive warfare with the Persians and a new menace, the armies of the Muslim Arabs, added the finishing touches. Trade died, and the coastal cities withered and disappeared; the once-fertile farmlands around them reverted to empty malarial plains. After a millennium and a half of sophisticated civilized life, Asia Minor had been destroyed.

Throughout the 8th century, the Byzantines had been preoccupied with the **Iconoclastic** struggles, in which disputes over the desirability of painted icons demonstrated a tremendous confusion of religious, economic, and political conflicts (the example of rising Islam made the Greeks' love of divine images seem pure idolatry to many minds, but behind that stood a deeper discontent with the power of the monks and the Church hierarchy). The prohibition of icons began with a Church council of 754, and lasted until 843. Attacks from the surrounding Arabs, Avars, Serbs, Bulgarians and Petchinegs brought the Byzantines to their senses, and under emperors Basil I (867–86), Basil II, 'the Bulgar-slayer' (976–1025), and Nicephorus Phocas, the 'Pale Death of the Saracen' (963–9), Byzantium achieved a cultural revival and a level of political stability. This was little relief to devastated Anatolia; such culture as survived existed only in Constantinople.

1071–1243: The Selcuks Lead the Turkish Invasion

In the emptiest of Asia's empty spaces, north of Manchuria, the Chinese chroniclers note a 'hill shaped like a helmet', the ancestral home of the *'Tu-kueh'*—the Turks; they first appear in history *c.* 500 BC, making trouble for the Chinese emperors. In about AD 800, a confederation of tribes called the Oğuz was gradually heading towards Europe. By AD 900, many of the tribes had become Muslim, warrior clans that helped the central Asian states as they infiltrated them, just as the various 'barbarians' had done in Rome. Though not the first Turks to find their way into the desolated bear-pit of Asia Minor, the Selcuks, under their chief Alp Arslan, were the first to do it in style, gobbling up the Armenians and ending Byzantine rule over much of Anatolia once and for all with a resounding victory at Manzikert, north of Lake Van, in 1071. They called their state, centred at Konya, the Sultanate of Rum—to the peoples of distant Asia, Rome was still a magic name. As soon as they settled down, the Selcuks transformed themselves with amazing speed into gifted rulers and patrons of the arts. At the height of their power, under the early 13th-century Sultan Alâeddin Keykubad, they were the strongest and most civilized state of the eastern Mediterranean, one considerably influenced by the culture of Persia, then under the rule of a separate Selcuk clan; Selcuk architecture, seen in the schools and mosques of Konya and so many other Anatolian cities, marks not only the beginning of Turkish art but one of its greatest achievements.

The Selcuks were only the first wave of a huge migration from central Asia. As well as the other Turkish tribes who set up petty emirates across the Middle East, the **Mongols** came, ending the Sultanate of Rum at the Battle of Kösedağ in 1243 and once more returning Turkey—we may now call it that—to anarchy. The most important result of their invasion was to push other Turkish tribes westwards, into the wastelands still nominally ruled by Constantinople. The first Turks to settle the Aegean coast, the Menteşe, founded a little emirate around Milas and Bodrum in the 1260s. By 1300 the situation had stabilized with the Karamanlı emirate ruling central Anatolia, the 'six emirates', including the Menteşe, Hamitoğulları and Germaniyids, in the southwest, and a number of tribes in the northeast.

Even before 1243, the Selcuks had been beset on all sides, not only by Turks, but also by the **Crusader States** founded by the Franks in the 12th century. The greatest of these in Anatolia, the County of Edessa (Şanlıurfa), survived for over a century, and orders such as the Knights of St John controlled much of the southern coast throughout the Middle Ages. The Crusaders soon learned to leave the Selcuks alone, and not wishing to tackle the other Muslim nations either, decided to go after the heretics in Constantinople. A new Crusade in 1204, serving the ends of Venice and the Pope, took advantage of the absent Byzantine army to storm and sack the city for the first time, humbling its pride, violating most of the women, and carrying off nearly every bit of its 900 years of accumulated treasure.

The Byzantine empire ends here. Although a government in exile was set up at İznik (Nicaea), from which Emperor Michael Paleologos chased out the Italians and reclaimed the city in 1261, it was an impoverished, enfeebled Constantinople that survived until 1453 behind its impregnable walls. In 1359, Emperor John Paleologos gave in and became a tribute-paying vassal to his son-in-law, Sultan Orhan, leader of a new and growing Turkish tribe, the Osmanlı, or **Ottomans**.

1300–1453: The Coming of the Ottomans

According to legend, these Turks were riding across Anatolia when they chanced upon a battle being fought on the plain beneath them. Under their chief, Ertuğrul, they chivalrously decided to join the losing side, and soon turned their defeat into victory. The lucky victors were the Selcuks, who rewarded their new allies with lands in western Anatolia. About 1300, Sultan **Osman** laid the foundations of the state and dynasty that was to bear his name. Equally talented in war and government and virtuous to an extreme, Osman made his state a power in the region. All his successors were girded with his sword in place of a coronation, and the cry that went up was not 'Long live the Sultan' but 'May he be as good as Osman!'

Orhan (1324–59), his son, conquered Bursa in 1326 and made it his capital. His marriage to a Byzantine princess was not a rare case; by the 14th century Greeks and Turks had come to know each other very well. Anatolia's gradual process of 'turning Turk' had begun with the Selcuks. Gradually, many of the Greeks had converted to Islam, often entire towns at a time; most of the rest, considering their alternatives, saw the tolerant Turkish Muslims as a lesser evil than the schismatics of Europe and their hated pope. (The average Turk of today probably has far more Greek and native Anatolian blood in him than Turkish.) Orhan, an able and liberal ruler, increased the Ottomans' prestige as he widened their boundaries. Early in his reign, a group of adventurers called the Catalan Grand Company, paid to defend Constantinople, had ferried Orhan's army across the Bosphorus to help. The Ottomans took one look at Europe and decided they wanted to keep it; Orhan conquered Thrace, and his son Murat I (1359–80) added Serbia, Bulgaria and Macedonia.

The Turks, changing from nomadic warriors to an imperial aristocracy, suffered from a shortage of women and, consequently, a shortage of Turks for a state with such big ambitions. They solved this problem with the *devşirme*, a harvest of five per cent of the infant boys from captured Christian provinces (first-born sons were excluded). All were educated and brought up as Muslims; the best became the sultan's generals and vezirs (ministers), while the rougher were enrolled in the Janissaries (*yeniçeri*, 'new troops'), a corps of highly trained soldiers that were to be the terror of Europe. The Janissaries were kept under the control of the Bektaşi dervishes, from whom they inherited an unusual tradition of rituals and titles based on soup. To show their displeasure with a sultan, for example, they would turn their large kettle upside down and refuse to eat. In later years, as the Janissaries became a law unto themselves, they did this whenever they felt like deposing a sultan. As long as discipline was maintained, though, they were the finest fighting force in the world.

For Beyazıt I, 'Thunderbolt' (1389–1403), they destroyed the flower of French chivalry at Nicopolis in 1396, finally damping the crusading urge. Beyazıt, a young hothead, addicted to battle even more than to wine, met his destiny in the person of Tamerlane in 1403. The invincible Mongol destroyed the Ottoman force at Ankara and took Beyazıt prisoner, and then mysteriously turned around and went back east. Mehmet I (1413–21) and Murat II (1421–51) picked up the pieces and carefully rebuilt, finding time in 1444 to win undisputed control of the Balkans at the Battle of Varna, after which the head of King Ladislas of Poland and Hungary ended up on the top of a pike in Bursa.

1453: The Capture of Constantinople

Almost from the beginning, this was the Ottoman goal. Earlier attempts against the city had failed, and it was left to **Mehmet II** (1451–81) to take the prize. Mehmet, perhaps the most remarkable sultan, was a poet and scholar who had mastered six languages and, unthinkable for a Muslim, had his portrait painted, by Gentile Bellini. He saw himself as a man of destiny, sent to fulfil Mohammed's prophecy about the capture of the city, and went about the task methodically. By 1453, he had an enormous army, the biggest cannons in the world and a fleet. Inside the city, whose population had dwindled from over a million to under fifty thousand, an Italian *condottiere* named Giustiniani led 8,000 Greeks and mercenaries for the defence. Against the odds, they held out for two months. The tide turned with Mehmet's brilliant trick of dragging his ships over land, around the famous chain across the Golden Horn, to the exposed side of the city. On 23 May Giustiniani died, and the disheartened mercenaries fled. The few Greeks remaining beat back a furious attack, but in their excitement left open a postern gate; some Turks found it, and the empire breathed its last. Mehmet ordered that the usual three days' pillage should spare all the buildings; he walked in awe through the Aya Sofya and the abandoned palaces, and remembered a bit of Persian poetry:

> *The spider weaves the curtain in the Palace of the Caesars,*
> *The night-owl keeps the watch in the Tower of Afrasiyab.*

To the Turks, Mehmet is *Fatih*, the Conqueror. He knew what the city meant, and rebuilt it as fast as resources allowed. In 1461 he added the Empire of Trebizond to his conquests, the last free Greek state, founded by refugee noblemen after the sack of 1204.

1454–1700: The Height of the Ottoman State

Mehmet's son, Beyazıt II, 'the Mystic' (1481–1512), seldom disrupted his reading for further conquests, but Selim I (1512–20) made up for him by swallowing up Egypt (thus gaining the Caliphate) and much of Mesopotamia. *Yavuz* Selim, as the Turks call him, is an honorific meaning 'the Formidable', but historians like to call him Selim the Grim for his frequent massacres of Shiite heretics (he was the first Ottoman to trouble himself about religious orthodoxy), and his habit of beheading his grand vezirs at an average of one a year. His son, **Süleyman the Magnificent** (1520–66), presided over the glorious noonday of the Ottoman state; under him the empire reached its greatest extent with the conquest of Hungary and North Africa. His title comes courtesy of his close allies, the French; to his own people he was 'the Lawgiver' for his thorough reforms of the legal code and commercial regulations.

Unfortunately, he also began the empire's slow decline. The trading concessions he granted to François I were the first step in the Ottomans' loss of control of their own economy. From his weakness for his scheming harem-favourite Roxelana, he brought the harem into the palace itself and inaugurated the period of palace intrigue that was eventually to ruin the state. The sultans that followed show clearly how far the decay had already penetrated. Selim the Sot (1566–74), and İbrahim the Mad (1640–8) lead the parade of wastrels, drunkards, sex perverts and imbeciles that decorated the latter-day Ottoman throne. Directly upon Süleyman's death the real power had passed to the Janissaries, the eunuchs and the ladies in the endlessly changing factions in the harem. Osman II (1618–22), who wanted reform, was murdered; his successors until 1832 were virtual prisoners of the Janissary guard.

In the *Divan* (cabinet), meanwhile, a remarkable dynasty of grand vezirs of Albanian descent, the Köprülü family, did their best to hold the leaderless state together throughout the 17th century. By the 18th, decadence had progressed so far that the European powers had to keep the Ottoman corpse propped on its throne to keep the Russians from occupying the straits.

1700–1910: The Empire Crumbles

For three centuries, the Russians kept the pressure on with 43 declared wars while, in the 19th century, some of the empire's captive nations, the Greeks, Serbians, Bulgarians and Egyptians, successfully gained their independence. Attempts to reform were too few and too late. Under Mahmut II (1808–39), the Janissaries were massacred in what the Turks call the 'Auspicious Event' but the empire was too far behind the Europeans militarily and technologically for it to make much difference. Mahmut's successors, Abdülmecit I (1839–61) and Abdülaziz (1861–76), proved too stupid and indifferent to keep his reforms going, and the paranoid Abdülhamid (1876–1909) sold his nation to European economic interests while ruthlessly stamping out any progressive thinking at home.

Despite his efforts, underground attempts to bring Turkey out of its political nightmare continued, especially among circles in the army. In Salonika, now Greek Thessaloniki, a group of discontented army officers formed the Committee for Union and Progress, known in the west as the **Young Turks**, led by Enver Paşa. Their manœuvrings within the upper echelons of the Ottomans led in 1909 to the fall of the hated Abdülhamid and the creation that same year of a constitutional monarchy, governed by an elected parliament.

1911–19: The War Years

During this period, the 'Sick Man of Europe' finally expired. The Italians started the final collapse when in 1911 they invaded the Turkish colony of Tripoli (Libya) and took it with ease. Encouraged by this, Montenegro, Serbia, Bulgaria and Greece joined forces to drive the Ottomans out of Europe in the First Balkan War (1913). A truce was negotiated by İstanbul before too much territory was lost, but Enver Paşa and the Young Turks seized power in a *coup d'état* and restarted the war. More defeats followed. Crete was lost; so too were the Dodecanese, and by 1913 Turkish domains in Europe consisted of just İstanbul and half of Thrace, the latter only because Bulgaria and Greece could not agree who should have it.

All of this should have put Enver Paşa off wars for good. It did not. When the Great War exploded in 1914, the Ottomans threw their fez in with the Germans, whom the Paşa hoped would help him realize his pan-Turkish dream of an empire extending to the shores of the Caspian Sea. Immediately, the Turks found themselves fighting on two fronts, at Gelibolu (Gallipoli) in the west and against the Russians in the east, while their empire fell apart, country by country. Sultan Mehmet V announced a *jihad* against the Triple Entente, hoping that all Islam would rise in his support, but the Ottomans had done the Arabs no favours when ruling them and now all blithely turned a deaf ear. By autumn 1918 Enver Paşa and others of the Young Turk *junta* had fled the country in disgrace, smuggled out on a German destroyer. By November of that year, British warships were at anchor in İstanbul.

In May 1920 the Triple Entente handed down their judgement on the old Ottomans, in the form of the Treaty of Sèvres. It carved up the country: İstanbul and a few surrounding areas were retained, but İzmir fell to Greek jurisdiction, an independent Armenia and an autonomous Kurdistan were to be set up in the east and any remaining areas of Anatolia handed out to France and Italy as spheres of economic influence. The Greeks saw their opportunity to put their long-dreamed-of *Megallo Idee* ('Great Idea') into practice—the recapture of Constantinople and the recreation of the Byzantine Empire. Encouraged by the British, the Greek army advanced from İzmir into Anatolia. Old, silly Mehmet VI, the last of the sultans, sat in his palace and wondered what would happen next.

1919: The Turkish Revolution

What happened was astounding. Throughout the Ottoman Empire, as under the Byzantines, Anatolia had been a neglected backwater of the empire, which saw its heartland more as Thrace and the Balkans. To be called a 'Turk' was something of an insult among the aristocratic Ottomans; the patient Turkish peasants and townsmen of Anatolia put up with as much scorn and as little help as any minority of the empire. Now, for the first time, Anatolia made a stand. Opposition to the Sèvres treaty centred around a brilliant, difficult general, **Mustafa Kemal**, with a military reputation from Gallipoli and a head full of nationalist ideas. He escaped from the intrigues of İstanbul on 19 May 1919, and landed at Samsun with the force of a Napoleon returning from Elba. Nationalist congresses were soon held at Sivas and Erzurum, and a provisional government set up for the deliverance of the nation.

Somehow a new army was created. Under Kemal the Turks chased out the French and Russians and decisively defeated the Greeks at the two battles of İnönü in January–March 1921. The Greeks burnt and pillaged their way back to the coast; by September 1922, the country was clear of all foreign troops. A republic was declared one year later, with Mustafa Kemal as its first president and Ankara, right in the middle of Anatolia, as its capital. A new treaty was negotiated at Lausanne to replace the redundant Treaty of Sèvres; it included the ghoulish 'Exchange of Populations', by which some two million Greeks were forced out of Anatolia, where Greeks had lived for nearly 3,000 years, in return for pushing a few hundred thousand Turks out of Greece. In retrospect, it seems a historical turning point. Neither Mustafa Kemal nor the Greeks probably had any idea of the evil they were loosing on the world. It was the beginning of the tribal politics and 'ethnic cleansing' we know today, the insistence that people must not be allowed to get on together if politicians and propagandists find it inconvenient. In all the bloody 20th century, few greater crimes were committed— yet, at the time, the whole world believed they were doing the right thing.

1922–60: The Westernization of Turkey

Few nations have ever had the will or unity to effect as many reforms as the Turks did in the 1920s and '30s, trying to make up for so many centuries of lost time. Mustafa Kemal's republic was to be thoroughly secular: the Caliphate was abolished, education and marriage secularized, the wearing of the fez banned. Turkey adopted the Christian calendar and made Sunday the day of rest. The language was also reformed. Arabic and Persian words were rooted out, and the Roman alphabet replaced the Arabic. As the simplest way of westernizing its laws, Turkey simply adopted the entire Swiss Legal Code, almost word for word. Women acquired equal rights. International time and measures were adopted, and the government worked with its meagre resources to improve industry and communications. To crown it, the President decreed that every Turk should have a Western-style surname. Mustafa Kemal's was chosen for him by the nation—Atatürk, 'Father of the Turks'.

It was only his moral authority as the nation's hero that enabled the changes to be accepted with so much enthusiasm and so little resistance. In politics, Atatürk began what has become a modern Turkish tradition by establishing a dictatorship to make reforms, while constantly and sincerely telling his people that their first aspiration must be democracy. After his death in 1938, his right-hand man from the War of Independence, General **İsmet İnönü**, took over with a pledge to bring democracy. The Second World War, in which the Turks remained neutral, postponed the experiment, but free elections in 1949 resulted in the victory of the new opposition Democratic Party and its charismatic leader **Adnan Menderes**. For the coastal areas, the most important event in over a millennium was something that few histories even bother to mention—the anti-malaria campaign of 1948, made possible by the invention of DDT and American aid. DDT may be murder on birds (that's why it's outlawed in most countries now), but by cutting down drastically the number of anopheles mosquitoes, it made possible the resettlement of places that had been wastelands since Byzantine times. Without it, much of Turkey's coastline would still be empty today.

The Democrats' corruption, mishandling of the economy and attempt to create a one-party dictatorship resulted in an **army coup** in 1960, after which Menderes was executed. The memory of this complex character is still alive in his political stronghold, the farming lands of western Anatolia. In the last two decades nearly every town has named a street after him, something that would have been unthinkable earlier. Every Turkish populist party in the decades since has been more or less the Democrats under a different name.

1960 to the Present: Three Coups, Three Constitutions

Democracy was restored the following year, under an extremely liberal constitution proposed by the coup's leader, General Cemal Gürsel, and a new coalition government bumbled along under the watchful eye of the army. In 1965 the Justice Party (the old Democrats), led by **Süleyman Demirel**, achieved a working majority but his government was beset throughout its term by the Cyprus crisis; domestic issues, including a rapidly worsening economy, took second place. By 1970 the mild civil unrest that marked the preceding years had exploded into bloody riots and once again the army stepped in.

It was not until 1973 that a new civilian government took office, led by Bülent Ecevit of the Democratic Left Party, but it was to fare no better than its predecessor, the war in Cyprus and the OPEC oil-price hike dominating its attention. Amidst the economic troubles, political violence between left and right threatened to turn into civil war. In 1980, after a year that saw over 3,000 politically inspired murders, the army stepped in once more, with a coup orchestrated by a real martinet, General **Kenan Evren**. All opposition to the new regime was stamped on, firmly. Political leaders from both sides, including Demirel and Ecevit, were jailed, sharing their cells with journalists, student leaders and trade unionists. In 1982, Evren proposed a new constitution, providing for a strong presidency. A referendum was passed—with the support of the vast majority of the country—which included an election for the new office of president with only one candidate, Evren. He was to hold the post until 1988.

Parliamentary elections the next year were won by the new Motherland Party (**ANAP**), led by **Turgut Özal**, an economist from Malatya. A typically Turkish paradox, Özal was a modern, Western-trained technocrat, a believer in democracy and a devout Muslim—the first prime minister of the republic to have made the pilgrimage to Mecca. His skill in mastering the moribund Turkish economy and his diplomatic treatment of the army started

Turkey on the longest period of freely-elected government it has yet enjoyed—17 years, so far. In 1988 he stepped into Evren's presidential shoes and lasted until his death in 1993, popular abroad for his ready support of the United Nations during the Gulf War and at home among those who can remember the condition their country was in before he achieved office. Support for Özal, however, was not transferred to the Motherland Party in the 1991 elections, when that old stager Süleyman Demirel gained a working Parliamentary majority for his centre-right True Path Party (**DYP**), in coalition with the mildly leftist SHP.

After Özal's death Demirel became president and the economics minster, **Tansu Çiller**, became Turkey's first female prime minister. A friend of Margaret Thatcher, she sought to bring similar free-market policies to Turkey. Although fêted by some business leaders for her efforts to privatise Turkey's moribund state enterprises, her government's currency manipulations contributed much to the runaway inflation, and accusations of gross governmental corruption filled the press. In late 1995, disillusioned Turks gave vent to their indignation and frustration at the ballot box, with the Islamic **Refah** (Welfare) Party, led by **Necmettin Erbakan**, gaining the largest share of the vote. In a desperate bid to prevent Refah from forming a government, ANAP and DYP pieced together a shaky minority governing coalition. This was brought down in the summer of 1996, and Turkey, an avowedly secular republic, witnessed Erkaban, a veteran Islamicist, becoming Prime Minister. By embarking on a series of visits to Libya and Iran, he hardly endeared himself to the National Security Council, Turkey's all-powerful guardian of secularism, made up of the military top brass and President Demirel. After just 11 months, the Council let its displeasure be known. Erbakan was forced to resign and Refah was dissolved on the dubious grounds that it was mixing religion with politics. Refah party members soon reconstituted themselves into **Fazilet**, the Virtue Party; they continue to exert pressure on the succession of secular governing party coalitions that have muddled through into the new century. Whilst fundamentalist detractors see Turkey today as some sort of velvet-gloved authoritarian state, secular apologists prefer to see it as a 'guided democracy'. Until both sides start speaking the same language, the volatile nature of Turkish politics is unlikely to calm down in the near future.

Turkey Today

Modern Turkey stands between the developed and developing countries. Any statistics relating to economic development are affected by millions of Anatolian farmers, only just now working their way out of primeval poverty; some stay on the land, others migrate to İstanbul, Ankara, or the cities of Western Europe (they joke that Berlin has become the 68th Turkish province). Their fertility is startling: the 63 million Turks today have one of the highest rates of population growth in the world. Despite this and other drawbacks—high inflation and a creaky and bureaucratic government among them—the Turks are determined to push their way into the developed world. They were finally admitted to the European Customs Union in 1995, and the pressure is on for Turkey to join the **European Union**.

Opinions and priorities may yet change on this: as an EU member Turkey might once more be the sick man of Europe, bossed around and buoyed up by grants, and this realization is sinking in among many Turkish politicians. Some urge the government to look to the east, to the new states of Azerbaijan, Uzbekistan, Turkmenistan and Kazakhstan, all Turkic-speaking, all with predominantly Muslim populations, who see Turkey as an economically successful, capitalist, modern Muslim role model. Let us form a Near-East Community, say these politicians. Better to be king of your own castle than doorkeeper to another's in the West. '

Internal problems are much more pressing. Industrialization and modernization brought huge waves of migrants to the big cities, and a host of social problems. Unemployment is high, and the Brazilian-style inflation, while helping along the export boom, is an increasing liability. The massive **earthquake** that struck the İzmit region in August 1999 brought to the surface many of the underlying problems facing Turkey. Emerging from the rubble of the devastated towns was evidence of corruption, illegal building practices and government ineptitude. Many more than the official estimate of 17,390 people died in the earthquake, and over 200,000 were left homeless. In the crucial days that followed, the government seemed paralysed by the scale of the disaster, inviting the scorn of the press, who condemned Ankara's callous disregard for those trapped in the debris. Ordinary Turks who had always looked to *devlet baba* (daddy state) for leadership now had to rely on their own efforts. Volunteers and equipment poured in from all over Turkey and abroad. One of the first countries to send help was Greece, causing an immediate thaw in Turkish-Greek relations which may yet improve Turkey's chances of joining the EU. In the weeks that followed, the dazed government faced not only the human and financial costs of the disaster, but also the political fallout. One junior minister frankly admitted that 'lying under the rubble is the Turkish political and administrative system'. The system may survive the quake, but it will take years before the government will be able to regain the trust and respect of the Turkish people.

1999 was also the year in which the **Kurdish** question came to a head. Some 20% of the population are Kurds, spread across the whole country, but concentrated in the southeast. They are a proud people with their own distinct language, culture and history who have never had their own state (though Saladin, who turfed the Crusaders out of the Holy Land, was Kurdish). Most Kurds are scornful of the Atatürkian creed that a Turk is a Turk and nothing but. Denied their own homeland by the 1923 Treaty of Lausanne that negated the Treaty of Sèvres, the Kurds have always seen themselves as second-class citizens of Turkey, and with some justification. For decades their aspirations to autonomy and to the practice of their culture were suppressed, sometimes with horrible violence, as in the rebellions of 1925 and 1939; speaking Kurdish was not decriminalized until 1991.

There was little the Kurds could do about this while Turkey was under military or semi-military rule, but as the nation emerged into democracy, they made their voice heard, most sinisterly in the form of the terrorist Kurdish Workers Party, the PKK. Financed and trained by a rogues' gallery of Turkey's enemies—Syria, the Palestinians and formerly the Soviets—the PKK has survived by extortion and racketeering, killing everyone it can who disagrees with it, occasionally entire villages at a time. Much of the southeast has been under martial law for decades, and the skirmishes between the PKK and the army turned into full-scale warfare in the late 1980s. The government's response has been witless and nearly as destructive as the guerrillas: hundreds of villages in unsafe zones have been forcibly evacuated, and Turkey's already hard-pressed cities have filled up with Kurdish refugees. Half the people who work in Turkish hotels and restaurants are Kurds; ask them about it and you'll get an earful. Ten years ago they would have been reticent, but the one ray of hope in a continuing tragedy is an increasing openness about the situation. Prime ministers from Özal onwards have made tentative steps to address the problem, and the scores of new private television and radio stations are telling people things they never heard over the old state networks.

In 1999 the PKK leader Abdullah Öcalan was arrested and quickly sentenced to death. The Turkish authorities blame him for 30,000 deaths. At the time of writing he remains in prison. If he escapes the gallows it will be due to pragmatic considerations on the part of the authorities. Since his arrest Öcalan has called his campaign of violence a 'mistake' and ordered his fighters to cease fire and leave Turkey. Calls for Kurdish autonomy have been diluted into appeals for cultural concessions. Turkey's politicians are well aware that carrying out the death sentence would end Turkey's chance of admission to the EU and elevate him to martyrdom, even in the eyes of many Kurdish opponents of the PKK. Whether or not Turkey can find a peaceful solution to the Kurdish crisis depends above all on the nation's ability to change the more authoritarian aspects of the army-designed 1980 constitution. Through much of the 1990s, the State Security Courts sent journalists, writers and even members of Parliament off to prison wholesale on the flimsiest of charges. These courts, run by grim hard-liners working closely with the nastier spooks in the security services and the army, are accountable to no one, and few politicians have the courage to speak up against them.

Behind all the political troubles is an economic situation bordering on total anarchy. Twenty years of market economics have greatly widened the gap between Turkey's rich and poor; the resulting discontent did much to put votes in the column of the fundamentalist Refah (usually translated as 'Welfare Party', but *refah* really means luxury, affluence—they tell the peasants they'll make them all rich). Its successor, Fazilet, only staggered into a poor third place in the national elections of April 1999, but has a solid base of support among the old Democratic supporters in rural districts, as well as the vast numbers that have moved to the cities. Surprisingly, they also draw much support from the generally non-fundamentalist Kurds—it's the only possibility the latter have for a protest vote. Much of the rest of their support may be protest also: disgust with the outrageous corruption of the political cliques, and with squabbling parties that all look much the same, is at an all-time high.

The fundamentalism that peaked during Erkaban's premiership in 1997 has manifested itself outside politics too. Proselytizers and preachers run as thick as in North Carolina, ugly new mosques are going up everywhere, and many women have been compelled to wear the baggy coats that mark them as male property. For now, the fundamentalists turn their most moderate face to the world, claiming that all they want is morality, and help for the poor. Islamicist calls for Turkey's withdrawal from NATO and for the establishment of an 'Islamic Common Market' are things of the past, they say. The Islamicists have a long way to go to convince the generals, Turkey's unelected guardians of democracy, of their sincerity.

But there is a deep and responsible side to the strange currents that have been flowing through Turkey lately. Having got a noseful of Western market madness from the policies of Özal and Çiller, many educated, modern Turks are convinced they do not want to see their country travel down the same road, even if it means mosque on Fridays and fewer electronic gadgets. A sense of community, and one of continuity and tradition, are two things very important to Turks. In conversation, you will hear many of them express the hope that there might be some 'middle way' that would give them Western prosperity and democracy, while keeping their country a place where they can feel at home. May they find it.

Topics

People in the West who are unacquainted with Turkish history have probably never heard of him, but in Turkey his face is everywhere: in statues, in the portraits that adorn all public places and most businesses, on coins and banknotes, on banners and even in neon lights. The best ones try to emphasize his sharp features to make him into a kind of mythological hero; instead he comes out looking like the Wizard of Oz.

At first he was just Mustafa, a sullen, red-haired, blue-eyed boy from Salonika (no doubt with a lot of Celtic blood, like so many Turks). His house there still stands, next to the Turkish consulate, and woe to the Greeks if they ever knock it down, as they threaten to whenever they feel the urge for Turk-baiting. A teacher who recognized his abilities gave him the name Kemal, meaning 'perfection'; by the time he and his crack 57th Division were helping whip the British at Gallipoli, he had become General Mustafa Kemal Paşa, a leader with a reputation for putting himself in the thick of the battle—a habit that got him wounded at Gallipoli.

Emerging from the disastrous war as the only general with a record of victory, Mustafa Kemal was the man of the hour, at a time when the Ottoman Empire had collapsed and the Turkish lands were descending into total anarchy. The Allies, particularly Lloyd George, had decided on a cynical rape of Anatolia, meaning to parcel it out among themselves and the Greeks. No novice to political affairs—he had led one of the units that occupied İstanbul in the Young Turk coup of 1909—the general found himself in the same position as de Gaulle in 1940, and he made the most of it. Even more than de Gaulle, Mustafa Kemal was able personally to lead his hastily-rebuilt army to victory against the Greeks, defy the will of the Allied powers, and force the British, French and Italians to leave the country.

With that accomplished, there was still the task of dragging a proud but woefully backward and disorganized nation into the twentieth century. Make no mistake, without him not a tenth part of it would have been accomplished as quickly or as successfully. All the important initiatives of Turkey's unique cultural revolution came from Mustafa Kemal: a republic, a Westernized legal system, women's rights, language reforms, economic modernization, educational reforms and the divorce of religion from politics. Nowhere in history is there a comparable example of such rapid, radical change in a nation's life and institutions—only the reign of Peter the Great in Russia comes remotely close.

Atatürk, or 'Father of the Turks', was the surname he assumed by general acclaim during his campaign to westernize Turkish names in the 1930s. Cults of personality were all too common in those days, and we might easily dismiss Atatürk as just another strongman. On the contrary, he has earned a place among the very few great statesmen this century has produced. One of the famous photos of Atatürk shows him in European formal attire, demonstrating Roman letters to a crowd of his earnest but probably bewildered countrymen. It wasn't just what a modern politician would call a 'photo opportunity'; he did it many times all over Turkey. He took his job seriously, and after so many centuries of decay, the job couldn't have been done any other way.

Atatürk thoroughly deserves all the statues and tributes, but they are more than just a memorial to a leader. They stand as a symbol of the revolution he began, and of the modern, secular nation that is still the aspiration of most Turks today. Though he died in 1938, Atatürk is still in a way the bulwark against fundamentalists, terrorists and all the other bogeys that threaten the peace of Turkey today.

The Evil Eye

You'll notice them everywhere; hanging from necklaces, on babies' cradles, dangling from the rear-view mirror of a dolmuş, over the front door of a home, wherever there is anything of value and importance. The *boncuk* ('bead', sometimes called a *göz boncuğu*, or 'eye bead') is easily recognizable; sometimes big, sometimes small but always a circle or oval of blue, centred with two other circles to represent an eye. They are worn to guard against that unseen, most nefarious of forces, the evil eye.

Folklore dictates that some people, either knowingly or otherwise, have in their eyes an evil spirit that can do untold harm. The blue 'eye' medallion reflects this wicked spirit back to the originator, so that he or she who displays one has nothing to fear. The medallion can be made from any substance—usually glass, but sometimes stone, bone, shell, even silver and gold—the important thing is that it's there. One newspaper prints a *boncuk* in colour in the top corner of the front page, perhaps to protect readers against all the malevolent influences emanating from the news. Most of Turkey's evil-eye medallions are manufactured near İzmir, at the villages of Karabağler, Karşıyaka and Kadifekale. This is perhaps suprising, for this region is one of the most prosperous and developed in the country. But it is also a region that was Greek, not so long ago, and the *boncuk* is really Greek in origin.

In ancient times, the Greeks feared the mysterious influence of the eye, particularly the eyes of serpents or snakes, which they believed had the power of hypnotizing their prey. They called this power Βασκανια, a word that passed through Latin into modern languages as *fascination*. Some people have it too; you'll know you do, if you go to Greece, and old women cross the street when they see you coming. Something very similar to the snake's eye, surprisingly, is flattery. Any unsuspecting person can be the bearer of the evil eye in this manner. Compliments of any sort induce pride, and so invite Nemesis—especially where children are concerned.

Not only in folk customs, but in music, cuisine and nearly everything else, much of what you see in Turkey comes from the Greeks (the average inhabitant of western Anatolia has as much Greek blood in him as Turkish). The influence works both ways, of course; you'll still hear old men in Greece greet each other with *selam aleyküm—aleyküm selam* (peace be with you—with you be peace), like any good Muslim would. The two peoples lived together so long, and have so much that is similar—from worry-beads to coffee—it is often hard to disentangle them and puzzle out who influenced whom the most. In fact, the more time you spend in this part of the world, the more you'll think that Greeks and Turks are really the same people, divided only by language and religion. Maybe that is why they love each other so dearly. It's fortunate at least that both have their blue beads. With politicians on both sides constantly making the evil eye at each other, both peoples need them.

East and West

William Butler Yeats, in his murky meditation *A Vision*, wrote of east and west eternally contending. He saw them as alternately fertilizing each other with new cultures in successive ages. However you choose to interpret this aspect of the world's secret history, it undoubtedly exists, and Turkey is its battleground. The Aegean coast, in fact, has usually been the front line ever since the rise of the ancient Greeks. It may go back even further, to Mycenaean times, when early Greek people occupied the Aegean islands and part of the coasts. The Greeks do get credit for inventing Western civilization, of course, and looking back beyond them means looking into a glass that is very dark indeed. But remembering that both the Hittites and the Phrygians probably invaded Anatolia from Europe, it just might be possible that this old quarrel goes back even earlier.

As far as we know however, it begins with the Trojan War (of which there is still no reliable historical record—but sometimes legend can be more significant than mere fact). The next round, some 700 years later, was what the Greeks knew as the Persian Wars, an attempt by the greatest empire of its day to squash a minor but troublesome nuisance on its far western border. It was the Greeks' finest hour, and in victory they began to grow conscious of their strength. A century and a half after that, Alexander the Great carried Greek culture and philosophy triumphantly eastwards through Anatolia, and pushed the boundaries of the west as far as India—for a short time. His successors brought back roses, astrology and, among a hundred other things, the Persian concept of the divine ruler, without which the cult of the deified Roman emperors could not have been.

Christianity began its drive westwards in Asia Minor, in a score of towns and churches mentioned in the New Testament; from the Sufi poets, the Crusaders adopted the cult of chivalry; the troubadours, alchemy and many themes found in medieval literature owe their beginnings to Islamic culture. Today, the Republic of Atatürk heads the incursion of our secular, mercantile culture into the Middle East.

Somehow, Homer's epic had the power of summing up all this to-and-fro, and evocations of Homer fill the pages of Turkey's history. Like Alexander, Mehmet the Conqueror took time to visit Troy. In 1453, he declared that by taking Constantinople he had avenged the 'peoples of Asia' on the arrogant Greeks. On his entry into the city after the conquest, Mehmet, according to tradition, knocked off with his sword one of the serpent heads of the old bronze column that stood in the Hippodrome. This monument had been brought to the city by Constantine the Great, who had looted it from Delphi. There is probably no way Mehmet could have known that it commemorated the victory of the Greeks over the Persians at Plataea in 479 BC—almost 2,000 years before.

Eleven Days at the Pera Palace

Even if only to sip tea with pinky extended in its splendiferous lounge, try to visit the grand old Pera Palace Hotel in İstanbul. Walking in, you may feel time-warped, rushed back to the days when Europe's elite carved up the crumbling Ottoman Empire on paper and stroked their moustaches as a grand piano tinkled gently in the background. The Pera Palace was founded in 1892, to provide travellers on the Orient Express with suitable accommodation in İstanbul after their trying journey, and the original fittings are still here: the chandeliers dripping wealth, the antique carpets, the elaborate electric-powered elevator, the piano. It may be a five-star no longer—there is no swimming pool and the service is not what it once was—but few hotels have a better pedigree or are richer in charm.

Atatürk stayed here often, as did Edward VIII, the last Shah of Iran, Mata Hari, Greta Garbo, Tito and Jackie Onassis. Agatha Christie wrote *Murder on the Orient Express* here. In fact, there is an unusual tale concerning Agatha Christie and the Pera Palace. Christie 'lost' eleven days in her life. Neither she nor anyone else could account for her whereabouts during this time. In their film of her life, Warner Brothers accounted for the missing days as best they could. Their best wasn't good enough and the film was savaged by the critics. Affronted, Warner Brothers took the rather bizarre step of consulting a medium, Miss Tamara Rand, requesting her to call up the soul of Agatha Christie and solve the 'missing days' puzzle once and for all. Which is what happened—well, almost. Agatha Christie told Miss Rand that the key to the mystery could be found in room 411 of the Pera Palace Hotel, İstanbul.

On 7 March 1979, with the world's press gawking, a search of room 411 was made, aided by a telephone connection to Miss Rand in the States who gave the searchers long-distance directions after consulting Agatha Christie. Eventually, they found the key—literally. Under a wooden panel near the door was a large, rusty key. Warner Brother's representatives were ecstatic; they grabbed telephones to babble the good news to their bosses Stateside. As they did so, Hasan Süzer, chairman of the Pera Palace, quietly pocketed the key. Later, at a press conference, Süzer announced that he would give the key to Warner Brothers in return for $2,000,000, to be spent on sorely-needed refurbishments to the hotel.

Warner Brothers decided to go back to Miss Rand who called up Agatha Christie and told her their woes. She told Miss Rand that if the medium were to hold that key in her hand, she would be told the location of the long missing and long sought-after diary of Agatha Christie, in which would be the secret of the missing days. Warner Brothers hot-footed it back to İstanbul and begged the loan of the key. Negotiations were held. Eventually it was agreed that Tamara Rand would come to the Pera Palace on 20 August 1979, to hold the key and to reveal the site of the diary.

Unfortunately, on 30 June that year, staff at the Pera Palace began a year-long strike and the visit had to be postponed. During that year further negotiations collapsed and the two sides decided that they disliked each other enough not to care about unlocking the past. So it is that the key to the eleven missing days in the life of Agatha Christie now lies in a safety deposit box in a bank in İstanbul.

The Fatal Glass of Beer

After another hot day tracking down Phrygian ruins or Selcuk medreses in a small Turkish town far from the tourist trails, you might think a glass of beer would be a good idea. Depending on the town, you may unfortunately expire before you find one. These days, the influence of the Islamic equivalents of the bluenoses and prohibitionists that often plague America are having an effect. As in some rural county in Kentucky or Tennessee, there will be plenty of alcohol all around you, but you may have to ask a man with a red nose if you want to find any. Bars tend to be tucked away behind curtained windows, or upstairs, or in hotels; look for the blue and yellow *Efes Pilsen* sign. Most small towns also have at least one outdoor beer garden on an obscure side street. In any case, the availability of beer will always provide a convenient index of the mood and morals of the place you're in. The fundamentalists may wish to get rid of bars altogether, but in the secular Turkish Republic they must be content trying to keep them out of sight, so that innocent lads who never yet tasted beer need not suffer constant temptation.

Ever since Plato recommended mixing wine with three parts water, alcohol has been an issue in this part of the world. Ironically though, this recurring monster of Temperance exists in a land that has developed a great drinking culture. In the cities' cafés and restaurants, you'll see parties of men at their *rakı* sessions, with a bottle of the 'lion's milk' in the centre of the table. It goes down very slowly, interspersed with plates of mezes or snacks and plenty of lively conversation. Such an evening is a Turkish ritual, an art, and getting too drunk would be very bad form. The best place to do it is in an old-fashioned *meyhane*, or tavern, a smoky den that stays open late; you'll know you've found the right joint if someone produces a lute or other instrument and begins some impromptu music.

It is entirely possible that great ages of creative drinking go hand in hand with great periods of art. Certainly the Ottoman Empire was at its best during the 'Tulip Period' of the early 1600s. Encouraged by the example of the decadent sultans, İstanbul at that time was quite a swinging place. The famous Turkish traveller and writer Evliya Çelebi wrote of the hundreds of *meyhaneler* in the cosmopolitan quarter of Pera with amazement. Though these were largely patronized by infidels, notably sailors, Turks began to catch on. They had, after all, just introduced coffee to Europe, and the Europeans were returning the favour with beer and gin. There was already plenty of wine and *rakı*. The Greeks never stopped making it, and they ran most of the bars.

All things considered, the current trend for prohibitionism, or closed-curtainism, should only be taken as one more example of the tenacious continuity of history. All through the Ottoman centuries, it seems that periods of serious public tippling alternated with waves of reaction. Whenever a serious-minded sultan, prodded on by the imams, decided to clean up the Empire, the curtains would appear for a while, or the *meyhaneler* would be driven upstairs. The Turkish Republic so far has been a golden age for drinkers. Partially inspired by the example of Atatürk himself, who died of cirrhosis of the liver, drinking was respectable— also Western, and therefore a sign of modernity (not to mention the fact that the state monopoly was bringing in bushels of lire from its alcoholic products, in a country where more direct sorts of taxation have always proved problematical). There's a story that Atatürk once heard that one of his provincial governors went out drinking every night with his cronies, behind curtains in a hotel. 'Pull them down!' he ordered. 'With curtains up they'll think you have girls dancing on the tables too!'

Futbol

Not really a topic, more of an obsession. Turks are football fanatics, pure and simple, and if there's a game scheduled on TV, they'll cancel all else to watch it. They are very good at watching and are always keen to point out solemnly the deficiencies of a team, a manager, or an individual player. They're not so good at playing it, however, and the national team regularly gets trounced by all comers. The Turks are nothing if not good losers, and when reminded of their national team's woeful shortcomings, they just smile ruefully, tilt their heads back and raise eyes and palms imploringly upwards to Allah. Besides 1453, the capture of Constantinople or the various battles of the War of Independence, there's one historical date every Turk knows by heart. Ask any man when Turkey was last in the World Cup, and he will look down at the ground and mumble '1958'.

Of the Turkish teams, Galatasaray are currently the best. The most consistent winner, though, and by far the coolest, is Beşiktaş, in Juventus-style black and white stripes. Beşiktaş is an İstanbul team, as is the third perennial contender, Fenerbahçe. A good provincial team is Trabzon, from the Black Sea coast. Football matches are played from September to April on Saturday and Sunday afternoons; even if you are not especially interested in the sport, going along can make for an enjoyable excursion.

Despite their love of the game, the Turks still have a lot to learn about football, as exemplified by the reply of one young hotel porter when asked his opinion of the great English striker, Gary Lineker: 'Gary Lineker? Well, yes, he was alright. But all he could do was score goals!' But no one would deny the Turks have the proper sporting spirit. We caught a bit of a recent World Cup from a hotel balcony in a small Turkish town; in the evening, the owner of an electronics shop across the street pulled one of his new colour sets out onto the pavement, and brought out some chairs for his friends and anyone else who chanced to be passing by. Now and again someone would whistle for the boy from the bar down the street to bring tea. Greece was playing that night, and whenever the woebegone Greeks did something right, which wasn't often, the crowd that had gathered broke out into cheers—it wasn't the home side, but at least the next-door neighbours, so everybody wished them well against those foreigners from far-off Colombia. Try and imagine Greeks doing the same thing, if cruel destiny should ever be moved to let Turkey in the Cup again.

The Green Man

The vast spaces of the Anatolian interior pull at the heartstrings. Almost all of it is wonderfully lonely and wonderfully beautiful, with a hint of paradise and a hint of the Waste Land, sometimes side by side. So much time and history: the Turks often seem innocents to it, relative newcomers who've been in the neighbourhood a mere 800 years.

Somewhere, dozing off by a bus window driving through these endless landscapes, you may catch a fleeting glimpse of a man in green, riding a grey horse. *Khidr* (the 'green one') is a character of pre-Islamic mythology, though his origins remain unknown. There seems to be a mention of him in the story of Utnapishtim in the Sumerian *Book of Gilgamesh*, the world's oldest written epic. As Khizr, he is mentioned in the Koran as the 'unknown'; some old legends say he was vezir to a Persian king in the 6th century BC, who was blessed by God with eternal youth. Muslim Sufi mystics mention him often; his sudden and unpredictable appearances are a symbol for the inspiration or enlightenment that comes without warning. In a way, Khidr is a kind of patron saint for the Sufis, and he made his way into Europe with so many other tales and legends in the early Middle Ages, the time of the Crusades and the troubadours, when the influence of the more civilized Muslim world was extremely strong, much stronger than you will ever read in conventional Eurocentric histories.

Christian stories taken from Islamic sources sometimes transform him (God knows why) into the prophet Elijah, or St George. Reminders of this mysterious character turn up in unexpected places, in the 'Green George' of Gypsy and Slavic spring festivals and, some scholars contend, the 'Green Man' of so many English pub signs. We might see Khidr also in that greatest of medieval allegorical poems, *Sir Gawain and the Green Knight*, a profoundly mystical work whose meanings have never been completely explored. And there is little in Professor Tolkien's *Lord of the Rings* that doesn't strike an echo from somebody's mythology; we shouldn't be surprised to find the Green Man turn up here too, in the person of Tom Bombadil. Khidr has been with the Turks since they first rode off the far Asian steppe into Anatolia. He is mentioned in the *Legends of Dede Korkut*, the collection of epic tales from the Oğuz Turks' nomadic days that was first written down in the 1400s. In the *Tale of Boğaç Khan*, he appears out of nowhere to save the life of the wounded hero; miraculous cures, often involving the 'water of life' are often attributed to him.

The Turks of today, besides being wonderfully meticulous farmers and gardeners, must also be among the most manic tree planters on the globe. The first thing you'll notice in İstanbul, if you haven't been there for a while, is the trees—a few hundred thousand of them, in a belt of brand-new parks that line the Marmara shore and the Golden Horn. Someone comes out to water the younger ones nearly every day, and they all look green and thriving despite the city's notoriously bad air. In many parts of the interior, the *Orman Genel Müdürlüğü*, the national forestry service, has done wonders with scant resources in preserving forests and reclaiming land wasted by millennia of deforestation and neglect. We have an entirely unconfirmable suspicion that Khidr spends a lot of his time in Anatolia. Travelling west from Beyşehir to Konya, through some of the bleakest and emptiest spaces Turkey has to offer, your eyes will fall on a vision: tiny young pines planted over the hillsides for miles and miles, stretching belief as they stretch on and on. This is the Atatürk Centennial Forest, a wonderfully quixotic and uneconomic attempt at creating a huge forest on what was previously barren land. In all there must be several million trees already planted. Look closely; you might catch sight of him there.

Music

Music is an important part of the Turks' cultural heritage and still one of the things they do best. Western travellers unsympathetic to it have given Turkish music a bad name, calling it monotonous; even if you don't go out of your way to find it, you'll hear enough of it on radios and in buses to get accustomed to it and make up your own mind. What you hear most of, unfortunately, is something called *oryantal* ('oriental') or *arabesk*, a noxious Arab-influenced pop style. Irritating as it is, the vocal strength and feeling of the performers, especially the women, makes Western popular music sound like a nursery school pageant.

Western classical music came into fashion with Atatürk, although the last sultans had cultivated opera and kept large dance orchestras. Today it is quite popular, and several Turkish singers and musicians have made names for themselves abroad. The Turks have their own classical tradition, however, and you hear what they call *sanat müziği*, 'art music', anywhere, even in night clubs. At first, this was heavily influenced by the Mevlevi dervishes; its main instrument is the lute (our word comes from the Arabic *al ud*). The lutes hanging in

Turkish music shop windows differ in no respect from those in medieval tapestries and illuminations; the Crusaders brought them back from Anatolia. To this the Mevlevis add the *ney*, a ghostly, reedy flute. Both types of music are ruled by modes (*makamlar*), like ancient Greek music. Their subtleties will require all your attention and goodwill.

The real treat, however, is Turkish folk music, which Béla Bartók said was the richest he had ever experienced. The *âşıklar*, rural troubadours who improvise to a stringed instrument called the *saz*, similar to the lute, can still be found (there may be one seated next to you on a bus) and folk music and dancing are still practised widely (the Black Sea and Aegean coasts, Konya, Kars and Silifke are especially known for them). Wild dances for men like the Aegean *zeybek* and the *horon* of the northeast are its most spectacular manifestation, along with popular, mainly improvised dances like the *çiftetelli*, traditionally performed at weddings. Besides the *saz* and lute, other instruments are the clarinet and accordion, a two-headed drum called the *davul*, the *kanun* (a 78-stringed dulcimer related to the Hungarian cimbalom), the *kaval* (shepherd's pipes), the *kemençe* (a tiny violin played like a cello) and the *cura* (a sort of zither that has been traced back to the Hittites).

Finally, there's the inimitable *Mehter* music played by the Janissaries under the walls of Vienna and a thousand other towns to dishearten the defenders. With the aid of enormous drums carted around in their own wagons, the 60-piece Mehter bands made grand and gloriously noisy music (you can hear a Mehter concert any afternoon at three, at the Soldiers' Museum in İstanbul). Though its art and melodiousness were probably lost on the besieged garrisons, Mehter is the ancestor of all our military music and marching bands; it has also found its way into western classical music through the Turkish bagatelles of Mozart, Beethoven and Weber.

Perusing the *Polis*

There are certainly plenty of other things to do on Turkey's coasts, but as far as sightseeing goes one item stands out above all—ruins. No place around the Mediterranean, possibly no place in the world, has so many once-thriving cities that simply became abandoned and disappeared. Thanks to the earthquakes that regularly shake down all the products of human vanity in this part of the world, not too much of these cities is left standing. To get anything at all from your visit requires a little imagination, and a little knowledge. Here is a very brief primer on Greek cities, so you'll know your way around when you visit one.

A Greek city was more than just a convenient place for people to live and work. It was the sacred *polis*, from which we get words like politics and politeness (the Romans carried on the idea in their *civitas*; to be 'civilized' was to live in a city). The Greek *polis* was a noble creation, unlike anything the world had known. These little walled towns, self-governing and self-sufficient communities of free citizens, were the seeds from which our Western culture grew. As its living heart, each had its *agora*, much more than just a central square. At first only an open stretch of ground at the centre, with a platform for speakers at the citizens' assemblies, the agora also served as a marketplace, and there were also religious shrines or images, and many statues of civic benefactors, victorious soldiers and athletes (and later, the reigning Roman emperor; often they'd just knock off the head and stick on a new one when a new emperor was proclaimed). Greeks did not compartmentalize the various aspects of their public life the way we do: the political, the sacred, civic monuments and day-to-day business shared the same space, a symbol of how life in the *polis* was a seamless whole.

To define the agora, the Greeks came up with an invention perfectly suited to their climate and their way of life: the *stoa*, a long, colonnaded portico, usually closed by wings at the ends. The 'stoic' philosophers took their name from the stoa, because that is where they liked to gather—along with the rest of the population, it seems. At all hours of the day, the stoa gave citizens an attractive place to spend their idle time and talk about the weather or argue about politics. Greek stoas were infinitely adaptable; some excavated examples show stone tables for meat and fish stands. The same ones might have been used at other times by bankers and merchants, or by the city's courts to hear cases. You'll have to go to Athens to see the reconstruction of a stoa, but they were always mentioned as among a city's major architectural works, often with famous frescoes on the inner wall; Pergamon, always the flashiest of cities, had some that were two storeys tall.

The two important public buildings of the *polis* will also be found around the agora: the *bouleuterion*, or council house, usually in the form of a small, enclosed theatre; and the *prytaneion*, the city's 'common house'. Here a perpetual fire was kept on the sacred hearth, as a symbol of its communal life of the city; a separate room served as a dining hall, in which the city could offer hospitality to distinguished visitors, ambassadors, or citizens who brought home victories from war or the games.

In Hellenistic times, planners began to think symmetrically, and when there was a chance for rebuilding they started making perfectly rectangular 'peristyle' agoras surrounded on all sides by stoas (there is a good example at Ephesus; the same idea was used in the Imperial Forums of Rome). Originally stoas would also be built that closed off one side of the agora, and continued from there down one of the main streets—a pretty trick of town design to make a gradual transition from the private spaces of the residential districts to the public space of the agora. In the opulent conditions of the 1st and 2nd centuries AD, this idea grew into the **colonnaded street**, the main status embellishment of any town of the Roman Empire. These often extended as far as the town gates. Towns that had two or more of them, such as Side, Perge or Ephesus, were really doing well. Whenever you're exploring a ruined city in Turkey, it should be remembered that most of what you see dates from this period, when the economy of Asia Minor reached its height; it was then that the most impressive public buildings, the basilicas and the gymnasia were built. Only towns, like Priene, that did not flourish in Roman times give the full effect of what a classical Greek or Hellenistic city was like.

The greatest temples, however, were raised in the 5th–3rd centuries BC. Before Roman rule, when the ethos of the Greek city-state was at its height, individual towns competed to build the most impressive temples, as the towns of medieval France vied to build the biggest cathedrals, or American cities the tallest skyscrapers. A Greek temple did not have to be in the centre of town: its site was usually determined by ancient tradition, some place that had been holy for centuries or even millennia. The temple itself was a relatively late idea, and never the centre of religious observance, the way a church or a mosque is. It housed a cult image (usually a statue), as well as ex votos and other gifts to the sanctuary; architecturally it served as a kind of stage backdrop for the sacrifice and other rites. In the sophisticated, secular age of the Empire, temples were little more than glorified art museums.

The important business of Greek religion was the sacrifice, and this took place in the open air. The *temenos*, or sanctuary, dedicated to a god, is the holy ground where sacrifices were performed, and it could be in or near the agora, or anywhere else, even out alone in the countryside. The temenos would usually be walled off, and it would contain the altar for sacrifices, with the temple façade behind it to the east, as well as a home for the priests or priestesses, and often a sacred grove; important sanctuaries might be entered by a monumental gateway, a *propylaea* or *propylon*. Originally the altar itself was just a simple slab or even a heap of stones—every passer-by would add another to the pile. But by Hellenistic times these often grew into magnificent buildings, such as the Altar of Zeus at Pergamon.

Of the Greeks' homes, you will see almost nothing. It would be surprising how simply they provided for themselves, did we not know how all-important was their communal life. There were neither sharply defined wealthy districts nor slums. The Greeks never minded rubbing elbows with their fellow citizens, of whatever condition; and their houses differed little in outward appearance or in any other way besides size. Few details of Greek houses are well known, only that the fancier ones were built around courtyards. In Roman times these often developed into impressive peristyle courts, with a fountain or pool at the centre.

Where the outlines of streets survive, as at Priene, you'll notice they usually run straight as arrows. The first town planner whose name has survived is Hippodamus, an Ionian who redesigned the port city of Piraeus in a gridiron plan for the Athenians in the 5th century. Hippodamus did not invent this sort of plan, but brought it back from his home city of Miletus, which had recently been rebuilt on a grid plan after its sacking by the Persians. Rectilinear street plans came naturally to the geometrically-minded Greeks; in the colonies of Asia Minor, this form was the easiest way to lay streets, measure land accurately, and get a new town started, just as it was in 19th-century America.

The Greek ideal of *paideia*, intellectual and physical education, treated as one, is symbolized in the *gymnasion*, usually a large complex of buildings that included an enclosed *palaestra*, or exercise ground, but also classrooms and lecture halls (Plato's Academy was a gymnasion). If space permitted, there would also be plane trees for shade (any kind of greenery was very rare in a Greek city), a spring or fountain, and often a temple, perhaps dedicated to Hercules or Hermes. In Roman times the gymnasion grew much more luxurious; palestrae became monumental colonnaded courtyards, and often a bath complex was added on—Pergamon, as usual, gives the most lavish examples. Occasionally, where there was room for it, there would be a *stadion* too, a course for footraces so called from the measure of length (about 200 yards). Classical stadia were simple open spaces with an earthen bank on one side for spectators; real stadia, with marble seats, colonnades and elaborate entrance gates, did not arrive until Roman times.

The first Greek theatre was the agora itself; in archaic Greece the open space of an agora was often called the *orchestra*, a word that means a 'dancing place'; it is a reminder of how classical theatre grew up out of the rites and dances that attended the cult of Dionysos. To accommodate growing populations, cities began to build proper theatres wherever there was a natural slope, with a banked, semicircular area for spectators called the *theatron* (or *cavea*), sited wherever possible with a grand panoramic view for a background to the play. When the classical plays were first performed, the orchestra (generally circular or trapezoidal, and unpaved) was still the centre of the action. Only in later centuries was a *skene*, or stage, built; this logical and adaptable feature served much the same functions as the simple, two-level stages we usually use for productions of Shakespeare. Again, only in Roman times did impressive columned stage buildings appear, and they were never universally popular in Greek towns. Neither were the Romans' barbaric gladiatorial games, which explains the lack of amphitheatres in Greek cities—though in many places you can see the Greeks slipping, and building walls around an orchestra to protect spectators at such games. It's a sad sight: theatres meant for the works of Euripides and Aeschylus being transformed into arenas for butchery. Nothing could illustrate more clearly the decay at the heart of that opulent age.

Religion

In the *hadis*, the collection of traditions and stories from the days of Mohammed that serves as a commentary on the Koran, it is recorded that the angel Gabriel, disguised as a Bedouin, confronted the Prophet one day and demanded to know the practices of the true belief. Mohammed's five answers satisfied the angel, and, as the 'five pillars of Islam', they continue to guide Muslims today, a solid foundation for the simplest of the world's great religions.

One of the pillars is the professing of the simple formula 'There is no god but Allah and Mohammed is his prophet.' This is painted or inscribed in elegant Arabic calligraphy over all the mosques of Turkey. Another pillar is the pilgrimage to Mecca, for all who are able. Giving alms to the poor is a third; however, begging is frowned upon and the mendicant dervishes and kalenders have been outlawed since 1925, so this duty is performed discreetly.

Muslims are also expected to keep a total fast during the daylight hours of Ramazan, the holy month of the Muslim calendar. In public, at least, the fast is well observed. During Ramazan a mood of peaceful contemplation occupies the faithful. Much of radio and television airtime is given over to religious programmes, and every evening at sunset in many towns a cannon booms out the signal that the fast has ended. Mosques are often gaily decorated with coloured lights, nowhere more so than in İstanbul where Koranic messages are spelled out in strings of lights between the minarets of the great imperial mosques.

The most conspicuous of the five pillars is the obligation of saying prayers five times a day, at hours proclaimed by the muezzins from the minarets (often now via loudspeakers attached to the minarets). It is permitted to perform these anywhere, and although Muslims usually go to the mosques for the midday Friday prayers, there is no Mass or ritual in the Christian sense. In the main, Islam avoids ritual and ceremony. The imam (priest) is present merely to lead the prayers; the formulaic discourse he declaims afterwards is hardly a sermon.

Mosque architecture illustrates the simplicity of Islam. Most are large halls furnished only with the mimber (pulpit), and the mihrab (the niche in the wall facing Mecca), which concentrates the thoughts and prayers of the faithful like a lens. Non-believers are allowed inside Turkish mosques, except during prayer time. Leave your shoes at the door, dress sensibly (no shorts, short skirts, or bared arms and shoulders) and don't make a nuisance of yourself, but don't feel unwelcome either. Muslims themselves enjoy coming to the mosque for meditation and quiet, and they are pleased to share them with you. To miss the interiors of the Ottoman mosques of Bursa and İstanbul and the Selcuk 'Great Mosques' of the cities of Anatolia would be to miss much of the finest in Turkish art and architecture.

One Islamic ceremony you may encounter accompanies the rite of circumcision: a small parade with a bravely smiling nine-year-old in a costume, crown and cape. Most weddings in Turkey are civil and the ballyhoo and decorated cars differ little from those in other lands; the busy marriage chapel next to İstanbul's city hall is a good place to watch them.

Most Turkish Muslims are Sunnis, the majority, orthodox creed, but all around the country you'll find a substantial minority of Alawis (or Alevis), a fascinating sect who have no mosques. They do have a refreshingly relaxed and tolerant attitude about religious matters, combined with a practice of equality of the sexes and often radical political beliefs. Alawis include groups around the Black Sea, the Bektaşi dervishes (see p.453) and entire villages inhabited by the nonconformist *Tahtacılar* in the southern mountains. They are also strong among Turkish intellectuals.

According to the last census, 99.04 per cent of Turkey's population are Muslim, but there are no figures on how many practise their religion seriously. During the 1930s, when Turkey was hell-bent on reform and secularism, religion became unfashionable, at least in the cities. Today, Turkey, like many of its neighbours, is experiencing an Islamic revival. The late President Özal was a *hacı* (the title for someone who has made the pilgrimage to Mecca), and in many towns, mosques that were once almost empty for Friday prayers are now almost full. Big money pouring in from Saudi Arabia and elsewhere finances not only the fundamentalist Refah Party, but scores of rabble-rousing preachers and tract publishing houses; you'll notice the stands they set up on weekends outside the main mosques.

Much like what is happening now in the United States, a strange and shadowy battle is currently underway in Turkey for the hearts and minds of the people. The fundamentalist forces, well organized and well financed, have so far been able to manipulate the masses, portraying any and all political issues as a struggle between good and evil. Those who support the secular republic of Atatürk seem confused and divided amongst themselves. They have yielded ground for many years, but there seems now to be a stalemate. No one knows how this struggle will end, but the spectre of the radical side of fundamentalism should not blind the visitor from the diversity—and beauty—of Islam in this country. Religion's moderate voices here have some interesting points to make, and they show a sincere concern for Turkey's future. More than in most Muslim countries, a gentler and more tolerant side of Islam has always flourished in Turkey, a long tradition best symbolized by the figure of Celâleddin Rumi, the Mevlâna.

The Sultan of Scholars

Islam has no saints, but Celâleddin Rumi, poet and Sufi mystic of Konya, approaches as nearly to that exalted state as is allowed. For Westerners who have never been able to take Islam seriously, he is the man to know. Born on 30 September 1207 in Balkh, Afghanistan, Celâleddin and his family—his father Bahaeddin Veled was a renowned scholar—fled before the Mongol invasions to Anatolia, where they took refuge in the Selcuk capital, then in its heyday under Sultan Alâeddin Keykubad. Here he remained as a teacher in the city's mosques, withdrawing more and more into his meditations and his poetry until his death on 17 December 1273. The Mevlevi order of dervishes—the 'whirling dervishes'—he founded was tremendously influential throughout the Middle East, and the hereditary line of its sheikhs, descended from the Mevlâna (literally 'our master'), even intermarried with the Ottoman dynasty during the reign of Beyazıt I.

Few poets in the world have been more prolific. His greatest work, a subtly arranged medley of lyric poetry, mysticism and anecdotes called the *Mesnevi* (or *Mathnavi*), runs to some 25,000 couplets (longer than the *Faerie Queene*, the longest poem in English), and there are 44,000 more couplets in the anthology called the *Divan of Shems-i Tabriz*. The title of a third work, *Fihi-Ma-Fih*, 'in it what's in it', clearly expresses the Sufi informality and disdain of dogmas and church establishments. All were written in Persian, the language of court and culture in Selcuk times (good translations of selections exist, notably by Professors Nicholson and Arberry).

The Mevlâna's poetry has been described as an ocean; vast and boundless, encompassing all the systems and creeds of lesser men within it. In truth there is no readily discernible philosophy in his work that does not state the obvious; the Mevlâna wanted it to appeal to all men at all levels. The unity of God and of creation is a recurring theme, consistent with Islam and the teaching of the Sufis. It is the revelation of divine love that sets his work apart, and the spiritual allegory of the 'lover' and the 'beloved', the soul and its dissolution into the infinite, is the core of his thought. On this rarefied plane of understanding, the claims of the various religions seem mere games of language, and issues such as predestination or free will simply cease to be relevant.

As for the whirling dervishes, the Mevlâna and his followers believed as much in music and dance as forms of spiritual expression as they did in poetry. The *sema*, the ritual dance still performed annually in Konya on the anniversary of the Mevlâna's death, 17 December, is his teaching of the abandonment of the self set into motion. The dervishes' tall hats represent their own gravestones, the jackets, which they shed, their graves. As the dancers spin around the floor, symbolically reflecting at once the movements of the cosmos and the soul's search for God, the dancers themselves attain a controlled mystic communion. With one hand raised and the other extended towards the ground, they '…take from God and give to man, keeping nothing for themselves…'

Language Quiz!

You may well know more Turkish than you think. Try and puzzle out these common words:

şoför	küaför	şantöz	komplo	şofben
org	otogar	fayton	şanjman	pardesü

Partly thanks to the *Lise* (*lycée*) of Galatasaray, where the late Ottoman Empire's elite was trained, French cultural influence has always been strong here, and hundreds of French words insinuated themselves into the language, mostly for modern inventions and innovations. After Atatürk's revolution all of these were spelled out phonetically in Turkish, so they may not look familiar at first glance. The answers: chauffeur, coiffeur, chanteuse, *complot* (a conspiracy), *chauffe-bain* (a water heater), *orgue* (organ), autogare (the bus station), phaeton (the horse-drawn carriages they still use on the Princes' Islands), *changement* (gearshift), *par-dessus* (those ugly overcoats pious Muslim women have to wear).

İstanbul

Just to vex the Turks, the Greeks still insist on calling it Constantinople, and print it that way on all their maps. The Ottomans never really meant to change the name; they probably thought of themselves as the successors of the Romans, just as the Byzantines had, and they did their best to keep Constantine's column in good repair. But, through centuries of trade and diplomacy with the Greeks, they had often heard this fabulous remnant of antiquity referred to as *stin poli* or 'in the city'. Turkish has no prepositions, and to their ears it must have sounded like one word.

The name stuck, and what could be better for such a place than to be called, simply, The City. To the Turks, the Mongols and other peoples of distant Asia, this was a kind of half-mythical land of dreams, known more through poets than historians or travellers, just as Cathay and the Indies were for medieval Europeans. All these Asian peoples migrated west to the 'Land of Rome' and its golden capital, and one day made it their own.

For sixteen centuries, İstanbul was the metropolis of the eastern Mediterranean. The Byzantines had a word for their legitimate heirs to the throne, those sons of emperors born in the famous Purple Chamber of the palace: Porphyrogenitus, or 'born to the purple'. This we can take as a title for the city itself, whose location astride both the land and sea routes between east and west guaranteed its long rule. There is a sinister aspect to this. İstanbul, under both the Byzantines and the Ottomans, was the most predatory city the world has ever known save Rome itself, sucking the economic lifeblood out of hundreds of provinces—even entire nations. For a long time, its matchless fortifications protected, even encouraged, the kind of decadence that nature and history usually root out of societies. Only now is the city just waking up from the terrible Ottoman hangover; it can take its place as a modern commercial emporium, realizing what a blessing it is to have the burden of governing lifted from its shoulders.

Its new burden, and one it gladly accepts, is carrying the Turkish economy; one-third of the nation's factories are here, and more than two-thirds of İstanbul's population of over 12 million are recent migrants from Anatolia, come to try their luck in what may already be the largest city in Europe. The old diversity of peoples remains, even increases; added to the long-established Greeks, Armenians and Jews are vast numbers of new arrivals from Eastern Europe, the Middle East and Turkophone Central Asia.

İstanbul will not disappoint. It is inexhaustible, pleasant to walk around, full of surprises. You could take your old aunt here on holiday or have a Bohemian dream vacation, live like a tycoon or a tramp. For those who have already been to İstanbul, if your last visit was more than a few years ago it's time to have another look—you'll hardly know the place today. İstanbul is booming, perhaps blossoming, a mildly schizophrenic metropolis of skyscrapers and street vendors, where some women wear veils and others the latest in Italian designs. All the energies of the nation seem concentrated in it now, as the millennary City transforms itself, while doing its best to drag the rest of Turkey with it into the 21st century.

History

Byzantion was already a sizeable town when the decision was made to transform it into an imperial capital. Set on the Bosphorus, bridging Europe and Asia, it was certainly the logical site for one, and it's surprising that no one took better advantage of its strategic position before Constantine the Great. The town's acropolis stood roughly where the Topkapı Palace is now, and archaeologists have uncovered fragments going back to Mycenaean times. The Greeks had a legend, though, that the city was founded by a certain Byzas of Megara in the 7th century, the great age of Greek expansion and colonization.

By the 3rd century AD, decadent Rome had already been largely abandoned by the emperors. Concerned above all with maintaining the two key strategic fronts, the Danube and the Euphrates, many of them kept their court at Milan, or at places like Sirmium and Serdica (Sofia) in the Balkans. The Balkan region, in fact, was one of the most important of the late Empire. Most of the army and its generals came from there, and more than a few emperors, including **Constantine** himself. As soon as he had consolidated his hold on the empire, Constantine began work on his new capital, in AD 328.

Like Rome, the new city was said to have seven hills (*see* p.93). It was given its own lavish dole, a racetrack, a Forum and its own Senate. The fleets of ships that had previously brought Egypt's bounty of grain to fatten Rome were now rerouted to Constantinople. Constantine meant the new capital not only as a base to defend the two hot edges of his realm and as a monument to himself, but for a third purpose too: creating a specifically **Christian city** as the capital for his new Christian Empire. No pagan temples were allowed to be built. Facing the new Forum, the Augusteion, rose one of Constantine's great basilicas, later rebuilt as the **Aya Sofya**. Constantinopolis' official date of birth was 11 May 330, the day the city was consecrated by Christian priests.

With the rich imperial subsidies and building programmes, Constantinople rapidly grew into the metropolis of the eastern empire, drawing population and economic life from the older cities of Greece and Asia Minor and beginning their fatal decline. A second wave of growth and embellishment of the city came with the reign of Justinian (527–65). As the booty rolled in from Byzantine conquests around the Mediterranean, Justinian found the money to rebuild the Aya Sofya, the imperial palace and much else. The beginning of his reign, however, saw the most serious outbreak of civil strife in the city's history: the **Nike Riots** of 532, really a full-fledged popular revolt against the emperor's oppressive rule, crushed by the army with tens of thousands of deaths.

After Justinian's bloody but glorious reign, Constantinople hung on for almost a thousand years as the capital of a venerable, declining, somehow unsinkable empire. For all that, it has surprisingly little history of its own. By the 12th century, appearances were still kept up but both empire and capital were mere shadows of their former selves. The new quarter of **Galata** was growing up across the Golden Horn, largely inhabited by the Italian merchants —Genoese, Pisans, Amalfitani and above all Venetians—who had seized control of the empire's economy. So resented were the predatory Italians that in 1180 a Greek mob massacred those they could catch; the state exiled the rest soon after.

In 1203, the Venetian fleet ferried the largely French troops of the **Third Crusade** down to Constantinople on their way to the Holy Land. The Crusaders couldn't pay their passage, and so the Venetians arranged a clever intervention into the empire's affairs. Alexius, the rightful heir to the Byzantine throne whose father had been deposed in a coup, agreed to pay the bill if only the Crusaders would get him back his throne. That was easily done, but the empire was broke and Alexius could not come up with the money. Another coup drove Alexius out, and in February 1204 the Crusaders and Venetians decided to take the undermanned city. After a siege of two months, they smashed their way in, the first time anyone had done so in 900 years. The sack that followed may well have been the richest in all history. The Westerners took their time and methodically looted everything, nailed down or not, and the Venetians, who had masterminded the whole affair and completed the Italians' revenge for 1180, got the lion's share—including the famous bronze horses of St Mark's, which originally stood in the Hippodrome.

Constantinople would never be the same. For the next forty years, the city endured life as capital of a ludicrous French-run 'Empire of Romania', and when the Greeks retook the city in 1246 under Emperor Michael Paleologos, they had neither the cash nor the energy to restore it. Constantinople's last two centuries were a sad affair, with much of the city centre in ruins; even the court deserted the old palace for the newer Blachernae Palace out by the Theodosian walls. It was those incomparable **walls**, besieged so often by Bulgars, Avars, Arabs and Turks, that kept the dilapidated capital and the pathetic empire in business for another two centuries, while the Ottoman Turks were gradually grabbing all Anatolia and the Balkans and eventually even building castles on the Bosphorus.

The end finally came in 1453, with the determined Sultan **Mehmet**, along with his matchless army, modern fleet and the most advanced artillery in the world. Largely empty, and defended by a handful of Greeks and Venetians, Constantinople fell after a siege of two months. Getting the city back on its feet again proved to be a much greater task than capturing it, but Mehmet proved as capable a ruler as he was a Conqueror. The presence of the court itself helped in the economic revival, but Mehmet also moved quickly to re-establish the Covered Bazaar, the cornerstone of the city's economy, while pumping in lots of money for public works: fixing up the walls, streets and water supply, and building the **Topkapı Palace** and scores of mosques. Incentives were given to get people to move back into the city and improve property. His successor, Beyazıt II, resettled thousands of Jewish refugees, who had fled from Spain after 1492, starting the city off on its new career as a polyglot, cosmopolitan city where Turks, Greeks, Armenians, Jews, Arabs, Slavs, Albanians and every other nationality lived side by side. Beginning with Mehmet, each Sultan in turn embellished the city with new mosques, pavilions and religious foundations. 'The City' was back in business.

From the 17th century to the First World War, The City did not share fully in the Ottoman decay; it monopolized whatever art and architecture, modernity and economic progress there was. Non-Turks, particularly Greeks, dominated both business and culture, and the Greeks' Phanar (**Fener**) quarter grew into a city within the city. İstanbul really opened to the West after 1839, the year of the Tanzimat reforms. Foreign businessmen poured in to take advantage of the empire's weakness, and **Beyoğlu**, or 'Pera', transformed itself into a proper European city where French was more commonly heard in the streets than Turkish.

All this was a mixed blessing. The reign of **Abdülhamid** especially (1876–1909) was a disaster for İstanbul, as it was for the rest of the empire. With the state desperately in need of foreign investment and technology, the city was completely at the mercy of the foreign interests Abdülhamid's vezirs invited in. The beautiful shore of the Golden Horn was degraded into an industrial nightmare, while the new railroad line to Sirkeci Station devastated the equally scenic Marmara side.

In 1919, British and French troops occupied İstanbul. The British government hoped to prop the gormless Mehmet V on the Ottoman throne as a puppet, while gaining de facto control of the straits for itself, plans that came to naught with the victory of **Atatürk**'s nationalists. Much of the Greek population fled though, like Mehmet, Atatürk took pains to reassure those who stayed behind. Though no longer a capital, İstanbul remained the economic heart of Turkey and its window to the West. One of the saddest, and least remembered, events in İstanbul's recent history was the **anti-Greek riots** of 1955. The whole story has been pretty well buried by now, but from the evidence it seems that local elements of the Menderes government and Democratic party had plotted to whip up sentiment against foreigners to distract attention from the country's economic problems. For a week, mobs burned out churches and monasteries, and attacked businesses belonging to Greeks, Armenians, Jews and others. When it was over, a majority of İstanbul's already dwindling non-Turkish population quickly decided to move elsewhere.

İstanbul Today

Over the last two decades, the big story has been the tremendous surge of **migration** into the city. Mostly rural folk, some 400,000 a year from every corner of Turkey, come to try their luck. İstanbul is where the jobs are. The newcomers have been a tremendous burden on the city's resources; water and public health head a long list of serious urban problems. Even so, the immigrants are contributing their hopes and hard work to a city that is changing faster than at any time since Mehmet the Conqueror—a city alive, exploding with energy.

You'll see the new İstanbul clearly if you arrive from the east; after the car passes over the Bosphorus Bridge you're on the ring motorway, the Çevre Yolu; for miles you'll look down on vast new neighbourhoods, full of attractive blocks of modern flats. Amidst these are **shopping malls** as modern as anything in California, and over it all rises a new crown of **skyscrapers**. The two tallest are the headquarters of the Koç and Sabancı holding companies, the two giants that between them now run much of the Turkish economy.

There's a new **metro**, progressing slowly, two new **tramways**, a ring motorway, and a second suspension **bridge** over the Bosphorus. New **suburbs** have gobbled up almost all of the countryside along the Bosphorus, and for sixty miles down the Asian shore. In the 1980s major infrastructure and slum clearance programmes were begun under Mayors Bedrettin Dalan and Nurettin Sözen. Much of the impetus for all this came from İstanbul's as yet unsuccessful bids to host the Olympics. Because of that, a large part of the effort has been devoted to cosmetics—most spectacularly, the ambitious plan to reclaim all of old Stamboul's **waterfront**. Already over half the Golden Horn and Marmara shores have been cleared and turned into parkland. It may not look too impressive for a few decades, until the tens of thousands of trees have grown up, but people then will be praising the Stamboullu for their foresightedness and care for their city.

Getting There
by air

They're building a metro line out to **Atatürk International Airport**, but no one has any idea when it will be finished. In the meantime, your options are a **taxi** ride, which should cost about $14 from the centre, or the inexpensive **HAVAŞ bus** connection, from the THY Turkish Airlines office near Taksim Square in Beyoğlu. This runs every 30mins until 9pm, and less frequently at night. The bus also stops on Mustafa Kemal Caddesi in Aksaray—and if you ask the driver he'll probably let you get off anywhere else you like. This bus also serves as the only connecting link between the airport's foreign and domestic terminals, which are about a mile apart. If you need to **change money** when you arrive, the bank offices in the foreign terminal give as good a rate as anything you'll find in town.

Atatürk International Airport, ✆ 0212 663 6400
THY Turkish Airlines, Atatürk Airport, ✆ 0212 663 6363
Atatürk Airport domestic terminal (**Yeşilköy**), ✆ 0212 573 2920

by train

The days of the Orient Express are long gone, but just in case you should be riding the Turkish rails, know that European destinations are served from **Sirkeci Station**, ✆ 0212 527 0050, at the tip of Stamboul's peninsula; besides international arrivals the main event here is the daily train to and from Edirne. Trains for Ankara and everything else on the Asian side (also to Russia) begin at **Haydarpaşa Station**, in Kadıköy (✆ 0216 348 8020). The express runs to Ankara (the Fatih Ekspres and the overnight Yataklı Ekspres) have the most comfortable cars and best services in the country, and are the only train runs in Turkey that come close to competing with the buses in speed and price. The only way to get from one station to the other, besides a ludicrously long taxi ride over the Bosphorus Bridge, is to take the ferry from outside Haydarpaşa to Karaköy, by the Galata Bridge, and then walk or take a taxi to nearby Sirkeci. The ferry and taxi combination is also the quickest and cheapest way to get from Haydarpaşa to the touristic heart of İstanbul in Sultanahmet.

by coach

Every traveller will agree that the new main coach station, **Büyük İstanbul Otogarı**, at Esenler, out in the far western suburbs, is one of the most gratifying of the city's many recent improvements. Instead of the old Topkapı Station, a vast, chaotic and sometimes dangerous mudflat outside the walls, there is a completely modern facility, a bizarre, space-age architectural apparition among the grim concrete *gecekondu* ('put up overnight') suburbs. Every bus that comes to İstanbul uses it. If you're heading for any big town there will be no need for a reservation; just turn up and you'll probably be on a bus within ten minutes. Getting there is no problem. The new **tram/metro** from Aksaray Meydanı pulls right into the middle of the station (about a half-hour trip), or else you can take a **taxi** for about $9 from Sultanahmet (which includes the $1 fee the taxi driver has to pay to leave the bus station again). If you're arriving in İstanbul from anywhere in Asian Turkey, your bus is likely to stop at the **Harem Otogarı** in Asian İstanbul before continuing to the main coach station. The quickest way to Sultanahmet is to get off at Harem and catch the **ferry** across to Sirkeci, from where it is a short taxi ride to Sultanahmet.

Getting Around

Many travellers take one look at İstanbul's medieval street plan on a map and surrender to despair, a feeling that is confirmed after the first attempt at reaching a destination on foot ends in utter bewilderment.

It isn't really so bad; as in most old cities, remember that the streets are laid out to make sense to your eyes, more than to be read on a map. After walking for a while through old İstanbul, you'll learn to orientate yourself to the major landmarks. Public transport in all forms is refreshingly inexpensive. If you are staying in İstanbul for more than just a few days, you may consider buying an **Akbil tab** (a small plastic keyring with a magnetic button in the end) which gives you discounted travel on most buses, trams, subway trains, ferries and seabuses, and more importantly saves you the trouble of buying tickets or tokens each time you need to get somewhere. These can be bought for $2.50 at kiosks with the sign '*Akbil satışı*' and can be topped up with credit at booths with the sign '*Akbil satılır*'.

by bus

İstanbul's transit system, the İETT, doesn't publish a route map, so until you learn your way around the best thing is to walk over to the nearest main station, as all lines begin and end at one of these: **Beyazıt Square**; **Eminönü**, in front of the Spice Market by the Galata Bridge; **Karaköy**, on the Beyoğlu side of the Galata Bridge; **Sirkeci Station**; **Taksim Square**; **Beşiktaş**; and on the Asian side **Harem**, near Haydarpaşa Station. Unless you have an Akbil tab, you'll need to buy tickets beforehand. You can buy books of them at the unmarked orange kiosks at these stations; more conveniently, men in the street will sell tickets to you for a few pennies extra. Aypa publish a quite detailed city map which includes a bus map and a list of the İstanbul buses and their routes, though the map can be hard to find. Buses are efficient and cheap, but they will usually be indecently crowded. Tickets, at time of writing, sell for 50¢. The word for bus stop is *durak* or *otobüs durağı*; signs are usually painted orange.

In distant parts of the city you'll also encounter *Halk Otobüsleri*, 'people's buses', a special service provided by suburban councils; these usually have a conductor to sell tickets.

İstanbul has the beginnings of a modern rapid transit system. Don't expect an underground—just imagine the difficulties of digging one here, with all the world's archaeologists looking over the workmen's shoulders. Instead, there are two inexpensive above-ground tram lines, which run underground where they can. One, the **Çağdaş** line, or **Metro**, starts from Aksaray Meydanı underground, then surfaces and heads out to the coach station in the distant suburbs on the European side. This will eventually be part of a metro network; work on a second line heading north from Taksim Square is under way. The other line, the **Hızlı** ('speedy'), is an above-ground tram that starts at Eminönü near the Yeni Cami, runs to Sultanahmet Square and then down the Divan Yolu, Stamboul's main street, ending up at Zeytinburnu, past the Topkapı Gate. (A third line runs from Sirkeci Station around the tip of the peninsula and along the Marmara shore, but it isn't much use to visitors.) The tram/metro lines use different (equally cheap) tickets from the buses; every stop has a booth that sells them but they aren't always open: carry a few around. İstanbul's most entertaining public transport is on the Beyoğlu side. If you're travelling from Galata Bridge to Taksim, you'll first meet the **Tünel**, the world's shortest underground (and one of the oldest) with the world's smallest tokens, sold in booths at either end. The Tünel is an inclined railway, which gets you from the bridge up the steep hill to the bottom end of İstiklâl Caddesi. From there, you can take the delightfully named **Nostaljik Tramvay** up İstiklâl to Taksim Square—real turn-of-the-century streetcars, carefully restored, with conductors in costumes to match.

by taxi

All the taxis are yellow, all have meters, and you'll have no trouble finding one on any major street. In the day, the meter should read *gündüz* (daytime). After midnight fares go up, and the sign reads *gece* (night). Drivers often stick resolutely to the main thoroughfares to avoid traffic jams, even if this seems to go out of your way. Taxis are inexpensive—less than $3 for an average trip in the city—and invaluable when you get hopelessly lost. If you're staying in a small hotel or in an out-of-the-way street, be sure to write the name down, as well as any nearby main streets or landmarks, as the drivers often don't know the city as well as they might—especially when you try to pronounce your destination in Turkish. One strange custom here—if you cross over one of the Bosphorus bridges, you'll be expected to cough up the toll.

by dolmuş

The bad news for anyone who loves İstanbul is that dolmuşes seem to be on their way out. The other means of transport—minibuses, İETT buses and trams—work well enough that it is becoming hard for the individual dolmuş driver to make a living. Nevertheless there are still a few operating around the centre, especially around Taksim. The dolmuş is a communal taxi. Getting into one is easy; just wait near one of the red, white, and black dolmuş signs, or hail one from anywhere on the street, see if the destination sign on the roof of the car is anywhere near your own, and pile in. In some outlying parts of the town, they're simpler to use than the buses, and equally inexpensive.

by minibus

These work much like the dolmuşes, and operate mostly from the city walls, going down the main streets of İstanbul; few penetrate further in than Beyazıt Square. Above all they'll be helpful if you mean to do some exploring around the Theodosian walls and the outlying quarters of old Stamboul. Like the dolmuş they have destination signs. Don't mistake Topkapı Gate for Topkapı Palace.

by boat

Outside Venice, there's no city in Europe better for messing about in boats. For many Stamboullu, a ferry ride with this remarkable cityscape for background is just a part of the daily commute. Ferries for all points depart either from docks on either side of the Galata Bridge, or the Kabataş landing near Dolmabahçe Palace. Cruises up the **Bosphorus** (Boşaziçi) depart from the Stamboul side of the bridge (pier 3, just to the right of the bridge), usually twice a day; you can get off where you please, or stop for lunch and catch the boat on the return trip, from any of its stops along the straits.

Ferry-boats to the **Asian side** go up to four times an hour from Galata Bridge (the docks nearest Sirkeci Station; departing from pier 1 to **Üsküdar**, or from pier 2 for **Kadıköy** and **Bostancı**), and from Kabataş for **Üsküdar**. Other boats for **Kadıköy–Haydarpaşa Station** leave from Karaköy landing, on the Beyoğlu side of the bridge (City Ferry Lines Information © 0212 244 0207).

For the **Princes' Islands**, several boats a day (more in the summer and at weekends) leave from both Galata (pier 5, behind Sirkeci station) and Kabataş landings. Some are express, getting to Büyükada in about an hour; others call at all four islands and several Asian ports as well. Note that you only pay for the trip to the islands—the return fare is included in the price. The shortest trip to the islands is from Bostancı landing on the Asian side. Another, less frequent, boat from pier 5 goes to **Yalova**, across the Marmara; there are also boats from Kabataş to Yalova. From the pier to the left of the Galata Bridge on the Stamboul side (pier 6), a boat leaves every half-hour to go up the **Golden Horn** (Haliç) to Eyüp and beyond.

Other boats leave from the docks near Tophane Square for **Marmara Island** (five hours) and **Avşa Island** (six hours) in the Marmara, and for Mudanya, the port of **Bursa**. Ticket booths are never clearly marked; in some cases you cannot buy tickets in advance, but most lines run on tokens that can be used anytime. Don't expect to find timetables posted, or any sort of system; the chaos of the İstanbul ferries is of Byzantine complexity. Just go and ask; with luck, someone behind a window will sell you some sort of ticket or token. Then, when you see a crowd gathering around a boat, try and push your way to the front.

car hire

If you're willing to risk the İstanbul traffic, and ridiculously high rates, the major car hire chains are here:

Avis: airport, © 0212 663 0646; Taksim Square, © 0212 241 78 96
Budget: airport, © 0212 663 0858; Taksim Square, © 0212 237 2919
Europcar: airport, © 0212 663 0747; Taksim Square, © 0212 254 7799

The tourist office has a long list of (often cheaper) local firms. At a pinch, try:

Er Rent, Topçu Caddesi, Taksim, ✆ 0212 235 5990
Oscar, Mustafa Kemal Paşa Caddesi, ✆ 0212 588 3057

For anyone driving in İstanbul, some explanation is in order. First of all traffic is nowhere near as insane as many would have it; from end to end of the town, it hardly ever moves fast enough to let the Turkish driver express himself. Parking is the real problem. Don't worry so much about parking tickets—but if you leave your beast in a really dumb place it could well be towed.

Tourist Information

Sultanahmet: facing the Aya Sofya, ✆ 0212 518 1802.
Beyoğlu: Meşrutiyet Caddesi 57, ✆ 0212 245 6875.
Taksim Square: in the Hilton Hotel lobby, ✆ 0212 233 0592.
Karaköy: at the cruise ship dock, ✆ 0212 249 5776.
Yeşilköy: Atatürk airport, ✆ 0212 663 0793.
Tourist Police: Yerebatan Caddesi 2, near the Aya Sofya, ✆ 0212 527 4503.
TTOK: Halaskârgazi Caddesi 364, ✆ 0212 231 4631.

post offices

There are branches all over town, including one in the Covered Market and one in İstiklâl Caddesi, Galatasaray, but the big one is near Sirkeci Station, on Yeni Postane Caddesi. This is where you should have *poste restante* mail sent: Post Restante, Büyük Postane, Yeni Postane Caddesi, İstanbul. All big offices have telephone services, which usually stay open until 10pm or even midnight.

laundry

Behind the Aya Sofya on Caferiye Sokak is Hobby Laundry which, in addition to offering a fully automatic washing and drying service, will serve you tea and coffee while you wait. *Open daily 9am–8pm.*

maps and publications

All the usual rules for Turkish cities apply here: there are very few street signs, streets are known by different names to different people, and many people know nothing of the city outside their own neighbourhood. Although the map handed out by the tourist office is perfectly adequate for most needs, if you plan to do any detailed sight-seeing, you'll want a better one; of the several available, the best are published by the Turkish Automobile Club (available at their offices) and by Keskin Colour (from hotels, news stands, and shops in the tourist centres).

Currently, the indispensable reference for events in the city is a monthly publication in English called *The Guide*, available from any of the bookshops below. *Hello İstanbul*, a free monthly guide to the city, is available from hotels. The best selection of books in English about İstanbul and Turkey will be found in the booksellers' stalls of the **Sahaflar Çarşısı**, on the Beyazıt Square side of the Covered Bazaar. Another good place is the bookshop in the lobby of the **Sheraton Hotel** on Taksim Square. Other shops offer rather less: most of these can be found along İstiklâl Caddesi, just north of the Tünel: **Haşet, Sander** and **ABC**. They also sell the previous day's editions of Europe's leading quality papers, plus *Time* and *Newsweek*. For the British tabloids, try the **kiosk** at the Yeni Cami end of the Spice Market.

money

Those needing a bank over the **weekend** will find one open, 9.30am–4pm, at the entrance to the Topkapı Sarayı. İstanbul also has two 24-hour post offices, one near Sirkeci railway station (the main PTT on Postane Caddesi), the other at Kadıköy in Asia. The Galatasaray office, on İstiklâl Caddesi, has fax facilities and is open until 8pm. Local post offices close at 6pm. Most people change money at the little *döviz* offices that have sprung up all over the city; you'll generally get a better rate, and with some asking around you'll find one that takes travellers' cheques.

Credit Card Hotlines

American Express: ✆ 0212 283 2201
VISA/Mastercard/Eurocard: ✆ 0212 225 0080
Diners Club: ✆ 0212 212 0800

youth discount card

Good value for **under-26s**, this can be bought from the front desk of the Interyouth Hostel on Caferiye Sokak behind the Aya Sofya. It grants free admission to most government-maintained museums, such as the Topkapı Sarayı and the Aya Sofya, and pays for itself after two or three visits. The card is valid throughout Turkey.

Orientation

A brief orientation will help in sorting out the complexities of the layout. Note that there are three parts. On the European side, the triangular peninsula south of the estuary of the Golden Horn is **Stamboul**, the old town (formerly Constantinople and Byzantium) which rises like Rome on seven hills, surrounded by the largely intact Byzantine walls; most of the sights—the Aya Sofya, Topkapı Palace, the Covered Bazaar, Süleymaniye Camii and the Blue Mosque—are concentrated within the square mile of its tip. We mention this only because you may not notice. Whether you're on foot or in a cab, the impenetrable maze of meandering streets makes them seem to be in different parts of the city. Study the map before you set out.

Two bridges span the lower end of the **Golden Horn**: the Atatürk and the famous, newly-rebuilt Galata, connecting old İstanbul with **Beyoğlu**, the 'European quarter' ever since Italian merchants colonized it in the latter days of Byzantium. Its outer fringes have been fashionable for two centuries now. Galata Bridge, and the Eminönü Square behind it in the old town, are the nearest thing İstanbul has to a centre; the busy comings and goings here were a feature of İstanbul life before there was a bridge, going back to the days of the Byzantines.

Ferryboats from Galata Bridge go to the districts of the Asian shore: **Kadıköy, Haydarpaşa** and others. The Bosphorus protects them, and has kept them quiet residential suburbs for centuries. Up the Bosphorus, İstanbul's metropolitan area has absorbed the picturesque villages on both sides, almost as far as the Black Sea.

Central İstanbul

N

500 metres
500 yards

1 Gate of Salutations
2 Harem
3 Gate of Felicity
4 Audience Chamber and Library
5 Wardrobe and Treasury
6 Revan Köşkü and Bağdad Köşkü

Golden

to Cistern
of Aspar

HALİÇ CADDESİ

ABDÜLEZEL PAŞA CADDESİ

UNKAPANI EMİNÖNÜ

Church of
Christ
Pantepoptes

CİBALİ CADDESİ

BOSTAN HAMAMI S.

Pantocrator
Church

HAYDAR CADDESİ

ATLAMATAŞI CAD.

FATIH

to
Fatih Camii

HACIKADIN CAD.

FATİH TÜRBESİ S.

İTFAİYE CADDESİ

BULVARI

Kilise
Camii

VEFA CAD.

to Amcazade
Külliyesi

MACAR
KARDEŞLER CAD.

Municipal
Museum

M

CEMAL YENER

KİRAZLI MESCİT S.

Süleymaniye
Camii

SÜLEYMANİYE C.

Aqueduct
of Valens

TOSYALI CAD.

Marcian's
Column

HORHOR CADDESİ

ŞEHZADEBAŞI CADDESİ

Şehzade
Camii

Burmalı Minare

Kalenderhane
Camii

İstanbul
University

DARÜLFÜN

ATATÜRK

AKSARAY

Valide Camii

GENÇTÜRK CADDESİ

Lâleli
Camii

LÂLELİ

CAD.

Beyazıt
Camii

MİLLET CADDESİ

ORDU CADDESİ

YENİÇERİLER CADDESİ

Beyazıt
Square

Mireláon
Convent

MESİH PAŞA CADDESİ

LİVAN

KOCA RAGIP CAD.

VAHYA

PAŞA

SOKAĞI

NAMIK KEMAL CADDESİ

MUSTAFA KEMAL CADDESİ

KÜÇÜK LANGA CAD.

HAYRİYE TÜCCARİ CAD.

KURBAN SOKAĞI

TÜRKELİ CADDESİ

KUMKAPI

ÇİFTE GELİNER S.

FLORYA SAHİL YOLU

KENNEDY

CADDESİ

to **Balıkpazarı**

Şişhane Square

BEYOĞLU

KUMBARACI YOKUŞU

Tünel

Museum of Divan Literature

İSTİKLAL CAD.

YOLCUZADE CAD.

OKÇUMUSA CAD.

AIRZIYA PAŞA CAD.

Tophane Square

to **Nüsretiye Cami**

Sokullu Camii

St Benoit Church

YÜKSEK KALDIRIM

Kiliç Ali Paşa Camii

Galata Kulesi

KEMERALTI CADDESİ

NECATİBEY CADDESİ

GALATA MUMHANE

Arap Cami

VOYVODA CAD.

TERSANE CADDESİ

Atatürk Köprüsü

Tünel

Yeraltı Camii

Karaköy Square

Horn

to **Üsküdar**

Bosphorus

Galata Köprüsü

İNKAPANI EMİNÖNÜ

TAHTAKALE CADDESİ

Rüstem Paşa Camii

Eminönü Square

HASIRCILAR CAD.

Seraglio Point

Atatürk Monument

SİMAVİDAĞAS SOK.

EMİNÖNÜ

Yeni Cami

Ferry Docks

HAMİDİYE CADDESİ

SİRKECİ

KENNEDY CADDESİ

Spice Market

YENİ POSTANE CAD.

CADDESİ M. HÜDAVENDİGAR CAD.

Sirkeci Station

Goths' Column

HESPÇEŞME CAD.

FİRİNCİLAR YOKUŞU

Main Post Office

EBUSSUT CAD.

HATUNI CAD.

Archaeology Museum, Museum of the Ancient Orient, Çinili Köşkü

UZUN ÇARŞI CADDESİ

MAHMUT PAŞA

TÜROCAĞI CAD.

Vilâyet

ANKARA CADDESİ

6

Beyazıt Kulesi

FUAT PAŞA CAD.

Mehmet Paşa Camii

BEZCİLER SOK.

Cağaloğlu Baths

4

5

2

Sahaflar Çarşısı

Covered Market

Nuruosmaniye Camii

NURUOSMANİYE CAD.

YEREBATAN C.

Sublime Porte

Gülhane Parki

3

Topkapı Sarayi

Beyazıt Camii

CAĞALOĞLU

Çemberlitaş

1

Aya İrene

Çorlulu Ali Paşa Medrese

Atik Ali Paşa Camii

DİVAN YOLU CADDESİ

ALEMDAR CAD.

SOĞUK ÇEŞME SOK.

Karamustafa Medrese

PİYERLOTİ CAD.

KLOT FARER

BABIALI CAD.

SULTANAHMET

Kaiser Wilhelm II Fountain

Yerabatan Sarayi

Bab-i Humayun

Fountain of Ahmed III

TİYATRO CADDESİ

TÜLCÜ SOK.

Firuz Ağa Camii

Museum of Turkish and Islamic Arts

Sultanahmet Sq.

MİMAR MEH. MET CAD.

Aya Sofya

ÇORLU PAŞA CAD.

Mehmet Paşa Camii

Binbirdirek Cistern

Blue Mosque

Aya Sofya Baths

KABASAKAL CAD.

KUTLUGÜN SOK.

KADIRGA CADDESİ

TERZİHANE SOK.

Hippodrome

TAVUKHANE

Küçük Aya Sofya

S. KÜÇÜK

AYASOFYA CAD.

MUSTAFA PAŞA S.

Mosaic Museum

CANKURTARAN CAD.

Bucoleon Palace

KENNEDY CADDESİ

Sea of Marmara

91

The Streets of İstanbul

You may come to this city for the monuments and museums, to see the sultan's jewels or the gold of the Byzantine mosaics, or simply to watch the sunset over the skyline of minarets and domes. The fantasies you entertain may be out of the Arabian Nights or an Eric Ambler spy thriller of the 1930s. Whatever your particular purpose, take care that you keep your eyes and ears open to the life in the streets. This is the real İstanbul, for which the mosques and palaces are merely decoration, and the people of the city have had centuries to cultivate this life of İstanbul into an art form.

Especially in the small things, İstanbul has sacrificed little to modernity. If your hotel is in one of the older residential districts, like Aksaray or Sultanahmet, you are likely to be awakened to the cry, *Nefis...simit, simit...*—'exquisite *simitler*'—and the man who carries these sesame-encrusted circles of bread, on a stick or in a glass box, may differ only in dress from those in 16th-century prints. If you were a Stamboullu, you might drop down a basket on a long rope for one. After the *simit* man comes the tinker's rattling empty cart, and his long unintelligible cries seem less a plea for trade than an eternal rambling monologue on God's unfairness to tinkers.

Of course there are street markets: some of the old quarters are named after the day of the week on which they would occur. In İstanbul, though, in the Middle Eastern manner, every street is an actual or potential market. Some have permanent sites: by Galata Bridge each morning housewives and stray cats circle around tired fishermen, angling for their share of the day's catch, while, opposite, in the narrow maze of streets climbing to the Covered Bazaar, the metal doors bang open to reveal thousands of tiny shops, segregated into streets according to their trade: an avenue of baby clothes, a street of copper pots, a cul-de-sac of used Korans. More money probably changes hands on the bridge itself than in a large department store. On Galata Bridge, on any given day you may spend a few lira on socks, wind-up monkeys, copies of the Turkish Highway Code, contraband blue jeans, clothes hangers, pastel knickers, aubergines, spanner sets (Imperial or metric), bicycle mirrors, hamsters, or portraits of Mehmet the Conqueror.

To all these, add the shoeshine boys: young apprentices with cheap wooden boxes and old paint tins to sit on, and dignified professionals with dozens of cut-glass bottles in gold-plated cases, embellished with scenes of Mecca and autographed pictures of overripe chanteuses. Sellers of sherbet, *ayran*, unidentifiable pastries and even water abound. The fellows with the jingling sacks and packs of untaxed Marlboros are on the lowest rung of Turkish organized crime; you choose a number, pick a numbered token from the sack, and if you click, the Marlboros are yours. You can try your hand at shooting with the young men who have invested their capital in an air rifle and target, or patronize the poorest of all, those whose business consists of a single rusted set of bathroom scales, waiting to weigh all comers—perhaps 10 people a day, when business is good.

As background, add the beggars (more than in Paris, fewer than in Philadelphia), military policemen, hosts of shabby-genteel cats and pigeons, farmers on donkeys, tourists from Iran and Indiana, seven hills, 1,300 minarets, gypsies, ferryboats, Roman cisterns, and the strangest Art Nouveau buildings east of Palma de Mallorca.

The older neighbourhoods have no monopoly on all this; it is the everyday ambience the Stamboullu takes for granted, varying in degree from the venerable precincts of Eminönü and Sultanahmet to the newer streets around Taksim Square and those on the Asian side, but never especially dirty or dilapidated. The old town is the real surprise. Following Turkish rather than European ideas of town planning, there are lots of trees, and the houses are as spread out as land values permit. Many of the outlying districts are really suburbs within the Theodosian walls, or better, aggregations of villages.

The Seven Hills

Constantine very consciously meant to make his foundation the New Rome; that was its name at first, until the emperor's vanity overcame him. Like the old Rome, it had a golden milestone, a Senate House and a Forum; to govern it, Constantine divided it up into fourteen wards, just as Rome had been divided, and, most importantly for imperial continuity, he declared that it had seven hills.

Finding some of these requires an effort of the imagination. Only three reach any height: the **First Hill**, where the Topkapı Palace and Aya Sofya stand; the **Fifth Hill** along the Golden Horn with the Fener and the Selimiye Cami; and the **Third Hill**, crowned by the Süleymaniye. None of the others will strain your legs: the **Second Hill**, roughly north of the Burnt Column; the **Fourth Hill**, around the Fatih Mosque; the **Sixth Hill**, at the Topkapı Gate, the centre of the land walls; and the **Seventh Hill**, in the southwest corner of the city.

Old İstanbul (Stamboul)

Sultanahmet Square

Most visitors begin their tours of İstanbul in the old city in **Sultanahmet Square**, the lovely garden of fountains and flowers between Aya Sofya and the Blue Mosque. A pavilion housing a very helpful **Tourist Information Centre** is here, near the **Kaiser Wilhelm II Fountain**, a small gift from Sultan Abdülhamid's big brother in Berlin, in the days when Germany was the declining Ottoman Empire's greatest ally. The low buildings along the southern edge, the **Aya Sofya Baths**, are among the few that survived the modern reconstruction of the square, when acres of Ottoman buildings were cleared (*see* below, p.97).

If you could have stood here in Byzantine times, however, you would have been in the city's grand ceremonial square, the **Augusteion**. Just to the left of Aya Sofya, the main street of the city passed through the Bronze Gate. A tall column bearing a golden statue of Justinian stood in front of the church, and near it was the golden milestone from which all distances in the empire were measured. The baths of Zeuxippos, a domed structure probably not unlike the modern Turkish hamams, occupied the western edge of the square, and, next to this, the bulk of the Hippodrome could be seen behind the towers of St Stephen's. The south edge fronted the Senate House, where the last remnant of the Roman Republic survived as a rubber-stamp council almost until the end of Byzantium. The emperors could be seen in this square at their accessions, and on the feast days of the Church. After the sack of 1204, when the Crusaders looted the square of its gold and ornaments, the area drifted gradually into ruin. Already the emperors had moved to the Blachernae Palace in the suburbs, and the restored empire after 1261 lacked the resources to keep up the church. One 14th-century traveller wrote of finding the great church eerily empty, its doors lying on the ground.

You may feel the same, and may hear the ghostly echo of Justinian's 'Solomon, I have surpassed thee!', as you walk under the dome of the denuded church, once glowing with golden mosaics and chandeliers, a golden altar and iconostasis.

The Aya Sofya

Open Tues–Sun 9–4, later in summer; adm.

Since 1933, the Aya Sofya has been a museum, and lacks even the prayer rugs and mihrab to relieve the tremendous desolation. Even so, in its present state, the lack of ornamentation perhaps makes the beauty and audacity of the architecture easier to appreciate. Undoubtedly this is the greatest dome in Christendom, though St Peter's in Rome and St Paul's in London are larger. In the 6th century, nothing like the Aya Sofya had ever been built, or even imagined, and even today the impression that it makes cannot be experienced anywhere else.

The original Aya Sofya, which the Byzantines called simply the Great Church, was built by Theodosius II in 415, on the site of an even earlier church built under Constantine the Great. Theodosius' Aya Sofya burned during the street battles of the Nike Revolt at the beginning of Justinian's reign (*see* p.108). To provide a symbol for his dreams of imperial grandeur, and to a certain extent to justify them, Justinian determined to rebuild as quickly and on as large a scale as possible. The cornerstone of his new church was laid exactly 40 days after the suppression of the revolt.

Building Aya Sofya

The two men chosen to design the church were not really architects. Not long before, the emperor had decreed an end to the Athenian Academy, the centre of learning of the classical world, and the last stronghold of philosophy untainted by the Gospels. In doing so, he put two of the greatest mathematicians of the age, Anthemius of Tralles (modern Aydın) and Isidore of Miletus, out of work. Between them, they accepted the job, and got it built in only five years. The imperial treasury had been strained to the limit, but the new Great Church was consecrated in solemn ceremony on 26 December 537, St Stephen's Day.

The difficulties in the construction were manifold; no architect alive had experience of a task of such magnitude. Improvisation was a daily necessity. The four massive piers on which the entire structure is hung have stones held together not with mortar, but with molten lead. The distinctive shape of Aya Sofya's capitals is no mere design conceit, such as those of the classical Greeks; it is absolutely necessary to the structure. The 'impost capital', as it is called, had already been invented to give proper support to arches and vaults, but here it was perfected. One of the problems was reconciling the strengths and weaknesses of so many different types of stone. Just as the emperor spared no expense in getting in the best architects and workmen, every variety of stone in the empire is represented here: green marble from the Peloponnese, yellow from Libya, rose from Phrygia and Lydia, great slabs of porphyry that were floated down the Nile from upper Egypt. Ancient buildings were looted for tall columns; of those in the galleries, the red are from the Temple of the Sun in Baalbek, the green probably from the Artemision of Ephesus.

In the Church

One enters the church just as a Byzantine commoner would, through side gates in the outer porch (the exonarthex). The centre gate was for the emperor alone, and it continues through a long thin hall to the narthex. Here, where the emperor passed into the church itself, one of the surviving gold mosaics portrays Emperor Leo IV kneeling before a seated Christ. Below, on the brass lintel, the Holy Spirit descends with a book, open to the words, 'The Lord said, "I am the door of the sheep: By me if any man enter in...he shall find pasture."' An empty throne stands concealed behind.

You can usurp the emperor's privilege and walk right in. The central gate opens at the rear of the great nave. As you pass through, turn and look up at the best-preserved **mosaic** of the church, the Virgin Mary cradling the infant Jesus. To her right, Constantine offers her the city of Constantinople; to her left, Justinian proffers the Aya Sofya. More mosaics, mostly geometric and floral patterns, cover the rest of the narthex roof. Though many of these have not yet been restored, they will give you some idea of how the decoration of the church's interior must have looked. One of the first things Atatürk did after converting Aya Sofya to a museum was to arrange for the restoration of the mosaics. The work was done over the next two decades by the Byzantine Institute, a private organization in Boston. Justinian's church had no mosaics: they were a later fashion, and those that remain—of the original estimated four acres—date mostly from the 9th century or later, after the defeat of the Iconoclasts.

As you approach the centre of the church, you realize the particular architectural problem Anthemius and Isidore faced, and their brilliant solution. For reasons of grace and symmetry, with a little bit of geometric mysticism mixed in as well, the emperor wanted a central plan, symmetrical on two axes. The forms of Byzantine ritual, however, required a basilica-plan church with a long nave. To accomplish this, Anthemius flanked his dome with two semi-domes along the axis of the nave and enclosed the space under the lateral arches with solid walls full of windows. Underneath these, the mass is distributed down to the ground through a network of smaller semi-domes (exedrae), vaults and columns, thus opening to the light a space six times the area of the dome. This conquest of gravity is the magic of Aya Sofya. Sixth-century chroniclers tell of visitors and citizens afraid to enter lest all collapse, or becoming dizzy trying to look at the top of the dome, 181ft above the floor. The Byzantines always spoke of this dome as being suspended from heaven by a golden chain.

Artistic details in the interior are few; little survived the Iconoclasts, the Crusaders and the Muslims. The bronze doors of the narthex are original, and the monograms of Justinian and Theodora can be seen on many of the capitals. The largest mosaic, on the apse above the place where the altar stood, is a portrait of the *Virgin Mary with the infant Jesus*; below it, figures of the Archangels Michael and Gabriel can be made out. In place of the altar and iconostasis, only the Muslim mihrab and mimber fill the void, along with the raised loge built for the prayers of the sultans, with İznik tiles and fine carved wood details. The four huge medallions on the columns, painted calligraphically with the names of Allah, Mohammed and the early caliphs, were removed by Atatürk but have recently been replaced as a gesture to the Muslim fundamentalists (also, they have recently started broadcasting the call to prayer from Aya Sofya's minarets). Above the medallions, four sinister-looking Byzantine seraphs stare down from the pendentives.

The Muslims, like the Greeks, segregated their women, putting them upstairs in the spacious galleries around the nave, making them climb about 50ft of ramps to get there. It's worth the walk, for the view and for the best of the remaining mosaics. In the centre of the galleries, at the far end of the church, two green columns from Ephesus mark the place where the empresses worshipped. The ladies, in fact, had only the **North Gallery**; the **South Gallery** was reserved for the rest of the imperial family—the Turks gave the lovely screen that partitioned it off the fanciful title of 'Gates of Heaven and Hell'. A celebrated series of the 13th-century mosaics, one of the last improvements to the church under the Byzantines, can be seen around the gallery: Emperor John Comnenus and his family, Empress Zoe and her third husband (his face painted over that of number two) and Jesus with Mary and John the Baptist. On the floor near this last one is a slab inscribed with the name Henrico Dandolo, the aged, bitter Duke of Venice who led the Sack of 1204. Surprisingly, the Greeks never disinterred him when they recaptured the city; the Turks did, within weeks of Mehmet's conquest. This south gallery often served for the transaction of church business; two General Church Councils, the second and the sixth, were held in it. High on a wall of the adjacent gallery is a faded mosaic of the Emperor Alexander who ruled only from 912 to 913. The inscription above his diademed head reads: 'Lord help thy servant, the orthodox and faithful Emperor Alexander.' Lord help him indeed. He was a habitual drunkard who died of apoplexy after a particularly heavy session.

You may be disconcerted to see that very few of the columns of the galleries are actually in plumb. Some list at alarming angles, many are cracked and bound with iron rings, and the impression of a house of cards is inescapable. Even before Atatürk, the Turks kept a constant vigil over this fabulous patient, on and off the critical list for 14 centuries. Anthemius and Isidore, for all their skill, could not make their church perfect. The dome, shallow enough now, was originally 20ft lower, and had to be reconstructed when a 40-day series of earthquakes toppled it in 558. In the 10th century, the next thorough restoration kept the church closed for 10 years. Again in the 14th century, a collapse seemed imminent; the emperors scraped the bottom of the treasury to construct the four colossal buttresses that so mar the exterior. No more money could be found to complete the repairs, and by the time of the Conquest, the church was no longer in use. Mehmet added more buttresses and the first minaret, and Mimar Sinan himself tore down much of the ruined old imperial quarter to get stone for further strengthening. Seven thorough restorations since have accomplished the preservation of the mosaics and the reinforcement of the dome with steel; specialists are still on guard for any further signs of weakness. The galleries, they say, are in no danger now—though yet another extensive (and expensive) restoration programme is now under way; expect the interior to be graced with plenty of scaffolding for years to come.

The theology of the Muslims would, on the whole, have seemed almost acceptable to a man like Justinian, and, as fate would have it, the Muslims were to be the vehicle for preserving his symbol and his dream over the centuries. Justinian must surely have thought the building of his church would mark the advent of a new world age. His choice of men from the Academy to put it up was as much symbolic as practical. Here, the entire harvest of classical science and philosophy was to serve the ends of the Christian God. The Muslims, who already had taken their own deep draughts of Greek thought, felt entirely at home after 1453. More than any other place in the Christian or Islamic worlds, this is the great house of monotheism, the place where human understanding and accomplishment were recognized as the Divine Wisdom, the *Hagia Sofia* both faiths believed it to be.

Around Aya Sofya

Just outside the main entrance, recent excavations have uncovered the foundations of the portico of Theodosius's church; an architect's reconstruction posted by the door shows an elegant classical building, architecturally a bit old-fashioned. Some bits of the columns and the cornice have survived, with reliefs of the Lamb of God.

The Muslims had more of a sense of humour than the Christians. In the **mausoleums** they built around Aya Sofya's garden were interred nearly all the worst of the worst Ottoman sultans: Mustafa I, an imbecile and tool of the Janissaries, İbrahim the Mad, the ultimate libertine who picked off his subjects from the Topkapı walls for target practice, and Selim the Sot, whose honorific tells us all we need to know. His mausoleum, decorated with fine İznik tiles, is a work of Mimar Sinan. Facing the row of mausoleums is the pretty, covered **Fountain of Mehmet II**, and a primary school built by the same Sultan in 1742.

Behind the Aya Sofya, adjoining the walls of the Topkapı Sarayı, the indefatigable restorationists of the Turkish Automobile Club have rebuilt an entire street of characteristic Ottoman wooden houses, **Soğukçeşme Sokak** ('Cool Fountain Street'), many of which are now in use as guest houses. This is only one part of their plan for beautifying the centre of old Stamboul. South of the Blue Mosque, they have a complex including shops in a restored medrese and the lovely wooden **Yeşil Ev Hotel**, one of the best-restored examples of Ottoman vernacular architecture in İstanbul.

Also behind the church, a famous monument of the Tulip Period (*see* p.102) can be seen as introduction to another aspect of Turkish architecture. The **Fountain of Ahmed III**, built in 1729, really a small pavilion, is covered with a wealth of green and blue tiles painted in floral motifs, and with verses of the emperor who built it. Yet another beneficiary of cosmetic surgery, its tiles and gilt trim shine with their original splendour, highlighting one of the finest works of the Ottoman 18th century, one that captures perfectly the super-refined and delicate sensibility of the 'Tulip Period'. There is much more of this behind the walls of Topkapı; the outer gate, the **Bab-i-Humayun**, stands only a few yards away.

Between the Aya Sofya and the Blue Mosque, the **Aya Sofya baths** have become the Turkish Handwoven Carpet Sales Centre. Don't let the name fool you. Once Sultanahmet's most elegant, most regal hamam, this was built by Sinan in 1556 on the orders of Süleyman the Magnificent to honour his favourite wife, the cunning and perfidious Roxelana. The first room is domed, and adorned with 16 lovely arched stained-glass windows. The baths lead on through three rooms into the central steam room, with numerous cubicles secreted away around it for more personal bathing, and continue onwards for its full length. This was a double, mixed-sex hamam, men bathing at one end, women at the other. Ignore the carpets draped everywhere and picture the place as it once was, a haven of refreshment for the empire's most illustrious. Or if you're crazy for carpets, compare what is on offer here with the fine antique works in the **Museum of Turkish Carpets and Kilims** or Halı ve Kilim Müzesi (*open daily exc Sun and Mon, 9–4; adm*), just around the corner on Mimar Mehmet Ağa Caddesi.

The Blue Mosque (Sultanahmet Camii)

Across the square from Aya Sofya, Sultan Ahmet in 1619 constructed the Sultanahmet, or the Blue Mosque, like a matching bookend—not so much to compete with the old church, but because all the other available sites already had big mosques on them. Even then, he had to knock down the palaces of several of his ministers to make space. None of the city's other monuments has occasioned more argument; some critics claim it is the finest work of architecture in the city, while others say it is overdone and uninspired. Certainly there are no new departures in the plan; just another copy of the Aya Sofya, only more rigidly symmetrical than the others. Like Mimar Sinan's mosques, the plan is an almost perfect square.

The main attraction here is the interior with its 21,043 blue İznik tiles, predominantly painted with the blue arabesques that give the mosque its familiar name. Each one of these tiles set Ahmet back 18 *akçeler*—twice the daily wage of a teacher in the palace school. The great dome, 70ft across, stands on four semi-domes, each of these on three exedrae and each of the exedrae on two arches; it doesn't hang, magically suspended, like the dome of the Aya Sofya and if you've seen the Byzantine church first, this may well disappoint. Also, the columns tend to crowd out all else, an effect worsened in season by the press of fellow visitors. At any time, two-thirds of the mosque will be given over to Muslims at prayer and a rail zealously watched by a mosque official separates the faithful from the flummoxed. The imperial loge is a lattice of pure marble, and the window shutters are of exquisite design, inlaid with ivory, mother-of-pearl and tortoiseshell. The windows, all 260 of them, are not original and could be better. As the Ottoman Empire was collapsing, so were the windows of the Blue Mosque, and their replacements do little to complement the marvellous tiles.

Ahmet was sure he was building for the ages, and with an arrogance possible only from a Commander of the Faithful he had his architect, Mehmet Ağa, build six minarets instead of the two or four customary in Ottoman imperial mosques. Previously, only the shrine of the Ka'aba in Mecca had been allowed six, and after a shrill chorus of protests from the divines of Islam, Ahmet was forced to send Mehmet Ağa down to Mecca to build a seventh. Don't forget this; knowing that the Blue Mosque is the one with six minarets may come in handy sometime when you're good and lost in old Stamboul. Also unusual in this mosque are the rows of great doors around the lovely courtyard—36 of them, all leading nowhere.

Ahmet died young at 27 and was buried near his creation; his *türbe* stands in the square between the mosque and the Aya Sofya. Buried with him are his wife and his sons, two of whom, Osman II and Murat IV, went on to the sultanate themselves. As in the great mosque, the tiles on the walls are from İznik.

Topkapı Palace (Topkapı Sarayı)

Buildings and museums open daily 9–4.30; closed Tues in winter; adm. There is a separate admission charge for the Harem buildings, with guided tours offered hourly 10–4 in various languages—check ahead for times of tours in English. A few rooms in the palace complex are usually closed for restoration at any one time.

Immediately after the Conquest, Mehmet Fatih built his first palace on the hill north of Beyazıt Square. In 1468, he began a summer palace on the beautiful and largely unoccupied hill at the tip of the peninsula, where the Golden Horn joins the Bosphorus. Later sultans favoured the site, and Süleyman the Magnificent was the first to move here permanently. Most of the present buildings are from the 18th century; by then the sultans had made themselves captives in this lovely soap-bubble of a world. Some of them spent more of their revenues here than in all the rest of the empire. Even though much of the Topkapı's treasure was sold off in the 19th century, when the Empire was constantly facing bankruptcy, the hoard that survives is incredible, including the richest collections of porcelain and emeralds in the world. There's hardly enough space to display all the trinkets the Sultans squirreled away here—the curators say they can only show about three per cent of it at a time.

The hill had been the acropolis of ancient Byzantium, with two theatres on its slopes overlooking the Bosphorus, several temples, a stadium, and an arsenal and drill field called the Strategion. Just inside the Bab-i Humayun stood the little city's main square, the Tetrastoon. Not a trace of any of this remains, and we know surprisingly little of the use the quarter was put to after Constantine.

First Courtyard

The **Bab-i Humayun**, a simple stone gate, looks to have been more for defence than decoration, and it was. The many revolts and skirmishes of the empire's decadent years put it to the test. Mahmud II hid here from his bloodthirsty Janissaries. Whatever the outcome, the gate would usually be adorned with the heads of the losers. Through it, one enters the **First Courtyard**, a large park. Two centuries ago, it was full of the palace outbuildings: the imperial mint and, most importantly, the barracks of the Janissaries. From this spot this praetorian guard was able to keep a constant watch on its sultans, standing between them and any hope of aid from the outside world. Mahmud demolished their buildings soon after their demise in the Auspicious Event.

In the same year Aya Sofya was completed, Justinian and Theodora dedicated a smaller church, the **Aya İrene**, just behind it. The two churches shared a common sanctuary, but were cut off from each other when the Turks enclosed Aya İrene in the First Courtyard. The site may have originally been occupied by a temple of Aphrodite; like the Aya Sofya, the church you see now replaced a work of Theodosius burned down in the Nike Riots. Aya İrene, the Divine Peace, was never used as a mosque: Its keys were given to the Janissaries who, following the precepts of the Bektaşi order of dervishes, were never allowed to enter a mosque. Instead, they used it as their arsenal, and kept it in surprisingly good shape over the centuries. The church is a basilica in form, but with a small dome and transepts, a very unusual plan for a Byzantine work. On the apse where the altar stood, a simple black and gold mosaic of a cross is believed to be original. For a while under the republic, Aya İrene was kept open as a military museum, making use of the curiosities accumulated over the years by the Janissaries. The church is now closed to the public, but occasionally used for concerts during the İstanbul festival and for exhibitions during the İstanbul Biennial.

Bab-üs Selâm

At the end of the First Courtyard stands another wall and the **Bab-üs Selâm** or **Gate of Salutations**, the entrance to the official part of the Saray (for which permission was required to enter); now it's where you buy your ticket. The medieval air of this gate, with its conical spires, is no accident. Süleyman was so taken with the castles and churches of Hungary when he campaigned there that he brought back Hungarian architects to build it for him. One of the customs of this gate was that no one except the sultan and his mother might pass through it on horseback. The head gardener of the Saray had his office here; this is a good example of the Turkish fancy for euphemism, for the 'gardeners' were really armed guards who shared fully in the palace intrigues, and the 'head gardener' was none other than the sultan's chief executioner. The block, and the fountain in which he washed his blade, can be seen near this gate, along with the 'warning stone' on which severed heads would be displayed *pour encourager les autres*.

Second Courtyard: Court of the Divan and Harem

The next courtyard, the **Court of the Divan**, was divided between the highest council chamber of government and the palace kitchens; this arrangement would never seem silly to an Ottoman, for whom all real government was embodied in the person of the sultan. For Divan, understand the sultan's cabinet; the vezirs met once a week in the Divan hall, under its tower on the left-hand side of the courtyard. The earlier sultans would have been present at these meetings, where the affairs of the government were discussed. Süleyman introduced the screen to keep his vezirs honest; they could never know if he were behind it listening or not. His successors hardly went to the Divan at all.

Unfortunately, most of the Divan chambers are usually closed, but they may let you in to see the lovely, thoroughly restored 16th-century council chamber. Other rooms house a collection of arms and armour, including the swords of many of the sultans. From a distance, the landmark of the entire palace complex is the Divan's **tower**, built in 1825 by Mahmut II as a watchtower, and strangely reminiscent of a New England church steeple.

The Divan is attached to the **Harem**, a group of buildings and courtyards that cover one-sixth of the total area of the Saray. Süleyman began its construction when his favourite wife Roxelana convinced him he could not live without her; as power devolved upon the ladies and their eunuchs, later sultans expanded it into the labyrinthine complex we see today. After Abdülmecit moved to the Dolmabahçe Palace in 1853, the surviving favourites of his predecessors lived on here, lonely and forgotten, some well into the 20th century.

Birds in a Gilded Cage

 Harems are good business, as the Turkish Culture Ministry well knows; not only do they make a fair amount of the money needed for the palace's upkeep from Harem tours, but nearly every summer, as part of the İstanbul Festival, they put on a production of Mozart's *Entführung aus dem Serail* in the Harem courtyard. Tickets sell out fast. *Harem* is really an Arabic word; the Turks called this place the Darissade (and, as you may have guessed, *seraglio* is a corruption of the Turkish saray, or palace). It isn't a barbarous oriental innovation; Turks and Arabs both learned the joys of confining women from the Greeks, who from their beginnings right up to the end of Byzantium were possibly the champion male chauvinists of all time.

Ottoman sultans led normal private lives up to the time of Yıldırım Beyazıt. When he and his family were captured by Tamerlane, the sultan's wife was forced to serve dinner naked to the conqueror and his generals. After this ultimate humiliation, no sultan ever legally married again—save only Süleyman the Magnificent, besotted with his Roxelana. The others had their collections of concubines, though they were only shut up in a harem after the conquest of Constantinople. When Roxelana brought the harem inside the palace, she intended only a means of getting closer to Süleyman and increasing her influence over affairs of state, but over the next two centuries the Harem became established, gradually building up its famous institutions and peculiarities. The cast of characters included the girls, or 'odalisques', as many as 800 of them, who lived in drab dormitories; apparently status was the only reason for having so many. The 'Favourites', including the 'First Four Women' (the first to give birth to sons) rated luxurious apartments. To watch over the girls, and more often after themselves, there were the Black Eunuchs. These ugly creatures (the sultan's slavemaster picked out the ugliest, to avoid any chance of arousing the girls) were usually given names like 'Hyacinth' or 'Daisy'. With the silver tubes that assisted them in trips to the WC perched nattily in their tall turbans, the Black Eunuchs became, in the latter days, a power unto themselves. Their chief, the Kızlar Ağası or 'Lord of the Girls', was after the Ağa of the Janissaries the most useful ally any scheming lady could have. (The White Eunuchs, by contrast, looked after the Selamlık, the sultan's quarters, and the education of the pages brought in by the *devşirme*, or boy tribute.) The only other men allowed in the Harem were the 'Tressed Halberdiers', whose job was to bring in the firewood. They had to wear their long hair in coils, hanging over their faces so they would be less likely to catch a glimpse of the women.

Sultans prefer blondes. Many of the women were slender, fair Circassians, Slavs, Armenians or Georgians. All of them, of course, were slaves, and despite the little courtesies of Harem life it is not likely that many of them ever had any illusions about their true status. The vast majority of them led wretchedly dull lives here, chaste as any nuns, except for the few who managed to catch a sultan's fancy. Even these were left only with a thank-you, a small present and the fervent hope that they might conceive a male child. It is pretty certain they did not get up to many high-jinks; the eunuchs installed old women to sleep next to their beds, to keep an eye on them at night, and, as an astonished Venetian ambassador once noted in his memoirs, care was taken even to ensure that all cucumbers were sliced before being brought in.

If you wish to visit the Harem—after the big jewels, it's the most popular attraction in the palace—make sure you stop beforehand at the booth by the Harem gate to buy a ticket and check the times for English-language tours, usually every half hour. Just inside the gate are the apartments of the eunuchs, including the **Court of the Black Eunuch**, all rebuilt after a fire in the 1660s. From here the *Altın Yol*, the 'Golden Road', the corridor down which the Harem women would walk to meet their rendezvous with destiny when a sultan called, leads to the rest of the Harem, beginning with the **Courtyard of the Sultan Valide** (the Sultan's mother), adjacent to the eunuchs' quarter. Considering the bizarre issues of Harem politics—the steering of the right girls into the sultan's bed, the manipulation and sometimes murder of prospective heirs—it becomes clear how only the greatest schemers of all could attain the glorious position of Sultan Valide. Their suite was usually the vortex of all palace intrigues. The next courtyard to the west housed the women servants, again mostly black, and beyond them lay the damp, chilly, unadorned quarters of the beauties themselves.

Perhaps the greatest attraction of the Harem quarters, now that you're thoroughly disillusioned, will be the rooms of the northern half of the Harem, the chambers where the sultans came for their pleasures. Several of these, the **Bedroom of Murat III** and the **Library of Ahmet I**, for example, are adorned with some of the most beautiful painted tiles to be found anywhere in Turkey. The **Dining Room of Ahmet II**, the most famous room of the whole Topkapı Palace, is lined with wood panelling painted with colourful flowers and fruits, the apotheosis of the gentle art of the Tulip Period. The designs may have violated Muslim taboos against images, but then few imams or members of the Ulema, the Muslim hierarchy, were ever invited in to see them.

Tulips, Tiles and Turtles

The Great Tulip Speculation of the 17th century is one of the oddities of European history. In Germany, France and Holland, these flowers briefly became an obsession, pursued with the kind of fervour we now devote to gold bullion and commodity futures. The bulbs of some exotic varieties actually brought more than their weight in gold; great financial houses and canny opportunists rose and fell with the fortunes of their favourite blooms, and tulip quotes filled coffee-house conversation as stock market closings do today. The Turks can take all the credit. Tulips, like cherries, pizza, parchment and angora wool, are among Anatolia's contributions to civilization.

A century later, it was the Turks' turn to get silly over tulips. What Ottoman historians call the 'Tulip Period' is generally associated with the reign of Ahmet III (1703–20). Here the sultans and their court reached their most Chinese extreme of abstraction and contrived refinement, while their empire careered into decay. With their wedding-cake turbans, layers of silk and brocades, and turned-up slippers, the bizarrely decorous Ottomans made a picture that fascinated contemporary Europe. Night garden parties among the tulips were the rage, illuminated by candles on the backs of wandering turtles.

Tulip art—for the sultan interested himself in little else—can best be seen in the lovely tiled chambers of the Topkapı Harem. If you want to see what started all the hubbub, there are wild tulips in the national parks around Ankara and Yozgat.

From the Dining Room, the tour guides may take you to see the swimming pool put in by Murat III, and the chambers of the Favourites, on a pretty terrace. Some of the rooms on the upper floors are thought to have been the location of the notorious *Kafes*, or **Cage**, the most thoroughly perverse of all the perverse customs of the Ottoman throne.

Beyazıt II, a scholarly, peaceful sultan, had his reign plagued by his younger brother Prince Cem, a romantic adventurer who caused plenty of trouble trying to seize the throne for himself. When Beyazıt caught him, he sent him off to exile in Italy, where it seems he was eventually poisoned by his keeper, the Borgia Pope Alexander VI. After that, sultans began murdering their brothers as soon as they were able. Eventually, the Cage was decided upon as a more humane solution. Younger brothers were simply locked up, with a few harem girls for company and a few deaf mute slaves for servants. They stayed there the rest of their lives unless the death of their reigning brother should make them a sultan (if any of their concubines got pregnant, they would be bundled up in a silk bag with some stone weights and dropped into the sea). A few of these unfortunates actually did make it out of the Cage and onto the throne. All of them turned out to be both insane and dangerous; the most notable of these was İbrahim the Mad, who had spent 22 years in the Cage. In his short reign it is estimated that he ordered the deaths of over 4,000 of his friends, relatives and servants.

Carriage Room and Palace Kitchens

After the Harem there are two more sections of the museum you may wish to visit before passing through to the third courtyard. The **Carriage Room**, once the sultan's stables, is full of the various conveyances of the 19th-century rulers, who apparently were as fond of fancy phaetons and landaus as modern autocrats are of shiny new cars. The **Palace Kitchens** across the courtyard, partly designed by Sinan, were ready, at the sultan's command, to whip up almost anything, from a snack for one to a dinner party for five thousand. In the 17th century some 1,200 people worked here, and the archives record as many as 22,000 sheep being turned into kebabs every week. The kitchens contain some of the largest soup pots ever constructed on this planet, and a tedious infinity of silver and china from the 19th century. The sultans accumulated these as presents from foreign rulers, in greater numbers than even a dinner for five thousand could require. The collection of **Chinese porcelain** is world-famous and priceless; note especially the celadon ware, a favourite of potentates everywhere, since it was reputed to change colour in the presence of poison.

The Third Courtyard

This is a wonderful park of plane trees and poplars. Visitors are often surprised to see how open and airy old Turkish palaces are. A love of nature, the necessity of having more than a bit of green around, was something the Ottomans never lost, even in their years of decay. They copied the form of the Saray—three successive courtyards of increasingly greater isolation—from the Byzantine imperial palace that once stood nearby (curiously the Hittite palace at Boğazkale also had the same plan). However, where the Byzantines probably had small, paved squares in the classical mode, the Turks built gardens like this, squeezing their buildings into thin quadrangles between them and the forested slopes of the Topkapı hill, for a view of trees on both sides.

To match this setting, the Turks evolved an architectural style very different from the grey mathematics of their mosques, a unique 18th-century concoction of distinctive, very oriental shapes and forms, limited perhaps to the Topkapı and the now-vanished gardens and palaces that once lined the Golden Horn and the Marmara shores. One of the finest examples is in this courtyard: the **Bab-üs Saade** or **Gate of Felicity**, the entrance to the *Selamlık*, the sultan's quarters. Very few outsiders were ever allowed the privilege of using this gate. On ceremonial occasions, such as a new sultan's accession to the throne, the Bayram festival, or the commissioning of a new general, the sultan would meet the assemblage seated directly under it, on the same portable bejewelled throne that went with him on campaigns. The Chief White Eunuch had his rooms here in the buildings around the gate, from which he and his fellow castrati oversaw the smooth operation of the Selamlık.

The **Audience Chamber**, a pretty parlour just inside the gate, served for the sultan's meetings with his grand vezir and foreign ambassadors. Its ambience is thoroughly Turkish; perhaps for the sultans it recalled the tents of their nomadic ancestors. The fountain in this chamber wasn't just for decoration; its running water made it difficult for anyone to overhear the Sultan's conversations. The coloured tiles and lovely hearth were added to Mehmet Fatih's original building by Ahmet III, but the Baroque ceiling came much later. Ahmet also built the **Library** just behind it, a marvellous small pavilion with lots of glass and window seats, to be envied by all serious readers. Before the 17th-century fire that damaged much of the Selamlık, this space was occupied by the Great Hall, a building that housed the *Enderun*, the school for pages where the Christian children collected in the *devşirme* round-up were converted into the ministers and generals of the empire. Before the decline, it had a reputation as the finest school in Europe, counting all the great Turkish poets and scholars among its instructors. The Enderun was the special preserve of the Chief White Eunuch, and any of these who was fortunate enough to serve under a sultan who liked boys better than girls would find himself, and not the Chief Black Eunuch, top dog around the palace.

Treasures of the Sultans

Most of the fabulous treasures of the sultans, the gold and jewels and the holy relics, are exhibited in the halls around the third courtyard. The spirit of the Topkapı was never to throw anything away, and one result is that extraordinarily well-preserved costumes of every sultan after Mehmet Fatih can be seen in the **Wardrobe**, from the gaily coloured flower-printed robes of Mehmet to the dreary European monkey-suit of Abdülhamid. Osman II, most tragic of the sultans, is represented by the blood-splattered caftan in which he was murdered. These costumes bring the sultans to life more than any other exhibit, and provide a few surprises along the way: the bright pink caftan covered in huge yellow polka dots belonging to Selim I is garish enough to put most jockeys to shame. Decked out in such garb, it's hard to believe that Selim could have been as intractably grim as the history books claim.

It may prove difficult to get excited over the riches of the **Treasury** next door, simply because it's hard to convince oneself that they're all real. The four rooms of bejewelled vessels and weapons, coffee sets and cabinets, as well as famous gems like the 86-carat Spoon Diamond, make up the richest hoard in the world, particularly if you include the additional warehouseful they haven't room to display. Other stars of the collection include the Emerald Dagger, made famous by the film *Topkapi*, and a golden casket supposedly containing the head of John the Baptist.

At the far end of the courtyard, the collection of **Miniatures** displays examples of another very Turkish art form; it seems the first portraitists of Islam felt guilty about breaking the law, and so made their paintings very, very small. One two-volume set of these, the *Hünername* or *Book of Talents*, ranks among the greatest works of Turkish painting and calligraphy. The celebrated **clock collection** occupies the next room. Byzantine historians often wrote of their emperors' love of mechanical contraptions, like the famous golden tree full of singing birds, and like them, the Ottoman sultans were always pleased by gifts of clocks and music boxes. Again, those on display are only a small part of the whole collection.

When Selim I conquered Egypt, whose ruler at the time was the Caliph, the head of all Islam, that title fell to him and his successors. The later emperors' oriental inapproachability had not a little to do with the fact that now they were Commander of the Faithful and the Shadow of God on Earth. In token of this great office, the Sherif of Mecca sent Selim the keys to the Ka'aba, and here at Topkapı they remain in the **Hırka-i Saadet**, the hall of holy relics to which Muslims make pilgrimages, located near the clock collection.

Under a great silver dome added by Murat IV are Mohammed's sword, bow and standard, and the famous cloak he once bestowed on a poet who converted to Islam. Other relics include the Prophet's seal, a broken tooth, a cast of his footprint, hairs from his beard and a letter he sent with an embassy to the Copts of Egypt—a bullying letter, full of threats. The sword of Osman, symbol of the Ottoman state, is also kept here.

Sultan's Residence

Next to this chamber, a fourth and final gate connects with the residence of the sultan, this a group of individual **pavilions** (the Turkish word for pavilion, *köşk*, is often translated as **kiosk**) around a courtyard, all with the best views of the Bosphorus and the Golden Horn. Two of these, the **Revan Köşkü** and the **Bağdad Köşkü**, must be accounted among the very greatest works of Turkish architecture for the simple magnificence of their form and decoration. Murat IV built them both, to commemorate his conquests of Erevan (now capital of Armenia) and Baghdad, and here he drank himself to death in the increasing revels of the last years of his reign. Among the marble terraces and roses of the Revan Köşkü is a marble fountain of three basins that approaches perfection more nearly than any other work of art in all the halls of the Saray.

To leave Topkapı, you must retrace your steps to the First Courtyard; from here instead of returning through the Bab-i Humayun, you can take the other route, around Aya İrene and down a shady cobbled lane towards the Gülhane Park and the imperial museums.

The Imperial Museums

All three museums open Tues–Sun, 9–4.30, adm. A board at the entrance shows which of the nine departments are open on a particular day. Due to staffing shortages, up to a third of the exhibitions may be closed.

Osman Hamdi Bey, by the standards of the late 19th century, was one very unusual Turk. A painter by trade, his knowledge of the ancient Greeks got him a job under Sultan Abdülhamid looking after the empire's antiquities. So well did he perform his duties, and with such panache, that he revolutionized the affairs of archaeology and museum-keeping, not only in Turkey but in the rest of Europe. Personally responsible for the first law anywhere governing the export of antiquities, he also made patriots of all the nations under Ottoman control work hard to keep their own archaeological discoveries from being shanghaied to the new **Archaeology Museum** that he had talked Abdülhamid into building. More often than not, they failed. Among the many excavations he oversaw was the one that uncovered the famous Alexander sarcophagus in Sidon. During the lengthy process of transporting this block of several tons to İstanbul, Hamdi Bey literally bound himself to it to impress upon the sailors that they had better take good care of it. On one later occasion, the sultan proposed presenting the sarcophagus to the visiting Kaiser Wilhelm II. Hamdi Bey had the effrontery to inform the sultan that this would only be accomplished by dragging it over his dead body, and the Kaiser went home empty-handed.

Archaeology Museum (Arkeoloji Müzesi)

The collection he and his successors piled up in this tasteful eclectic building—the very image of what his generation thought a museum should look like—is one of the greatest in Europe. Sarcophagi were Hamdi Bey's speciality, and there's not enough room for them all; many more line the square in front of the museum. The *Alexander sarcophagus*, not actually that of Alexander, but decorated with scenes from his conquests, is perhaps more bombast than art, but it's considered one of the finest examples of late Roman sculpture. Two other sarcophagi, one Hamdi Bey called '*des Pleureuses*', and the other a barn-roofed Lycian model, are in the same room, along with a famous bust of Alexander.

The museum's other attractions include bronze pedestals that once supported statues in the Hippodrome, carved with scenes from the games; coats of arms of various states and knightly orders from the old walls of Galata; Egyptian works; Greek and Roman bronzes; the famous statue of a young man called the *Ephebos of Tralles*; a mosaic of Orpheus and the wild animals; and a remarkable 12-foot statue of the Phoenician god Bes—the Greeks know him as the 'Cypriot Hercules'—toying with a lion.

Museum of the Ancient Orient (Eski Şark Eserler Müzesi)

Across from the Archaeology Museum, the government has more recently created the **Museum of the Ancient Orient**, an equally impressive cache of pre-classical finds from Turkey and the Middle East. Some of its best works are from Babylon: the city's Ishtar Gate is largely reconstructed here with its glazed reliefs. In the Assyrian Room are reliefs from the palace of Assurbanipal; nearby, two 3,600-year-old copulating Kassites (from Northern Mesopotamia) may well be the world's oldest erotic art.

Also in the Assyrian room the museum has assembled a collection of 'interesting documents' from ancient civilizations, with translations: love poems and tables of astronomical events in Assyrian cuneiform, laws and penalties for various crimes ('two-thirds of a mina of silver for cutting off someone's nose with a copper knife'), and the King of Lagash describing his struggles against his own government bureaucracy. The Treaty of Kadesh is here, an agreement of 1269 BC between the Pharaoh and the Hittite King Hattusilis which was found in the state archives at Boğazkale; it's the oldest treaty ever discovered.

Museum of Turkish Ceramics (Çinili Köşkü)

The third building in the square is the **Çinili Köşkü**, an exquisite small palace built by Mehmet Fatih in 1472 as part of the original Topkapı Sarayı. Its painted tiles show the lingering influence of the Selçuks in their design. Fittingly, the pavilion now houses a museum of Turkish ceramics from Selçuk times up to the present.

Sublime Porte and Gülhane Park

Head down from the Çinili Köşkü towards Gülhane Park for the north gate of the palace, the **Sublime Porte** that became the metaphor for the Ottoman government during the 19th century. Built into the walls here is the **Alay Köşk**, the Saray's window on the outside world where the sultan would review his troops and be seen by the people—on very rare occasions. **Gülhane Park**, a part of the Saray, was converted to a public garden in 1913. This lovely oasis, with a pond and woebegone zoo, stretches all the way to Sarayburnu, Seraglio Point. Here İstanbul keeps its **Atatürk Monument**, perhaps the only one in Turkey not on a main square. Across the road, just under the walls of the sultan's quarters of the Saray, you can see the stump of a granite column that is the oldest monument in the city: the **Goths' Column**, commemorating the victory of the Romans over the invading Goths in AD 269.

Yerebatan Sarayı

Returning to Sultanahmet Square down Alemdar Caddesi, just across the street from the Aya Sofya stands the unprepossessing entrance to the **Yerebatan Sarayı**. No one has yet proposed old Constantinople's water supply for associate membership in the Wonders of the Ancient World, but this perhaps is only because this network of underground cisterns is so little known. The 'Underground Palace', as the Turks call it, is a great hall 230 by 460ft, supported by ranks of columns and vaults. Though the largest, it's only one of several in the city. Two more have recently been discovered near the Aya İrene, and it is possible that some others remain unknown. By the 16th century, although the old aqueducts were still in use, these reservoirs had been quite forgotten. A French antiquarian named Petrus Gyllius spent weeks looking for this one in 1545, until he had the good fortune to find a resident of the quarter who had a trap door in his house. Down in the cistern, this gentleman kept a boat and used it daily to catch fish, which he sold to his puzzled neighbours. No one suspected the cistern existed, even though the wells of their houses led directly into it.

Each of the 40ft columns—there are over 300 of them—has a capital to bear the arches, and some of these are carved as if they had been part of a church, instead of a reservoir. Justinian, who was responsible for most of these works, was forced to demolish an old basilica that stood above the cistern, and simply reused the capitals. Two of the columns are supported by massive reused carved heads: one is upside down, the other on its side.

The Hippodrome

In Byzantine times, the site of the Blue Mosque held the Golden Hall, the outermost building of Justinian's palace where the throne was kept and the affairs of government transacted. A private corridor connected this part of the palace with the *Kathisma*, or imperial box of the **Hippodrome**, which once stood just to the west. No stadium, ancient or modern, was ever so famous in its time, or played such an important role in its city's public life. Much more went on here than just chariot races and athletic events. Emperors celebrated their victories here, and executed their enemies. Even the games should not be taken as simple entertainment; during the Roman period, they had evolved into a strange sort of mystic communion between the emperor, who of course picked up the bill, and his people. Everything about the games became a symbol, reflecting some aspect of the politics of the day.

Blues, Greens and Purple

Construction of the Hippodrome began in 203, the same year Septimus Severus was building the Circus Maximus in Rome, but it remained unfinished until the reign of Constantine. Subsequent emperors improved and enlarged it, and by the time of Justinian it was nearly a third of a mile long, with seats for 100,000.

Much has been made of the Hippodrome factions, the Blues and Greens, that caused so much trouble in Constantinople in the 6th century. It would, however, be giving the Byzantines more credit for decadence than even they deserved to suppose that the course of the empire was governed by militant sports fans. Originally, there were four factions, the Reds and Whites later merging into the others. They were nothing less than the organized *demes*, or tribes, traditional in any Greek city. (Rome had the same four colours and factions, though it is likely that the Romans adapted the idea from the Greeks or the Etruscans.) They had both military and civilian functions; it was they who built the city walls, and their leaders received salaries as officers of the state. Gradually they came to identify with socio-economic divisions within the city (exactly how the historians can't tell, though it seems the Greens were somewhat more proletarian and politically radical), but when the Blues and Greens joined forces in the Nike Revolt, they were fighting for the city's liberty, and their own, against imperial absolutism and all its aggression abroad, its cops and spies, and its unbearable taxes.

Nike means Victory, the battle cry of the rebels; the revolt began in 532, five years after Justinian's accession to the throne. The rebels soon gained control of the city: chroniclers paint a picture of the young emperor staring helplessly from the palace balcony, too amazed and terrified to act. The story goes that Theodora, the low-born dancing girl who had so captivated Justinian that he made her an empress, finally snapped him out of it and put a little steel in her man's soul. When he proposed to flee the city, she refused, insisting that he should stay and fight, telling him 'The purple [the imperial colour] is the noblest winding-sheet'. The rebels were defeated when the great General Belisarius, at the head of an army of Goths and Alans—the Greeks could not be trusted—surrounded the rebels in the Hippodrome and massacred them all: 60,000 of them if contemporary sources are to be believed.

The Crusaders in 1204 thoroughly laid waste the Hippodrome and, as the restored empire had little spare money to spend on games, the great stadium gradually fell into ruin. Under the Turks, most of its stones found their way into new building projects, but the sultans always left the surviving monuments alone, and kept the ground clear for practising their game of *cirit*, a form of polo. From this, the square where the Hippodrome once stood came to be known as the At Meydanı, Horse Square, and this name is still sometimes heard. In the late 1960s the square became something of a hippie encampment, until Turkish patience finally ran out.

The Monuments of the Hippodrome

The present square, though it follows the contours of the Hippodrome's field, is less than half as big. Its centre line can be traced through the three surviving columns. This line was the *spina*; the Byzantines liked to call it the 'Axis of the Empire'. Originally its two ends were marked by golden columns representing the sun and the moon—the symbolism of the games was astronomical as well as political. These were the pylons around which the charioteers raced; between the two columns, the *spina* boasted an almost unbroken line of monuments. The Crusaders carried away or wrecked most of these when they sacked the city, most famously stealing the bronze horses of Lysippus that now adorn St Mark's in Venice. The three that remain were too heavy to move.

In the case of the first, the **Column of Constantine Porphyrogenitus**, the Crusaders had to settle for melting down the bronze plates that covered it. The second monument, the **Serpentine Column**, a twisted stump of bronze, retains little of beauty or interest to remind us of its fascinating history; from faint inscriptions on its base, it has been determined that this column was the monument dedicated by the united Greek cities to celebrate their victory over the Persians at Plataea in 479 BC. After transporting the column in joyous ceremonies through all the towns that shared in the victory, it was erected at the Temple of Apollo at Delphi, where it stood until Constantine the Great stole it to embellish his capital. Before it toppled, sometime around 1700, the column had the form of three intertwined serpents, their heads supporting the legs of a great golden tripod dedicated to Apollo.

The third monument, the **Obelisk of Theodosius**, was acquired by that emperor in 390 especially for the Hippodrome; an obelisk was something no stadium could be without. This one came from Heliopolis, and the hieroglyphic inscriptions on its sides record the victories of the mighty Pharaoh Thutmose III. Like most of the Egyptian obelisks that have found their way to the world's capitals, this one is in surprisingly good shape for its 3,400 years; all the hieroglyphs still stand out clearly.

The marble base on which the obelisk was raised has been called one of the finest works of 4th-century sculpture; its reliefs portray Theodosius and his family in the Kathisma, viewing the games, the emperor with a wreath in his hand ready to crown the victor. Another relief shows the transporting of the obelisk; the inscriptions on the sides, in both Greek and Latin verse, recall the difficulties of erecting the heavy stone and the praise due to Proclus the prefect for accomplishing it. The wells in which these monuments are sunk gives you an idea how much the land has risen since the Hippodrome was last in use. A group of British officers on leave excavated the bases of the three monuments during the Crimean War.

North of the Hippodrome, back near Kaiser Wilhelm's Fountain, stands a small mosque that is one of the oldest in İstanbul. The **Firuz Ağa Camii**, built in 1491, has nothing of the grandeur of later imperial mosques, but its architecture definitely points towards them, in a transition from the old, plain Ottoman style, the masterpieces of which you can see in Bursa. Five times a day, a real muezzin climbs up the short minaret to give the call to prayer. The big mosques usually have only loudspeakers, but with the renaissance of Muslim piety in Turkey, many mosques have gone back to the old-fashioned way. The unexcavated ruins near this mosque belonged to a nobleman's palace, converted in the 7th century to the **Martyrium of St Euphemia**.

West of the Hippodrome

Just across the street from the monuments of the Hippodrome, the palace of İbrahim Paşa, a grand vezir first favoured then executed by Süleyman the Magnificent, has recently been restored to house the **Museum of Turkish and Islamic Arts** or Türk ve İslam Eserleri Müzesi (*open daily exc Mon, 9.30–4.30; adm*), with a well-arranged collection of ceramic and brass works, carpets and carved lecterns, some dating from the first centuries of Islam.

Over the last decade this museum has grown into one of the best planned and presented in Turkey, as well as one of the most comprehensive collections of its kind anywhere. Objects on display go back to the earliest times: peculiar mosaics from the Abbasid Caliphate, along with acanthus-leaf capitals that show a Greek influence. There are some fine Selcuk ceramics, with figurative representations of people and animals (and one relief carved with warriors and griffins in a way that suggests the sculptor had been looking closely at the monuments of the ancient Assyrians). Beyond these there are Persian miniatures, lovely geometrically carved doors and window shutters, and early Korans. Ottoman works, not surprisingly, make up the best parts of the collection: 16th- and 17th-century silver and brass work, İznik tiles, tulip art, inlaid wood chests and Koran stands. There is a 'magic shirt' that belonged to Beyazıt I (it didn't help him against Tamerlane) and several examples of the *mülkname*, state decrees in exquisite calligraphy, adorned with the Sultan's personal *tuğra*. On many old Ottoman buildings, such as the Sublime Porte, you will have noticed this unusual symbol, made of Arabic characters in a scroll of concentric loops. The tuğra was the mark of the Ottoman Empire from the early days. It originated with Murat I, who, like his predecessors, was illiterate and signed documents with his thumbprint.

It's easy to overlook the the museum's basement, entered by a small door off the courtyard. This section is devoted to traditional Turkish life, and the star exhibit is a complete *toprak ev*, or yurt, the sort of tent used by the Turks' nomadic ancestors, along with some fascinating dsiplays on the natural dyes and other crafts that went into making it. There is also a 'black tent' of goat hair (the *yörükler*, nomads of eastern Turkey, still use these today), and tableaux of an Anatolian village house and 19th-century homes, complete with authentic costumes and furnishings.

All of the area west of the Hippodrome is built over another of Justinian's underground cisterns, though the entrance is difficult to find. From Divan Yolu, the main street of the city, head three blocks south on Klodfarer Caddesi to a playground where bits of a large retaining wall are visible. Here you'll find the entrance to the **Binbirdirek Cistern**—the 'thousand and one columns', the name a familiar Turkish hyperbole. This one, though smaller than the Yerebatan Sarayı, is dry, and you can explore its entire extent. In Byzantine records it was known as the Cistern of Philoxenes.

Sultanahmet District

In İstanbul, the Blue Mosque is more commonly referred to as the Sultanahmet Camii, after its builder, and in this form the mosque has given its name to the quarter west and south of it, one of the most interesting old residential neighbourhoods of the city. Some parts of the Sultanahmet near the Marmara shore, with street after street of characteristic Ottoman wooden houses, do not even have a modern water supply, and the women of the district can be seen gossiping around the corner *çeşme* (fountain), just as they are pictured in engravings of centuries ago—although the plastic jerricans make the scene somewhat less picturesque. The lower parts of Sultanahmet are charmingly schizophrenic these days, with half the Ottoman houses restored as hotels in pretty pastel colours, and the other half falling to pieces; poor children playing football share the narrow streets with bewildered-looking young tourists.

The plumbing was probably better when this part of the town was the **Palace of the Byzantine Emperors**. Since no excavations have ever been made, it's impossible to tell much about the layout. The palace began to decay already in the 12th century, when Alexius Comnenus abandoned it for Blachernae out by the city walls. From contemporary accounts we can expect there were plenty of golden domes and towers, and that its three divisions, the Chalce, the Daphne and the 'Sacred Palace', covered an area not much smaller than the Topkapı Sarayı. The **Arasta Bazaar**, a restored shopping arcade opened in 1985, is southeast of the Blue Mosque. It was built by Sultan Ahmet to provide revenues for his mosque and lies on top of remains of the Byzantine palace (*see* 'Shopping', p.144). Among the shops can be found the new **Mosaic Museum** or Büyüksaray Mozaikleri Müzesi (*open daily exc Mon, 9–4; adm*), opened in 1987, housing 6th-century floor mosaics from the large peristyle court of the palace. These mosaics are largely *in situ* and the museum winds underground several yards beneath the shops of the Arasta Bazaar. Much still remains to be excavated. Otherwise, all that is left of the palace is a small court, believed to have been part of the stables, that housed another mosaic museum before its removal to the Aya İrene, and a section of the sea walls to the west where Justinian built his Bucoleon, the seaside pavilion. The area between the Blue Mosque and the Marmara, apparently, was devoted to the imperial polo grounds. Throughout the history of the empire, polo was the top snob sport, and most of the emperors, if not too debilitated by their lifestyles, indulged in it.

Küçük Aya Sofya

If you follow the twisting side streets south of the Hippodrome, where you can see the stone walls that supported the closed end of the stadium above the slope, with luck you will find the **Küçük** ('little') **Aya Sofya**, the name the Turks give to the 6th-century **church of St Sergius and St Bacchus**. Emperor Justinian's first major building project in his capital, modelled after the famous church of S. Vitale in Ravenna, begun the year before, can be seen as an experiment on the way to the big Aya Sofya, with its semi-domes, exedrae and two levels of arcades around the central space (on the map, you can see how the Aya İrene, the Aya Sofya, Hippodrome, Palace and Little Aya Sofya are laid out in a line—the main axis of old Constantinople's plan). This church, like S. Vitale, is square with an octagon of piers and columns inside it, supporting a dome just small enough to avoid the need for pendentives. Many of the capitals are finely carved, and like those of Aya Sofya they bear the monograms of Justinian and Theodora. Some vine motifs can be seen in playful allusion to Bacchus, who with his comrade Sergius was the first Christian soldier in the Roman legions to suffer martyrdom. Sergius and Bacchus were the patrons of soldiers, and especially meaningful to Justinian, preoccupied in the early years of his reign with one war after another. As an adjunct of the imperial palace, Küçük Aya Sofya was given the role of occasional Catholic church, where embassies from the pope were allowed to say Mass according to their own usages. Pope Gregory the Great, before his election, was long the papal legate to Byzantium, and he must have prayed here often. Today it is Muslims who prostrate themselves on the patchwork of carpets laid out under the dome.

Prayer alone is not enough to stop the spread of huge cracks across the building's dome, damage caused by both man and nature. Vibrations from the train tracks five yards behind the church have compounded the subsidence caused by water from the nearby Bosphorus seeping into the church's foundations. Donations to combat the damage are welcome.

The Divan Yolu and Cağaloğlu

On your way back to the Divan Yolu, try to find Kadırga Sokak and the **Mehmet Paşa Camii**, built in 1571 for one of the Sokollu grand vezirs. This small mosque, along with its courtyard, porticoes and school complex, is one of the most beautiful of all the works of Sinan, though few people trouble to see it in its out-of-the-way location.

The **Divan Yolu** was and is the main street of İstanbul. Though today it changes its name every few blocks—to Yeniçeriler Caddesi, and then to Vezneciler Caddesi after Beyazıt Square—in Byzantine days, the whole stretch as far as the Adrianople Gate was known as the *Mese* (the Middle), lined with arcades on one side, and on both where it passed through the choicer districts.

Cağaloğlu, the area north of Divan Yolu, takes its name from the **Cağaloğlu Baths** on Yerebatan Caddesi, built in the 18th century and still popular. This is one of the prettier parts of old Stamboul, where mostly 19th-century buildings are interspersed with fine mosques and institutions endowed by the sultans and their courtiers. It is also the home of most of the national newspapers and book publishers—in the years of political troubles its streets were often a battleground. The Press Museum, or Basın Müzesi, is on the Divan Yolu here.

Çemberlitaş

Çemberlitaş, the 'bound monument' further up Divan Yolu, commemorates the very beginnings of the Byzantine Empire. The Column of Constantine, as it was called, was the first monument erected by that emperor on his refounding of the city; with the modesty for which his house was so renowned, Constantine had a golden statue of himself bolted on top. The Forum of Constantine, of which the small square you see today is the only remnant, was the business centre of the city, and the monument served as the site for many public festivals, including the annual ceremony on the anniversary of the foundation. A storm in the 11th century brought the old emperor down to earth, and the golden cross with which Manuel Comnenus replaced it did not survive long under the Turks. The sultans left the column standing, however, contributing the bronze bands that have held it together since a fire in the 18th century; it took its name from these. The fire gave rise to the scorched monument's other popular name, the **Burnt Column**.

Immediately before the Burnt Column, on the same side of the road, is the **Türbe of Sultan Mahmud II**, a dull and ugly building set behind high steel railings within an Ottoman cemetery. Beneath the outrageous glass chandelier rests Mahmud II, with his son, Sultan Abdülaziz, and his grandson, Sultan Abdülhamid, plus family members of each and their favoured ministers. Across the road is the **Köprülü Kütüphanesi** (library), built in 1661 by members of the distinguished Köprülü family of Albania, which contributed five grand vezirs in the 17th century. There is little of interest inside apart from a few dusty tomes. Next to the Burnt Column itself is the 17th-century **Çemberlitaş Hamamı**, commissioned by the wife of Selim II and still open for bathers.

Just past the Burnt Column, still on Divan Yolu, is the **Atik Ali Paşa Camii**, built for that gentleman in 1497 by Beyazıt II in honour of services rendered as grand vezir. It is a peaceful mosque, plain and simple, set in a lovely garden with lots of Christmas-tree firs. The larger mosque behind it, the **Nuruosmaniye Camii**, the 'light of Osman', is one of the better examples of Turkish Baroque. By the 18th century, the religious architecture of the Ottomans had lost all the momentum built up in its earlier inspirations. The result, an attempt to maintain the form while prettifying it in a bastard half-Italian, half-Persian style, seems sensible enough here, but the greatest horrors were still to come. The main entrance to the Covered Bazaar leads through the tout-patrolled courtyard of the Nuruosmaniye. Near the Nuruosmaniye, the **Mehmet Paşa Camii** is the oldest in İstanbul, built just 10 years after the Ottoman conquest. **Nuruosmaniye Caddesi**, leading from here back towards Aya Sofya, has recently been given a complete facelift; lined with graceful plane trees, it is the fashionable shopping street of old Stamboul.

Back on the Divan Yolu, the **Külliye of Koça Sinan Paşa**, grand vezir under Murat III and Mahmud III, stands just beyond the Atik Ali Paşa Camii. The complex was erected by Davut Ağa, who had the unenviable task of succeeding Sinan as chief architect to the sultan. Nearby is the **Çorlulu Ali Paşa Medrese**, built in 1711. Across the road to the left, the **Karamustafa of Merzifon Medrese** was built in 1690 in honour of the Grand Vezir Karamustafa by Mehmet IV. It has an octagonal plan, unusual in a mosque. Now it is a research institute named for the 20th-century Turkish writer, Yaşar Kemal. Here the Divan Yolu becomes Yeniçeriler Caddesi, lined with buildings from the 1960s breezeblock-and-cement school. Signs point the way to McDonalds.

Sirkeci and Eminönü

Crossing Nuruosmaniye Caddesi, one of the main thoroughfares of Cağaloğlu is Babıâli Caddesi; if you follow it north to where it becomes Ankara Caddesi, passing the most conspicuous of İstanbul's consulates—the Iranian—and the provincial government house, the **Vilayet**, you'll end up in the **Sirkeci** quarter, a scrofulous twilight zone of cheap hotels and auto parts shops around the ornate Victorian **Sirkeci Station** (1885). Foreign companies built the first railway into İstanbul, and they and Sultan Abdülhamid are responsible for the greatest act of municipal vandalism in the city since the Sack of 1204: for the tracks, they destroyed the entire Marmara shore and many of the gardens and woods of the Topkapı hill.

Eminönü, the area just west of Sirkeci along the Golden Horn, was in the last century the business district of old Stamboul, as opposed to the European-dominated Beyoğlu across the Golden Horn. Its streets are still lively, its property values the highest in the city, and if you must pass through to visit the monumental **Main Post Office**, take time to admire this and the many other outlandish works of *c.* 1910 eclectic architecture. Two of the best Art Nouveau works, grimy fantasies with cast-iron flowers on their balconies and pseudo-Ottoman painted tiles, are the small business block on the square opposite the post office and the **Büyük Vakıf Han**, an enormous landmark just two blocks away, in the direction of **Eminönü Square**, old Stamboul's window on the Golden Horn. From the square, the famous Galata Bridge crosses over to Beyoğlu, carrying the life of the city back and forth.

The Galata Bridge

Just after the Conquest, Mehmet's army engineers built the first bridge here, of boats lashed together and covered with planks. One of the succeeding sultans, the Turks say, invited Leonardo da Vinci to design a permanent structure, but he declined, and none was constructed until 1845. The present, like its companion the Atatürk Bridge further up the Golden Horn, is a floating metal drawbridge. Caissons could only have been planted into the mud bottom with great difficulty, and so this unusual method was adopted. German engineers built it in 1912 but the Turks had to reconstruct it almost from scratch after a fire in 1992. Both bridges are opened only in the early morning hours, when long lines of ships pass in and out. In the days of the sultans, they were also opened at the least sign of trouble in the city, in order to prevent insurrection from spreading outwards. The 1992 fire began in one of the little fish restaurants housed on the bridge's lower level. For the rebuilding, there was much talk of making a proper modern bridge, instead of the incredible floating café and jumble sale the old one always was. In the end, fortunately, custom and sentiment won out—the new bridge looks exactly like the old one, with plenty of room on the pavements for hawkers to sell their wind-up turtles and polyester negligées, and of course spaces underneath for the restaurants.

The docks on either side, from which you can catch ferry boats to Asia, the Bosphorus or the Princes' Islands, once were the busiest part of the commercial waterfront. Old travellers always remarked how close the city's life was to the life of the sea; any trip through town was likely to involve elbowing your way past deck hands and stevedores, and staring into the cannons of the ships-of-the-line. Today, besides the creaky ferries, the maritime experience is limited to the informal fish market on the Beyoğlu side, and the cafés on the lower deck of the bridge, where you can sit and sample the notorious aromas of the Golden Horn. All this lies in the shadow of one of the great imperial mosques, the **Yeni Cami**.

Yeni Cami and Spice Market (Mısır Çarşısı)

This mosque, a landmark more for its location than for any special virtue of its architecture, was begun by a Sultan Valide (mother) named Safiye, a wife of Murat III, in 1597. Three different architects had a hand in the work, only finished in 1663. Of the original *külliye* of foundations, only two fountains and the Sultan Valide's *türbe* remain, along with the **Spice Market** (*closed Sun*), whose rents still go to the upkeep of the mosque. Most of the locals call this market the **Mısır Çarşısı**, the 'Egyptian market', since most of the herbs and concoctions traditionally sold here came from the banks of the Nile. Today, in the long, L-shaped hall, a smaller version of the Covered Bazaar, you may purchase anything from jewellery to electric tin-openers to caviar, but at a few of the old stands it's still fun to guess just what the hundreds of items displayed in barrels, bags, and jars could possibly be. 'Spices' to the Turks, as to the rest of Europe, once meant not simply herbs for cooking, but drugs, dyes, preservatives, cosmetics and any other useful substance that grows. One of the biggest sellers today is *kına*, or henna, for ladies' hair.

The **Eminönü Market**, a green and crowded yard between the Spice Market and the Yeni Cami where caged birds, seeds, bulbs, and garden tools are sold, was also the traditional home of the city's scribes, the placid gentlemen with typewriters on little stands, who composed letters for the unlettered and filled in government forms for the bewildered. Perhaps it is a sign of progress—on our most recent visit we didn't see a single one.

Rüstem Paşa Camii

As seen from the bridge or from Beyoğlu, the Yeni Cami stands in the shadow of the great Süleymaniye, on the heights to the southwest. Between the two, the little mosque called **Rüstem Paşa Camii** is hardly even noticed. A closer look will reveal one of Sinan's most elegant works, built in 1550 for Süleyman's grand vezir. The real surprise, though, is within; the mosque is almost entirely covered with the very best İznik tiles, in a spectacular variety of colours and patterns. For all these Ottoman creations, it will never do to ask where the funds came from. Rüstem Paşa was a son-in-law of Süleyman the Magnificent and Roxelana, and the sultan's favourite, in her endless intrigues, determined to make him grand vezir. To accomplish this, all she had to do was to convince Süleyman to have his old friend the Vezir İbrahim murdered. She had little trouble; İbrahim was soon strangled by the palace mutes, and Rüstem distinguished himself by inaugurating the practice of putting government offices up for sale, an Ottoman tradition ever after.

The Covered Bazaar (Kapalı Çarşı)

Open Mon–Sat 8.30am–6.30pm.

It seems likely that Constantinople had some kind of market on this spot; over one of the arches of this vast and rambling structure, a Byzantine eagle can be made out clearly. Long before the days of shopping malls, covered markets like this were an Eastern tradition, not only for convenience but to discourage burglars. No one disputes İstanbul's claim that theirs is the largest in the world. Since Mehmet Fatih built the two *bedestenler*, or stronghouses, in the 1460s, street after street of shops, covered with simple barrel vaults and skylights, have grown up around them, always well maintained and promptly rebuilt after such disasters as the earthquake of 1896 or the fire of 1954. Today, the Kapalı Çarşı, as it is called, is a city unto itself, with five thousand shops, a mosque, a school, even its own post office and police station.

It isn't just for tourists—far from it. Though you'll see plenty of trinkets and little signs proclaiming the owner's proficiency in English or German, the Covered Bazaar has its more prosaic side, as the purveyor of all manner of goods to the Stamboullu, from diamonds to dustpans; note that Mehmet built it before embarking on either his mosque or his Topkapı palace. The market was the key to bringing the half-abandoned city back to life. Even today, despite the advent of industrialism and high finance in Turkey, what goes on here, and in the seemingly endless maze of wholesalers, warehouses and workshops to the north of it, still carries some weight in the nation's economy.

This mighty citadel of the independent businessman also stands ready to give any perceptive visitor some advanced lessons in a free-market economy. The location of shops, for example, will tell you all about everyone's profit margins; the jewellers will be found in the centre and around the entrances, of course, while the dealers in raw leather or children's mittens are tucked away in low-rent alleys where you'll never find them.

Most of the street names tell what trades were followed long ago—for example, the Fezmakers' Street or the Avenue of the Slippers—though the locations gradually changed with the years. Atatürk put the fezmakers out of business long ago, and now their street sells mostly blue jeans. Other names are more colourful, like the Louse Bazaar. You may wander its broad avenues and dim cul-de-sacs, recently renovated and cleared of their ugly thicket of electric signs, and look for bargains to your heart's content. Don't miss the **İç Bedesten** at the centre, devoted to copper and rare antiques; they glitter in Mehmet's dim hall like the treasure in the Cave of the Forty Thieves.

If the Hat Fits…

On the whole, Turks are sharp dressers, and always have been. What is unusual, however, is the way in which matters of dress manage so frequently to insinuate themselves into matters of state: hats, for example.

Most of us have heard of Atatürk's famous Hat Law of 1925, outlawing the wearing of the fez, the conical felt hat with a tassel that Egyptians call a *tarboosh*. Here, what the Father of the Turks had in mind was to do away with one conspicuous symbol of pious reaction; in public, he always wore a fedora or smart cloth cap to set an example. Ironically, the fez itself had been introduced during the 19th-century Tanzimat reforms for the same purpose: to replace the then disreputable old Turkish turban.

Hats in politics go back much further. As far back as the 1460s, Mehmet the Conqueror was enacting a hat law, governing the colours of turbans that could be worn at court: green for vezirs, red for chamberlains, white for muftis, red, yellow or black for everyone else except infidels, who weren't allowed a turban at all. Mehmet followed this up with a shoe ordinance: black for Greeks, blue for Jews, violet for Armenians, and so on.

The Hat Law of 1925 accomplished its purpose in a roundabout way. Today most Turks have given up and don't wear any hat at all, except for the Kurds with their inevitable flat grey caps. Meanwhile, street hawkers go on selling fezes to tourists in front of the Aya Sofya every day.

Stamboul's market district really stretches as far as the Golden Horn, and the Kapalı Çarşı is only its glamorous retail end. Many of the surrounding streets, like those inside, have a particular function. One of the most interesting is the **Sahaflar Çarşısı**, the old Booksellers' Market, just outside the Beyazıt Square entrance to the Covered Bazaar. This lovely courtyard full of tiny shops, with its fountain and large population of cats, is believed to have been around in one form or another since Byzantine times—it's the best place in İstanbul for books and souvenirs. North of the Covered Market, around Uzunçarşı Caddesi, are a number of old *hanlar*, no longer performing their old functions as merchant hotels, but still buzzing with porters and handcarts, the whirr of old machinery, and decorous transactions made over tea.

Beyazıt Square and Beyazıt Camii

An old story relates that, when Beyazıt II was building the mosque that bears his name (the oldest of the Ottoman imperial mosques still standing), a pious old woman offered a pair of pigeons—Turks are fond of pigeons—for the courtyard and gardens. Their descendants rule **Beyazıt Square** today, and you'll earn yourself some credit in Allah's bank of grace for spending a few liras on them; someone will always be there to sell you a plate of seeds. The square, entirely redone several years ago, apparently by some berserk minimalist architect, has become an outstanding piece of modern urban design with few admirers apart from the pigeons, who seem happier than ever even if there are fewer trees. This is what the critics would call an architectural square, a vast expanse of grey granite blocks on different levels; it is a veritable symphony in grey, between the pavement, the pigeons and the subtle variety of grey tones in the **Beyazıt Camii**, the grand and beautiful mosque that the square was designed to show off.

Whether or not this was the mosque that set the pattern for later imperial foundations we have no way to tell. The mosque of Beyazıt's father Mehmet, the original Fatih Camii, was destroyed in an earthquake. Its architect was a Greek named Christodoulos; the Beyazıt Camii, completed in 1504, is the work of his sons. They built their mosque after the plan of the Aya Sofya, only without the upper gallery, and endowed it with a particularly fine courtyard and fountain.

Also on the square is what is claimed to be the world's only **Museum of Calligraphy**, the Beyazıt Hat Sanatları Müzesi (*open daily exc Sun and Mon, 9–4; adm*), concentrating on the art in the Ottoman era.

İstanbul University

Across the square, the monumental gateway in some sort of Persian rococo is the entrance to **İstanbul University**. The date over the arch, the Roman numerals 1453, is a sorry deception. That was the year of the Conquest, but the university was not founded until 1845, as part of the reforms of Abdülmecit. Since Atatürk, the university has expanded greatly, taking over the buildings of the old *Seraskeriat*, the War Ministry, in the large park behind the gate. If you want to meet the students, the wonderful, tree-shaded open-air **café** behind the Beyazıt Camii, at the entrance to the Sahaflar Çarşışı, is full of them.

Mehmet II built the 200ft **Beyazıt Tower** on the campus in 1823 as a watchtower for fires (or insurrections); it is the tallest structure in old Stamboul. Along Yeniçeriler Caddesi, on the south side of the square, the recently excavated ruins lying about belong to the Forum of Theodosius—Beyazıt Square's ancestor on this site.

Süleymaniye Camii

Mimar Sinan, in the last years of his life, is supposed to have said that the Selimiye in Edirne was his favourite among all his scores of mosques; the great architect chose to live, however, near his Süleymaniye (1557), and nearby also is his tomb.

If you have the chance to visit only one of the imperial mosques, your time would be best spent here. No features of the construction are unique or original; the same elements of the classic design will be found in the same places. The building's only excuse for existing is perfection. Just as a mathematician can sometimes look at a complex equation and understand it by what seems to be intuition, so when we look at the Süleymaniye we have no need of measurement or analysis to know that each proportion and line is nothing either more or less than right. The outstanding features are subtle: the excellent stone porticoes on either side, the courtyard and the smooth plain hierarchy of domes, to which we could add the surviving stained glass, the work of a legendary artist called İbrahim the Drunkard.

No mosque in İstanbul, and certainly not the Aya Sofya, has such a feeling of openness within. For a moment, it's easy to forget the reality of columns, arches and vaults and imagine the Süleymaniye as a great stone tent, hung on the four square solid piers at the corners of the dome. Just as Süleyman's reign marked the high noon of the Ottoman state, so does this mosque that Sinan built for him declare the zenith of his nation's art. Time would show that neither had much more to give.

Almost alone among the imperial mosques, the Süleymaniye retains almost all of its *külliye* (complex of religious and educational institutions). This is the grandest *külliye* ever built by the Ottomans, an integral part of Sinan's perfect composition, and no one has dared to tamper with it. The eight low buildings, with over 200 domes between them, have all recently been restored, and several are creatively reused, one as a library and another as a clinic, to benefit the people of the neighbourhood, just as their builders intended. In the courtyard of the mosque, you can see the separate *türbeler* of Süleyman and Roxelana, both done in fine İznik tiles. A smaller tomb, at the narrow angle of a street in the northernmost corner of the complex, is that of Sinan himself.

The Master Builder

Not all Christian boys pressed into the Janissary corps ended up as soldiers. One young Greek, born about 1489, worked his way up through the military engineering branch to become the head architect of the Ottoman state. At the age of 59, Sinan built his first mosque, the Şehzade in İstanbul, for Sultan Süleyman the Magnificent. It was the beginning of a brilliant collaboration that created scores of mosques, schools, bridges and fortifications—the launching of the Ottoman imperial style, as well as its greatest achievements. For the Turks, his profession became a title; they call him Mimar Sinan: Sinan the Architect.

It would have been impossible for one man to have accomplished the tremendous output with which Sinan is credited, several hundred buildings in all. Like the Renaissance artists who attached their names to everything that came out of the workshop, even if all the details had been handled by students, Sinan must really be thought of as head of a huge public works collective. All these works (most are in İstanbul) are distinctive and gracefully proportioned, but those that most clearly bear the stamp of the master are the Selimiye in Edirne, the little Sokollu Mehmet Paşa Mosque and the Süleymaniye.

Just west of the Süleymaniye, in a small courtyard off Kirazlı Mescit Sokak, stands the small Kilise Camii, formerly the **church of St Theodorus**; although much was rebuilt in the 12th century, the foundation and much of the structure are from the 5th, making this the oldest religious structure in İstanbul.

Returning to Beyazıt Square, and continuing west along Vezneciler Caddesi, still following the route of the old *Mese*, we pass reminders of the Ottoman or Byzantine eras on almost every block. The **Kalenderhane Camii**, at the corner of the Büyük Reşit Paşa Caddesi, where six streets meet, was originally the church of the Akataleptos Monastery; 13th-century frescoes have recently been discovered inside, but they have been removed and cannot be seen. A *kalender* is a kind of dervish, and it appears that the function of this and many other monasteries changed little after the Conquest.

Şehzade Camii

Many consider the **Şehzade Camii** (1548), two blocks further east, to be one of the finest of the Ottoman mosques, but its lofty dome conceals a great crime—also, perhaps, the secret of the decline of the Ottoman Empire. Süleyman the Magnificent had a son named Mustafa by one of his concubines, an intelligent and virtuous young man who gave every promise of being an excellent soldier and ruler. All that stood between him and a brilliant reign was the unfortunate matter of his mother's name not being Roxelana. The sultan's favourite had sons of her own, younger than Mustafa, and she was determined to do anything to see them on the throne. She had already driven Süleyman to murder once, in the case of the Grand Vezir İbrahim, and now, on the evidence of forged letters that suggested that Mustafa was planning to stage a revolt, she persuaded the sultan to do him in.

Mustafa, called back from the province he was governing, went unsuspectingly to his doom; it is said Süleyman watched from behind a curtain while the mutes and the bowstring went to work—spilling royal blood was an unthinkable crime, and garrotting with a bowstring was the custom for such necessities. Roxelana, ironically, never lived to enjoy the power of a Sultan Valide, but her son Selim II, called the Sot, was to reign for eight years as the first dissolute Ottoman before succumbing to cirrhosis. It is said Süleyman built the Şehzade Camii, the 'Prince's Mosque', out of remorse. Sinan used the opportunity to experiment, bestowing upon his mosque one of the most unusual exteriors to be seen in İstanbul, with plenty of Persian and Moorish-inspired detail on the minarets, domes and windows. Later Turkish architects were to draw on these, especially during the Baroque era, but Sinan himself returned to his accustomed austerity just in time to design the Süleymaniye.

Just behind the Şehzade, a small mosque called the **Burmalı Minare** was built by an Egyptian paşa two years after its larger neighbour. The name refers to the 'spiral' minaret, unique in the city. All this area around the intersection of the *Mese*—called Şehzadebaşı along this stretch—and Atatürk Bulvarı was developed into a park as part of İstanbul's first ambitious planning scheme in the 1940s. Across the street, the steel and glass City Hall was its centrepiece, and broad **Atatürk Bulvarı**, designed for cars, its major improvement. Amazingly, in 1,600 years this was the first ever street laid out to form a direct connection between the Marmara and the Golden Horn.

Aqueduct of Valens

The park was opened up partly to expose the **Aqueduct of Valens**, supported by an arcade over half a mile in length between the Third and Fourth Hills, and nearly 60ft tall where it passes over Atatürk Bulvarı. The 4th-century Emperor Valens really only expanded and repaired an older aqueduct, but the popular name credits it to him even though most of what you see was constructed by, of course, Mimar Sinan, who rebuilt the city's water supply for Sultan Süleyman. The aqueduct was in use well into the 20th century; today you can follow its crumbled end into a street of car mechanics in the Fatih district. In its shadow, next to the boulevard, the early 17th-century Gazanfer Ağa Medrese was restored in the 1940s as İstanbul's **Municipal Museum**. The humble and dusty collection includes maps and views of the city, expropriated relics from the dervish orders, imperial firmans directed to the city, portraits, Karagöz puppets and other bric-à-brac.

Church of the Pantocrator

A walk a few blocks north along Atatürk Bulvarı will take you past the Zevrek Kilise Camii, once the **church of the Pantocrator**, built in 1124, its history intertwined with that of the empire in its last centuries. John Comnenus, 'Good John', who presided over the last spell of peace and prosperity for Byzantium, built it, and was buried here along with his Hungarian wife Irene, a great patroness of the arts. During the occupation of the Crusaders it became a Catholic church, the seat of the Venetian Bishop Morosini; ironically, later it was to be the church of Gennadius, the prelate who worked so fervently in the 1440s to avert the proposed union of the churches, Constantinople's last hope for aid from the west against the Ottomans. Mehmet rewarded Gennadius after the Conquest by making him the first patriarch under the new dispensation. The monastery of which this church was a part has completely disappeared; the retaining walls of the huge cistern that served it and the neighbourhood are all that is left.

After passing Atatürk Bulvarı, the old *Mese* changes its name one last time, to Fevzi Paşa Caddesi. The *külliye* here, a fine example of Turkish architecture, is the 1698 **Amcazade**, built by one of the grand vezirs of the Köprülü family. Two blocks south of Fevzi Paşa, the most complete surviving Roman monument in İstanbul stands on a quiet street of apartment blocks: the **Column of Marcian**, built *c.* AD 450. The tall granite shaft, surmounted by a Corinthian column and a much-effaced winged symbol, once bore a gold statue of this vain emperor, an intriguer with no real successes to commemorate. Traces of the reliefs on the base can be made out.

Lâleli District and Aksaray

East of Marcian's column, the quarter around Atatürk Bulvarı south of the *Mese* is called **Lâleli**, named after the **Lâleli** (tulip) **Cami**, on busy Ordu Caddesi, a famous work of the Turkish Baroque built under Mustafa III in 1760. The high stone platform on which the mosque stands now contains a little bazaar of shops added in the 1950s. Long ago, before the mosque was even built, it was the central hashish and opium den of İstanbul, a distinction it seems also to have had under the Byzantines. Murat IV, a tremendous drunkard, closed it down for the good of the nation.

Across Ordu Caddesi, **Aksaray** is a bustling, thoroughly modern district packed with hotels and foreigners. A decade ago there was a large Arab and Persian influence; now in a transition that native Stamboullu find amazing and amusing, the quarter has become home to thousands of Russians, Poles and other East Europeans. Many of them are in the textile and fashion trades, and their boutiques can be seen along every street. Aksaray and Lâleli have become the most frenetic corner of the city, a raucous street scene, day and night, that includes wall-to-wall street vendors, *hamallar* (porters) struggling under enormous burdens, Slavic prostitutes (Turks call them 'natashas') and suspicious-looking folk from all over the world. It explodes into total confusion several times a day when lorries packed with cloth pull in from the docks, or from Adana, centre of the cotton country of the southeast. Brokers and shopkeepers descend on them like locusts, and impromptu auctions start in the middle of the street. Here too, tucked away on Mesihpaşa Caddesi, is the **Bodrum Cami**, originally the **church of the Mirelaon Convent**, rebuilt and renovated so often since the 6th century that no one knows to whom to credit it.

The Lâleli Cami may be the place where Turkish Baroque went over the edge, but the indescribable **Valide Camii**, on Aksaray Square, must be the supreme example of the preciosity of a decadent nation carried to its wildest extreme. The Turks were as eclectic as anyone in 1870, and the idea here was to invent Turkish neo-Gothic.

Fatih District

North of Lâleli, **Fatih**, the enormous quarter named after Mehmet the Conqueror and the great complex of religious buildings he erected at its centre, is home to over 100,000 of Stamboul's working people; plain and honest, it has survived both urban decay and creeping modernity. At present, it has a reputation as the stronghold of the fundamentalists in the city. When Mehmet built his **Fatih Cami** here in 1463, this Fourth Hill was one of the choicer districts of the city. Here stood the church of the Holy Apostles, the church second in size and importance only to Aya Sofya. Mehmet demolished it, one of the few instances of wanton destruction of Christian buildings on the part of the Turks. Eighteen of its columns can be seen in the mosque's courtyard. It should not be too hard to imagine how the Holy Apostles looked; St Mark's in Venice was modelled on it. The church is also said to have had a unique conical dome; underneath it for a time lay the remains of the city's founder and 'thirteenth apostle', Constantine.

Mehmet's mosque, which we know had two equal domes in the fashion of the earlier Ottoman mosques of Bursa, was shaken down by an earthquake in 1766. The reigning Sultan Mustafa III had it rebuilt even bigger in the classical style, but the result is just another uninspired copy from the same mould. The *külliye*, an enormous complex elevated on a platform that turns a vast blank face towards Fevzi Paşa Caddesi, is even larger than that of the Süleymaniye; its institutions and foundations still provide important services for the people of the Fatih. Yet another small, inconspicuous Byzantine building can be seen a few blocks to the north on Küçük Mektep Sokak, the 12th-century **church of Christ Pantepoptes** built by Alexis I Comnenus. Now it's the **Eski İmaret Camii**, though much of its attractive exterior survives, decorated with patterns of tiles and bricks.

Outlying Areas to the West: the Exokionion

On the map (*see* pp.124–5), you can follow a line of avenues—Haliç Caddesi, Akdeniz Caddesi and Kızıl Elma Caddesi among others—starting at the Golden Horn and winding an irregular course behind the Fatih complex and across the peninsula. These generally follow the line of the original long-vanished walls of Constantinople, paced off by Constantine himself after a vision showed him how best to defend the city. Even after the Theodosian walls were built further west, this area beyond the older line had the legal status of an extra-mural district, and during the various conflicts over church dogma heretics were allowed to hold religious services here. The Greeks called this wide swathe of land between Constantine's and Theodosius' Walls the *Exokionion*. Today it is home to hundreds of thousands of Stamboul's poorer residents, in a disorganized conglomeration of villages and market gardens with some dense concentrations of flats, all up and down the Fifth, Sixth and Seventh Hills.

With the help of the dolmuş and minibus, those with a real interest in tracking down the wealth of Ottoman and Byzantine monuments here can start their expeditions. Doing it properly will require some walking, and some climbing—around the Fifth Hill in particular, the only one of the seven that truly deserves the name. Your troubles will be rewarded by an endless supply of curiosities past and present, as well as insights into the working life of the more prosaic corners of the fantastical city.

The neighbourhood directly north of the Fatih, along Darüşşafaka Caddesi, gets the travelling market on Wednesday (*Çarşamba* in Turkish), which has given the quarter its name. From here Yavuz Selim Caddesi ascends the Fifth Hill to the **Sultan Selim Camii** or **Selimiye**, begun by the conqueror of Egypt but not completed until 1522, in the reign of his son Süleyman. Selim built his *türbe* in the garden behind this austere and beautiful mosque. From here, you can look out over the rooftops of one of Stamboul's oddest neighbourhoods, a pretty sunken village built around crags of antique masonry at the bottom of the **Cistern of Aspar**, a 5th-century addition to Constantinople's water supply.

Fener Quarter

Progressing any further will require a stout heart and shoes, for the streets that introduce you to the quarter of the Fener are the steepest and roughest in all İstanbul. The old ladies storm up and down like mountain goats, and the children play vertical tag, but you may be hard pressed. The Fener takes its name from the old Phanar (lighthouse) Gate, a part of the Theodosian walls along the Golden Horn. After the Conquest it became the district allotted to the Greeks, and some live here to this day. Since 1923, however, most have either returned to Greece or moved to newer parts of the city across the Golden Horn.

The Fener today, with its melancholy, half-empty streets wrapped in the silence of the tomb, stands in sharp contrast to past centuries. Even after the Conquest, the talents of the Greeks in the arts and in commerce, and the natural disinclination of the Ottoman élite to earn an honest living, ensured that the more accomplished of the infidels would find many doors open to them. Throughout the empire, the Greeks controlled shipping, finance and many of the trades, and provided the sultans with most of their officials and tax collectors. The capital

İstanbul: Outlying Sights

Stamboul
- **A** Greek Orthodox Patriarchate
- **B** St Mary Mouchliotissa
- **C** Fethiye Camii (Pammakaristos Church)
- **D** Kariye Camii (St Saviour in Chora)
- **E** Dungeon of Anemas
- **F** Palace of Constantine Porphyrogenitus
- **G** Mihrimah Camii
- **H** Koca Mustafa Paşa Camii (St Andrea in Crisal)
- **I** Altımermer Cistern
- **J** Cerrahpaşa Camii

Beyoğlu
- **K** Soldiers' Museum
- **L** Naval Museum
- **M** Çırağan Palace

In Asia
- **N** Selimiye Barracks
- **O** Mihrimah Camii
- **P** Yeni Valide Camii
- **Q** Şemsi Pasa Çamii

Bosphorus
- **R** Ortaköy Camii
- **S** Beylerbeyi Palace

Inset map
- **T** Küçüksu Palace
- **U** Anadolu Hisarı
- **V** Rumeli Hisarı
- **W** Emirgan Park
- **X** Genoese Castle

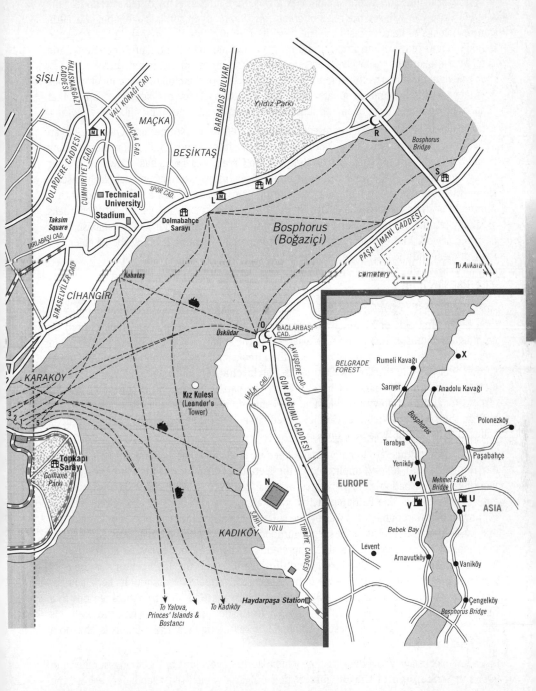

of this conspicuous and favoured community was here, and on many of the streets near the Golden Horn you will see the ruins of great houses, and even some fashionable late 19th-century blocks of flats, to testify to the wealth and influence the Phanar—as it was then called—once enjoyed. The stranglehold they maintained over the empire's economy, and thus over the sultans themselves, was notorious; the monopolies they effectively held in many fields contributed as much to the economic decline of the empire as the incompetence of the government, and so great were their exactions from the subject peoples that 'Phanariot' became a term of opprobrium used by Slavs, Turks and Arabs alike.

Most historians have chosen to present the struggle of the Byzantines and Ottomans as an apocalyptic battle of two faiths, both incapable of either understanding or showing any sympathy at all for each other. On the contrary, the Greeks and Turks had known each other for so long before 1453—four centuries of alliances, intermarriages and scholarly discussion—that when the end came for Byzantium, the transition was accomplished with a minimum of hysteria. After the pillage Mehmet had promised his troops, life for the Greeks gradually returned to normal, and even improved, as the sultan's efforts to re-establish trade began to pay off. In the Phanar, the heirs of the imperial Byzantine families, the Paleologues, the Comneni and the rest, were reported still to be around as late as the 1900s.

The Patriarchate

Letters in [ ] refer to the map of İstanbul on pp.124–5.

One of the first acts of Mehmet after the Conquest was to co-opt the Greek church by naming Gennadius patriarch, as much a servant of the sultan as was the Sheikh ul-İslam, and meant to act as an intermediary between the Greeks and the Ottoman state. Gennadius' successors live on in the **Greek Orthodox Patriarchate** [A] on a steep hill just above the Golden Horn. Old St George's Church, where the patriarchs sat on the throne of St John Chrysostom, burned down in 1941, and the centre of the complex is now a huge tower—built in the 1880s, in Victorian Gothic, incredibly enough. The Patriarchs' throne inside is believed to date from Byzantine times.

The main gate of the Patriarchate has not been opened since Easter Sunday 1821. On that day the Patriarch Gregory, implicated in the Hetairist conspiracy of the Phanariot Greeks working for their nation's independence, was hanged from it. All those with business here enter from the side. The Patriarchate today has a lonely and forlorn air. The Greek school, supported by the republic as it was by the sultans, appears almost empty. Few Greeks, for that matter, seem to be left in the neighbourhood, if the faces of the inhabitants and signs in the shops are any indication. The tiny, unpretentious chapel a block away has great meaning for the remaining Greeks: **St Mary Mouchliotissa** [B], from the 13th century, is the only surviving pre-Conquest church never to have been converted to a mosque. Its benefactress, 'Saint Mary of the Mongols', was a Byzantine princess married off for political reasons to a Khan of the İlhanlı Mongols in 1282. After his death she returned to the city and built this church as part of the great monastic complex in which, long before, the Empress Theodora had spent her last days.

Just a few blocks away, overlooking the Golden Horn, have a look at the strangest church in İstanbul, **St Stephen of the Bulgars**. When Bulgaria gained its independence from the

Ottoman Empire in 1871, the Turks weren't sore losers. They allowed the Bulgarians of İstanbul to build this church in celebration of the event. A church that defies all attempts at architectural classification, St Stephen's is made entirely of cast iron. A foundry in Vienna cast it, then shipped it down the Danube and Black Sea on barges to İstanbul, where the pieces were assembled. Each Orthodox New Year's Day, an ancient ceremony is held here in which the priest tosses a cross into the frigid waters of the Golden Horn, while the young men of the congregation (there can't be many these days) leap in and try to retrieve it.

With luck, you'll be able to pick your way through the tortuous lanes towards the walls to see two other important Byzantine monuments. The 11th-century **Pammakaristos Church** [C], quite near the Patriarchate, has one of the most unusual and most elaborate exteriors of any church in the city, in patterns reminiscent of those on the apse of the famous Greek-Norman cathedral of Monreale in Sicily, built at the same time. One distinctive feature is the delicately carved window mullions, unique to this church. Inside, a fine 13th-century mosaic scene of the baptism of Christ has recently been restored, along with a large number of mosaic figures of saints. The Pammakaristos ('most blessed') was the seat of the Patriarchate from 1456 to 1586. If you ask for directions, try using its old name of **Fethiye Camii** even though it's been a museum for some years. Unfortunately, it is now closed, but if you really want to see the mosaics ask at the museum office of the Aya Sofya, © 0212 528 4500, which has charge of it. Permission, if granted at all, may take up to a week.

Church of St Saviour in Chora (Kariye)

Open daily except Wed, 9–4; adm.

From here, Fethiye Caddesi, changing its name to Draman Caddesi, will bring you to the **church of St Saviour in Chora** [D], or Kariye. This is nothing less than the finest collection of Byzantine mosaics and mural painting in Turkey. You'll find the trip worth the trouble, especially since Çelik Gülersoy and his Automobile Club have transformed the surroundings—in the middle of a very shabby neighbourhood—into a small oasis with a garden café and a number of restored Ottoman houses. The art inside, like that of the Aya Sofya, was restored by the Byzantine Institute.

Originally built by Justinian, and completely rebuilt by the Comneni in the 11th century, it is always associated with the name of Theodore the Logothete, a high official in the late 14th century who fell victim to political intrigue and ended his days as a poor monk in the church he had restored and beautified. In the latter days of the empire, when the Aya Sofya was falling into decay and the emperors had moved to the Blachernae Palace nearby, the Chora became the city's fashionable church, where the imperial family usually attended services. An icon of the Virgin kept here, one of those supposedly painted by St Luke, was credited with saving Constantinople from the siege of Murat II in 1428; the Turk's final attack failed shortly after the icon was carried solemnly around the walls.

Architecturally, little in the Chora is outstanding; the major attraction is its wealth of frescoes. Byzantine painting has always been undervalued by the critics, their eyes dazzled by the gold of the less expressive, less articulate mosaics. The restoration of the frescoes in the **Paraecclesion**, or mortuary chapel, of the Chora, as well as those in other late Byzantine churches like the Aya Sofya in Trabzon, has already gone a long way towards correcting this.

In these paintings, it is easy to see the influence and the inspiration without which the Italian Renaissance would not have been possible.

Of these, the greatest perhaps is the spectacular version of the *Last Judgement*, in which Jesus raises the dead over a shower of broken locks and keys; Adam and Eve are shown redeemed, along with the unbaptized kings and prophets of the Old Testament. The remainder portray various Biblical scenes, the Burning Bush and Jacob wrestling with the angel, as well as a whole catalogue of Orthodox saints and some unusual *trompe l'œil* borders. Theodore the Logothete himself appears in one of the mosaics, presenting his rebuilt church to Christ. A figure of the Christ Pantocrator and other mosaics with scenes from his life and portraits of apostles and saints cover the outer and inner nartexes; unfortunately few have survived in the nave of the church.

Theodosian Walls

The **Theodosian Walls** can be seen just a few blocks west of the Chora. In their own right, they are among the greatest monuments of İstanbul. No city has ever had better; without them, the Byzantine capital could easily have succumbed on scores of occasions to Huns, Avars, Bulgarians, Russians, Arabs, Goths or Turks; with them, even in its darkest and most decadent moments, the empire was able to maintain itself as the bulwark of Christendom and the heir of Rome.

Fully 17 miles in length, the walls stand almost intact between the Golden Horn and the Marmara, but in fragments along the shores. The inland walls, the easiest to attack, are the most impressive. Anthemius, Theodosius's prefect, made them invulnerable by doubling them, with a raised inner wall looking down over and protecting the outer, and a deep ditch in front of that. For most of their length, you can walk between them or even on them. A word of **caution** is in order, though; some of the areas around the walls, particularly in the Topkapı Gate area, have a reputation as being a bit dangerous, and a lot of Turkey's drug manufacturing business is said to go on here.

Where the wall meets the Golden Horn, two towers stand as remnants of the **Dungeon of Anemas** [E] where the Byzantines kept unsuccessful schemers and political prisoners. These walls are actually not part of the original work, but a long loop added around the **Palace of Blachernae**, the huge suburban garden palace of the late emperors. Very little of it remains; the palace encompassed all of what is now the green district called **Ayvansaray**, its houses and gardens betraying occasional traces of an old wall or a bit of carved stone. The **Palace of Constantine Porphyrogenitus** [F] adjacent to the Blachernae still stands, a stony pile, literally a shell of what it once was, without roof, floors, or even its marble façade.

Edirne Gate (Edirne Kapı)

Just inside the **Edirne Kapı**, the old Adrianople Gate, is another fine mosque built by Sinan for Süleyman the Magnificent, the **Mihrimah Camii** [G] (1562), named after the sultan's favourite daughter. The section of the walls to the south, in the dangerous spot depressed by the valley of the Lycus stream, saw much of the heaviest fighting during the siege of 1453. Here Mehmet's cannons pounded away relentlessly for days. Giustiniani, the Venetian commander, was wounded there, and although the wall was not breached, his loss greatly disheartened the defenders and contributed much to the fall. The postern gate of Charisius, the one accidentally left open that caused the defeat, is just north of the Mihrimah. The tallest of the towers is at the old Roman Gate, now the **Topkapı** ('cannon gate'), the major entrance to the city by road.

On the Marmara shore, the **Marble Tower** at the end of the inland walls was a famous Byzantine landmark. Just to the north was the **Golden Gate** where all the emperors, on their accessions or their triumphs, entered. Most of its legendary embellishments are long gone, including the famous golden doors, but the Crusaders could not remove the marble triumphal arch at the centre of the gate, built to commemorate Theodosius' victory over the pretender Maximus in 391. To its four towers, Mehmet II added three more and an inner wall, creating the **Yedikule** (seven towers) **Castle**, recently restored and now open to visitors (*open daily exc Mon, 9.30–5; adm*). Here Osman II was murdered by the Janissaries. Later sultans used it for incarcerating foreign ambassadors when the mood struck them; many of these, along with other prisoners, have left interesting inscriptions on the walls.

Southwestern İstanbul

This part of the city has little to offer. Byzantine churches like those of the monastic complex at Studion and the Peribleptos Monastery have long ago been battered out of recognition by earthquakes and subsequent rebuildings. Under the Byzantines, the Studion was the centre of learning of the Greek world, the prototype of the university. All that is left of it today is one of its churches, **St John in Studion**, now the **İmrahor Camii** on İmrahor İlyas Bey Caddesi. Even this has little to show from its past: just a few capitals and a 12th-century patterned pavement. Another church, that of **St Andreas in Crisal** [H], is still substantially intact, just to the north at the western end of Koca Mustafa Paşa Caddesi; now it is the **Koca Mustafa Paşa Camii**. Many Armenians live in this area, and their mostly 19th-century churches are still in use, including the **Armenian Patriarchate** in Sarapnel Sokak near the Marmara end of the Atatürk Bulvarı. The largest of all open cisterns, the **Altımermer** [I], may be seen in the quarter of the same name, and the 1593 **Cerrahpaşa Camii** [J] is the most interesting of the area's mosques.

Rather than visiting these, take yourself to Adnan Menderes Bulvarı, one of the broad empty boulevards driven through Stamboul in the 1940s, and see the ancient metropolis from the top of the Ferris wheel in the little amusement park there. Not long ago this street was called Vatan Caddesi; they changed it, ostensibly to commemorate the deposed prime minister of the 1950s, whose name was still taboo only a few years ago—but also perhaps because this was the lowest-rent street in the Turkish version of Monopoly; the highest, by the way, is Barbaros Bulvarı in Beşiktaş.

Eyüp

Once upon a time, the Golden Horn was the most beloved of all the embellishments of İstanbul. From Eminönü Square all the way up the estuary, both banks were lined with *yalılar*, the wooden mansions of the paşas, set among gardens and groves of plane trees and cypresses. Marble quays brightened the shores, and the only boats to be seen were pleasure craft and water taxis. Then, in the 19th century, Abdülhamid the Damned—Abdülhamid II, the sultan of whom not even the Turks will speak kindly—let in the foreign syndicates and industrialists, and in no time at all the Horn became a seamy polluted waterfront, the black sewer of İstanbul.

Just beyond the inland walls at Ayvansaray, the little village of **Eyüp** was, before Abdülhamid, a rare jewel of the waterway. Set on a height, enjoying the best view of the domes and minarets of the city, Eyüp was a garden suburb of lovely modest houses, favoured by the most influential artists and public men of the Ottoman Empire. Also, it was a holy place, a traditional spot for pilgrims to stop on the way to Mecca. Today, surrounded by factories and *gecekondu* sprawl, Eyüp has become a poor district and somewhat bedraggled, but still tries its best to keep its head above the miasma.

Although it is believed the spot has been holy ground since ancient times, Eyüp acquired its sanctity for Muslims during the Siege of 1453, when Mehmet or one of his vezirs had a dream directing him to the unmarked grave of Eba-Eyüp el-Ensari, the standard bearer of the Prophet Mohammed, who had died here during the first Arab attack on Constantinople in the 7th century. Eyüp—the name is the Arabic form of Job—was found just where the dream had promised. Mehmet built a *türbe* and mosque, and when an earthquake knocked it down in 1800, Sultan Selim III replaced it with the **Eyüp Camii** you see today. It was here that the sultans, upon their accessions, were girded with the sword of Osman, which served them in place of a crown as the symbol of sovereignty.

All around, between the blocks of small shops selling Korans and a strange assortment of Islamic trinkets, the living village shares the space with acres of beautiful cemeteries, their marble headstones laid out in walled gardens with names like the Pavilion of Idris and the Valley of the Nightingale.

Beyoğlu

In Byzantine times, there was no bridge over the Golden Horn—there was no reason to cross it. The little settlement on the opposite shore called Sycae never played much of a role in the life of the city. Galata, the port of Beyoğlu on the tip of the Golden Horn, began as a Genoese trading colony in the 9th century. As the Italian control of trade routes strengthened, Constantinople's economic power declined, and by the 14th century Galata was a large and prosperous town; such trade as passed through the Bosphorus landed here, not at the impoverished capital.

Italians had long played a role in the city, not only the Genoese, but Pisans, Venetians and Amalfitani. At one point in the 12th century, some 60,000 of them were reported to be living within the walls. Their commercial arrogance, not to mention their heretical Christianity, infuriated the Greeks, and in 1180, a mob—among whom we may guess were many of the Italians' debtors—massacred thousands. Diverting the Fourth Crusade to sack Constantinople was the Italians' way of returning the favour.

When the Greek emperors returned in 1261, Galata began to build walls against the possibility of another such debt moratorium. The restored empire, weak as it was, became entirely dependent on the Genoese. The Genoese nonchalantly declared their neutrality during the siege of 1453, and kept some of their privileges under the Turks for as long as Genoa remained a maritime power. Under Ottoman rule, Galata maintained its role as a foreign compound; the Genoese were gradually replaced by the French and others, who were granted their first commercial privileges, or 'capitulations', by Süleyman the Magnificent in 1525.

Life in Stamboul was perhaps too unsettling for the ambassadors of the European powers, and they soon began to construct large embassy compounds on the lovely hills of **Pera** (Beyoğlu) above Galata. Fashion and influence followed, and enough money flowed into the capitulations to build Galata and Pera into the real centre of the city. As the Turks and their government became increasingly impotent and irrelevant, eventually even the sultan joined the migration, building a new palace, the **Dolmabahçe**, on the Bosphorus in the 1850s. Most of the recent growth of the city has occurred on the Beyoğlu side of the Golden Horn. While in many places you can still look out over open countryside from the Theodosian walls of Stamboul, new districts have spread for miles northwards from Pera; today even the villages along the Bosphorus are considered part of the metropolitan area.

These streets were once legendary throughout the world for their scenes of ostentatious wealth mixed with age-old grime and squalor, their Levantine mix of a hundred nationalities and languages, their excesses and their intrigues. The departure of the embassies, after Atatürk moved the government to Ankara, simply let all the air out of them, and now they display a kind of decayed grandeur that only cities like Naples and Palermo or certain parts of New York can approach. Nothing urban is as romantic as the capital of a vanished empire— think of Vienna or Venice—and in its decay this quarter really blossomed, the natural habitat of Joel Cairo and Casper Gutman from *The Maltese Falcon*, and every other sort of spy and adventurer, real and fictional.

About a decade ago, this neighbourhood had hit rock bottom. İstiklâl Caddesi, its main thoroughfare, was a grimy, degraded shadow of its former self, lined with sordid night spots and porno theatres; few of its buildings were occupied above the ground floor. Since then the change has been dramatic. İstiklâl has been scrubbed up and polished and closed to traffic, embellished instead with the charming (and also totally practical and efficient) Nostaljik Tramvay, to carry people between the Tünel and Taksim Square. Businesses have moved back in, and the renewal is starting to spread to the side streets.

Karaköy

Coming across the Galata Bridge, you meet first the grey mess of warehouses, workshops and office blocks of **Karaköy**, or 'black village', the modern name for Galata. If the gritty surroundings suit you, walk around: İstanbul's oldest Catholic church and other odd relics of Galata's past are tucked away in corners where it will take you some effort to find them.

Just a block east of the bridge, the **Yeraltı Camii** or 'underground mosque' originally occupied the cellar of a defence tower believed to have been built by the Romans. The more conventional mosque building over it was added in the 1750s. To the west, off Tersane Caddesi, the **Arap Camii** started as a Byzantine church, and was rebuilt as a Dominican chapel in the early 14th century; in 1492 Beyazıt II converted it into a mosque for Arab refugees expelled from Spain.

Voyvoda Caddesi takes its name from the redoubtable 15th-century Voyvode of Transylvania, Vlad Dracul, stalwart enemy of the Turk and inventor of a hundred novel ways of disposing of captives and indiscreet ambassadors. His metamorphosis into the blood-sucking Count Dracula at the hands of novelist Bram Stoker is well known. The Turks say they caught him and stuck his head on a pike; it is supposed to be buried somewhere along this street. The Romanians, and most of the historians, maintain Vlad was never defeated. Come around some night and look.

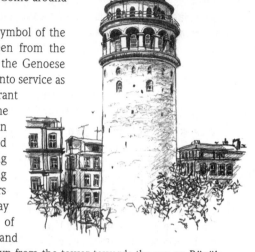

The **Galata Tower**, the most conspicuous symbol of the quarter and the centre of its skyline as seen from the Stamboul side, was built in 1350 as part of the Genoese fortifications. Under the Ottomans, it was put into service as a fire tower. Recently restored, it has a restaurant on the top floor with a fine view of the city. The streets surrounding the Galata Tower are an enticing tangle of steep and crumbling steps and narrow walkways, flanked by old, looming apartment blocks. Workmen's hammers clang from within dark and musty workshops and cars hoot ceaselessly as they try to squeeze their way through. This area houses a small section of İstanbul's Jewish population, and a plain and modest synagogue can be found 100 yards down from the tower towards the sea on Büyük Hendek Caddesi. Called the **Neve Shalom**, it is identifiable only by the row of Stars of David above the glass doorway. It was here that Palestinian terrorists massacred 21 worshippers one terrible *Shabbat* in 1986.

Nearby, on Galip Dede Caddesi, the **Museum of Divan Literature** or Divan Edebiyatı Müzesi (*open Tues–Sun 9.30–4.30*) is really the subtle Turkish republican way of preserving İstanbul's Mevlevi House, the *tekke* (lodge) of the whirling dervishes, after the order's dissolution in 1925. While the *tekke* began here as early as the 1490s, most of what you see now are the contributions of the 19th-century sultans, traditionally the friends of the Mevlevis. There are exhibits of musical instruments and other dervish paraphernalia, a smaller version of the Mevlâna Museum in Konya. This is also part of a working monastery; performances of the dervishes' dances are given on 17 December and other dates.

Kemeraltı Caddesi

As a perfect counterpoint to the dervish house, İstanbul has long kept its **red-light district** in a compound of shabby blocks off Kemeraltı Caddesi, guarded by a policeman at the front gate to keep out unlicensed females and anyone with a camera. This is a highly organized, officially sanctioned operation. Kemeraltı continues westwards, past the 15th-century **St Benoit Church**, tucked awkwardly between two warehouses. Long the church of Pera's French community, St Benoit holds the remains of Ferenc Rakoczy, the 18th-century Hungarian patriot who fought not the Turks, but the Habsburgs of Austria, and ended his life in exile in Turkey after the defeat of his revolutionary army.

Kemeraltı ends at **Tophane Square**; the name commemorates the first Turkish cannon foundry built here in the early 19th century by Sultan Selim III. The **Kılıç Ali Paşa Camii** here is a noteworthy late work of Sinan; the larger mosque to the east, the 1826 **Nüsretiye Cami**, was completed just as Mehmut II won his death struggle with the Janissaries—hence its name, 'Victory Mosque'.

The Tünel

No trip to İstanbul would be complete without a ride on the world's shortest underground, the **Tünel**, which will take you from the environs of Galata Bridge some 600 yards up the modest slope to İstiklâl Caddesi. The motives for building this little inclined railway in 1877 are unclear; some say its original purpose was to move livestock through to İstanbul avoiding the crowded streets of Pera. Affectionately known as the 'Mouse Hole', it was built by the Frenchman Henri Gavand in 1873, and if it takes longer than 90 seconds to hurtle through the 2,034ft of its length, then it's travelling slowly. From Tünel Square, where it ends, you may start up İstiklâl or go back to **Şişhane Square**, one of the few real tragedies of İstanbul's recent redevelopment. Once a frilly, cobbled Italianate piazza with its radiating avenues and overdressed buildings, and the site of the city hall, it has been almost totally obliterated to make more room for cars. Walking up the hill from the square, along Meşrutiyet Caddesi, you will come to one of the city's great institutions, the **Pera Palace Hotel** (*see* p.68).

İstiklâl Caddesi

İstiklâl Caddesi was once known as the *Grande Rue de Pera*, where the ambassadors rubbed elbows with the city's commercial élite. In the 19th century it became heavily built up with European-style apartment and business blocks. Many of these are glorious Art Nouveau works from the turn of the century, their balconies dripping cast-iron vines and flowers over the street; one of the best is at No.479 (more good ones are on Kemeraltı Caddesi and other streets in Pera). Another feature of the street is the old embassies, now reduced to the status of the world's fanciest consulates. Many of the embassy compounds included churches; today you'll need to peek behind the shops into their quiet courtyards to find them: two especially fine ones, both Italian, are the church of **S. Maria Draperis** (1783) and **S. Antonio di Padua** (1725) at Nos.431 and 331 respectively.

The antique trams run every 10 minutes up İstiklâl Caddesi to Taksim Square but it is more interesting to walk, taking care that the trams—stealthy, quietly whirring contraptions—do not flatten you along the way. Starting from the Tünel entrance, the first noteworthy consulate is the **Swedish**, on the right hidden behind big gates. Two hundred years old, it exudes a lofty elegance. Just beyond it is the **Russian consulate**, splendidly overblown, all neo-Grecian columns and carved cornices, painted a purple that is, oddly enough, quite fetching. Designed by the Fossati brothers, the Italian architects of Czar Nicolas I, it was completed in 1837. S. Maria Draperis is a short way up from here, still on the right.

If the **Dutch consulate**, very white and very pretty, looks familiar, it's because you've just seen its big brother: this too is the work of the illustrious and prolific Fossati brothers. Just before the consulate a narrow street declines sharply to a **Dutch chapel** which today is the base of the Union Church of İstanbul, a Protestant congregation which embraces all nationalities. Sunday services are held in English. Back on İstiklâl Caddesi, S. Antonio di Padua, imposingly Gothic, is the last church in this sector. A daily Mass is held here at 6pm.

İstiklâl is full of arcades (*pasajlar*), dim covered alleys or grand follies like the Avrupa Pasajı, serving many purposes. Most famous is the one devoted to beer, the narrow **Çiçek Pasajı**. Despite all the good things that have happened to this neighbourhood in recent years, we can still shed a tear for the 'flower arcade'. Not long ago this was the most beloved and atmospheric watering hole in Turkey, four feet wide and lined with crowded cafés and stand-up joints with sawdust on the floor. You would get a beer in a huge glass called an 'Argentine', and the barman would dump a depth charge of vodka in it if you looked like you needed it. A dancing bear might come in to entertain. All that's gone now. Well-painted and cheerful, the arcade shelters a few colourless new cafés and fish restaurants. The building in which the Çiçek Pasajı is located is itself part of the İstiklâl scenery, a florid, incredible pile with iron letters proclaiming CITY OF PERA on the cornice. Now beautifully restored, for decades it was a burned-out, empty shell. Across the street, the school behind the big gates is the **Galatasaray Lisesi**, once the most prestigious in the empire, where instruction was carried on, naturally, in French. At the end of a side street near the school is the **Galatasaray Hamam**, built by Beyazıt II in 1481 and still the city's most opulent.

Behind the Çiçek Pasajı, İstanbul's liveliest market, the **Balık Pazarı** (fish market) covers a maze of streets; most of the *meyhaneler* (bars) chased out of the Çiçek Pasajı by restoration have taken refuge here, on Nevizade Sokak and other streets. Immediately to the right of the entrance to the market is the Armenian church of **Surp Yerrortutyun**, its doors adorned with two distinctive Armenian *katchkars*, raised crosses, in wooden relief. Inside, the church is long and arched and graceful; incense hangs in the air. The street to the left of the market leads down to Meşrutiyet Caddesi and the **British Consulate**, built by Sir Charles Barry, co-architect of the Houses of Parliament. If you keep straight on past the consulate, you reach a large iron gate on the left. Through the gate is a courtyard, centred on a tree twisted around an old Victorian lamppost; to the right, a short flight of steps leads up to the Greek Orthodox church of **Panaya Isodion**. The church will be locked but the narthex will be open; it is hung with silver icons and gloomy paintings, the best of which is a serene Madonna set high inside the central dome. From the church, retrace your steps to the Balık Pazarı and turn left. A few strides away is the small **Avrupa Pasajı**, the European Arcade, now serving as a second-hand book bazaar. The books are mostly in Turkish but some shops sell old newspapers and colourful prints from the Ottoman era and you may pick up a curio or two.

Continuing down İstiklâl Caddesi, you pass on the left the **Ağa Camii**, a small and peaceful mosque constructed during the reign of Mahmut II. At the low, elegant French consulate, marked by a gargantuan tricolour, a narrow street opposite leads to another Greek Orthodox church, the **Aya Triada** or Holy Trinity. Built in neo-Gothic style, it is set in a well-kept garden and the narthex contains a gentle mosaic of the Virgin cradling the baby Jesus.

Taksim Square

When İstiklâl finally gives out, it leaves you stranded in **Taksim Square**, the centre of Beyoğlu, a dull place full of cars where the dilapidation of Pera fades into the well-painted concrete of the newer areas. The *taksim* itself, a water distribution point housed in a squat building with a pointed roof, is at the very end of İstiklâl Caddesi. İstanbul's fresh water was once piped here direct from the Belgrade Forest, and distributed throughout the city from the *taksim* via a smaller, more intricate piping network. The **Atatürk Cultural Centre**, a bland block of glass and stone, was completed in 1962 as the home for the Opera and a showpiece of the city's cultural life. Grand opera has had a home in İstanbul since Donizetti Paşa, brother of the famous composer, conducted the Palace Symphony in the 1840s. There is also a small Municipal Art Gallery on the square itself, with exhibits of mostly contemporary Turkish artists. On the northern fringes of Taksim, really more a large park than a square, are the two oldest of the city's fancy chain hotels, a Hilton and Sheraton, looming above the trees. Both are isolated, self-contained compounds, seemingly the last survivals of the days of capitulations and trading colonies.

Soldiers' Museum (Askeri Müzesi)

The modern neighbourhoods beyond, Harbiye, Şişli and Maçka, are bright and busy, with little to see. If you're anywhere near, stop in at the **Soldiers' Museum** or Askeri Müzesi [K] (*open daily exc Mon and Tues, 9–12 and 1–5; adm*), housed in an old barracks in the hill-side park near the Hilton Hotel a half mile north of Taksim. The Janissaries, like the sultans, never threw anything away, and the vast hoard of souvenirs and curiosities they piled up on their tours of Europe and Asia and stored in the Aya İrene church armoury made this natural museum collection: Crusaders' swords, Byzantine battle flags, Tamerlane's coat of mail, flags of the '16 historical Turkish Empires' (including Tamerlane's and Attila the Hun's), the famous chain the Byzantines used to close off the Golden Horn, a whole hall of wax dummies of the sultans and Janissaries—the whole crazy hierarchy from the Ağas through the Makers of Soup and Water Carriers down to the dwarfs, the *soytarılar*, who, as their card explains, 'do funny things for sultan'—and a table-and-chair set made entirely out of rifles, a gift of Kaiser Wilhelm. If you come at 3pm, you'll be treated to one of the best shows in İstanbul, a performance of the **Mehter Band** in all its glorious cacophony. The early Ottoman armies marched to this music, the precursor of all band music in Europe.

Dolmabahçe Palace

Open 9–4, closed Mon and Thurs; adm. To book tickets call© 0212 236 9000.

At the end of the park, where it descends towards the Bosphorus, your view of the water will be blocked by the **Dolmabahçe Palace** (1852). No better monument to the spirit of the later Ottomans could be imagined. Abdülmecit, the reforming sultan of the Crimean War, was acutely aware of, and sensitive to, the growing backwardness of his nation, compared to the rest of Europe. To restore Turkey to its place in the sun, he emptied his treasury—literally putting the Ottoman Empire into receivership—not on armies, or railroads, or factories, but on this preposterous Versailles, all marble and only about half a block shorter than the Tünel. Ahmet Fethi Paşa, the Ottoman ambassador to France, scoured the luxury workshops of Europe to furnish the place, and persuaded the stage designer of the Paris Opera to come to İstanbul and put it all together. Here Abdülmecit could receive ambassadors in a proper frock coat, hold grand balls, even indulging in a waltz or two himself, or treat his guests to a private performance of Donizetti Paşa's orchestra. The empire was now officially up to date.

The real tragedy is that to make room for this pile, Abdülmecit tore down a lovely expanse of gardens and pavilions that probably included some of the finest works of Tulip Period architecture, wood and tile pavilions like those at Topkapı and Yıldız Parkı. Eighteenth-century sultans such as Ahmet II and Mahmut III spent much of their time here. Anyhow, take the tour; you've never seen anything like it before. More bad taste is concentrated in this one building than in Napoleon's Tomb, the Great Hall of the Soviets and the Vittorio Emanuele Memorial all combined, with still enough left over to balance all the funeral homes in Los Angeles. All the gold and silk and crystal are real, of course, and there's plenty of Czech and Baccarat crystal, Venetian glass, Sèvres vases, Belgian carpets (not Turkish, naturally; that would be too easy). No particular style predominates; it probably occurred to the architects and decorators early on that the sultan only desired that they should lay it on thick. Czar Nicholas sent polar-bear rugs, and a present of elephant tusks came from the governor of the Hejaz. The British, though, knew what the Ottomans really liked; Queen Victoria sent him the biggest chandelier in the world.

The Dolmabahçe has lots of clocks, all of which have been stopped at the same time, 9.05am, the hour that Atatürk died here on 10 November 1938. To his credit, the Turkish leader occupied only a small room on his visits here; he converted the rest into a conference centre and exhibition hall. Today, the city uses it to put up whatever kings, sheikhs and presidents happen to visit.

Beşiktaş and Yıldız Parkı

Beşiktaş, the neighbourhood directly east of the palace, further up the Bosphorus, begins the fashionable quarters of the modern city. Where its main street, Barbaros Bulvarı, meets the Bosphorus, Turkey's **Naval Museum** [L] (*open daily exc Wed and Thurs, 9–12.30 and 1.30–5; adm*) contains not only ship models, elaborately carved figureheads and other relics, but entire ships: pretty things like the 1876 gilded barge used by Abdülaziz's harem for outings, and a 144-oar naval galley from the 18th century. The point is to remind you that the Ottoman state was, in the early 16th century, the leading sea power of Europe. The **Tomb of Barbarossa**, just outside, honours the brutal Greek-born corsair who, in the service of Süleyman the Magnificent, made that pre-eminence possible.

In 1863, 11 years after Abdülmecit built Dolmabahçe, his successor Abdülaziz grew tired of it and built a new one half a mile up the Bosphorus. **Çırağan Palace** [M] is only a third as large; presumably that was all the great powers and their Ottoman Debt Commission would allow. A fire in 1910 left only the four enormous exterior walls standing, and Çırağan was for years a ghostly shell before being converted into a luxury hotel.

In another 13 years, Abdülaziz was gone—deposed for his reckless extravagance—and his successor Abdülhamid, finding the treasury even emptier, could only build the small pavilions in **Yıldız Park**. These were left to rot after the deposition of the sultans, but recently the Automobile Club has restored both the buildings and the grounds to their original appearance, adding open-air cafés and terraces with a view over the Bosphorus. Altogether the park is one of the most beautiful in Turkey, and the restoration of the **Malta Köşkü** has won an architectural award. Another pavilion, the **Şale Köşkü**, was a residence for guests of the sultans, and is now open for visits (*open daily exc Mon and Thurs, 9.30–5; adm*).

In truth, the Asian side is older. The Delphic oracle had told Byzas the navigator to settle 'opposite the land of the blind'; when his Argive expedition arrived at the Golden Horn, they found a colony of Megarans already established near what is today the suburbs of Kadıköy. Byzas knew who the blind were; the advantages of the European side for building a city were plain. In the Roman and Byzantine eras, Kadıköy was the sizeable town of Chalcedon, the site of many councils of the early Church. The emperors never favoured Chalcedon; on the contrary, they sealed its fate when they took most of the stone from its walls to rebuild their own aqueducts after various sieges. Chalcedon dwindled to nothing in the last days of the empire, and the Turks took the rest of its stones for their own projects; columns from its famous Church of St Euphemia can be seen in the courtyard of the Süleymaniye.

On the ferry from Eminönü or Karaköy, you pass **Leander's Tower**, a landmark in the Bosphorus since Byzantine times, with its lighthouse and customs house. You can also see the two main landmarks of Asian İstanbul, Haydarpaşa Station and the Selimiye Barracks.

Kadıköy and Üsküdar

The Stamboullu claim that the Asian side of the city is very different to the European side. It's calmer, they say; so much more relaxed. They're right, and you'll notice the change the minute you alight from the ferry, probably at **Kadıköy** (the destination of most boats from Europe), to set foot in another continent. It's the space that does it; ahead is a wide, uncluttered square with only a statue of a benevolent Atatürk stretching out his hand to Turkish youth. The extravagant blue building across the square (Buckingham Palace meets the Blue Mosque) is another 19th-century disaster of Ottoman architecture, now housing the local government offices. The mosque near the dock is the 1761 **Sultan Mustafa III Camii**, simple and appealing. In the streets around Kadıköy there are snazzy clothes shops, while at the port at least a dozen boot-blacks line up in a row, semi-pornographic pictures pasted to their elaborate gold-painted foot rests.

A five-minute walk along the dock leads to the most elegant railway station in Turkey, the **Haydarpaşa**. Sirkeçi is nice but this is quite remarkable. Built in 1908 by Sultan Abdülhamid's friends, the Germans, it is named after an old general of Selim III. The ceiling is vertiginously high and twistingly ornate, the windows colourfully stained and the waiting room a revelation: wood-panelled, with chandeliers and a huge rubber plant. There is a police station, a restaurant of considerable repute, a barber shop and a post office; you can catch a train as well. A plaque outside gives more information on the station's history, in a head-scratching sort of way: 'Since putting into service the station building has the large (gross) restoration up to date (now)'.

Further along, up a gentle hill on the road to Üsküdar, are the **Selimiye Barracks** [N]. Built as part of the military reforms of Selim III, this was the home of the new model army the reformers hoped would replace the Janissaries—until the Janissaries ordered it to be disbanded. During the Crimean War (1854–6), when Britain was allied with Turkey against Russia, it served as a hospital and it was here that Florence Nightingale made her name. Her work room and personal quarters have been converted into a small and simple **museum** (*best to phone ahead to check it's open,* © *0216 343 7310*) by the Turkish Nursing Association (she is as big a heroine in Turkey as she is in the UK). A selection of the books she wrote and published are on display, their titles holding clues as to her formidable personality: *Notes on Nursing: What It Is and What It Is Not.* Tours of the museum are conducted by a courteous young officer.

The Selimiye Barracks are now the headquarters of the Turkish First Army, charged with the defence of Thrace and the Dardanelles. At their entrance is the **Selimiye Camii**, built by Selim III for the spiritual health of his ill-fated army and set in a charming garden. At the top of the street, over the road, is the immense, haunting **Karaca Ahmet**, the largest cemetery in İstanbul, prettified with shady cypress trees.

From here **Üsküdar** is a five-minute dolmuş ride away. Like Kadıköy, it is a bustling yet relaxing place. To the Byzantines it was Chrysopolis, 'city of gold'; today it is more a 'suburb of food' with a lively fish, fruit and vegetable **market** held daily and lots of good, inexpensive restaurants where the menus are in Turkish, not English. No one takes much notice of tourists here and you can stroll amongst the noisy shoppers and traders enjoying an anonymity impossible to achieve in, say, Sultanahmet.

Two large and beautiful mosques decorate the open space around Üsküdar landing. Sinan was responsible for the **Mihrimah Camii** [O] (1547), which, like the other Mihrimah, was built in honour of Süleyman's favourite daughter. Standing opposite it is the 18th-century **Yeni Valide Camii** [P], built by Ahmet III. Up the hill from the dock is another work of Sinan, the **Şemsi Paşa Camii** [Q].

The Bosphorus (Boğaziçi)

Even if you have only a little time in İstanbul, you will probably want to invest some of it on a trip up this lovely waterway. Roads follow both the European (*Rumeli*) and Asian (*Anadolu*) sides, but the best way to see the Bosphorus is by boat. Regular ferries from Galata Bridge traverse its length, most taking a zigzag course up and down the straits and giving you the chance of a fine fish dinner in one of the villages before your return. Unfortunately, in the last decade almost all of the Bosphorus shore has been swallowed up by the relentless growth of the city. On both sides of the straits, as far as Rumeli Kavağı and Anadolu Kavağı, villas and blocks of flats have been built on every square inch where the slope isn't too steep.

It's Only a Shanty in Old Shantytown...

Under Turkish law, the authorities may not remove a squatter's shack if the roof can be raised in one night. As country people flocked to İstanbul and Ankara in the last 30 years, in search of modern life and good jobs, the outskirts of these and other cities filled with *gecekondu* ('put up overnight') neighbourhoods. They are the outward manifestation of Turkey's continuing social revolution. Most of them, as you will see if you travel out into the vast suburbs beyond the Theodosian Walls or on the Asian side, by now have grown into real neighbourhoods with real houses, as their hard-working inhabitants gradually make their way into urban society. Turkish planners once looked upon them as their greatest problem, and their populations are still a tremendous strain on the city's budget; but by the curious and immutable laws of urban economics, it seems their resourceful, upwardly mobile people may be one of the nation's great resources. Big cities in western Europe and America went through stages like this in the 19th century, and it was just as rough for them.

In İstanbul, though, the poor aren't the only ones who can enjoy the delights of the *gecekondu*. Largely because of the ludicrous bureaucracy involved in getting a building permit, some 70 per cent of all construction in the city is now illegal, a figure probably much higher than even Naples. About 300 new buildings get started every night, and some Turkish genius has invented a concrete that sets in half an hour to help them along. İstanbul's boom involves not only penniless migrants, but an exploding class of nouveaux riches; they need houses too. More money is flowing around İstanbul these days than at any time since the days of Süleyman the Magnificent, and a sizeable proportion of it is being invested in real estate. The ultimate status symbol in İstanbul today is a villa with a balcony overlooking the straits. Nearly all of them are *gecekondu*—even if they're worth a million dollars or more.

Nothing—not the best efforts of the few, underpaid city building inspectors, nor the outcries of Turkey's small environmental preservation groups—has been able to stop the tidal wave of villas and flats that has irrevocably ruined the Bosphorus shores. There is simply too much money at stake. A new class of building speculators has rapidly become the richest and most powerful interest in the city. Often tied to organized crime, it has its ways of corrupting local governments and muscling common people off desirable plots of land they own. Sarıyer (*see* below) is at the storm centre of the building boom these days.

The Bosphorus Bridge

Just as you leave the built-up areas of the city, you will pass the **Bosphorus Bridge**, a new symbol of İstanbul often seen on souvenirs and brochures these days. It's the fifth largest suspension bridge in the world, the longest in Europe and the only one to link two continents. It was completed in time for the fiftieth anniversary of the republic, and the Turks like to think of it as an emblem of the great progress they have made. The tolls on this bridge have already paid for the construction of another, the **Mehmet Fatih Bridge**, positioned further up the Bosphorus at the point where the waterway was first spanned, in 512 BC by King Darius of the Persians, using a bridge of boats. The Mehmet Fatih Bridge was opened in 1988, exactly 2,500 years after Darius first made the connection.

Two symbols of the bad old days are underneath the Bosphorus bridge: the 1854 **Ortaköy Camii** [R], on the European side, a mosque with Corinthian columns, looks even more like a 1920s American movie-palace than the others of its ilk; on the Asian side Sultan Abdülaziz found the money for yet another marble pile, the **Beylerbeyi Palace** [S] (*open daily exc Mon and Thurs, 9.30–7; adm*). Napoleon III's wife, the Empress Eugénie, spent a few weeks here in the 1860s, and she must have felt right at home. The Beylerbeyi's other famous occupant was Sultan Abdülhamid, who was allowed to stay on at the palace by the Young Turks after they deposed him. Abdül the Damned lived out his life here in a simple room with simple furniture; he brought none of his wives or servants with him—just his cat, the only creature he trusted. On the hills above Beylerbeyi, Turkey's tallest structure, the TRT television tower, stands atop **Çamlıca Hill**, a popular resort in the old days, with a wonderful prospect of the city and the straits. There are cafés and carriage rides, part of the recent rehabilitation and relandscaping of the hill by the TTOK.

Arnavutköy and the Rumeli Hisarı

Back on the European side, **Arnavutköy**, the 'Albanian village', was once the prettiest town along the Bosphorus, with tall, elegant 19th-century houses built right up to the water's edge. A few of these are still left, but Arnavutköy has suffered more than any of the villages from creeping urbanization. A little further on, the straits open up into **Bebek** ('baby') **Bay**. The little palace across the way, a cupcake compared to the over-frosted wedding cakes down the straits, is the **Küçüksu Palace** [T] built by Abdülmecit (*open daily exc Mon and Thurs, 9.30–4; adm*). This is often called the **Palace of the Sweet Waters of Asia**, for the lovely stream that flows down from Çamlıca. In Ottoman times, the rivers that led into the Golden Horn were called the 'Sweet Waters of Europe'.

Just after Bebek Bay, the straits close to their narrowest point, guarded by two Turkish castles that antedate the Conquest. Sultan Beyazıt I built the **Anadolu Hisarı** [U] in 1393 to choke off Constantinople's Black Sea trade. Across the straits, Mehmet tightened the grip with the **Rumeli Hisarı** [V] in 1452. It's difficult to believe the latter could have had any military purpose; draped languidly over the slopes, with its neat crenellations and perfect round towers, the Rumeli Hisarı is the most picturesque castle imaginable. Once it had wooden towers inside, but these have been cleared out and, instead of old cannons and dust, the castle is filled with flowers and trees; it also has an open-air theatre where plays and concerts are presented in the summer.

From Emirgan to the Two Kavağıs

Emirgan [W], on the European side, was a garden-palace compound the sultans used for captured or exiled potentates in their care. The grounds and pavilions have been restored (by the Automobile Club, of course), most notably the lovely **Yellow Pavilion**, an outstanding example of the Turkish talent for fairy-tale architecture. An annual Tulip Festival is held here in April–May. All the land west of this section of the Bosphorus is İstanbul's famous and beautiful suburban park, **Belgrade Forest** (Beograd Ormanı), originally a hunting preserve of the Ottomans. The name comes from the Serbian prisoners of war that the sultans settled here; they and their descendants formed a tight little community charged with the responsibility of keeping up İstanbul's aqueducts and reservoirs, until the paranoid Abdülhamid had them expelled for fear they would poison the water supply. Much of the city's water still comes from here, transported via a graceful **aqueduct** built by Mimar Sinan.

The oldest surviving wooden *yalılar* can be seen at **Kanlıca** on the Asian side, hanging gracefully out over the water. A few miles north, in the hills above Çubuklu, you can see a very different kind of house, the **Hıdiv Kasrı**, an Art Nouveau palace of an exiled Khedive of Egypt, now restored with a restaurant and tea salon. From nearby Paşabahçe, you can get to **Polonezköy**, some five miles (8km) to the east. This weekend resort, famous for food and scenery, has been, as its name implies, a thoroughly Polish village since 1842, when refugees from the freedom struggles against Russia settled here. The land was a present from the sultan, in return for the Poles' services in the Crimean War. (Having a common enemy in the 18th and 19th centuries, the Poles and the Turks were quite close, and devotees of Polish

culture will be interested in the **Adam Mickiewicz Museum** on Tatlıbadem Sokak in Beyoğlu, the home in exile of Poland's greatest poet.)

More towns on the European shore are **Yeniköy,** where a small Greek church overlooks the waterfront, **Tarabya,** a quite ritzy corner of the Bosphorus with a yacht harbour, and **Sarıyer**, where cafés and fishing boats crowd each other along the tree-lined waterfront. South of Sarıyer at Büyükdere, the **Sadberk Hanım Museum** contains a small but beautifully displayed collection of ancient Anatolian arts and Turkish handcrafts (*open daily exc Wed, summer 10.30–6; winter 10–5; adm*). The last two towns the ferry visits are **Rumeli Kavağı** and **Anadolu Kavağı**, a pair of perfect bookends on either side of the Bosphorus, both relatively quiet and pleasant. Beyond these, much of the land is given over to the military; it's very discreet and you'll never see them, but these straits are well guarded now, just as they always have been, as several ruined fortifications testify, including the **Genoese Castle** [X] north of Anadolu Kavağı: a half-hour's climb up from the port, to a castle with medieval inscriptions and great views over the Bosphorus.

At the end of the straits, where the Symplegades, the clashing rocks of Greek mythology, were defeated by Jason and the Argonauts, all is quiet and still; two old lighthouses, the Anadolu Fener and the Rumeli Fener, wait to guide ships into the channel.

The Princes' Islands (Adalar)

There are nine of these in the Sea of Marmara, and ferries from the Galata Bridge, Kabataş or Bostancı call at the four largest, inhabited islands—Kınalı, Burgaz, Heybeliada and Büyükada. The first two are inhabited mainly by Armenians who commute to jobs in İstanbul, while the last two, especially Büyükada ('Big Island'), have long been favoured as summer retreats from the city, with their lovely pine groves, often dramatic cliffs dropping into a clean azure sea, colourful flower gardens, and lanes plied by horse-drawn carriages called *faytonlar* instead of cars. All the islands are car-free, and despite moves to 'modernize' and bring in traffic, the friends of the islands have so far been able to keep the beasts at bay.

Their name seems to derive not from any son of the sultan, but from the fact that from the earliest days of Byzantium up until the 15th century, they were a place of royal exile, as well as a popular spot for monasteries and, occasionally, pirates' nests. A few ruined churches and monastic buildings remain, but far more impressive, especially on Büyükada, are the grand old wooden summer houses, in all their pastel, 'gingerbread' Victorian-Gothic splendour. Another advantage of taking a trip out to the islands is the twilight return, 'sailing to Byzantium', when the great domes and minarets of the imperial mosques glow in the rosy dusk, creating one of the most rarefied and poetic cityscapes in the world.

Büyükada, *Prinkipo* in Byzantine times, is as its name implies the largest and most populous of the islands. Sights include the Anatolia Club, originally built by British residents as a yacht club a century ago, and a number of Greek relics, churches and monasteries, on the hill above the town. Carriage-taxis offer tours up to these, or you may walk or rent a bike and have a picnic; like the other islands Büyükada is largely covered with pines, planted a century ago. The most interesting, but the hardest to reach, is the **monastery of St George** on the southernmost hill, dating in part back to Byzantine times. There are small beaches at Yörük Ali and Dil Uzantısı.

The next-largest island, **Heybeliada**, lies just a mile or so to the west of Büyükada. The Turkish Naval Academy is here; on their grounds is the last church of the Byzantine Empire, the last one to be built before 1453, the **Kamariotissa** (you'll need to get permission from the naval authorities to visit). Overlooking the village from the top of the island is the **Aya Triada Monastery**, now closed but once the most important orthodox school of theology. As on Büyükada, you can easily find a *fayton* to take you around the island, and there are some decent beaches, the biggest of them at Değirmen, and others on the undeveloped western half of the island.

Two more islands are served by the ferries: **Kınalıada**, small and rather barren, is the closest to İstanbul, and largely inhabited by Armenians. **Burgazada** is steeper and greener, with ruins of another old monastery at its summit.

Shopping

You can get anything you want in İstanbul, from a 30¢ *boncuk* (anti-evil eye charm) to a full-size 20ft granite replica of a Hittite relief. For those born to shop, it's the best and the worst of all possible worlds. All the treasures of the Orient at your feet—but at a much higher price than out in the provinces. Those Kütahya plates seem a bargain at $9; a few hours' bus ride away in Kütahya, they can be one-third the price. The finest antique Ottoman-era jewellery is on display in the *bedestenler* of the Covered Market—but you might not be able to take it out of the country with you.

fashion & clothing

Metropolis İstanbul has another trump: *haute couture*, Turkish style, the logical development of a very talented nation with a very large textile industry. A few of the newer districts have concentrations of shops where you can find not only Turkish surprises but well-known designer labels at prices lower than you'll see them at home (Benetton and Levi's for example; almost everything they sell in the UK is actually made in Turkey). Such fashion strips include **Rumeli Caddesi** and surrounding streets in Nişantaşı, **Bağdat Caddesi** in Erenköy on the Asian side, the **Galleria** mall in Ataköy, and the incredible **Akmerkez Shopping Mall** on Ulus Caddesi in Etiler:

a totally colour-coordinated experience on four levels, with glass elevators, Wendy's, Dairy Queen and Buffalo Wings, and all the Italian designer clothing chain stores; you might as well stay at home.

İstiklâl Caddesi in Beyoğlu, since its recent facelift, is once again becoming a fashionable shopping street; plenty of new addresses have joined old established clothing stores like **Beymen** and **Vakko**. The latter, with many other branches around town, is currently tops in Turkish fashion for both men and women, with clothes in beautiful fabrics often employing colourful, traditional Turkish motifs. Beymen tends to be more traditional, with an emphasis on simple elegance and fine materials in clothing, shoes and accessories; they also have a big department store in Akmerkez. Some other style leaders include **Mudo**, for men and women, at Akmerkez, Rumeli Caddesi and 162 İstiklâl Caddesi, **Vekem**, for women's clothing, on Kuyulu Bostan Sokak in Nişantaşı, and **Gazellini**, on Gazi İpekçi Caddesi in Nişantaşı. **Zeki Triko**, 64 Rumeli Caddesi and sold in many other shops, is internationally famous for its range of swimwear.

The **Silk & Cashmere** shop in Akmerkez has unusual things in those materials at bargain prices—it all comes from Mongolia and central Asia. Cheaper still is the shop opposite the Galatasaray Lisesi on İstiklâl Caddesi called simply **İpek** ('silk'), where quality is high and the prices are low. For leather, a Turkish speciality, the latest can be seen at **Derishow** in Nişantaşı and on Bağdat Caddesi, **Modello**, on Nispetye Caddesi in Etiler, and **Desa** on İstiklâl by the Beyoğlu Cinema. For shoes, Beymen is good; there are also many shops in Nişantaşı, especially **Hotiç**, on Teşvikiye Caddesi, and **Demirel**, on Akkavak Sokak.

jewellery

The obvious choice is the Covered Market, where tons of it are on display, but there are other fine shops around the city: **V-22**, on Teşvikiye Caddesi; **Artisan** and **Ayşe**, both on İskele Caddesi in Ortaköy; **Bazaar 54** and **Lapis**, both on **Nuruosmaniye Caddesi** in Cağaloğlu. This tree-lined street, running from Yerebatan to the Covered Market, has recently been refurbished; rapidly becoming old Stamboul's only fashionable shopping strip, it has jewellery, clothing and other speciality shops.

antiques and carpets

As you may imagine, these are big business, and there will be exotic trinkets to take home in all sizes and price ranges—just keep in mind Turkey's tough laws about exporting things of genuine value (*see* p.16). İstanbul doesn't exactly have flea markets. It has *bit pazarları*, literally 'louse markets'—not much difference. The word came from a street in the Covered Market called the Bit Pazar that now serves other purposes. Today, the biggest and most popular one sprawls around **Çukurcuma Caddesi** (east of İstiklâl, behind the Galatasaray Lisesi), a great place for every kind of Ottoman-era trinket and offbeat souvenir. Another big louse market takes place on the Asian side in **Üsküdar**, indoors in a rambling old building at 30 Büyükhamam Sokak; mostly furniture. The same description goes for the **Horhor Bit Pazarı**, a big indoor market on Kırık Tulumba Sokak in Aksaray. However, the address for the real treasures is still the **Covered Bazaar**, particularly in the enclosed İç Bedesten and Sandal Bedesten: the choicest in antique jewellery, silver and gold work, even Byzantine icons and medieval astrolabes.

As for **carpets**, their buying and selling is the national pastime, and İstanbul is not necessarily the best place to do it if you are concerned about price. Carpet shops around the Aya Sofya in Sultanahmet come as thick as flies, and some of the country's finest productions are brought to them. If you're experienced in the carpet game you may get a correct price there; otherwise, the carpet avenues of the Covered Bazaar or on the side streets off İstiklâl may be a better bet.

If time is short, the **Arasta Bazaar** behind the Blue Mosque has an arcade of select shops specializing in porcelain, Kütahya and İznik tiles, jewellery and, of course, carpets. Whilst prices may be slightly higher than elsewhere, this is reflected in the quality of the merchandise.

galleries

For art galleries and exhibitions, the Tünel end of İstiklâl Caddesi in Beyoğlu is promising. On İstiklâl Caddesi itself, the **Borusan Culture and Art Centre** has five floors of pictures executed to a variable standard as well as a wide range of art books. Opposite the St Antoine Catholic Church at No.256 is **Elhamra Sineması**, a former cinema now housing a huge art gallery. More intimate in scale is the **Asmanlımescit Art Gallery and Café** at Sofyalı Sokak 5/1 which has new exhibitions of pictures and sculpture every 3–4 weeks. Bean fiends should note that its café also serves real espresso coffee. For those who want to see beyond the canvas, visit the small gallery of **Neriman Oyman**, off Sofyalı Sokak at Asmalımescit Şehbender Sokak 8/2, ✆ 0212 243 0173. There's little to indicate its presence on the street, just a small black nameplate and bell next to the front door. Neriman's work is displayed in the front gallery, and she paints in the studio at the back. If her paintings are not to your own taste or your bank manager's liking, her enthusiasm and energy alone make the effort of finding her gallery worthwhile.

bargains

Depending on the room in your suitcase, you might take advantage of Turkey's peculiar economy and rotten exchange rates to pick up some familiar items at prices much less than at home—Turkish-made jeans and other Western duds, eyeglasses, lace and curtains, children's clothing (or anyone's clothing, really)—or spend a Sunday touring one of the dozens of suburban fields where people sell cars. For a small admission fee, you get a look at '49 Cadillacs, '50 Mercurys, '55–'59 Chevys and Chryslers, all with no rust and for a pittance; all you have to do is work them through the government bureaucracy, and then figure out how to drive them home.

food

If you're cooking for yourself or planning a picnic, **food** will prove no problem at all. The **Balıkpazarı** in Beyoğlu isn't just a fish market, you can get just about anything there, and in the delicatessens and speciality shops in surrounding streets. Polish-run **Sütte**, on Duduodalar Sokak, is one of the few places where you can get ham and other pork products; or try **Konyalı**, near Sirkeci Station. For health foods, there is **Zencefil** on Kurabiye Sokak. Most of the better delicatessens are out in the newer districts, such as **Abant Ciftliği**, on Valikonağı Sokak in Nişantaşı. The **Spice Market** has plenty of food stands, with fruits and vegetables outside, and there are weekly markets in all of the city's neighbourhood high streets. An especially big and popular one takes place in **Kadıköy**, Tuesdays and Fridays; also **Cihangir** (downhill from Galatasaray) on Tuesdays, and the big daily market in **Beşiktaş**. In the **Spice Market**, you can get the finest caviar: not from Russia any more, but from the Azerbaijani Republic.

other shopping

As in the quarters around the Covered Market, some of the older streets in Beyoğlu are devoted to particular trades and kinds of shops. **Galip Dede Caddesi**, right at the top of the Tünel, is lined with **music** shops where you can find lutes, *neyler* and other traditional Turkish instruments, along with books on how to play them, CDs, records and cassettes. For the best selection in recorded music though, look in the myriad little shops around the Stamboul side of the Atatürk Bridge. For **books** in English, and books in general about Turkey, the booksellers in the **Sahaflar Çarşısı**, between the Covered Bazaar and Beyazıt Square, have by far the best selection (*see also* p.88). They are also probably the best place to pick up inexpensive **souvenirs**: old prints and watercolours of the city, hand painted boxes and other trinkets. There is a **flower market** on the side streets off Taksim Square.

Sports and Activities

One thing you couldn't do in İstanbul ten years ago is shoot a round of **golf**. Now there are two nine-hole courses open to the public: the İstanbul Golf Club in suburban Ayazağa, ✆ 0212 264 0742, and the new Kemer Golf and Country Club, a serious development in the beautiful Belgrade Forest (how'd they get permission to build there?). You can golf, ride a horse, etc. with views of Mimar Sinan's aqueducts. Call ✆ 0212 239 7913 for information about opening hours for non-members.

Some of the luxury hotels are pretty liberal about letting folks in to use their **tennis**, **handball** and **racketball** courts, **gyms**, etc; try the Hilton on Taksim, ✆ 0212 231 4646, or the Swissotel, ✆ 0212 259 0101, first.

The Merit Hotel on Ordu Caddesi, ✆ 0212 513 9300, has one of the few **swimming pools** in Stamboul; again, most of the big hotels around Taksim and the Bosphorus let the public use their pools. There's even a place to **ice-skate**: the Galleria Shopping Mall in Ataköy, open daily until 10pm.

Most of Turkey's top **football** clubs call İstanbul home, and you can watch them get battered regularly by foreign competition at Beşiktaş (İnönü Stadium); Fenerbahçe (in Kiziltoprak), and Galatasaray (in Mecideyeköy).

Hamams

Altogether, this is a wonderful town to take a bath. All of the luxury hotels and a number of the less pretentious establishments (*see* under 'Where to Stay') have their own hamams. Wherever you stay, there will be one nearby. Some of them are historic landmarks, heating the water by traditional means; in the larger hamams more than thirty tons of wood and coal go up in smoke each month. Perhaps the poshest and best-known is the **Cağaloğlu Hamamı**, on Yerebatan Caddesi, a palatial 18th-century hamam that even has its own bar. *Open for men 7am–10pm and women 8am–8pm.* They are accustomed to tourists and, though it's expensive, this may be a good place for first-timers to take the plunge. Nearby, and slightly less expensive, is the 16th-century **Çemberlitaş Hamamı**, on Vezirhan Caddesi near the Burnt Column. It's patronised by Stamboullu as well as tourists, and the massages here tend to be more thorough than in establishments catering solely to tourists. *Open 6am–midnight.*

One of the nicest is the **Çinili Hamam**, in a very out-of-the-way location on İtfaiye Caddesi, just off Atatürk Bulvarı north of the Aqueduct of Valens. This 'tiled' hamam was built in the 1600s for the pirate admiral Barbarossa, and it retains some of its original décor, with baths for both men and women. Because of its location it has avoided becoming touristy.

Where to Stay

The subject is inexhaustible; besides the ones you'll find listed in the official tourist literature, there are literally hundreds of unclassified establishments—so you shouldn't have trouble finding a place even in summer. Prices naturally tend to be a bit higher than elsewhere in Turkey, but there is still plenty of room for bargaining in all categories.

The first thing is to decide where you want to stay. For seeing the sights, the most logical locations by far are the **Sultanahmet** and **Cağaloğlu** districts around the Aya Sofya and Blue Mosque. Sultanahmet has a dizzying array of hotels to welcome tourists. In recent years many of the ramshackle wooden buildings propping up this area's character have been restored into plush hotels. Critics argue that Sultanahmet is succumbing to theme-park tendencies, becoming an Ottoman Disneyland complete with open-top bus tours and illuminated monuments at night. Others see this as progress. Whatever the case, while the heart of İstanbul today beats across the Golden Horn in Beyoğlu, Sultanahmet is the beautifully made-up face that the city presents to the world at large.

Another large concentration of hotels, mostly in the moderate range, can be found in **Aksaray/Lâleli**, a noisy, modern district about a kilometre to the west, but still convenient for most of the sights. And there are still plenty of inexpensive hotels in the **Sirkeci** area around the rail station, though this thoroughly dismal quarter will not make your holiday any happier.

For businessmen and travelling paşas, most of the luxury hotels are on the Beyoğlu side, on or near the **Bosphorus coast** south of the bridge, and around **Taksim Square**. Some of the older ones, along with less expensive choices, can be found on and around **Meşrutiyet Caddesi**, a street that runs parallel to İstiklâl Caddesi through Beyoğlu.

luxury

İstanbul probably has as many really posh hotels as anywhere in Europe, Paris included; quite a few have opened up in the last few years. Counting up all the royal and presidential suites, this city could accommodate about 85 kings and presidents at once.

Sultanahmet

A former prison is an unlikely location for İstanbul's most exclusive hotel, the **(S)Four Seasons**, Tevkifhane Sokak 1, ✆ 0212 638 8200 ✉ 0212 638 8210. This Ottoman building must surely have been the prettiest prison in the world, painted yellow ochre and decorated with turquoise and cobalt-blue floral painted Kütahya porcelain tiles. These features were preserved during its recent conversion into a hotel, although the architects deemed it necessary to add some space-age smoked glass walkways to the façade. Many of the 65 luxurious rooms look onto the courtyard, planted with an inviting garden. Doubles cost upwards of $320, although candidates for a night in the presidential suite should have in the region of $2,000 in their slush fund.

Beyoğlu

Near the Dolmabahçe Palace at Beşiktaş, the ★★★★★**Çırağan Saray**, Çırağan Caddesi 84, ✆ 0212 258 3377, ✉ 0212 259 6687, *reserve@ciraganpalace.com.tr*, is a one-time palace built by Sultan Abdülaziz which gives the Four Seasons in Sultanahmet a run for its money as the city's most sumptuous hotel. Everything you could possibly require from a hotel is here: rooms overlooking the Bosphorus, sauna, hamam and deluxe suites in the sultans' apartments (all the furnishings are modern; the palace was gutted by fire long ago). Doubles from $300, up to $7,500 for the Sultan Suite.

For those who like their hotels modern, spotless, comfortable and international, there's the ★★★★★**Marmara Oteli**, ✆ 0212 251 4696, ✉ 0212 244 0509, *marmara@verisoft.com.tr*, on Taksim Square. It was once the tallest building in İstanbul, and has a swimming pool, as well as television, air-conditioning, refrigerators in every room and a baby-sitting service. Doubles $260. The ★★★★★**Hilton Oteli** on Cumhuriyet Caddesi, ✆ 0212 231 4650, ✉ 0212 240 4165, has the same facilities, as well as tennis courts, a hamam, sauna, squash, tennis and, if you need it, a chopper pad.

Among the newer competitors, there is the ★★★★★**Swissotel Bosphorus**, ✆ 0212 259 0101, ✉ 0212 259 0105, a striking modern building across from the Dolmabahçe Palace. Many rooms have a view of the straits. There is a wide choice of bars and restaurants on the premises, including a roof garden, a hamam, two pools and tennis courts. Or for some outrageously flash architecture straight from Dallas or LA, there's the 27-storey ★★★★★**Holiday Inn Crowne Plaza**, Sahil Yolu, Ataköy, ✆ 0212 560 8100, ✉ 0212 560 8157, with 'fitness centre' and gargantuan pool; satellite TV and trouser press built into every room.

Far more convenient for the sights, and affording a lavish view over the Golden Horn, is the outwardly magnificent ****Pera Palace** at Meşrutiyet Caddesi 89/100, Harbiye, ✆ 251 4560, 🖷 251 4089 (*see* p.68). The Pera Palace is the city's most famous hotel, a great Edwardian pile built by the Wagons-Lits Company for their passengers on the Orient Express. It has changed little over the years, and has provided the setting for several novels about the city. Its bar is legendary, its restaurant excellent; you can ask for a free tour of the suite, now a museum, that Atatürk used when staying here. On the down side, a satellite dish now sits unceremoniously on the roof, there is no swimming pool, and we've had complaints about the service. Rooms are very large and bright, but hardly luxurious by modern standards. Traffic noise may also be a problem. The $220 per double pays for the hotel's illustrious past, not its present.

Lâleli

The *****Merit Antique**, Ordu Caddesi 226, ✆ 0212 513 9000, 🖷 0212 512 6390, is the only luxury hotel near the sights, with rooms more like small apartments than anything else; it has all the amenities but can be a bit noisy.

The Asian side

The pick of the bunch is the *****Hıdiv Kasrı** (Summer Palace of the Khedive), in the village of Çubuklu on the Bosphorus, ✆ 0216 331 2651, 🖷 0216 322 3434, built at the turn of the century by the King of Egypt as a holiday home, and restored by the Automobile Club. It's lovely, set in its own peaceful park with immaculate gardens; and there's a restaurant.

expensive

Sultanahmet

The best hotel around the $100 mark in Sultanhamet is also the most difficult to find. The ****Arena** is tucked away on a quiet street in one of the few remaining traditional Stamboul neighbourhoods near the Sokullu Camii, at Küçük Ayasofya Mah., Şehit Mehmet Paşa Yokuşu Üçler Hamam Sokak 13, ✆ 0212 458 0364, 🖷 0212 458 0366, *arena@arenahotel.com*. The hotel was once a grand mansion where the present owner was born. An oil portrait of her grandfather complete with fez hangs in the reception, sizing up potential customers. The Arena has created an easy elegance and unforced intimacy that most hotels spend a fortune trying to manufacture. The comfortable en suite rooms are tastefully decorated, and the service is excellent; $90.

The ****Yeşil Ev,** Kabasakal Caddesi 5, ✆ 0212 517 6785, 🖷 0212 517 6780, is another 19th-century mansion, once the home of an Ottoman paşa. This was one of the first restoration projects of the TTOK, and is a blissful bolt-hole of tranquillity between the Blue Mosque and the Aya Sofya, with a back garden; all rooms have period décor. Reservations are essential. Doubles $160, $140 in low season.

In the same spirit, but somewhat cheaper and, some might feel, over-restored, are the old Ottoman houses called the ***Aya Sofya Pansionları** on Soğukçeşme

Sokak behind the Aya Sofya, ✆ 0212 513 3660, ✉ 0212 513 3669; a couple of the rooms have their own private hamam. Doubles are $120 for streetside rooms, $100 for those facing the palace walls. Behind the Arasta Bazaar at Dalbastı Sokak 14 is the ★★★★**Blue House Mavi Ev**, ✆ 0212 638 9010, ✉ 0212 638 9017. Unparalleled view of the Blue Mosque from its rooftop restaurant; well-appointed doubles $130.

The nearby ★★★**Sarı Konak**, Mimar Mehmet Ağa Caddesi 42–46, ✆ 0212 638 6258, ✉ 0212 517 8635, *sarikonak@superonline.com*, is a smaller and better value alternative. This is a good choice for those who like spending serious time in the bathroom: some of the bedrooms are a little on the small side, but the bathrooms are huge. As with many of the hotels in this area, the Sarı Konak has a roof terrace offering panoramic views of the Bosphorus; doubles $80. Just north of the Hippodrome is the ★★★**İbrahim Paşa**, Terzihane Sokak 5, Adliye Yanı, ✆ 0212 518 0394, ✉ 0212 518 4457, *pasha@ibm.net*. With its air of quiet sophistication, this makes a refined refuge from the bustle of the city; doubles $95.

For an alternative to the restored clapboard mansions, try the ★★★★**Sultan Ahmet Sarayı**, set in pleasant gardens behind the Blue Mosque at Torun Sokak 19, ✆ 0212 458 0460, ✉ 0212 518 6224. Although the hotel claims to be a fusion of Byzantine and Ottoman styles, its profusion of heavy mouldings and coloured glass skylights would be enough to make Holmes and Watson feel at home; doubles $140.

Sirkeci

A strange sight in the backstreets of Sirkeci is the brand new ★★★★**Prince**, Nöbethane Caddesi Kargılı Sokak 5, ✆ 0212 513 2550, ✉ 0212 522 4359, *info@hotelprince.com*. Comfortable but anonymous rooms cost $120; there's also a sauna and fitness centre. For the same price (or less if you fax in advance requesting a discount) there's more atmosphere at the ★★★★**Yaşmak Sultan** Ebusuud Caddesi 18–20, ✆ 0212 528 1343, ✉ 0212 528 1348, *yasmaksultan@yasmak.com*.

Kariye

The ★★★**Kariye**, Kariye Camii Sokak 18, ✆ 0212 534 8414, ✉ 0212 521 6631, *kariye@kariyeotel.com*, is another tremendous renovation job by the Automobile Club, in a converted Ottoman mansion across the street from St Saviour in Chora. $80, although the neighbourhood is an unlikely location for such a hotel.

Beyoğlu

Across the Golden Horn, the only hotel on İstiklâl Caddesi is the ★★★★**Richmond**, at No.445, ✆ 0212 252 5460, ✉ 0212 252 9707. It is a thoroughly modern establishment; there are fine rooms with air-conditioning and other amenities, but nostalgia is still the selling point here—no traffic to keep you awake, just an occasional antique tram rattling by. Posted rates are a steep $165 per double, although this soon drops to $135 or less. On Meşrutiyet, the second choice to the Pera Palace in the old days was the ★★★**Büyük Londra** (né 'Grand Hotel de Londres' in 1892), ✆ 0212 245 0670, ✉ 0212 245 0671. Now it's a similar faded beauty, completely unrestored, worthwhile if you can get one of the front rooms with a balcony and a view over the

Golden Horn, although the side rooms are quieter. The reception and hallways are filled with a collection of old cast-iron stoves. Doubles are priced at $80, less if you employ some old-world charm.

There are any number of hotels in the middle range around Taksim Square, but most of these are purely for businessmen, and not distinguished in any way.

Princes' Islands

One serendipitous alternative to city hotels, for anyone who doesn't mind a ferry ride commute for sightseeing, is to stay on Büyükada, largest of the Princes' Islands. The domed ★★★**Splendid Palas**, 23 Nisan Caddesi, ✆ 0216 382 6950, ✆ 0216 382 6775, has pretty, old-fashioned rooms with balconies, and a small pool; built in 1908, it's nice though a bit faded. Doubles $90. On Heybeliada, the ★★★**Merit Halkı Palas**, ✆ 0216 351 8890, ✆ 0216 351 8483, used to belong to the Orthodox seminary; now it is a pretty, restored hotel with lovely rooms and a pool. $100.

moderate

Sultanahmet

Novelty in Turkish hotels often borders on the tasteless, but not at the ★★**Poem**, Akbıyık Caddesi Terbıyık Sokak 12, ✆ 0212 638 9744, ✆ 0212 517 6836, *hotelpoem@superonline.com*, where each small but tastefully furnished room is named after a Turkish poem, a translation of which hangs inside each bedroom door. Set in two buildings in one of Sultanahmet's quietest back streets, the hotel has the added bonus of a mature garden at the back; $65. Hardened nostalgia seekers should head for the **(S)Turkuaz**, near the Küçük Aya Sofya at Kadırga Cinci Meydanı 36, ✆ 0212 516 0862, ✆ 0212 517 3380. The wooden Ottoman building oozes charm, although the tacky reproduction furniture spoils the effect somewhat. All rooms have bathroom facilities, costing from $60.

A better-furnished alternative is another restored house, the ★★**Turkoman**, north of the Hippodrome away from the tourist ghetto at Asmalı Çeşme Sokak 2, ✆ 0212 516 2956, ✆ 0212 516 2957, *info@turkomanhotel.com*. Real antique furniture is dotted about the place and many of the rooms have brass beds. The breakfast room has views of the Blue Mosque. $60 a double, less if they're not busy. The best of the many Best Western hotels in Sultanahmet is the ★★★**Sokullu Paşa**, Küçük Ayasofya Mah., Şehit Mehmet Paşa Sokak 5/7, ✆ 0212 518 1790, ✆ 0212 518 1793, *sokullu@superonline.com*, an old Ottoman house which still retains many original features such as its wooden ceilings. Posted rates are $110, although they may settle for as little as $60.

The **Berk Guesthouse** Kutlugün Sokak 27, ✆ 0212 517 6561, ✆ 0212 517 7715, *reservations@berkguesthouse.com*, is run by a very friendly family, offering well-kept but slightly outdated rooms for $50. Located in a car-free street near the Bosphorus is the relaxed ★★**Şebnem Hotel** Akbıyık Caddesi Adliye Sokak 1, ✆ 0212 517 6623, ✆ 0212 638 1056, *sebnemhotel@superonline.com*. Mornings get off to a good start with a big breakfast on the terrace overlooking the Bosphorus; $50.

On the main Divan Yolu opposite the *türbe* of Mahmut II, the ★★★**Pierre Loti**, ✆ 0212 518 5700, ✆ 0212 516 1886, has bright and keen staff; comfortable if charmless rooms for $65, with air-conditioning and TV. Just off Divan Yolu, the ★★★**Nomade** at Ticarethane Sokak 15, ✆ 0212 511 1296, ✆ 0212 513 2404, offers very good value at $50 for en suite doubles. Although the hotel itself is modern, the marble floors and old furniture lend it a pleasant atmosphere.

Next door is the brand new ★★★**Ambassador Hotel** Ticarethane Sokak 19, ✆ 0212 512 0002, ✆ 0212 512 0005. Its alabaster and wrought iron decoration may be a little over the top for some people's taste, but the management is very eager to please. Some rooms are equipped with jacuzzis and, at $75, are much cheaper than equivalents in more fashionable parts of Sultanahmet.

Sirkeci

An Armenian house from 1903 near the railway tracks at Nöbethane Caddesi 30 has recently been converted into the **(S)Grand Seigneur Hotel**, ✆ 0212 512 1034, ✆ 0212 520 8910. The décor of this family-run place is on the fussy side, but all rooms have private bathrooms, offering great value at $45.

Lâleli

Just a short tram ride from the main sights is the ★★★★**Prestige**, Koska Caddesi 8, ✆ 0212 518 8280, ✆ 0212 518 8290. It's very popular with Russian tourists; the rooms lack both character and views, but where else in İstanbul can you find a four-star room for $50?

Beyoğlu

Well, Beyoğlu for one, where rooms at the ★★★★**Grace** in Tepebaşı at Meşrutiyet Caddesi 38, ✆ 0212 293 3955, ✆ 0212 252 4370, *info@gracehotel.com*, can be as low as $50. The hotel's trump card, however, is its indoor oval swimming pool, which may tempt even the most unadventurous to stray away from the cosy bubble of Sultanahmet.

inexpensive

Don't expect wonders here. By comparison with the rest of Turkey, hotels on the lower end of the scale tend to be higher-priced, and proprietors do not worry themselves as much about keeping them attractive. At least there's plenty of choice. These days, the place to look first for an *inexpensive* or *cheap* room is the Sultanahmet district, south of the Aya Sofya and Blue Mosque. In the last decade, scores of places have opened up in the old residential parts of the neighbourhood—a funky and amiable place, about evenly divided between run-down flats and the hotels. In general, the further you are from the Aya Sofya, the cheaper the hotel.

Sultanahmet

Located directly across from the Four Seasons Hotel, the **Ali Baba Guesthouse**, Tevkifhane Sokak 12, ✆ 0212 518 0030, ✆ 0212 517 1783, is a bargain, with spacious rooms costing $30—less than a tenth of the cost of rooms in the Goliath opposite. Its terrace has views over the Bosphorus. The nearby **Side Pansiyon**, Utangaç Sokak 20, ✆/✉ 0212 517 6590, gives you the full range of options. Its tile-lined top floor has the best rooms, which are clean if basic; $35 with shower, $25 without. Next door is the **Side Hotel**, under the same management, offering far superior wooden-floored en suite rooms for $50.

The owners of the **Hanedan Guesthouse**, Akbıyık Caddesi Adliye Sokak 3, ✆ 0212 516 4869, ✉ 0212 517 4524, have gone to some lengths with the decoration, putting down colourful carpets in many of the hallways, although the big rooms with correspondingly large bathrooms are only kept in so-so condition; $25. The nearby **Şah Konak**, Akbıyık Caddesi Bayramfırını Sokak 13, ✆ 0212 638 2608, ✉ 0212 458 1829, has a small garden and breakfast room to the rear, with comfortable if characterless bedrooms for $40 in summer, $30 in winter. Choose a room at the back to avoid noise from the weekly market in a nearby street.

In the unfashionable backstreets off Divan Yolu is **Hotel Legend**, Peykhane Caddesi 16, ✆ 0212 518 3348, ✉ 0212 638 6476, newly opened and eager to please. Doubles are quoted at $35, although the price may creep up once the hotel becomes established. Another good place to save your lira is the **Ema**, north of the Aya Sofya at Yerebatan Caddesi Salkım Söğüt Sokak 18, ✆ 0212 511 7166, ✉ 0212 512 4878. Unimaginative rooms with private facilities cost $25.

Beyoğlu

Of the many unappetizing choices near the İstiklâl Caddesi, the **★Villa** at Balıkpazarı Topçekenler Sokak 10, ✆ 0212 252 2637, is better-kept than the rest, which isn't saying much. Tiny bedrooms with private bathrooms big enough for one leg at a time are $20.

cheap

Sultanahmet

Most of İstanbul's cheap hotels can be found in Sultanahmet, places with long experience of catering to student backpackers such as the friendly, well-heated **Sultan Tourist Hostel**, Akbıyık Caddesi Terbıyık Sokak 3, ✆ 0212 516 9260, ✉ 0212 517 1626; $8 per person. A quieter alternative, popular with Japanese travellers, is the **Konya Pansiyon**, Akbıyık Caddesi Terbıyık Sokak 15/2, ✆ 0212 638 3638. Dorm beds in this basic family-run concern are $5 per person. Doubles are $14, except for the one where the bath is almost as big as the bed (for budget honeymooners?), which costs $30.

The **Yücelt Interyouth Hostel**, Caferiye Sokak 6/1, ✆ 0212 513 6150, ✉ 0212 512 7628, is bristling with facilities—a bar and terrace, laundry, internet, billiards, table tennis and even a DVD machine. Very cheap meals are also served up, and it is often bulging with backpackers. Dorm beds are $7. Double rooms with basins are $22, almost as much as the lower priced hotels. The **Arsenal Youth Hostel** just off Divan Yolu at Dr Eminpaşa Sokak 14, ✆ 0212 513 6407, is a hard-core sleepery. Four-person dorms with en suite shower and toilets cost $6 per person. Anyone who finds their roommates' socks a little on the mature side can always slip the basement laundry into conversation.

Other cheap hotels abound in Sultanahmet and you'll have no trouble finding a place to stay; if you don't find them, they'll find you.

Sirkeci

In Sirkeci, the cheapies tend to have monolingual staff and revolting rooms. An exception to this is the **Gezginci Hostel**, Hüdavendigar Caddesi Serdar Sokak 5, ✆ 0212 527 8516. Rooms are very clean but basic and can be a little noisy at night; toilets and showers are communal; $6 per person.

Beyoğlu

None of the budget hotels around Taksim can be recommended with any confidence; if you want to stay in Beyoğlu on the cheap, try Meşrutiyet Caddesi, where there are a few tolerable addresses, such as the **Dünya** at No.79, ✆ 0212 144 0940.

campgrounds

There are a few places to camp, all located west of the old town near the airport. **Ataköy Kamping**, on the Marmara, is a good one, with a pool and other facilities, and convenient bus service into the city: Orbay Caddesi in Ataköy, ✆ 0212 556 000. Also by the sea, near a small beach, **Florya Turist Camping**, on the coastal road in Florya, would be perfect if not for the noise from the airport, practically next door; very close to the commuter rail line into İstanbul; ✆ 0212 574 0000.

Eating Out

Eating in İstanbul is a pure delight; the city has attracted the best of the country's chefs and many places still serve old Turkish specialities, almost impossible to find elsewhere in the country. It's true that most of the finest restaurants are now out in the newer quarters north of Taksim Square, or along the Bosphorus, places where tourists have little other reason to travel. But you're not likely to starve in old Stamboul or Beyoğlu.

Do note that İstanbul is not a wonderful town for hotel restaurants. Places that have them are either catering to businessmen or tour groups, and it often seems they're only spreading a table out of some vague sense of obligation. Ask the desk clerk where he'd go if he were you; maybe he'll tell you. And if you're looking for something special, beyond what we offer below, you'll probably have to ask somebody, because restaurants in this city—beyond simple lokantas—are surprisingly hard to find. They're all around, only a bit inconspicuous, often tucked away on back alleys and in second-storey rooms.

But who needs restaurants in İstanbul? It is entirely possible (and if you like to eat, almost inevitable) to spend the whole day grazing out on the pavements. There are the ubiquitous *simit* vendors—and with experience you'll learn that no two *simitler* are alike; some are divine, others can be taken home as souvenir door-knockers. *Büfeler* ('buffets', another French word) and street vendors decorate every street corner; they offer tasty döner, sandwiches, nuts and pumpkin seeds, bowls of lentil soup, *börekler*, puddings, cookies, baked potatoes with dressing or roast corn on the cob (two new fads), not to mention an infinity of kebabs, fish sandwiches around the docks, and lots more. Between each indulgence you can sit down for a fast glass of tea. And then there are the pastry shops—start frequenting these and it's all over.

expensive

Most of these accept credit cards; *moderate* or *inexpensive* places hardly ever will.

Sultanahmet

It's hard to find anything really distinguished in Sultanahmet. The best fresh fish can be had at the **Balık Sabahattin**, near the Cevriağa School in Cankurtaran, ✆ 0212 458 1824; $25 for a full meal. The Turkish/continental restaurant at the **Yeşil Ev**, Kabasakal Caddesi 5, ✆ 0212 517 6786, is pleasant and peaceful, offering meals in a charming conservatory; $20–25.

On Soğukçeşme Sokak behind the Aya Sofya is **Sarnıç**, ✆ 0212 512 4291, a truly remarkable restaurant sited underground in what was once a Byzantine cistern. Converted by TTOK, it is furnished in a strange baronial style with much wrought-iron work and an open fire big enough to roast a Volkswagen. Such surroundings don't come cheap—but one comes here more for the setting than the cuisine. The same is true for a number of İstanbul's old standbys, such as the Greek-Turkish **Pandeli's**, above the Spice Market at the Yeni Cami end, ✆ 0212 527 3909, with high prices (lunch only, about $20) to match its old reputation.

Kariye

The **Asitane Restaurant** attached to the Kariye Hotel has an understated elegance. Waiters pad up to the tables with exotic Ottoman meat and fish dishes (and some vegetarian options) costing upwards of $20.

Karaköy

By the cruise ship dock, the **Liman Lokanta** is a longtime seafood favourite; it's upstairs in the Turkish Maritime Lines's terminal building, ✆ 0212 292 3992. An old-fashioned place with a marvellous view of Stamboul, it has recently been restored to its Art Deco glory. $20, more for fish.

Beyoğlu

More expensive dining can be had at the lavish dining room of the **Pera Palace**, though here the real pleasure is dressing up and playing spy; about $25. At the landmark **Galata Tower** in Beyoğlu, ✆ 0212 245 1160, the attraction is the view, and the evening belly-dancing and music. Dinner $30 and up.

At the Tünel end of İstiklâl Caddesi, the **Four Seasons** (*Dört Mevsim*, not to be confused with the hotel of the same name in Sultanahmet), ✆ 0212 293 3941, has charm, sophistication, French onion soup and a very English sweet trolley. Further out, a fine lunch in sumptuous surroundings overlooking the Yıldız Parkı can be had at the **Malta Köşkü**, an Ottoman pavilion. $20, closed evenings.

Along the Bosphorus

Next to the fish market in Sarıyer on the Bosphorus, the **Urcan Restaurant**, ✆ 0212 242 1677, has been a seafood favourite with locals and visiting celebrities for over fifty years (one recent visitor was Helmut Köhl, but they've restocked the kitchen since). Another one with a view, and lovely seafood *börekler*, is the **Körfez**, near the Bosphorus bridge at 78 Körfez Caddesi, Kanlıca, ✆ 0212 413 4314. Both these places, as well as the myriad other seafront restaurants along the straits, pride themselves on local favourites such as sea bass baked in salt (not too salty when it's done, don't worry); expensive as they are ($40 or so), they're always crowded.

On the Asian side

There are a number of seafood restaurants on the coastal Sahil Yolu in Usküdar: the **Salacak**, ✆ 0216 341 2089, serves excellent grilled fish, with windows overlooking the Bosphorus, for $25 and up; and the **Kız Kulesi**, ✆ 0216 341 0403, just across from Leander's tower, has outdoor dining in summer and occasionally live music; about $15 and up.

Princes' Islands

On Büyükada, try the long-established **Milano**, ✆ 0216 382 6352, on the waterfront, which serves a truly delectable prawn casserole and other dishes: prices $15 and upwards.

moderate

Sultanahmet

In the Covered Market (western side, on Gani Çelebi Sokak), **Havuzlu Lokanta**, next to the post office, has a good range of Turkish food, and is open 11am–6pm. *Havuzlu* means 'with pool', for the small marble pool outside the restaurant.

Sirkeci

Konyalı's, on Ankara Caddesi 223 opposite the railway station, is long established in İstanbul and has a fine reputation for kebabs and *börekler*, serving good food for around $12 and up. There is another branch in the Topkapı Palace (the only restaurant in the Saray). **Borsa** (next to the walkway over Reşadiye Caddesi near the Galata bridge) is a chain, but it works hard to present typical kebabs and other dishes, such as *lahana dolma* (stuffed cabbage), with a little more care than the usual lokantas; especially good with soups and desserts (around $9), they are becoming quite popular—and they take credit cards. Other branches are on Taksim Square, in Fenerbahçe and in Osmanbey.

Kumkapı

In Byzantine times, the Kumkapı quarter was the fisherman's port of the capital. Today, just by coincidence, this busy neighbourhood on the Marmara, south of the Covered Bazaar, has become popular with the Stamboullu for its seafood restaurants. There are dozens of them on the pedestrian streets around Telli Odalar Sokak and

Arapzade Ahmet Sokak at Kumkapı's centre. None really stands out, but at most you can get a fine fish dinner for $18 or under; strolling around looking for something that catches your fancy (all the seafood will be on display in glass-fronted coolers) is a pleasant way to build up your appetite. Some of the less expensive places are on Gedik Paşa Caddesi, such as the **İstanbul Restaurant**; outside tables amidst swarming street life and convivial waiters. Pick a good fish out from the cooler for $12, or dine for much less on soup and kebabs.

When you visit the Süleymaniye Mosque, try and plan it to make lunch or dinner at the **Dârüzziyâfe**, ✆ 0212 511 8414; housed in the Süleymaniye's *külliye*, this is a thoroughly modern place with some extremely refined cooking. The speciality of the house is a spicy chicken in pastry dish called *tavuklu kolböreği*; about $15.

Outside town, there's always the enormous **Beyti** at Orman Sokak 8 near the airport, ✆ 0212 663 2990, with its heliport, three kitchens, and the much-imitated *Beyti kebap*; open until midnight and reasonably priced, around $12 for a full meal.

Beyoğlu

Hacı Baba, İstiklâl Caddesi 49, is now approaching its 80th year and still serves delectable Turkish cuisine at around $15 a head. Competition is not far away, however. This area has plenty of other choices, though they're often hard to find. The easiest thing is to take yourself to **Nevizade Sokak/Kalyoncukulluğu Caddesi**, behind the Balıkpazarı, where there are scores of simple restaurants with outside tables in the $9–15 range, most of which specialize in seafood. **Kalyoncu**, on Kalyoncukulluğu, is a nice one for grilled fish. **Asır**, on the same street, is one of the most authentic surviving *meyhaneler*, offering plates of mezes and fish along with the drinks. The newly-restored **Çiçek Pasajı** is full of restaurants, their benches and tables jostling so much for the limited space under the vaults that the whole place feels like one huge bawdy refectory. The **Pavyon** on the inside corner at No.11 is the oldest establishment, now run by two of the founder's grandsons, although the food and ambience elsewhere in the *pasaj* are equally good.

On a backstreet towards the Tünel area, the gravel-voiced Refik Arslan has been holding court since 1954 at the **Refik Restaurant**, Sofyalı Sokak 10. During his reign, the walls have been covered with sketches, notes, posters and obscure photos which you could spend all evening trying to make some kind of sense of. You're better off concentrating on the overflowing drinks and excellent dishes from the Black Sea Region; $10. A good option for sophisticates on a budget is the **Çatı** at Orhan Adlı Apaydın Sokak 20/7, an easily missed turn off İstiklal Caddesi. The restaurant is in the Lawyer's Association Building and, as the name implies (*çatı* means 'roof'), it's on the top floor with partial views over İstanbul. Although the menu offers examples of world cuisine, Turkish dishes predominate. You can even order that most patriotic of Turkish vegetables, aubergine, for dessert (in the form of *patlıcan tatlısı*). Somewhat syrupy live music is also served up most nights, and a dancefloor beckons for romantics.

Ortaköy

In the shadow of the Atatürk bridge is a bar and restaurant area popular with young Turks. Leading off from the Ortaköy Camii, a sickly-sweet mid-19th century confection, is a network of pedestrianized roads packed with restaurants. Amongst the best is the **İlhami'nin Yeri** at Osmanzade Sokak 6, where the mezes and fish are always fresh and the chicken kebabs are amongst the most succulent you'll savour. $12 for the full works including wine, less if you let your tongue loose on a *şalgam suyu*—a crimson tang of turnip juice—instead.

On the Asian side

If you have a car, try to make it up to the Çamlıca hill park and the **Çamlıca Café**, ℰ 0216 329 8191; good, typical Turkish cooking with the grandest view of all views of İstanbul. One of the best spots for *mantı* and *börekler* is up the Bosphorus, on the coast road in Istinye: the **Armağan Mantı Evi**, offering a wide choice of fillings, sweet and savoury, and suitable quantities for a snack or a full meal. At **Yedigün**, İskele Caddesi 13 in Sarıyer, you can get a nicely grilled fish and mezes for much less than most of the places in this swank area; $10.

If you want to see what the other Bosphorus villages were like twenty years ago, take the ferry to the end, to Anadolu Kavağı, the only one that hasn't been totally swallowed up by villas yet (though by the time you read this it may be too late). All around the waterfront are small fish restaurants with outside tables where you can get a sweet and simple dinner for about $12.

While in Asia, you could do a lot worse than dine at the unnamed restaurant at the **Haydarpaşa railway station**, with its tiled and panelled walls and respectful, uniformed waiters. You may never dine at another railway station like it. And if you're anywhere nearby, it's well worth an evening excursion to Kadıköy, the neighbourhood south of Haydarpaşa, for a dinner at the wooden **Kadife Chalet**, on Kadife Sokak, ℰ 0216 347 8596. The restaurant shares space with an art and crafts gallery in an old Ottoman house.

cheap

Sultanahmet

Cheap lokantas and kebab stands abound in Sultanahmet, most of them on or near the Divan Yolu. The **Paris Lokanta**, on the south side of the strip, serves tasty stews on marble tables—Turkish diner paradise for about $5, the going rate for the area. Second choice is the **Vitamin**, on the north side of Divan Yolu, a lively place where an idiosyncratic chef stands in the window, surrounded by tempting dishes, and tries to entice tourists in with forceful cries of 'Yes!'. Near the Vitamin, the **Can Restaurant/Pudding Shop** was the old 1960s international rendezvous point for hippy travellers on the overland route to Asia. It's inexpensive, and you'll get a free postcard, but it's lost a lot of its character. There's a wide choice of dishes; the *sütlaç* is an absolute dream.

Slightly more expensive than the average lokanta in the area, **Buhara** at Nuruosmaniye Caddesi 7, a block from the Aya Sofya, is a classic meat and kebab restaurant; $6. Vegetarians won't find much here.

The perfect place to refuel before or after plunging into the nearby Covered Bazaar is the **Çemberli Safran Sofrası**, opposite the Burnt Column at Vezirhan Caddesi 18, offering a wide selection of stews and kebabs at lunchtime only; $4. Alternatively, try lunch at **Subaşı**, on Nuruosmaniye Caddesi near the market gate; the tasty lokanta cooking means it's always crowded.

For a snack or light lunch after sightseeing or shopping, there is **Cennet**, on the north side of the Divan Yolu at Çemberlitaş: touristy but atmospheric, decorated with kilims, and offering a wide choice of pastries with cheese, spinach or meat, *mantı*, *börekler*, puddings and desserts. The best lokanta around the Spice Market is also the hardest to find: **Küçük Hüdadad**, hidden inside the Şapçı Han directly across from the market on Kömür Bekır Sokak. A complete dinner of soup, kebab and dessert is $7.

Sirkeci and around

In Sirkeci, the lokanta under the Gezginci Hostel is popular with locals, with meatballs and kebabs costing $3–4. Along the nearby İbni Kemal Caddesi is a strip of good-value restaurants, such as the **Özler** at No.29, where prices are half what they would be in Sultanahmet.

There are several good *börek* houses near the railway station, where a plate of *börekler* and a cup of tea make a lovely mid-morning snack. At the time of writing, the lower deck of the new Galata Bridge isn't open yet, but several of the inexpensive fish restaurants and cafés for which the old bridge was famous plan to move back as soon as they can. At any rate, you can still find fishing boats tied up along the docks on either side, where they grill the fish right after they catch it, and sell you a very tasty and very filling sandwich for next to nothing. If your stomach is rumbling out at Lâleli, the **Murat** at Ordu Caddesi 212A, near the Antique Merit Hotel, has solid stews to fill the void for $5.

Beyoğlu

Elsewhere in İstanbul, cheap eating is reduced to the simple lokantas that are everywhere. Beyoğlu and Taksim have plenty—one on every corner on busy streets. At the Taksim end of İstiklal Caddesi is **Bereket Halk Döner**, where for $3 you can sink your teeth into a plate of whatever that thing grilling in the window is (a brontosaurus leg?). **Fehmi Baba**, on the northern end of Meşrutiyet Caddesi, has tasty *İskender kebap* and other kebabs for $6. **Yakup 2**, on Asmalımescit Sokak near the upper end of the Tünel, is a lively, fun place, a combination neighbourhood lokanta and *meyhane* for the artsy Beyoğlu set; $7.

The venerable **Hacı Abdullah Lokantası**, founded in 1888 when Atatürk was still just a lad in Salonika, can be found near the Ağa Camii off İstiklâl Caddesi at Sakızağacı Caddesi 17. This bastion of traditional Ottoman cooking has kept its prices low, with a good selection of vegetarian options to offset the meat dishes; $7 and upwards, no alcohol.

Tucked away in the backstreets nearby are some of the most characterful places that tourists rarely stumble upon. At Jurnal Sokak 1 is the **Kelif**, run by three women serving excellent home-made food for only $5; no alcohol. Opposite the Kelif at No.6 is **Lay**, with a few simple tables and chairs which spill out onto the pavement in good weather. Regular customers are drawn by the traditional Turkish dishes such as *yuralma*, small meatballs with pasta, costing $5. No alcohol.

On the Asian side

Üsküdar and Kadıköy are both full of good chow houses. In Üsküdar, **Kanaat**, Selmanıpak Caddesi 25, has a wide menu and since 1933 has specialized in gorgeous, sticky desserts; $8. The coastal road in Salacak just south of Üsküdar, facing the Kızkulesi (Leander's Tower), is a good place to look for restaurants. Just off it, at 20 Salacak İskelesi, **Arabın Yeri**, ✆ 0216 333 3157, is a favourite neighbourhood seafood spot, with a view over the straits; open until midnight.

The Islands

It's hard to find anything more than a simple lokanta on the Princes' Islands; on Büyükada, at 10 Gülistan Caddesi, **Birtat** offers kebabs and some seafood at relatively cheap prices.

alternative cuisines

If the delights of Turkish cuisine wane, there is a wide range of alternatives. The most famous of these is **Russian: Rejans**, a favourite of Atatürk's, is hidden away on Emir Nevruz Sokak, off İstiklâl Caddesi near the Panaya Isodion, ✆ 0212 243 3882. Founded by White Russians in the 1920s, and once the most fashionable spot in town, Rejans has declined a bit, but the Russian cuisine, the vodka and the tatty ambience keep it popular. For the fine wood-panelled interior and the pre-Great War atmosphere of hushed stealth, you pay around $15. İstanbul's other famous Russian restaurant is in İstinye, up the Bosphorus: **Süreyya**, İstinye Caddesi 260, ✆ 0212 277 5886. Serious bortsch and caviar, as well as Turkish food; expensive and usually crowded. **Café Wien**, on Atiye Sokak in Teşvikiye, ✆ 0212 231 8963, serves **Austrian** food on its garden terrace: schnitzel, lavish pastries and *kaffee mit schlag*.

French and Italian restaurants are very popular, though there are few in the old city. Try **Ristorante Rosa**, Cumhuriyet Caddesi 131, ✆ 0212 241 2827: good for pizzas, about $18 for a full dinner.

Oriental restaurants are becoming popular in the modern neighbourhoods. The poshest, with arguably the most refined and authentic cuisine, is the **Dynasty Asian**, in the Merit Hotel, on Ordu Caddesi in Lâleli, ✆ 0212 513 9300, about $30 maximum—they also do a much less expensive *dim sum* lunch. **China Restaurant**, on Lamartin Caddesi near Taksim Square, was the first in Turkey, in the 1950s, and has become an institution. It's still good and reasonably priced: average dinner about $20. For **Indian** grub there is **Awara** at Köybaşı Caddesi 76.

With all this on offer, philistines can still be satisfied: the **world chains** now have many links in İstanbul, including a **McDonalds** in Beyazıt and in Taksim, and now Turkey's first drive-in, on the E5 at Merter; a **Wimpy** on İstiklâl Caddesi and a **Kentucky Fried Chicken** near the airport in Ataköy. **Pizza Hut**, at the Taksim end of Cumhuriyet Caddesi, ✆ 0212 251 8998, will deliver.

pastry shops

Don't forget to save a major part of your calorie budget for these, for İstanbul is one of the world's capitals of sweet indulgence. You'll never be more than a block away from a place where you can sit down with a glass of tea and a slice of baklava at almost any hour of the day. In addition, the big hotels here have always had a tradition of keeping a master pastry chef in the kitchens of their elegant cafés. It isn't just about baklava and other Turkish treats. With its cosmopolitan tradition (and its incurable sweet tooth), this city has embraced everything that's tasty, from Central European tortes to French pâtisserie and chocolates or American cheesecake.

Top of the list, and still an essential part of the İstanbul experience even though it's often crowded with tour groups, is the **Pâtisserie de Pera**, in the Pera Palace Hotel: a marvel of Victorian cosiness with antique décor and silver, and a view. In the Hotel Richmond, the **Café Lebon** is locally famous for its fruit pies. The **İnci**, at 124 İstiklâl, is renowned for profiteroles (they claim to have invented them).

Some of the luxury hotel cafés roll out their finest confections for a five o'clock tea: the Çırağan Palace's **Gazebo Café** and the **Café Marmara**, in the Marmara Hotel on Taksim Square. For overwhelming cream and chocolate spectaculars with the Central European touch, there is the **Café Wien** (*see* above), or the **Pâtisserie Gezi**, on İnönü Caddesi off Taksim Square.

Entertainment and Nightlife

arts

İstanbul is well endowed with **cinemas**, and each district has at least one, usually with several screens; most of the film palaces are on İstiklâl or around Taksim Square. English-language films, though, are almost invariably dubbed. Try to check what's showing just before setting off, lest you fall prey to the irritating habit of last-minute programme changes. İstanbul has a full schedule of **concerts**, **opera** and **ballet**; the two big venues are the **Atatürk Cultural Centre** (known to locals simply as AKM—Atatürk Kultur Merkezi) on Taksim Square and the **Cemal Reşit Rey Concert Hall** in Harbiye. Genuine **Turkish traditional and classical music** is a bit harder to find; you'll get some on TRT3, 88.2 FM; beyond that consult *The Guide* or the tourist office for schedules of concerts.

The big cultural centres plus other spots, including historic sites like the Aya İrene church at Topkapı, host events during the **İstanbul Festival**. Although not yet in the league of Edinburgh or Salzburg, this has an impressively ambitious programme and tickets cost well under half what you'd pay for equivalent performances in London or New York. The İstanbul Festival begins in the second half of April each year with a **film** festival showing over 150 movies in two weeks. **Theatre** takes over in the second half of May, when the curtain is raised on 40 plays. **Dance** follows in June, mostly of the western classical variety, but with some performances of Turkish dancing. A **jazz** festival rounds off the proceedings in the first half of July. As if this weren't enough, the **İstanbul Biennial** is held from mid-September to mid-November on odd years (2001, 2003), and has a growing reputation for bucking trends and showcasing new artists. The Festival and the Biennial are both run by the İstanbul Foundation for Culture and Arts, ✆ 0212 293 3133, ✉ 0212 249 7771.

nightlife

Forget the images of Turkish Delight advertisements, forget the Thousand and One Nights and 'Eastern promise'; night-time entertainment in İstanbul is disappointing. What there is is largely found across the Golden Horn in Taksim, the modern and international part of the city. There are many nightclubs and discos along Cumhuriyet Caddesi, where the atmosphere is so muted and antiseptic you would be happy to take your mother or to let your daughter go alone.

Nevertheless, a pleasant evening can be spent at **Kervansaray**, Cumhuriyet Caddesi 30, ✆ 0212 247 1630 (*open 9pm–3am*). The cost, with a meal, all drinks, a belly-dance show, a singer, dancing and maybe a magician, will be in the region of $50. **The Grand**, at Bella Limana Caddesi 80 in Rumeli Hisarı, offers more of the same. Similar, and the only cabaret on the Stamboul side, is **Orient House**, on Tiyatro Caddesi near Beyazıt Square, ✆ 0212 517 6163.

At the top of the **Galata Tower**, ✆ 0212 245 1160, is a restaurant which puts on a floor show that includes folk dancing. The clientele is composed almost entirely of tour groups and the menu and floor show are only too clearly tourist-oriented, but at least the view from the tower is good. The restaurant opens at 8pm, and the programme starts at 9.50 and finishes at midnight. The fixed, all-in price is about $70 with show, $17 without.

The **Çiçek Pasajı** (*see* p.134) has long been the traditional place to start an evening's revelry, and many people still turn up in the early evening before moving on to a nightclub. Just as popular now are the *meyhaneler* of neighbouring Nevizade Sokak and Kalyoncukullüğü Sokak. You'll also find lots of bars, some with live rock or Turkish folk music, in the streets off İstiklâl Caddesi. Rockers should swing by the **Asparagus**, a small dark bar off İstiklâl Caddesi at Büyük Parmakkapı Sokak 32A, with free entry and live rock music that might blow your mind but certainly will blow your eardrums.

A sort of coffeehouse, also just off İstiklâl on Büyük Parmakkapı Sokak, **Hayal Kahvesi** has rock and jazz groups until 2am. Jazz is king at the **Café Gramophon**, near the Galata Tower at Tünel Meydanı 3, with live bands five nights a week. Night-owls can listen to live popular Turkish and Circassian music three times weekly from 10pm at the **Karma Café Bar**, on the first floor at Orhan Adlı Apaydın Sokak 31–33.

For an evening at a lower volume setting, head for the **Kaktüs Kahvesi** at İmam Adnan Sokak 4, where, as in cafés the world over, customers sip coffee and wine whilst poring over newspapers and magazines. There's wine by the barrel at **Pano's**, near Çiçek Pasajı at Kalyoncu Kulluğu Caddesi 4. It frequently resembles a *bon viveurs'* convention and is cacophonous when heaving—which is most nights.

Some of the luxury hotels around Taksim and the Bosphorus, such as the Hilton and the Marmara İstanbul, have rooftop bars with a view; the latter's **Tepe Bar** is one of İstanbul's top jazz venues. The **Lâleazar Bar** atop the Hilton offers a view and a happy hour from 6.30 to 8pm. **Babıâli,** one of the city's few proper wine bars, is in the Merit Hotel on Ordu Caddesi in Lâleli; happy hour from 5 to 7pm.

Around Sultanahmet, options for an evening's entertainment shrink. On fine evenings, the outdoor **Café Meşale** near the front entrance to the Blue Mosque along the Hippodrome can be enchanting. Its low chairs and tables under the trees offer a refuge for *nargile* smokers and postcard writers alike. You'll find many Turks sipping tea and coffee and swaying to the live music alongside the foreign tourists. Opposite the Hippodrome, the **Sultan Pub** tries hard to create a dimly lit 'Rick's Bar'-type ambience that is spoiled by Humphrey Bogart having to share the wall with James Dean and Marilyn Monroe. **Rumeli Café**, just off the Divan Yolu behind the Vitamin restaurant, is a quiet and serendipitous place for a drink, with outside tables and occasionally live music.

If you completely want to forget that you're in Turkey, there's no place better than İstanbul's state-of-the-art discos. **Memo's**, with live music on Salhane Sokak 10 in Ortaköy, is currently the trendiest place to go, if you've got the clothes for it. Ortaköy, for that matter, is quite the hot spot these days. Other bars include **Night Calls**, nearby on Vapur İskelesi Sokak, with live rock most nights after 11pm; and **Yelkovan**, one of the few places offering alternative music, on Muallim Naci Caddesi. For techno-madness, try **19/20**, Tanimhane Belediye Dükkanları 73, near Taksim, and the **Paşa Beach**, overlooking the Bosphorus on Muallim Naci Caddesi in Kuruçeşme.

A **word of warning** for males only. In the side-streets of İstiklâl Caddesi are 'night-clubs', usually called *gazinolar*, that advertise steamy belly-dance shows. Don't go into any, no matter how ingratiating the tout who tries to entice you may be. It's the old, old story; you'll be entrapped, required to buy 'champagne' for some repulsive whore at 100 times the going rate, and you'll leave with your wallet empty and your ego in shreds. Don't imagine you can sweet-talk your way out of this with a few smiles and protestations of innocence. You can't.

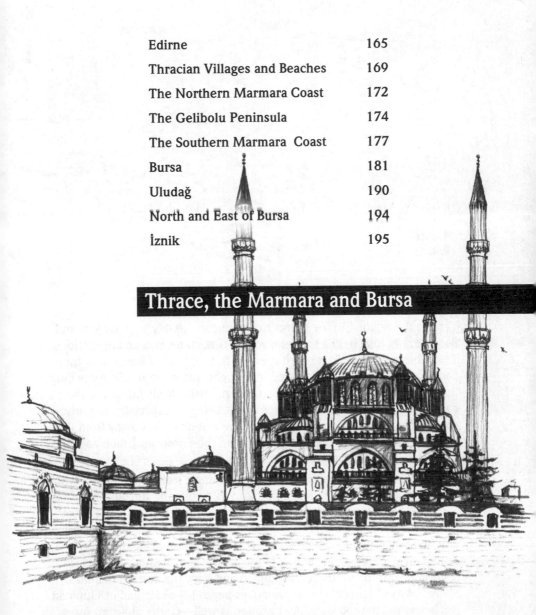

Thrace, the Marmara and Bursa

Thrace, the region Turkey shares rather uncomfortably with Greece and Bulgaria, has long held a special place in Turkish dreams and aspirations. The tribes out of the East called it Rumelia, the 'land of Rome' that they had heard so much of and so ardently sought. Although it comprises only three per cent of Turkish territory, modern Turks, from Atatürk to the current government, pin their hopes on it being an especially magnetic chunk of real estate, capable of pulling the rest of Turkey away from the insoluble squabbles of the Middle East into the European Union and the democratic traditions of the West.

Ancient Thrace was occupied by antiquity's most skilled horsemen, who had a special knack for splendid barbaric goldwork and uncouth religious practices. Unfortunately for them, Thrace was on the principal highway of conquerors bent on Europe or Asia. Xerxes and Alexander came this way, while the Romans, who went about their conquering more systematically, bisected it with a highway, the Via Egnatia (the modern Londra Asfaltı) to speed their legions to and from the eastern marches. Many towns of Thrace's three provinces began life as Roman or Ottoman garrisons, and have known other armies as well—Goths, Bulgars, Avars,

Crusaders, Russians and Greeks. Battles that have changed history have taken place here, or offshore in the Dardanelles, from the days of Homer to the First World War. Until recently, much of Thrace was an off-limits military zone.

Yet Thrace is a quiet, almost lonely place, with few monuments to show for the great events that have occurred on its soil. Most of the land is a rolling plain, emerald green in spring, but hot and humid in summer, and snow-blasted in winter. As for the Marmara, it looks promising on the map, but don't expect anything like the sunny blue Aegean. In this part of the world, every corner seems to have its own climate, landscapes and moods, and the Marmara's tend to be somewhat sombre, more like the Black Sea than the Mediterranean. Nevertheless, there is some agreeable scenery in out-of-the-way places: the little-known Marmara Islands, around Lake İznik, and especially up on Mount Uludağ, where there is good skiing, just a cable-car ride away from the centre of one of Turkey's most engaging cities, the old Ottoman capital of Bursa.

Edirne

Thrace's one real attraction is its largest town, **Edirne**, old Adrianople, four hours from İstanbul, near the Greek and Bulgarian frontiers. If you're driving from the north to Turkey, it's on the way; if you're coming from Greece, it's worth the detour from the main coastal route, for you won't find a better introduction to Turkey and its architecture—and greased wrestling, the one thing that keeps Edirne's juices flowing these days. Although the city once served as the Ottoman capital, it has few modern industries to keep it growing and prosperous, and today looks more or less the same as it did a hundred years ago.

History

Hadrian founded Adrianople in AD 125, on the site of Thracian *Uscudama* (Hellenistic Oresteia). Almost exactly 200 years later, his successor Constantine the Great fought a major battle nearby, a prelude to his capture of Byzantium; a thousand years later, history repeated itself when Murat won it for the Ottomans in 1361. Since the seat of the Ottoman Empire in its early days was wherever the sultan had his divan, Edirne hosted the Ottoman court while the sultan waited for Constantinople to fall into his hands. If there was trouble in the east, the sultan stayed in Bursa; if he was interested in expanding the boundaries of Rumelia, he stayed in Edirne. Although this shuttling about ended when Mehmet the Conqueror took Constantinople, the sultans continued to bestow lavish imperial monuments on their first European capital until it reached the height of its beauty and importance in the late 16th century, before later wars and natural disasters took their toll.

Getting Around

Edirne is linked to İstanbul by a recently completed **motorway**. Several coach lines compete on the Edirne–İstanbul run, and both frequency and service are excellent;

this is the run on which you're most likely to get tea and cakes and television. Travelling on Lux Express or Radar buses takes 2½ hours via the motorway, whilst Edirne Birliği buses take 3½ hours to trundle along the old E5 highway.

However, it's rather difficult to get anywhere else from Edirne. There are two **buses** a day for Çanakkale. Bus connections to Tekirdağ are more frequent, although the onward trip by boat to Marmara is erratic in winter. Ring ahead to the Tekirdağ tourist office. To reach the isolated beaches at Erikli or Enez, catch a bus from Edirne or İstanbul to Keşan. Minibuses and local buses run from there to these proto-resorts.

The **rail** service from İstanbul's Sirkeci Station somehow takes 6 hours; the bus is by far the best bet. The daily Balkan Express from İstanbul stops in Edirne on its way to Sofia. Edirne's rail station is out near the otogar to the south-east of the centre.

Both the stations are too far to walk with luggage, and you may want to take a **dolmuş** or **taxi** into the centre, although be warned that the metered taxi fares in Edirne come as a shock after İstanbul. Edirne has Bulgarian (on Talatpaşa Caddesi) and Greek (next to the police station on Cumhuriyet Caddesi) consulates to help with any anticipated border difficulties.

There is an hourly dolmuş service from the centre of Edirne to Kapıkule on the **Bulgarian** border. For **Greece**, take a dolmuş or city bus (both from the bus stop opposite the post office at Saraçlar Caddesi) to the small village of Karaağaç from where it is a 2½-mile (4km) taxi ride to the frontier at Pazarkule. According to the locals the Greeks have been behaving themselves lately and border hassles, which used to be commonplace, are now infrequent. On occasion the border may only be open 9am–noon; check with the Edirne tourist office to avoid being stranded.

Tourist Information

Edirne: Hürriyet Meydanı 17, ✆ 0284 213 9208. The provincial directorate is at Talatpaşa Caddesi 76a, west of the town centre, ✆ 0284 225 5260.

Kapıkule: at the Bulgarian border, ✆ 0284 238 2019.

İpsala: at the Greek border, ✆ 0284 616 1577.

Selimiye Mosque

The crowning achievement of the sultans' 16th-century building spree, itself set like a crown over Edirne, is the grand **Selimiye Mosque**, built by Mimar Sinan for Selim II. Sinan finished the mosque, which he considered his finest, in 1575, when he was over 80 years old. According to legend it has 999 windows and its dome is slightly larger than the Aya Sofya's; its four identical 225ft minarets, girdled with three balconies, are the tallest outside Mecca, and were supposedly aligned to appear as a single one from the distance, to deceive enemy artillery. Unlike most mosques of its stature, the Selimiye is uncluttered with a large complex of religious foundations, and those it does have are all on one side, allowing impressive views of the mosque itself from three sides.

But it was in the interior that Sinan worked his best magic. The great dome hovers at 145ft on eight massive piers over a marble fountain symbolizing the waters of a legendary source called Zem-Zem, while at floor level the eye is drawn towards the exquisitely carved marble mimber and mihrab, the latter set back in an apse with walls adorned by İznik tiles; it is perhaps the only one in Turkey with a window opening towards Mecca. An even lovelier display of İznik tiles decorates the **imperial loge**; if you weren't able to get into the harem of the Topkapı Sarayı, here's a chance to see what you missed.

The medrese, in typical cloister style, now houses Edirne's **Museum of Turkish and Islamic Art** (*open daily 8–noon and 1.30–5.30, closed Mon; adm*), with items from the local *tekke* of whirling dervishes, calligraphy and charming photographs of great greased wrestlers from Edirne's past. A new **Archaeological and Ethnographic Museum** (*open daily exc Mon, 8.30–12, 1–5.30; adm*), with a small collection of costumes, kilims and carpet saddle bags, artefacts from Trakya (Thrace) and ancient coins, is behind the Selimiye. The arcade of shops along the west flank of the mosque, the **Kavaflar Arasta**, was built exclusively for Edirne's cobblers; as with so many other arcades, the idea was to put the rents towards the upkeep of the mosque.

Other Mosques

Just below the Selimiye, off central Cumhuriyet Meydanı, are two older imperial mosques, textbook examples for studying the development of the classical Ottoman style. The **Eski Cami**, a plain square encompassing nine vaults, was begun in 1402 by the three sons of Yıldırım Beyazıt after their father's collision with Tamerlane; during the next 11 years, as the mosque was erected, the three brothers fought for control of the empire. The winner, and sole survivor, Mehmet I, had the honour of dedicating the mosque. One distinct feature of the Eski Cami is the inscription in great Arabic letters painted on the outer walls, giving the mosque a curiously primitive appearance.

The second mosque, the innovative **Üç Şerefeli Cami**, was built in 1447 by Murat II; its name of 'three balconies' derives from one of its asymmetrical minarets, which at 218ft was the tallest the Ottomans ever built—until Sinan's slender rockets went up around the Selimiye. Each of the mosque's minarets is a delicately carved work, and each is different— one straight, one spiral and one in zigzag patterns. Üç Şerefeli, the last great imperial mosque built prior to the capture of Constantinople, is covered with the largest central dome the Ottomans had yet dared and a clutch of smaller domes; inside, the architect achieved a surprising airiness. Although its other foundations lie derelict, the mosque's **Sokullu Hamam**, built by Sinan in the 16th century and one of Turkey's most elegant, has been restored and still serves as a bath today (*open daily 8am–10pm, bath only $3, massage and scrub $5 extra, women's entrance at the rear*). Remains of the mosque's medrese can still be seen clinging to the façade of the hamam; fireplaces which once welcomed theological students after their lessons in the chilly mosque are now exposed to the windswept street. Sinan's finely restored **Rüstem Paşa Kervansaray**, adjoining the Eski Cami, has also regained its original function as a hotel (*see below*).

Other Monuments

In the Cumhuriyet Meydanı, Atatürk has to share space with a peculiar statue of two wrestlers, each of whom has two faces, so the work has no 'back'. Also here are the two covered bazaars, the *bedesten* (1405) and Sinan's **Ali Paşa Çarşısı**, from 1569. Its mesmerising arches of brick and plasterwork stretch on for over 600ft. After a devastating fire in 1992 it was extensively restored, and now looks indecorously new. Both bazaars are fun to visit, especially if you need a plastic bucket or saucepan.

Besides these, Edirne contains literally hundreds of other Ottoman buildings in its cobbled lanes. Especially interesting (and especially in danger of collapsing) are the great wooden Ottoman houses, typically unpainted, but adorned with folk motifs carved on the gables and balconies. Edirne is one of the few places outside İstanbul where you see many of these; a couple have been converted into rather shabby pensions, in the back streets behind the Ali Paşa bazaar. When built, however, each had separate quarters for men and women.

If you haven't yet seen enough mosques, one of the best is up on the hills above the Selimiye, off Mimar Sinan Caddesi: the charming **Muradiye**, a landmark visible from almost everywhere in Edirne. Murat II founded the mosque in 1435 for the Mevlevi dervishes and spared no expense on its exquisite İznik tiles. Like the Green Mosque in Bursa and many others, the Muradiye is built in a T-shape; the two rooms on either side of the mosque proper were for travelling dervishes to spend the night.

Ottoman Monuments on the Periphery

Several other imperial mosques lie on the outskirts of Edirne, mostly along the willowy banks of the **Tunca**, a tributary of the Meriç (the Greek Ebros), the river that forms the border between Greece and Turkey. A walk around them on a nice day is one of the most pleasant things you can do in Edirne; there are several good picnic spots around the riverbank.

Start the tour by walking to the end of Talatpaşa Caddesi. The **Gazimihal Bridge** over the Tunca, an Ottoman work on Byzantine foundations, commemorates a Greek who turned Turk and became a redoubtable general for the Ottomans; at the end of the bridge, the 1421 **Gazimihal Mosque** has a graceful portico and carved minaret. Further down the road is the 1361 **Yıldırım Camii**, but you may wish to turn right, following the riverbank; not far away stands the **İkinci Beyazıt Külliyesi**, founded by Beyazıt II in 1484 and endowed with a record number of religious foundations, now mostly empty but occupied in part by a small museum of medicine. It includes a hospital and *timarhane* (an insane asylum) considered among the most progressive and well equipped of their day, with a sumptuous therapy ward (*darüşşifa*), a medical school, bakery, two hospices, and baths. Architecturally the complex is an important stepping-stone towards the grand imperial style of İstanbul: a lovely ensemble including a square mosque, decorated with simple patterns of windows, surrounded by an asymmetrical arrangement of domed buildings, set off with attractive small lanterns and chimneys. The six-arched **Beyazıt Bridge**, built at the same time, connects the complex to Edirne. Several other fine 15th-century Ottoman bridges span the Tunca and Meriç; two of them connect Edirne with the island in the Tunca called the **Sarayiçi**, just north of the Beyazıt Külliyesi. The name comes from the *Edirne Sarayı*, or sultan's palace, a pleasure dome built here by Murat II but blown to bits by the Turks in 1877 to keep the explosives they had stored there out of the hands of the invading Russians. Today the island is home to Edirne's biggest annual event, the **Greased Wrestling Tournament** (*Yağlı Güreş*), which is held in late June–early July, depending on Ramazan.

The Greased Wrestlers of Edirne

The Turks call the tournament the *Kırkpınar* ('forty spring'); according to tradition, the bouts began in the 14th century, when Süleyman Paşa, son of the second Ottoman sultan, Orhan Gazi, brought his forty heroes to campaign in Europe. In between battles, they amused themselves by wrestling. Two contestants were so equally matched they wrestled to death and were buried by their companions. The next day a spring appeared by the tombs, which became known as the 'spring of the forty'.

The Kırkpınar (now caged up in a modern stadium) attracts thousands of competitors from around Turkey. The contestants, dressed only in their leather breeches, or *kispet*, rub their skin with olive oil and warm up to drums and a wailing oboe. Next the announcer, or *cazgır*, leads a prayer and introduces the pairs of wrestlers; part of the Turks' enjoyment of the matches is hearing the *cazgır*'s recitation of each wrestler's claim to fame and his best tricks. The free-style bouts last until one contestant is pinned down or simply keels over. Wrestlers compete in four categories, classed by age and prowess. A grand champion (*Baş Pehlivan*) who retains the title for three years straight is awarded the highest honour, the Golden Belt. One who won it around the turn of the century, Koca Yusuf ('Enormous Joe'), has become a legend in Edirne: he went on to challenge and defeat the greatest champions of Europe and the US, but was drowned on his return voyage from America when his ship sank, finally, as the Turks sigh, 'beaten by his own bad luck'.

North of here, in an unmarked battlefield, Visigothic horsemen devastated Roman infantry in one of the climactic battles of history, the 378 AD **Battle of Adrianople**. The Visigoths had peacefully settled much of Thrace in the 4th century, and they were only rising up in revolt against the oppression and taxes of Roman rule. But the battle was a landmark in military history, demonstrating conclusively the superiority of cavalry over the Roman legions: the Roman Empire was sadly lacking in horses, while the Germans had plenty. Adrianople was the first big crack in Rome's defences, and the beginning of the end for the empire; after it, the Visigoths went on the move, raiding through Greece and the Balkans. In 410, they would sack Rome itself.

Thracian Villages and Beaches

The Thracian interior isn't holiday country—rolling, featureless farmland full of wheat and sunflowers that turns golden-brown in late July and August. The villages offer few sights, but on the whole they are happy and prosperous places. Two things you'll come across are tumuli, the preferred mode of burial of the ancient Thracians (some can be seen from the E5 around Lüleburgaz) and Ottoman-era bridges. The roads here were crucial to the 15th-century sultans, consolidating their hold on the Balkans. The most impressive of their works is in **Uzunköprü**, a village near the Greek border, the name of which means 'long bridge': a 174-arch, 4,400ft span completed in 1444 that was probably the longest in Europe at the time. South of Uzunköprü on the Gulf of Saroz are long sandy beaches around **Erikli** and **İbrice**. Although they contain a number of simple *pansiyonlar*, these seaside villages remain undeveloped compared with resorts closer to İstanbul, such as Şarköy and Silivri. If you're really intent on getting away from it all, **Enez** on the Greek border is as good a candidate as any. A port has been on this site since the 12th century BC, and though there is a picturesque castle to keep watch, it's the beach with clear water that people come for today.

The Yıldız Mountains mark the boundary between Bulgaria and Turkey. Local beauty spots in the area include the frontier post of **Dereköy** and the Black Sea village of **İğneada**, both surrounded by forests. A new road has been built here, and İğneada's port, the village of Limanköy, has beaches and a number of family *pansiyonlar*.

Inland, each of a triangle of small towns in central Thrace has its Ottoman ornament: **Kırklareli**, with its 1407 Hızır Bey Cami and old hamam; **Babaeski**, with its Cedit Ali Paşa Mosque, built by Sinan; and **Lüleburgaz**, ancient Arcadiopolis, with another of Sinan's works, the Mehmet Paşa Mosque and its large collection of religious foundations, including baths and a soup kitchen.

Edirne and Around **Where to Stay**

Edirne

moderate

The conversion of a historic *han* into a hotel created the **(O)Hotel Rüstempaşa Kervansaray**, in the centre on İki Kapılı Han Caddesi 57, ✆ 0284 225 7195, ✆ 0284 212 0462. The service and furnishings can't match the auspicious surroundings, windows are on the small side and front-facing rooms can be noisy; but this is your only chance to stay in a building by Mimar Sinan. Prices go as low as $40; amenities include a disco, two bars and a hamam that stays open 24 hours a day.

Edirne not being much of a tourist destination, you can usually get a room for about $40 in a nice hotel that would be twice as much in İstanbul or on the coast. The best choice is the **★★Şaban Açıkgöz**, ✆ 0284 213 0313, ✆ 0284 213 4516, near the Kervansaray in the Tahmis Çarşısı (look for the yellow sign): pleasant airy rooms with television (though all you can pick up is MTV). Similar rooms may be had for the same price at the **★★Balta Oteli**, Talat Paşa Asfaltı 97, ✆ 0284 225 1011, inconveniently situated out of town on the road to the bus station. At Talatpaşa Caddesi 170, near the tourist office, the **★★Sultanotel**, ✆ 0284 225 1372, ✆ 0284 225 5763, has a gloomy restaurant but comfortable en suite rooms for $50.

inexpensive–cheap

The family-run **★★Efe** lies on the relatively quiet Maarif Caddesi 13, ✆ 0284 213 6166, ✆ 0284 213 6080. Ask for a room on the top floor and you'll be sure to avoid any interference from the basement 'Efe English Pub'. Doubles for $38 are bright and comfortable with a private bathroom. Just up the road at No. 7 is the inferior **★Park**, ✆ 0284 225 4610, ▤ 0284 225 4635, where the redeeming feature is its cosy fireplace in the middle of the lobby; doubles $35.

The only cheapie worth laying your hat in for a night is the **(O)Aksaray**, on the corner of Maarif Caddesi and Alipaşa Ortakapı Caddesi. This 100-year-old clapboard house with a fretwork balcony looks like it has just been vacated by the Waltons. Inside, the rooms offer further evidence of the Turks' love affair with the colour brown, but all have phones and TVs. Rooms cost $18 with bathroom facilities, $14 without. There is a bar downstairs with a loyal local clientele.

camping

Several campsites dot the area, the best of which is the **Fifi Motel Camp**, ✆ 0284 235 7908, next to Edirne College, five miles out on the old E5 road to İstanbul. Camping facilities are available in summer only; motel rooms are open all year round.

Erikli

Simple *pansiyonlar* open in season only are the norm on this stretch of coast, such as the *cheap* **Erikli Oberj**, ✆ 0284 737 3181. The only hotel of any note is the *inexpensive* **★İşçimen** in Erikli, ✆ 0284 737 3148, ▤ 0284 737 3126.

Edirne	*Eating Out*

As every Turk knows, Edirne is famous not only for wrestling, but for liver, especially meatballs—*ciğ köfte*. Done properly, they're nearly raw and very spicy; aficionados say they're only right if you throw them at the wall and they stick. Many will find them an acquired taste, but be brave; the centre of town is full of *ciğer* (liver) parlours where the proprietors will be happy to initiate you—they also like liver kebabs, fried liver, and Allah only knows what liver else.

Outside of that you're not likely to find anything unforgettable in Edirne. The best restaurants are out by the Meriç River, a good 25min walk from the centre, across two narrow bridges which don't have the benefit of pavements to protect you from the local show-em-who's-boss roadhogs. A better bet is to become one yourself (if you have your own transport) or to get a lift with one (in any dolmuş heading for Karaağaç). Furthest from the road is the **Lalezar Restaurant**, with huge windows overlooking the river and an even bigger TV screen dominating one end of the dining room. Meat and fish dishes are served for $8 and upwards, although you'll find a better fish selection next door at the **Villa**. This is open every night until 3am, with intriguing 'live Turkish pop and arabesque' music served up alongside the food from 8pm onwards. In summer there is also a large terrace opening out onto the river.

In the town centre, there are plenty of cheap lokantas around Şaraçlar Caddesi, such as the **Polat**, across from the Şaban Açıkgöz Hotel (a favourite of soldiers in from the nearby base—poor devils who can't get more than a $1.50 lunch on Turkish Army pay), and just around the corner, truly good döner at the **Sini Kebab**. The **Saray** lokanta near the main post office gets crowded at lunch time with locals filling up with ready food chosen from trays in the window. The **restaurant** under the Park Hotel serves up an array of kebabs and *pide* for around $5.

Sweet teeth need not go unindulged in Edirne; there is a wide range of delicious southeastern-style pastries at the **Gaziantep Baklavacısı** on Balıkpazarı Caddesi, and two more tempting pastry shops across from the post office on Şaraçlar Caddesi, the **Roma** and the **Zogo**. Alcohol isn't that hard to find either, though Turkey's only entirely European city is a surprisingly conservative place. Just look up; around the central squares bars are everywhere, on the first or second floors.

The Marmara Coast and Gelibolu Peninsula

Getting Around

Buses from İstanbul and Edirne go to Tekirdağ, and there is also a frequent service to Çanakkale via the Eceabat ferry. Tekirdağ's bus station is on the coastal road, just over a mile (about 2km) north of the centre, but for some İstanbul–Çanakkale runs you'll have to flag down the bus on the road; they don't come into the station. In summer, there are weekly Turkish Maritime Lines **ferries** from Tekirdağ to Marmara Island and Erdek, with other competing car ferries making the trip daily.

The two **car ferries**, Eceabat-Çanakkale and Gelibolu–Lâpseki, cross the Dardanelles every two hours until midnight.

Tourist Information

Tekirdağ: Rüstempaşa Çarşısı, 45 Atatürk Bulvarı, © 0282 261 1698.

The Northern Marmara Coast

Tekirdağ, ancient Bisanthe, is the largest town on Thrace's Marmara coast, and one aspiring to become a resort, with nearby beaches at Kumbağ and Değirmenaltı. Although mostly concrete and modern, Tekirdağ is spread attractively over the hills, and has two works by Sinan: the Covered Bazaar and **Rüstem Paşa Mosque**. On the seaside promenade stands one of the best Atatürk statues, depicting the father of his country with his famous chalkboard and pointer, teaching two earnest citizens their vowels. A mile to the west of here lived the Hungarian patriot, Prince Ferenc II Rakoczy, who spent a career leading his countrymen against the Habsburgs in the Hungarian War of Independence; in 1717, the Ottomans granted him political asylum in Tekirdağ, where he lived until his death in 1735. The song Rakoczy's troops sang in battle, the *Rakoczy March*, has roused Hungarian patriots ever since; once, when Liszt played it as encore to a recital, it caused a riot. In 1932 the Hungarian government made the house into the **Rakoczy Museum**, on Barbaros Caddesi, containing Rakoczy's flag, documents, Hungarian weapons, and paintings from the era.

East of Tekirdağ, there's a beach at **Marmara Ereğli**; to the west, the road to the Gelibolu peninsula becomes ever rougher as it passes through vineyards to other beaches at Barbaros, Mürefte and **Şarköy**. The latter, with an especially fine broad, sandy beach, has grown into the biggest resort on this part of the shore; it's quite a lively place when it fills up with İstanbul families in the summer.

On the narrowest neck of the peninsula, **Bolayır** overlooks both the Dardanelles and the Saros Gulf; here Şüleyman Paşa, son of Orhan Gazi, and leader of the forty heroes who captured Gelibolu fortress in 1354—the Ottomans' first handful of Rumelia—is buried in a *türbe* at one end of the village. Next to him is the grave of the 19th-century poet Namik Kemal, a native of Tekirdağ and leader of the movement to reform the Ottoman Empire at the end of the 19th century.

The Dardanelles

Gelibolu, the Turkish name for Gallipoli, is a pleasant fishing village, though one usually full of soldiers. Its **castle** has long guarded this entrance into the straits; the walls you see today date from the 14th century, when the Ottomans captured the town. One of the two Dardanelles ferries crosses here, to **Lâpseki**. If you're driving, the road to Çanakkale along the Asian shore is more pleasant, but the peninsula route has more tales to tell: from Protosilaus, the first casualty of the Trojan war, to battles in the Crimean War, the First World War and the Turkish War of Independence. Some nine miles (14km) south of Gelibolu, at the mouth of the stream Aegospotamos (modern **İnce Liman**), Lysander and his Spartans clobbered the Athenian fleet in 405 BC, in the decisive and final battle of the Peloponnesian War.

A little further south stood **Sestos**, across the strait from ancient **Abydos**. Nothing remains of either of these but stories. Here in 480 BC, Xerxes' army, marching to invade Greece, crossed the strait on a pontoon bridge of boats while the Persian King of Kings watched from the heights of Abydos, sitting on the marble throne he had had carted along with him, and wept because none of the men labouring below would be alive in a hundred years. Here lived the famous lovers Hero, a priestess at Sestos, and Leander, a resident of Abydos, who would swim the strait every night to visit his love, guided by her lamp. One night, a storm blew the lamp out, and Leander got lost and was drowned; when his body was discovered the next morning, Hero flung herself into the sea and drowned herself too. Romantic-minded travellers can make the swim as well, taking care to avoid the many steamers that ply the strait; Byron did it in 1810.

The car ferry crossing to Çanakkale departs from **Eceabat**, near a village called **Kilitbahir**, located where the Dardanelles are at their narrowest and most defensible. The trefoil **castle** on the shore, a striking and unique design, was constructed by Mehmet the Conqueror to cut off Constantinople before he besieged the capital. Never one to leave matters to chance, Mehmet built another castle, across the water at Çanakkale, and slung a heavy chain between the two thus sealing the straits completely and giving Kilitbahir its name, 'Lock of the Sea'. Kilitbahir is now empty, and can be explored.

Jason and the Argonauts

So many and tangled are the influences and sources of this cycle of myths that its origin can hardly be found. Homer only mentions Jason once, indirectly, and the earliest versions of the tale have Jason sailing not to the Black Sea but up the Adriatic in search of the Golden Fleece.

Pelias, the usurper of the throne of Iolcus, would have murdered the infant heir Jason, but his mother took him secretly to Mount Pelion, where he was raised by Chiron the Centaur. When Jason arrived to regain his kingdom, Pelias promised to relinquish it on completion of this quest. The fleece had belonged to a flying golden ram sent by Zeus to rescue an ancestor, Phrixus, from execution; the ram carried him to Colchis, the farthest eastern land known to the Greeks. Jason accepted the job, and got Argus the Thespian to build him the famous *Argo*. The list of companions he collected included heroes from all over the Greek world: Heracles, Castor and Polydeuces, Mopsus the Lapith, who later founded so many cities on Asia Minor's southern shore (an inscription bearing Mopsus' name has recently been discovered in Cilicia, making him the first Greek hero to be documented as a historical person), Atalanta the speedy virgin, even Orpheus the poet .

After dallying with the women of Lemnos (who had murdered their husbands) and repopulating the island, the Argonauts sailed through the Hellespont. Heracles' squire Hylas disappeared on the coast of the Marmara near Bursa, and Heracles, who had just defeated Jason in a rowing contest, was marooned there by the captain as he searched for his friend. At Salmydessus in eastern Thrace, the Argonauts chased off the harpies that were plaguing King Phineus, and received in return advice on how to navigate the Symplegades, the 'clashing rocks' (probably ice floes that floated down from Russian rivers), that destroyed all ships attempting to pass the Bosphorus.

Along the Black Sea, they stopped at Mariandyne (somewhere near Akçakoca). Had Heracles still been with them, he could have shown them here the opening into Hades, from which he had dragged out the captured dog Cerberus on his twelfth labour. At Sinope they picked up new crew members, and from there they passed into the lands of the iron-smelting Chalybians, the Amazons and the promiscuous Mosynoecians. Soon afterwards, they crossed the Georgian border (Colchis lay north of modern Batum) where destiny and Medea awaited. Their journey had only begun.

One source of the tale was the Greek voyages of exploration in the Black Sea c. 1000 BC. The fall of Troy had probably opened up this new trade route, and they went in search of amber, iron and furs from the east. Every Greek city in classical times wanted its trading sites there justified, and no doubt a few paid off the early poets to make sure their heroes were in the Argo's crew.

The best version of the tale comes in the 3rd-century BC poem by Apollonius of Rhodes—the *Argonautica*. There are several good translations in English.

The Gelibolu Peninsula

There is a sad, melancholy loveliness to the lush and undulating Gelibolu peninsula. Over 200,000 young men lie buried in this thin pine-clad strip of land. In spring, the hills here bloom with wild flowers; appropriately, the most numerous are poppies.

The Battles of the First World War

It is easy to forget that behind the ill-fated Allied attack on the Dardanelles in April 1915, there existed a sound strategic rationale; had it succeeded the Great War might well have ended that same year. The seeds of the assault were sown only a few months after the assassination at Sarajevo in June 1914: on the western front both sides were already dug in for the four terrible years of stalemate trench warfare that were to follow. On the eastern front, however, the Czarist Russian army was crumbling before the power of the Kaiser's well-disciplined, well-equipped forces. In desperation, the Russians called for a mammoth resupply of arms and equipment from their British and French allies.

Britain and France were anxious to comply but this was no easy request. The way overland to Russia was blocked by the German army, the way by sea from the north by the German navy. Only the sea route from the south remained viable—from the Aegean through the Dardanelles and Bosphorus to the Black Sea ports on the Crimea. The route was blocked by Turkey, Germany's ally, but it was the only option open to Winston Churchill, First Lord of the Admiralty. Moreover, success would not only resupply Russia; capturing Constantinople would enable Allied troops to drive north through the Balkans, leaving the Central Powers fighting an ultimately hopeless war on three separate fronts. So, in November 1914, Churchill ordered the ships of an Anglo-French fleet to charge the Dardanelles.

The assault was a disaster, the naval equivalent of the Charge of the Light Brigade. The Turks had mined the straits. Three warships were sunk, three crippled; thousands of sailors died. Later attempts to sweep the straits of mines were foiled by Turkish heavy guns positioned on the peninsula. To Churchill and his generals it was clear; the Dardanelles could not be breached by sea until the Turkish army was removed from the Gelibolu peninsula.

To achieve this, two simultaneous amphibious landings on the peninsula were planned, one at Cape Helles at the entrance to the straits, the other at Kabatepe beach eight miles north. An Anglo-French army was to conduct the former, an ANZAC force (Australian and New Zealand Army Corps) the latter. The two were to drive inland, link up and together push the Turks and their heavy artillery off the peninsula. Allied troops were assembled in huge numbers on the Greek island of Limnos, and at dawn on 25 April 1915 the first landing boats hit the beaches.

By noon of that same day the Allied strategy had gone horribly awry. At Cape Helles the Anglo-French contingent had encountered massive opposition and established a beachhead only after horrific losses; the ANZAC force was hit even harder. A signals failure had directed their boats not to wide, spacious Kabatepe but to a small, narrow cove backed by sheer, towering cliffs. ANZACs died in their thousands before gaining a tentative toe-hold but that was all that was needed. More troops were landed. The push inland began. Some small advances were made. Then they were stopped.

The Gelibolu campaign was to last eight months, conducted in the steal-a-yard, lose-it-again manner of the Western Front. Much of the fighting was centered around Çonkbayırlı Hill, the peninsula's highest point, and it was here that Lieutenant-Colonel Mustafa Kemal, the commander of the elite Turkish 57th Regiment, acquired a reputation as a brilliant, tireless leader, not afraid to risk death by his men's side—a reputation that was to serve him well when Kemal metamorphosed into Atatürk.

In January 1916 the Allies pulled out. Ironically, their retreat was the most successful manœuvre of the campaign; tens of thousands of men were evacuated under the cover of night without a single loss. Czarist Russia was never resupplied and in 1917 fell first to the

Germans and then to the Bolsheviks. Churchill was dismissed and was not to hold government office for another 24 years. Yet his moment was to come, as was that of his adversary, Atatürk, the man who, quite rightly, had the last words on the Gelibolu campaign:

> *Those heroes that shed their blood*
> *And lost their lives*
> *You are now lying in the soil of a friendly country*
> *Therefore rest in peace*
> *There is no difference between the Johnnies*
> *And the Mehmets to us where they lie side by side*
> *Here in this country of ours*
> *You the mothers*
> *Who sent their sons from far away countries*
> *Wipe away your tears*
> *Your sons are now lying in our bosom*
> *And are in peace*
> *Having lost their lives on this land they have*
> *Become our sons as well.*

Touring the Peninsula

Although the village of Gelibolu sounds like the logical place to stay when visiting the Gallipoli peninsula, most visitors find it more convenient to stay across the Dardanelles at **Çanakkale** (*see* p.205), which is nearer to the sights.

It is impossible to see all the monuments, museums and battlefields by public transport alone; so, unless you have a **car** or are prepared to hire a **taxi** for the best part of a day, a **guided tour** is the only real option. These are instructive although tour operators tend to concentrate almost exclusively on the ANZAC-related sites. Hopefully, this will soon change.

With one of the finest beaches on the peninsula, **Kabatepe** is the best place to begin any tour. Here a small, spaceship-shaped **museum** (*open daily 8.30–5; adm*) overlooks the beach and contains a sad collection of memorabilia, from an English Tommy's last letter home to the skull of a Turkish soldier ('martyr' in the Turkish vernacular), with a bullet still embedded in the centre of his forehead. From here it is a short drive to **ANZAC Cove** where you can see just why the landings were doomed from zero hour one. The hills above are dotted with ANZAC cemeteries and memorials, all immaculately maintained by the Allied War Graves Commission. Trenches remain intact at **Lone Pine**, the main Australian cemetery, and on the heights of **Çonkbayırlı Hill** where five huge Turkish monoliths recount the crucial battles fought there, each stone positioned so as to represent the fingers and thumb of a man's hand, raised, pleading to God.

At **Cape Helles** the British memorial towers high, in memory of the 20,761 men of the empire who have no known grave. There are six British and French cemeteries in this area and two significant **Turkish monuments**, the First Martyrs Memorial and that huge, *pi*-shaped structure, at once a **museum** and the headstone of the literally countless Turks buried on the peninsula. Unlike the Allies, the Turks kept no records of their dead; the slain were simply shovelled into mass graves, unmarked and unknown.

Silivri

A remarkable establishment on the Marmara shore, east of Tekirdağ—close enough to İstanbul to attract the city's elite—is the *luxury* ★★★★★**Klassis**, ✆ 0212 727 4050, ✆ 0212 727 4049, a striking ensemble of neo-Ottoman buildings set high over a huge, dreamy pool. They lay it on thick here: private beach, casino and disco, every sport from squash to water skiing. The same company has opened the **(S)Klassis Golf and Country Club** ✆ 0212 748 4600, ✆ 0212 748 4643, 17km from Silivri, offering everything from an 18-hole golf course to volleyball.

Tekirdağ and around

In Tekirdağ, the new and modern ★**Yat Oteli**, Yali Caddesi 8, ✆ 0282 261 1054, has sea views and single rooms for $20. Right in the centre, the cheaper ★**Akbulut** on Muraltı Caddesi offers little more than balconies above the traffic. Kumbağ beach, five miles to the east, has the most hotels including the comfortable **Bilge**, ✆ 0282 283 4104, which has its own stretch of beach; doubles $25. Pensions are easily found at both Tekirdağ and Kumbağ beach.

Gelibolu

There is *inexpensive* accommodation near the ferries, such as the friendly **Yılmaz Otel**, Liman Meydanı 6, ✆ 0286 566 1256, charging around $25 for a double. Like most of the hotels in Gelibolu, they can arrange inexpensive tours of the battlefields.

camping

There is a wide choice of campsites around the Gelibolu peninsula, including the big **Patiş Kum Motel Camp**, ✆ 0286 814 1466, ✆ 0286 814 1917, at Kum Limanı, with all the facilities, and $45 motel rooms on hand should you want to wriggle out of the tent option.

The Gelibolu Peninsula **Eating Out**

In **Tekirdağ**, try the spacious **Sahil Dörtler**, near the waterfront, across from the tourist office, with fish and meat specialities averaging around $7.

Gelibolu's eateries are mostly gathered around the harbour; the **Gelibolu** has outside tables, and will provide a satisfying dinner for $6, slightly more for fish. A similarly priced selection of meat and fish dishes is served at the **Yelkenci Restaurant**. Located near the ferry port, its double terrace overlooking the straits is a relaxing place to observe the maritime comings and goings.

The Southern Marmara Coast

Although the scenery along the south shore of the Sea of Marmara is quite beautiful and blessed with beaches, it doesn't feature on many foreign visitors' itineraries. As far as Biga, you'll see lush green countryside with muddy fields and mules, broken by little villages lost among the trees, their presence betrayed by a single minaret sticking up. Most of its ancient sites have little to show for themselves today; nothing remains of ancient Abydos or Lampsakas (modern **Lâpseki**, the second ferry crossing), although to the east two famous battles of antiquity occurred: **Biga**, where Alexander first defeated the Persians in 334 BC at the mouth of the River Granicus (Biga Çayı), and further east at **Edincik** (ancient Cyzicus), where Alcibiades and the Athenians defeated the Spartans in the Peloponnesian War. **Bandırma**, the biggest town before Bursa, is a sorry industrial settlement that was largely ruined in the war of 1922; you'll have to pass through it in order to get to Erdek and the Marmara Islands.

Alexander the Great

Before moving on to Egypt, Persia and India, Alexander polished off the Persian King Darius's satrapies in Asia Minor for practice. With some 40,000 men, including 5,000 cavalry, he crossed the Hellespont in the spring of 334 BC, sacrificing a bull to Poseidon in mid-passage. After visiting Troy and paying homage to the Homeric heroes, he and his men were immediately confronted by an army commanded by the Persian satraps of Phrygia and Ionia. At the River Granicus, they stormed across the water into the Persian lines and routed them, setting the tone for the rest of the campaign.

Then the Macedonians marched down the Aegean coast, taking Sardis, Ephesus and Miletus. In Ephesus Alexander threw out the pro-Persian aristocracy and restored democratic institutions, and by so doing made himself popular with all the Greeks of Asia Minor not in the Great King's pay. Taking auguries at Miletus, Alexander saw an eagle flying towards the shore, and took it to mean he would conquer the Persians by land, not by sea. Accordingly, he sent his Greek navy home—he couldn't afford it anyway—and marched across the Mediterranean coast to take the Persians' naval bases away. Termessos alone refused an alliance, and survived when Alexander decided it wasn't worth a siege. Perge, Aspendos and Side were brought into line, and then the Macedonian force split up, the great general Parmenion taking half the force to assault the Cilician coast while Alexander headed north to chase the Persians out of Phrygia. Here, as recorded by his chronicler Arrian, he cut with his sword the famous Gordian knot. The two forces met again at Tarsus, where the always fragile Alexander took ill from a swim in the cold River Cydnus. He recovered just in time to meet Darius, the Great King himself, at Issus near today's İskenderun. The Macedonian victory, at a disadvantage of perhaps five to one, opened the way for the conquest of Persia and Egypt.

South of Bandırma is the **Kuşcenneti** (Bird Paradise) **National Park**, a sanctuary for migratory waterfowl, especially pelicans, grey and white herons, and cormorants, who come to nest along the willow-shaded banks of Lake Manyas between February and October, and then fly south to India and Africa in the winter. In all, 239 different species of birds have been spotted in the sanctuary. Just west of here, at **Gönen**, other airborne creatures—namely, tens of thousands of bats—have taken up residence in the Dereköy Caves. Gönen also has one of Turkey's major thermal spas for rheumatism.

Towns on the south Marmara shore are easily reached by **buses** travelling between Bursa and Çanakkale, a trip of about 4hrs. From Bandırma and Erdek **minibuses** serve the surrounding towns and beaches. Note that Bandırma has two **otogars**. The main one, south of town, serves Bursa–Çanakkale and other main line buses. To get from there to the waterfront station where the Erdek and Gönen buses start, you can take a taxi or die waiting, possibly, for a city bus or dolmuş.

As any local will tell you, boat timetables to the islands often seem to change from one week to the next. Avşa and Marmara islands are served by **ferry** from İstanbul, daily in the summer, and usually twice a week in the winter depending on weather conditions. Boats operate from Tekirdağ with similar frequency. Services also run from Erdek: in summer there are daily boats to Avşa and Marmara, and a twice-weekly crossing to Paşalimanı. In all the ports, look out for the fellows with boats who run informal private ferry services, or ask anyone. On these very laid-back islands, the locals use these much more commonly than the infrequent Turkish Maritime Lines service; they are much more convenient and somewhat cheaper.

Tourist Information

Erdek: Nafiye Sıtkı Caddesi 31, 4th floor, ✆ 0266 835 1169.

Avşa Island: a booth in summer by the docks at Türkeli.

Erdek and the Kapıdağı

The road into the Kapıdağı peninsula is not promising at first, passing scrapyards, gravel pits and, most impressive of all, a festering sulphuric acid plant. But persevere; it gets better. **Erdek**, the capital of the Kapıdağı, is a very modest though very agreeable resort, popular with the people of Bursa. In the lively village centre, cafés in shady gardens cluster around the shore; from here a pretty pedestrian walk leads out to the beach and the strip of modern hotels that follows it. There are less crowded beaches to the north at Ocaklar and Narlı, both with small but growing collections of cheap *pansiyonlar* and restaurants (and, for all the industry nearby, the water seems clean enough). Another beach, one of the few accessible by paved road, is north of Karacabey at **Bayramdere**.

The Marmara Islands

Before 1923, this miniature archipelago was largely inhabited by Greeks. They are nearly all gone now, and like much of the area around the Marmara the islands have a slightly rough, just-settled air to them. Lately, people from the capital have been buying or building houses as summer retreats, but outside of Avşa Island don't expect much of the trappings of tourism. There are a few small beaches and secluded coves, and absolutely no sights to visit. The peace and quiet is seamless when the cement mixers aren't going, and your creditors will never find you here.

Of the four inhabited islands of the Marmara, **Paşalimanı**, with its five small villages, is nearest to the mainland. There is a ferry from Erdek to its tiny capital, Balıklı (which means 'fishy'), and private boats make regular crossings from Narlı, which can be easier. Paşalimanı welcomes few visitors; there's really very little there, not even a beach, but at least you'll be guaranteed a peaceful stay. **Avşa**, the next nearest, is its antithesis. Loved by Turks from the cities, it is green and undulating and has some good beaches, particularly around its capital Türkeli (Avşa appears on many maps as Türkeli Island). Avşa has become a bit overbuilt in the last two decades—at least there'll be no problem finding a place to stay, although many of these establishments have a 'resort-that-time-forgot' feel to them. **Ekinlik**, north of Avşa, is the smallest of the islands, no more than a village, where there's even less to do than on Paşalimanı. The largest of the group is **Marmara** (Greek *Elafonisos*). As its name suggests, Marmara is famous for its marble, which has been quarried here since ancient times. Despite thousands of years of mining, supplies of this stone have yet to be exhausted. Today, the industry is centred around Saraylar on the island's northern side. It is from here that white marble softly veined with blue and grey originates—you will see and feel it all over Turkey: it is the preferred covering for the interiors of the nation's bathhouses. Despite being stonier than Avşa and lacking that island's beaches, Marmara is nevertheless well-patronized by Turks on vacation. There is a beach four miles north of Marmara village at Çınarlı, reachable by dolmuş or boat. Çınarlı's tea garden is protected from the sun by a gnarled monster of a tree which has been the venue for village gossip for centuries.

Erdek and Around   **Where to Stay**

Most accommodation in this region is open June–September only.

Erdek

inexpensive

In Erdek, the ★★**Gül Plaj Moteli** on Kumlu Yalı Caddesi 86, ✆ 0266 835 1053, is clean and on the beach, with half-board doubles for $35, all with private bath (open June–Sept). Similarly priced on the shorefront nearby is the ★★**Alevok**, ✆ 0266 835 1116. Erdek has many other hotels, though hardly any are open all year.

cheap

Erdek's cheaper establishments are clustered around the port, most in the form of pensions charging around $7; one of the nicest is the **Ümit**, ✆ 0266 835 1092, on Balıkhane Sokak, a quiet backstreet near the port. There are also cheap choices along the beach strip, including the clean and well-kept **Yat Otel**, closest to the centre, and the **Gün Motel**, where all rooms have a shower or bath, for $12.

On Ocaklar beach, north of Erdek, the **Arseven Pansiyon**, ✆ 0266 835 1464, is slightly more expensive but still good value for money, offering spotless rooms with en suite facilities.

Outside Erdek

Hotels near the thermal baths in **Gönen** are open all year, such as the ★★★★**Yıldız Kaplıca Otel** on the appropriately named Banyolar Caddesi, ✆ 0266 762 1840, where in addition to the baths there's a sauna and hamam.

In **Marmara**, the **Marmara Otel**, ✆ 0266 885 5476, is the best the island can do, though open in season only. Double rooms with private bath go for $12. There are a number of pensions in Marmara town and a bigger choice around the beach at Çınarlı, such as the basic **Gül Pansiyon**.

The height of luxury on **Avşa** doesn't go very high—just to the rooftop bar at the ★★**Ayberk**, ✆ 0266 845 5151. This is located two miles north of Türkeli, and has light, airy rooms with balconies overlooking the beach; half board doubles with bath are overpriced at $60.

The **Otel Temizel** on Avsa, ✆ 0266 896 1134, is pleasant, and more typical of what's on offer; $12.

Being stuck in **Bandırma** need not be miserable; the ★★**Asuhan**, on Atatürk Caddesi near the main otogar, has comfortable rooms and a passable restaurant; there is also the less expensive and tidy **Özgür**, next to the mosque by the ferry landing.

Erdek   ***Eating Out***

There are several small lokantas along the coast and on the islands, though many close in the winter. In Erdek, you'll have a choice of seafood places with outdoor tables around the port; **Kafkas Restaurant**, not Kafkaesque at all, will bring you out some *börek* and a fine grilled fish for $8 and up, depending on the fish. The **Rıhtım** on the seafront esplanade serves good fish at similar prices.

Bursa

> All of us old people here dream that one morning we will open our
> eyes and all the factories and cars will be gone, and Bursa will be as
> it was before.

So said the elderly gentleman we met in the tourist office, lamenting the fate that has overtaken this most refined of Turkish cities. In the last decade or two, prosperous, well-run Bursa has become a victim of its own success. They wanted industry, and they got it: Türk Fiat and Renault plants and scores of others. The jobs they provide have attracted vast numbers of migrants from all over Turkey, especially the Black Sea area and the northeast. The population has more than doubled in the last decade, and now stands at over a million.

All these people, necessarily, have to stuff themselves into a ribbon-shaped medieval city built on the side of a mountain. Atatürk Caddesi, the only big street through it, has become a boiling, deafening motorway capable of giving anyone a headache after walking only one block. Everywhere else, crowds of people and cars make life pretty much unbearable. They have started building a metro (currently delayed by lack of funds), but it won't be enough. Bursa is faced with the task of redesigning and rebuilding itself from the ground up, which will take decades.

Not that we want to discourage you from coming. On the contrary; for all the commotion, Bursa is still an obligatory stop, with its medieval Ottoman monuments, a covered market second only to that of İstanbul, and its friendly, alert population. Bursans in many ways seem to be a step or two ahead of the rest of the Turks. Not the least of their virtues is a resolute civic pride, which manifests itself in surprising ways even in these difficult times. Another reason for coming is Uludağ, a breath of fresh air both figuratively and literally. This 8,300ft massif is just a cable-car ride away from the centre of the city. With the snow on its peaks lingering well into the summer, the traffic and noise seem far away. Added to this Muslim alpine setting are famous thermal baths, a huge and lovely park and plenty of trees. Bursa is the only city we have ever seen where the town council operates a flower shop. Its citizens call their town *Yeşil* Bursa, 'Green Bursa', a title, unfortunately, that Bursa will have to struggle to hold on to.

History

King Prusias I of Bithynia founded Bursa—then *Prusa*—in the 2nd century BC. Although today Turkey's sixth-largest city, in ancient times Bursa was never more than a minor provincial centre. What little is known of it comes from the letters of Pliny the Younger, the governor under Emperor Trajan. To the Byzantines, the town was a fashionable resort for its baths, but the Ottomans put Bursa on the map. Sultan Orhan captured it in 1326 and made it his capital, a position it held on and off until 1453. Here the Ottomans began to sponsor great religious architecture. Drawing on the traditions of the Selcuks and Byzantines to develop a style that would be a fit heir to the past, and complement the ambitions of the sultans, their architects crowned Bursa with mosques, schools and mausolea, solidly and honestly medieval, possessed of an austere but very present spirituality that earns them a place beside the more elaborate creations of İstanbul.

Throughout the centuries of Ottoman rule, Bursa lived quietly and polished its arts and manners; culturally it has always been the second city of Anatolia, after İstanbul. The city's career as a thermal resort blossomed under the Turks, and a spin-off, the manufacture of bath towels, grew into a fully-fledged textile industry that is still important today. Particularly, the city is known for silk and for its beautifully embroidered linens (the silk industry probably goes back to Emperor Justinian, whose spies managed to steal some cocoons from the Chinese and break their monopoly). Serious industry came only after 1950. Now, along with the towels, Turkey's second-largest industrial centre ships out tons of soda-pop, bathtubs, clothing, knives, cars and trucks, cannons for the army and hosts of other products.

Getting Around

Bursa is often described as a day trip from İstanbul. This is possible but not much fun—four or five hours one way by road. Bursa deserves more than one day anyhow. Most **coach** companies have 'express services' that make use of the Topçular–Eski Hisar ferry; these are comfortable, but only about 45mins faster. Bursa has a huge new bus station six miles north of the centre on the Yalova road. Known to one and all simply as 'Terminal', the station can be reached from the city centre by any bus with the sign 'Terminal' in its window. You'll never have to wait long for a bus to İstanbul or any other western city; if you want to plan ahead for any trip, talk to the Bursa-based *Uludağ* company, a good line which has the most connections in this part of Turkey (and which uses flash double-decker buses on some of their runs).

Fortunately, the main sights are within easy walking distance of each other in the centre; the other old quarters, the Hisar, Muradiye and Yeşil, are removed a bit from the traffic and still fun to walk. Atatürk Caddesi, even though it changes its name several times (*see* map), is the main axis of Bursa, and the route of many **buses** and **dolmuşes**; terminus for most routes is the *Heykel* ('statue'), the Atatürk monument on the western end of Atatürk Caddesi. As in İstanbul, bus tickets are purchased at the kiosks by the major stops. Buses for the Uludağ *teleferik* (cable car) start from Heykel (route 3A). The *teleferik* itself runs every half hour, weather permitting, until 10pm, 9pm in winter. Taxis are easy to find anywhere in the city centre.

Bursa — Tourist Information

Orhan Gazi Parkı, Atatürk Caddesi, © 0224 220 1848. They are competent and helpful, as ever in Turkey, though the otherwise good city map they hand out pictures the city upside down, which can be a bit confusing. In summer a branch is open just outside the bus station.

Seeing Bursa: The Market Area

A good place to begin a tour of Bursa is at the **Ulu Cami Parkı** (also called Koza Park), focal point of the city, with the tourist office and the entrance to the covered market. Facing these is Bursa's first Ottoman mosque, the **Orhan Camii**, built by that sultan in 1335, and restored after a Karaman invasion damaged it in 1413. This small but lovely mosque is the pattern for later works in Bursa; its best features are its simple but graceful porch and fountain. Inside, the central dome is supported, not by pendentives, but by semi-domes in the corners. In some ways, this is the structural system of older buildings like the Aya Sofya turned inside out; it would not work with a larger dome. The outlandish geometry that decorates the semi-domes is just that, decoration, not part of the structure. Such polygons run amok are a recurring conceit in Bursa's mosques.

Just across the street, Bursa's **Belediye** (City Hall) is not in tourist brochures, but it's probably the largest piece of folk art in Turkey, and the prettiest city hall. Its construction of half-timber, with horizontal, vertical and diagonal beams in a seemingly haphazard manner, and bricks in between, is common in the older village homes. Here, with its painted designs of flowers and trees, and occasionally illuminated with strings of coloured lights, it's one of the unexpected delights of Bursa. Also here, on Atatürk Caddesi, is the Grand Mosque, the **Ulu Cami**, completed in 1396 by Yıldırım Beyazıt and twice restored. Here twenty domes, two graceful minarets and the more than usual austerity of the outside give way to a virtuoso display of Arabic calligraphy and a famous carved mihrab within.

Next to the Orhan Camii on the northern side of the park are two lovely 15th-century *hanlar* that mark the entrance to the bazaar, the **İpek** ('silk') **Hanı** and the adjoining **Koza** ('cocoon') **Hanı** with a little *mescit* built over a fountain at the centre. Under the Ottomans Bursa was famous for silk; the trade is experiencing something of a comeback today, and each year in late June there is a big silkworm-cocoon market here. The rest of the year, this is the fancy end of the market, largely given over to leather and designer clothing shops; the jewellery and serious antiques await nearby in the *bedesten*.

The rest of the market district encompasses everything north of Atatürk Caddesi, nearly a square kilometre in size. The network of covered bazaars and *hanlar* is not quite as large as İstanbul's, with less jewellery, and more bath towels and tea sets. However, it's tidier and has better bargains. You can find just about anything you want here, but the real prizes are the embroidered bed linens, bathroom sets, etc. Whether hand-embroidered on silk or done on a machine, it is some of the most beautiful work you'll see anywhere, and quite inexpensive; save some room in your suitcase.

Like any good Turkish bazaar, this one is a labyrinth, a web of long arcades, with streets and *hanlar* tucked in between. Many of the arcades were destroyed in a 1955 fire, but the Bursans have rebuilt them exactly as they were. As in İstanbul, many of the surrounding streets are given over to a particular trade; Demirciler Caddesi, as its name implies, is a whole street of smiths, hammering away in ferrous harmony.

The Citadel

To the west, Atatürk Caddesi curves around the old **citadel**, which is in an extremely strong position. Undoubtedly it had much to do with maintaining Bursa's peace and quiet over the centuries. Not much remains of the old walls built by the Ottomans, but on the slopes down to Atatürk Caddesi, modern Bursa has turned the old fortress into a modern-day version of Nebuchadnezzar's hanging gardens, called **Timurtaş Paşa Parkı**; the slopes, with stairways and terraces full of trees and flowers, and bits of Byzantine arches, give ever-changing views over the old city. There are also many cafés, in which the people of Bursa practically live; wherever there's a beautiful view, common enough in the neighbourhoods on the heights, you'll find a pleasant spot to sit and reflect.

The citadel area contains the oldest houses in the city. Many are in disrepair, but more than other cities, Bursa has made an effort at historic preservation, noticeable in such streets as

Kale Caddesi, lined with homes of the 17th to 19th centuries. Near the **clock tower**, a landmark visible from most of Bursa, are the tombs of the first two great Ottoman sultans, the **Osmangazi Türbesi** and **Orhangazi Türbesi**, both restored after heavy damage in the earthquake of 1855. Orhan's sarcophagus lies beside that of his wife, Nilüfer Hatun, a Byzantine princess married off for reasons of political expediency who became the first of the great ladies of the Ottoman Empire; the building she founded for travelling dervishes in İznik now contains that city's municipal museum.

Two routes lead down from the citadel, one through the meandering streets westwards to Kaplıca Caddesi, leading eventually down to the Kültür Parkı and suburb of Çekirge (discussed below), the other going back through the hanging gardens. From here, the abominable **Atatürk Caddesi**, the modern business street, continues eastwards around the market district. Just beyond Atatürk's statue, the street goes over a small bridge that crosses the narrow chasm of the **Gök Dere**. Small cafés overlook the stream, with lawns and flowerbeds arranged in patterns and scrolls, but you can't get to them from the cliffs. Just beyond, in a little square overshadowed by an enormous plane tree, a road branches off to the left for the **Yeşil** ('the Green'), one of the loveliest of Bursa's neighbourhoods though it too is somewhat tarnished by the traffic. This road, the Yeşil Caddesi, goes to the Green Mosque and the Green Mausoleum. Even the street signs here are green.

The Green Mosque (Yeşil Cami)

The **Yeşil Cami** (Green Mosque) stands among the finest mosques in Turkey, a marvel not only in the perfection of its form and decoration, but for the way these two elements, the simple structure and the lavish stonecarving and coloured tiles, are combined into a harmonious work of art. We read in the history books of the early Ottoman Turks as grim and resolute Gazi warriors, still attached in many ways to the kind of life their nomadic forefathers led out on the Asian steppe just a few generations before. Their detractors, historians like Gibbon and the Byzantine apologist Steven Runciman, paint them as semi-barbarians who could build an empire but didn't know what to do with one. Such a building as this makes us pause to reconsider. Mehmet I had the Yeşil Cami built in the second decade of the 15th century, at a time when all the Ottomans' resources must have been needed for the reconstruction of the state, so soon after Sultan Beyazıt's disaster at the hands of Tamerlane. Nevertheless, the necessary money and attention were found to construct this masterpiece.

Mehmet's architect, Hacı İvaz Paşa, attempted no radical departures here; the Ottomans had been building in this style for half a century already, in Bursa and elsewhere. Rather, this mosque represents the perfection of that style. If the Ottomans had met an early end like the Selcuks, if they had never captured Constantinople and acquired the resources to build so many copies of the Aya Sofya, the Yeşil Cami would have its page in the art histories as the greatest work of the deceased nation; we would mourn the Ottomans as we do the Selcuks, thinking, 'If only they had been around to build more.' Decadence is a subtle disease; nations do not always reach their political and artistic peaks at the same moment.

Most visitors come down Green Avenue to the place where the Green Mosque and the Green Mausoleum face each other across the street and immediately head for the latter, their eyes caught by the masses of green tile. The very same beautiful sea-green tile from İznik is used around the windows of the mosque, though sparingly, to call attention to the excellent carved stonework. No windows like these exist in İstanbul and certainly nothing like their flowery decoration, an inheritance from the Selcuks, as is the fine gateway with its concave 'stalactite' recess. Similar entrance gates are the principal adornment of most of the older Turkish mosques.

Inside, any impression that Mehmet was being cheap with the İznik tiles is immediately dispelled. The mihrab, the ceilings, the upstairs galleries, and all the walls up to six feet are covered with them, in blue and green, many with floral designs. The plan is a simple one: a central hall under two shallow domes, one slightly higher than the other, a common form for the smaller early Ottoman mosques, as in the Orhan Camii. The Islamic fascination with geometry is here on display, from the unusual three-dimensional shapes that support the domes to the intricate patterns, carved into the walnut doors, shutters and mimber, and the geometric medallions intertwined with Koranic calligraphy along the walls.

Some features are unusual. The ribbed interior of the domes shows a Greek influence, recalling the İstanbul Byzantine churches like the Kariye. In the dome near the entrance an oculus sends down a sunbeam at high noon over an exceptionally beautiful fountain, carved from a single piece of marble. The galleries around it, with some of the best İznik tiles, were meant as private boxes for the sultan and his harem. Two *eyvanlar*, or chambers, flank the central hall, once used for the reception and repose of travelling dervishes.

The Green Mausoleum (Yeşil Türbe)

Open 8.30–12 and 1–5.30.

Mehmet I, who put up the work, did not command the respect of the other early Ottoman sultans, preoccupied as he was through most of his reign with defeating the intrigues of his brothers and cousins, and with reunifying and rebuilding his shattered state. His conquests were few, but his achievements, in the worst of times, should have earned him more credit than he usually gets. His grandfather, Murat I, had been illiterate, but Mehmet can be accounted the first cultured man among the sultans. He wanted to be buried beside his great mosque, and during the reign of his son Murat II the Yeşil Türbe was built for his remains.

If the mosque had been for Allah, this was for the family. The architect was the same, Hacı İvaz Paşa, but although he and Murat were not able to confer the same perfection of spirituality upon this tomb, at least in the best family manner they spared no expense, pouring in the rich İznik tiles in numbers exceeded only in the Blue Mosque in İstanbul. There are almost as many inside, sheathing Mehmet's immense sarcophagus, painted with sayings of the Prophet in a bold flowing calligraphy.

The Green Medrese (Yeşil Medrese)

A third and equally worthy member of this complex stands just a block away on Yeşil Cadde; the old theological school called the **Green Medrese** has lately been restored and converted to house Bursa's **Museum of Turkish and Islamic Arts** (*open daily exc Mon, 8.30–12, 1–5; adm*). The large ethnographic collection occupies the students' cells and the central courtyard; outside there's a pretty garden with a view over the Gökdere stream and the rest of Bursa. Inside are fine silver, carpets, and swords, İznik ceramics, Selcuk architectural decoration, books and almanacs, and some very unusual 19th-century pottery from Çanakkale, a centre of the ceramic craft after it had died out in İznik. Overhead in some of the domed ceilings around the cloister is more first-class tile work.

One speciality of the museum is figures from the old Turkish shadow play, *Karagöz*. Bursa likes to claim Karagöz and Hacivat, the traditional Punch and Judy of this ancient entertainment, as its citizens; their 'tomb' is in the suburb of Çekirge. On one puppet you can see the mechanism whereby Karagöz's hat pops up when he is surprised, revealing his bald head.

Yıldırım Beyazıt Camii

Continuing beyond the Yeşil into the eastern edges of Bursa, there are two mosques of the same era, both set up on hills among the rambling cottages and stone walls of this delightful area. The **Emir Sultan Camii** (1431) stands on the street of the same name, off Yeşil Caddesi; it was built by one of the daughters of Yıldırım Beyazıt in honour of her deceased husband. From here, head northward some ten blocks to that sultan's own complex of religious buildings, the **Yıldırım Beyazıt Camii** (1395). In both of these, it's interesting to make architectural comparisons with the Green Mosque, but we can only guess at their original decorative scheme. Like the tombs of Osman and Orhan, and indeed almost everything else in Bursa, these mosques were hit hard by the 1855 earthquake; apparently the city only had resources enough to do a complete job of restoration on the Green complex. As a result, Beyazıt's and Emir Sultan's foundations were left with plain interiors that go well with the structure's formal simplicity but are no substitute for the original.

Beyazıt's mosque may have been especially good. Its *eyvanlar* and uneven twin domes recall the Yeşil Cami, and its arched portico and single slender minaret are fine elements. Before the earthquake, this mosque was the centre of a well-endowed *külliye*, a complex that included a hospital, schools and dervish communities. Of the original eight buildings only the mosque, medrese and Beyazıt's tomb are left. This tomb, small and severe, is probably the most fitting memorial to the most ambitious and least cautious of the Ottoman sultans. Undoubtedly, it would have been grander had not Beyazıt's 14-year reign ended so ignominiously at the Battle of Ankara; here, the mercurial warrior, who expected to become the lord of Europe and Asia, instead ended up as lunch on Tamerlane's table. The Turks accepted it, as the Greeks would have, as divine punishment for hubris—how could the Mongols have been explained, but as a scourge of God? Later sultans, for a while, took the lesson to heart.

The Muradiye

Returning to the citadel, and beyond it to the west end of Bursa, you may visit the works of a more fortunate monarch, Mehmet II, the Conqueror, at the **Muradiye Complex**, along Kaplıca Caddesi just off the main street which, at this point, has changed its name to Çekirge Caddesi. Among the eleven buildings are a mosque, tombs and schools, all plain, all made of sandstone and narrow brick. There is none of the marble and fine sculptural detail of the earlier mosques here; this no doubt reflects the attitude of Mehmet, always with his eye on Constantinople. If he did not choose to embellish his *külliye*, at least he had himself buried here, next to his father, Murat II, who is interred in a simple *türbe* supported by ancient Corinthian columns with a wide oculus in the dome; Murat had requested that his tomb be open to the sky. The most elaborate tomb here, ironically, belongs to the celebrated upstart

Cem Sultan, Mehmet's younger son, who rebelled and intrigued for years against Beyazıt II, his brother. Cem's career as Ottoman pretender would have been an ideal subject for a novel by Sir Walter Scott, but one with a sad end for his partisans. Beyazıt finally managed to pack him off to exile in Italy, in the care of Pope Alexander VI. Even though Beyazıt was paying huge sums for his brother's room and board, the Borgia pope eventually tired of his exotic guest, and had him poisoned. As if in compensation, the sultan brought him to this beautiful mausoleum, with its tiles and painted details in fairyland colours.

Çekirge

'Çekirge' means 'locust' in Turkish, and there are certainly enough of them in the woods that cover this slope of Uludağ. In the days of the sultans, Çekirge, with its famous therapeutic baths and lovely views, was the favoured residence of the imperial families. Today it's Bursa's wealthy suburb, with two miles of hotels and smart new apartments spreading westward from the city. The people of Bursa like to come here to play at the **Kültür Parkı**. Turks in the big cities use their parks the way Westerners would have a century ago: it's charming to see the families in their Sunday best dragging their children along and they, in turn, dragging their balloons; all coming to see and be seen, to eat ice cream and inspect the flower beds. There is a blue lagoon with a fountain where young couples paddle canoes, an amusement park that must have half the neon in Turkey (its two giant Ferris wheels are among Bursa's landmarks), a football stadium and acres of garden paths. Bursa's **Archaeological Museum** (*open daily exc Mon 8.30–12, 1–5; adm*), in the centre of the park, has a smattering of mainly Roman artefacts and a large jewellery and coin collection.

In the same Victorian atmosphere are the fine homes built a century ago in the streets across Çekirge Caddesi. Most are in the typical old Bursa style, in pastel plaster with enclosed wooden balconies, but a few, like the summer houses along the Bosphorus, could easily pass for American Queen Anne-style homes of the 1880s, with more than a touch of Hansel and Gretel thrown in. The city put President Atatürk up in the best of them whenever he came to town, and it has been preserved as the **Atatürk Museum**.

If Çekirge has been the fashionable end of the town ever since Roman times, the springs and thermal baths are the reason, widely prescribed for all manner of ailments and for general well-being besides. Most of Bursa's tourist trade comes for the waters, and several hotels in the district have their own springs. Two Ottoman foundations, called locally the **Eski Kaplıca** (old spring) and the **Yeni Kaplıca** (new spring), the latter in a nice garden next to the Kültür Parkı, are open to the public and are quite popular. Even if you aren't troubled by rheumatism or gout, these are worth a visit. The Yeni Kaplıca was last rebuilt by Süleyman the Magnificent; parts of the Eski Caplıca go back to Byzantine times. Both are open all day for both men and women.

Further west in Çekirge Caddesi, you pass a little monument called the **Tomb of Karagöz and Hacivat**. One story from old Bursa relates that these incorrigible clowns (the shadow-play figures) were workmen in the service of the sultan, helping to build the Birinci Murat Camii; not only did they never do their own jobs, but with continual arguing and joking, they so distracted the other workers that the sultan was eventually obliged to put them to death. In fact Karagöz and his friend could probably trace their origins back to the ancient

Greeks, and they have a surprising amount in common with their 14th-century contemporaries, Harlequin and Puncinello of the Italian *commedia dell'arte*. There was a time when it looked as if VHS machines and computer games would zap all before them, including Karagöz, but tradition in Bursa is tenacious. Şinasi Çelikkol runs an antique shop in the Eski Aynalı Çarşısı of the *bedesten*, but his passion is for puppets. His infectious enthusiasm has led to a renewed interest in the Karagöz art form. He recently founded the **Karagöz Art House** (Karagöz Sanat Evi) across the road from the Tomb of Karagöz. Shadow play performances are staged on Wednesday and Saturday mornings. In mid-November each year, devotees from around the world gather in Bursa for the four-day Karagöz Festival, a puppetting jamboree, with workshops and some quite hilarious public performances.

At the very end of the city, stands the oldest of the imperial mosques, the 1367 **Birinci Murat Camii** (Birinci means *the First*). At that time, Turkish architects had not yet found their classic style; this building, good as it is, can be considered an experiment on the way. Roughly square, the mosque occupies only the first floor, with one squat minaret in a corner. The second floor, behind a graceful loggia, was a theological school. The tomb of Murat I in the grounds has been restored too often to be of much interest, though Murat himself was a great soldier and statesman who contributed much to the growth of the Ottoman state with his Balkan conquests and rationalization of the government. A Serbian prisoner stabbed Murat in the back in the Battle of Kosovo, his greatest triumph, and his son Beyazıt brought him here to this *türbe*.

Uludağ

If not for the waters, or the charms of the city itself, visitors come to Bursa to see **Uludağ**, literally 'great mountain' (8,300ft), the tallest peak in north-west Turkey. From Bursa, the mountain may not at first seem impressive, only a steep emerald ridge enfolding the city and stretching to no great height. Take either of the roads around it, however, towards Eskişehir or Kütahya, and you'll see the true Uludağ, standing high above the surrounding plain in the same manner as the much taller mountains of eastern Anatolia. The peak visible from Bursa is only the first of a series, stretching peak after peak into the southeast, with forests, meadows and mountain streams in between. The highest will be covered with snow well into the summer. Uludağ is a national park, with alpine scenery, hiking trails, ski resorts with properly alpine lodges (the season runs roughly from December to March), and several hotels. Due to its proximity to İstanbul, Uludağ is one off the most popular reports in Turkey, although the skiing at Palandöken near Erzurum (*see* p.473) is more varied and demanding. You can get up Uludağ either by the road off Çekirge Caddesi that runs for 20 miles (32km) almost to the highest summit, or by the long **funicular railway** (the *teleferik*), with a continuous service from the eastern edge of Bursa.

The ancients called Uludağ Mount Olympus, the Mysian Olympus, one of eight or so peaks around the Mediterranean with that name. The religious syncretism of the sophisticated Hellenistic world led men of letters to look for similarities in all the local cults and myths that soldiers and travellers brought back to them from the ends of their rapidly expanding world. Any mountain credited with being the home of the gods by the natives, as Uludağ was, became an 'Olympus', less a name than a category.

The tourist office lists two prices for the city's *expensive* and *moderate* range hotels, regular and 'reduced'. Theoretically these are for the off-season, but in many cases you can get the reduced rate anytime, from a quarter to a third off the price. It doesn't hurt to try—though don't expect much from the five-star places, which get a steady business from İstanbul and from the Arab world.

Central Bursa

expensive–moderate

Opposite the tombs of Osman and Orhan at Orta Pazar Caddesi Arka Sokak 4 is Bursa's most atmospheric hotel, the **(S)Safran**, ✆ 0224 224 7216 ✇ 0224 224 7219. Its wood-timbered, mustard-coloured exterior is of traditional Bursan design, but inside the en suite rooms are all up to date, with phones, TV, minibar and air-conditioning. The 10 rooms are often booked up in advance; call ahead. Doubles $80. A more conventional hotel in the city centre is the **★★★Kent Oteli**, Atatürk Caddesi 69, ✆ 0224 223 5420, ✇ 0224 224 4015, big and bright, a typical businessman's hotel with prices for doubles posted as $100, although they will settle for $60. A slightly cheaper alternative, away from the main drag, is the **★★★Dikmen**. This is to be recommended above all because it is on a relatively quiet side street: Maksem Caddesi 78, just north of Atatürk, ✆ 0224 224 1840, ✇ 0224 224 1844. It has a pleasant garden terrace and rooms have TV, minibar and balcony for $45.

inexpensive–cheap

There is a dearth of cheap hotels in the centre of Bursa, a situation made worse by the closure of the city's youth hostel. A reasonable option is the pleasant **Otel Çamlıbel** at İnebey Caddesi 71, ✆ 0224 221 2565, quiet and well run with en suite rooms costing $30. One street away, near the covered bazaar, is the **Çeşmeli**, at Gümüşçeken Caddesi 6, ✆ 224 1512, run by a friendly Turkish lady who charges $25 per double. You could also try the **Saray Otel**, Osman Gazi Caddesi, Matbaa Sokak 1, ✆ 0224 221 2820, next to the main square and very noisy.

The biggest collection of *cheap* rooms in town are near the minibus station; a good one is the **Terminal**, Garaj Batısı 6, ✆ 0224 254 7220—a bit old and raggedy perhaps, but friendly enough and they do their best to keep it up; baths in most rooms, and a hamam downstairs. Slightly more expensive is the **Kardeş**, Santral Garaj Batısı, ✆ 0224 272 1770; friendly and well kept; $18, slightly more with bath.

Çekirge

luxury–expensive

Most of the finest establishments are near the hot springs in the Çekirge suburb, a mile west of the centre. Many of these boast thermal baths; the oldest and most renowned is the **★★★★★Çelik Palas** at Çekirge Caddesi 79, ✆ 0224 233 3800, ✇ 0224 236 1910. Its name, 'Steel Palace', comes from the great steel dome over the baths. It also has tennis courts, an indoor pool, a disco and nearly every other amenity for $140 a double. The ultramodern **★★★★★Hotel Kervansaray-Thermal**,

Çekirge Meydanı, ✆ 0224 233 9300, ✉ 0224 233 9324 is more opulent still, with a health centre amongst its attractions; all rooms have air-con and satellite TV. Posted prices are $170 per double; if business is slow this may fall to as low as $95.

moderate

The ★★★★**Dilmen Oteli**, Murat Caddesi 20, ✆ 0224 233 9500, ✉ 0224 235 2568, has fewer luxuries than other four-star places. It has no main thermal bath complex, but all rooms have en suite baths with mineral water running from the taps. $65 per double, reduced rates for children. The ★★★**Termal Otel Gönlüferah**, at 1 Murat Caddesi 24, ✆ 0224 233 9210, ✉ 0224 233 9218, has thermal baths and well-appointed rooms with TV for a pricey $70.

inexpensive

The ★★**Adapalas**, Murat Caddesi 21, ✆ 0224 233 3990, ✉ 0224 236 4656, has thermal baths and charges a good-value $35 for a double. The **Medine Tuğra Termal Hotel**, 1 Murat Camii Yanı 2, ✆ 0224 234 3740, ✉ 0224 233 0324, set well back from the noisy main road, is dwarfed by the monumental Hüdavengar mosque next door. Its brightly decorated rooms push the boundaries of taste with their questionable line in technicolour landscapes, but have all the mod cons including air-con and mineral water piped to all rooms, for only $35 per double.

Of the few budget hotels in Çekirge, the **Yeşilyayla**, Çekirge Caddesi, Selvi Sokak 6, ✆/✉ 0224 239 6496, is the most appealing. Set slightly back from the main road, the wooden building is painted green throughout; old-fashioned double doors open onto the bedrooms from the large central hallway. Although toilets are communal, guests do have use of a small hamam in the basement; $22.

Uludağ

Most establishments on Uludağ are closed outside the winter months and full board is usually mandatory. Accommodation is mostly in chalet-style ski lodges, the grandest of which is the ★★★★**Kervansaray**, 1 Gelişim Bölgesi, ✆ 0224 285 2187 ✉ 0224 285 2193. Situated with immediate access to the ski lifts, the hotel has any number of activities to keep you busy pre- or post-piste, from an indoor pool and squash to a disco. After all that exercise, you may not care that the bedrooms themselves are comfortable rather than appealing; $90 on weekdays, but as much as $140 on busy weekends. The ★★★**Beceren**, ✆ 0224 285 2111 ✉ 0224 285 2119, has a more 'Heidi's Heimat' feel to it, although Heidi might have had problems working out what to do with the satellite TV and hair dryer in each room. Full board for two costs $80 on weekdays, $120 weekends during the ski season, $60 at other times.

One of the least expensive hotels is the **Kar Oberj**, in the national park, ✆ 0224 285 2121. It's $50 for two people on full board out of season; this almost doubles in season.

Bursa   *Eating Out*

Bursa is the home of the *İskender kebap*, a mixed grill with a tomato-based sauce, and you can sample it at the restaurant that claims to have first created the dish, the **İskender Kebapçı** at Ünlü Caddesi 7. Founded in 1867, it's an odd-looking place, with an exterior like a Wild West saloon and an interior like the Blue Mosque, but you'll eat well for $9 with a soft drink. Other *İskender kebap* places are all over town, charging an average price of $5. The **Hacı Bey** chain is very good, with branches in Çekirge and on Atatürk Bulvarı, west of the post office. There is also an inexpensive local favourite, the **Nazar Restaurant**, $3, in the İç Koza Han in the bazaar area.

Bursa's answer to İstanbul's Balıkpazarı is **Sakarya Caddesi**, known to locals as Arap Şükrü Sokak (you'll understand why when you get there). As you follow the main street, here called Altıparmak Caddesi, as it curves around the Hisar, Sakarya branches off to the left. This pedestrian street, lined with restaurants and bars with outside tables, is one of the two places to go in the evening. As you wander up the narrow alley, you'll see five restaurants all named after the man who put this street on the culinary map several decades ago—Arap Şükrü. Outside each establishment stands an experienced waiter casting out his rudimentary English line to the tourists drifting past—'Tasty fishes. Look! Look!' One glance at the displays of fish and before you know it you'll be reeled in for dinner. Many other restaurants also specialize in seafood: try the **Havuk**, where you can get a grilled fish and mezes for $8 and up. Outside dining hours there will be plenty of places open for beer and snacks.

The other place to go is the **Kültür Parkı**, where half of Bursa comes on any given night to row boats around the lagoon and inspect the pavilions of the permanent industrial exhibition, featuring Turkish-made cars, eggbeaters and double-glazing. There are a number of agreeable outdoor restaurants, doubling as beer gardens in the off hours. One of the best-priced is the **Ocakbaşı**, near the lagoon, with a wide choice of kebabs, delicious, thin home-made *pide* and a pretty fruit plate for dessert; $6. For a bit more you can enjoy the wide choice of mezes at the **Akarsu**, overlooking the lagoon—come on a Saturday night and there may well be a wedding party in the place, which can be a lot more entertaining than you would expect.

Even the corner diners of Bursa keep high standards. In the home of *İskender kebap*, you needn't pay more than pocket change for the genuine item at lunchtime—look for places like the excellent **Çarşı Kebabçısı**, near the Atatürk Caddesi entrance to the covered bazaar: genuine ambience of shiny formica tabletops, Coca-Cola and a huge plate of meat drenched in melted butter for $2; two or three of the owner's sons wait to see who can light your post-prandial cigarette first. If you find yourself near the minubus station, you won't do better for $3 than the **Lezzet Lokantası** on Çelik Sokak, serving tasty soups and *İskender*; open until 11pm.

As you would expect, Bursa has its share of fancy pastry shops. At the **Ulus**, by the post office on Atatürk Caddesi, you can pick out dainties from a wide assortment of sweets, from chocolates to chestnut cakes and pastel-coloured *lokum*, and wash it down with a glass of kiwi-fruit juice.

Çekirge

The **Çırağan** restaurant on the main street is where the beautiful people of Bursa go for a meal and a beer and to watch the sun go down over their city; $9.

Few cities enjoy such a paradisical hinterland. To the south there's Uludağ and its mountain forests and lakes; any other direction takes you through landscapes so green and lush they will make you drowsy looking at them (Uludağ stops all the weather fronts pouring down the Black Sea and Marmara and catches all the rain). Turkey's careful farmers have made good use of this land; all along the main roads they have set up stands to sell you incredibly colossal and juicy peaches, perfect sour cherries or whatever else is in season.

Getting Around

Regular **buses** from Bursa make the one-hour trip to İznik, taking the scenic route along the southern shore of the lake. If you're **driving**, consider carefully any trip from Bursa east to Yalova and points west; traffic can be as intense as in Bursa's centre. Mudanya has infrequent **car ferries** and summer **hydrofoils** to İstanbul, though for car and coach travellers it will usually be more convenient to take the short Topçular–Eski Hisar ferry to get to the city.

Tourist Information

İznik: Kılıçaslan Caddesi 130, ☎ 0224 757 1933.

Yalova: İskele Meydanı 5, ☎ 0226 814 2108.

Directly north of Bursa is **Mudanya**, a large, gloomy port that saw the signing of the armistice ending the Turkish War of Independence in 1922. Further on, past Gemlik and Gemlik Bay, you'll come to **Termal**. Emperors Constantine and Justinian enjoyed the thermal baths from which the town draws its name; you can do the same, although there's no other reason to stop. The road continues north to meet the sea at **Yalova**, from where ferries cross to İstanbul. It's a bright and breezy town, with yet another product of the Atatürk statue factory in its square; this one is more dramatic than most, depicting the Great Man in strident pose, arm upraised as if to strike. Should you wish to risk swimming in this less-than-clean stretch of the Marmara, there are beaches at **Çiftlikköy**, **Koruköy** and **Çınarcık**, all west of Yalova. The water at **Armutlu**, on the western edge of the peninsula, is clearer but the beach is nothing special.

Ancient *Mysia* was the province stretching from Bursa towards the east, including much of the southern shore of the Marmara and the city of Balıkesir, the ancient Paleokastro. Ancient geography, as is usual in Asia Minor, was never too clear about boundaries; for a while the Romans were wont to call the area around Bursa *Phrygia Minor*, and the city itself, along with the territory to the east, *Bithynia*. Today these lands along the valley of the Sakarya River, the ancient Sangarius, are in one of the more fortunate corners of Turkey, even if they no longer have a sense of being a distinct region. The countryside is green and good, and obviously cultivated with loving care; the villages, with their characteristic brick and timber dwellings, drift through the decades in a permanent state of genteel dilapidation. **Bilecik** would have been the most interesting, had it not been destroyed in the War of Independence. Of its early Ottoman monuments only the Karasu Bridge, reputed to be the work of Mimar Sinan, remains.

İnegöl, to the west, is an agricultural town famous throughout Turkey for spicy meatballs, *İnegöl köfte*, while in Söğüt, you may visit the **tomb of Ertuğrul**, the father of Osman, founder of the Ottoman dynasty. In a way this Sakarya valley is the original Ottoman home-land, a secure and uncontested spot in the 13th century, a perfect place for an ambitious band of roving warriors to await its opportunities with patience. The Byzantines were too feeble to trouble them, and no serious enemies appeared from the east either; despite all the talent of the early Ottomans, one can perhaps attribute much of their early success to a lucky choice of locations. Maybe the spot is always lucky for the Turks; just a couple of miles south of Söğüt, the climactic battle of their War of Independence was fought at **İnönü** in 1921. A few years later, when Atatürk decided that all Turks should have Western-style surnames, he himself conferred one upon the general who had won the battle and halted the Greek offensive. İsmet Paşa now became İsmet İnönü, later to be the second president of the Turkish Republic.

İznik (Nicaea)

Between the Sakarya and Gemlik Bay, an inlet of the Marmara, a circle of wooded hills isolates a large lake, **İznik Gölü**, named after the ancient city on its eastern shore. İznik, the ancient Nicaea, was founded in the 4th century BC. For a while it was the capital of the Kingdom of Bithynia, before the Romans swallowed it up, but it wasn't until the Christian era that the city achieved its fame, or perhaps its notoriety, as seat of the two great church councils. First in the 4th century and again in the 8th, the querulous bishops and bureaucrats of early Christianity met here to argue, anathematize their enemies or smash them with bats, and run up uncollectable bills at the local hostelries.

The Church Councils

Constantine first summoned the church councils in 325 to decide the insoluble conflict between the Arian and Athanasian sects. His favourite, St Athanasius, came all the way from Alexandria to lead his partisans in the attack, demanding that every Christian admit both the divine and mortal natures of Christ. Arius, who has been called a 'unitarian', wanted to avoid having the godhead cluttered with extra, inessential 'essences', and got himself murdered here for his trouble, though his party won a short-lived victory. Nicaea, a beautiful resort city in a strategic location, central for the eastern half of the empire, had already been a residence of Emperor Diocletian; the Church Fathers found it a wonderfully agreeable locale for conventions and they came often, most importantly for the great council of 786, when the bishops codified rituals and beliefs into the form still observed by the Greek Church today.

Empress Irene, who almost married Charlemagne but could not bear to part with the intrigues and luxury of Constantinople, may have been an outrageous tart, but she is remem-bered fondly by the Orthodox for calling this council to put an end finally to the Iconoclastic struggles that had so bitterly divided the empire. Convening at Nicaea's church of Aya Sofya, the bishops from as far away as Italy decided once and for all that holy images 'stimulate spectators to think of the originals', and therefore deserved an indirect sort of adoration, though not worship.

Nicaea's finest hour, however, came in the dark days following the Sack of Constantinople in 1204. A die-hard, Theodore Lascaris, brought the remnants of Greek resistance here and became emperor-in-exile; he and his successor, John III Vatatzes, reconstituted the empire, rebuilding its finances and army for the day when Constantinople would again be theirs.

The Selcuk Turks held the city and made it their capital for a brief period in the 11th century, and it fell again, finally, to the Ottoman leader Orhan in 1331. As a Turkish city, Nicaea, now İznik, gained fame throughout the Islamic world for its hand-painted ceramic tiles, made with a quality of colour and design that cannot be imitated today. Expensive though they must have been, all the early Ottoman sultans demanded them in enormous quantity for their mosques, and today they can be seen on buildings across Turkey wherever earthquakes and decay have spared them. They can be approximately dated by colour and pattern. Until 1520, all İznik ceramics were exclusively dark blue and white. About that time, turquoise was added. A kind of red, always difficult in glazing, was achieved in the 1600s. Throughout the 17th and 18th centuries, designs grew less abstract and more naturalistic; floral designs predominated in the Tulip Period and after, and even human and animal figures were appearing near the end in the early 1800s.

As the finances of the empire declined, the market for these tiles disappeared, and the city with it. İznik had reached its peak of prosperity in the 17th century with 300 workshops turning out thousands of tiles a week; by the 19th century only a dismal village was left inside the old Byzantine walls and even that remainder suffered grievous damage in the fighting of 1922.

İznik Today

Today, some leftover grace from its days of greatness keeps İznik free of the usual sadness that accompanies ruins. The town is simply too full of roses and children and green gardens to be melancholy. Indeed, the modest agricultural centre that İznik has become cannot nearly fill the square mile or so within its Byzantine walls, and its people wisely use the remaining space for vegetable plots and olive groves. Until recently, whatever talent was left from the long-gone ceramic industries was devoted to making cinder blocks and roof tiles. Not a jot of documentation had survived from the golden age of tilemaking: the master craftsmen of the 16th and 17th centuries had taken their secrets with them to the grave—or so they thought. The **İznik Foundation** was set up in 1993 to re-learn the lost techniques. Archaeological excavations of the İznik kiln sites had already yielded much practical information. Scientists from as far away as M.I.T. in the US analysed the tiles, revealing that they contained up to 80% quartz. Even with this knowledge, it took another two years of hit-and-miss experimentation before the Foundation could come up with something approximating the original 400-year-old tile recipe. Commercial production was finally begun in 1995, but it was decided not to produce exact copies of the 16th-century designs, for fear they would be sold on to hapless tourists as originals. The Foundation is situated on the lake road at Sahil Yolu, Halı Saha Arkası; the Tourist Office should be able to facilitate a visit. Unlike the disappointing tiles in the stack-em high, sell-em cheap shops nearby, those on display at the showroom of Eşref Eroğlu on the main Kılıçaslan Caddesi are masterpieces, each one signed and dated. His designs are both figurative and abstract, but at $150 apiece, you won't find them gracing many bathroom walls.

Even though the foundation of the city predates the Romans, İznik has the plan of a typical Roman provincial town: two broad main streets meeting at right angles in the centre,

connecting the four main gates. Nearly all of
İznik's **walls** can still be seen, in various
stages of decay, and along the garden
paths and sheep trails you find the occasional arch or Greek inscription, towers,
sally-ports and storage rooms. Two of the
gates, the northern or **İstanbul Gate**
and the western or **Lefke Gate**, survive,
with Roman triumphal arches between
their inner and outer parts, inscriptions in
Greek and Latin commemorating the visit of
the Emperor Hadrian, and remains of marble
reliefs. The Lefke Gate is the better preserved,
and near it are parts of a much-weathered
decorative frieze. Also carved, inconspicuously,
on the inside of the gate is something that is obviously a layout for the game of Nine Men's Morris

(others can be seen on the steps of the Basilica Julia
in the Roman Forum, the Basilica of St John at Selçuk
and in scores of sites across the Mediterranean; this must have been the favourite game of
classical antiquity for people with time on their hands). Outside the gate, the **Byzantine
aqueduct** has suffered little from time, although it is no longer in use.

Inside the walls, little remains of ancient İznik. Near the ruined Yenişehir gate at the south
entrance, the half-excavated ruins of the **Roman Theatre** are visible behind a fence. Amidst
one of Turkey's best-kept public gardens in the centre of the town stands the derelict **church
of Aya Sofya** (*open daily exc Mon 9–12, 1–4.30; adm*), an 11th-century structure that
replaced the earlier church from the era of Justinian that hosted the two ecumenical councils. Some fragments of mosaics and frescoes can still be seen. The conquering Ottomans
added a minaret, and its stump is currently the home of one of İznik's numerous storks.

Storks, surprisingly, spend their summers in Turkey. This kind have little to do with their
North European cousins, and spend their winters in eastern or southern Africa. Minaret
stumps make perfect bases for their nests, combining good drainage, peace and quiet, and
inaccessibility to weasels. A favourite nesting place for storks is atop the ruined minaret near
the İstanbul Gate, next to the Nilüfer Hatun İmareti, a 14th-century hospice for travelling
dervishes that now serves as the **İznik Museum** (*open daily exc Mon, 8.30–12, 1–5; adm*).
Here a selection of artefacts, from recent Turkish crafts going back to Paleolithic tools, proves
the long continuity of this site; more interesting are the grave steles and architectural fragments arranged in the garden outside. Ranging from the early Hellenistic to the late
Byzantine, the steles provide a kind of glossary of symbols, a complete guide to the inexhaustible iconography of death that so long occupied the Greek world's fancy.

Not surprisingly, the most important part of the museum's collection is devoted to ceramics,
some as old as 2500 BC, as well as the best Islamic work. Don't hold your breath, however:
there is less on display than you would imagine for such a renowned ceramics centre. A city

map on the wall of the museum helps in finding your way through the village to the ancient sites and around the walls. Ask at the museum about a possible excursion to the **Yeraltı Mezarı**, north of town, a 6th-century Byzantine tomb with some fine frescoes; they have the keys. Across the street from the museum, the **Yeşil Cami**, built in the 1380s, will catch your eye with what may be the prettiest minaret in all Anatolia. The blue and green tiles that cover it are not original İznik work, however; during restorations in the last century it was necessary to replace them all.

There are no good **beaches** on İznik's lake shore, but people still come here, particularly from Bursa, to walk along the promenade outside the town's ruined **Lake Gate**, and to eat fresh fish in the restaurants on the water's edge. If you come on just the right day in the spring, you can ski down Uludağ in the morning and swim in Lake İznik or the Marmara in the afternoon.

İznik and Around   ***Where to Stay***

İznik

cheap

The **Çamlık Motel**, © 0224 757 1362, 📠 0224 757 1631, is the best available, right on the lake shore at Göl Caddesi 1. It's a friendly family motel where rooms are clean but modest at $20 for a double with bath; there's also a good restaurant. If you prefer to stay in the centre, the **Hotel Babacan**, Kılıçaslan Caddesi 104, © 0224 757 1211, somehow manages to retain a friendly atmosphere, despite the gloominess of its huge corridors. Its double rooms are spacious too, and a little brighter, at $12 without bath, $16 with. Nearby is the welcoming **Kaynarca Pansiyon**, M. Günden Sokak 1, © 0224 757 1753, 📠 0224 757 1723. The corridors here are a riot of colour, decked out with naïve paintings of Aya Sofya frescoes and İznik tile designs. En suite doubles are good value at only $14. The management tries hard to please, offering free use of the kitchen facilities; there's also an internet café downstairs.

Yalova

The **Otel Fatih**, Cumhuriyet Caddesi 27, is cheerful, comfortable and good value at $18; there's also a wide choice of *cheap* pensions, all near the ferries.

İznik and Around   ***Eating Out***

In İznik fish are easy to come by in a number of restaurants along the lakeside promenade, including the excellent **Balıkçı** at the northern end. A wide range of fish is on offer, including *yayın* (local catfish), but if you want to move away from the normal school of fish dishes, try the spicy fishsteak kebabs coated in paprika, expensive but memorable at $4 a skewer. In the town, on Kılıçaslan Caddesi between the tourist office and the Aya Sofya, the **Bülbül Lokanta** is cheap, clean and friendly.

There are several basic restaurants by the harbour in Yalova; most stay open late.

The North Aegean Coast

100km
50 miles
● International Port

N

After İstanbul, Turkey's Aegean coast has long been the country's main attraction, originally for scholars and philhellenes who came to stroll through the ruins of cities renowned in antiquity, and nowadays for holiday-makers who combine a tour of the archaeological sites with the pleasures of the Mediterranean. The climate is pleasant, tempered by the sea in the summer and winter; olives and vineyards cover the fertile valleys and coastal plains. Mountains are never far away, nor are beaches—some in the throes of becoming major resorts, others quite deserted. Of all Turkey's regions, the Aegean coast has the best hotels, and more sprout up every year.

The northern part, Mysia and Lydia in ancient times, is a bit less touristy than the south—no fleshpots like Bodrum and Marmaris, but serene, laid-back resorts such as Behramkale (Assos) and Ayvalık. The major attractions are archaeological: Troy, of course, and Pergamon (Bergama) one of the great cities of the Hellenistic Era.

Troy and Çanakkale

Getting Around

Çanakkale is connected by **bus** to İstanbul, Bursa, İzmir, and Edirne; the **ferryboat** crosses the Dardanelles from Eceabat hourly between 6am and midnight. The crossing takes 25 minutes and is ridiculously cheap, and it carries the very regular **dolmuş** from Kilitbahir, as well as buses to Tekirdağ and İstanbul. There are also informal ferries between Çanakkale and Kilitbahir, if you want to have a look at Mehmet II's unusual castle. These are small, usually unmarked boats that go whenever there are enough people; ask around.

From Çanakkale's otogar, a few streets south of the port on Atatürk Caddesi, frequent **minibuses** go to Troy and the neighbouring villages; naturally buses from across the straits stop in the centre too, on İskele Meydanı. Çanakkale is the most popular base for exploring both the Gelibolu **battlefields** and ancient Troy and two travel agencies offer tours of both, **Troy-Anzac**, ✆ 0286 217 5847, and **Ana-Tur**, ✆ 0286 217 5482. Both can be found near the clock tower and both charge the same rates, about $18 per person. Be wary of unlicensed guides at both sites, who may or may not know the first thing about them.

Tourist Information

Çanakkale: next to Abdülhamid's clock tower at İskele Meydanı 67, the main square by the port, ✆ 0286 217 1187.

Troy (Truva)

From the time of Alexander the Great, travellers have come expressly to see **Troy**. No place is so highly charged in the Western imagination; after two and a half millennia, the wrath of Achilles, the beauty of Helen, the death of Hector, the ploy of the wooden horse, the sack of the high-walled city and the misfortunes that dogged the victors in Homer's *Iliad* and *Odyssey* have retained their poetic resonance, each character and event an evocative, ambiguous symbol deeply embedded in our culture. For the ancient Greeks, the *Iliad*'s account of the Olympian gods was the source of their religious beliefs. And who can argue with Herodotus, who saw the Trojan War as the root and mirror of all later antagonisms between East and West?

Few ancients doubted the veracity of Homer's Troy; Alexander even exchanged some of his own armour for trophies from the Trojan War still hanging in Athena's temple. But by the 6th century AD the city was abandoned, its port silted up, the Anatolian dust thickening over it until the physical Troy vanished from all memory. Outwardly the site resembled a hill, which the Turks called **Hisarlık**; scholars argued over where the city might have stood, had it really existed. Byron was one of many who visited the Troad (the region around Troy), and one of very few who left believing in more than its poetic truth. In *Don Juan* he wrote,

> *I've stood upon Achilles' tomb,*
> *And heard Troy doubted; time will doubt of Rome.*

Another believer was Heinrich Schliemann, a merchant who made a fortune from the California Gold Rush and the American Civil War. In 1868, 46 years old and tired of wheeling and dealing, he came to the Troad, where he met an Englishman named Frank Calvert who had dug a trench in Hisarlık and showed Schliemann his finds: part of a classical temple and, deeper down, signs of older civilizations, layered one on top of the other. Schliemann was hooked, and the former businessman became the greatest dilettante archaeologist of all time, one destined to unearth Troy, Mycenae and Tiryns, a series of spectacular finds that electrified the world. Subsequent archaeologists, especially Schliemann's assistant Dörpfeld and the American Carl Blegen, uncovered further proof that Hisarlık is indeed the site of the ancient city of Troy.

Recent Theories

As Calvert had brilliantly surmised, Schliemann found layer upon layer of civilization, which he numbered from Troy I—the oldest, dating back to 3600 BC—to Troy IX, the Hellenistic city of Ilion, founded by Alexander's general Lysimachus. Although Schliemann's aim was to discover the Troy of Priam and Hector, he uncovered a fascinating chronicle of people building over and over again on the same site. Was one of these Troys the Troy of Homer? Most scholars date the Trojan War to *c.* 1250 BC, just before the decline of the Mycenaean empire; Troy VII coincides rather neatly with that date, and it perished in a terrible conflagration. However, the city preceding it, Troy VI, was far more imposing and better fits the epithets Homer used in the *Iliad*—but it was destroyed by an earthquake.

Turkish archaeologists resolve the contradiction by seeing magnificent Troy VI as the citadel that Agamemnon's Achaeans unsuccessfully besieged for ten years; rebuilt shoddily after the earthquake, it was then easily captured. The Wooden Horse, it follows, was an offering by the Achaeans to Poseidon, the sea god and earth-shaker, whose assistance proved crucial in their sack of Troy. Others believe the *Iliad*, composed some 500 years after the traditional date of the war, recalls not one particular event but several Mycenaean raids on the Anatolian coast; or perhaps even the last great twilight expedition, recited for latter-day kings by their bards to evoke the good old days.

In any event, no definite proof has ever been discovered in Troy that the Trojan War took place, although many recent discoveries, especially in Miletus, prove that the Mycenaean Greeks were in Asia Minor as early as the 15th century BC; in 1984 some of their tombs were discovered on an ancient beach at Besike Bay, one of the possible sites of Troy's long-vanished harbour.

But what has kept the debates on the Trojan War on the front burner since Schliemann is the finding of references to Troy in the dead languages of Anatolia. In the 1920s, scholars read about the Ahhiyawans—probably the Achaeans—when translating tablets from the 15th-century BC Hittite archives at Boğazkale. The archives also refer to a place called Wilusa, believed to be Ilios, Homer's other name for Troy.

Then, in 1984, some very suggestive evidence turned up in Luvian—an ancient Indo-European language, possibly the language of the Trojans—referring to 'steep Wilusa' and men named Priya-muwas (Priam?) and Paris. Add the fact that linguistically some lines of the *Iliad* have been shown to be older than the traditional date of the Trojan War (1250 BC), and the problem becomes even more complicated. Scholarly symposiums in England and America and Michael Wood's excellent BBC series on Troy heightened interest in the question: did the Trojan War take place as Homer recounts?

The Site

The Trojan horse is certainly still there, or at least its modern Turkish descendant. It's the first thing you see at Troy and the only thing most tourists take pictures of. For, in all honesty, the site itself is bewildering, 'a ruin of a ruin' as some call it, a victim of 19th-century archaeology. The University of Cincinnati archaeological team determined that Schliemann's original nine layers contained some 46 substrata. What you see as you walk through the excavations are fragments of a *millefeuille* pastry of Troys.

The tall Mycenaean walls of Troy VI are the most impressive sight and among the most beautiful of the ancient world. They fit the Homeric descriptions of 'beetling' and 'steep', and at one point in the *Iliad* (Book XVI) Homer refers to their most unusual feature—angles or offsets that divide the wall into several sections. Here, too, are the foundations of a mighty bastion, perhaps Homer's 'great tower of Ilios'. Yet as splendid as these walls still are, they are not of any great extent: this eminence was the citadel of Troy, not the city. The South Gate (Homer's Scaean gate?) facing the plain was the most important; the so-called **Pillar House** above it is the most popular candidate for Priam's Palace.

Troy

Near the entrance you can walk up a surviving section of the old Hisarlık mound, for a view that evokes Homer perhaps even better than the old stones. There, on a clear day, is Mount Ida to the southeast, from where Zeus watched the war; to the west, on a *very* clear day, you can make out Mount Fingari (Moon Mountain) on the island of Samothrace, where Poseidon sat. In the plain below wanders the Scamander River, whose god tried to drown Achilles for turning the water red with the blood of the Trojans. The two mounds near the river's mouth at Sigeion Point are by tradition the tombs of Achilles and his friend Patroclus, whose death at the hand of Hector finally roused Achilles from his sulking wrath to return to the battle-field. On most days, you are also aware of another Homeric epithet—'windy'. Much speculation has gone into determining the location of Troy's harbour, where the 'beaked ships' of the Achaeans were beached for the duration of the war. Certainly much of what is dry land was once a shallow bay or flood plain and marsh; if the Argives had had to commute to the battlefield every day from any contemporary harbour, they would hardly have had time to fight.

The Chariot Ramp

The path through the excavations leads past the ruins of the temple of Athena, last rebuilt by the Romans, to the great flagged **chariot ramp**. It was near here that Schliemann unearthed the controversial 'Jewels of Helen', the one really splendid treasure found on the site. The jewellery convinced many sceptics that this was indeed the Troy of Homer, and Schliemann was so proud of his find that he couldn't resist smuggling the baubles out of Turkey to adorn his wife at Athenian parties. Finally he gave the jewellery to the Berlin Museum, from where it disappeared in 1945. Many thought it had been destroyed during the attack on Berlin, others that it had been pillaged by Soviet occupation forces. Not until 1994 was the mystery solved, when the jewellery surfaced in Moscow's Pushkin Museum, with the German identification tags still attached. Both the 'Jewels of Helen' and the chariot ramp, however, date back to Troy II (2600–2300 BC), which, though a glorious city in its day, predates the commonly accepted date of the Trojan War by a thousand years.

The Romans

The other prominent remains belong to Troy VIII, the Greek Ilion (700–300 BC), and Troy IX (300 BC–4th century AD), respectively the Hellenistic and the Roman New Ilium. You can see a partially restored shrine, Roman theatre and bouleuterion. Neither of these cities was very large, although as the successors of Troy they enjoyed a certain renown. Julius Caesar, like many modern visitors, was disappointed by the meagre ruins; Emperor Julian the Apostate was delighted to find that Christianity in AD 354 had not yet done away with sacrifices on Achilles' tomb. Yet it was the voice of the East that has had the last word. After conquering Constantinople, Mehmet II came to Troy and declared:

> *It is to me that Allah has given to avenge this city and its people...*
> *Indeed it was the Greeks who before devastated this city, and it is*
> *their descendants who after so many years have paid me the debt*
> *which their boundless pride had contracted—and often afterwards—*
> *towards us, the peoples of Asia.*

Troy, or *Truva* as the Turks call it, is 17 miles (27km) from **Çanakkale**, which most visitors use as a base for visiting the excavations. On the way you can stop at **Tevfikiye**, the only oasis of tackiness Troy has produced, with its trinket shops and fake 'House of Schliemann'; actually, the whole village was built of materials quarried from Schliemann's dig.

Çanakkale, at one of the Dardanelles' ferry crossings, is a pleasant, slightly faded provincial capital, the ancient Greek Abydos, successor to Troy. Its name in Turkish means 'saucer castle', 'saucer' recalling the town's old ceramics industry which once produced florid Turkish Art Nouveau—though the town lives more from tourism and tuna fishing today. The **castle**, one of several built by Mehmet the Conqueror to hem in Constantinople, still guards the Hellespont, housing soldiers and a small **Military and Naval Museum** (*open daily exc. Mon and Thurs, 9–12 1.30–5; adm*) with a special display devoted to the heroics of Atatürk during the Gelibolu campaign. Outside the castle is a mock-up of the *Nusrat*, the Turkish minelayer that sealed the straits to Allied destroyers, thus precipitating the landings. (One bit of naval history they missed is that Çanakkale was probably the spot where the Persian King Xerxes made his famous bridge of boats in 483 BC, when his vast horde was marching to invade Greece.) The excellent **archaeological museum** (*open 8.30–5, closed Mon; adm*) is a mile from the centre, and stars finds from the Dardanos Tumulus. This, dating from the 4th century BC, was discovered six miles south of Çanakkale in 1959 and produced golden diadems, ivories, gold jewellery, votive statuary and the remains of a wooden harp.

The best thing about Çanakkale is its lively waterfront, where the whole town along with the visiting ANZACs comes each evening for a promenade and a fish dinner. The nearest beach to Çanakkale is the thin strip of sand at **Kepez**, four miles (6km) west of town. The beach at **Dardanos**, three miles (5km) further on, is better. **Güzelyalı**, a small fishing village-cum-resort 11 miles (18km) south-west of Çanakkale, also has a beach.

Turkey's Aegean Islands

Getting Around

Kabatepe, on the Gelibolu peninsula, is the port for Gökçeada, though in summer there are also services from Çanakkale. Boats for Bozcaada depart from Odun İskelesi south of Çanakkale; it's a trip of less than half an hour, but first you need to get to Odun İskelesi, an hour's minibus ride from Çanakkale. Services to both Aegean islands can be infrequent, particularly in the winter.

Gökçeada and **Bozcaada** are Turkey's sole possessions amongst the Aegean islands, both of them wrested from the defeated Greeks in 1923. Strategically, they are important, guarding the mouth of the Dardanelles, and both are heavily militarized, staring across the sea at the equally well-defended Greek islands of Samothraki and Limnos. Historically and ethnically, the islands are more Greek than Turkish and were exempted from the population exchange. Since the Cyprus conflict, many of the indigenous Greeks have left, driven out by years of nagging Turkish oppression (mirrored by the treatment of ethnic Turks in Greek Thrace). Only in the last few years have the islands become accessible to foreigners

Gökçeada (the Imbros of the Greeks and Imbroz of Homer) is a green, lumpy island whose few visitors tend to head straight for **Kale** in the north where there are beaches, pensions and restaurants. The island is the birthplace of Bartholomeos, the current Greek Patriarch in İstanbul (patriarchs are required by law to be Turkish citizens). Above the village is a ruined Ottoman castle, built by Süleyman the Magnificent. There's not much else, save for a prison and some pleasant walks.

Bozcaada is flatter and smaller, and fringed with beaches. Its one town seems very Greek, with whitewashed houses, overhanging upper storeys and narrow, serpentine streets. Its **castle**, vast and explorable, has been there since Byzantine days, and now guards the islanders' goats and sheep. Bozcaada (ancient Tenedos) was, according to epic tradition, the Achaean base where the Greeks hid their ships, waiting for Odysseus to emerge from the belly of the wooden horse and signal that the sleeping Troy was theirs for the taking. Up until the 15th century, Greeks living on the island acted as tour guides for foreigners seeking Troy.

Çanakkale and the Aegean Islands   **Where to Stay**

Çanakkale

expensive

In Çanakkale the most comfortable, and most expensive, hotel is the ★★★★**Akol Hotel** on Kordonboyu, ✆ 0286 217 9456, 🖷 0286 217 2897, where $90 buys a plush double room with air-conditioning, TV, balcony and so on.

moderate–inexpensive

On Kordonboyu the ★★★**Büyük Truva**, ✆ 0286 217 1024, 🖷 0286 217 0903, is nice if not wonderful; about $60. The ★★★**Otel Anafartalar**, İskele Meydanı, ✆ 0286 217 4454, 🖷 0286 217 4457, is closer to the centre and is correspondingly noisier, but has rooms with balconies that gaze across the Dardanelles to Kilitbahir; doubles $40.

The ★**Kestanbol**, just around the corner from the bus station at Hasan Mevsuf Sokak 5, ✆ 0286 243 0466, has pokey rooms with balconies and television for $30. Better rooms for the same money can be had at the ★★**Anzac Hotel** (not to be confused with Anzac House, *see* below), in front of the clock tower at Saat Kulesi Meydanı 8, ✆ 0286 217 7777, 🖷 0286 217 2018. The carpets may be grimy, but the blue and white tiled bathrooms are a delight.

A long way from the harbour action is the **Aşkın**, İsmet Paşa Mah., Hasan Mevsuf Sokak 53, ✆ 0286 217 4956, 🖷 0286 217 7541. The rooms are so tiny that the TVs are kept like medieval prisoners in metal cages suspended from the ceiling, but are good value at $20 for an en suite double with balcony.

cheap

Çanakkale can seem like a 1960s time capsule in summer, loaded with bright-eyed, clean-cut backpackers. The vast majority, as you will soon discover, hail from the Antipodes, and there are plenty of places that specialize in accommodating them. Descending from the coach you will most likely be met by an employee of the **Anzac House**, Cumhuriyet Bulvarı, ✆ 0286 217 1392, 🖷 0286 217 2906. Rooms can be a bit musty and almost half of them don't have windows, though there are fans to compensate for this. Shower and toilet facilites are shared. The friendly and very helpful staff serve up beer and Vegemite sandwiches (would we lie?) and show battle documentaries on video; everyone has a good time. Like many other Çanakkale hotels, they arrange tours of the battlefield. Doubles $12, dorm $4 per person.

Çannakale's best choice by far is the **Hotel Efes**, ✆ 0286 217 3256, with its peaceful garden complete with gurgling fountain. It is quieter than most too, set back from the main street, with its own parking spaces, on Aralık Sokak 5. Run single-handedly by the house-proud and delightfully chirpy Mrs Yetimoğlu; spotless doubles with private shower cost only $16. If the Efes is full, another good option nearby is the **Yellow Rose Pension** in a quiet backstreet at Yeni Sokak 5, ✆ 0286 217 3343, *yellowrose1@mailexcite.com*. $12 for a basic en suite double.

camping

There is certainly no shortage of campgrounds around Çanakkale, from the large and well-equipped **Truva Mocamp** at Güzelyalı, ✆ 0286 232 8025, which has a restaurant/canteen, to the simpler **Paradise Camping**, ✆ 0286 263 6178, near the beach at Dardanos. At Kepez, 5km from Çanakkale, the **Şen Mokamp**, ✆ 0286 263 6888, has campsites under the pines on the beach.

Güzelyalı and Tevfikiye

moderate

Güzelyalı, 18km from Çanakkale, has several comparatively swanky hotels, popular with holidaying Turks. The best is the ★★★**İris Oteli**, Mola Caddesi 48, ✆ 0286 232 8100, ✉ 0286 232 8028, where doubles with breakfast cost $52. It boasts the town's only disco, as well as its own stretch of beach, and water sports. The ★★★**Tusan Oteli**, ✆ 0286 232 8210, ✉ 0286 232 8226, in a pretty setting in the woods, is new and bright and slightly less expensive, also with a private beach, windsurfing and water-skiing, etc. *Closed Nov–May*.

cheap

A simple choice at Güzelyalı is the **Taşkın**, ✆ 0286 232 8138; $12. Güzelyalı has a handful of *pansiyonlar* and there are campsites at Kepez and Dardanos.

If you are mainly interested in Troy, as an alternative to Çanakkale you might stay in **Tevfikiye**, though it has only a few very modest *pansiyonlar*, plus a lokanta.

Gökçeada and Bozcaada

cheap

On Gökçeada the **Gökçe Otel**, Fevzi Çakmak Caddesi 14, ✆ 0286 697 1473, is pleasant and eager to please, charging $8. The ★★**Koz Otel**, ✆ 0286 697 8189, on the waterfront in Bozcaada town, charges $18, breakfast included. Like most of the hotels and pensions on the Turkish Aegean islands, both are open June–September only. Outside these months, you may be able to find a room to let in a private house.

There are two modest **campgrounds** on Gökçeada.

For proof of just how good lokantas can be, search out the **Gözde** in a street leading inland from the clock tower at Kemalpaşa Mah., Kemalyeri Sokak, Akyurt Apt 31. One customer liked the food so much that he married the lady who owned it. Now they run the place together and have gone to town on the décor, with tables and chairs covered in matching material and wrought-iron fittings made by the husband. The *tabldot* (fixed menu) at lunchtime is incredibly cheap: at $2 for three dishes, it's little wonder that half the students and workers in the area descend on the place each day. Chemists, goldsmiths and others who can't leave their shops send out for their food. The *à la carte* menu has tempting alternatives, not least the *soyasoslu tavuk*: chicken in soy sauce and honey. Last orders 9pm, closed Sundays, no alcohol.

Çanakkale is a great place for a fish dinner: there are a number of good restaurants competing for your trade, all in a row near the castle, and all with outside tables facing the harbour. Most locals prefer to splurge at the **Liman Yalova**, with its breezy rooftop terrace. You can snack on the excellent seafood mezes for $3 per plate, or splash out on a full fish meal for upwards of $12.

For excellent value, try the **Entelektüel** further along the harbour front, with fixed-price menus including grilled fish, chips, salad and a beer for as little as $6. It's all a matter of what fish, of course; you could spend as much as $15. Also good is the very similar **Rıhtım Restoran** next door.

Less expensively, you can get tasty kebabs and köfte, and sometimes grilled fish, at the **Ömur Köfte Salonu**, on the waterfront near the Hotel Bakır. The **Trakya Restoran**, a good and inexpensive lokanta across from the Anzac House, is more than used to entertaining tourists, as is the **Aussie and Kiwi Restaurant**, recommended by readers both for the food and the proprietor, around the corner on Yalı Caddesi. For a filling *mantı* lunch, there is the **Tutku Mantı Salonu**, just down the street from the Trakya on Demircioğlu Caddesi.

The Troad

The bulging peninsula south of Troy to Mount İda is known as the Troad, famous in ancient times for horse breeding. Highlights include the awe-inspiring walls of ancient Assos and the sumptuous Gulf of Edremit. It's a dreamy, beautiful country, full of maples and olive trees; farmers set up stands all along the roadsides selling olives (some of Turkey's best), olive oil and homemade relishes. The best time to come is June, when the deep red blankets of poppies make an unforgettable sight.

Getting Around

Buses and **minibuses** between Çanakkale and İzmir serve the coast well, and there should be no difficulty getting to and from Assos or anyplace else (Assos is also known as **Behramkale** and minibuses always bear the latter name on their destination signs). During the day, minibuses run continuously along the northern edge of the gulf to Edremit. To reach Ören you may have to take a **dolmuş** from Edremit to

Burhaniye and then a local bus to the coast. In summer, Ören is linked by **boat** to Ayvalık (*see* below), with four crossings a day.

Travelling between this part of the coast and the Marmara shore or points east will require a bus change in Balıkesir (where, if you get tired of lemon cologne, the bus station has a shop that will sell you cologne in a few dozen other flavours).

Tourist Information

Akçay: Edremit Caddesi, Karabudak Apt 20, ✆ 0266 384 1113.

Ören: town centre, ✆ 0266 422 2870.

Alexandria Troas

South of Troy lie the ruins of the city that superseded it in Hellenistic times, **Alexandria Troas**, a few miles south of the sandy beach at **Geyikli**. Many early travellers to the Troad mistook its ruins for Troy itself. The city was founded by Antigonus the One-Eyed at the end of the 4th century BC, but achieved its greatest glory after another of Alexander's generals, Lysimachus, killed Antigonus in battle and renamed it in memory of his old commander. He made it the main port in the Troad and one of the richest commercial centres on the entire coast. In Hadrian's time, Herodes Atticus, the Rockefeller of his day, endowed it with a monumental bath complex and aqueduct. Its convenient position on the main sea route later brought about its demolition, as the builders of İstanbul's imperial mosques cannibalized it, block by block. Today the most impressive remains, besides the baths, are the great broken stones scattered on the beach.

Before you get to Assos, the dolmuş from Çanakkale passes through **Ayvacık**, a ramshackle village worth a stop only if you're hunting for Turkish carpets: Ayvacık is the home of DOBAG, a cooperative run by weavers dedicated to doing things the traditional way.

Assos (Behramkale)

South of Alexandria Troas, on the north shore of the lovely Gulf of Edremit is the imposing site of ancient **Assos**, known to locals as **Behramkale**. Take the paved road from Ayvacık, crossing a charming 14th-century Ottoman bridge, from where you can see the town hugging the top of an extinct volcano, some 785ft over the sea. This part of Assos is known as the **Kale**. Far beneath the ruins is the **İskele** (wharf), Assos' tiny harbour, whose old stone houses and acorn warehouses have now been converted into atmospheric hotels. Several kilometres east of Assos itself is **Kadırga**, which is becoming increasingly popular— perfect (especially if you have your own transport) for a day or two on the beach and a look at the ruins; enterprising locals are already getting up day trips to Troy from here.

History

Some archaeologists believe the Hittite King Tudhaliyas IV established his colony of Ashachuva on the commanding height, in the 13th century BC, to keep an eye on the Mycenaeans troubling his western frontiers. Greek Assos was founded by Aeolians from Methymna, Lesbos, in the 1st millennium BC. The city was famous for its great archaic Doric temple of Athena (540 BC) that once crowned the very summit of the acropolis.

Assos passed through several hands—Persian and Athenian—and was once governed by a banker and once by a eunuch. The latter was Hermias, a student of Plato at the Academy, who had a chance to apply his teacher's theories of an ideal city-state to his own realm of the Troad and Lesbos. He invited other students of Plato to found a branch of the Academy in Assos, and for three years Plato's greatest student, Aristotle, lived here, founding the sciences of biology and botany, and marrying Hermias' niece. Aristotle's pupil Alexander later captured the city; after that it came under the kings of Pergamon.

In the Middle Ages, several Crusaders' battles took place nearby, until the Ottomans captured Assos in 1330, and at once began to quarry the site to build a mosque and bridge over the Tuzla. The villagers of Behramkale took up the stones when the Ottomans left off; one anonymous Turkish writer describes Behramkale as 'a rusty dagger piercing the walls of Assos'. Perhaps because of this Assos is one of the more dishevelled gardens of weeds along the coast; be prepared to scramble through the prickles to see the remains.

Walls of Assos

Most remarkable, especially in light of the quarrying on the site, are the **walls**, among the best preserved in the whole eastern Greek world. Stretching some two miles, they stand 46ft high in places; they include some excellently preserved gates, each done in a different style. They date back to the mid-4th century BC, perhaps built under the rule of Hermias. Inner walls surround the acropolis and the **Temple of Athena**. Of this once magnificent structure little remains but its platform and a few decorative elements; its Doric friezes are scattered in museums in Paris, Boston and İstanbul. In keeping with the current vogue for the tarting up of Turkey's architectural treasures, the temple's fallen columns are in the process of being re-erected. Where the original fluted stones are missing, hollow concrete replacements have been inserted: just tap to prove it. The bird's-eye view of Lesbos and the Gulf of Edremit on one side and the valley of the Satnioeis on the other makes the climb worthwhile.

Other Hellenistic remains, all in the lower town, include two stoas of the agora (3rd century BC), an agora temple, a bouleuterion, gymnasium and theatre. Architecturally, they resemble the Pergamon style—note the location of the temple in relation to the agora, and the unusual mix of Doric and Ionic orders in the decorative scheme. Outside the main gate in the Hellenistic-Roman **necropolis** are numerous broken sarcophagi; Assos exported similar ones throughout the ancient world. If you're energetic you can hike down to the fine white pebble beach for a swim and a look at the remains of the ancient breakwater.

Gulf of Edremit

The **Gulf of Edremit** is one of the loveliest places in the whole of Turkey. Here are fine sandy beaches, writhing olive groves, dark pine forests and sparkling white seaside villages. To the east loom the bosky slopes of Mount İda (Kaz Dağ) and in the gulf the emerald Alibey islets float in a crystal sea, with the shapely green outline of Lesbos as a backdrop.

Unfortunately the beach resorts that line the gulf have grown so much in recent years that in many places they have now joined up together into a single ribbon of concrete. The first, **Küçükkuyu**, looks idyllic from afar, its harbour filled with bobbing fishing smacks, but closer inspection reveals a grubby, ramshackle little town with little to boast of save a small beach to the west. **Altınoluk**, six miles (10km) east, is a slight improvement. Cleaner and brighter, it has a nice, if small, beach. Halfway between Altınoluk and the next resort, Akçay, the village of **Güre** soothes your aches away in warm, mineral-filled waters, for a small fee.

Above Akçay looms **Mount İda**, venue of the world's first beauty contest, where the judge, Paris, chose Aphrodite as the fairest of the goddesses after she bribed him with the promise of Helen, an ill-fated selection that led ultimately to the Trojan War. **Akçay** itself is another Altınoluk, open and breezy with a welcoming aura, a resort that, whilst it has certainly been 'discovered', has so far refrained from the mass, crass commercialism that so bedevils **Ören**, 15 miles (25km) south at the gulf's epiglottis. The reason for Ören's overdevelopment is quite simple; the beach is the best along the gulf, huge and wide and sandy, backed by a grassy verge that billows with flowers in spring.

Inland between Akçay and Ören, the humble town of **Edremit** can at least pride itself on its antiquity. This was ancient Adramyttium, sacked by Achilles in one of his raids along the coast. It was in Adramyttium that Achilles captured Chryseis, daughter of the priest of Apollo, and gave her as a prize to Agamemnon. The *Iliad* begins with Agamemnon's refusal to accept the father's ransom for the girl. The main road east from here will take you to **Balıkesir**, the equally humble provincial capital of all this area, a city with a grumpy air that seems to be wondering why it is stuck out in the middle of the pine-wooded mountains while all the other towns in the province are having fun on the beach. Balıkesir was the ancient Greek *Paleokastron*, though most of its monuments are Ottoman mosques and tombs from the 14th and 15th centuries.

The Troad **Where to Stay**

Kadırga

expensive

Quite a bit of top-quality accommodation has opened near Behramkale in recent years. Six miles (10km) to the east at Kadırga is the palatial ★★★★**Assos Eden Gardens**, ✆ 0286 764 0290, ✆ 0286 764 0298. It's right on the beach, and offers a huge pool, hamam, jacuzzi, gym and every other conceivable amenity. Almost all the rooms have a sea view; doubles cost $100. The same management also runs the less expensive ★★★**Assos Eden Beach**, ✆ 0286 721 7039, also on the beach 4km from Assos, with windsurfing and sailing on offer; $80 for a double.

Assos

expensive–moderate

With no more space to build on, the hotels along Assos' diminuitive harbour, all converted from old stone houses, cash in on their stunning location. At the western end of the harbour, two old stone houses have been converted into the ★★★**Nazlıhan**, ✆ 0286 721 7064, ✆ 0286 721 7387; its rates are steep at $90, but the rooms are tastefully decorated. Although there's very little difference in quality between them all, the ★★★**Kervansaray**, ✆ 0286 721 7093, ✆ 0286 721 7200, is perhaps the best, with air-con and an outdoor pool for summer, and stone fireplaces and a sauna for winter; doubles with half board $60. The smaller **★★Assos**, ✆ 0286 721 7017, ✉ 0286 721 7249, comes a close second; a little noisier than the Kervansaray, but cheaper at $45 for half board.

inexpensive

Şen Pansiyon, ✆ 0286 721 7076, in a stone house set back from the water's edge, fits the bill for those happy with a plain room for $35. Under the same management is the **Antik Pansiyon**, ✆ 0286 721 7001. Rooms are small and dark with no sea view, hence the price of $24.

The best *pansiyonlar* in Assos are to be found up on the hill, in the village proper (known to dolmuş drivers as Kale). Just a few metres from the entrance to the Athena Temple is the **Timur Pansiyon**, ✆/✉ 0286 721 7449, *www.hitit.co.uk./ timur/*. Some parts of this unpretentious and welcoming place are over 200 years old, with walls over a metre thick. The terrace is perfectly placed for panoramic sunsets: the two owners—a brother-sister team—have never seen the sun set in the same way twice. Be warned: the breakfasts are truly special, different each day and using local ingredients such as village butter. With only five rooms, reservations are recommended; $30–40. Nearby, the **Eris Pansiyon** is another haven, ✆ 0286 721 7080. While it lacks views of the sea, it is one of the calmest lodgings you'll find, overlooking craggy hills of bushes, rocks and poplars. From the breakfast terrace you can hear the tinkling bells of the sheep grazing in the walled pasture below; $26.

Behramkale seems determined to become an upmarket resort, and the cheaper choices are few: the **Plaj Pansiyon** at the eastern end of the harbour, ✆ 0286 721 7193, is about as low-priced as you'll get, with frontier-like rooms for $20 or more.

camping

Next door to the Plaj Pansiyon is **Çakır Camping**, ✆ 0286 721 7048, right by the sea, but with limited space for pitching tents.

Ören

In Ören the **★Otel Urut 2**, ✆ 0266 416 3173, ✉ 0266 412 5250, has a swimming pool, a bar and a restaurant; rates for a double room are $25.

Edremit

Only a malevolent twist of fate would condemn you to a night in Edremit, but at least there's a good hotel there, the **★★Otel Bilgpiçler**, across the street from the pretty town park at Menderes Bulvarı 63, ✆ 0266 374 2255; $24. The only *cheap* option in Edremit is the wretched **Otel Sato**, Park Karşısı; as a rule, any hotel in Turkey called the Sato should be avoided, though don't ask us why.

Akçay

moderate

On the road to Edremit, the **(TK2)Turban Akçay Holiday Village**, ✆ 0266 422 1217, offers many sports facilities, tennis, swimming pool, and water-skiing, and reductions for children; $55, or you can rent your own beach house for $80. There is also a fully-equipped campground as part of the complex.

inexpensive–cheap

On a quiet section of the beach a short walk from the centre of Akçay is the **Yavuz Motel**, Leman Akpınar Caddesi, Sarıkız Mevkii, ✆ 0266 384 3380, ✆ 0266 384 3078. Cool, simple rooms with attached bathrooms cost $35. For activity seekers there are pedaloes, canoes and speedboats for hire. If you want to be in the centre, nestled amongst the cafes and ice cream stands is the ★**Otel Özsoy**, ✆ 0266 384 1190, ✆ 0266 384 2190. Each en suite room has a phone and TV, but much of your time may well be spent on the balcony with its great sea view; $26.

There are pensions galore, all charging in the region of $15 for a double room with en suite facilities. A good choice is the **Denizler Aile Pansiyon**, ✆ 0266 384 1011, with a shady green terrace opening onto the beach, and a few rooms with a sea view. Alternatively, the **Hayat Aile Pansiyon**, ✆ 0266 384 1097, is further back from the sea, but the rooms have large balconies with sea views.

Küçükkuyu

Just east of Küçükkuyu is a strip of campsites, including the shady and quite inexpensive **Truva Camping**, ✆ 0286 752 5206.

The Troad   **Eating Out**

As a rule, restaurants in the region are simple though the food is often delicious.

Assos

Up on the hill, the **Timur Pansiyon** is excellent: the food is always fresh and the menu always changing; $6. Down at the harbour, the seafront hotels all have restaurants full of customers on half-board deals. The food is good and there's often gentle live music to accompany your meal. For a more lively evening, head to the western end, where the open-plan interior of the **Fenerlihan Restaurant and Dance Bar** is filled with voluminous soft rock music.

Edremit

Edremit's favourite since 1924 is the inexpensive **Omür Lokanta** on Menderes Bulvarı, with a wide choice of stews and kebabs for $4.

Altınoluk/Akçay

In Altınoluk, the **Doba** restaurant serves fine fish meals for $8 or less if you haggle hard, and likewise the **Beyaz** restaurant in Akçay.

Küçükkuyu

The **Nür Motel** behind the harbour in Küçükkuyu has a restaurant where you can eat well and cheaply for around $6, while admiring the décor: flying ducks pinned to the wall.

The southernmost of the gulf resorts, **Ayvalık** tends to be largely bypassed by visitors from overseas—inexplicably so. The town has excellent beaches close at hand, several local curiosities to view and the loveliest setting on the gulf, surrounded by an entourage of 25 islands and islets, most uninhabited, all verdant, all rising from the sea like the lost cities of antiquity. Beyond them, its pine-draped cliffs bristling on the horizon, looms the Greek island of Lesbos.

Getting Around

Ayvalık's **bus** station, 1km outside the centre, opposite the new harbour on the road to Edremit, has services to most major towns in western Turkey. Most minibuses to local destinations, however, start from the central square by the old port. In season there are also very frequent minibuses to the beaches around Sarımsaklı.

The **boat** service to Greek Lesbos operates three times a week in summer but only sporadically in winter.

Ayvalık   Tourist Information

In a booth by the harbour, © 0266 312 3158. The extremely helpful office here has deals including a 20% discount on rooms, camping and rental cars if you contact them in advance.

The **Ceylan Bookshop**, in the Süner Pasajı on Talatpaşa Caddesi, has English books and books about the area. The **White Knight Tourist Bazaar**, a tiny shop behind Atatürk's statue, sells a wide range of English newspapers and magazines.

Ayvalık itself was predominantly Greek before 1923 and still retains a faintly Hellenic aura, particularly in its churches, even though most have since been converted into mosques. Unlike most of the other resorts on this stretch of coast, it is an old and sizeable town, with a charming centre of narrow streets of brightly painted houses, and little squares with plane trees. Most of the tourist activity is confined to the port area, lined with cafés, restaurants and excursion boats; from here you can see the long peninsula of **Sarımsaklı** to the left, where the best beaches are, and to the right the conical island of Alibey, Greek Lesbos and, on a reasonably clear day, Mount İda.

Two of the churches in particular are worth a glance, if only to see what a neo-Gothic church looks like with a minaret attached: the **Çınarlı Cami** (once Agios Ioannis) and the **Saat Camii** (Agios Georgios). The latter is the 'clock mosque', so named for the large timepiece that adorns its exterior. Another church, the **Taksiyarhis**, contains a unique collection of icons painted on dried fish skins although, since its doors are permanently locked, there seems to be little hope of ever seeing them. If you pester the tourist office enough, they might—just might—be able to arrange a visit. Make an effort to see the icons now, if you can, for plans are under way to claim this church, too, for Islam. Ayvalık has an organization dedicated to the preservation of its old quarter and the churches, but resources are scant and little can be done.

Try to be in Ayvalık on Thursday, for one of the busiest and most colourful **markets** on the Aegean coast—few tourist trinkets, but dozens of back streets lined with gorgeous produce; all the country folk for miles around come in to see and be seen.

Around Ayvalık

A dozen or so cruise boats permanently haunt Ayvalık's harbour, waiting to carry tourists and trippers off to the dozen or so islands and a number of good beaches. These boats can offer very good value, with all-day trips including a lunch of fish, salad and fruit for $8. If you're lucky, live music may also be thrown into the bargain. One of the prime attractions is **Alibey Island** (also called Cunda Island by the locals), the largest of the island group (for this you really don't need a boat; the island is also connected to the mainland by a causeway). Opposite Ayvalık, it curves around from the north in the shape of a badly drawn treble clef. It furnishes the town with a perfect sheltered harbour and is a popular spot with day-trippers. You can see the island's old Greek houses, now in a desperate state of repair, but most people come here for the beaches.

Two miles south of Ayvalık, the leafy suburb of **Çamlık** is also blessed with a beach but the first prize for sea and sand epiphanies goes to **Sarımsaklı**, three miles (5km) beyond Çamlık. Sarımsaklı may not be to everyone's taste—lots of breezeblock hotels and overpriced restaurants—but its beach is monster-sized and utterly enticing. Yet another huge beach is at **Altınova**, a further five miles (8km) to the south.

A short dolmuş ride from Ayvalık or Sarımsaklı, a couple of geological oddities lie in wait: the **Devil's Dinner Table** (Şeytan Sofrası), a large, flat, round rock on a promontory protruding into the Aegean, and, on the hill adjacent, another flat rock from which two slender outcrops rise vertically to a height of 13ft. They look like **rabbit's ears**, hence their name. Inland from Ayvalık, on the road to Bergama, you'll be skirting the truly imposing massif of the Madra Dağı, a beautiful and totally unspoiled area (if you have a car that can take it, consider continuing on to Bergama via the bad, partially unpaved mountain road through it instead of the coastal route).

Lesbos

Greece's third-largest island, Lesbos is also commonly called Mytilini after its capital, the destination of the little ferries from Ayvalık. The island has its charms, but it isn't really the place to go for a day trip unless you simply want a taste of Greece—it's fine for that, being one of the less touristy islands; Lesbos is more concerned with its olive trees, of which there are about eleven million. **Mytilini**, under its Byzantine-Genoese castle, is an attractive town, with antique shops, a Hellenistic theatre and a number of interesting museums, including one dedicated to the works of Theophilos, Lesbos's famous naïve artist.

Most visitors to Lesbos stay a few days and tour the quiet rural parts, where sights include ruins of a Roman aqueduct, several beaches, yet another Mount Olympos, a few Byzantine churches and monasteries and, of all things, a petrified forest, at **Sigri** in the northern part of the island.

Ayvalık

inexpensive

Ayvalık has plenty of good hotels at very reasonable rates, but none that is truly outstanding. The ***Kaptan** at Balıkhane Sokak 7 near the harbour, ✆ 0266 312 8834, ✉ 0266 312 1271, is the best of the mid-range hotels, with a patio butting right up against the Aegean. Private parking, views of Alibey Island and double rooms with bath for $22; the friendly proprietor speaks English. Ring ahead to reserve one of the three rooms with a sea view, and look out for the wonderful photo of local bigwigs in the 1920s posing in front of a flying boat in Ayvalık harbour.

cheap

After the Kaptan the best deal in town is the **Kıyı Motel**, Gümrük Meydanı, ✆ 0266 312 6677. Each small room is packed with the full list of requisites for much grander hotels: tiny en suite shower, TV, minibar, hairdryer, phone—it just leaves little space for you and your things. Rooms at the front have views of the sea, but also of a car park, which makes the Kıyı a noisier option than the Kaptan; great value, though, at $15 per double. Seekers of space can stretch out or swing cats to their heart's content at the rather soulless **Ayvalık Palas** next door to the Kıyı, ✆ 0266 312 1064, ✉ 0266 312 1046; doubles with private shower $18. The local diving school, offering PADI courses and scuba hire is based downstairs.

Almost all the cheap accommodation is found in the centre of Ayvalık where you are spoilt for choice. Near the harbour, the **Yalı Pansiyon**, ✆ 0266 312 2423, is a charming, family-run establishment. Housed in an old Greek mansion, with a garden leading out to the sea, a grandiose staircase and delicate ornamentation, its cavernous rooms go for $7 per person. There are only eight of them, however, so it's best to phone ahead. Bathroom facilities here are shared.

In the backstreets leading up the hill from the seafront are three pensions that are so atmospheric you'll be tempted to spend a night in each one. All have shared bathroom facilities and cost about $7 per person. The first of the three, the **Taksiyarhis**, next to the church of the same name at Mareşal Çakmak Caddesi 71, ✆ 0266 312 1494, is run by an Austrian-Turkish couple. It is really three old stone houses knocked into one, creating a warren of old wooden staircases and secluded rooms, popular with backpackers and families alike. Follow the signs directing you to **Chez Beliz**, a grand old house with its top floor jutting out into the street, also on Mareşal Çakmak Caddesi, ✆ 0266 312 4897. Run by Beliz, an ex-actress with a passion for cooking, it's an experience not to be missed. The imposing **Bonjour**, Mareşal Çakmak Caddesi, 5.ci Sokak, ✆ 0266 312 8085, has a genuine reason for indulging in French nomenclature: it was the 19th-century home of a French priest who did a bit of work on the side as French ambassador to the Sublime Porte. Lovingly restored into a pension in the mid-1990s, its courtyard is so relaxing that you may find that breakfast drifts into lunch, followed by an afternoon pick-me-up—oh, alright, just one more...

Sarımsaklı

moderate–inexpensive

The plush hotels here are all out by the big beach at Sarımsaklı. One especially nice one is the **★★Büyük Berk Otel**, ✆ 0266 324 1045, 🖷 0266 324 1194 (the name means 'the Big Strong Hotel'). It's set pleasantly on the beach, with double rooms with balconies for $45. Most of Sarımsaklı's hotels are hastily slung-up budget constructions that suffer from over-exposure to tourists. The **★★Ankara Hotel**, ✆ 0266 324 1195, 🖷 0266 324 0022, is one of the better ones, with a terrace bar and television in some rooms; $25. For a little bit more, you can get a pool and rooms with balconies at the **★★Billurcu**, ✆ 0266 324 1188, 🖷 0266 324 1751.

cheap

Anything under $15 is hard to find in Sarımsaklı. You could try the **Zafer Pansiyon**, north of the PTT building, ✆ 0266 324 1168.

Alibey Island

moderate

The attractive **★★★Cunda**, ✆ 0266 327 1943, 🖷 0266 312 9638, is a low, motel-style place with balconied rooms right on the beach. The hotel offers opportunities for water sports. Doubles £50.

inexpensive–cheap

The **Ortunç**, ✆ 0266 327 1120, 🖷 0266 312 1271, is a simple place hidden away in spacious grounds between a pine forest and a quiet beach on the far side of the island. Rooms cost about $30. It also has a campground. There are a number of *pansiyonlar*, including the *cheap* **Günay Motel**, by the port, which also has a nice, simple restaurant; ✆ 0266 327 1048.

camping

In a peaceful, isolated setting on the far end of the island is the **Ada Camping**, ✆ 0266 327 1211, with shade, a restaurant and a beach.

Altınova

Near the beach, the **Kazan Motel**, ✆ 0266 343 7100, is quiet, comfortable and set in a pleasant garden; $15 with bath.

Ayvalık and Around   **Eating Out**

Ayvalık

There are several good restaurants clustered around the Atatürk statue, at the angle of the port. The best of these is the **Şehir Club**, a private establishment on the tip of the harbour which is nevertheless open to foreigners. With a clientele of demanding local businessmen, the Şehir always has an impressive range of mezes, as well as meat dishes and fish charged by the kilo (agree on the price before you order it); $8 and upwards.

Also good for fish, but at slightly higher prices, are the **Öz Canlı Balık** at Sahilboyu 3 and the **Kardeşler** next door, both with tables overlooking the harbour and fish meals from $9. For landbound fare, try the traditional Ottoman soups, stews and kebabs at the **Osmanlı Mutfağı**, near the Ayvalık Palas Otel; $4.

Leading off inland from the main street 50m north of the Atatürk statue is **Tenekeciler Sokağı**, 'tinmakers' street', now heaving with *meyhaneler* and cheap lokantas. Dining here can be a smoky, raucous experience, especially when the soccer's on. **Hüsnu'nün Yeri**, with no-nonsense Hüsnu at the helm, offers the perennial lokanta favourites, as well as small fish, calamari and prawn dishes (again, check what you're getting for your money before ordering); $5. But don't forget the 'big Turkish dinner' that beckons at **Chez Beliz** (*see* 'Where to Stay').

Alibey Island

The causeway between the mainland and Alibey Island is one long row of bright fish restaurants. On Cumhuriyet Caddesi in the village, the **Lyra** offers a wide choice of mezes and seafood and an outdoor terrace; $7 and up. On the harbour front, the **Canlı Balık** restaurant (not to be confused with the Öz ('real') Canlı Balık in Ayvalık) is the perfect place for fish from $9.

Otherwise, the **Papalina** on the old road into Alibey from Ayvalık is very popular with locals and holidaying Turks, set in an atmospheric wooden building with fish nets hanging up outside and in; $9.

Aeolia

The Aeolian Greeks came from Thessaly or Boeotia, perhaps as early as the 12th century BC, and until the Persian conquest Aeolia survived as a quiet little nation, with its capital at Mytilini on Lesbos. Aeolia was famed in antiquity for the fertility of its soil, so fertile, it seems, that the early Greek colonists spent all their labours tilling it, with little time left over for the intellectual pursuits and adventures that preoccupied the Ionians to the south. But it is here in Aeolia that we find Bergama, ancient Pergamon, a city that rivalled Athens and Alexandria as a cultural centre in its day.

Getting Around

Bergama is the **minibus** transportation hub of the area, although if you go there on any bus that doesn't end its run there, you'll be left on the highway 4½ miles (7km) from town and have to catch a minibus in, which can be a problem. If you mean to come here on a day trip, arrange your transportation back in advance, or you may be stranded in the evening.

From Bergama's otogar there are minibuses every half-hour to Dikili; Dikili has a weekly **ferry** to Lesbos in summer. Direct **buses** from Bergama and İzmir also serve Eski Foça but they are infrequent. You may have to take an İzmir-bound bus from Bergama: ask to be let off at the Eski Foça junction and trust to either luck or a **dolmuş** to carry you the remaining 16 miles (26km).

Bergama: Hükümet Konağı, B Blok, Zemin Kat, ℗ 0232 633 2851.

Eski Foça: Atatürk Bulvarı, on the entrance to town, ℗ 0232 812 1222.

Pergamon (Bergama)

In the last two centuries BC, Pergamon may well have been the most beautiful and sophisticated city in the Mediterranean world. It was not an original Aeolian foundation, but rather a Hellenistic city state, a creation of Alexander's heirs. Although inhabited before Alexander, the site never amounted to much—a minor Greek-Persian satrapy, first mentioned in 399 BC in Xenophon's *Anabasis*. Doubtless, had it been nearer the sea, it would have thrived much earlier, for few cities could boast such a splendid defensible site, a citadel 1,300ft above the surrounding plain, with streams flowing below on two sides. When Alexander's general, Lysimachus, came into a fabulous fortune—9,000 talents, the spoils of war in the Troad— Pergamon seemed the perfect place to safeguard the treasure. Lysimachus died without an heir in 281 BC, and the man he set to watch over the loot, a certain Philetairos, simply kept it, using the money to wine and dine friends and build monuments in Pergamon. His adopted son Eumenes is the first of the famous Kings of Pergamon; Eumenes' adopted son Attalus (ruled 241–197 BC) gave the rulers their dynastic title, the Attalids.

Attalus I

Attalus I was audacious and spent much of his reign fighting for more territory; most notably, he stood up to the bellicose Gauls of Galatia, who were running a proto-protection racket in Anatolia. Upon his refusal to pay they came to collect, a fierce crew, outnumbering the Pergamene defenders, who were reluctant to fight against the odds. However, Attalus ordered a sacrifice to the gods, and miracle!—plainly written on the victim's lungs was the word 'Victory'. Inspired, the Pergamenes soundly thrashed the Gauls. Only later was it discovered that the priest offering the sacrifice, or more probably Attalus himself, had written the word backwards in ink on his hand and pressed it on the entrails when no one was looking. But even if the augury was a cheat, Attalus had freed western Anatolia from a serious threat, and in honour of the victory over the barbarians his successor, Eumenes II, erected the famous Altar of Zeus.

Eumenes II

Eumenes II ruled Pergamon at the height of its power and influence. But just as the city owed its initial prosperity to the luck of a treasure deposit, it owed its great rise in prestige to a second lucky break. Attalus had kindly sent the superstitious Romans the meteorite-cult statue of Cybele, the Great Mother Goddess of Asia (the Romans hoarded cult statues of their conquests, to keep the gods of conquered provinces in line), and in return the Romans, upon defeating Antiochus the Great at Magnesia (190 BC), gave Pergamon Antiochus' provinces of Asia Minor, stretching from the coast to Konya. Relations between Rome and Pergamon became even closer as Eumenes assisted Rome militarily against its enemies, including the most worrying, Hannibal, who ended up in Bithynia after his defeat at Zama and, according to tradition, died and was buried in İznik. Eumenes' brother, Attalus II, continued his policy of helping Rome, especially in the subjugation of Greece.

Attalus III

But it was his nephew, Attalus III, who recognized the inevitable, and amazed the classical world by willing Pergamon to Rome when he died in 133 BC. Some accounted it a Roman trick, and, perhaps as a result, a body of stories has grown up attesting to Attalus III's eccentricities: that he loved his mother so well that he took the title 'Philomater', that he was obsessed with poisonous plants, which he fed to condemned criminals to try out his antidotes, and that he never went out in public except to tend to his mother's tomb, where one day, in the heat, he fainted and died, only five years into his reign. Rome had no problem in accepting Attalus' bequest, and according to the terms of the will left Pergamon a free city. This state of affairs lasted until 88 BC, when Mithridates Pontus came to 'liberate' the Greek states from Rome and ordered all Romans massacred, an order the Pergamenes carried out with great zeal.

When Rome, in return, defeated Mithridates, Pergamon lost all its rights; 40 years later it even lost its greatest treasure, its library, when Antony looted its 200,000 volumes and gave them to Cleopatra, ending once and for all the rivalry between the libraries of Alexandria and Pergamon. Pergamon gradually dwindled after that. Up on the acropolis, any walls of cheap mixed brick and stone you see probably date from Byzantine or Selcuk times.

The Site

Open daily 8.30 until sunset; adm.

The average visitor is attracted first to Ephesus, where the ruins are more substantial, or Troy, where there's a story everyone knows. But use your eyes and your imagination a bit, and you may find Pergamon the most totally captivating site of all classical cities. The key to everything is the tremendously high acropolis. Try to catch sight of it from wherever you are in the town or on the plain, and imagine it as it was under Eumenes or Attalus, crowned with spectacular marble temples, and with a plume of smoke continually rising from the Altar of Zeus.

At its height, Pergamon had a population of well over 100,000. It spilled down the precipitous slope, making nearly every building visible from the valley and creating the impression of a single work of architecture. The city was blessed not only with its natural setting, but also with unreasonable portions of wealth and talent. Its architects and sculptors were among the finest in the Hellenistic world. To see the best of their creations you have to go to the Pergamon Museum in Berlin (where much was damaged in the last war), but the assiduous Germans left enough behind for us at least to conjure up an image of this fantastical city of dreams.

To see the ruins of Pergamon in a day without a car, you'll probably have to invest in four taxi trips: to the acropolis and back, and to the Asklepieon and back. If you only have one day, the best thing to do with it is to take a taxi up to the acropolis, then walk back down along the ancient main street. It isn't easy finding the path, but it can be done and it's worth the attempt.

Pergamon

Acropolis

- Arsenals
- Barracks and Hellenistic Tower
- Temple of Trajan
- Temple of Dionysus
- Library
- Palace of Attalus I
- Palace of Eumenes II
- Temple of Athena
- Theatre Terrace
- Theatre
- Heroon
- Altar of Zeus
- Agora

ACROPOLIS

1000metres
1000yards

N

Acropolis
parking
mid town
ancient road

1 2
3
4
5

6

aqueduct

Asklepieon
parking
10 7
11
9
13
12

BERGAMA
military zone

military zone

1 Temple of Demeter
2 Temenos of Hera Basilica
3 Upper Gymnasium
4 Middle Gymnasium, stairway e
5 Lower Agora
6 Temple of Serapis (Kızıl Avlu)
7 Colonnaded Street
8 Theatre
9 Temple of Asklepieos
10 Library
11 Fountain
12 Round Building
13 South Stoa/Latrine

Acropolis

The majestic **acropolis** looms behind the modern town, from where there is a paved road to the top (it's a stiff climb of over 3km, so you may want to spring for a taxi). Since 1878, when a German railway engineer and amateur archaeologist named Karl Humann began digging here, the Germans have completed four major excavations in Pergamon, and currently a fifth is under way. One project in progress is the reconstruction of the columns of the **Temple of Trajan**, at the highest level of the acropolis; it is the only structure dating wholly from Roman times. Both Trajan and his son Hadrian were remembered here; their two huge marble heads, found in the temple, are now in Berlin. Hadrian, one of the most cultured of the emperors and a great friend of Pergamon, built the Temple as centrepiece of an important complex, modelled after the great Forum of Hadrian in Rome. It may have included a library, as in Rome—perhaps intended as recompense for the Roman theft of the original. The pseudo-Egyptian capitals around the stoa are an unusual touch.

Directly behind the temple stood the Hellenistic **barracks** and **tower**, which were perfectly located for the view over the plain. Adjoining the barracks to the south were the two **palaces**, peristyle mansions of the kings of Pergamon, of which not much remains except walls and cisterns. Water was always a headache in the citadel, and anyone caught polluting the reserves was punished.

Up on the acropolis, you'll notice one telling piece of evidence of Pergamon's early decline. The tops of the walls, built under Roman rule, use plenty of recycled marble from earlier Greek buildings.

Library

Southwest of the palaces stood the renowned two-storey **library** begun by Attalus II, which at its height had some 200,000 volumes. Eumenes II in particular was obsessed with acquiring books, and had a naughty habit of borrowing and not returning. For books by Aristotle and Theophrastus he is said to have paid their weight in gold.

The Pergamene library became so great that it excited the jealousy of the Ptolemies in Egypt, whose library at Alexandria was its only serious rival. As a result Egypt banned the export of papyrus. All books at the time were written on long scrolls of this brittle stuff; but Eumenes, undeterred, offered a large reward to anyone who could come up with a replacement. A certain Crates of Smyrna recalled the old Ionian custom of writing on sheepskins treated with lime and dried. This 'Pergamon paper' became known as parchment and, as it was too thick to roll up like papyrus, the codex or modern paged book was invented. Pergamon's library survived in Alexandria until the 7th century; the Christians have a story that the Arabs used the books to stoke the fires in their baths after they conquered the city, while Muslim historians say that Christian fanatics had torched them all long before.

The Theatre

A **temple of Athena** stood next to the library, of which little more than the foundations remain. The Athena of this temple was Athena Nikephoros, or 'she who grants victory' and it is thought that the original of the famous 'Dying Gaul' now in the Capitoline Museum in Rome once stood in its precincts. From the temple a narrow stair-passage descends to the

Greek Theatre. It's not unusual to find ancient theatres carved into hillsides, offering spectators not only a view of the stage but a panoramic backdrop as well, but this is an extreme case; nowhere will you find a theatre so dizzyingly steep and dramatic, resembling an immense fan cut into the rock. Its 80 rows of seats could hold 10,000 spectators. A **Temple of Dionysus**, the god of wine and theatrical festivals, stood off to the audience's right, closing one end of the long promenade of the **Theatre Terrace**; since the stage of the theatre was portable, it could be removed at the end of a performance to permit access to the terrace (where the post holes for the wooden set can still be seen). Architecturally, the Dionysus Temple (also known as the Caracalla) is considered a landmark—set high on a platform, closed on three sides, it is the prototype of many later temples in Rome.

Altar of Zeus

As you walk over the acropolis, consider the method behind the Greek planners' seemingly haphazard arrangement of monuments. The great **Altar of Zeus** stood on the terrace below the temple of Athena. Built during the age of Eumenes II, this was one of the outstanding monuments of the Hellenistic age, shaped like a horseshoe and covered with the famous high reliefs portraying a battle between the Olympian gods and the Titans, symbolic of Pergamon's (or civilization's) victory over the barbaric Gauls. There was another connection. With the presumption possible only to the heirs of Alexander, Eumenes and his family pretended that Telephos, the son of Hercules (who figures prominently in the reliefs), was the founder of their dynasty. These reliefs are in Berlin; all that remains on the acropolis are the altar's foundations. The Turkish government and the city of Bergama have been trying to get them back for decades, without much success.

To the south of the altar, on a lower terrace, are the remains of the **Upper Agora** and its temple, in a mixture of Ionic and Doric orders, a common trait of Pergamene buildings that spread throughout the Mediterranean world. The Altar of Zeus was Karl Humann's greatest discovery (he found it incorporated into a Byzantine wall); a life-size reconstruction, along with those reliefs, is the star attraction in the Berlin museum. Humann is buried here, just below the Upper Agora.

Mid-town Pergamon

Recently much of the **ancient road**, connecting upper Pergamon to the **mid-town area**, has been cleared. While the acropolis was reserved for the kings, nobility and officers, regular citizens lived in the mid-town, which also has several important public buildings. Excavations in 1973 uncovered the **Odeion** and a 'Marble Hall' which have both been reconstructed—a fascinating sight few visitors to Pergamon ever see. Further on, mysteries (initiations) similar to those at Eleusis took place in the enormous **Temple of Demeter**, erected by Philetairos and later enlarged by the wife of Attalus II, Apollonia. The temple—with its pit for the blood of sacrifices, fountain, and rows of seats for spectators of the mysteries—has unusual archaic palm leaf capitals. Near here are three terraces, each with a gymnasium. Young men trained and studied in the huge **upper gymnasium**, which doubled as an auditorium for ceremonial occasions with its small theatre; Attalus II created it, though what you see is largely a Roman-era rebuilding. The **middle gymnasium** was reserved for adolescent boys, and the third served as the children's playground. The

stairway entrance connecting the lowest level to the second is one of the finest pieces of workmanship in all Pergamon, an early and well-preserved example of vault and arch construction.

The main street through the mid-town was remarkably narrow, though paved with massive blocks, worn by pedestrians and scored by chariot wheels. Along it are the ruins of shops and houses. Especially interesting here is the peristyle **House of Attalus**, a fair example of how the upper classes of Pergamon lived. Beyond the house in the **Lower Agora**, the famous head of Alexander, now in the İstanbul museum, was discovered.

If you've made it this far down, you'll already see the edge of modern Bergama below. The rest of the ancient street is unexcavated and unmarked, but steep as it is, you should be able to pick your way down, finally ending up in some woebegone, cobbled back streets near the Temple of Serapis where the children and dogs will stare at you as if you had just dropped down from Mars.

Remains in the Modern Town

Modern Bergama has engulfed lower Pergamon, with one monumental exception. The Turks call it *Kızıl Avlu*, the Red Courtyard. This red brick mastodon originally served as a **Temple of Serapis**, or Osiris, the resurrected Egyptian god. According to legend, the thousands of bricks in the temple were relayed to the site from hand to hand in a great human chain, so they would be neither on earth nor in the sky; indeed the whole temple is built over the Selinos stream, which still runs through an ancient tunnel below. Other underground chambers and tunnels had a religious significance. One of the temple's two massive towers now contains a mosque. The whole building was converted into a basilica by the early Christians. The church of Pergamon was one of the seven churches of Asia addressed by St John in his *Apocalypse* (*Revelations*), singled out as possessing the 'throne of the Devil'—interpreted as the Altar of Zeus, or more probably as the seat of Roman authority.

Modern Bergama itself is a shabby and dusty sort of town; at first glance you would guess it was built around a factory rather than a major tourist attraction. It does have a fine little **Archaeology and Ethnographic Museum** (*open 8.30–5.30, closed Mon; adm*), where there is a small model of the Altar of Zeus and some finds from the site, including two statues of hermaphrodites. The courtyard is filled with reliefs and other architectural fragments; look out for a wonderful figure of Cerberus, the three-headed hound of hell, and another relief with a poppy. Inside, there are some lovely terracotta ex votos to Asklepieos, the god of healing—an ear or a finger to show what part the god cured—and a Roman mosaic with the head of Medusa. Also present is that staple of all Mediterranean archaeology museums, a big nude statue of Emperor Hadrian (one of the greatest and most useful of all Roman rulers; unabashedly gay, and *such* a tease).

Asklepieon

A few arches of an aqueduct remain in the modern town; if you walk up the maze of streets towards them you'll eventually find the short cut to ancient Pergamon's **Asklepieon**, the sanctuary of healing (*open daily 8.30–5.30, until 7pm in summer; adm*). You can drive there: take the road that branches off next to the tourist office, passing a large military base.

Pergamon had the most renowned Asklepieon in Greek Asia, and produced one of the best physicians of the ancient world, Galen (AD 131–201), personal doctor of Marcus Aurelius. Asklepieos, the god of healing, was the son of Apollo, and his priests, like Galen, treated the faithful with surprisingly modern methods—diet, baths, music and exercise in a lovely environment, combined with dream interpretation and auto-suggestion. Over the entrance of the sanctuary were inscribed the words, 'By order of the gods Death may not enter here'.

The sanctuary in Pergamon predates the kings of Pergamon and reached its greatest extent in the 2nd century AD, when the hellenophile Emperor Hadrian endowed it with most of the structures you see today. The **Sacred Way**, a wide colonnaded street that led to the Asklepieon from the Roman town, leads you to the entrance gate, or **Propylon**, of which only a few steps remain. Within an open space is the circular **temple of Zeus-Asklepieos**, at one time covered with a dome, modelled after the Pantheon in Rome, which was yet another of Hadrian's works.

Beyond lie the main grounds of the Asklepieon itself, encompassed by three long stoae; there patients could sit in the shade or be sheltered from the rain. When bored, they could use the library, a square building north of the temple. The sanctuary's theatre, off the end of the north portico, could seat 3,500 and is believed to have been used to entertain both patients and locals. A sacred spring flowed in to the nearby fountain with marble steps. Such water was very important in the healing process: an analysis in the 1970s found it to be mildly radioactive. There are two other fountains in the sanctuary: a drinking well near the entrance of the sacred Tunnel, and a carved rock pool near the west stoa, used for the frequently prescribed mud baths.

The Sacred Tunnel

The **Tunnel**, 266ft long, leads from the centre of the sanctuary to a mysterious two-storey brick structure, built in Roman times, and believed to be a **Temple of Telesphoros**, a minor medical deity. Another treatment centre, it was added on to the original Asklepieon rather like a modern hospital annexe. The tunnel itself was more than a passageway: while patients walked through its shadows, the doctor-priests would whisper healing suggestions.

The **south stoa** near here had to be supported on columns to attain the level of the rest of the sanctuary, producing a cryptoporticus you can walk through; at the far end is a luxurious marble **latrine** for men, and a small, less well-appointed one for the women; both, however, had to use mussel shells in lieu of toilet paper. The central Asklepieon proper had shrines to the several gods of healing, Hygiea and Apollo among them, and incubation chambers where patients slept, hoping for a dream from the god to guide them in their cure.

Dikili

Cruise ships call at **Dikili**, the port of ancient Pergamon and the nearest beach which is safe for children. Though it's a growing resort, there's not much else to Dikili, other than some mildly attractive back alleys, a simple monument erected in memory of the assassinated Swedish Prime Minister Ölaf Palme (who visited Dikili in 1968) and a string of waterfront bars. South of Dikili, there is a quieter, smaller resort at **Çandarlı**, set under a Genoese castle that has been so enthusiastically restored it seems a stage prop.

Between Bergama and İzmir, the coast is dotted with Aeolian cities, of which little remains beyond their names. **Pitane**, the northernmost city of the Aeolian Confederacy (modern **Çandarlı**), has a picturesque 13th-century Venetian castle next to the small beach. To the south stood **Gryneion** (**Temasalık Burnu**), once renowned for its temple and oracle of Apollo, of which only a mound in a field remains. Continuing south, **Myrina** was said to have been founded by the Queen of the Amazons, and beyond that, on the coast, stood the once-great **Cyme**. Both contributed too much building material to modern **Aliağa** to be of any interest today.

Eski Foça (Foça)

In the *Odyssey*, Homer tells of the Sirens, whose beautiful songs lured sailors to their death. They would sail towards the wonderful voices and be shipwrecked on the sharp rocks on which the Sirens sat. The cunning Odysseus, who had to sail past the Sirens on his voyage home, managed to evade disaster yet still enjoy their singing by ordering his crew to bind him to the mast and then to block their own ears with beeswax. Of the many places across the Mediterranean that claim the Sirens, **Eski Foça** (Old Foça, often called just Foça) puts in one of the better bids with its jagged **Siren Rocks** just off the shore that whine and howl when the wind blows through them. How the sailors could have found such a banshee-like wailing so enchanting is another question entirely, but that's Eski Foça's story and they're sticking to it.

Today, tourists sunbathe on the Siren Rocks, as they do on most of the beaches near Eski Foça, for this little town, occupying a promontory between two deeply indented bays, has now become an attractive resort. The town has not been swamped, however, and still retains a workaday atmosphere, thanks to the good fishing off its shores. The fishermen are not the only ones who appreciate the rich fishing grounds off Eski Foça: it is one of the last remaining habitats of **monk seals**, and in 1991 the town and its sea were declared a protection zone for these lively but reclusive beasts. Eski Foça's inhabitants take this responsibility seriously, to the extent that the obligatory statue of Atatürk in the main square has been replaced by a stone seal. In spite of all their best efforts, however, fewer than a dozen monk seals remain in the area.

Eski Foça was ancient **Phocaea**, the northernmost Ionian city, and unlike its Aeolian neighbours always looked to the sea, boasting one of the best harbours in the area. The seafarers of Phocaea founded numerous colonies, most famously Marsalla (Marseilles) and Elea in Italy (where Zeno wrote his nasty paradoxes). Again, almost all the stone that remained of ancient Phocaea went into the medieval castle on the shore. Still standing, oddly enough, is the so-called **Taş Kule**, a mysterious 8th-century BC tomb, believed to have been built by the Phrygians or Lydians. It's along the Eski road, where you just might mistake it for an Art Deco petrol station.

Yeni Foça (New Foça), little sister of Eski, is some 12 miles (20km) to the north, a pleasant village with pleasant beaches that attracts the likes of the Club Méditerranée.

Bergama

expensive–moderate

Bergama has a few good hotels—but when it's crowded in summer the best way to do the sights might be as a day trip from Ayvalık. Nearly all accommodation in the town is near the main road, so traffic noise can be a problem. Clustered on the İzmir road just out of town are a number of hotels, the best of which is the ★★★**Berksoy**, ✆ 0232 633 2595, ✉ 0232 633 5346, with balconied rooms facing a park, pool and tennis, and satellite TV in each room; $65. If they're full, settle for the ★★★**Asude** opposite, ✆ 0232 633 3179, ✉ 0232 632 0512. Rooms at the back are relatively quiet, some with bathtubs. For more intensive aquatherapy, a sauna and hamam await downstairs. Doubles $50. Conveniently located in the centre of town in a side street opposite the museum, is the ★★**Anıl**, Hatuniye Caddesi 4, ✆ 0232 631 1830. Opened in 1999, it has a good rooftop restaurant and very colourful rooms with air-con, TV and en suite bathtubs; $45.

inexpensive–cheap

Next to the Berksoy and under the same management as the Anıl is the ★★**Efsane**, ✆ 0232 632 6350, ✉ 0232 632 6353; its rooftop pool makes up for the outdated rooms at $35.

As with Bergama's hotels, most of its pensions are prey to street noise, two exceptions being the Athena and the Nike *pansiyonlar* in the old quarter. You could follow the helpful signs egging you on to them, but this may result in hours of wandering down the narrow back lanes in a fruitless search. From the main road through the centre of town facing the Acropolis, turn left at the Sağlam 2 restaurant. When you reach the picturesque old bridge, look around until you see the **Athena** at Barbaros Mahallesi İmam Çıkmazı 5. It's well worth the effort of finding, offering good views of the Acropolis. The main building is 160 years old, with rooms full of character: one has a built-in safe by 'Les Fils de S.O. Nicolaidis, Smyrna'. Other facilities of a lesser vintage include a satellite TV and washing machine. Three rooms have en suite facilites, costing $7 per person; rooms without are $5. Across the stone bridge, the 300-year-old **Nike**, Tabak Köprü Çıkmazı, ✆ 0232 633 3901, has recently been restored, with large rooms and a courtyard full of flowers; $8 per person.

On the other side of town, just off the main road, is the **Böblingen**, Asklepion Caddesi 2, ✆ 0232 633 2153, a friendly, modern family pension that serves up an excellent breakfast. The cool rooms in the annexe to the rear escape most of the road noise; $8 per person with private bathroom facilities, $7 without. The **Berksoy Hotel** (*see* above) has a well-equipped campground, ✆ 0232 633 2595—you get to use their pool, too.

camping

A few metres up the road, the less expensive **Caravan Camping**, ✆ 0232 633 3902, has a restaurant and pool.

Dikili

Right next to the otogar in Dikili is the ★★★**Ünmetoğlu**, ✆ 0232 671 9030; comfortable rooms with air-con and balconies, but the only views of the sea are from the top floor; $40. For a little more, you can do much better at the ★★★**Mysia Hotel** with a pool, watersports and its own private stretch of beach 3km outside Dikili at Geren Mevkii, ✆ 0232 671 7010, ✉ 0232 671 4987.

cheap

Dikili has some nice pensions north of the bus station and some filthy flea-pits on the main road towards the harbour and in the old town. The **Halat Pansiyon**, ✆ 0232 671 4825, and the **Dikili Pansiyon**, ✆ 0232 671 2454, are both on the road into town, hardly romantic hideaways, but clean and good value at $7 per person.

Eski Foça

moderate

Eski Foça is awash with hotels, *pansiyonlar* and restaurants, although the best rooms with the sea views are often booked out in summer. The **Karaçam**, Sahil Caddesi 70, ✆ 0232 812 1416, ✉ 0232 812 2042, offers nice rooms in a restored old house facing the sea, with trawlers tied up out front; $46. For a more modern alternative in the same price range, you could try the ★★**Hanedan**, ✆ 0232 812 1515, near the beach with its own restaurant.

inexpensive

If being off the busy main strip is more important than a sea view, head for the **Hotel Amphora**, İsmet Paşa Mah., 208 Sokak 7, ✆ 0232 812 2806, ✉ 0232 812 2483, *amphorah@superonline.com*. The lobby is decorated with, you guessed it, amphorae, and there's a small terrace and pool at the back; $28.

Eski Foça has some lovely pensions, the best of which is the **Huzur**, with its perfect seafront location next to a small strip of sandy beach at İsmet Paşa Mah., 139 Sokak 5, ✆ 0232 812 1203, ✉ 0232 812 6647. The basic, clean rooms have balconies on the seaward side covered in foliage. The shady breakfast terrace edges onto the sea; doubles $20. If this is full, the nearby **İyigün**, Sahil Caddesi 155 Sokak 1, ✆ 0232 812 1182, has rooms with huge sea windows and balconies for $24.

cheap

If you're on a tight budget, the **Zeki** on Hükümet Caddesi, ✆ 0232 616 1280, owned by Zeki, a friendly Kurd from Erzurum, has very plain and simple en suite doubles with large balconies for $12.

Bergama to Eski Foça   ***Eating Out***

Bergama has a pitiful few inexpensive lokantas, almost all just south of the bus station on İzmir Caddesi, such as the **Ozan 2**, with decent *pide* and soup. A few gruesome locations try to tempt tourists with signs like 'Flat Bread with the Soup; Meatball in the Tile!' But just when you think you're going to starve to death here, you find the **Pergamon Pansiyon** on Bankalar Caddesi (the main street's name in the town centre), and one of the most gratifying dining experiences to be had in these parts, for about $7. The restaurant is in an enclosed courtyard, with two fountains and lots of cushions everywhere, Ottoman-style. The menu, in Turkish and English, enigmatically offers 'Ladies' Things' for a very reasonable $2. Otherwise *börekler* and other mezes are excellent, the kebabs are damn spicy all right, and they serve beer. All Bergama seems to come here in the evenings, and upstairs there's a primitive bar/disco in winter.

Dikili has a good selection of waterfront restaurants serving fresh fish. Being a resort, **Eski Foça** provides good fare, particularly at the **Ali Baba Restaurant** ($8) near the otogar on Büyükdeniz Sahil Caddesi, and at the **Pizza Milano** at Kücükdeniz Sahil 58 (pizza and a glass of wine $5). On the same road, the **Celep Restaurant** on the waterfront, with a good selection of fish dishes and grills, is well placed for watching the sun sink below the waves.

İzmir

Of all the ancient Greek cities on the coast of Asia Minor, only **İzmir** (old Smyrna) has survived as a city into modern times. Why İzmir, and not Sardis or Pergamon or Ephesus or Miletus? Partly because of a good deep harbour that can't silt up, and partly simple luck of the draw; while the city has suffered much from history and earthquakes, it has never been completely destroyed like so many others. Few cities can boast such a splendid situation, at the head of a long narrow gulf, spread out beneath the flat-topped hill known as Mount Pagus by the Greeks and more picturesquely as the Velvet Castle (Kadifekale) by the Turks.

Now Turkey's third city, with over three million people, İzmir is still a new, rough creature, rebuilt from the ground up after the fire and population exchange of 1922. Understandably, it is still a city in search of an identity. To get an idea of what up-to-date, hard-working İzmir thinks, ask someone there what they think of Ankara or especially İstanbul. You'll learn a new word in Turkish: *yaramaz*, or useless. 'İstanbul *yaramaz!*' Similarly, ask for a *simit* on the streets of İzmir and you'll get one; but if you use the local word, *gevrek*, you'll get one with a smile.

History

Surprisingly, when the Aeolian colonists arrived in the 10th century BC, they chose not the present site of İzmir but a small peninsula at the end of the gulf, called Bayraklı. One day, while the entire city was out celebrating the Dionysia, Ionians from Colophon sneaked in and took over. According to one ancient tradition, Ionian Smyrna was the birthplace of Homer, said to have been born on the banks of the River Meles (*Halkapınar Suyu*). Ancient Smyrna was plagued by the Lydians and never thrived until Alexander the Great, while hunting on Mount Pagus, dreamt that Nemesis told him to found a city there. The inhabitants on the peninsula moved to the hill, and the new Smyrna prospered and was eventually welcomed into the exclusive confederacy of Ionian cities as its thirteenth member. Strabo and many other ancient authorities referred to the city's charms, and 'beautiful Smyrna' is a name that has stuck through the centuries, despite frequent disasters.

In the late Ottoman Empire, Turks referred to the city as *gâvur İzmir*—'infidel Smyrna', for its overwhelming majority of Greek and Armenian Christians and Jews. In those days it was the unquestioned cultural and good-time capital of the eastern Mediterranean, full of blooming Art Nouveau buildings, buzzing with deals being made in a score of different languages, and quite seriously looped on hashish and opium; among the city's creations was the intense, heavy style of Greek popular music called **rembetiko**, born in Smyrna's bars and drug dens. All this came to a tragic end in 1922, when Atatürk's defeat of the Greek army led to a mass exodus of Greek civilians from the city. As is traditional, the Greeks blame the Turks and the Turks blame the Greeks, but for whatever reason, while hundreds of thousands of Smyrna's citizens waited on the docks for transit to Greece, the city caught fire and over eighty per cent of its buildings burned to the ground.

Atatürk's government wasted no time in rebuilding it, in a dreary modern plan of wide, straight boulevards and traffic circles. After the last war it became the headquarters for NATO's southern command. Trade has returned, and the new all-Turkish İzmir is flourishing, the most thoroughly modern and Westernized city in Turkey, and its busiest port. Seagoing vessels are casually moored to the seafront pavement of Atatürk Caddesi, as if the captains have just left them for a minute while popping across the road for some cigarettes.

Getting Around

After years of city centre public transport chaos, İzmir municipality dug into its pockets and built the new main **bus terminal** (İzotaş), about 10km from the centre in Pınarbaşı. The 502, 601 and 602 buses shuttle back and forth from the city centre to this shiny new satellite. While waiting you may succumb to the tempting honking of the cab drivers, who charge $6 for a one-way trip. Another terminal, serving Çeşme and other nearby southern destinations such as Çiftlik, is in suburban Üçkuyular; to get there, take the 86 or 169 bus from Alsancak Station, Lozan Meydanı or Konak.

The new **Adnan Menderes airport**, 25km south of the city, is served by frequent flights from İstanbul and Ankara, as well as weekly direct THY flights from London, and numerous charters from abroad. The THY office is next to the Tourist Office on Gaziosmanpaşa Caddesi, and is connected by Havaş bus to the airport, taking 40mins subject to traffic. From İzmir's central Basmane Station, at the head of Fevzipaşa Bulvarı, there are **rail** links with Aydın, Denizli, Konya, Ankara and beyond (e.g. Adana). The overnight *Mavi Tren* special to the capital is a relatively fast and luxurious run if you're headed that way (though still not as good a deal as the bus).

The Yeni Liman (new harbour) at Alsancak, on the northern tip of the city, is the port for **ferryboats** and the Turkish Maritime Lines cruise boats; in İzmir their address is Atatürk Bulvarı 125. Once a week (on Wednesday at 4pm), a car ferry leaves for Venice; the return leaves Venice on Saturday night and may stop in İstanbul to pick up extra passengers. It arrives in İzmir on Tuesdays. Boats to İstanbul leave at 2pm on Sundays; boats from İstanbul to İzmir leave at 2pm on Friday. Ferries for the short ride to **Karşıyaka**, İzmir's suburb across the bay, leave regularly from the Konak docks (Konak İskelesi) and Alsancak İskelesi, on the Kordon.

İzmir

1000 metres
1000 yards

N

Yeni Liman
(new harbour)

Ferries to Karşıyaka

Alsancak Rail Station

Alsancak

ATATÜRK CADDESİ
ATATÜRK BULVARI
ŞEHİTLER CADDESİ
CUMHURİYET CADDESİ
KIBRIS ŞEHİTLER CADDESİ

1455 SOK.

1464 SOK.

MAHMUT ESAT BOZKURT CAD.

Atatürk Museum

TALAT PAŞA BULVARI
PILEVNE CADDESİ
ŞAİR EŞREF BULVARI
ALI ÇETİNKAYA BUL.
ZİYA GÖKALP BUL.
DR. MUSTAFA ENDER CADDESİ
MIMAR SİNAN CAD.

1420 SOKAK

1425 SOKAK

1435 SOKAK

Lozan Meydanı

İzmir International Fair

Kültür Parkı

Cumhuriyet Kapısı

1396 SOKAK

CUMHURİYET CADDESİ
ATATÜRK CADDESİ
VASIF ÇINAR BUL.

Cumhuriyet Meydanı

ŞEHİT NEVRESBEY BUL.
GAZİ OSMANPAŞA BUL.
AKDENİZ CAD.

Büyük Efes Otel

Montrö Meydanı

CUMHURİYET BULVARI

BOZKURT BULVARI

Luna Park

Passenger Dock

ATATÜRK CADDESİ
CUMHURİYET CADDESİ
ŞEHİT FETHİBEY BUL.
HALİTZİYA BULVARI
NECATİBEY CAD.

GAZİ BULVARI

9 Eylül Meydanı

MÜRSEL PAŞA BULVARI

Basmane Rail Station

To Denizli & Selçuk Rail Stations

Ferries to Karşıyaka

1369 SOKAK

İNÖNÜ CADDESİ ANAFARTALAR CAD.

GAZİLER CADDESİ

To Baths of Artemis

27 Mayıs Meydanı

FEVZİ PAŞA BULVARI

1326 SOK. 1294 SOK.

902 SOK.

Bazaar

Clock Tower

Konak

Konak Camii

938 SOK.

ANAFARTALAR CADDESİ

1282 SOK.

1021 SOK.

ANAFARTALAR CADDESİ

920 SOK. 933 SOK.
816 SOK.

952 SOK. 953 SOK.

BALLIKUYU CADDESİ

Roman Agora

825 SOK.
803 SOK.
823 SOK.

974 SOK. 681 SOK. 1029 SOK.

794 SOK. ALİ EFENDİ CADDESİ

1011 SOK.

1012 SOK.

5312 SOK.

Opera

Archaeology

Ethnography

ESREFPAŞA CADDESİ

742 SOK. 741 SOK.

714 SOK. ELKUTLU

HACI ALİ EFENDİ

Kadifekale

MUSTAFA KEMAL SAHİL BULVARI

MİTHATPAŞA CADDESİ

RAKIM

CADDESİ

731 SOK.

To Balçom

Gaziosmanpaşa Bulvarı next to the Büyük Efes Hotel, ✆ 0232 489 9278; there is also an office near Pasaport Pier, on the Akdeniz Caddesi, ✆ 0232 483 5117.

The main **post office** (and poste restante pickup) is on Cumhuriyet Meydanı; there is another big office on Fevzipaşa Bulvarı near Basmane station. For English **books**, the best bet is the **Dünya Bookshop** on Akdeniz Caddesi, off Gaziosmanpaşa, or the **Net** bookshop, Cumhuriyet Bulvarı 142/B.

A Tour of the Town

İzmir's pride and its symbol is the **Kordon** (Atatürk Caddesi), the shorefront boulevard where the waves of the Aegean beat almost against the doors of swank blocks of flats and cafés. At its centre, **Cumhuriyet Meydanı**, stands the big Atatürk Monument and the Büyük Efes Hotel, which thanks to a peculiarity of the 1920s plan has the role of being the focal point of the city.

To the south, especially on and around Necatibey Bulvarı, you can see some of the remains of old Smyrna, lovely buildings like the restored **Kızlar Ağası Hanı** on 902 Sokak, at the southern end of Necatibey. One of the few blessings the planners left İzmir is the great green expanse of the **Kültür Parkı**, İzmir's fairground. Like the similar Kültür Parkı in Bursa, this one is the place to go on weekend evenings, with outdoor restaurants, dance halls, horse-drawn carriages and a 'Luna Park' with some good rides. The İzmir International Trade Fair is held from the end of August to mid-September (a time when it is harder to find hotel rooms). The fair showcases Turkish technology both old and new, from traditional pottery to the latest machinery for pasteurising milk. Whereas in the West the public flocks to watch artisans practising dying crafts, in Turkey the opposite is true: rarely will you see such genuine enthusiasm for the most obscure apparatus—from saline pumps to gizmos for putting stoppers in olive oil jars—all concrete proof of Turkey's rapid industrial progress.

Of course, no Turkish city worthy of the name would lack an **Atatürk museum**: İzmir's is on (where else?) Atatürk Caddesi towards Alsancak and contains the usual assortment of Atatürkish knick-knacks. **Alsancak** itself, centred on Kıbrıs Şehitler Caddesi, is a calm pedestrianised oasis in a city notorious for its roaring traffic. With some of İzmir's more upmarket shops in the vicinity as well as dozens of restaurants with chairs and tables spilling onto the street, it makes for a pleasant stroll at any time of the day or evening.

Back on the seafront, at the southern end of the Kordon is **Konak**, the name of both of a district and also of its central square distinguished by its lovely **clock tower**, built in the 19th century by Sultan Abdülhamid the Damned, and the small but ornate 18th-century mosque, **Konak Camii**. From the square an underground passage leads to the shore and the ferry docks; if you have time to kill in İzmir one of the best things to do is take the ferry across the bay from here to **Karşıyaka**, not only for the views around the bay from the boat, but for the suburb's very pleasant water-front park, full of snack stands and cafés.

Everything inland from Konak is İzmir's **bazaar district**, a maze of narrow streets and cul-de-sacs that predate the great fire. Anafartlar Caddesi is the main drag, and while İzmir's market can hardly compare to İstanbul's or Bursa's, it's still worth a visit for unexpected things like the Şunnet Çarşısı, a pretty courtyard next to an old *han* where garden supplies are sold, or the huge glass-roofed arcade at 913 Sokak and Gaziosmanpaşa Bulvarı, a pre-1922 monument now come down in the world and selling cheap clothes.

Just south of the bazaar (take 938 Sokak south of Anafartlar) are the excavations of the **Roman agora**, a rebuilding financed by Emperor Marcus Aurelius after a terrible earthquake (*open daily 8.30–5.30; adm*); here you can see two rows of colonnades and three statues discovered on the site: Poseidon, Demeter and half of Artemis.

The Museums and Kadifekale

South along the waterfront from the clock tower a new three-storey building houses İzmir's **archaeology museum** (*open daily 8.30–12, 1–5; adm*), with an extensive collection of artefacts from the region. If you're on your way to Ephesus, you should definitely stop in here first; there are models and plans of the Meryemana Kilisesi and St John's, and a number of finds from the sites. In any case, this museum is worth the trip, a treasurehouse of expressive sculpture from archaic times through the Classical and Hellenistic periods. In the latter, especially, you may appreciate the soft reflectiveness of the portraits of a *Nun of Isis* and *Aspasia*. Some of this sensibility carried on into Roman times; there's a basement full of fine Roman portrait busts, though all are larger than life and a bit Felliniesque. Some of the best works are outside in the gardens: grave steles with the common motif of death's door, friezes from Aphrodisias and a fanciful, delightful Roman frieze from Miletus, showing almost naïve hunting scenes with grinning goats, dolphins and ostriches.

Next door, the **ethnography museum** (*open daily 9–12, 1–5; adm*) has more to offer, with well-thought-out displays on Ottoman life ranging from a feature on camel wrestling to a mock-up of a Turkish boy's circumcision ceremony, complete with a mannequin of a suitably anguished adolescent. Almost directly above the Roman agora looms Mount Pagus, or **Kadifekale**, the Velvet Castle, crowned with fortifications begun by Alexander the Great, and rebuilt in turn by the Byzantines and Ottomans. On your way up, you may see friendly gypsies or Kurdish women scrubbing their household rugs on the pavement. Once at the castle, the view of İzmir from the walls or one of the nearby cafés is vertiginous.

East of the central city, on Gaziler Caddesi, the *Halkapınar Gölü* has been identified as the ancient **Baths of Artemis**, where a statue of the goddess was discovered. This spring-fed pool, which lies in what are now the grounds of the İzmir water company, supplies the entire city, and is believed to be the source of the ancient River Meles. A Homeric hymn refers to a pool of Artemis in the vicinity, and, according to tradition, Homer sat on its banks and composed his iambic verse. The pool is still a charming, poetic oasis in the big city, and visitors are welcome.

luxury

In İzmir, the ★★★★★**Büyük Efes**, ✆ 0232 484 4300, ✉ 0232 441 5695, is an institution, its enclosed garden occupying a large wedge of the city's most expensive real estate, on Cumhuriyet Meydanı. Although ageing, it has all the amenities, from sauna to tennis courts, television to refrigerators, Turkish bath to swimming pool.

In recent years the Hilton chain has trumped this with a hideous but inescapable 500ft skyscraper, visible from almost anywhere in town; the ★★★★★**İzmir Hilton**, at Gaziosmanpaşa Bulvarı 7, ✆ 0232 441 6060, ✉ 0232 441 2277, has two presidential suites, in case two presidents happen to pass through at the same time, a non-smoking floor(!), 24-hour room service, pool, health club, sauna, tennis and squash courts, and on and on. At Mithatpaşa Caddesi 128, the ★★★★**Mercure Konak**, ✆ 0232 489 1500, ✉ 0232 489 1709, is another top-class establishment, to the south of the Konak clock tower.

A recent challenger to the title of hotel with most on offer is the ★★★★★**Termal Princess Otel**, ✆ 0232 238 5151, ✉ 0232 239 0939, in Balçova, five miles to the southwest of the city centre. On top of the usual embarrassment of amenities, it also has a thermal spa which claims to have restorative effects on every ailment ranging from stomach pains to rheumatism, with dolmuş fatigue and archaeological overkill somewhere in between.

expensive

The ★★★★**Marla**, Kazım Dirik Caddesi, off Gaziosmanpaşa, ✆ 0232 441 4000, ✉ 0232 441 1550, has posh air-conditioned rooms and a health club downstairs. It's in a striking post-modernist building decorated with a bizarre sort of totem pole of goddesses all the way to the roof. If you don't stay there, at least have a look. $80.

Nearby, in a quiet location off Gaziosmanpaşa Bulvarı, is the ★★★**Karaca Oteli**, 1379 Sokak 55, ✆ 0232 489 1940, ✉ 0232 483 1498, modern and stylish, at about $100 per double. For about the same, you can stay outside town at Balçova at the ★★★**Balçova Thermal Hotel**, Hüseyin Öğütçen Caddesi, ✆ 0232 259 0102, ✉ 0232 259 0829. This resort complex built around hot springs is a more affordable alternative to the nearby Princess and has air-conditioning, tennis, two big pools and plenty of other sports activities.

moderate

Near the city centre are the ★★★**Anba Oteli**, Cumhuriyet Bulvarı 124, ✆ 0232 484 4380, ✉ 0232 484 4383, and the ★★★**İzmir Palas Oteli**, Vasif Çınar Bulvarı 2, ✆ 0232 421 5583, ✉ 0232 422 6870; both have air-conditioned rooms with balconies and TV for about $65. The İzmir Palas is on the Kordon and some rooms have sea views. Prices may be lower in the off season.

Most hotels in this category are rather drab modern places intended for travelling salesmen. The nicest is the ★★**Tanık**, on 1364 Sokak off Gazi Bulvarı, ✆ 0232 441 2007, ✉ 0232 483 1119: fine rooms with bath and TV (quieter if you ask for a room away from the boulevard); $52. Next, the ★**Babadan** at Gaziomanpaşa Bulvarı 50, ✆ 0232 483 9640, charges about the same rates (it's a bit noisy though). For a quiet night's sleep, a good option is the ★★**Baylan**, on a quiet street a few minutes' walk from Basmane station at 1299 Sokak 8, ✆ 0232 483 1426, ✉ 0232 483 3844. The staff are friendly and the rooms clean, if on the small side, but some of them can be gloomy: ask for one facing the Kadifekale. Ignore the posted prices of $70 per double—you should be able to stay for half that. Drivers will be glad to know that the hotel has a private car park in which their metal beasts can take refuge from the chaotic İzmiri traffic.

cheap

Rather than pay more for one of the above, you'll do just as well in one of the perfectly acceptable inexpensive hotels on **1369 Sokak**, the traveller's best friend in İzmir. The street is located in the Basmane area near the rail station, just north of Fevzi Paşa Bulvarı, and it holds everything you will ever need (*see* 'Eating Out', below). First choice is the **Oba** at No.59, ✆ 0232 483 5474, the furthest hotel from the station but one with clean, modern rooms with bath, some with TV, for $16 (and not to be confused with the similar-sounding Oya nearby, an establishment that even Mae West would have considered a bit overpowering). At the opposite end is the **Özcan Oteli**, 1368 Sokak 3, ✆ 0232 483 5052, very much the same in quality and price. Tolerable places for slightly less on the strip include the **Kent** and the **Güven Palas**, and the **Fatih**, around the corner on 1366 Sokak.

One step lower than 1369 is the street on the other side of Fevzi Paşa Bulvarı, 1294 Sokak. Hotels here are the cheapest in town; there are loads of them, some nice and some a bit rough. Two of the best-kept are the **Yıldız Palace**, at No.50, ✆ 0232 425 1518, and the **Balıklı**, at No.20, ✆ 0232 484 2560. The **Güzel Konya**, not quite as good, has more character, set in a ramshackle wooden pre-fire building.

For a different look at İzmir, stay in the **Yeni Şükren Oteli**, on Anafartlar Caddesi, a very basic but friendly establishment in the middle of the bazaar.

İzmir **Eating Out**

Do as the locals do and take yourself to the trendy district of Alsancak, where most of the restaurants are. These tend to be agreeable, informal place with tables out on the pavement; on any evening, and particularly on weekends, it's the best scene İzmir has to offer. **Kıbrıs Şehitler Caddesi**, a pedestrian street of surviving pre-1922 houses just off the Kordon, is one of the first places to look. One of its offshoots is the **Gazi Kadinlar Sokak**, lined with attractive Greek houses whose bay windows have been largely restored. Many of them now house seafood restaurants, most with simple menus of mezes and the day's catch of fish, such as the **Cipa Restoran**; $12. For kebabs and typical Turkish fare the **Sardanya** will set you back $10.

The fancy places are along the waterfront on and around the Kordon, where seafood is the speciality. You could try the **Remzi Baba** at No.282 or the **Golden Restaurant** at No.314. Both have music, dancing and set meals for around $20 a head, wine included.

Almost every big street corner in Alsancak seems to have some sort of outdoor fast-food joint, Turkish-style, with big Coca-Cola signs to prove they're hip. Some of these can be surprising, such as the **Fil Kafeterya** on Ali Cetankaya Bulvarı, offering pizza on a plank, fresh-squeezed orange juice, soft ice cream, burgers and kebabs; a quite acceptable pizza and a drink costs less than $4. One step up from this is **Recis**, on 1382 Sokak 31 near the Lozan Meydanı. Students are drawn here by the keen prices, their parents' generation by the healthy Turkish and European food served up by waiters fresh from charm school. A large salad with 'Recis sauce' and fresh orange juice costs $5 and hits the spot on a hot day. On a side street at the southern end of Kıbrıs Şehitler Caddesi is **Altın Kapa**, which looks for all the world like a chain restaurant, but is a firm local favourite nevertheless; kebabs and so on for $9.

The obvious place to look for inexpensive chow is around the **Basmane railroad station** and that ever-friendly **1369 Sokak**. On this pedestrian street, plenty of bars put out tables and grill kebabs outdoors (some have live music on weekends); chestnuts and mussels are on offer, and violinists and girls with roses ply the tables. There are also proper restaurants, notably the **Dört Mevsim**, with truly good kebabs and incredible homemade *pide* blown up like a balloon; $5. Directly across from the station, the **Basmane Kebab Salonu** packs them in for a wide choice of grills at low prices; they offer chicken too. Among a score of steam-table lokantas on the station square, the **Nazar Lokanta** benefits from the shade. Next door the **Alu Ulvi** café is the place to draw on a *nargile* and watch the locals play cards and gossip, probably about your bungled attempts to tame the smoke pipe.

Finding something cheap and decent around Gaziosmanpaşa Bulvarı can be a problem. The **Amazon Bar-Restoran**, hidden away next to a playground behind the Hilton, offers seafood, pizza, roast chicken and such; $5 for a full meal. On weekdays the **Büyük Efes Hotel** has a very good all-you-can-eat buffet in their garden, 12 noon–3pm, for $6, with live classical music playing to help your food glide down. For seafood there is the simple, popular **Çanlı Balık** on Cumhuriyet at Kemalettin; $6. The **Deniz Restaurant**, on the seafront at Atatürk Caddesi 188B, one block north of Cumhuriyet Meydanı, is famous for its seafood and with good reason. The service may only be lukewarm but the fish more than compensates; it's so succulent that it literally melts in the mouth. $25.

For something different, try the inexpensive and highly rated **Vejetaryen Restoran**, on 375 Sokak in Alsancak near the American Hospital. The rather unimaginatively named **Chinese Restaurant** at 1379 Sokak 57, off Gaziosmanpaşa Bulvarı near the Hilton, will set you back about $20, for a full dinner; lunch menus are less. At **La Folie** restaurant, behind the Efes hotel on Kızılay Caddesi, the globe-trotting menu has everything from curries to pizzas and Chinese sweet'n'sour dishes, but not a kebab in sight. The huge salads are a vegetarian's dream. $20 for a major blow-out.

For the simple **lokantas**, search in the area between Konak and the market. Many of the city's *meyhaneler* are on or around Akdeniz Caddesi, dark dives with outside tables under a canopy, which provide some of the cheapest fare in town—it's good for lunchtime refuelling and they usually grill some kebabs in the evening. **Ora** serves up wooden platters of wafer-thin *lahmacun* with salad and a drink for only $2. Also here is the **Café İzmir**, on Akdeniz, where you can puff on your *nargile* in a strangely modern setting. On Anafartlar Caddesi, the main street of the bazaar neighbourhood, the **Şükren Lokanta** provides a welcome oasis amidst the bustle; the food's nothing special but you won't do better here. An equal choice just nearby is the **Meşaret Kafeterya**, in the courtyard of an old *han* with a marble fountain.

Plenty of **street-front stands** in İzmir specialize in *börekler* and other sorts of Turkish savoury pastries that everybody's mom makes, but you'll hardly ever see in restaurants. Some of the best come from a tiny local chain facetiously named **McZeki's**; there's one on Fevzi Paşa Bulvarı near the post office.

To unwind in the company of İzmir's well-heeled young set, find your way to the pleasant tree-lined Mustafabey Caddesi near the 9 Eylül Üniversitesi, where **Cafés Plaza** and **Biyer** nestle together under the trees. Both have Turkish and European dishes on the menu for about $6, as well as a wide choice of alcohol, but everyone really comes for the people-watching.

Inland from İzmir

Getting Around

Both Manisa and Sardis are connected to İzmir by **rail** and **bus** (1½ hours). For Sardis, take any **bus** or **minibus/dolmuş** for Salihli or Sartmustafa.

Tourist Information

Manisa: 3rd Floor, Doğu Caddesi 8, Eylül Işhani, ℰ 0236 232 7541.

Manisa

East of İzmir is **Manisa**, ancient Magnesia ad Sipylum, which began its life as the westernmost outpost of the Hittites. Much later, as a Greek city, Magnesia was mentioned in Homer and in mythology—though it *isn't*, sorry, the Magnesia that gave its name to magnesium and magnets; that one is a region in Thessaly. Magnesia was, however, the birthplace of our forebear Pausanias, whose scholarly *Guide to Greece*, written in the reign of Trajan, was probably the world's first travel guide. Manisa became an Ottoman possession in the early 14th century, and was favoured under the sultans, particularly Süleyman the Magnificent, who served as governor here before his accession to the throne. In 1922, retreating Greek troops destroyed most of the city, leaving this provincial capital modern and a bit dull, with little to show the visitor.

Finds from ancient Magnesia and Sardis can be seen in the **Manisa museum** (*open 8.30–12, 1.30–5, closed Mon; adm*), among them a fine Roman statue of a young girl and inscriptions from a synagogue discovered in Sardis in 1962. The museum is located in the medrese of the **Muradiye Cami**, a work of Mimar Sinan and noted for the tiles and goldwork in the interior. The 14th-century **Ulu Cami**, halfway up to the derelict Byzantine fortress on the ancient acropolis, has a Selçuk-style minaret, with coloured tiles and columns from an ancient temple. A third mosque, the 1522 **Sultan Camii**, built by the mother of Süleyman the Magnificent, is the most famous in Manisa, for here, at the end of May, the

Mesir festival takes place. *Mesir* is a kind of paste, a concoction of some 41 ingredients and spices, reputed to be a cure-all. It is tossed in paper wrappers from the top of the minaret. According to popular belief, it only works if you scramble for it, and hundreds of people do so every year.

Food of the Gods

 Just east of Manisa, at Akpınar, there is a carved relief of the great Mother Goddess Cybele on the side of Mount Sipylus. This region is closely identified in mythology with Tantalus, his sons Pelops and Broteas, and his daughter Niobe. Broteas, the ugliest man in Greece, is credited with carving the Cybele, while Pelops, less talented, ended up on the other end of the knife and was chopped up in a soup at the banquet Tantalus prepared for the gods on top of Mount Sipylus. The gods (except for the earth goddess Demeter, who was mourning for her lost daughter Persephone and carelessly ate a bit of shoulder) recognized the meat for what it was and punished Tantalus in Hades with eternal thirst and hunger, always keeping water and fruit just out of his reach (hence 'tantalize'). Zeus put Pelops back together again (with an ivory shoulder), and he went on to conquer southern Greece and give it his name—the Peloponnese.

It's difficult to know exactly what to make of all this, but we have definitely hit a nerve; the story of Tantalus is one of the myths where the ghosts of ancient belief and ritual glare out from behind the civilized veneer laid down by the mythologizers of the classical era. A 'Feast of Tantalus' was an important midwinter holiday in western Asia Minor, celebrated by an *eranos*—a pot-luck banquet, like the one Tantalus threw for the gods. It may contain a memory of an actual human sacrifice and even cannibalism, rites suppressed in the later stage of religious evolution represented by Zeus and the Olympian gods; there are plenty of dark hints toward this in Arcadia, in Pelops's own Peloponnese. Or else the fate of Pelops may have been strictly metaphorical. We may think of him as the typical sort of sacred king, whose career, representing the sun's, begins at midwinter (the New Year's baby of popular art is a survival of this). His death and rebirth recalls the cycle of the year. Somewhere on the slopes of Mount Sipylus is a small ruin of a *tholos* tomb that the ancients called the 'Tomb of Tantalus'.

As for Tantalus' unfortunate daughter Niobe, she had seven daughters and seven sons, but was rash enough to boast that she was a better mother than Leto, who had only two children, Apollo and Artemis. These two stern archer gods avenged the insult to their mother by slaying Niobe's fourteen. Niobe's grief was so great that Zeus took pity on her and turned her to stone. A natural rock formation southwest of Manisa is believed to be the Niobe referred to by ancient writers; it lies along the road to Karaköy, near a picnic ground, one of the many scenic spots in the region.

Almost two hours' east of İzmir (take the bus for Salihli from İzmir) is the 20th-century village of Sart, built over the ruins of the ancient capital of Lydia, **Sardis**. Situated below the steep Mount Tmolus, dominating the fertile plain of the River Hermes (the *Gediz Nehri*) and located on the great Royal Road of the Persian Empire (the western part of the road may go back to Hittite times), Sardis from the 7th to the mid-6th century BC was the world's richest city. A good part of its wealth was in gold washed down from the mountain by the River Pactolus, which the Lydians collected in sheepskins spread in the shallows—perhaps the source of the legend of the Golden Fleece.

The Lucrative Lydians

The Greeks were fascinated by the Lydians, and their fame went as far as the Assyrians who called them the *Luddi* in their inscriptions. The Lydian race was a mixture of native Anatolian and Western invaders; their language used many Greek letters and was related to Phrygian and, perhaps, Etruscan (Herodotus writes that Etruria was a Lydian colony, and the mysterious Etruscans claimed to have originated in Asia Minor). Besides building giant mounds for their deceased rulers, the Lydians were also famous for condoning prostitution; it was the way a good Lydian girl earned her marriage dowry.

There were three Lydian dynasties. At the end of the second, the Heraclid, the Lydians gained ascendancy as the Hittites in the region declined. The last Heraclid king was Candaules (700 BC), who, it is said, was so proud of his wife's beauty that he contrived for his trusted minister Gyges to see her naked. The queen, however, saw the unwitting voyeur and the next day gave him a choice: either kill her husband and marry her, or die on the spot. Gyges chose the more pleasant alternative, and founded a new dynasty, the Mermnad, that brought Sardis and Lydia, literally, a golden age. By the time of Croesus (563–546 BC), Sardis controlled the whole of Asia Minor, which Croesus ruled with a very benevolent hand. Lydia had been the first nation in the world to mint coins, and Croesus the first to issue them in pure gold and pure silver. His reputation for wealth has come down to us, but did little to impress the visiting Athenian lawgiver Solon, who, after touring the fabulous treasuries, merely commented, 'No man can be reckoned happy until the end'.

A few years after Solon's visit, the Persians under King Cyrus menaced Lydia's borders. Croesus asked the Delphic oracle whether he should attack and the oracle coyly replied that if he crossed the River Halys he would 'destroy a great empire'. Encouraged, Croesus took the offensive, only to meet defeat. Cyrus chased the Lydians back to Sardis. After a two-week siege the city fell, and Croesus realized too late that he had destroyed his own empire. Condemned to be burnt at the stake, Croesus groaned 'Solon, Solon!' as the fire was lit, and Cyrus asked what he meant. Croesus told him what the Athenian had said and, moved, Cyrus ordered his life to be spared.

Cyrus made Sardis the capital of a satrapy and, as such, it was sacked when the Ionian cities revolted against the Persians in 499 BC. It recovered in the Hellenistic era, until the earthquake of AD 17 flattened it. Tiberius had it rebuilt, and it became an early centre of Christianity, one of the seven churches of Asia and an important bishopric under the Byzantines. In 1401, Tamerlane destroyed Sardis so thoroughly that it was never rebuilt; when excavations began in the early 20th century, the archaeologists had to dig down 30ft in places, so thickly had the soft rock of the acropolis silted down over the lower city.

The Site

One thing the excavators have discovered is that Sardis was at its most extensive during the rule of Croesus, and it takes some walking to see it all. The **Temple of Artemis**, the most famous of ancient Sardis' monuments, is about half a mile up the Pactolus valley; although the sanctuary was founded in the 5th century BC, the temple wasn't begun until the 3rd. Its two Ionic capitals are among the finest anywhere; thirteen others have been re-erected to give an idea of the temple's shape. In Roman times the temple was divided into two, one half dedicated to the worship of Artemis, the other half to Faustina, wife of the Roman emperor Antoninus Pius. Along the road to the centre of Sardis, an altar to Cybele was discovered, as well as the workshops where the Lydians worked the gold they 'fleeced' from the river (*see* above, p.239).

Equally impressive are the Roman gymnasium and baths from the 2nd century AD, just off the highway; shops and a synagogue complete the complex with the **Marble Court** in the centre. Nearby, part of the Royal Road has been uncovered, and, most interestingly, what appears to be a sort of prototype bazaar dating back to the 7th century BC, giving rise to the theory that wealthy Sardis was the first city to practise organized retail trade. Next to this, the **House of Bronzes** (6th century AD) was perhaps the residence of the bishop of Sardis.

If you're reasonably energetic you can walk up the acropolis, one of the most dramatic in Asia Minor, its sheerness accentuated by the dagger-shaped rock formations around it. The walk from the valley takes less than an hour; on top the surviving fortifications are mostly Byzantine. Six miles (10km) north of Sardis are the *Bin Tepe*, or **Thousand Hills**, actually some 100 earthworks built by the artisans, merchants and prostitutes of Sardis. The largest is the **Tomb of Alyattes**, the father of Croesus. At three-quarters of a mile in circumference and 260ft high, it's the largest mound in Turkey, perhaps in the world.

Kemalpaşa

Between Sardis and İzmir, **Kemalpaşa** is the ancient town of Nymphaeum, where Andronicus I Comnenus built the **Palace of Nymphaeum** in 1184, the ruins of which are just outside town. In **Karabel**, on the main road south of Kemalpaşa, there is a second **Hittite relief** similar to Manisa's Cybele, this one of a large warrior. Herodotus referred to it, although, like all Greeks in the classical era, he knew nothing of the Hittites, and assumed it was Egyptian. Incidentally, for workmanship of a more recent vintage, you could head to Kemalpaşa on a Sunday, when people come to buy and sell cars. If you're tired of riding buses, here's your chance to pick up a 1952 Chevy and do the coast in style.

Getting Around

There are frequent **buses** (lines 86 and 169) from İzmir's Cumhuriyet Meydanı and Konak Meydanı to Üçküyülar bus station from where buses leave regularly for Çeşme. From that town's tiny otogar, on the port, **minibuses** depart for the beaches and villages around the peninsula.

Between November and April there are usually one or two **boats** a week between Çeşme and the Greek island of Chios; in season they go every day. They can only take about five cars. A round trip costs $35; if you're staying in Chios beyond 24 hours, you'll have to pay a tax of $10. For details of ferries, contact Ertürk Travel Agency, Beyazıt Caddesi 7/8 in Çesme, ✆ 0232 712 6768, *info@erturk.com*.

Tourist Information

Çeşme: İskele Meydanı 8, at the harbour, ✆ 0232 712 6653.

The peninsula west of İzmir has several popular beach resorts and thermal spas. **İnciraltı** is the closest to İzmir and thus the most crowded; just to the south in the modern suburb of Balçova, the **Baths of Agamemnon**, in use since antiquity, are noted for treating rheumatism. Further west, near **Urla** and another beach, a causeway leads out to an islet where once stood the ancient city of **Clazomenae**. The original causeway, constructed by Alexander the Great, can be seen just below the surface of the sea; otherwise little remains of this Ionian city that produced the great philosopher Anaxagoras, the precursor of Socrates, in the early 5th century BC.

Sığacık

You can go south from Urla to Seferihisar and from there to **Sığacık**, the prettiest village on the peninsula, its old houses clustered around an old Genoese fortress and small port. Here, by the lovely white beach of **Akkum**, stood ancient **Teos**, one of the wealthiest Ionian cities on the coast. Teos was the birthplace and home of the lyric love-poet Anacreon; it is also the site of a famous Hellenistic **temple of Dionysus**, with an unusual trapezoidal enclosure. Some columns have been re-erected, to make a picturesque tableau in the olive grove. Nearby is the **theatre** which, though in poor condition, offers a fabled view from its upper seats. Better preserved is the **Odeon**, with its eleven rows of seats, where concerts would have been performed.

Çeşme

At the tip of the peninsula, facing the Greek island of Chios is **Çeşme** ('fountain'), named after its numerous hot springs. It is the westernmost town in Turkey, a distinction that has an added significance during Ramazan, when the pious Muslims of Çeşme have to wait longer than anyone else to eat supper. Çeşme makes its living as a resort, though one totally lacking in the glamour or intensity of resorts further south. It is a serene family spot to sit on the beach; that's all.

An attractive town, with red tile roofs, Çeşme is dominated by a large, sloping Genoese **castle**, captured and restored by Yıldırım Beyazıt in 1400. Beyazıt's engineers evidently discharged their duties well; the castle is in good shape and housed within the crenellated walls is a theatre, a restaurant and a small **museum** displaying the finds from ancient Erythrae (*open daily 8.30–12, 1.30–5; adm*). Two important naval battles took place off Çeşme: the decisive Roman defeat of Antiochus III in 190 BC, which gave the Romans a free hand in Asia Minor, and the destruction of the Ottoman fleet by the Russians in 1770.

Çeşme faces the Greek island of Chios, much favoured by the sultans for its breath-sweetening mastic, some of which went through the **caravanserai**, built in a U-shape by Süleyman the Magnificent in 1529; it has been restored and is now a hotel (*see* below). As in all Turkish resorts, the port is lined with cruise ships, pretty wooden sailing craft waiting to take you away on a trip around the peninsula and its islets; going rate for a half-day excursion with lunch is about $10.

Around Çeşme

Çeşme has a small beach but better bathing is to be had elsewhere. South of town there are beaches at nearby **Çiftlik**, much better ones at fast-developing **Altınkum** (not to be confused with the megabeach of the same name further south) and more at **Ovacık** and **Güverçinlik**. For real seclusion head for tiny **Alaçatı**, a village 4½ miles (7km) east of Çeşme, and then walk south two miles (3km) to find the beach. With strong, steady winds blowing reliably all year, it's a windsurfer's paradise, and the facilities here reflect this: surf school, board rental, surf boutique, camping ground and café. At offshore **Donkey Island** (Eşek Adası), so named for its population of wild donkeys, there are several nice swimming spots; Çeşme's travel agents regularly organize day trips.

Dalyan, a fishing village north of Çeşme, is pleasant and pretty but its beach is small and poor, unlike the mammoth stretch of white sand that can be found at **Ilıca** to the east. Fronted by four large windmills, and famous for its thermal springs, Ilıca has pretensions to becoming a popular resort in its own right, with holiday homes replacing ancient vineyards, unfortunately leaving the impression that the town is just one big building site. Other beaches are at **Şifne** and **Ildırı**.

Ildırı is near ancient **Erythrae**, a member of the Ionian Confederacy, set at the foot of the rugged Karaburun peninsula. Unfortunately the site was so well quarried in the 19th century that little remains in the picturesque spot beyond some well-built walls and a ruined theatre. In ancient times Erythrae was famous for a statue of Heracles which floated on a raft from Egypt to a point between Chios and Erythrae. Both wanted it, but the raft couldn't be budged until a blind man in Erythrae dreamed that the statue could only be towed away with a rope of women's hair. The women of Erythrae refused to part with their locks, but their Thracian slaves used theirs to make the rope that did indeed pull the raft to their city. The statue restored the blind man's sight, and in the sanctuary subsequently built for it, no women were allowed except Thracians. It's now impossible to tell which of the remains was Heracles' sanctuary, but a stream that tastes bitter still flows in the walls and, according to Pliny—a notorious story-teller—it causes hair to grow all over the body.

A Trip to Chios

There's plenty to see on this island if you want to cross over for a day or two. Chios (*Sakız* in Turkish) is famous for its rich shipping magnates and for the mastic chewing gum, made from local lentisk bushes. **Chios** town, impressively modern and prosperous, is the capital, with an excellent white sand beach just to the north at Karfas; or else you might take an excursion up into the mountains to **Nea Moni**, a fascinating 11th-century monastery in a beautiful setting, with Byzantine mosaics. Chios does not see vast numbers of tourists; it's especially fun to bicycle around, exploring picturesque medieval villages such as **Pirama** or **Pitios**, which like İzmir claims to be the birthplace of Homer. Aound **Sklavia**, there are a number of villas and gardens from the time Chios was ruled by the Genoese. The most memorable sight Chios has to offer is undoubtedly **Pirgi**, a village with a long-standing custom of decorating its buildings with complex, geometrical *sgraffito* façades in black and white (this was a habit in many of Anatolia's Greek villages too, before 1923, and you'll see a few forlorn examples as you travel around the coast).

Çeşme Peninsula   **Where to Stay**

Çeşme

Çeşme's **Hotel Cooperative** has booths at the entrance to town and near the otogar and tourist office; they can help you find a room in summer when things are packed.

expensive–moderate

Around Çeşme, the top beach resort hotel is the Golden Dolphin, in Turkish the **(TK1)Altınyunus Tatil Köyü**, ✆ 0232 723 1250, 🖷 0232 723 2252, with 515 bungalows and nearly every possible recreational facility, including horse riding, water-skiing and thermal baths; $80 for a double. The peaceful ★★★**Kervansaray Hotel**, ✆ 0232 712 7177, was once the town's caravanserai; it has been completely redone although it's already starting to look a little scruffy.

inexpensive

Next to each other near the harbour at Çeşme on Cumhuriyet Meydanı are the ★★**Ertan**, ✆ 0232 712 6795, 🖷 0232 712 7852, and ★★**Ridvan**, ✆ 0232 712 6336, 🖷 0232 712 7627, very much alike, with private sections of beach and double rooms for about $27. The **Kaptan**, Adnan Menderes Bulvarı, ✆ 0232 712 6186, is owned by Mustafa Denizli, trainer of the Turkish football team; it has a pool.

cheap

Just follow the signs for Çeşme's cheap pensions—there are over 100 on the peninsula. If you're looking for accommodation in this category, though, try to avoid arriving in Çeşme over the weekend in summer, when the town fills up with holidaymakers from İzmir. Most of the *pansiyonlar* are located on the hill above the port, pleasant, family-run places such as the **Tani**, ✆ 0232 712 6238, in a lane behind the Kervansaray, run by the delightful Mrs Tani, with a rooftop terrace overlooking the port; doubles $12. Otherwise, there's the **Begovilya**, ✆ 0232 712 8120, and the **Sahil**, ✆ 0232 712 6934, both also overlooking the port. Another one nearby is the **Koroğlu**, ✆ 0232 712 6086. In the centre of Çeşme, top choice is the **Alim Pansiyon**, near the hamam, ✆ 0232 712 7828, where a sparkling-clean room with private shower awaits you for only $7.

Dalyan

The ★★★**Çeşme Ladin**, ✆ 0232 724 8327, ✉ 0232 724 7039, offers a private beach and a pool, and rooms with TV and balconies, most overlooking the sea. The emphasis is on sports, with a pool, gym and all imaginable water sports offered.

Ilıca

Among the many small hotels with thermal establishments is the pleasant ★★★**Delmar Hotel**, ✆ 0232 723 4300, ✉ 0232 723 4103, on the beach, with helpful staff and its own thermal spa and swimming pool.

camping

There are camp sites near the town and on the peninsula, notably the rather deluxe **Vekamp**, in a pleasant location near the beach at Ilıca; it also has a swimming pool fed by natural hot springs; ✆ 0232 717 2224. A very simple and inexpensive campsite is the **Altın Kum**, on Altınkum beach. **Tursite Camping**, ✆ 0232 722 1221, five miles (8km) from Çeşme on Tursite beach, has its own restaurant as well as 56 simple, inexpensive bedrooms

---

Çeşme Peninsula   ***Eating Out***

Çeşme

You can get all the kebabs and sandwiches you need, but whether in Çeşme or anywhere else on the peninsula anything above the tourist common denominator is hard to come by. At any rate, there will be no problem finding good seafood; the **Rıhtım Restaurant** on the harbour in Çeşme offers *midye dolması* (stuffed mussels), and uncommon treats like octopus ($10), the best deal among the generally over-priced harbourfront places. Next door, the **Dolunay Café** has an $8 set menu including a fish or kebab plate and wine. Popular with tourists, the **Castle Restaurant** is unusually located within the precincts of the castle itself; $8. On Yalı Caddesi, the **Buhara**, with outside tables, specializes in spicy Gaziantep-style kebabs and other grilled meats; $6.

Around Çeşme

Among the many restaurants in **Ilıca**, the **Anılar** has good food ($8) and, as night falls, music and dancing. **Dalyan** has several good fish restaurants, although on the rest of the peninsula you'll be fortunate to find anything beyond the basic lokanta.

The South Aegean Coast

This section of the coast encompasses most of ancient Ionia, where much of western civilization was born in the 7th and 6th centuries BC. But the region is blessed with more than the remains of great cities and past glories. As Herodotus, a native of the region, wrote, the climate of Ionia is the fairest in the world, and it is endowed with a light-filled Aegean beauty—'all repetitive variations, outline beyond outline, like the tones of a voice beyond words', as Freya Stark put it.

Names like Kuşadası, Bodrum and Marmaris, only a few years ago sounding strange and exotic, now roll off the tongue of many a travel agent, yachtsman (the jagged coast is exceptionally well suited for sailing) and even the most timid package-tourist. Yet, as modern and trendy as the south Aegean coast has become, it is paradoxically the only place in Turkey where you're likely to see a camel or, in winter, that most exotic of Turkish sporting events, camel wrestling.

Kuşadası Bay

This gently curving bay, *Kuşadası Körfezi*, has become one of the hot spots for tourism on the Aegean coast. Its two poles, Kuşadası and Selçuk, maintain a neatly symbiotic relationship to keep all the visitors happy; together they do their best to fill the shoes of neighbouring Ephesus, one of the great metropolises of the ancient world and now one of its most evocative ruins. Kuşadası, an improbable, noisy and overbuilt resort, supplies the beaches and seafood; Selçuk, an amiable modern town, offers itself as the most convenient base for seeing Ephesus and the other classical remains in the area.

Getting Around

Selçuk and Kuşadası can easily be reached by **bus** from anywhere, and there is also a typically slow **rail** connection to Selçuk from İzmir. Selçuk's bus terminal is in the town centre, on Atatürk Caddesi (the main İzmir–Muğla road), although it is to be relocated away from the centre in the near future, once the builders have extricated their blueprints from red tape. Through buses from either direction do not usually stop in the station, but just outside it on Atatürk Caddesi facing the town park.

From Selçuk there are frequent connections to **Pamukkale** and to **Aphrodisias**; there are ten buses a day to the village closest to the latter, Karacasu. There is an infrequent dolmuş for **Belevi**. There's no problem exploring **Ephesus** from Selçuk; you could take a dolmuş but the two-mile walk is very pleasant and passes the Temple of Artemis. The only way to get to the House of the Virgin Mary, three miles (5km) from town, is by taxi. If you want a look at the ancient **Carian cities** to the south, ask at Selçuk or Kuşadası; bus arrangements change frequently and in summer there are often tours on offer. **Colophon** and **Claros** are hard to reach by minibus from Selçuk or Kuşadası, but it can be done—it's better if you have your own transport and can combine the ruins with a spell on the isolated beaches in the area.

Tourist Information

Selçuk: in the park in the town centre, facing Atatürk Caddesi, opposite the museum, © 0232 892 6945.

Colophon

One Ionian city splendid in its own day but almost forgotten now is **Colophon**, most easily reached by heading directly south from İzmir. It was the only city built far from the sea, and the home town of Plato's courtesan Archeanassa ('Even upon her wrinkles there rests a bitter passion'). Colophon was renowned in antiquity for its horses and mighty cavalry, and for its fierce dogs trained to fight in battle; it was also one of few places in the ancient Greek world where dogs were sacrificed (the only deity that demanded dogs was Hecate, the underworld deity who may have originated in Caria). Because its land was incredibly fertile and its fleet powerful, it became so wealthy that the men wore kingly purple robes daily, drenched their hair with musk and ate 12-course meals. Lavish living made them soft, and Colophon was one of the first Greek cities to fall to the Lydians. In the Hellenistic age, it became a backwater as Ephesus stole all the trade; eventually it was destroyed by Lysimachus, and its inhabitants relocated to his newly-refounded Ephesus. Today little remains of Colophon except a few scanty walls.

Notium and Claros

Notium nearby was the port of Colophon and, although mainly visited these days for its sandy beach, it has some well-preserved sections of wall, the foundations of a temple and stoa and a small theatre. What really makes the trip worthwhile are the excavations at

Claros, a 20-minute walk from Notium. Here stood the famous temple and oracle of Clarian Apollo, visited from as far away as Britain and southern Russia. If excavation work is in progress, you may find that you have to view the ruins from behind a fence.

The valley of the temple floods every year, and over the ages the temple disappeared in the mud. In the 1960s it was rediscovered and excavated by the French, although in the winter large parts of it will be underwater. The lower chamber, to which the priest would descend to drink the sacred water and utter the oracles, is all flooded, but you can make out the purposely disconcerting maze-like corridor that led to the Adyton, the sacred oracle chamber. The temple was built in the Doric style, surprisingly, because Doric was usually reserved for temples on heights, where it showed to better advantage. A sacred way led to the entrance from the monumental **Propylaea**, or gate. Around the temple, fragments of three colossal statues—of Apollo, Artemis and their mother Leto—lie strewn about; Apollo's leg alone measures over 10ft. The **altar**, just east of the temple, is some 60ft long, half dedicated to Apollo, and half to Dionysus, who, as at Delphi, took over the temple during the winter months, when the sun god went to frolic with the Hyperboreans in Britain. Near the temple there's a **sundial** dedicated to Dionysus; a smaller **Ionic temple** dedicated to Apollo's twin, Artemis, lies northwest of the main temple. Although the structures date from the Hellenistic age, Claros had been a sacred spot for hundreds of years before. The weary, pregnant Leto stopped here as she fled the relentless jealousy of Hera, before giving birth to Apollo and Artemis on the island of Delos; here also the famous Sibyl, Herophile, predicted that both Asia and Europe would be destroyed because of Helen.

Selçuk

Selçuk, the small but attractive successor to ancient Ephesus (Turkish *Efes*), is a happy town, grown prosperous on its proximity to some of the finest attractions of western Turkey. Ephesus is an easy walk away, bustling and overripe Kuşadası a 30min drive. Priene, Miletus and Didyma can all be seen by day trip. Add that to the sites and charm of Selçuk itself, and after a day or so you may not want to leave. Because of the area's religious associations—which include the home of the Virgin Mary herself—it is extremely popular among Christian tourists and groups; everybody comes here, even the pope (1979). Giving the Popemobile a run for its money are some of the local taxis, heavy metal Fifties floaters that glide majestically along the streets, beaming aboard Americans in search of the heady days of youth.

Selçuk has an exceptionally fine **archaeology museum** (*in summer open daily 8.30–12 and 1–6.30, in winter 9.30–12 and 1–5.30; adm*). Besides the two famous cult images of Ephesian Artemis (*see* below), look for a dramatic tableau of Odysseus blinding the Cyclops, some lovely carved ivory furniture, erotic statuary from the brothel and a frieze from the altar of the Temple of Domitian in a style that can only be called Roman Art Deco. From Domitian's statue in the temple a weird colossal head and arm have survived, looking like lost props from a Fellini film. Note the 6th century AD statue of the city's consul Stephanos. His head is only the most recent occupant of the body; the townspeople would change it whenever a new one was elected.

Out in the courtyard is more sculpture, including a memorable 2nd century BC stele with a relief of a sexy Dionysus, and a sarcophagus with the nine Muses on it.

Moods of a Goddess

The star attractions of the Selçuk museum are undoubtedly the two statues of Ephesian Artemis, so covered with hanging, breast-like thingumabobs that she resembles a pine cone. No one knows what they really were intended to represent, but they certainly aren't breasts—the image of Zeus Stratius at Labranda had them too. The earliest cult images in Greek temples were weird, primitive objects dating back to remotest antiquity: conical wooden figures, shapeless stone lumps or even meteorites. The Selçuk statues, products of a very sophisticated age, nevertheless offer plenty of clues to the primeval sources; they rank among the most striking images of a deity ever produced in antiquity, and are worth looking at in detail. One Artemis wears a *polos*, a kind of crown suggesting a wall and towers that is often worn by Athena, or by the tutelary goddess of any city, which was certainly Artemis's status in Ephesus. The other has a necklace with the signs of the Zodiac, pictured just as we know them today. Astrology first came into the west in Hellenistic times, brought back from Babylon after Alexander's conquest, and it was the fascination of the age.

Note the animals, in ranks of three, that adorn much of the statues' surface, betraying this Artemis's true meaning as just a Hellenized, up-to-date name for the primeval Anatolian goddess, the mountaintop *potnia theron*, or 'mistress of the wild things'. One statue has plenty of bees on it, which to a Greek mind would be more appropriate to Aphrodite—but then this lady does not have much to do with the tenets of classical Olympian religion. An outlandish but currently popular theory says that Artemis's 'breasts' are really testicles. Cybele, another aspect of the same Anatolian goddess, presided over an orgiastic cult whose priests offered her the ultimate ex voto: they castrated themselves. (This cult eventually spread as far west as Gaul. In the last centuries of ancient Rome it was quite popular among the city's poor.)

The consciously sanitized version of Artemis that we see in Greek mythology—the virgin huntress revelling with her nymphs—may be unpredictable and a bit dangerous, but she's never a serious threat to the reasoned order of Zeus and her brother Apollo. She is the poetic creation of a very civilized age. But as the aspect of the Great Goddess who delights in untamed nature, and rules the hunters who live from it, her origins may go back as far as the Paleolithic. As Artemis, she first appears in a Linear B inscription from Minoan Crete. The Greek colonists in Asia Minor melded her image onto the transcendent goddess already worshipped everywhere in Anatolia. Everywhere, though, her rituals carry dark hints of a violent, half-remembered past. In many Greek cities, they included the drawing of human blood, likely a sublimation of what was once human sacrifice. More commonly, Artemis would demand a vast sacrifice of living things, hung on trees or columns and incinerated in a great bonfire. As Pausanias described one,

> *...all manner of victims, also wild boar and deer and fawns and some even bring the cubs of wolves and bears, and others full grown beasts... Then they set fire to the wood. I saw indeed a bear and other beasts struggling to escape from the first force of the flames and escaping by sheer strength. But those who threw them in drag them up again on the fire. I never heard of anyone being wounded by the wild beasts.*

In any case, not a goddess to be taken lightly. You'll meet her everywhere in Anatolia, as Cybele or Artemis or Aphrodite—originally it's all the same. And in one form or another she will always be around. Currently, the people of Selçuk are so taken with their Artemis that they have reproduced her in larger-than-life marble on a fountain facing Atatürk Caddesi, just north of the town hall. That will give future archaeologists something to think about.

Dominating Selçuk is the old acropolis of Ephesus, which Justinian crowned with the **Basilica of St John**. The Apostle John spent his last years in Ephesus writing his Gospel, and his burial spot is marked by a slab of marble. The church was in the form of a cross, covered by a large central dome with several smaller domes forming the arms—before the whole was shattered by earthquakes. Today the entrance is through the **Gate of Persecution**, a Christian misinterpretation of a relief of a battle scene: the baptistry and apse with some surviving 10th-century frescoes have been reconstructed. Directly above towers the **Citadel of Ayasoluk,** with its Byzantine-Turkish fortifications and grand views (*closed for restoration until Judgement Day, it seems*). Just below the church stands a key work of the Selçuk Turks, the **İsa Bey Mosque** (1375). İsa Bey was a prince of the Aydın Turks who briefly ruled western Anatolia, and his mosque was the first to be built with a courtyard and stalactite vaulting, anticipating the later Ottoman style. The mosque was devastated by an earthquake in the nineteenth century and remained an empty shell until 1975, when a new wooden roof was built. They did not add one innovation of the Ottomans, a special balcony for women's worship: this Selçuk mosque still makes do with cotton sheets strung up between pillars to segregate the sexes. The present imam, Mustafa Koçyiğit, is a softly-spoken ambassador of Islam and may be on hand to show you around. When he became imam in 1986, only half a dozen people turned out each Friday during Ramazan. Now, more than 3,000 crowd into the mosque during prayer time in the fasting month. Local people donated the carpets that cover the floor in a sea of colour, with crude woollen flatweaves lapping up against intricate silk masterworks.

Ephesus (Efes)

Thanks to its proximity to the coastal resorts, more tourists come to visit Ephesus than any other site in Turkey. Yet it isn't a genuine city of classical Greece you'll see here, but a relative late-bloomer, a conveniently situated city that the Romans transformed into the capital of their Province of Asia. That was an opulent time for Ephesus, and most of the ruins on display are the magnificent public buildings of the 1st–2nd centuries AD. Compared to the older sites, such as Priene or the Carian cities, Ephesus can seem strangely modern and familiar. Its remains are those of a rich, comfortable place, living on the crest of the wave of classical civilization, centuries after the great period of Greek cultural achievement. When you get to know it, you'll certainly notice a kinship with the cities we live in today.

History

Ephesus was first settled by the Lydians and Carians who worshipped the great Anatolian goddess Cybele. When the Ionians arrived, around the 10th century BC, they combined the ancient cult of Cybele with their own of Artemis, a syncretism that had unusual success. But Ephesian Artemis has little in common with the virgin goddess of the hunt; she is a mysterious oriental fertility figure. From the start the cult attracted devotees from across the Mediterranean, and its temple was the one constant in the city's history, for Ephesus itself moved no fewer than four times. The early Ionian settlement was on the slopes of Mount Pion (*Panayir Dağı*), above the theatre, and its harbour was near Selçuk. The greatest of all the pre-Socratic philosophers, Heraclitus, was born here. Croesus, King of Lydia, conquered Ephesus in 550 BC, but refrained from destroying it when the artless Ephesians tied a rope around the town and bound it to the temple of Artemis. He did however force them to relocate to the defenceless plain near the temple. Lysimachus, Alexander's general and heir to Ionia, noticed that the River Cayster was silting up the port and induced the Ephesians to move again by building new houses downstream and flooding the old ones with tons of sewage—a convincing argument for those who had wanted to stay put.

In its new location, in the valley between Mounts Pion and Coressus, Ephesus became the boom town of Asia Minor. The population doubled when Lysimachus removed the people of Colophon and Lebedos to Ephesus. In Roman times, it became a provincial capital of the province of Asia, the banking and trade centre of the east, and, with some 500,000 inhabitants, the largest city in Anatolia; as Philostratus wrote in the 1st century AD, it was

> devoted to dancers and taken up with pantomimes, and the whole city was full of pipers, and effeminate rascals and noise.

Or as Heraclitus, Ephesus' native son, had earlier put it: 'May wealth never leave you, Ephesians, lest your wickedness be revealed.' Four different Roman emperors granted the Ephesians permission to construct a temple for their own worship—a great state honour. Yet Ephesus' prosperity was undermined by one constant vexation: the silting up of its harbour. Several dredgings and other solutions were attempted, with only temporary success; today the sea is more than five miles away.

St Paul

Ephesus in its prime witnessed some of the events that marked the great religious conversion from the goddess Artemis to the new God of the Christians. The Apostle John converted many of the natives even before St Paul came to live in the city. After three years, his preaching had attracted so many adherents that the local silversmiths, who made cult figures of Artemis, felt their livelihoods threatened and started a riot, packing the great theatre with people shouting, 'Great is Artemis of the Ephesians!' St Paul left shortly afterwards. With the decline of Rome and the silting of its harbour, Ephesus dwindled, and in the 6th century the city was abandoned for a new site—modern Selçuk.

The Temple of Artemis

Most of what remains in Ephesus today is Roman, except for the melancholy remains of the **Temple of Artemis**, about half a mile from the excavations on the Kuşadası–Selçuk road. This, one of the Seven Wonders of the Ancient World, is now marked by a single column re-erected on a ruined foundation in the middle of a swamp, its tip a favourite nesting place for storks. At least three temples have stood on the site. The original, built around the 7th century BC, was replaced in the 6th with a far grander edifice (significantly bigger, for the sake of status, than the temple of Hera under construction on the nearby island of Samos). The temple measured 179 by 374ft, larger than a football field and four times the size of the Parthenon, surrounded by a forest of 129 columns. For all their sophistication, the Greek cities loved to compete in the same boosterish way American cities do with their skyscrapers today. The Artemision was undoubtedly planned to be the biggest temple in the world, just a few feet longer and wider than the then-reigning champ, the 175 by 367ft Temple of Olympian Zeus in Akragas (Agrigento, Sicily). Amazingly, the whole thing was made of marble, except for the wooden roof and inner architrave. In 356 BC, on the night of Alexander the Great's birth (so they say), a mad arsonist in search of fame burned it down. It lay in ruins until Alexander himself came and offered to pay for its restoration. The Ephesians politely declined, with the excuse that one god should not build a temple to another. They then rebuilt it themselves on the same massive scale, and filled it with treasure and statues.

Gigantic as it was, by the mid-19th century, when the British railway engineer J.T. Wood tried to find it, not a trace remained: Justinian had quarried most of its marble for the Basilica of St John (*see* below) and the rest had receded into the mud. For nine years Wood searched for the temple, until 1874 when an inscription was discovered, giving directions to the Sacred Way. Wood excavated the road and followed it to the great temple.

The Main Excavations

Excavations of Lysimachus' Ephesus were begun in 1895 by the Austrians and continue to this day. Along the road from the parking lot lies the vast **Gymnasium of Vedius**, built in AD 150 by a prominent citizen, Publius Vedius Antonius; the structure includes well-preserved baths and a latrine. Next to it is a partially excavated **stadium**, much quarried by the Selcuks for their castle. Across the road are the few remains of a temple from the time of Croesus; south of this are ruined Byzantine baths and the long, narrow **church of Agia Maria**, built in the 2nd century as a bank and market. In the 3rd century it was converted into a church dedicated to the Virgin Mary—the first church anywhere consecrated to the Mother of God. In 431, the Emperor Theodosius II convened the Third Ecumenical Council here, which declared Jesus to be both the son of Mary and the Son of God.

The Theatre

Beyond the parking lot and the ticket booth are the remains of the **Harbour Gymnasium**, **Palaestrae** and **Baths**, the largest surviving structure in Ephesus, only part of which has been uncovered. It gives on to the **Arcadiane**, the street to the harbour, named for its builder, the Byzantine emperor Arcadius (d. 408). Paved with marble and lined with colon-nades and stoas, this was one of the few thoroughfares in antiquity to have street lamps. At the end of the street rises the majestic **theatre** carved into the flank of Mount Pion, built in the Hellenistic era and remodelled by the Romans under Claudius and Trajan. In classic Greek theatre, all the action took place in the orchestra, but by the Hellenistic age the actors performed on a small raised stage, leaving the orchestra to the increasingly irrelevant chorus. By Roman times, fashion had moved all the drama to the stage, which reached grand operatic proportions in Ephesus—three levels with an ornate façade, adorned with statues and columns. The theatre seats 24,000, and has been restored with a heavy hand for the annual Ephesus Festival. The top seats offer a fine view of the ruined city.

Along the Marble Road

From the theatre, the **Marble Road**, grooved with deep cart ruts, was the main street of Ephesus. Following it will bring you to a 1st-century **Doric stoa** and, the most elegant of Ephesus' buildings, the **Library of Celsus**, with its lovely white marble façade, fine carvings and statues. This was built in 110 by the consul Gaius Julius Aquila as a temple-tomb for his father, Gaius Julius Celsus, whose unopened lead casket is still in its sarcophagus in the grave chamber. The reading room of the library had three floors; as in Pergamon, niches in the walls mark former shelves for the scrolls. Although the reading room was burned by the Goths in 262, the façade survived unharmed, and in the 5th century the depression around it was filled with water to make a reflecting pool. Behind the **agora** (currently being restored) stood the **Temple of Serapis**, built in the 2nd century, perhaps by the Egyptian residents of the city, although the god Serapis had a cult following among Greek and Roman alike and provided serious competition for Christianity in its early days. Like the Temple of Serapis in Pergamon, this one was massive; each of its eight monolithic columns weighed 57 tons.

Street of the Curetes

At the library the street turns and becomes the **Street of the Curetes**. According to the Ephesians, Artemis was born nearby, at a place called Ortygia; her mother the goddess Leto, pursued by Hera, was able to deliver her here thanks to the Curetes, the young men who frightened the vindictive Hera away by banging on their shields. The Curetes had performed a similar service in Crete, at the cradle of the infant Zeus, where their banging kept his cannibalistic father Cronos from hearing Zeus' cries. Their presence in Ephesus, and the fact that an order of priests in the Artemision were called the Curetes, suggests that the cult of the Ephesian Artemis long predates her first temple.

The **Baths of Scholastica** (2nd century AD) were renamed after a Christian who remodelled them in 400. Her headless statue still presides over the entrance; inscriptions indicate that the baths also served as the town brothel. Much of the stone Scholastica used for her remodelling came from the neighbouring Corinthian **Temple of Hadrian**, which had partially collapsed in an earthquake. Part of it has been reconstructed, and with its four reliefs (the originals are in the museum), this shrine to the good gay emperor is one of the most attractive in the city. Opposite, on the slopes of Bülbüldağ (Mountain of the Nightingales), a large **residential quarter** (*separate adm*) has recently been excavated, bringing to light many luxurious mansions owned by Ephesian merchants, complete with mosaics and frescoes.

Curetes Street continues to the fountain of Trajan, or **nymphaion**. A colossal statue of the emperor once stood over the fountain, and what remains—his giant feet, one resting on the world—suggests a Rome already too big for its britches. The street continues past numerous small buildings, some reliefs and fountains, to Domitian Street, leading to the ruined **Temple of Domitian** (1st century AD), the first of the four temples consecrated to imperial worship. A huge statue of the sporty but paranoid Domitian stood within, enjoying a splendid view from the temple's platform. Little survives of the **state agora** next to the temple. Adjoining the north stoa of the agora is the **prytaneion**, or city hall, and the **odeon**, which was probably used for government meetings rather than concerts. An eternal flame was kept burning in the prytaneion and it was here that the museum's two statues of Artemis were found, carefully buried—perhaps by a secret worshipper to hide them from the Christians.

The Seven Sleepers

The road continues past a great fountain, another bath and the **East Gymnasium** (all 2nd century AD) on its way to the ruined **Magnesian Gate**, one of the two main gates built by Emperor Vespasian *c.* AD 75. The Sacred Way to the Temple of Artemis passed through here and around Mount Pion. Following the track, you pass a large, early Christian cemetery that surrounds a church and the graves of the **Seven Sleepers**, a popular motif in Christian and Turkish folklore. In the mid-3rd century, seven young Christians of Ephesus hid in a mountain cave to escape the mandatory imperial worship. They fell asleep, the cave was sealed up, and when they were shaken awake by an earthquake, they discovered that they had slept for 200 years. When they died the Ephesians buried them here, and a church was built over their graves that became a popular pilgrimage site—an echo of the myth of Endymion (*see below*). In fact there were really eight Sleepers; one of them had his dog with him.

The track continues to modern Selçuk. (The track to the right from the Magnesian Gate leads to the **Walls of Lysimachus**, well preserved in many places.)

The House of the Virgin Mary

In a municipal park five miles (8km) southeast of Selçuk is the Panaya Kapulu, or **Meryemana**, the house where Mary, who accompanied St John to Ephesus, is said to have lived and died c. AD 37–45. While the site has always been associated with the Virgin, the house was unknown until a German invalid called Catherine Emmerich (1774–1824), who had never been to Ephesus, had a series of visions which enabled her to give exact directions to the house and a detailed description of its appearance. In 1891, the Lazarist order of İzmir found it exactly where and as she had described it: a brick house of the 6th century, its foundations dating back to the 1st. (The story curiously parallels Mehmet Fatih's dream discovery of the grave of Mohammed's standard-bearer Eyüp near İstanbul.) In 1967 Pope Paul IV gave the house its certificate of authenticity, and it was recently visited by Pope John Paul II. The Virgin's tomb, according to Catherine Emmerich, is about a mile from the house, but has never been found. The house is a busy pilgrimage site; both the Orthodox and Catholics (as well as many local people) gather here to celebrate the Assumption of the Virgin on 15 August. Mass is celebrated every Sunday, at 10.30.

The Church does tolerate some competition in Virginal abodes. In Loreto, the famous pilgrimage site in central Italy, you may visit Mary's original home from Nazareth. As the story goes, the house was divinely transported to a hill in Istria (in Slovenia today), but God changed his mind and airmailed it to Italy in 1294, just coincidentally at a time when the pope was trying to drum up interest in a new Crusade.

Belevi

Ten miles (16km) northeast of Selçuk, on the İzmir road, the village of **Belevi** has two unusual monumental tombs. One, known as the **Belevi Mausoleum**, is just off the road; it stands on a massive square base carved from living rock, topped by a chamber of marble, surrounded by columns and reliefs of the battle of Lapiths and centaurs; the sarcophagus, however, was hidden in the base in an effort to foil grave robbers (it is now in the Selçuk Museum). Many believe the man buried here was the Seleucid King Antiochus II who died in Ephesus in 246 BC, poisoned by his wife. The other tomb, a hilltop tumulus surrounded with a wall of fine masonry, probably dates from the same century.

Selçuk	*Where to Stay*

Accommodation in Selçuk is more than ample, though there is little that really stands out. If you really want to see the sights in style, it can be done just as conveniently from one of the resort hotels at Pamucak, on the way to Kuşadası (*see* below). Although the situation has improved greatly in recent years, some places in Selçuk still seem to be in the business of exploiting tourists, so be a bit selective about letting someone lead you away from the bus station.

The pick of the bunch is the **(M2)Kalehan**, Atatürk Caddesi 49, ✆ 0232 892 6154, a renovated, charmingly decorated stone inn with a swimming pool; $50, for a bit more there are four luxury suites.

There are more than 30 pensions, the vast majority being clean, comfortable and cheap. Most convenient for Ephesus are those in the back streets behind the museum. One of the most atmospheric is the **Naz Hanı** near St John's basilica on St John Caddesi, ✆ 0232 892 8731, ✆ 0232 891 4011. The pleasant courtyard is cluttered with plant pots and old brass hanging scales. Although not cheap at about $30 per double, with only five rooms, it's often full. An otherwise unremarkable hotel facing the aqueduct is very popular with tourists for its rooms with views of the nesting storks along the way: the **★★Victoria**, ✆ 0232 892 3203, with double rooms for about $35. The hotels **★★Atadan**, Atatürk Caddesi 6, ✆ 0232 892 6297, and **★★Mekan Hotel Villa**, Atatürk Mah., 1067 Sokak 11, ✆ 0232 892 6299, are both newer buildings with balconies and charge about $22, breakfast included.

cheap

Very near to the entrance to Ephesus, and set in an attractive garden, the **(M1) Tusan Efes Moteli**, Efes Yolu, ✆ 0232 892 6060, is convenient for the site although prey to traffic noise and somewhat isolated; double rooms go for $15.

Even cheaper alternatives are not hard to find: try the **Australian Pension** at Prof Miltner Sokak 17, ✆ 0232 892 6050: $8 for a double room with a free ride to Ephesus thrown in. It fills up fast in the summer with backpackers and can be noisy when the overland truck hits town. The **Australian Pension** is run by a Turk who spent 12 years down under; the nearby **Outback Pension**, on Turgut Reis Sokak, ✆ 0232 892 2452, is run by an Aussie who downed his backpack here in 1987 and has stayed ever since. Rooms are spartan but clean, and there's access to a roof terrace and the internet; doubles $8. Next door is the quainter **Barım Pansiyon**, ✆ 0232 892 6923, an 18th-century Greek house with a secluded courtyard and a stork on its chimney. Doubles cost $8, or more for rooms with showers.

camping

Camping choices are limited; it seems a toss-up between the simple **Garden Camping**, ✆ 0232 892 2489, out near the İsa Bey Cami, which has a pool but little else, and the better equipped **Pamucak Dereli Turistik Tesisleri**, just off the beach in Pamucak, ✆ 0232 893 1206.

Selçuk   **Eating Out**

The pedestrian streets in the centre of Selçuk make a lively scene on summer evenings; there are a number of restaurants geared towards the tourist trade, of which the best is the one with the attractive kilims spread over the tables out on the street, the **Tat Restoran** on Cengiz Topel Caddesi, run by a friendly young fellow from out East; a very good selection of mezes, and *saç kavurma* done at your table for $6 or less. One of the nicest places to dine is the **Park Restoran**, in the park at the town centre: outside tables under the trees, and kebabs and moussaka for about $5.

Across the street from the Ali Bey Mosque at the edge of town is the **Karameşe Restaurant**. Despite its touristy appearance, this is also a favourite with local families. Children bring carrots to feed the pet rabbits. Rabbit is not on the menu, which may be a relief to parents who've had enough of giving awkward explanations to inquisitive youngsters. You can gorge yourself on the Anatolian village staple of *gözleme* for only $2.

Kuşadası and Around

In the early 1970s, **Kuşadası** was still a sleepy little port town; today it holds the dubious distinction of being one of Turkey's slickest and most expensive resorts, where seven or eight cruise ships call each day, and luxury yachts under many different flags bask in the marina. New geometric holiday homes have been griddled onto the hills surrounding the town. More than any other resort in Turkey, this town has been built by package tourism.

Getting Around

To reach Kuşadası, take a direct **bus** from İzmir or a **minibus** from Söke or Selçuk. Minibuses trundle continually up and down the coast, linking the resort to all the beaches. You'll be able to catch one on Atatürk Caddesi near the harbour for nearby Kushtur Beach. Minibuses to the other beaches, as well as Selçuk, Dilek National Park and more distant points begin from the station on Adnan Menderes Bulvarı, three short streets east of İnönü Bulvarı. The big buses, for İzmir and more distant points, use the Yeni Garaj, south of the centre on Çevre Yolu (the road for Söke).

Most of the coastal and Greek Island **cruises** stop here, and Kuşadası is also linked year-round with the Greek island of Samos. This is probably the busiest of the cross-border ferries; except Sundays, there will usually always be a morning and afternoon boat, and more if demand warrants it. In the summer as many as five boats make the crossing each day—often tiny, cabin cruiser-type boats with room for just a few people. With the bizarre winds that frequent this part of the Aegean, this can be an exciting crossing, even in summer.

Tourist Information

Kuşadası: Liman Caddesi, near the quay, © 0256 614 1103.

Kuşadası

Kuşadası means 'bird island' in Turkish; off the shore is an islet called Pigeon Island, the site of a Genoese castle, where cafés and the garden are dotted with pigeon houses. The town itself has grown up into a rather unlovely city, with the resort strips stretching out for miles in either direction. At the centre, the **Kale**, most of the streets have been taken over by *pansiyonlar*, souvenir shops and such; the best indication of what Kuşadası has become is the incredible thoroughfare renamed **Barlar Sokak**—Bar Street—where hordes of indistinguishable t-shirted north Europeans stumble about aimlessly until 3am any summer night. The city has an entertaining and not at all touristy market on Friday mornings.

Ancient Anatolia had its amphitheatres; modern Turkey has its aquaparks. If you are experiencing a touch of ruinitis or are accompanied by children showing symptoms of the disorder, Kuşadası offers an antidote in the form of three aquaparks, the largest of which is Adaland,

© 0256 618 1252, on the hill overlooking Pamucak beach; the full water works will set you back $12 (half price for children). If this doesn't do the trick, then Kuşadası's better hotels offer every imaginable type of watersport, from paragliding to windsurfing. Scuba diving costs about $35 per day. Several outfits offer the five-day PADI beginners' course for $300–$350. The nearest beach is **Kadınlarplajı**, 'Ladies' Beach', two miles (3km) south and backed with all the usual trappings of mass tourism. Further on is the aptly named **Long Beach** and beyond that **Silver Beach**. **Kuştur Beach** and **Pamucak Beach**, probably the best and least crowded of them all, are north of town off the road to Selçuk.

In 1985 the forests above Kuşadası and Ephesus were hit by a devastating forest fire, but beautiful **Dilek National Park** on the peninsula 20 miles (32km) to the south was spared (*open daily 8–5, later in summer; adm*). The park encompasses beautiful Mount Mycale (modern Samsundağ), its 4,082ft plunging down into the strait facing Samos; it has abundant wildlife, caves, beaches, springs and a castle. There are camp sites and picnic grounds and paths up the mountain (although visitors are advised not to go walking alone because of the bears). The beaches on the peninsula's northern coast are quieter than those at the resort; they can be found at **Aydınlık**, **İçmeler** and **Kavaklı**, and also near the village of **Güzelçamlı**, the closest village to the park.

Samos

Now, as in ancient times, Samos holds its place as the richest and most important Greek island after Crete. Back then, the island produced famous men such as Pythagoras and the astronomer Aristarchus; its great Temple of Hera was known across the Mediterranean— fittingly so, as the goddess herself was born on Samos. Lush and green compared to other islands, Samos sees plenty of tourists throughout the season, so prices can be high. In July or August there will usually be a festival in one of the villages, along with the Wine Festival in August; Samos has been known for its wines since antiquity.

Samos is also the name of the island's capital, the destination of the ferries from Kuşadası. This slick and modern town can offer a **museum** of archaeology, and good **beaches** just to the south at Possidonion and Psili Ammos. **Pythagoria**, not far from Samos but on the southern shore, is the biggest draw, with ruins including Hera's temple, walls and a unique half-mile tunnel, built in the 6th century BC.

Kuşadası   ***Where to Stay***

There are quite literally hundreds of hotels and pensions in Kuşadası and finding a room is rarely a problem. However, many of the more up-market establishments tend to be block-booked by tour operators in summer, and closed in winter.

luxury–expensive

The really exceptional places are not in Kuşadası itself, but on the beaches to either side. At Pamucak, 6km to the north, near Selçuk, the ★★★★★**Ephesus Princess**, © 0232 893 1011, @ 0232 893 1039, offers plush air-conditioned rooms, an enormous pool, sauna and hamam and all sports facilities imaginable; in addition to the main building there are also rooms in separate bungalows and some self-catering accommodation. Very similar in amenities and style, the ★★★★**Ephesus Richmond**,

℡ 0232 893 1051, 🖷 0232 893 1055, is slightly less expensive, and offers a good restaurant on its rooftop terrace. Other self-contained pleasure palaces on the periphery include the ★★★★★**Korumar**, ℡ 0256 614 8243, 🖷 0256 614 5596, a Miami Beach-style complex on a cliffside facing two small coves with beaches. There is a casino and disco, hamam and sauna, two pools and water sports.

The ★★★★★**Fantasia Hotel**, Söke Yolu, ℡ 0256 614 8600, 🖷 614 2765, is three miles (5km) out of town on the road to Söke and has restaurants, bars, a disco, recreational facilities and everything else you would expect for $115. Slightly less expensive, on one of the busier parts of the beach, the ★★★★**Tusan Oteli**, ℡ 0256 618 1088, 🖷 0256 618 1096, offers a wide range of recreational facilities and in-room satellite TV; about $95.

Staying in the centre of Kuşadası isn't much fun, unless you do it at the elegant ★★★**(S)Club Caravanserai**, ℡ 0256 614 4115, open April–Oct, located in the centre of town in a 17th-century caravanserai, with a beautiful garden restaurant in the courtyard; doubles $70. At the same price, the ★★★★**Atinç Oteli**, Atatürk Bulvarı 38, ℡ 0256 614 7608, is swish but rather soulless.

In an isolated setting (by Kuşadası standards anyway) 3km from the centre, the ★★★**Zinos**, at Eski İçmeler Mevkiki, ℡ 0256 618 0761, has a private beach, restaurant, pool and sports opportunities; motel-style rooms with balconies are simple but comfortable. Somewhat similar, with plenty of trees and its own marina, is the ★★★★**Kısmet**, at Akyar Mevki, Türkmen Mah., ℡ 0256 614 2005, 🖷 0256 614 4914. The hotel has the added cachet of being run by a princess of the Ottoman imperial line; one up, at least, on the White Russian emigrés working as waiters in Paris after their revolution.

moderate

These can be a pretty undistinguished lot: an endless supply of concrete chunks with only the names to tell them apart. In the town, and open year-round is the ★★**Efe Oteli**, at Güvercin Ada Caddesi 37, ℡ 0256 614 3660, where a double with bath goes for $35; some fancier rooms cost more. On a hill overlooking the harbour, the ★★**Stella Oteli**, Bezirgân Sok 44, ℡ 0256 614 1632, has a lofty charm; double rooms with breakfast cost $42.

If you'd prefer something nearer the beach, the ★★**Minay**, Alitepe Sitesi at Kadınlar Beach, ℡ 0256 614 8804, 🖷 0256 614 5302, is open all year and a good bargain: air conditioned rooms, some with TV, a hamam and gym. Close to Kadınlar Beach, the ★★**Turkad**, ℡ 0256 614 2866, has a garden and tennis courts.

cheap

As is so often the case in Turkey, most of the cheap hotels and pensions are clustered together in the same area; in Kuşadası this is one block south of the post office on and around Arslanlar Caddesi. Along this street are the pensions **Su**, ℡ 0256 614 1453, and **Rose**, ℡ 0256 614 1111, both clean and charging about $8; both have shared bathroom facilities. On Bezirgân Sokak, the **Hasgül**, ℡ 0256 614 3641, has clean simple rooms, some with balconies overlooking the harbour; $15 double. In the centre of town, the **Bahar Pansiyon**, Cephane Sok 10, ✆ 0256 614 1191, is colourful and has a restaurant on the roof; $18.

Another happy hunting ground for cheap digs is in the streets behind Kadınlar Beach. In this area, the **Emek Pansiyon** (follow the signs from the beach road), ✆ 0256 614 1731, offers good value for money—very clean and airy rooms with private shower and toilet at only $6.

One surprisingly nice alternative to Kuşadası is to spend some time at the village of Güzelçamlı, on the boundaries of the Dilek National Park. A number of *pansiyonlar* have opened here, including the **Aydın**, ✆ 0256 646 1203.

camping

The most pleasant of the campsites around Kuşadası is out on the İzmir road, **Önder Camping**, ✆ 0256 614 2413, which also offers cabins and a restaurant.

Kuşadası **Eating Out**

Kuşadası has many expensive fish restaurants on the waterfront, but nothing particularly distinguished. Generally, the further you go from the sea, the less you will have to pay. At the harbour, the **Kazım Usta Restaurant** has a fish tank out front from which you select your hapless dinner; it's not cheap, a full meal with wine costing around $20. In a similar price bracket is the much-praised restaurant at the hotel **Club Caravanserai** (*see* above). A good, inexpensive restaurant with a more authentic Turkish ambience (a rarity in Kuşadası) is the **Konya Pide Salonu** at Kahramanlar Caddesi 65, where a meal of grilled meat, rice, salad and a soft drink should come to no more than $6.

A restaurant where you pay for the food, not the frills, is the **Albatross**, on Emek Street behind the town hall. Locals refuel on simple food prepared by Mrs Yucel in large pans; her doleful husband doles it out for a flat rate of $5 per piled-high plate. Hearty vegetarian fare such as okra and spinach features regularly on the menu.

The Cities of Ionia

In ancient times, the heartland of this most gifted province was the valley of the Maeander (modern Menderes), the largest and most important river of western Asia Minor. Its often-changing course gave us the word 'meander'; yet, much though the river contributed to trade and the fertility of the soil through its annual, Nile-like flooding, it proved as much a curse as a blessing to Priene and Miletus, the two cities at its mouth. Like Ephesus, both once stood on the coast, but the tons of silt the Maeander carried down to the sea each year filled their harbours, and caused them to be abandoned. Today both are miles from the sea.

From the Coast to Lake Bafa (Çamiçi Gölü)

Getting Around

The village of **Söke**, with regular connections to Kuşadası, is the transport hub for the coastal area, with frequent minibus services to **Priene** and **Didyma**.

There's no public transport to Miletus, though a Söke minibus goes to Yeniköy, 5km away. To reach **Lake Bafa**, take any bus from Söke to Bodrum and ask to be let off at the lake (Bafa Gölü, also called Çamiçi Gölü). From the campgrounds, you can take a boat to Heracleia. The requisite half day's hire is expensive at $25 but each boat has room for 25 people.

For seeing Priene and Miletus, transport is convenient enough (via Söke) if you use Kuşadası or Selçuk as a base. Another possibility, especially if you have a car, is the resort at Altınkum, near Didyma.

Tourist Information

Altınkum: a booth on the beach at the centre of town is open irregularly in summer.

Priene

Priene was never a large city; estimates of its greatest size range from 4,000 to 6,000 free citizens. Nor did it play much of a role in the politics of the age. In late Roman times, as its harbour gradually became unusable, the city dwindled, and after the 6th century nothing more is heard of it. Even so, you may well find its ruins more alive, more evocative of the ancient world, than any other city in Asia Minor. Despite its small size, Priene had a reputation for accomplishment. The site, largely excavated, reveals a well-built and beautiful city, especially its residential quarters. Also, Priene's very lack of prosperity under the Romans make it, in one sense, unique. Unable to build on the scale of Ephesus, Priene changed little after the 4th century BC; it remains the best example of a Hellenistic city outside Greece.

Nothing remains of the first Priene, founded at the same time as the other Ionian cities. Its site on the muddy Maeander hasn't even been found. By the 4th century, the advancing coastline made a new foundation necessary, and with the support of Athens, a new Priene was laid out on the slopes of Mount Mycale. Following the precepts of the geometer Hippodamus of Miletus, the steep and difficult site was forced into a strict gridiron plan of narrow streets, with a broad central avenue connecting the major buildings and agoras. The plan has an elegant simplicity, but it's a matter for conjecture whether the Prieneans used it for art's sake or simply to make land surveys easier.

The Site

After a fair climb up from the parking lot, you enter Priene through the northwest gate. Continue across the unexcavated portion of the town to one of the finest extant examples of a classical Greek **theatre**. Unlike the theatres elsewhere in Turkey, built or remodelled under the Romans, this one is small and horseshoe-shaped, leaving ample space for the orchestra and chorus, the centre of attention in a classical Greek play. The seats around the orchestra were for the nobles of the city, a kind of ancient dress circle. At the centre is an altar, dedicated to Dionysus. Also unlike later works, there is no elaborate stage building. The small colonnaded structure, the **proskenion**, dates from the 2nd century BC. Originally, the three doors were used for the entrance of actors, and the spaces between them covered with painted boards for scenery. The roof of the proskenion, used for the *deus ex machina*, took more and more of the action as drama evolved; eventually it came to hold the action,

Sanctuary of
Demeter and Kore

Theatre

Temple of
Athena

Bouleterion

Sacred
Stoa

House of
Alexander

N

300 metres
200 yards

Gymnasium

Stadium

and the proscenium became what we know as the stage. Facing it, at the right-hand end of the first row of seats, is a square stone base that held a water clock; as Greek theatres also served for political meetings, and occasionally for important trials, the water clock controlled the time allotted to each speaker.

Immediately below the theatre are the foundations of a Byzantine church and a gymnasium. Below these lie the **agora** and centre of Priene. On its north side, the **sacred stoa**, according to its inscriptions, was built as a gift of King Ariarthres VI of Cappadocia. Behind it, the well-preserved **bouleterion** or council hall (200 BC) was the subject of a beautifully drawn reconstruction that appears in most books on ancient Greek architecture. Even among its ruins, you can gain an insight into the public life of an ancient Greek democracy. In the bouleterion were seats for 600–700 citizens, who discussed matters not crucial enough to submit to the entire citizen assembly. Speakers stood next to the altar that held an eternal flame, symbolizing the purity and continuity of Priene's civic life; as they spoke, their peers, on three sides, were close enough to look them in the eye. Next to the bouleterion is the **prytaneion**, where committees delegated by the council dealt with routine city business.

The Temple of Athena

The agora was the central square of Priene, devoted to commercial and religious affairs as well as political issues. The small square just to the east was the city's food market, while the sanctuary of Zeus Olympios, now gone, occupied the square's eastern face. Just to the northwest of the agora, stairs from another stoa lead up to the most important building of Priene, the **Temple of Athena**, a classic example of the Ionian order. Its architect, Pytheos, also designed the Mausoleum of Halicarnassus, but thought more of this temple, so much so that he wrote a book about it which was used as a textbook by architects throughout the Mediterranean. Several of the columns have been re-erected, and it's not hard to imagine how the temple must have appeared looming over the agora, Priene's most conspicuous landmark, visible for miles around. Here, as in all the city's buildings, the grey weathered surface of the stone hides a luminous cream-coloured marble from Mount Mycale, which the Greeks painted in bright colours.

An inscription on the temple of Athena relates that Alexander the Great financed its completion. For this, and for their liberation from the Persians, the Prieneans devoted a small shrine to him, in the company of the other gods. The **House of Alexander** is near the western gate of the central avenue. Along the way, you'll pass the excavated residential district of Priene. Although this was laid out in a rigid grid plan, there was a remarkable individuality in the inner plans of the houses: nearly all had a central courtyard and columnar porches, and many had second floors. The finest ones are just a few squares west of the theatre.

Other sites on the north and south sides of town require some climbing. In the northern heights, not too far above the theatre, is the oldest temple in Priene, the **Sanctuary of Demeter and Kore**, where the *temenos* wall, benches to hold votive statues, and the sacrificial pit can be seen. To the south, just below the agora at the city's walls, are the **gymnasium**, with its well-preserved washrooms where the water poured out of lion-headed spouts, and the **stadium**. Like the theatre, this is a rare example of the earlier Greek style, and was never remodelled into a Roman extravaganza. Seats are on one side only, and the course is a short and simple one-way track. Remains of the starting gate are near the entrance from the gymnasium: the Greeks started their runners as we do horses.

Miletus

Priene stood on the northern edge of the Latmian Gulf, the inlet now filled by the advancing delta of the Maeander. On the southern shore was **Miletus**, first among the Greek cities until the rise of Athens in the 5th century BC. Few cities have ever achieved such power and brilliance, and left so little to show for it. The river again is to blame. Of the original Miletus so few traces remain that scholars still dispute its precise location. The present ruins date from the second foundation, after the original city was devastated by the Persians in 495 BC.

History

Miletus' origins are shadowy, though recent excavations have produced finds that go back to *c.* 1600 BC. Ancient writers claimed its founding as the work of Carians, Lycians or Cretans. The city was probably the *Millewanda* that appears in Hittite records of the 14th century, a thorn in the side of Hittite King Mursilis II. Millewanda was the capital of a people known as the Ahhiyawans—probably the origin of the 'Achaeans' in Homer. Mythology credits an eponymous founder, a mortal son of Apollo who sailed from Minoan Crete and made Miletus an important seaport. With the collapse of the Minoans, Miletus was occupied by the Mycenaeans; when the Ionians seized the town, they killed the Cretan men and married their wives, lousy but typical behaviour for the period. By 700 BC, Ionian Miletus began to prosper, controlling the Aegean trade routes and sending out more colonies than any other Greek city—90 of them, from Naukratis on the Nile delta to Sinope on the Black Sea.

Miletus' greatest colony, however, was the human mind. The Milesians were the first to look at the world from a detached, universal viewpoint. Thales, foremost among the Seven Sages and the first philosopher, suggested that water was the origin of all life; his follower Anaximander declared all things were infinite in substance, that the earth hung free, only one of infinite worlds; while the third great Milesian philosopher, Anaximenes, understood everything to be made of air, either rarefied or condensed, which encompassed the world like a human soul.

As the Persian menace grew, Ionian thinkers started moving to the growing city of Athens, keeping philosophy alive after Miletus suffered its fatal defeat in 495 BC. It broke the heart of the ancient world: when a play called *The Fall of Miletus* was performed in Athens, it caused the audience to burst into tears, for which the dramatist was fined a thousand drachmae.

Miletus was rebuilt immediately after the Persians flattened it, on a new site and on a new grid plan according to the precepts of its native son, the geometer Hippodamus. Its arrangement of agoras and public buildings was a triumph of Greek urban design, but you can't see that from the ruins. If Priene is the most evocative Greek city, Miletus is the biggest archaeological disappointment of Turkey. So thoroughly has the Maeander scrubbed away and silted over its ruins that little beside the theatre remains. It is even difficult to tell where the coastline was, and the city that contributed so much to western civilization has become a creepy desolation of muck and prickly weeds. In Aristotle, we read that the great Miletan philosopher Anaximander believed that the water was gradually drying up from the earth—it has been suggested he got the idea from watching his city's harbour gradually silt up.

Philosophy Starts Here

According to Aristotle's follower Eudemus, Thales, one of the 'seven wise men' of antiquity, brought geometry into Greece from Egypt, and showed how to use angles to find the distance from the shore to a ship in the harbour. Besides Egypt, he may also have visited Babylon, or perhaps he learned his astronomy only from contacts with the east, connections for which the cosmopolitan trading city of Miletus was well placed. His famous trick was to predict the solar eclipse of 585 BC. Though other peoples, the Chinese and the neolithic Britons, had done this long ago, it was quite a stunt for a 6th-century Greek, and it made his reputation for wisdom. 'The man's a Thales!', says a character in Aristophanes' *Birds*, written two centuries later.

Thales' successor, and possibly his student, was Anaximander, who drew the first maps among the Greeks and built the first model of the heavens and the first sundials. His student Anaximines, yet another Milesian, speculated on the cosmos and the nature of matter. From nearby Samos came Pythagoras, whose monumental contributions to mathematics are familiar enough; his brand of mathematical mysticism, in which all things could be reduced to numbers, dominates the thinking of scientifically-minded people today. All of these founders of philosophy wrote in verse, and only tantalizing fragments of their work remain—as with Heraclitus of Ephesus, the deepest and strangest of all, who left behind fascinating epigrams in the spirit of Zen :

> *This most beautiful cosmos is a pile of things poured out at random.*

> *It is not possible to step twice into the same river... it scatters and again comes together, and approaches and recedes.*

The lives of the Ionian philosophers covered only a few generations. By the 5th century the leading lights of philosophy, such as Zeno and Empedocles, were coming from the distant colonies in southern Italy and Sicily. Until the time of Plato and Aristotle, very few Greek thinkers came from Greece itself. Ionia, like Italy, was the 'new world' for the Greeks, a wide-open society of booming cities where free thinking was considerably easier than in the tradition-bound homeland.

The genuinely subversive contribution of the Ionian thinkers comes through in their attitude towards religion. As Xenophanes of Colophon put it, in one of the few surviving bits of his poetry:

> *Ethiopians say their gods are flat-nosed and dark,*
> *Thracians that theirs are blue-eyed and red-haired...*
> *If oxen and horses and lions had hands*
> *and were able to draw with their hands and do things the same as men,*
> *horses would draw the shapes of gods to look like horses,*
> *and oxen to look like oxen...*

Never before had anyone looked upon sacred things with such a critical eye. But the first philosophers were not trying to destroy religion, but to make faith square with what could be understood by reason. Their consensus was that God is one. Ideas make their way slowly, and the Ionians could not know they were paving the way for the acceptance of Christianity many centuries later. But that, however significant, was only a small part of their achievement. The Ionian philosophers' great discovery was a perception of order at work in the world, an order comprehensible to the human mind. Their speculations marked the beginnings of philosophy and science—the start of western civilization, no less.

The Site

With a map from the small **museum** half a mile south of the ruins (*open daily 8.30–12.30 and 1.30–5.30; adm*), you can locate a few landmarks. Miletus' great **theatre**, then as now the most conspicuous landmark, rises on a hillside above one of the city's five harbours, well preserved above the floods of the Maeander. The Roman theatre, with seats for 15,000, was built around the earlier work of the 4th century BC that seated only a third as many. The columns that marked the 'royal box' still stand. Scanty ruins of an agora and the stadium occupy the former harbour's opposite shore. From this side of Miletus, you have a good view of the island of Lade, now a mere lump in the Maeander Plain. Here, in 495 BC, the Persian navy destroyed the combined fleets of the Ionian cities and put an end to their rebellion. As leader of the revolt, Miletus' destruction was assured. Ironically, the Persian garrison later took refuge here when Alexander the Great stormed the town.

Climbing over the hill of the theatre will bring you to the **city centre**, a network of stoas, avenues and agoras around the narrow **Bay of Lions**. In wartime this harbour had special significance; it needed no fortifications on the shore, as a chain could easily be extended across it to protect both the town and the fleet. Some searching among the weeds will reveal the two stone lions that stood on either side of the harbour. Inside the harbour, a large triangular base once held a **monument of Augustus**, commemorating his victory over Cleopatra and Mark Antony at Actium in 31 BC.

Around the harbour, the only structures of interest lie along the wide processional avenue; the first, the **Temple of Apollo Delphinius**, has the foundations of a colonnaded sanctuary with statue bases and a curious circular temple. On the same side of the avenue are the **Capito Baths**, the **gymnasium**, a **nymphaion** and a 5th-century **church**. If you follow the avenue south through the enormous **south agora**, you'll find a fine 15th-century mosque, **İlyas Bey Camii**, made of coloured marble salvaged from Miletus, belonging to the nearby village of Yeniköy. The low hill beyond the city's southern walls called *Kalabak Tepe* was the acropolis of the original Miletus founded by Crete, where a few old stones have been found.

Didyma (Didim)

If Miletus disappoints, **Didyma** won't. Didyma, south of Miletus and in its territory, is a temple complex and not a city. Yet few in western Asia Minor are so well preserved or as impressive.

Didyma was a holy site before the Ionians ever arrived, and was believed to be the oldest of the 19 oracles in Asia Minor. The Greeks rededicated the Anatolian cult to their own god Apollo and continued the oracle. When Croesus, the King of Lydia, was considering his invasion of Persia, he wanted the advice of an oracle, but first decided to put three of them to the test. He sent ambassadors to ask each of them, on the same day, 'What is King Croesus doing?' Only Delphi knew he was boiling a lamb and tortoise stew; Didyma failed. When the Persians sacked Miletus they burned the temple and carried off its statue. The oracle fell silent for 150 years, until it predicted Alexander the Great's victory at Issus. Then the sacred spring suddenly flowed again. A grateful Alexander sent some money, his lieutenant Antiochus brought the statue back, and the oracle declared Alexander to be the son of Zeus.

Seleucus I of Syria and the Milesians started to rebuild the temple on a massive scale, planning to make it the largest in the world. Work continued in fits and starts for some 500 years but was never completed. As with so many other things in the time of Alexander and his successors, the ambition of the original work seems to have overreached all common sense; the technical difficulties in building column-and-lintel architecture on such a scale might well have doomed it from the start. Completed, it would have surpassed even the Artemision at Ephesus. As it is, the temple provides a wonderful lesson in the transience of glory. You may never have heard of Seleucus I, but he ruled an empire that stretched from the Aegean nearly to India, building it a piece at a time with lands snatched from the other generals of

Alexander, his former comrades-in-arms. Undoubtedly Seleucus' interest in the temple was in part as political propaganda, and as a monument to himself. Soon after it was begun, Seleucus moved to expand his empire westwards. He landed in Greece, and was assassinated as he stepped out of his boat.

As it was, the unfinished temple was considered by the ancients as one of their greatest works of architecture. In design it is comparable to the Artemision in Ephesus, encompassed by a double row of columns, some 120 in all. The cella, with its 70ft walls, was too large to be roofed over, so the cult statue of Apollo was kept in a smaller temple behind the cella. Many columns have been re-erected by the excavators. Because the temple was never completed, some are unfluted, and many stone blocks still bear their masons' marks. Every five years the Didymeia—sports, drama, and music contests—was held at the sanctuary and in the **stadium** next to it; names carved in the steps of the temple are those of spectators with reserved seats.

Lake Bafa and Heracleia (Kapıkırı)

Near Didyma are a pair of beauty spots. On the tip of Didyma's peninsula, **Altınkum** boasts fine sandy beaches, and an ambition someday to usurp Kuşadası as the coast's busiest resort. On the main north–south highway, the lake of **Bafa** was once part of the sea, but the silt-bearing Maeander dammed it off so long ago that its waters are more fresh than saline. In summer, the polarized blue, burnt gold and silvery green of the lake, grass and olive trees can be mesmerising. Overlooking the lake looms the jagged form of Mount Latmos (in Turkish, the 'Hill of Five Fingers'), where the beautiful shepherd Endymion slept. The moon goddess Selene fell in love with him, asking her father Zeus to grant perpetual sleep to the youth. This done, she visited him every night and eventually bore him 50 children. Few places in Turkey are so hauntingly beautiful under a full moon.

Beneath the mountain stood **Heracleia,** a Carian city (the Carians, like the Lydians and Lycians, were a native people of Anatolia Hellenized by the Greeks). Heracleia was never very important, but is a must for all romantics, who, for the full effect, should sail there across the lake from the camp site on the shore. A new road also leads around the lake to the site and the nearby village of **Kapıkırı**, which has basic accommodation. The ruins are impressive, especially the walls and defensive works built by Lysimachus in the 3rd century BC that twist and clamber up the slopes of Mount Latmos. The setting lends the towers, gates, stairs and parapets an other-worldly air.

In the city, the cella walls of the **Temple of Athena**, high on a bluff, dominate the other monuments. The **agora** behind the temple is also mostly intact, especially its fine south wall. The theatre, nymphaeum and bouleuterion have not held up so well, but in the southern part of Heracleia is an unusual temple, the **Sanctuary of Endymion**, partially cut into the rock, rounded in the back, with a row of columns in the front. In the 7th century, Christian refugees from the Sinai built monasteries and hermitages on the lake islets and around Mount Latmos, and venerated Endymion, a mystic who spent his life on Mount Latmos meditating on the moon, seeking the secret name of God. When he finally learned it, he died and was laid to rest here. Once a year the Christians would open up Endymion's coffin, and his bones would hum, trying to communicate the holy name. Further south, beyond the

Byzantine castle is a **Carian necropolis:** the economy-minded Carians used natural pits in the rock and covered them with crude stone slabs. Some lie under the surface of the lake.

Priene to Lake Bafa *Where to Stay*

Two decades ago, the swampy, formerly malarial wastelands at the mouth of the Menderes were one of the emptiest corners of the Aegean coast. Now the growing new resort on the fine beach at Altınkum ('golden sand') has over a score of hotels and *pansiyonlar*. Don't come expecting peace and quiet: its decibel count is fast catching up with the other coastal fleshpots.

Priene and Söke

Just a pleasant amble away from the ruins at Priene is the former Greek village of Güllübahçe, a haven of pomegranate gardens and orange orchards. Set amongst these is the **Priene Pansiyon**, ✆ 0256 547 1725, where the kindly hostess offers simple, spotless rooms with wooden ceilings for $16. She also welcomes campers. If you prefer hustle and bustle, there is a simple and quite comfortable hotel in Söke, the **Haymanalı**, near the bus station at 55 Santral Garaj Yolu, ✆ 0256 512 0322; some rooms with TV and balconies. After all the showiness of the coastal resorts, the workaday atmosphere in this warts-and-all small town may prove oddly refreshing.

Altınkum

To do Altınkum in style, stay at the *moderate* ★★★**Orion Hotel Didim**, ✆ 0256 813 5550, ✆ 0256 813 2041, a nicely flagrant piece of resort architecture right on the beach; all rooms have balcony, sea view and satellite TV. There's a pool and garden.

Altınkum's *cheap* pensions are gathered together behind the harbour: about a dozen family-run places, all charging roughly $6 and all much the same; take your pick.

Lake Bafa

Situated off the road to Milas in an olive grove sloping down to **Lake Bafa** is **Club Natura Oliva**, ✆ 0252 519 1072, ✆ 0252 519 1015. This German-owned club has received a World Wildlife Fund award for its sensitivity to the environment. Each of the 11 bungalows has a fireplace and terrace with stunning views over the lake. En suite doubles with wooden ceilings are priced at $48, $60 with dinner. The club is somewhat isolated, so venturing elsewhere for an evening meal without your own transport is difficult.

The village of Kapıkırı, near the lake, is set amongst the Heracleian ruins. The best of the rudimentary pensions here is the **Agora**, ✆ 0252 543 5445 ✆ 0252 543 5567. Its 14 rooms and three separate wooden bungalows are surrounded by a garden cascading with flowers. Included in the price of $16 per double is an excellent break-fast. Bathroom facilities are shared.

camping

On beautiful Lake Bafa there are several places to camp, the best being **Çeri'nin Camping**, ✆ 0252 519 1086; it is next to some Byzantine ruins and has a basic restaurant, as well as several rather spartan rooms to let for $5 per person. Boat tours of Heracleia can be arranged from here, as well as trips to the far side of the lake, where the seldom-visited island of Ekiz is strewn with yet more Byzantine ruins. If you are on the lake in April or May, you may be treated to a migrating flamboyance of flamingos and pelicans.

Priene to Lake Bafa   *Eating Out*

Right below **Priene** and next to the waterfall is the **Şelale** restaurant, a wonderful oasis after clambering over the ruins in the sun, where you can eat for around $6. In **Söke** the **Barış Salonu** is at Basmacılar Caddesi 18, a pedestrian street next to the Koca Cami. You can eat good *pide* and döner under a canopy of vines for under $3. At **Didyma**, occupying a tremendous spot overlooking the temple, is the **Kamaçi Restaurant**, renowned for its fish. There are many more restaurants and lokantas by Didyma, and at **Altınkum**—typical resort town seafood places here, none of which seem to stand out. Everywhere else, take what you can find; some informal outdoor places with lake fish open up in the summer around the shores of **Lake Bafa**.

Along the Maeander to Pamukkale

Getting Around

The nearest **airport** to Pamukkale is 45 miles away at Çardak from where THY service buses run to Denizli. Flights are daily in summer, twice a week in winter.

Trains run frequently from İzmir and Selçuk to Aydın and Denizli; the overnight 'Pamukkale Ekspresi' connects Denizli with İstanbul. Aydın's otogar is south of town on the E24 highway; **buses** run from here every 30mins from İzmir and there is a regular service from Selçuk too, as well as Denizli and Bodrum. Minibuses use the old station in the city centre on Gazi Bulvarı, and there is a dolmuş connecting service between the two. From Denizli, frequent minibuses go up to Pamukkale—some wait until they have a load of passengers. Denizli city buses also make the trip, from the big square south of the otogar. In summer there are services direct to Pamukkale from all the nearby resorts (as many as ten a day), and also from Selçuk.

Getting to **Aphrodisias** by public transport can be a problem. If you mean to do it as a day trip make sure you have return transportation arranged in advance. Minibuses provide a service to Aphrodisias from Nazilli, though most only go to the village of Karacasu, seven miles (12km) away, from which you would have to take a taxi. In summer you might find a direct bus from İzmir to Geyre, or to Karacasu, with a dolmuş service to Geyre. Even so, the easiest way to do it without a car is to get on a tour from Pamukkale.

Tourist Information

Aydın: Yeni Dörtyol Mevkii, ℭ 0256 211 2842.

Denizli: City Tourism Directorate, Turan Güneş Caddesi, Valilik Arkası, ℭ 0258 264 3971. There are also tourist offices (no phone) at the train and bus stations.

Pamukkale: Örenyeri, ℭ 0258 272 2077.

Myus and Magnesia ad Maeander

Up the Maeander from Lake Bafa's north shore are the scanty remains of one of the twelve Ionian cities, **Myus**, near the modern village of Avşar. Although it once had a harbour bristling with 200 warships, it was later best known for malaria and for having once been traded away by Philip V of Macedon in exchange for some figs given him by Myus' upriver rival, **Magnesia ad Maeander**.

Lying between modern Söke and Ortaklar, Magnesia ad Maeander, like Turkey's other Magnesia (now Manisa), was founded by settlers from Greek Magnesia, who lacked imagination when it came to place names. Under the Persians, Magnesia itself had been given away to their old enemy, Themistocles, hero of the great Athenian victory over the Persians at Salamis in 480 BC. Towards the end of his career Themistocles lost the favour of the fickle Athenians and went to Persia, where King Artaxerxes had offered a reward to anyone who brought him Themistocles. The charming Themistocles claimed and received the reward himself. Artaxerxes then gave him Magnesia (for his bread), Lampsacus (for his wine) and Myus (for the rest of his dinner). Themistocles lived in Magnesia; when he was forced to take sides between his native Athens and Persia's ally Sparta in the Peloponnesian War, he committed suicide by drinking bull's blood during a sacrifice at the **Temple of Artemis Leucophryene**, the only monument of Magnesia that has survived. The temple dates from the 2nd century BC, and was erected after the goddess herself made a miraculous appearance in the city. Because of this, Magnesia was considered sacred, and therefore had no walls until Byzantine times.

Tralles (Aydın) and Nyssa

Continuing up the fertile Maeander valley, the large town of **Aydın** is the descendant of ancient Tralles, which lies just to the west. A military installation now occupies the site, and it can only be visited with special permission. It had two claims to fame: the 'Tralles stone', the most complete record of Greek musical notation, and its son Anthemius, mathematician and co-architect of the Aya Sofya. Aydın has a 17th-century mosque, the **Bey Cami**, and a small **museum** displaying some of the finds from Tralles, but nothing else to detain you.

Some twenty miles (32km) to the east, a sign points the way to ancient **Nyssa**, lost in the olives a mile from Sultanhisar. The city, in a lovely, picturesque gorge beneath Mount Messogis, was founded by Antiochus I in the 3rd century BC; most of what we know about it comes from the geographer Strabo, who studied there. He described Nyssa as a 'double city', split half the year by a torrential stream; he also wrote that the water was so greasy that the young men could dispense with oiling themselves after bathing. The imperial Roman **theatre** and the semi-circular **bouleuterion** (2nd century BC) are the best-preserved monuments in the city. Strabo described the 350ft vaulted **tunnel** that helped to drain Nyssa's spring torrents and support the city's main square and the current parking lot. Two Roman bridges spanned the gorge; nearby, a pile of stones once formed a **stadium**, although its seats were destroyed by flooding—flooding that was an original feature of the building, for the staging of *naumachiae*, or simulated sea battles.

Ancient **Aphrodisias**, on a lofty plateau below the slopes of Mount Cadmos, now Babadağ ('Mount Dad'), is a 44-mile (70km) detour south of the Maeander, but well worth while. Dedicated to the goddess of love, and to art, this city is one of most exciting recent excavations in Turkey, begun in 1961 by Dr Kenan T. Erim and New York University, partially financed by the National Geographic Society, and still underway.

History

The site was always sacred, perhaps as early as the Neolithic age; two large hills on the site are tells, covering settlements that go back at least 8,000 years. Aphrodite's predecessor may have been the eastern goddess Enana, the equivalent of Ishtar or Astarte; the city's original name had been Ninoe, for Enana or for the legendary King Ninus of Assyria, founder of Nineveh, and it is believed the Assyrians at some remote date founded a sanctuary to the goddess here. By the Hellenistic age, the city's population was largely Greek, and Enana had become Aphrodite. History tells us little about classical Aphrodisias, except that Julius Caesar, whose family claimed descent from the goddess through Aeneas of Troy, preserved the sanctity of the great Temple of Aphrodite. In the civil wars that followed his death, Aphrodisias wisely chose the side of Augustus, and was rewarded with special privileges and exemptions from imperial taxes; the first Emperor was so impressed with it that he declared, 'I choose this city from among all those in Asia for myself...'

After three centuries as a pampered art centre, the first catastrophe to strike Aphrodisias was the coming of Christianity; besides shutting down the market for classical sculpture, the Christians added the indignity of renaming the town 'Stavropolis', the City of the Cross. Then came two major earthquakes in the 4th century, and another in the 7th. By Byzantine times, the town was known simply as Caria, as it was the chief town in the province, and by the 13th century it was probably abandoned. A Turkish village named Geyre (a corruption of Caria) later grew up over the ruins; the village was relocated over the last 30 years to make way for the excavations.

Though it was long known that Aphrodisias had been a centre of scupture from Augustus' day, scholars had always believed that its artists were mere copyists, redoing earlier Greek and Hellenistic works. But from the quantity of excellent statuary found, made of the fine blueish marble from Babadağ, it became clear that an important and strikingly original school of sculptors existed here, one that adorned Aphrodisias and exported works throughout the Mediterranean; signatures on statues found elsewhere are now identified with the 'Aphrodisian school'. The city's festivals featured sculptural competitions, something unique in the ancient world.

The Site

Open in summer 8.30–7, in winter 9–5; adm.

Still under excavation (no photos, no dallying off the prescribed path), Aphrodisias is little more than a third uncovered. The circular tour begins with the **theatre**, with a seating capacity of 10,000, dug into the flank of a tell, or mound, in which are buried layers of

Aphrodisias

400 metres
400 yards

N

Stadium

Northern Gate

Temple of
Aphrodite

Monumental
Gateway

Western Gate

Museum

Odeon

Entrance

Bishops
Palace

Agora

Baths of Hadrian

Agora

Theatre

Portico of
Tiberius

Acropolis
Hill

Baths

Eastern Gate

earlier settlements. Built into the theatre walls are a number of inscribed stones, recording Augustus's favours to the city and decrees of later emperors. An enclosed square, the **Tetrastoon**, with a round fountain at its centre, stood here, along with a bath complex, the **'Theatre Baths'**, while to the west are the much more lavish **Baths of Hadrian**, complete with huge galleries, heated rooms and a palaestra, still retaining some tiles and mosaics. Adjacent to these baths, on the opposite side of the hill from the theatre, the **'large basilica'** was decorated with some unusual reliefs of the city's history, including figures of Ninus, his famous wife Queen Semiramis, and King Gordius of Phrygia. Also on display here is a stone carved with Emperor Diocletian's *Edict of Prices* of 301 AD, the economic 'reform' that fixed prices, devalued the currency and locked sons into following their fathers' professions—altogether perhaps the most catastrophic error Rome ever made, and one that probably sealed the fate of the dying empire.

The **Portico of Tiberius** and the **agora**; both impressive colonnaded quadrangles, marked the centre of the city and its marketplace, now a poplar grove. To form a grand entrance for the agora, the Julio-Claudian emperors contributed a sumptuous embellishment called the **Sebasteion**, consisting of two parallel three-storey porticos that housed shops. Some of the finest sculptural work in Aphrodisias was created to decorate it, and some has been left *in* *situ*: mythological and Homeric scenes, and imperial propaganda reliefs including *Claudius subduing Britain* and Nero being equally rough with the Armenians.

To the north is the former palace of the Roman governor, a peristyle house converted in the 5th century into the **bishop's residence**. Next to it stands the **odeon**, a smaller, more intimate theatre; originally covered with a wooden roof, it was used for concerts and meetings of the town council. Behind it, the circular platform in stone was a **heroon**, the base of a tomb or monument to some local worthy; the surrounding area was occupied by one of Aphrodisias's sculpture workshops.

North of the agora, the **Temple of Aphrodite** was built in the reign of Augustus over a sanctuary at least six centuries older; 14 of its Ionic columns have been re-erected. The Byzantines made the whole into a basilica in the late 5th century. Hadrian added the most remarkable building yet discovered in Aphrodisias, the **Tetrapylon**, a monumental gateway that led into the *temenos*, or sanctuary area, which in Roman times took the form of a small park connecting the gate and the temple facade; subsidiary buildings filled the temenos on the other three sides. Now sustantially rebuilt from the stones on the ground, the Tetrapylon provides a wonderful example of the 'Baroque' tendency of classical architecture in the 2nd century AD, at the height of Roman-era prosperity, with a tall arch boldly cut into the pediment, Corinthian columns with spiral fluting, and lavish sculptural trim of acanthus scrolls.

North of Aphrodite's temple is the **stadium**, perhaps the largest, and certainly one of the best preserved ever discovered. It stretches 865ft from end to end and could seat 30,000; one side was enclosed in late Roman or Byzantine times for use as a theatre. The northern side of the stadium was incorporated into the **walls**, which may have been begun in the 5th century AD, or perhaps even as early as the 3rd, when the Goths made their great raid into Asia Minor. As a sacred city, like Magnesia, Aphrodisias had no need for defences in Hellenistic times.

A **museum** has recently opened on the site to house the marble goddesses, gods, satyrs and emperors found in the ruins of all the city's major buildings. Some of the outstanding works come from the **Monument of Zoilos**, a wealthy benefactor of the city who had once been a favoured slave of Augustus; others were found in the theatre, including a beautiful, damaged statue of *Melpomene*, muse of Tragedy, or in the odeon: a number of statues of philosophers and poets with their heads knocked off, no doubt by the Christians. The cult image from the Temple of Aphrodite was never found, but another statue of the goddess uncovered here may provide some clues to its appearance: a standing figure in a gown covered with religious symbols and attributes: a crescent moon, the Three Graces, beasts of land and sea, and winged *erotes* offering a libation.

Denizli

Returning to the main highway, the E24, you'll pass **Laodicea**, chiefly remembered today as one of the Seven Churches of Asia addressed by John in *Revelations* and as the last residence of Cicero. At the head of the Maeander valley is the major market town of **Denizli**, unremarkable except for two large statues of chickens, the bird to whom the city owes its present prosperity, one in the centre of town and one on the roundabout on the road to Pamukkale.

Pamukkale ('Cotton Castle') has a lot to live up to. It features in all the tourist brochures; posters of it cover up stubborn stains on hotel walls the length and breadth of Turkey. The familiar image is of a curtain of stalagmites and stepped shallow pools, merging into one another on dozens of different levels, a fairyland of cotton-white forms and pale blue water cascading gently down. Carefree holidaymakers are shown frolicking in the warm, glistening pools, with the lovely green valley of Maeander spread out far below.

But if you look closely at these pictures of people splashing about, their hairstyles may seem a little dated: the pools have been closed to bathers for several years. This UNESCO site has become a victim of its own popularity: too many hotels draining off the water in the 1980s and '90s and too many tourists tramping around the pools caused serious deterioration in the terraces. A drastic remedy was called for, and to its credit, the Turkish government swallowed its bitter pill unflinchingly: it had the hotels crowding around the lip of the great white plateau paid off and pulled down. A team of German scientists was brought in to devise a way of restoring the damaged travertines to their former glory. Their answer has been to ensure that all the water in a particular pool has evaporated fully (leaving behind the maximum amount of calcium necessary to strengthen the pool) before diverting spring water to fill up the pool again. As a consequence of this preservation work, the pools are cordoned off and many are empty. Signs put up at the top of the cliff say it all: 'Entering the travertines is certainly not allowed to protect this amazing natural beauty as it used to be.' This is undoubtedly good news for the site in the long term, but not for today's visitors brainwashed by the glossy poster images of old. Yet if visitors can put their wilder expectations to one side, then Pamukkale remains spectacular, rising irrationally from the valley like a glistening mid-summer snowscape.

Hierapolis

The charms of Pamukkale and its thermal springs also caught the eye of Eumenes II of Pergamon, who founded the Holy City, or **Hierapolis** on top of the plateau. Like Pergamon itself, Hierapolis was bequeathed to Rome in the will of Attalus III. An earthquake shattered it in AD 17, but it was quickly rebuilt and had its greatest prosperity in the 2nd and 3rd centuries. The Apostle Philip lived here and was martyred in the year AD 80: in the Byzantine era, the church of St Philip dominated the town.

The great **baths** near the parking area were constructed in the 2nd century and are so well preserved that they now serve as a **museum**, displaying the fine marbles unearthed by Italian archaeologists; many of the statues are now recognized to have come from the Aphrodisian school. At least three Roman Emperors visited Hierapolis and bathed in the portion of the bath especially reserved for them. Behind the bath stands a **temple of Apollo**, chief deity of the city, a **fountain** and a small grotto called the **Plutonium**, a sanctuary of Hades (Pluto), the god of the Underworld; a sign warns of poisonous vapours, the same that instantly killed sparrows in Strabo's day but were harmless to eunuchs.

The impressive and recently restored **theatre** dates from the 2nd century AD, and is especially interesting for the fine reliefs of Apollo's twin, Artemis. Behind the theatre and outside the Roman wall is the **Martyrium of St Philip the Apostle** of the 5th century. From the bath, the road leads to the other excavations: a **colonnaded street** erected by Domitian, a monumental **gate** of the same period, another **bath** and, stretching on for over a mile, the **necropolis** with a fascinating variety of tombs and sarcophagi dating from Hierapolis' foundation up into Christian times.

Visitors can still swim in the warm and slightly effervescent water of the ancient Sacred Pool, although there's little sacred about it nowadays, ringed as it is by tourist stalls and ice cream stands. Signs boast of the water's powers to heal everything from cataracts to obesity.

Aydın to Pamukkale **Where to Stay**

Aydın

There's little reason to overnight here: if you do, the **★★Orhan**, Gazi Bulvarı 63, ✆ 0256 225 1713, ✇ 0256 225 1781, is the best available; double rooms with private shower cost $24.

Aphrodisias

Staying near the site of Aphrodisias is possible at **Chez Mestan**, ✆ 0256 448 8046 on the Karacasu road. The Turkish owner and his French wife offer basic rooms for $15. If the 28 rooms fill up, their plan B is to send the touristic overflow to their more luxurious establishment up the road, the **Aphrodisias Hotel**, ✆ 0256 448 8132 ✇ 0256 448 8422, where rooms are twice as nice for twice the price.

Denizli

inexpensive–cheap

Denizli has several pleasant hotels although, again, there's no reason to stay here unless Pamukkale is packed—a common enough occurrence in summer. The best in town are the **★★★Pişkin**, 10 Atatürk Caddesi, ✆ 0258 264 5648, and the **★★★Palaz**, Kayalık Caddesi, ✆ 0258 263 0587; both have comfortable rooms with TV and air-conditioning. There are many options if you need to be near the bus station and its attendant decibel levels. Closest and most convenient is the **★★★Laodikya** at 630 Sokak 9, ✆ 0258 265 1506, ✇ 0258 241 2005. Although still clinging to its three-star rating, it's dangling from the third star like a latter-day Buster Keaton. However, its bright rooms with air-con are good value at $22. The best of the hotels orbiting the otogar is the **★★★Den Tur**, Saraylar Mah., Cumhuriyet Caddesi, ✆ 0258 241 7189, ✇ 0258 241 1969; $35 for well-equipped if impersonal rooms.

Most of the good *pansiyonlar* in Denizli are a fair walk from the otogar: the best is the friendly **Denizli**, ✆ 0258 261 8738, on Deliktaş Sokak. Rooms with private showers and toilets cost $16.

Pamukkale and around

moderate

The best hotels near Pamukkale are are in Karahayıt, three miles west of the northern entrance to the site. Karahayıt is currently more of a tourist shanty town than a village, all breezeblocks, cement mixers and half-finished roads. Most of the luxury hotels here have comfortable rooms, swimming pools and a tourist conveyor-belt atmosphere. An exception to that last comment is the ★★★★**Colossae Thermal**, ✆ 0258 271 4156, 🖷 0258 271 4250, *colossae@domi.net.tr*, an impressively stylish complex built around a courtyard with a huge pool: lavish rooms, a hamam and nightclubs and sports to keep you busy. Better value is the ★★★★**Thermal Pam**, ✆ 0258 271 4140, 🖷 0258 271 4097, set back from Karahayıt amongst well-kept gardens. Entry to the complex is via a road lined with palm trees. As well as two swimming pools there are also sauna and hamam facilities. Well-equipped rooms cost only $40 including breakfast.

inexpensive

Pamukkale village (Pamukkale Köyü) is a short walk away from the calcium formations. Although it's bursting with hotels, many of these became bloated and lethargic over the 1980s and 1990s on the rich tourist pickings. Now that drastic measures have been taken to preserve the Pamukkale pools, the site is no longer such an automatic tourist draw and the hotels suddenly need to work harder to hold on to their clientele. Clustering at the western edge of the village are a number of family-run hotels catering mostly to tour groups. The best of these is the ★★★**Koçak**, ✆ 0258 272 2492, 🖷 0258 272 2112. All rooms have air-con, showers and balconies, many of which overlook the swimming pool. There's also a jacuzzi for bubbly types and a sauna for sweaters; doubles with half board $35.

cheap

In the village below Pamukkale (Pamukkale Köyü) are dozens of cheap *pansiyonlar*. It's an inferno; their representatives will accost you the moment you clamber out of your car or off the bus. Most are fair for the price, and many have swimming pools (although some are no bigger than a fair-sized bucket), but this is a place where you can afford to be choosy. One of the nicest is the **Turku**, ✆ 0258 272 2181, located in a quiet back street off Atatürk Caddesi. It has a pleasant wooden façade and interior as well as the obligatory small pool. Its only drawback is the cramped en suite bathrooms; $15 including breakfast. The **Weisse Burg**, just off Menderes Caddesi, ✆ 0258 272 2064, may not be the most beautiful *pansiyon* in the village, nor the best kept or situated, but it is certainly amongst the most welcoming. It is run by one of life's enthusiasts, Hacer Yiğen, and her husband. Doubles with private bathroom go for $14; there is also a swimming pool actually big enough to swim in. For the same price, nearby on the opposite side of the street, is the well-run **Aspawa**, ✆ 0258 272 2094, where the family will even fetch you from Denizli bus station if you call them, any time day or night.

Many of the *pansiyonlar* have improved themselves into proper little hotels, where a room with bath usually goes for $14. Try the English-speaking **Kervansaray**, ✆ 0258 272 2209, 🖷 0258 272 2143, with a swimming pool and good restaurant.

Ali's, ✆ 0258 272 3123, is a famous institution, with everything from a campground to private rooms, a restaurant and a swimming pool filled with water from the hot springs. It offers uninterrupted views of the white cliffs of Pamukkale, but is also next to a main road; $10. Further along the same road is the **Özbay Hotel**,

℗ 0258 272 2720, ✆ 0258 272 2126, where smarter en suite doubles with balcony cost $18 including breakfast.

Aydın to Pamukkale
Eating Out

In **Denizli**, the place to go is the **Denizli Evi**, a beautifully restored Ottoman house on İstiklâl Caddesi: a wide choice of mezes, grills and seafood, and sometimes live classical Turkish music for accompaniment; well worth a splurge at about $12.

If you're driving, the **Doyurum Restaurant**, 10km out of Karacasu on the road to Pamukkale, is a nice place to break the journey, where you can eat very well for $6. In **Pamukkale**, nearly all the restaurants are attached to the hotels and are somewhat overpriced. On the other hand, most *pansiyonlar* offer filling meals at sensible prices. The **Aspawa** charges $5 for an evening meal of six dishes. You could climb up to the rooftop of the **Weisse Burg** for Hacer's excellent culinary creations, often including vegetarian options. If you want to dine at a restaurant proper, the **Han** on the main square offers the usual meat dishes and fish such as speckled trout for $3.

Caria

This section of the southwest coast, between Lake Bafa and Bodrum, once belonged to the Carians, yet another native people more or less Hellenized by the time history discovered them. Halicarnassus (Bodrum) was their largest city, the birthplace of Herodotus and capital of King Mausolus, who gave the world a new name for tombs.

Getting Around

It won't be easy to see any of these minor sights without a **car**. For Euromos, take any **bus** from Söke to Bodrum and ask to be let off at Selimiye, the nearest village; Selimiye is also served by infrequent **minibuses** from Milas. For Alinda, take the **minibus** from Aydın to the village of Karpuzlu, within walking distance of the ruins; this will be a rather long day trip. For Alabanda and Gerga, you'll have to make a deal with a **taxi** driver if you don't have a car. Labranda can be reached by **car** or taxi on a nasty dirt road from the village of Kargıcak, north of Milas.

To reach Güllük, take any Milas–Bodrum **bus** and get off at the Güllük junction, where you can either hitch or wait for one of the very regular **minibuses** from Milas dolmuş terminus to pass by. In Güllük, you can get a party together and rent a **boat** for an inexpensive day trip to Iasos. Ören is linked by **bus** to Milas.

Tourist Information

Güllük: in the Belediye on the harbour front, ℗ 0252 522 2776.

Muğla: Marmaris Bulvarı 24 (a 10min walk from the roundabout which encircles a statue of Atatürk), ℗ 0252 214 1261.

Inland: The Carian Heartland

Even in Roman times, cultural Hellenization of Caria was largely limited to the coasts. Come up to the heights between Aydın and Muğla, to the heart of this lost nation, and you will find a remarkable little flock of stone cities, testimony to a Caria that was prosperous and densely populated through Roman times, and has been a desolation ever since. The architecture—for the surviving ruins are substantial—and the entire feeling of the more isolated sites seems a world away from sophisticated Ephesus or Pergamon.

There are few good roads in these parts, and it's as easy to get lost in the hills as it is to become totally confused over all these sites with exasperatingly similar names. **Alinda**, near the village of Karpuzlu, about halfway between Aydın and Muğla, was once the outpost of Queen Ada, sister of King Mausolus (one that he didn't marry). She kicked up a fuss in the dynastic squabbles following Mausolus' death, and found her knight in shining armour in the person of Alexander the Great. Ada promised to support Alexander if he helped her capture Halicarnassus, and the two spent weeks plotting in Alinda.

Never excavated, Alinda is one of the most attractive ruins in which to explore. The ancient town is on a dominating height. In the centre, there is a market building the size of a department store bordering its agora (two of the three floors are still intact), a theatre and a watch tower, all in a good state of preservation. From the tower it is a short climb up to the second, upper acropolis, with walls and a gate in equally good shape; oddly, this one contained no temples but only houses. If you have more time for exploring there are necropoli all around the town, and the handsome arcade of an aqueduct, visible from the acropolis.

Less remains of **Alabanda**, five miles (8km) from modern **Çine**. This city was also briefly capital of Caria, and still has its fine wall and bouleuterion, but no trace of a temple of Apollo mentioned by Vitruvius. The river Çine Çay, with its gorge, is ruggedly picturesque, especially along the road between Çine and Yatağan Göktepe. In antiquity the river was called Marsyas, after the flute-playing satyr who had the audacity to challenge Apollo and his lyre to a musical contest, with the Muses as judge. When the god was proclaimed victor, Apollo, never known for his sense of humour, flayed Marsyas alive and hung his skin on a tree at Calaenae to the south, the source of the Çine Çay.

Southeast of Alabanda, on the opposite side of the Aydın–Muğla road, you can visit **Gerga**, no doubt the most bizarre ruin in western Turkey—but it won't be easy. Along the Aydın–Muğla road north of Çine, you'll see the ruined 16th-century İncekemer ('slender arches') Bridge; from here, it's a two-hour walk, not signposted, up to the village of İncekemer and from there to Gerga. The big mystery here is the endless Greek inscriptions on every monument and bit of exposed rock—'Gergas' or 'Gergakome' (Gerga village), as if the inhabitants wanted to make sure you know where you are. Some of these are in letters three feet tall; nothing similar is recorded in any other ancient town. In fact no one knows whether this was a real town, or perhaps an important Carian religious sanctuary, or whether Gerga was its name or the name of a deity worshipped here. The major attraction is a temple, almost perfectly preserved, that seems almost a parody of Greek architecture, with a stone roof carved to mimic a wooden one. Nearby is a huge fallen statue, also marked 'Gergas'. There is another fallen statue to the west, along with two oil presses and a pair of tall pyramidal monuments. Everything in Gerga most likely dates from Roman times. No ancient writers mention this town, neither has any part of it been excavated. What it was, and the meaning of its enigmatic monuments, remains a total mystery.

Muğla, and More Carian Cities

The road to Marmaris and its peninsula begins at the provincial capital, **Muğla**, a modern and surprisingly attractive city that seems a world away from the tourist fleshpots of the coast. Bureaucracy is Muğla's business. Like a mini-Bonn, it is full of civic pride and *bieder* prosperity, though this has come mostly from the tobacco and olive fields in the surrounding countryside. There is little to go out of your way for, but you can explore the pretty, well-maintained 18th-century residential neighbourhoods reminiscent of those in Bursa, clinging to the hillsides to the north of the bazaar. Market day is Thursday. In the second week of September each year, the nearby village of Yeşilyurt plays host to a bull-wrestling contest. The owner of the beast who can bring the opposing animal to the ground or chase it out of the ring wins $300, more than a government employee's average monthly salary.

Muğla is also the base for visiting the Hellenistic-Roman ruins of **Stratonikya** (*Stratoniceia*), 22 miles (36km) to the west, near to Eskihisar and to a lignite strip mine that has devoured the necropolis. This city began as Chrysaor, centre of the Chrysaoric Confederacy to which all Carian cities belonged. It was refounded by King Antiochus and named for his wife Stratonice, who had previously been his stepmother (a little present from his dad, Seleucus I; women didn't get much respect from Alexander's generals). The city belonged off and on to Rhodes before Roman rule, and it prospered greatly until Byzantine times. At the centre of the site stands a building that is often called the 'Temple of Serapis', but may really have been the bouleterion, bordering what was the agora. Other remains include parts of the walls and gates, a Roman gymnasium and a substantially intact theatre; there's a small **museum** of finds, and further excavations here are currently underway.

Lagina, north of Stratonikya near the village of Turgut, is the site of the **Hekateion**, an important Carian sanctuary to Hecate, the witchy Queen of the Night. Her sacred spring can still be seen near the ruins.

Another collection of lost Carian cities can be visited south of Lake Bafa. **Euromos**, the northernmost of them, is also the easiest to find, just off the road from Lake Bafa to Milas. It is notable these days for its majestic, magnificently preserved **Temple of Zeus** (2nd century AD), lying tantalizingly close to the highway (Route 525). Paid for by Hadrian, it's one of the few Corinthian temples along the coast, and one of the best-preserved in Turkey; 16 of its elegant columns and their architrave still stand in place. Other ruins include a theatre and Roman-era baths.

Much more substantial is **Labranda**, a town that usually belonged to neighbouring Mylasa. It was known for its sanctuary of the double axe (a *labrys*, as in ancient Crete) dedicated to Zeus Statius, where the oracle was a pool of tame fish who, if ancient writers are to be believed, wore golden earrings and necklaces. (The answer was favourable if the fish ate the petitioner's breadcrumbs. A similar oracle survives way out in eastern Turkey, at Şanlıurfa (*see* p.498); now it is an important Muslim pilgrimage site, but you can still feed the fish.) The remains here, tidily excavated by a Swedish team and marked on a placard, include the Temple of Zeus, adjacent priests' houses and well-preserved *androns* (palaces reserved for sacred banquets) notable for their unusual windows. Another excavated section to the east includes a monumental stairway leading up to a Byzantine church. Behind this, a small building is thought to be the location of the oracle.

Mylasa (Milas)

A Sacred Way ran the 10 miles between Labranda and the city of **Mylasa** (modern **Milas**) in the 4th century BC. Mylasa, long the most important of the Carian cities, was the home town and capital of Mausolus. In ancient times it had a reputation for its fine temples and public buildings, partly thanks to a nearby marble quarry. Milas has been continuously occupied since ancient times, the only one of these Carian towns to survive, and consequently little remains. Bits and pieces of its ancient buildings can be seen in the town's fine collection of medieval mosques, notably the **Firuz Bey Camii**, built by the Ottomans in 1394, shortly after they captured the city. Earlier mosques, the **Orhan Bey Camii** and the **Ulu Cami**, are the work of the Turkish Menteşe emirs, who founded a little state here a century before the Ottomans. Across from the Ulu Cami is a small **archaeological museum**.

The large **Baltalı Kapı**, the Roman-era 'gate of the axe', marks the beginning of the Sacred Way, around the corner from the Orhan Bey Camii. South of here on Tabakhane Caddesi, the site of the **Temple of Zeus** is marked by a single Corinthian column, currently occupied by a stork. This is the edge of Milas's charming bazaar district, a pocket of narrow streets that contains a wonderful medieval *han*, the **Çöllu Hanı**, just off Cumhuriyet Caddesi. The best time to visit Milas is a Tuesday, when there is a big farmers' market. Old streets around the edge of the bazaar and on the riverbank have a number of pretty Ottoman mansions from the 18th century, in varying states of decay.

West of the centre on Gümüşkesen Caddesi, a tomb called the **Gümüşkesen** (2nd century AD) is believed to be an exact miniature of the great Mausoleum of Halicarnassus. For a tip the caretaker will let you climb up to the roof for a view over the city. It's ironic that Milas was the only one of these cities to survive, because it is the only one on the plain, not on a defensible hilltop. A Roman governor once remarked that 'the people who founded this city must have known no fear'. The Mylasans' citadel, now called **Beçin Kale**, lies 5km east of the city. Its castle, built by the Byzantines and remodelled by the Menteşe Turks, now contains the ruins of a later Turkish village. The Menteşe governors built a complex of buildings further up the hill, including a mosque, a *han* and the 1375 **Medrese of Ahmet Gazi**, the last governor, who withstood an Ottoman siege of over a year and who is buried inside.

Back on the coast, **Iasos** (modern Kıyıkızacık), famous in antiquity for the best fish along the coast, has recently been excavated to reveal the best-preserved Carian city, although that's not saying a great deal; most memorable here is the restored Roman-era **mausoleum** on the outskirts. For a while splendid mausoleums were the fad in Caria, inspired by the great model in Halicarnassus. Excavations at Iasos have turned up pottery going back to Minoan times. An ally of Athens in the Peloponnesian War, the city was destroyed by a Spartan-Persian force and thereafter refounded. Its coinage showed a boy riding a dolphin, and there was a story to go with it of a boy who had befriended one, and was brought before Alexander and made a priest of Poseidon (similar legends were told in many Greek cities, such as Puteoli, near Naples). The scanty remains of the town itself, on a small peninsula, include a Roman-era bouleuterion, a colonnaded agora, walls and gates, a Temple of Demeter and Kore, and a Roman villa with some floor mosaics. Much of the rest of Iasos was cannibalized by the Ottomans; there are good views across the coast from the castle, founded by the Knights of St John when their headquarters were on nearby Rhodes.

Güllük and Ören

An oasis on its own small gulf, **Güllük** was for years the sole preserve of locals and Germans. Now it is fast learning to live with tourism, particularly as the nearby airport has been completed. This diminutive fishing village has been earmarked for development, and already the hulks of soon-to-be holiday homes fill the hills to its north. Recreation is limited to swimming off the minuscule beach or crossing the gulf to Iasos, an hour's sail away. In the evening you can fall into step with everyone else and promenade along the harbour front. The more adventurous amongst these evening strollers make it along later in the night to **Mythos**, a primeval disco bar in the unlikely setting of an old Ottoman storehouse on the harbour front. Bodrum's last experience of such places was in the late 1960s.

Ören, the only village on the northern coast of the gulf of Gökova, is much the better resort choice here, despite the smokestacks of several Polish-built power stations nearby. Yet it is pretty, with a good beach, and it sees very few foreign visitors. Even in summer, you may well be the only non-Turk in town.

Milas to Ören   **Where to Stay**

Most accommodation in this area is of a modest nature, clean and comfortable but with very few frills. It's mostly in Güllük but there are a few other options.

Milas has a handful of pensions, should you happen to be stuck there for the night. There are a few comfortable hotels in **Muğla**, such as the ***Yalçın**, ✆ 0252 214 1050, facing the otogar; $20 including breakfast. To reserve a room at the comfortable **Yiltur Pansiyon**, on the beach in **Ören**, call ✆ 532 2108; $14.

Güllük

moderate

Güllük plays host to what must surely be the oddest hotel arrangement in Turkey: two four-star hotels, just 30 metres apart, run by the same chain. Towering over the village on the northern side of the bay is the ******Corinthia Labranda Hotel**, ✆ 0252 522 2911, ✉ 0252 522 2009, where most of the brightly decorated rooms have a sea view; $65 for a double with full board. Marginally less luxurious is the ******Corinthia Güllük** just below, charging $50 for bed and breakfast.

inexpensive–cheap

Across from the Corinthia twins, on a hill at the southern side of the bay is the friendly *****İkont**, ✆ 0252 522 2427, ✉ 0252 522 2426. This unassuming place with a diminuitive pool is popular with holidaying Turks. Quiet, clean en suite rooms with balconies cost $30.

The **Kordon Motel** next to Güllük harbour, ✆ 0252 522 2356, has rough-and-ready doubles for $8.

Milas to Ören   **Eating Out**

Nothing in **Milas** is particularly wonderful, excepting the extremely cheap **pide salonu** at the bus station, useful if you're just passing through.

Attached to the motel, the **Kordon Restaurant** in **Güllük** is typical of the eateries here; good, friendly and inexpensive, charging $6 for a fish meal with a side dish and a drink. A short walk away along the quayside, the **Eski Depo** is also good.

Ören has several nice fish restaurants near the harbour and some simple lokantas further back.

Bodrum

Whitewashed and flower-decked **Bodrum** is the most sophisticated resort on the Aegean coast (even though its name means 'dungeon' in Turkish). Anchored to the southern shore of the Bodrum peninsula, it lies in a sunny region of spectacular scenery and sandy beaches; when approached by land, it makes an unforgettable impression, even at night when its great landmark, the Castle of St Peter, is bathed in a golden light.

Bodrum is big business. In the surrounding hills, dazzling white encrustations of Costa del Sol-style holiday villages and timeshares become more in evidence each passing year. Hundreds of advertising hoardings on the roads approaching Bodrum wink in the sun at passers-by. (Maybe it's the heat, but some of these signs invite irrational speculation: 'Carpet farm 15km' conjures up images of orchards full of fibrous flatweave fruits billowing in the breeze, awaiting a snip of the farmer's carpet scissors.) If you've booked a Blue Cruise from overseas, your voyage may well begin in Bodrum; if you'd like to initiate your own sailing

Bodrum and Marmaris

holiday while in Turkey, this is a good place to do so. The diving is excellent, and you can learn at one of several scuba-diving schools. What really sets Bodrum apart from the other resorts is its nightlife; it's the only town in Turkey that truly stays up all night, with a scene that is brasher and louder than anywhere.

History

Bodrum occupies the site of ancient Halicarnassus, a Carian city colonized by the Dorians from the Peloponnese *c.* 1000 BC. It belonged to the Dorian 'Hexapolis', a typical Greek confederacy of cities that included Kos, Cnidos and the three cities of Rhodes. In the 6th century BC, the other five members gave Halicarnassus the boot: it was too ambitious, and too susceptible to Ionian free thinking. Although the city soon came under direct Persian rule, the spirit of inquiry survived to inspire Herodotus (485–420 BC), the 'father of history', the first to chronicle events (the Persian wars) without resorting to the gods for an explanation. Halicarnassus' most glorious period came late, under the Hellenophile satrap Mausolus who made himself king of a powerful, independent Caria from 377 to 353 BC. He was so pleased with himself that he began the Mausoleum to himself, which his widow (and sister) Artemisia II finished as a tomb to beat all tombs, one of the Seven Wonders of the World. Artemisia declared herself Queen of Halicarnassus and militarily baited the Greeks so much that they put a price on her head, 'thinking it a matter of great shame for a woman to make war on Athens'. It was her younger sister, Queen Ada of Alinda, who became a good buddy of Alexander and encouraged him to attack Halicarnassus in 334 BC: for Ada's sake, Alexander spared the Mausoleum but little else.

When the Knights of St John lost their castle in Smyrna to Tamerlane in 1402, they came here; finding the Mausoleum toppled by an earthquake, they used it as material to build their Castle of St Peter. With further fortifications on the islands of Kos and Rhodes, the Knights dominated the southeastern Aegean, running a hospital for passing pilgrims and ruling the seas as privateers in their swift vessels.

One of the most interesting people to reside in St Peter's Castle was the Ottoman Great Pretender, Cem Sultan, younger brother of Beyazıt II. Cem thought the Knights would assist him in his frequent attempts to defeat and depose his brother, but the Knights, paid off handsomely by Beyazıt, had other ideas, and kept him as a hostage. They handed him over to Pope Alexander VI Borgia, who made a small fortune on the ransom before poisoning Cem. The Knights themselves were forced to move on to Malta when Süleyman the Magnificent captured Rhodes in 1523, making their citadel at Bodrum untenable.

Getting Around

Bodrum is easily reached by bus from anywhere on the coast, though it will always be a long and roundabout trip by way of Milas or Muğla. Minibuses serve most of the towns on the peninsula, and all of them leave from the otogar on the main Cevat Şakir Caddesi, a mile north of the centre. Some of the more tucked-away beaches are best visited by the boat taxis (*dolmuş motorları*) that depart from Bodrum harbour. Boats ply between Bodrum and the island of Kos regularly from spring to autumn, less frequently in winter, and it's a port of call for many cruise ships. In addition, the summer brings daily ferries to Rhodes, Datça and Altınkum, and at least two a week to Didyma, depending on demand. Occasionally there are even services to Patmos, Dalyan and Caunos; see any travel agent or Bodrum Express Lines on Kale Caddesi, © 0252 316 1087, near the port for details. Some of these take cars, but hydrofoils are increasingly used.

The Bodrum International **Airport** near Güllük has recently opened, receiving regular charter flights from across Europe as well as daily Turkish Airlines flights from Ankara and İstanbul.

Bodrum   ***Tourist Information***

İskele Meydanı 48, right on the harbour; © 0252 316 1091.

Bodrum Babylon

The town follows the classic Turkish resort plan closely: castle in the middle, next to a harbour lined with seafood restaurants and full of attractive excursion boats waiting to take you on cruises around the peninsula. Tickets for these can be bought for about $10 at the co-operative booth on the seafront. Day trips are offered to westerly beaches such as Bağla and Ortakent and the small cove known as Akvaryum, where the sea is so clear that you can watch fish from the boat. Boats also head for Orak Island and the quieter beaches to the east of Bodrum. Those who get a distant look in their eye whenever they look out to sea will be glad to know that crewed gülets can be chartered from Bodrum for two days and upwards.

Just north of the castle is the frenetic **bazaar district**, where mountains of gold and hecatombs of leather await the tourists. Shopkeepers keep a sharp eye on the arcades, ready to pounce on anyone who stops to look in the window. At the centre, with some of the swankiest shops, is the restored 18th-century **Hacımolla Hanı**.

The castle of St Peter, on its tiny neck of land, neatly divides the harbour into two. Dreadnoughts of the wealthy tie up at the yacht marina in the **West Harbour**, but the action is to the east, along pedestrianized **Dr Alim Bey Caddesi/Cumhuriyet Caddesi**. Here the real tourist inferno begins—a rather jolly one, as tourist infernos go, with more food and carpets and jewellery lurching out at you from every shop window, cosmopolitan crowds of happy campers, and a babel of signs like the one promising 'Constantly Hot Water Speaking English and Greek.'

On Thursday afternoons and Friday mornings, there is a busy and colourful (but more than a bit touristy) market.

The Castle of St Peter

The Knights' castle (*open daily exc Mon, 8.30–12 and 1–5.30; adm*) stands high on a small rocky peninsula over the original Carian settlement. Because the Knights ruled the seas, they concentrated their defences on the landward side. The first of seven gates to the castle is at the top of the ramp near the tourist office. This leads into the Northern Moat, site of the annual Bodrum Festival. Near the gate you will see the first of some 250 knightly coats of arms carved into the castle walls, as well as numerous reliefs and other architectural embellishments salvaged from the Mausoleum. A wooden bridge replaces the drawbridge leading into the outer citadel, where peacocks patrol the courtyard.

The castle now houses Bodrum's excellent **Museum of Underwater Archaeology** (*open daily exc Mon, 8.30–12 and 1–5; adm*), showcasing the best finds from the many ancient wrecks littering the Turkish coastline. As a sign at the entrance helpfully explains, 'Our museum is not under the water but most of the artefacts came from under the sea.' The small Gothic chapel of the Knights now contains a reconstructed stern section of a Byzantine ship which sank off the island of Yassıada in 626. The subdued lighting sets the mood; when you peer into the gloomy cabin to see how the crew would have spent their last days at sea, the smell of the wooden planks wrenches you back to the seventh century more effectively than a painting or film ever could. Another penumbral room contains glass exhibits brought up carefully from the Turkish seabed. An exquisite beaker from the 11th century AD is etched on its lower half with two primitive lions eternally chasing each other's tails. But the most unusual of the beautifully lit objects is a four-inch blue glass needle from the 1st-2nd century AD. Those who claim that we are now living through an age of unprecedented consumerism may have second thoughts when confronted by this evidence of the Roman's flourishing export trade in four-inch glass needles. Who bought them? What did they do with them?

Further chambers in the castle have been arranged to display collections of ancient and medieval glass, coins and jewellery; best of all is the **Hall of the Carian Princess** (*open for groups of 8 at a time, Tues–Fri 10–12 and 2–4; adm*). In 1989, a sarcophagus was discovered in Bodrum, belonging to a woman who was probably member of the Hekatomnos dynasty, the family of King Mausolus, sometime in the 4th century BC. Besides some rich jewellery and furnishings, enough of the body and clothing remained for a medical team from Manchester University to attempt a reconstruction of the poor girl in clay. They've got her standing up in a niche, wearing a rich Hellenistic ball gown and looking for all the world like Imelda Marcos.

Elsewhere in the castle grounds, the **Snake Tower** (named for the relief over the door) has a small theatre full of amphorae. Another room, containing a long-awaited **Bronze Age Shipwreck exhibition**, should be open by the time you read this.

The Knights of St John, or Knights Hospitallers, were most often the second and third sons of noblemen. They divided themselves into different *langues* (meaning nationalities), each one responsible for defending a certain area of the walls. St Peter's Castle had four *langue* towers. The **German Tower**, near the Snake Tower, has been restored, along with the nearby hamam, built for the prisoners when the castle was made into a state prison a century ago; the **Italian Tower** and the **French Tower**, the highest of all, offer wonderful views of the town and the harbours formed by the peninsula. The **English Tower**, on the south corner of the castle, has been done up to its medieval hilt, with tapes of medieval music and glasses of wine served by young Turks dressed as knights and ladies. On the west wall, notice the relief of a lion and the arms of Edward Plantagenet; inside on the marble windowsills are names and dates carved during many long hours of idleness. Perhaps they were relieved when England was expelled from the Order upon Henry VIII's divorce from Catherine of Aragon.

The Mausoleum

What remains of the **Mausoleum of Halicarnassus** (*open daily exc Mon, 8–12 and 1–5; adm*) is a bit outside the bustling trendy centre of Bodrum, on Turgutreis Caddesi to the west of the ancient harbour. Designed by the great Ionian architect Pytheos, only the massive foundations remain, capable of supporting a 200ft pile. Models on the site tentatively reconstruct the form of the Mausoleum, and there are a few copies of its reliefs—most of the originals were carted off to the British Museum in London.

The Mausoleum was the biggest tomb ever built by the ancient Greeks, and not just its name has come down to us: it has been imitated ever since (as in the Masonic Temple in Washington DC, a full-size copy). The best copy, however, is in Milas (*see* p.280). The only ancient monument of Halicarnassus to survive is the restored **amphitheatre**, with an original seating capacity of 10,000, north of the Mausoleum on Göktepe. This offers a grandstand view of the four-lane Kıbrıs Şehitler Caddesi, which snakes past just metres away from the first row of seats.

Bodrum Peninsula

As resorts go, Bodrum has everything—except a beach. But there are plenty of those minutes away around the peninsula. Shaped like a badly drawn map of Africa and Asia, the Bodrum peninsula contains several burgeoning resorts, some attractive fishing villages and the ruins of ancient Myndus. It can be toured by dolmuş or by chartering your own caique.

West from Bodrum: Gümbet, 3km outside town, is the closest and busiest beach resort, a rather characterless place with plenty of plastic hotels and evidence of more in the offing. The beach is good, however, and fitted out for every possible water sport, although windsurfers prefer **Bitez**, further west. The inland village of **Ortakent**, brooded over by the hulks of abandoned windmills above it, has a lazy charm; its beach, 6km south, is the peninsula's longest, 3,000 yards of sand and pebbles stretching westward. Even nicer are the beaches at **Bağla** and sheltered **Karaincir** to the south, with their lovely, fine sands and (usually) lack of crowds. At the southern tip of the peninsula, opposite the Greek island of Kos, a resort is fast being slung up around the fishing village of **Akyarlar**.

The western tip: In spite of its rather inconsequential beach, **Turgut Reis** is a heavily developed resort. It is named after the 16th-century Admiral Turgut (Dragut), who was born here to Greek parents; his mentor Barbarossa, another Greek who 'turned Turk', in a moment of unusual humility declared that Dragut was ahead of him 'both in fishing and bravery'. Together the two of them terrorized the Mediterranean through much of the 16th century. Dragut led the great siege of Malta in 1565 and died there, and Süleyman's fleet and army had to return empty-handed, the first important military setback for the Ottoman Empire. Two fine beaches lie on either side of Turgut Reis: **Akyar** at a fishing hamlet, and silvery **Gümüşlük**, the site of ancient Myndus. Development of Gümüşlük village has been deliberately restrained due to its proximity to ancient Myndus, and the village is perhaps the peninsula's most charming. Just south of here is **Kadıkalesi**, another attractive little village, with an abandoned Greek church on the hill above it.

The northern shore: This side of the peninsula is blanketed with pine forests that reach the shore in many places. **Yalıkavak** is a scenic settlement, where many windmills still function, but its beach is poor, typical of those along this mostly unspoilt stretch of coastline. The villages of **Gölköy** and **Türkbükü** do their best for bathers, making the most of their narrow strips of sand.

Off the southern coast of the peninsula lies **Karaada** or Black Island, where mineral waters flow into a sea grotto, popular with bathers. The island can be reached by boat trip from Bodrum, as can Cnidus, due south on the western tip of the Datça peninsula (*see* below).

Kos

Bodrum itself is so like a Greek island resort, it's a wonder that anyone would want to cross the border. Kos offers more of the same; its location near Rhodes has made it one of the busier tourist destinations among the islands. In season, everything will be just as crowded as Bodrum (and much more expensive). Nevertheless, Kos can invite you to some ancient attractions: another **castle** of the Knights of St John, a restored **Roman house** with mosaics, as well as other Roman-era ruins, all in Kos town, the island's capital. You can bicycle a few kilometres outside town to see the famous **Asklepeion**, a centre of ancient medicine and a reminder of Kos's great son, Hippocrates.

Bodrum   **Where to Stay**

Bodrum is blanketed in endless hotels and pensions; prices are on the high side, but that doesn't keep them from filling up in the summer. Plenty of new luxury establishments have opened in recent years, but though the trend is upmarket the overwhelming majority are still resolutely middle-range. Virtually every town and village on the peninsula has places to stay, although in some of the less-frequented villages on the northern coast, there may only be basic pensions.

If you're the type that sleeps nights, the important thing about staying in Bodrum is to find a place not too near the nightclub strip: Dr Alim Bey Caddesi/Cumhuriyet Caddesi, in Kumbahçe, which can be deafening until dawn. Most of the *pansiyonlar* are in this area, as well as more expensive places. Some of the noisiest places are quite nice and do their best to compensate. On the other hand, if you're looking for people who dance nights and sleep days, this is definitely the place. Also note that half pension is required in almost all of the three-and four-star places, and in some of the two-stars.

luxury

There are a few of these, most of them spread around the peninsula in peaceful settings. An establishment at the top of the status totem-pole, the ★★★★★**Club Hotel M**, Değirmen Mevkii, Haretman, ✆ 0252 316 6100, 📧 0252 316 6109, is a small and lavish place, designed with touches of Cecil B. De Mille (like the colonnaded pool); all imaginable amenities, disco, beach and water sports.

There's also opulence aplenty closer to the centre of Bodrum at the ★★★★★**Karia Princess**, Canlıdere Sokak 15 near the Myndos Gate, ✆ 0252 316 8971, 📧 0252 316 8979. Rooms have huge beds and marble bathrooms, with sufficient sports and fitness facilities to put a smile on even Arnold Schwarzenegger's face.

Twelve miles east of Bodrum at Yalıçiftlik is the ★★★★★**Sea Garden Hotel**, ✆ 0252 368 9015, 📧 0252 368 9048, a sprawling, self-contained complex boasting three swimming pools, a private beach and a vast range of activities and facilities, from archery to diving and from jacuzzis to catamarans.

In Bodrum itself, connoisseurs head for the **Antik Tiyatro**, Kıbrıs Şehitler Caddesi 243, ✆ 0252 316 6053, 🖷 0252 316 0825, *theatrehot@superonline.com*. With engaging staff and one of the most elegant pools in Bodrum, the Tiyatro provides a real haven from the hurly burly of the town. All 20 rooms have excellent views of St Peter's castle; doubles $110.

One of the longer-established holiday villages, the **(TK1)Club Ora**, four miles (6km) east of town on Milas Yolu, ✆ 0252 337 1350, with tennis courts, swimming pools and plenty of other recreational facilities. Half-board is compulsory. Also to the east, but closer to the town, is the ★★★**Manastır**, Mevkii Kumbahçe, ✆ 0252 316 2858, with a swimming pool, on a pretty terrace overlooking the sea, as well as a gym and tennis courts.

moderate

One of the most comfortable places in town is the ★★**Bodrum Maya**, Gerence Sokak, ✆ 0252 316 4741, 🖷 0252 316 4745, which offers a pool and its own parking, always a consideration in this crowded town; doubles $45. In the centre of Bodrum are a number of excellent, moderately priced hotels, including the **Emirhan**, Kumbahçe Mah., Adliye Sokak, ✆ 0252 316 6830, with a swimming pool. Two of the nicest are on the strip, and will be perfect if you're coming to Bodrum for serious partying: the **Karya**, 127 Cumhuriyet, ✆ 0252 316 1535, and the **Dinç**, next door at No.123, ✆ 0252 316 1141. The ★★**Seçkin Konaklar**, Neyzen Tevfik Caddesi, ✆ 0252 316 1351, enjoys an ideal location by the West Harbour—close to the action but not too entirely noisy. It's a low-rise complex with both rooms and apartments, and has a pool; doubles $40 and upwards.

For recreational facilities in Turgut Reis, try the holiday village **Gökçe Club Armonia**, ✆ 0252 393 6481, 🖷 0252 393 6318, on the beach at Akyarlar, at $60, typical rates for this category; there's a nice stretch of private beach, plenty of sports opportunities and a hamam; they arrange babysitting and entertainment for children.

Gümbet beach, 2km west of the centre, is lined with a wide selection of three-stars, good places to look for bargains when they aren't full of package tours. The ★★★**Anka**, Eskiçeşme Mah., ✆ 0252 316 8217, 🖷 0252 316 6194, and the ★★★**Club Hotel Flora**, ✆ 0252 316 8200, 🖷 0252 316 1462, are both air-conditioned and next to the beach, and both can set you up with equipment and lessons for windsurfing and other sports.

At Kumbahçe the ★★★**Hotel Naz**, Mümtaz Ataman Caddesi, ✆ 0252 316 5690, has a pool and a garden full of orange trees; it's close to the strip but not too noisy.

inexpensive

Relatively quiet is the **Ataer Pansiyon**, Neyzen Tevfik Caddesi 102, ✆ 0252 316 5357, a pleasant place run by a pleasant family and charging $24.

Gümbet has a few one-star places that are practically indistinguishable from the more expensive ones. The ★**Melisa**, Eski Çeşme Mevkii, ✆ 316 1044, has simple rooms and a pool for about $25.

Out on the peninsula, the **★★Toloman**, ✆ 0252 343 1226, @ 0252 343 1637, at Bitez is a pleasant and restful place directly on the beach. Besides the rooms there are a dozen apartments for rent.

The Turgut Reis area has several hotels in this category, including the **★★Yaprak**, at Kadıkalesi, ✆ 0252 382 2018, a very pleasant and well-run establishment.

On Ortakent beach, the **Yıldız Motel**, ✆ 0252 316 3195, has a pool and spartan double rooms with bath for $20.

cheap

Most of Bodrum's *pansiyonlar* are located in Kumbahçe, what seems a whole city of them on the back streets behind the bar strip of Dr Alim Bey Caddesi; there isn't a lot of difference from one to the other. Try the **Kemer Pansiyon**, Uslu Çıkmazı 30, ✆ 0252 316 1473, where rooms are basic but clean although they may be a little noisy; $10 with shower. Avoid the rip-off Burak Pansiyon on Dere Sokak, which always has a minion around the bus station.

Around the West Harbour area is another concentration, including the welcoming **İstanbul Pansiyon**, on 1017 Sokak. Near the main PTT building is the **Dönen** at Türkkuyusu Caddesi 21, ✆ 0252 316 4017. With its own car park and set amongst eucalyptus trees, this pension is quieter than most; rooms on the top floor are the most pleasant, with doubles costing $16 including breakfast.

In Turgut Reis, 15 miles west of Bodrum, the **Aydın Pansiyon**, ✆ 0252 382 3082, is attractive and comfortable; doubles $18 with breakfast. Gümüşlük has several very pleasing pensions, all charging $15–20.

camping

The region has a handful of camp sites, of which the best equipped are **Zetaş Camping** in Gümbet, ✆ 0252 316 1407, and the **İrem Motel Camping** at Bites Koyu; other, more informal places, often on far nicer sites, are near the beaches nearly everywhere on the peninsula.

Bodrum   *Eating Out*

Like the other resorts, only more so, Bodrum has a waterfront lined with outdoor restaurants. In general, these are the last place to go—expensive, tourist-orientated places cobbled together each season with temporary staff. Still, there are plenty of places to get a good dinner. The **Han** restaurant, in an 18th-century caravanserai at Kale Caddesi 23, ✆ 0252 316 7951, has the most original surroundings, and possibly the finest cuisine in town, with dishes like shrimp and avocado cocktail and chicken stuffed with pistachios; original desserts too, and a bar upstairs with live Turkish music; average $12. The restaurant at the **Antik Tiyatro** has a deservedly good reputation for its cuisine; the hotel's candlelit patio overlooking the harbour and castle makes dining here an experience for all the senses; $20 upwards.

One reliable place for seafood is the **Gemibaşı**, with outside tables facing Neyzen Tevfik Caddesi; $12 average. For something unexpected and memorable, head north from the town hall and seek out the **Buğday Vegetarian Restaurant** on Türk

Kuyusu Caddesi, a back street far from the tourist strip. Lovely cooking, all natural ingredients, and a pretty enclosed garden (occasional music and even art exhibits); $6 or a little more. Just off Kale Caddesi on Yeni Çarşı is the **Sakallı** ('the Bearded') **Köfteci**. For once the portrait staring from the wall is of the restaurant's founder, not the Republic's. Bearded Sakallı Bey started the restaurant 50 years ago and seems to have been the Colonel Sanders of Bodrum. His köfte and onions were so good that locals used to wolf them down for breakfast. His successors open from lunchtime; by evening the options are limited. Lentil soup, grilled aubergine and köfte costs $4.

Off Dr Alim Bey Caddesi on a side street (with no street sign), the **Eylül Restaurant** has outside tables just far enough away from the action on the strip; $8, more for seafood. **Sünger Pizza**, at the end of the strip near the Halikarnas disco, offers a wide choice of creditable Italian pizzas and beer for about $6. The name Sünger (sponge) derives from the family's former employment as sponge divers.

Restaurants on the peninsula range from the fancy at Gümbet and Turgut Reis to the plain at Ortakent and Yalıkavak. The popular **Vira Cafe** at Ortakent does pizza as well as the usual Turkish fare; $10 for a full dinner; they also have rooms to let. Bitez has some good simple places: the inexpensive **Çardak** near the Bitez Han hotel is popular for its chicken casserole. At Kadıkalesi, the **Kılçik** in the Yaprak Hotel offers mezes and grilled fish for $12. If you're staying at Gümüşlük, by all means stop in at the **Batı**, near the beach; everything from the best mezes on the harbourfront to full dinners for about $12; excellent lamb and seafood casseroles and outside tables.

Bodrum, at least, is one place where you can get a change from Turkish food: there are Chinese restaurants, such as the **Sandal**, the 'Authentic Thai and Chinese Restaurant', Atatürk Caddesi 74; its menu features no less than 139 items but those confounded by the agony of choice can always order the set meal for $12. Another, for slightly less, is the **Uzakdoğu** (means 'far east'), 146 Neyzen Tevfik Caddesi, with a branch at Gümbet; $15. **Picante**, a bar/restaurant with Tex-Mex cooking and margaritas, is at 8 Külcü Sokak; $12.

Entertainment and Nightlife

Almost everything is on the joyous pedestrian strip of Dr Alim Bey Caddesi/ Cumhuriyet Caddesi, which becomes one long funnel of love in the evenings, directing a steady stream of revellers towards the Halikarnas nightclub at the far end. It's a potent and concentrated mixture, with everything from slick discos to quiet bars with folk music, and watering holes that seem to be specially designed to attract northern lager louts and get them off the streets. Pool halls, hippie trinket dealers and sidewalk portrait painters decorate the streetscape. At the top of the list is the afore-mentioned Bodrum institution, the disco **Halikarnas**, which claims to be the biggest in Europe with a capacity of 5,500. You can't miss it; its laser light shows bounce off the castle and around the town all night, giving the impression of an invasion from Mars. Dress up; it's $15 to get in, which after a while in Turkey may seem like a fortune. Charging the same for entry is the **M&M Nightclub** on Dr Alim Bey Caddesi, in a former sponge warehouse on the seafront. This may not be as big as the

Halikarnas, but has outdone its rival in the novelty dance floor stakes. Moored out front is the huge M&M catamaran, an insomniac's dream. It slips anchor at midnight filled with nautical ravers, and returns to port at dawn.

Another flash disco, currently very popular, is the **Hadigari**. Closer in, you'll encounter the **West Side Bar**, one of the cooler places to be, with a shady courtyard and an up-to-date playlist. The **Red Lion Bar** is for serious guzzling, and it generates the highest decibel levels east of Mykonos. There are some agreeable holes-in-the-wall featuring whatever live folk, jazz or blues music floats into Bodrum, such as the **Club Mani**, and the **Jazz Cafe**, near the Halikarnas.

Marmaris

The scenery between Muğla and Marmaris is reminiscent of California and becomes spectacular as you descend to the lovely pine-clad **Bay of Marmaris**. The town itself was devastated by an earthquake in 1958, and little of architectural interest remains apart from the fortress built by Süleyman during his siege of Rhodes. However, its lovely setting on the deeply indented coast, its access to the bay's beaches and its fjord-like scenery have made it one of Turkey's major yacht ports and one of its most popular holiday resorts, though one where the concrete mixers have definitely got out of hand. Superficially, at least, Marmaris is practically identical to Bodrum. For you package trippers who can't tell which you're in, Marmaris is the one with the smaller castle, and the marina on the east side instead of the west.

History

The Carians were quick to appreciate the natural harbour of Marmaris, or Fyskos as it was then, and used it as a base from which to terrorize the Phoenicians on Rhodes. After the eclipse of the Carians, the town was passed around among various powers—Egyptians (Ptolemy's empire, after Alexander), Ionians, Dorians, Romans—before becoming part of the Ottoman Empire in 1425. It remained a forgotten outpost for nearly 100 years until Süleyman the Magnificent, irritated by the Knights of St John on Rhodes, who pillaged Muslim pilgrim ships and let Christians pass freely, followed the Carian example and used the town as his base to besiege the island. When the Knights finally surrendered, Süleyman was so pleased with his success that he ordered a castle to be built in the town. The result was a typically quaint Ottoman affair, almost cute, its battlements affording one of the coast's loveliest vistas. However, Süleyman didn't like it. '*Mimarı as*', he grumbled when he saw it—'Hang the architect'. Hence the town's name. Or so they say.

Getting Around

Marmaris has one of the most reliable **ferry** services to a Greek island—Rhodes, daily, most of the year round.

Dalaman **airport** at Muğla is the closest airport, about a 90-minute drive from Marmaris. Buses run every hour in season to Marmaris's main otogar. The airport has regular domestic flights from İstanbul, İzmir and Antalya, and an increasing number of international charters—including daily connections to London, Amsterdam and even New York, all via İstanbul.

Marmaris's **otogar** is located to the north-east of the harbour on the Mustafa Münir Elgin Bulvarı, though most buses also stop at the circle on Atatürk Caddesi, by the west harbour. There are frequent bus connections from Bodrum, and from İzmir and Fethiye; minibuses provide transport along the serpentine road to Datça and Cnidus. Those for İçmeler and points west begin from the centre of the harbour, by the Atatürk statue (one of the new model Atatürk statues, with a top hat), as do the seasonal **boat dolmuşes** for Turunç and the many fine beaches and islets around the bay. **Minibuses** for Yalancı and Boğaz beach leave from Mustafa Münir Elgin Bulvarı, behind the marina, but you can also catch them from opposite the Tansaş shopping centre on Ulusal Egemenlik Caddesi.

Tourist Information

Marmaris: İskele Meydanı 2, on the west harbour, ✆ 0252 412 1035; there is a hotel reservation booth open in season here, where you can also check information about boats to Rhodes.

Datça: Hükümet Binası, ✆ 0252 712 3546.

Around the Town

The Knights' **castle of St Peter** (*daily exc Mon 8.30–12 and 1–5.30; adm*) has since been restored and converted into an archaeological museum with the standard collection of kilims, daggers, etc, as well as a room given over to holiday snaps of Cappadocia. The castle is reached through a convoluted series of back streets that offer some hints as to what Marmaris was like 50 years ago, when the town's income was derived from that most hazardous of occupations, sponge-diving. The divers would set sail every spring and return several months later, usually minus a few poor souls. The women and children would see the boats coming in and gather anxiously on the quayside. The **statue** of the woman and child at the harbour commemorates those who looked in vain (currently, there are hardly any sponges to be had here or anywhere else in the Mediterranean, thanks to an epidemic of 'sponge blight' in recent years).

Nowadays the harbour is filled with boats offering **day trips** to the nearby beaches for $10 per person including lunch. The larger vessels can be chartered for week-long trips to Datça or Fethiye and beyond. As a yardstick, for every week on board, expect to pay about $250 per passenger, including meals. **Scuba diving** shops can also be found on the water front, offering a full day's diving at reefs near Marmaris for $30. Five-day PADI courses for beginners are cheaper in Marmaris than Bodrum, costing in the region of $200.

Set back from the quayside the town's **bazaar** begins, one of the more pleasing touristic markets in Turkey, bustling and cheerful. From here the town's spacious **beach** is a short walk away, to the west of town. Stalls set up at the seaside offer all manner of distractions, including one with a sign explaining 'we make holes in nails'; it's not clear who pays whom for this exercise in sado-masochism. Other stallholders offer five-colour tattoos that supposedly rub off after 20 days. Recipients are long since back at work in their home countries before they can discover whether 20 days really means 20 days or, as with most approximations of time in Turkey, somewhat longer.

East of Marmaris, over the wooden bridge, is **Günnücek Park**, a picnic spot within a grove of rare frankincense trees. You can swim off the small platform here. For better swimming, go to the islet of **Sedir** on the other side of the peninsula in Gökova Bay. The islet is only half a mile long but very popular for its unusual snow-white sand with perfectly round grains, shipped to the islet from the Red Sea some 2,000 years ago for Cleopatra. Then, a city called Cedrea stood on the islet; the ruins of walls and a theatre remain.

For yet more beaches, and for **thermal springs**, head south of Marmaris to **İçmeler**, a fast-developing resort with all the adrenalin-boosting activities that this entails, from paragliding to jet-skiing. Nearby is the village of **Turunç** where the beach is less crowded; across the bay are the **Phosphorescent Caves**, where the water glows when disturbed.

South of Turunç lies the **Rhodian Peraea**, the only mainland territory of that once-powerful island-state. The Rhodians made little use of this little peninsula, spreading between the islands of Rhodes and Kos, and there's little to see. A steep climb up from **Kumlubük**, another village with a sandy beach, leads to what remains of ancient **Amos**: fragments of some walls, and of a theatre and a temple. The ancient towns of **Saranda**, near **Sögüt** village, and **Bybassios**, on the road to small but teeming **Bozborun**, have scanty remains, likely to appeal to specialists only.

A Trip to Rhodes

The largest and greenest of the Dodecanese is also one of Greece's most flagrant tourist play-grounds—prices will be a shock after Turkey. Rhodes has had a fascinating history: a power in its own right in Hellenistic times, home of the famous Colossus. Like Bodrum, the island was controlled by the Knights of St John for two centuries after 1306, and the Italians ruled it from 1912 until 1945.

The ferry from Marmaris lands at **Rhodes** town, the island's capital, where there are the castle and walls of the Knights to explore, as well as architectural contributions from ancient times up to Süleyman the Magnificent and Mussolini. The town is a major resort, with a casino, busy nightlife and even a golf course. From the capital the most common excursion is to beautiful **Lindos**, the island's second city, with the ruins of its magnificent acropolis. A number of villages haven't yet been too spoiled by tourism, notably **Lardos**, on the coast near Lindos; **Embona**, up in the mountains above Rhodes, and **Kamiros**, the third of the island's Doric 'three cities'. Along the west coast are a number of resorts and a famous beauty spot, the **Valley of the Butterflies**.

Datça and Cnidus

West of Marmaris, the road makes quite a dramatic ascent up to the top of mountains, before dropping down to **Datça**, one-time Doric city, now a small-time Turkish resort popular with windsurfers because of its blustery location. Built around a horseshoe bay, Datça has beaches but there are better ones further west along the peninsula, and local tour operators will happily sail you to them. They'll also take you to ancient Cnidus.

Cnidus, at the very tip of the peninsula, was the headquarters of the Dorian Hexapolis (a loose confederacy of towns in Asia Minor that had been settled by Dorians). In ancient times, it was famous for a statue of Aphrodite by the great Praxiteles, modelled on the renowned courtesan Phryne (whose name means 'Toad', although she won a court case by baring her bosom before the judges). This first 3D female nude was originally commissioned by Kos, but the islanders were too prudish to keep such a bombshell, and Cnidus picked it up and made the 'Aphrodite of Cnidus' the main tourist attraction of the coast, set in a temple to be viewed from all angles and tended by a lusty crew of priestess-prostitutes. The base of the statue has recently been discovered in the circular foundations of a Corinthian temple in the city. The streets of Cnidus were laid out in a grid over a number of terraces; the walls and the Hellenistic theatre are the best preserved of the remains. The lovely statue of Demeter in the British Museum came from here, and although excavations are currently under way, no one has yet found the observatory of Eudoxus, a native of the city, student of Plato, and a pioneer in astronomy and geometry.

Marmaris and Around   **Where to Stay**

The only time of the year when it may be difficult to find a room in Marmaris is during the regatta, held in the second week in May.

luxury–expensive

The ★★★★★**Marmaris Altınyunus Oteli**, ✆ 0252 455 4100, three miles (5km) west of Marmaris, offers almost every form of recreational activity including a fitness room, swimming pools, private beach, nightclub and so on. At İçmelar the **(TK1) Martı Holiday Village**, ✆ 455 3440, ✉ 455 3448, offers more of the same but is somewhat cheaper. The emphasis is on water sports here; there are indoor and outdoor pools and a broad stretch of beach. In Marmaris itself, the ★★★★★**Merit Grand Azur** to the west of the centre at Kenan Evren Bulvarı 11, ✆ 0252 412 8201, ✉ 0252 412 3530, is the status address on the beach front with all the links of the perfect chain hotel: hamam, gym, nightclub, pools and all sorts of water sports.

moderate

To the west of the town, the ★★★**Lidya**, Siteler Mah. 130, ✆ 0252 412 2940, although aimed somewhat at packagees, is nevertheless one of the most ambitious establishments in town, with opportunities for all water sports and speedboat rental, a piano bar and a night club with a wild floor show. There is a variety of accommodation available, from rooms to apartments; half-board doubles $45. There are plenty of hotels near the beach, on Atatürk Caddesi and the back streets behind it.

The ★★★**Mare** in Datça, ✆ 0252 712 3211, has a solid reputation, a beachside location and a swimming pool. Turunç, with its long beach, has a number of adequate mid-range hotels; two that place a special emphasis on sports, with excellent facilities, are the ★★**Diplomat**, ✆ 476 7145, and the ★★**Mavi Deniz**, ✆ 476 7190. The Diplomat has a nicer section of beach; both also have apartments to rent.

inexpensive

At Atatürk Caddesi 10, the ★★**Yavuz Oteli**, ✆ 0252 412 2937 has a rooftop pool with terrific views; good value for money at $30. The ★**Ayce Oteli**, Çam Sokak 4, ✆ 0252 412 3136, has doubles for $21. It's off the main street and therefore quieter than most. One of the better bargains is the air-conditioned ★★**Çubuk**, 1 Konti

Sokak, ✆ 0252 412 6774. Right in the centre of the action on Hacı Mustafa Sokak, the family-run *Begonya, ✆ 0252 412 4095, with its wooden lattice shutters and well-furnished rooms, must be the prettiest hotel in Marmaris; the only drawback is noise from all the bars around it. If you're not set on staying at a seafront location, the family-run **Ünver, ✆ 0252 412 2968, ✆ 0252 412 2967, is a quieter option. Set in a back street near some garden nurseries at 112 Sokak 20, it has a small swimming pool and clean, cool rooms with balconies. If there are no partying Danish and Dutch groups in residence, you will be guaranteed a good night's sleep; doubles $20.

cheap

Marmaris does not have as many *pansiyonlar* as Bodrum, and it can be crowded in summer; it's best to arrive early in the day and check the hotel reservation booth by the tourist office. Otherwise, the best place to look is not in the old town, but in the new streets to the west behind Atatürk Caddesi. There, where the paint is hardly dry and the streets have no names, you'll find family-run places like the friendly, English-speaking **Maltepe**, ✆ 0252 412 1629; nice rooms with bath for $15.

The **Otel İmbat**, on Eski Çarşı 5, is a bargain choice, where a clean double room with private shower and toilet costs $12. For slightly less than the average pension, you can stay at the **Interyouth Hostel**, ✆ 0252 412 3687, near the sea front on 42 Sokak, not far from the PTT. It has a cafeteria, bar and laundry and is the best deal in town for $10 per double.

For budget accommodation in Datça, try the **Karaoğlu**, ✆ 0252 712 3079, among a number of similar places on the hill overlooking the bay.

camping

The nicest campsite in the region is **Camp Amazon**, ✆ 436 9111, 24 miles (39km) from Marmaris in the Bordübet National Park, with a pool, nearby beach and every essential facility.

Marmaris and Around　　　　　　　　　　　　　　　　　**Eating Out**

In Marmaris there is a solid block of restaurants along the yacht harbour. Most of them are quite expensive by Turkish standards, although the food is delicious, particularly grilled fish like the wonderful *mercan* (pandora) which can be had for about $15. The best of these establishments is the **Marina** on Barbaros Caddesi, 50ft short of the mermaid with the mohican hairdo (you'll know her when you see her). The restaurant has an inconspicuous entranceway at street level, leading upstairs to a haven from the madding crowds with panoramic views of the harbour. The owner's wife, Mrs Yatmaneş, does much of the cooking, serving a range of traditional Turkish cuisine; specialities of the house are *çiğ* and *içli köfte*, which must normally be ordered a day in advance; $10 and upwards. In an ancient back street near the castle is the **Ney Restaurant** at Kale Mah. 26 Sokak 24, ✆ 0252 412 0217. The sign outside proudly declares 'Turkish Home Cooking' and the aromas wafting out through the front door back up this claim. The irrepressible boss, Birgül Zülfikar, does all the cooking, using only fresh ingredients to create Turkish mainstays such as *börekler* and *mantı*. She has also infused this old stone house with a wonderful ambience. A *ney* (dervish flute) from which the restaurant takes its name hangs downstairs. Wooden chairs crowd around small tables upstairs; with room for only 20 guests, booking is advisable. A full meal with wine is a reasonable $10.

Down a side street opposite the Tansaş Shopping Centre is the brightly lit **Kırçiçeği** at Yeniyol Caddesi 15. From here the hooves of the herd on the beachside strip are out of earshot. Its *tandır* dishes are very popular, but the *karışık* (a mammoth mixed grill) is also delicious. The team of 11 waiters is very attentive, unless you catch them on a football night, when their attention drifts inexorably to the screen in the corner. They claim to be open 25 hours a day, with full meals costing $9. The **Yeni Liman Restaurant** in the bazaar has a nice selection of meats and sweets; a full meal, with a beer or glass of wine, should come to around $12. West of the castle, one street in from Atatürk Caddesi, the unassuming **Stop Restaurant and Bar** is a good place for a light lunch or snack; $6.

Hundreds of bars and restaurants belch onto the crowded beach strip west of the town centre. Chutzpah is of the essence for these places to draw in the customers; the **Garden Restaurant** has more chutzpah than most, with a male belly dancer and dancing waiters sallying forth to put bums on seats each night. More orthodox in approach are two nearby Chinese restaurants, the **Tai Pan** and the **Pagoda**, serving up western approximations of eastern cuisine for $10.

In Datça, the unprepossessing appearance of **Hüsnü'nün Yeri** by the Bodrum–Datça ferryboat landing, belies the fact that it serves the best fish for miles around, and is consequently often full; $12.

There are two small restaurants in Cnidus, and you can get food at any of the coves with a camp ground around Marmaris bay.

Entertainment and Nightlife

Marmaris is second only to Bodrum in this department, and the centre of the action is Hacı Mustafa Sokak, just behind and running parallel to the East Marina. The disco crowd fills up the attractive open-air **Backstreet** and popular **Casablanca** discos nightly. Along the seafront to the west is the **Beach Club**. All three offer free entry.

More subdued entertainments can be had at places like the small and refined **Bar Fendi** or the **David Jones Bar**. Open all year round is **Le Petit Bar** at Bar Sokak 39, which has another entrance on the harbour front where it is known as **Le Petit Café Bistro Bar**. Nearby is the **Ivy Reggae Bar**, serving up cold beers and syncopated rhythms until the early hours. Over on the harbour, the yacht set congregates at the **Scorpio Bar**.

Marmaris's best setting and view belong to the **Panorama Bar** on the height next to the castle, although its prices match its lofty position. Even higher up the hill, but with more sensible prices, is the **Castle Bar**. While you're pub crawling, watch out for the incredible stand on the harbour occasionally set up by **Lütfü Küçük**, a manic, talented caricaturist who has become locally famous from appearing on Turkish TV—the spirit of P.T. Barnum lives on.

The Southern Coast

ANTALYA MARINA

N

50km
25 miles

● Port

To Burdur & Isparta

To Konya

Selge

Karain Cave

To İzmir & Marmaris

Lycia

Köyceğiz

Perge   Sillyon   Aspendos

Kaunos   *Lake Köyceğiz*   Kadyandá   Termessos   Lara   Side   Manavgat

Ortaca   Antalya

Dalyan   Dalaman

Fethiye

Ermenek

Phaselis   *Pamphylia*   Alanya

Ölü Deniz   Kemer   Tlos

Xanthos   Olympos   *Gulf of Antalya*   Seydra

Letoon   Kalkan   Myra   Finike   Gazipaşa

Patara   Üçağız

Kaş   Anamur

Kastellorizo (Greece)   Kekova   Anemourion

The Lycian Coast: Köyceğiz to Antalya

In ancient times, when the indigenous Lycian people crowned this rugged stretch of coastline with a garland of lovely cities, the area was still something of a *terra incognita* for most Greeks and Romans. Even now the difficult mountainous terrain makes the interior hard to penetrate. Lately, however, the Turkish government has completed a coastal road, stretching around the Lycian bulge from Fethiye to Antalya. It was the last unfinished section of the coast highway, and its construction has opened to tourism a land that still retains its lazy charm, a transparent sea in every imaginable shade of blue and turquoise, magnificent scenery, and archaeological sites in varying stages of excavation, all in settings that would delight any romantic. The villages, strung around the coast, might as well be islands: on one side the sea, on the other an equally inhospitable sea of steep mountains and maquis. In such a setting, people here tend to be convivial even by Turkish standards—friendly and talkative, and never in a hurry.

Around Lake Köyceğiz

Getting Around

Köyceğiz is serviced by all **buses** travelling east or west along the coast. For Dalyan, coming from either direction, you must alight at Ortaca and take a **dolmuş** from there. Alternatively, there are **boats** to Dalyan from Köyceğiz several times a day. Kaunos can be reached by motorboat from Dalyan or Köyceğiz; in summer you'll always be able to find someone to ferry you across.

Köyceğiz: Atatürk Kordonu 1, © 0252 262 4703

Köyceğiz

Köyceğiz lives for the lake on whose northern shores it stands, and from which it draws its name. Ringed by a phalanx of foreboding mountains, with waters transparent in the shallower stretches, this lake has supported the town for millennia, its healthy stock of fish constantly being replenished via the meandering channel that connects it to the Mediterranean. Birds like the fish as much as the local fishermen do and 119 species have been spotted here, from storks to kingfishers and even, on occasion, the endangered sea eagle. Out on the lake at night, you may sight another rare creature, the softback turtle. Köyceğiz is also one of the last remaining places in the world you'll be able to see the *Liquidambar Orientalis*, a member of the witch-hazel family. The resinous gum it exudes from its bark has been used by perfumiers and physicians alike since antiquity. A few of these trees can still be found between Marmaris and Fethiye: there's a grove of them on the western edge of Köyceğiz.

Köyceğiz itself is a drowsy town and Monday, market day, is the only time of the week when it shakes itself from stupor. On other days there's little to do except stroll the leafy promenade, cross the lake to the muddy thermal baths on the southern shore of the lake and enjoy fresh fish at any one of several wonderful lakeside restaurants.

Dalyan

Dalyan represents all that is gorgeous about the southern coast of Turkey, yet it has so far been spared the more tawdry trappings of mass tourism. The village can be reached by road but it is far nicer to sail there from Köyceğiz, winding through the channel on the way to the open sea. Dalyan lies midway along this channel, a village of little more than one street, a square and a harbour, bounded to north and south by barely touched countryside. Across the water the first traces of ancient Kaunos (*see* below) can be seen, rock tombs built into the sheer cliff face. No structure in the village is higher than three storeys, by order of the *belediye*, who are anxious that Dalyan remains unsullied and who reinforce this policy with loudspeaker announcements exhorting locals not to 'pester the tourists' or drop cigarette ends in the street.

Dalyan **beach**, a 30-minute sail south, is one of the most visually stunning on the Mediterranean rim, a sand-based island at the mouth of the channel. It is totally undeveloped, thanks to the presence of giant loggerhead turtles, who have used it as a laying ground since time immemorial. Tourist development very nearly killed these turtles off. The female loggerheads would lay their eggs by night in the soft sand, in clutches of about 100; by day, sunbathers would turn up to stretch out on that same sand and poke sun umbrellas into it for shade. If the eggs managed to survive this treatment and hatch, the hatchlings were faced with a further problem; the bright lights from the hotels and bars on the beach would counteract the gleam from the sea that they would otherwise instinctively crawl towards. The baby turtles would set off in the wrong direction; inevitably, they died.

What was happening became common knowledge in the late 1980s and ignited a debate within Turkey that soon was to spread overseas. Influential environmentalists became involved and in 1991, the developers, who had previously been proposing that they and the turtles should have half the beach each, completely backed down. All structures on the beach were bulldozed and their foundations covered, and the entire area was ordered closed from 8pm to 8am, from May through to October, the main laying season. The beach is open during daylight hours but swimmers and sunbathers are asked to exercise special care.

Kaunos

Further down the channel from Dalyan is ancient **Kaunos**, the westernmost settlement on the Mediterranean coast, marking the border between that sea and the Aegean, and between Caria and Lycia. Its remains show the styles of both cultures, as well as of later civilizations: there are Lycian and Carian tombs, a wall built by King Mausolus of Caria, medieval walls on the acropolis, a Roman fountain and a Byzantine basilica. The city was eventually abandoned after its harbour silted up, a fate it shared with illustrious Ephesus.

Köyceğiz and Dalyan   **Where to Stay**

In both Köyceğiz and Dalyan you can save money on hotel bills. There is nothing at the costly end of the market, although the moderately priced places and pensions are, as a rule, very good indeed.

Köyceğiz

moderate

The **★★Hotel Özay**, Ulucami Mahalle, ✆ 0252 262 4300, 🖷 0252 262 1819, is tastefully furnished, has a swimming pool, and is on the lakeside; the management arranges sailing, sports and boat tours. The recently built **★★★Panorama Plaza**, ✆ 0252 262 3773, 🖷 0252 262 3633, at the western edge of town by the beach, is similar to the Özay but more stylish and expensive, at $60 for doubles in summer.

inexpensive–cheap

By the lake at the other end of town is the **Kordon Boyu Motel**, ✆ 0252 262 3993: clean doubles with shower and lake view balconies go for $30 in high season, much less if it's quieter. Near the main swimming pool, there's another, smaller, pool surrounded by high fences topped with barbed wire. Here the owner, Mr Özoğuz, keeps his pet trout, far too plump and numerous to leave unprotected and at the mercy of opportunist poachers.

Köyceğiz has a clutch of pensions, all good but mostly in the $20–24 price range. Try the **Tanya Pansiyon**, ✆ 0252 262 2501, half-way between the main square and the Panorama Plaza Hotel. The cheaper pensions tend to be the oldest—try the **Star**, ✆ 0252 262 1035, at $16 for a double with shower.

camping

Just beyond the Panorama Plaza is **Delta Camping**, wonderfully situated amongst the liquid amber trees, ✆ 0252 262 1480.

Dalyan

moderate

Dalyan has seen a number of new hotels open up in the last few years. The status address here is the **★★★Antik**, ✆ 0252 284 2136, a very attractive motel-style complex with a pool set in a garden full of oleanders; some rooms have air-conditioning. Another good choice, close to the centre, is the **★★★Dalyan**, ✆ 0252 284 2239, a similar complex right on the waterfront.

inexpensive–cheap

At the harbour, the **Göl Motel**, ✆ 0252 284 2062, is clean and has en suite rooms for $24. The street leading south from the square, adjacent to the channel, is filled with small pensions, all charging around the same rate. On Yalı Sokak, the **Onur**, ✆ 0252 284 3074, ✉ 0252 284 2787, is run by a friendly family; good value at $16 per double, with air-con but no pool.

Köyceğiz and Dalyan   ***Eating Out***

The cheerful staff at the **Şamdan** on Lake Köyceğiz serve fish (usually sea bass or grey mullet) fresh from the lake for around $8 a head, drink and side dish included.

In Dalyan, the harbourside **Denizatı** has perfected the art of grilling fish, and serves a full meal for $8. The less expensive **Çiçek** on Maras Mahalle has a fine selection of mezes. For a drink, try the **Han Bar** on Maras Mahalle, decorated with *nargileler*, kilims and Ottoman memorabilia.

Fethiye

Getting Around

Dalaman **airport** (50km from the town) has regular flights to İstanbul and weekly charters from abroad; there's an information office and taxis to Dalaman, from where minibuses run to Fethiye and everywhere else on the coast. All **buses** travelling this coast stop at Fethiye; the otogar is a mile east of the centre on Süleyman Demirel Bulvarı, at the intersection of the roads for Muğla and Antalya. **Minibuses** leave constantly in the summer for Çalış and Ölü Deniz from the central terminus on Çarşı Caddesi east of the castle where it intersects Atatürk Caddesi. In season there is also a **boat-dolmuş** to Çalış, every 30mins until at least 10pm.

Getting to most of the **ancient sites** is possible without a car, though not always easy. From Fethiye, you can take a minibus to Sidyma, Araxa, Tlos, Xanthus, Pınara and the Letoon; all will require some walking once you get there. For all those close to the coastal road, you can be fairly sure of finding some minibus or even intercity bus to pick you up on your way back.

Fethiye   ***Tourist Information***

İskele Meydanı 1, ✆ 0252 614 1527.

A modern town built over ancient Telmessos, **Fethiye** has Lycia's best harbour, protected by twelve islets. Telmessos means 'Land of Light' in Lycian, and is first mentioned in the 4th century BC. Most of it lies buried under modern Fethiye (itself rebuilt after an earthquake in 1957), with the exception of the **rock tombs** cut into the cliff near the bus station; these, especially the grand Ionic temple **Tomb of Amyntas** of the 4th century BC, are among the finest in Lycia. Here and there throughout the modern town you see large sarcophagi. The oldest and most interesting of these is the **Lycian Sarcophagus** next to the post office, carved from a single block of stone. The new **museum** (*open daily exc Mon, 8.30–5; adm*) is near the school, and has exhibits from Lycia and an interesting sculpture garden.

The Lycians

 The Lycians were a native Anatolian people. Homer says that they fought with the Trojans under their leader Sarpedon, brother of King Minos of Crete, which led Herodotus to write that they were the descendants of an ancient Cretan colony. Lycia first appears in the records of the Hittites as the 'Lukka Lands', in the 13th century BC. Most of the remains discovered along the coast, however, date back only to the 7th century BC at the earliest. Like Cilicia to the east, the rugged nature of the thickly forested terrain kept Lycia out of the pages of history, but by the time of Alexander—who captured the coast easily from its Persian satraps—its population had become more or less Hellenized, adopting many Greek letters into the alphabet, and adapting Greek sculptural and architectural forms.

The latter they used for their mortuary obsession, carving elaborate tombs with temple-like façades into the living rock, in some places so thick they resemble lost metropolises of the dead. Elsewhere, they made sarcophagi and tombs in the form of miniature houses of stone, remarkably graceful constructions with curving roofs. These, often on high platforms, and the beautiful tombs carved into the steep cliffs overhead are the most distinctive features of the Lycian landscape.

Below the castle is the **amphitheatre**, a 6,000-seater dating from the late Hellenistic period. Abandoned in the 7th century, it remained buried under a thick layer of earth until the early 1990s; appropriately enough, the local museum director lived in a house on top of it. Only in 1992 did excavations begin on the site (once the director was ensconced in his new house). The money and manpower for the dig all came from local volunteers: each day a group assembled at the site after work, with pickaxes and shovels in hand, to be put to work by the museum staff. Three years on, work on the amphitheatre itself was complete; meanwhile the concrete pavement that once curved around its base was left with a huge section missing. The council have yet to replace it, something that nocturnal strollers should bear in mind.

Fethiye, though modern, has a leisurely charm, and it is the best base for visiting the Lycian sites in the vicinity. After Marmaris or Bodrum, it may even look a bit down at heel; at least it has managed to side-step the blanket commercialism of some of the resorts on the southern coast. The leather and carpet merchants are huddled together in a relatively small area behind the harbour; in the hamlets outside town, life meanders on as it always has. From the harbour most of the sailboats will be offering 'twelve island tours'; some will go wherever you want.

The nearest beach is two miles (3km) away at **Çalış**, a suburb of Fethiye that is more obviously a 'resort'. It lies opposite the islet of **Şövalye** which also has a beach. Gümlük beach, just north of Fethiye, is in a grove of styrax (liquid amber) trees, like those at Köyceğiz. All of these, however, take second place to **Ölü Deniz**, the 'dead sea' to the south, a warm lagoon off the gulf of Belcekız backed by pine-covered mountains. Once the haunt of pirates, this is a perfect beach, two miles long with transparent waters and fine sand; you have to pay to use the best part. Ölü Deniz is extremely popular but is too large to be crowded and development is not yet dense. In the mountains above Ölü Deniz is tacky **Hisarönü**, several miles from the beach, a small town devoted entirely to tourism. A 30-minute walk from Hisarönü is the Greek ghost town of **Karmilassos** (Kara Köyü in Turkish), with forlorn houses and abandoned churches; as so often, when the Greeks left in the population exchange the Turks didn't move in, letting entire towns go to ruin. There are some ambitious plans for restoration of the village, but besides the efforts of some private individuals, little has happened.

Inland from Fethiye

Inland from Fethiye you can explore, literally, three seldom-visited Lycian cities. **Kadyanda**, northeast of Fethiye near modern Yeşil Üzümlü, has a well-preserved **theatre**, a Doric **temple**, and **baths**, as well as other remains. **Tlos**, on the slopes of Akdağ, the White Mountain, is 30 miles (48km) from Fethiye, near modern Kaleasar, on the other side of the River Xanthus, the modern Koca Çay. Tlos was one of the most important members of the Lycian confederacy of the 2nd century BC and remained inhabited through the Byzantine era; in the 19th century it served as the winter headquarters of the pirate Kanlı Ali Ağa. As well as Lycian **rock tombs**, there are remains of Kanlı Ali Ağa's **fortress** on the acropolis, a **Roman stadium**, baths and **walled necropolis**, and a **Byzantine church**. On the other side of the modern village lies the **theatre**.

Pınara, another important member of the confederacy, is closer to Fethiye, on the west bank of the River Xanthus, east of Kemer—the *western* Kemer (there are two villages of this name, one at each end of Lycia). Pınara is one of the more romantic sites, on a height beneath the mountains, the ruins overgrown. Pınara is especially notable for its Lycian **rock tombs**; a **Roman odeon** and a **Greek theatre** are also easy to find. **Sidyma**, nine miles (14km) off the coastal highway south of Pınara near Dodurga, has more rock-cut **tombs**.

Xanthos

Far more interesting, however, is **Xanthos**, the ancient capital and oldest city of Lycia, dating back to the 8th century BC and famous in antiquity for its great resistance to Cyrus' General Harpagus who attacked in the mid-6th century BC. Although they fought courageously, the Xanthians were outnumbered. According to Herodotus, when they saw they were doomed to defeat, they retreated to their citadel, gathering together their womenfolk, children and slaves. After locking them inside, they set fire to the building and burned it to the ground. They then swore to fight to the death, and did. Indeed, when Xanthos was excavated, a heavy layer of ash was discovered over the ruins of that period.

Rebuilt by 50 families who had been away during the siege, Xanthos prospered up until the Roman period, when it once again suffered a terrible devastation, this time at the hands of

Brutus in 42 BC; rebuilt yet again with the aid of Mark Antony and Emperor Vespasian, the city survived until the 12th century. Today it is one of the most revealing Lycian sites, most of it having been cleared to disclose the layout of the city and its imposing funerary monuments. Unfortunately they were stripped of their reliefs in 1838 but these can now be seen in the Lycian Room of the British Museum in London, along with the entire Temple of the Nereids. The Turks have replaced many of the reliefs with plaster casts.

The funerary monuments are all near the parking area, around the **Roman agora** and **theatre**; the **Tomb of the Harpies**, high on its monolith, is adorned with reliefs (plaster copies) of scenes from the Underworld. The winged female figures transporting souls, however, are not harpies but *kers*, who in true Greek religion, as opposed to the Olympian mythology, performed that function. Next to the tomb is a **Lycian tomb-sarcophagus** (4th century BC), high on its pillar. A similar tomb stands on the other side of the theatre. The **Inscribed Pillar** in the agora once supported the sarcophagus of a Lycian king; it bears writing in Lycian on all four sides, their longest inscription yet discovered, and although this has yet to be deciphered, other evidence has led scholars to believe it was the tomb of King Kherei, who defeated the Athenians in a battle of the Peloponnesian War. The Lycian acropolis was just south of the theatre; the palace of the Xanthian kings may have stood here, on the western end overlooking the river that locals call the '**Royal Terrace**', but the only ruins older than Byzantine times are those of a **Temple of Artemis**.

East of these ruins, part of a street can be made out, with another **agora** on one side and a **basilica** on the other; at the southern end of the street stood the **Temple of the Nereids**, which the malevolent Hyperboreans carted off to their capital a century ago as a cultural trophy. Across the path from this is an **arch** near the southern gate, donated to Xanthos by Vespasian. If you follow the street in the opposite direction, towards the northern walls, you'll come to more interesting **tombs** and a Byzantine monastery, and beyond the largely ruined walls, the city's **necropolis**.

The Letoon

Like the other ancient provinces of Asia Minor, Lycia had a federative sanctuary, a holy place shared by all the cities, the expression of their ethnic and religious unity. This was the **Letoon**, 2½ miles (4km) south of the main road (the turn-off is just north of the one to Xanthos), dedicated to Leto and her children, Apollo and Artemis. Although there was a small city here, the only remains are of the temples and a small but well-preserved **theatre** on the hillside. Even though foundations of only three temples remain (the **Temple of Leto**, the largest and easternmost of the three, the **Temple of Apollo and Artemis**, and a smaller unidentified one between them), the site is one of the most pleasant along the coast. The half-sunken ruins, including a huge and elaborate semi-circular **nymphaion** and a 7th-century **monastery**, have become elegant pools for the lazy turtles and fat white ducks that abound near Leto's ancient spring, which still flows as freely as in ancient times. These peacefully share the spot with other exotic wildlife, including clouds of magenta dragonflies, and frogs straight from Aristophanes croaking 'Brekekekex coax coax!' in the most correct classical Greek accents. On the floor of the twins' temple is a mosaic in the cella (inner sanctum) showing Artemis' bow and Apollo's lyre. Long inscriptions are everywhere; some have been removed to the nearby **museum**.

Apollo, surprisingly for a god of light and reason, proves a pretty shadowy character outside Greece proper. His mother Leto—etymologically and in religion the same as Leda, Latona, Lat, or other variations in mythology—seems to have been an old Middle Eastern version of the Great Goddess. Apollo, here, must appear in his role as god of the cult of Hyperboreans ('men from beyond the North Wind') centred at Delos, and extending, if the ancient historians are to be believed, from Britain to Palestine. At Patara, the next town along the coast (*see* below), an oracle of Apollo existed that functioned only in the winter, the opposite of the oracle at Claros. In the summer, Dionysus presumably took over the temple while Apollo removed himself behind the north wind, to England, specifically to the temple founded in his honour (under a different name) at Stonehenge.

Fethiye and Around   **Where to Stay**

Fethiye

moderate

A number of upmarket hostelries have opened near Fethiye in recent years. The most attractive is the ★★★**Asena**, ✆ 0252 616 6713, ✆ 0252 617 0487, 7km from town at Hisarönü Köyü. It's a lovely complex of low-rise buildings (pool, gym, hamam); riding and more on offer. The ★★★**Mendos**, 5km from town on Çalış beach, ✆ 0252 613 1130, ✆ 0252 613 1129, is a simple beach hotel with air-conditioned rooms.

In Fethiye itself, there is the ★★★**Hotel Mara**, Kral Caddesi, Yalı Sokak 2, ✆ 0252 614 9307, ✆ 0252 614 8039, where air-conditioned double rooms with breakfast on the rooftop terrace go for $45. The ★★**Hotel Se-Sa**, ✆ 0252 614 4656, ✆ 0252 614 4326, near the Mara on Akdeniz Caddesi, is similar to it and slightly cheaper, with en suite doubles for $40.

inexpensive

Next to the tourist office is the ★★**Hotel Dedeoğlu**, ✆ 0252 614 4010, ✆ 0252 614 1707; air-conditioned rooms with satellite TV for $25. At Çalış Beach the hotels tend to lack character but service is friendly and helpful, as at the ★★**Seketur**, ✆ 0252 622 1139; rooms with balconies, a lovely pool, disco and sports opportunities.

cheap

Fethiye is where to find one of Turkey's best pensions, the **Mer Pansiyon**, Dolgu Sahası Sahil Yolu 1, ✆ 0252 614 1177, which would put many a two-star hotel to shame. Rates for the spotless en suite rooms vary according to the view, averaging $18 per double, breakfast included. For families, there is a special lockable annexe with a separate room for the kids. Not as good but still nice, at a similar price, is the **Palmiye**, ✆ 0252 614 2140, on the shore west of the centre at Karagözler, with breakfast served on the roof terrace. The town's cheapest pensions can be found in the streets around the bus station, with an average price of $14; just follow the signs.

Çalış has *pansiyonlar* too, the best of which is the **Anıl**, on Barbaros Sokak, ℗ 0252 613 1192; all rooms with bath and there's a small pool.

Ölu Deniz

Directly on the beach, the **★★Meri Oteli**, ℗ 0252 617 0001, 🖂 0252 617 0010, is nice, set on a steep hillside among trees, with facilities for water sports and riding; very expensive for its rating at $115 per double for half board, but worth considering if you can afford it. Early reservations are essential.

Hisarönü has any number of hotels charging similar prices, all new and seemingly alike. This village is not to be recommended as a base unless all you are interested in is Ölü Deniz.

camping

There are plenty of scrappy campsites around Ölü Deniz; **Deniz Camping**, ℗ 0252 617 0045, has full facilities.

Fethiye   *Eating Out*

The **Rafet Restaurant** in Fethiye's harbour-front park is an old-established favourite but still good and very inexpensive: good kebabs, including fish kebabs, from $6 up, more for a full seafood dinner. The **Tahirağa** is also good, as is the **Meğri**, both on Çarşı Caddesi; the latter serves a mammoth collection of mezes, including stuffed aubergines drenched in cheese sauce. Both places charge around $6, drink included.

The lightest lunch in town is provided by the **Turkish Vegetarian Restaurant**, on Eski Mehri Sokak; very inexpensive omelettes, sandwiches and *plats du jour.*

For a splurge, if you can make it out to Ovacık Köyü, on the road to Ölü Deniz, the **Şadirvan** offers some delicate cooking in specialities such as trout with almonds and quail (*bıldırıcın*) cooked in butter, as well as the usual kebabs. A full dinner with mezes and wine goes for about $15, though you can eat well here for half that.

Entertainment and Nightlife

Nightlife here is not as frenetic as in the other resorts; most of the few places are in the old town above the harbour. The **Yeşilçam** is worth a drink at least for the view from its roof terrace, and the **Yasmin Bar**, set prominently in an elegant Ottoman building above the harbourmasters', has live rock and blues and occasionally performances of Turkish music. Unmistakable in the old quarter on Hamam Sokak is the **Car Cemetery** bar with the obligatory car fronts bolted above the entrance. Inside it's a dark grotto, usually heaving, in which you can get funky among the automotive parts until 4am. More dancing is to be had at the **Yes! Bar** at Cumhuriyet 9, a long-time local favourite.

Near the harbour, Fethiye's 16th-century **hamam** on Hamam Sokak has a sign up outside inviting you to 'be a sultan for one day'. Its clientele is mostly transitory and the high prices reflect this: $11 for 'Full Rub Down Soapy Bubbles Massage Services'. *Open 7am–midnight.*

Patara and Kalkan

The Fethiye–Patara–Kalkan–Kaş **bus** and **dolmuş** service is fast and regular, even out of season. In Patara, there are frequent **minibuses** from the village to the beach and the ancient city. Kalkan is a good place to base yourself if you are interested in archaeological sites; more than 25 can be reached within two hours by **car**. There is no proper otogar; all buses stop on the coastal highway at the top of the town.

Patara and Kalkan both have their own loyal fan base—people who have holidayed in Turkey for donkey's years but who always end up returning to one or the other of these tiny villages. Patara is a bit shabby but comfortable, warm and welcoming. Kalkan is showier and smarter but less home-like. Either makes a good base for visiting the nearby ruins.

Patara

There are two good reasons for visiting **Patara**, 46 miles (74km) east of Fethiye. The first is to explore the ruins of ancient Patara; the second is to enjoy the 11-mile sandy beach, the longest continuous strand in Turkey and one that is, save for one café, a small colony of umbrellas and some sun loungers, completely undeveloped. As at Dalyan, giant loggerhead turtles must be thanked for this. These immense amphibians have long used Patara beach as a laying spot, and it was the furore over Dalyan that raised concern in Patara as to the fate of their own turtles. Now the beach is closed off at night and daytime bathers are warned to be careful where they lay out their beach mats, lest the eggs be scrambled. Simple pleasures are the order of the day: canoes can be rented and there's a volleyball net in an egg-free zone, but otherwise it's a case of heading for the hills rising in the distance until you find a suitably deserted section of beach; you shouldn't have to go far. There is no development at ancient Patara either, in this case to protect the ruins. The village itself has remained very much the bonsai resort: whereas the growth of nearby coastal enclaves such as Olü Deniz continues virtually unchecked, Patara has been artificially stunted since 1988, when the government banned new construction. Perhaps because of this, there's little friction in Patara between the traditional and the modern: when they hear the call to prayer, barmen and waiters across the village turn down the volume of the western music serenading their customers.

Between sand, sea and pines, ancient Patara is altogether one of the most attractive sites in Lycia. Entering the ruins (*open daily 8–5.30, until 7 in summer; adm*), you pass some fine **Lycian tombs** on the right-hand side, and two apsed buildings, the **Roman baths** built by Vespasian and a later **Christian basilica**; new excavations here started in 1994. A three-gated monumental **arch**, stripped bare of its statues, adorned the town's main entrance, doubling up as part of the aqueduct carrying water to the baths. The **theatre** is in good shape, but partially covered by a tremendous sand dune, well over 100ft high. Be warned: squadrons of mosquitoes patrol the site in summer.

Kalkan

Although it has its devotees, there's nothing much to say about **Kalkan**, despite the magic of its location at the mouth of a crystal bay, and why it has grown into a small resort since a paved road was first built in 1982 is something of a mystery. It is certainly colourful enough, and has a definite charm, but if you walk from where the buses stop at the top of the hill down to the twee little harbour below, you will see all there is to see. There are no beaches here—for a swim, people go either to Patara or to **Kapıtaş beach**, 200 steps below a steep cliff 10 miles (16km) west of Kaş—and the nightlife is very low-key. Overall, Kalkan is a nice place to hole up for a day or two before boredom drives you on.

Patara

moderate

There is very little that's fancy here. The highest priced, thanks to its swimming pool and tennis courts, is the ★★★**Beyhan Patara**, at Gelemiş, ✆ 0242 843 5096.

cheap

In Patara, every other building seems to be either a cheap hotel or a pension. Most are very good, with mosquito nets and fans (more than a luxury in this former swampland). The **Apollon Motel**, ✆ 0242 843 5048, has a pleasant garden and a pool too and is well priced at $18. The **Otel Mehmet**, ✆ 0242 843 5032, is good and has a helpful English-speaking proprietor. All rooms have a balcony and private bath; $16 per double. Similar in both price and quality is the **Rose**, ✆ 0242 844 5165. The **Patara Viewpoint**, ✆ 0242 843 5184, has a wonderful setting on a hillside above the village and very friendly proprietors.

Kalkan

expensive

To compensate for the lack of a beach in Kalkan, the ★★★**Hotel Pirat**, by the marina, ✆ 0242 844 3178, 📠 0242 844 3183, has constructed a swimming platform only 200 yards distant. It's an elegant establishment, with air-conditioned rooms and two pools; $65. You'll need to book in advance if you want to stay.

moderate–inexpensive

There are several very nice pensions. At the harbour the **Akın Pansiyon**, ✆ 0242 844 3025, 📠 0242 844 2094, is drenched in bougainvillaea and charges $24 for doubles with bath, less if you don't mind sharing the common bathroom. A short stroll away, the **Balıkçı Han**, ✆ 0242 844 3075, 📠 0242 844 3641, was once a fishing captain's home, situated what must have been a pleasant commute away from work, directly above the harbour. Ottoman antiques are dotted about the front rooms, and there's an annexe of two old Greek houses nearby with quieter rooms than those in the Balıkçı proper; en suite doubles $35.

cheap

Kalkan's cheap pensions are few; you'll find what there is in the side streets at the top of the road leading down to the harbour. One good budget option is the **Kervan Han**, Yalıboy Mahalle 49, ✆ 0242 844 3684; small rooms with private bath and views of the harbour for $18.

In Patara's **Ali Baba Restaurant** at the top of the village, a meal of grilled chicken and salad and a glass of wine costs around $8. A little further into the village is the **Sofra**, run by a husband and wife team. She cooks and he serves a wide selection of Turkish dishes, including vegetarian options such as stuffed mushrooms; $6.

For good *pide* in Kalkan, try the **İlban** near the bus stop at the top of the village. Further down, the **Köşk** is good, though expensive, with all-you-can-eat meze buffets and the house speciality, swordfish steak, for $12; you can do just as well for half that at the **İlyada**, on the harbour.

Kaş to Antalya

Getting Around

Kaş is easily reached by **bus** from anywhere on the coast; the otogar is on the northern edge of town, on the road to Antalya (Atatürk Bulvarı). The **drive** from Patara to Kaş is one of the most spectacular—and stomach-churning—in Turkey. As you weave your way along the road cut into the cliff in the 1960s, islets bob invitingly out at sea, distracting you from that tortuous corner ahead. Here and there are tiny coves where you can stop off for a cool dip before pressing on to Kaş. Coming from inland, the only entrance is over the mountains from Isparta and Burdur, a long and tiresome journey.

The easiest way to explore the Kaş coastline is by day trip from Kaş, though there's nothing to stop you hopping off the boat in Üçağız, doing some hiking or some lazing, and picking up the boat the following day. Each morning at 10am a **dolmuş boat** leaves Kaş for Üçağız, returning early the following morning. To get to Aperlae, charter a fishing boat from Üçağız. It's an 80-minute walk from where the boat docks to the site. Also from Kaş, there are **minibuses** every half-hour in summer for Patara, Xanthos and Kalkan. 'Midi' buses depart regularly for Antalya.

For **Kyanaea**, take an eastbound bus from Kaş and ask to be let off at Yavu; from there, the ruins are a hard, one-hour climb away. Be sure to get good directions as it is easy to get lost; you may want to employ someone from the village as a guide. **Demre** can be reached by bus from Kaş, or more expensively by boat from Üçağız. Inexpensive tours of **Kekova** are arranged daily through the travel agents.

To get up to **Mount Olympos** without a car from Kaş, you'll have to take a bus bound for Antalya and get off at the Olympos crossroads to connect with a minibus to Olympos. Most coastal minibuses will take you at least within walking distance of **Phaselis**, though for the sites up in the mountains, **Limyra** and **Arykanda**, you'll need to take a minibus to Finike, then another minibus to get you to the site.

Tourist Information

Kaş: Cumhuriyet Meydanı 6, ✆ 0242 836 1238; faultlessly helpful.
Kemer: Belediye Binası (city hall), ✆ 0242 814 1537.

Kaş

Fifteen years ago the delightful fishing village of **Kaş**, huddled shyly under the lower peaks of 9,802ft Mount Akdağ, offered perhaps the ultimate in sunny Mediterranean languor. Of course it was too good to last—even then, Saudi Arabian interests were plotting the biggest resort complex in the world here, with no fewer than 10,000 rooms. That scheme fell through, thank goodness, but one or two of the hills behind the old town of Kaş have been more than overbuilt since. Don't be put off though; it's a happy, relaxed place, and still maintains more of its village character than most of the big resorts. Despite its small size, Kaş is one of the most cosmopolitan towns on the southern coast, with many of its inhabitants speaking four or five languages, and it's still the best base for seeing this delicious stretch of the Lycian coast.

Arching back from the sea, Kaş ('eyebrow') was given its name for obvious reasons. Before this, it was Habesa to the Lycians and Antiphellos to the Greeks; bits and pieces from the past survive both within the town and on the cliffs behind, where several tombs have been cut into the almost vertical face. West of the harbour are the ruins of a **temple** and a 1st-century **theatre** of medium size, with 25 rows of seats, weathered to provide a pleasing dappled effect. The location is simply stunning, with towering mountains behind the seats and tiny islands in the open sea behind the stage. The theatre commands a quiet spot on the edge of town, the voices of the original actors almost audible in the breeze. In the centre of town stands a **tomb**, as tall as the two-storey buildings surrounding it, and mellowed into a warm orange-brown. Its inscriptions are in a form of Lycian which has yet to be deciphered, even though many of the letters look uncannily modern. The hole smashed in the side was made centuries before by looters, robbing the corpses of the gold and the jewellery interred with them. Another tomb is on a hill just to the west on a narrow peninsula, and another at the harbour. All of these tombs (except the one at the harbour, which was moved by the municipality to make way for extensions), indeed all the tombs in the vicinity of Kaş, face the island of **Kastellorizo**: archaeologists and anthropologists alike are totally baffled as to why.

Just a mile offshore from the town, this lonely little island (also called *Megisti* in Greek, or *Meis* in Turkish) marks the easternmost boundary of the Greek republic, inherited from the Italians after the Second World War along with the rest of the Dodecanese. This quirky backwater, which once had a population of 16,000, is still recovering from 1944, when it was pillaged and burned by departing British troops in one of the more bizarre incidents of the war. The few Greeks who live there, heavily subsidized by the Greek government, come over to Kaş to do their shopping. A small company in the town runs unofficial day trips to the island, unofficial as Kastellorizo is not a port of entry into Greece; ask at the tourist office to find out how to get over, since conditions change all the time.

Around Kaş's **harbour** you'll find the usual array of cruise boats, offering day trips to Simena (Kale Köy), Uçağız and Kekova, and something unique, the **Aqua-alkım**, a glass-bottomed boat that does tours of the partially sunken ancient town of **Aperlae**, as well as night cruises when the moon is out and weather permits. A local travel agency, **Bougainville Travel**, Çukurbağlı Caddesi 10, © 0242 836 3142, *bougainville@superonline.com*, has more on offer than most, from dives and PADI dive courses to tours of some of the lesser known and more inaccessible local sites, as well as sea kayaking at Kekova. The town's other attraction is its farmers' market every Friday. Some of the farming families stay on into the evening, staring wide-eyed at the colonies of exotic foreigners in the outoor cafés.

Kaş's beaches may disappoint: two stony, ugly coves known respectively as Little Pebble Beach and Big Pebble Beach, next to the road to Fethiye. The nearest sandy beach is **Kapıtaş**, 10 miles (16km) to the west, created by the Kapıtaş stream which has cut a big chasm through the rock wall. By land, it is accessible only via an endless flight of stone steps. To save yourself this exertion, you can hire a motorboat from Kaş to take you there. Understandably, Kapıtaş gets very crowded.

Inland, 12 miles (19km) east of Kaş, are the ruins of ancient **Kyanaea**, which are renowned for the rows and rows of sarcophagi that dominate the site. These date back to Lycian and Roman times.

Kaş   *Where to Stay*

At the moment, Kaş is short on *expensive* and *luxury* hotels. This will change in the near future, however: establishments of this nature are already being built on the Çukurbağ peninsula outside town wherever there is a level stretch of ground.

expensive–moderate

Currently, the status address in Kaş is the ★★★★**Aqua-park**, four miles (6km) up the coast at Çukurbağ, ✆ 0242 836 1901, ⊕ 0242 836 1992. It's a beautiful complex, with pool, tennis, and a gym. At the extreme southern tip of the peninsula, three miles (5km) from Kaş itself, is the ★★★**Hadrian** ✆ 0242 836 2856, ⊕ 0242 836 1387, an isolated oasis clinging to the rocky coast with a pool and a sun terrace offering breathtaking views of Kastellorizo and the bay. Many customers first hear about it by word of mouth—a good sign in itself.

As the beaches in Kaş are poor, you may want a hotel with a swimming pool, in which case the ★★★**Ekici Oteli**, Hükümet Konaği Yanı, ✆ 0242 836 1417, ⊕ 0242 836 1823, is a good choice. It has a hamam too; air-conditioned rooms go for $45.

inexpensive

The ★★**Mimosa Oteli**, Atatürk Bulvarı, ✆ 0242 836 1272, is about $22 but has no pool. The **Limyra**, Meltem Sokak 5, ✆ 0242 836 1716, is a top-quality pension, with pine décor, in a quiet setting; doubles $24 with breakfast, and big discounts available off-season. On Bahçe Sokak, near the post office, the **Otel Çukurbağlı**, ✆ 0242 836 1760, has rather cramped doubles with private bathroom for $20. If you need a quiet setting, the ★★**Bolel**, ✆ 0242 836 1428, is out by itself at Çukurbağ. There's a pool, and rooms with satellite TV; some rooms have great views over the bay. Doubles $30.

cheap

Cheap pensions are all over town, particularly north of the bus station: their representatives will wave their cards in your face the minute you arrive in town. Nice ones include the **Linda**, ✆ 0242 836 3114, with rooms with a view at Küçük Çakıl Mahalle, by the Little Pebble Beach, and the **Yalı**, ✆ 0242 836 1132, on Hastane

Caddesi, run by a gentle old couple offering kitchen facilities and simple doubles for $12. Those at the back have panoramic views of the bay.

In the accommodation ghetto to the east of the centre, the second street back from Little Pebble Beach (Küçük Çakıl Plajı) is the quietest. The best of the pensions here are the **Defne**, ℐ 0242 836 1932, the **Cemil**, ℐ 0242 836 1554, and the **Antiphellos**, ℐ 0242 836 1136, all modern establishments with balconies, en suite bathrooms and breakfast for $15 per double. Being further up the hill, the Defne has better sea views, although only its top two floors have uninterrupted views of the bay. Also at Little Pebble Beach, the **Çakıl Pansiyon**, ℐ 0242 836 1532, is a low-priced family concern; $12 including breakfast.

camping

Among a number of campsites, the **Kaş Camping**, ℐ 0242 836 1050, on the road to Çukurbağ, stands out; it's right on the sea, and besides campsites it has bungalows to rent at $9 for doubles (without bath).

Kaş   Eating Out

Not many come to Turkey in search of fine French cuisine, but anyone who has dined at **Chez Evy** on Terzi Sokak will leave having tasted it. At the helm is the eponymous chef-hostess Evy, an effervescent Frenchwoman whose personality is as delicious as her cooking. Not surprisingly, her place has become a Kaş institution: locals and tourists alike soon get hooked on the relaxed ambience, with details such as the Camus quotation hanging in the toilet adding a dash of quirkiness. From the calamari Provençale to the magnificent pepper steak, the food is simply superb. Bring an appetite: one of Evy's portions is often sufficient to feed a small family. At $15 or so for a meal, prices are indecently low for what you get—but don't tell Evy.

Sun Café and Restaurant, near the harbour on Hükümet Caddesi, serves up a selection of jazz, Ottoman dishes and good fish for upwards of $15. Tucked away on Anıt Mezar Karşısı behind the Lycian tomb is the **Bahçe** ('garden'), set amongst lush greenery, offering the best mezes in town; a full meal costs $8. The **Oba** on Çukurbağlı Caddesi also has a pleasant shady garden, with indoor tables in case of inclement weather. Pick from the trays of freshly made food such as okra, spinach, grilled aubergine and beef goulash; $4 per plate, but make sure it is hot. For a break from Turkish food, **Ginarlar**, on Şube Sokak opposite the Kalamar Restaurant, will pull a crispy pizza from their wood-fired oven for $4.

Entertainment and Nightlife

This can be at least slightly more intense than Fethiye, but nothing like Bodrum. There are some wonderfully noisy dancing spots in town: the **Deniz Altı** and the **Mavi Bar**, on the waterfront. However, the **Redpoint** is the town's premier entertainment spot, always packed because of its mastery of the basics—a good choice of alcohol, communal outdoor benches and music that everyone can hear but that deafens nobody. For something a bit more refined, the **Sun Café** by the harbour plays jazz and occasionally live Turkish music.

Kekova Island and the Kaş Coastline

Heavily indented and full of isolated caves and islets, this part of the coast captures in equal measure some of Lycia's most spectacular scenery and some of its most intriguing ruins, many of which lie semi-submerged in a sea as clear as any in the world. The best are at the mysterious city that once stood on **Kekova Island**, east of Kaş; along its southern shore houses, walls and kilns can be easily identified and staircases descend from the cliffs to disappear into the ocean. On a small beach a large, arched structure stands erect, once part of a boatyard. Little is known of this city, not even the name. A local theory maintains that it was inhabited by pirates who, after indulging in the pillage and plunder that their occupation entailed, would then stash their loot in one of the many hidden caves. They lived here for centuries until divine retribution intervened in the form of a massive earthquake that shook the city into the sea and drove the brigands away.

The village of **Üçağız**, across the water on the mainland, began life in the 4th century BC as Teimiussa. What remains of Teimiussa is spartan but striking, a plethora of **rock tombs** huddled together, many rising picturesquely out of the water—again, all facing west to Kastellorizo. For the present, Üçağız itself exists in a time-warp, a barely touched village of fishing and weaving that until 1992 could be reached only by boat. Its setting is undeniably lovely, amidst the two bays and slender channel that give the village its name, Üçağız being a direct translation of its Greek name, Tristomo, or 'three mouths'. As a recent fixture on the day-trip itinerary from Kaş, however, Üçağız is fast becoming a 'real' village. Restaurants line the waterfront and the first carpet shop is already open. From here a boat can be hired to view ancient **Aperlae**, a mostly submerged Lycian city.

Further along the mainland, clinging to the side of a hill, is **Kale**, descendant of ancient Simena, another member of the Lycian League. Its **castle**, built by the Lycians and renovated, so it is said, by the pirates of Kekova Island, is in good condition, its crenellations showing a variety of styles. Inside it is the **theatre** of Simena, the smallest theatre yet discovered, with only seven rows of seats—an indication of the diminutive size of Simena and also of the value placed on culture in even the tiniest Greek towns.

Demre (Kale): St Nick's Home Town

Going northeast, the next modern town, **Demre** (which appears on many maps as *Kale*), stands on a little plain full of small farms, grown prosperous from citrus fruits and greenhouse tomatoes. Demre is the descendant of ancient Myra, home of jolly St Nicholas, a 4th-century prelate. He was actually born in Patara, but it was in Myra that he was bishop, sufficiently beloved for his generosity and good deeds to get himself canonized. Before he became Father Christmas, he was known as patron of sailors and pawnbrokers; and the Greek Church still knows nothing of the Christmas duties he has in the west. Travel brochures have lately appeared with pictures of an American-style Santa Claus in front of the ancient ruins. Indeed, a huge sign has been erected next to the St Nicholas church advertising the 'Santa Claus Foundation', complete with a smiling Santa looking a little overdressed for a Turkish summer. Let us hope this Santa fixation doesn't get out of hand. Follow the 'Baba Noel' signs in Demre to find the **St Nicholas Church** (*open daily 8–7.30 in summer, otherwise 8–5.30*), a 5th-century building with extensive 11th-century additions, including a large barrel-vaulted nave and cloister. In the original structure there is some fine marble inlay work and much carved stone recycled from earlier buildings. Of the later frescoes, only one unidentified saint remains. This may well be the oldest surviving church building in Turkey.

Myra

About a mile outside Demre, the ruins of **Myra** (*open daily 7.30–7 in summer, otherwise 8–5.30*) include an amazing collection of **tombs** cut out of the cliffs above the city, all in the form of temple façades. There are over a score of them, arranged on the cliff in an asymmetric jumble. Most are from the 4th century BC, and many contain funeral scenes in relief. Several façades have roofs carved to imitate wooden beams, suggesting that they were copied in form from wooden temples or other similar buildings that have not survived; the same is true of the Phrygian cliff-face façades west of Ankara.

Myra's other attraction is its **theatre**, a late Roman work with some uninspired sculpture. From its huge orchestra, we can guess it was used more often for games and animal shows than for classical drama. In the vicinity are a number of Byzantine structures protruding from the surrounding farms and greenhouses, and, a few miles to the southwest, a **Roman granary**, one of many in Lycia, decorated with a relief of Hadrian, who built it.

Around Finike

The coastal road east of Demre runs by a very long and scrubby beach, with its scattering of curious wooden holiday bungalows on huge wooden wheels. Keep on driving and you'll pass a number of small coves ideal for quick dips to break up long drives. From **Finike**, a nondescript agricultural town 19 miles (30km) east of Demre, you have the choice of continuing along the coast, passing by the 'Turtles Crossing' roadsigns, or striking inland through the mountains. Either way will take you to Antalya, though the recently built coastal route is considerably shorter. Travelling inland, you encounter first the ruins of **Limyra**. In the early 4th century BC, this was the most powerful city of Lycia under King Perikles, founder of the Lycian League of cities and a fighter for Lycian independence against Mausolus of Caria. The site is worth a visit for the tombs—if you haven't seen enough yet—spread all over the outskirts of the ancient town. Notable among them is the **Heroon of King Perikles**, in the form of an Ionic temple, although some climbing will reveal several others that rank among the best Lycian tomb architecture.

North of Limyra the road passes **Arykanda**, another ruined town. Its only distinction seems to have been a precocious and enthusiastic acceptance of Christianity, as reflected in its monuments, including remnants of an early Byzantine basilica and an even earlier temple that was converted to Christian use. The biggest ruins on the site, however, are a small **theatre**, well preserved and beautifully situated, with a view over the surrounding hills, and a **bath complex** with one of its 30ft walls still standing.

Beyond this come two lakes, **Avlan Gölü** and **Karagöl**, the 'Black Lake', its waters held back by a natural dam and overflowing dramatically through a chasm in the cliff. If you press even further inland, into the Ak Dağlar, you'll come to the only sizeable village in these parts, **Elmalı**, with some Selçuk remains and an attractive, tiled 17th-century mosque to match its neighbourhoods of old wood-frame houses.

Olympos and the Chimaera (Alev)

Along the coast, the road skirts the grand massif of the Bey Dağları, the 'Bey's mountains' around Cape Gelidonya, a familiar landmark to sailors ancient and modern. Heading northwards, **Olympos** is another ruined town in a pretty setting, though little remains of it. If you pass at night, you will see a small flame rising from the mountains above the town. All the ancient geographers mention it, and it takes its name, the **Chimaera**, from the myth of Bellerophon. The Lycian King, Iobates, sent Bellerophon to kill the fire-breathing monster, part lion, part goat, part serpent. With the aid of the winged horse Pegasus he succeeded, and returned, after completing other tasks set by Iobates, to Xanthos where he married the king's daughter and became heir to the Lycian throne. Carried away by his success, Bellerophon tried to ride Pegasus up to Mount Olympos. For his presumption, Zeus sent a gadfly to tickle Pegasus, who threw him to earth; Bellerophon landed in a thorn bush, which put out his eyes, and he wandered the earth, blind and lame, to the end of his days.

The real Chimaera isn't at all monstrous; in the daytime it isn't even visible. Whatever combination of gases causes it has never been satisfactorily explained, but if you care to make the half-hour climb up to the spot (on a well-marked trail), you will find it can easily be extinguished, only to relight itself after a few seconds. Apparently in ancient times it put on a better show. Nearby are the ruins of a temple (of Hephaestus of course) and the old writers describe it as only one of a number of fiery manifestations on the mountain's slopes.

Bellerophon didn't have to go far to reach the home of the gods. The Lycian Olympos, one of at least three mountains of that name and fame in Asia Minor alone, is now called **Tahtalı Dağ**, the highest peak of the Bey's mountains.

Olympos is noticeably wetter and greener than the rest of the southern coast and can provide a welcome sanctuary from the oppressive summer heat. Çıralı Beach, a short walk through orange groves from the ruins, is set against a dramatic backdrop of cliffs and peaks that seem more Thai than Turkish. The coarse sand beach plays host to the odd colony of wicker umbrellas and sun loungers as well as egg-laying turtles from May to September, in deference to whom organized watersports have been banned.

Phaselis

Beneath Tahtalı Dağ on the shore are the ruins of **Phaselis**, one of the foremost cities of Lycia. Founded by Rhodes in the 7th century, Phaselis often stood apart from its neighbours, even to the extent of supporting Mausolus against the Lycian League. The Phaselitians, like the people of Side, had a reputation as cut-throats and schemers; once, desperate for cash, they offered Phaselitian citizenship for sale to all comers. They met their match when a real cut-throat, the pirate Zenicertes, sacked the town and made it his headquarters, *c.* 90 BC. The ruins left today are all from the rebuilt city of Roman times. Its three harbours can easily be seen from the shore, and there is also a **theatre**, an **aqueduct** and a number of **tombs**. Now as in ancient times Phaselis, though lovely, is famous for being infested with nasty hornets. These may or may not be in the mood to annoy you when you visit.

Beyond Phaselis, the highway passes more wonderful corniche scenery through mature Mediterranean pine forests. The broad curve of the Lycian shore ends as it began, with a village called **Kemer**, its name fittingly meaning 'band' or 'arch'. From here, Antalya is just over the horizon; Kemer has absorbed much of the holiday overflow from that city, and grown into a big, brash resort built around a new marina—a startling contrast to the relatively unspoiled parts of the coast that precede it. Among the ranks of hotels are complexes like **Tukan City**, 4½ miles (7km) away at Çamyuva, with a shopping mall, parks, horseback riding, a huge, high-tech disco, pool and casino.

Üçağız

Üçağız has a woeful collection of *cheap* ramshackle pensions. The best is the **Koç**, ✆ 0242 874 2080, east of the centre by the shore, followed by the nearby **Onur**, ✆ 0242 874 2071, also by the shore.

Demre

Demre has a nice hotel near the Baba Noel, the ****Şahin**, ✆ 0242 871 5686, where doubles with private bathroom and breakfast cost only $16. There is a good selection of pleasant *cheap* pensions scattered around town; the **Noel**, ✆ 0242 871 2267, has its fans and is close to the ruins. Closer still is the **Kent**, ✆ 0242 871 2042, with friendly management and a garden to unwind in. Doubles $16. On the main road near the western entrance to the village is the modest **Kıyak Otel**, ✆ 0242 871 2092, which will do at a pinch; doubles $18.

Finike

You wouldn't think of Finike as a prime spot for a holiday, but if you end up there the **(S)Anadolu**, on Sahil Yolu, ✆ 0242 855 1665, can provide an agreeable stay by the beach; simple rooms with bath for $20.

Olympos

The closest base for seeing Olympos would be the village of Çıralı, where some very modest accommodation exists. The best is the **Orange Pansiyon**, ✆ 0242 825 7293, set in an orange grove just across from the tiny bridge; $20 with breakfast. More pleasant, though, would be to stay at the tiny, nascent beach resort of Adrasan, very near Olympos village. There are a number of *pansiyonlar* here, including the clean, family-run **Özcan**, ✆ 0242 833 5220.

To see the ruins at Phaselis there are a few *pansiyonlar* and a campsite at **Tekirova**, 3km to the north.

Kemer

luxury–expensive

Everything in these classes is in Kemer, which has somehow, inexplicably, become the poshest corner of the southern coast. The tone of the place is set by impressive, totally self-contained holiday complexes like the *******Favori Aqua Resort** at Çamyuva, ✆ 0242 824 6214, 🖷 0242 824 6210, where everything that has ever been devised for having fun in the water is on offer, from jacuzzis to banana sailing;

there's a casino, disco, gym, private beach, shopping mall and special entertainments for children. Something very similar, at Tekirova, is the **★★★★★Phaselis Princess**, © 0242 821 4070, ✆ 0242 821 4069: every luxury a resort could have, on a broad stretch of beach.

moderate

There are plenty of comfortable modern places in Kemer, such as the **★★Dragos**, © 0242 814 3022, with a small pebble beach and pool, and some rooms with a view, but for something a bit different try the **Erendiz Ranch**, outside Kemer at Aslancakbucak, © 0242 814 3742, where the accommodation is traditional and simple and the emphasis is on horse riding (it's run by and for Germans).

Üçağız to Kemer   ***Eating Out***

Üçağız has several restaurants, none of which stand out particularly, although their waterside settings are charming. In nearby Kaleköy the **Marina** is a good bet for seafood; about $10 and up.

Along the coastal road between Kaş and Demre, the popular **Çeşme** has a lovely garden terrace; its speciality, besides kebabs, is *gözleme*, or Turkish crepes; $9. **Demre** is full of plain lokantas of which the **İpek** on the road to Baba Noel is the best, serving good honest Turkish fare for $6.

Near **Olympos**, the beach at Çıralı has a fringe of rudimentary cafés and lokantas, where fish is good value at $7.

In **Kemer** and environs, you could easily spend as much for dinner as in Paris, especially in some of the hotel restaurants—but we doubt it would ever be worth it. A couple of alternatives popular with the Turks are the **Mimoza**, in the centre on Hastane Caddesi, with typical Turkish food for about $8; and the **Ulupınar**, just off the coastal road south of Tekirova: a beautiful view and excellent fresh-water fish (you can bet the trout is fresh; they raise them themselves). $9 and up.

Antalya and the Pamphylian Coast

In the twilight of the Aegean Bronze Age, a time when history passes into myth, the Greeks wrote of the 'mixed multitude of peoples' set in motion by the fall of Troy; many of these found their way to the land between the mountains of Lycia and Cilicia. Historians think it likely that settlement of this region actually preceded the breakdown of civilization in the 12th century BC. The Greeks later came to call this region **Pamphylia**, 'land of all tribes'.

Its ancient borders are marked by the two largest modern towns in the area, **Antalya** and **Alanya**. Its cities, Perge, Side and Aspendos, all prospered on the fertile plain, becoming rich and thoroughly Hellenized by the time Alexander came. Although their early history was more within the Hittite-Anatolian world than the Greek, they kept stories, some from Homer, of their foundation by the seers Mopsus and Amphilochus, who had been with the Achaeans at Troy.

The coastal plain begins at **Antalya**, the Lycian mountains ending abruptly to form a spectacular backdrop for the city. Ten years ago, Antalya seemed well on its way to transforming itself from a sleepy old Selcuk town to a charming Mediterranean resort city, the capital of what people back then were fond of calling the 'Turkish Riviera' or the 'Turquoise Coast'. Somewhere along the way, however, things got out of hand. There are plenty of palm trees, and broad, fine beaches stretching away from the city on both sides, but Antalya can hardly be called a resort any more—it's Turkey's wealthiest and fastest growing city (25% annually, in the last few years), with a population already over half a million. Antalya can still be fun: stay in a *pansiyon* in one of the restored old houses in the centre, and take a big city break after all those ruins and beaches.

History

Unlike so many of the coastal cities vacated by the Greeks, Antalya has been continuously occupied, and consequently very little is left to mark its history. King Attalus II of Pergamon, given this stretch of coast by the Romans for safe-keeping in 188 BC, founded the city when Side refused to acknowledge his authority. Called Attaleia, it soon surpassed Side and the other Pamphylian cities, gaining further impetus under the Romans when Augustus settled a colony here in 6 BC. When Mediterranean civilization collapsed, Attaleia showed more resourcefulness than other cities, setting up a fleet to defend itself against pirates, Arabs and occasionally the Byzantine taxman, and consequently survived in a reduced state despite the contraction of seagoing trade.

Recovery came with the Selcuks in the early 13th century; although various Turkish tribes had already held stretches of coastline, the Selcuks were the first to develop the area, rebuilding Attaleia and Alanya and linking them to Konya with a string of caravanserais. The sultans often spent their winters here. Had it not been for the disruptions caused by the Crusaders, and the stranglehold that Venice and Genoa kept on the eastern trade, the Selcuks might well have brought the old eastern Mediterranean world back to life with a Turkish-Muslim slant.

Getting Around

There is **no rail service** in the area. **Buses** between Antalya and all points are very frequent (even to İstanbul, a 13-hour trip). The **bus station** is located 4km north of the centre on Kepez Altı, the main road to Burdur. The bus station has two terminals. **Minibuses** to nearby destinations such as Alanya, Side or Kemer depart from the provincial terminal (*İlçeler Terminalı*) on the left. **Long-distance buses** depart from the intercity terminal (*Şehirlerarası Terminalı*) on the right.

The city's newly extended **airport** receives daily flights from Ankara and İstanbul and charters from abroad; it is connected to the centre (Cumhuriyet Caddesi) by THY airline buses; a taxi will cost about $9.

Dozens of cruise **ships** stop here in season, and there is also the Turkish Maritime Lines **steamer** to Venice, every Wednesday from May to October (© 0242 241 1120 in Antalya for details).

Within the city, most sites are within easy walking distance of each other; for the museum and Konyaaltı beach, it's easy to take a **dolmuş** down the main street, Konyaaltı Caddesi (called Cumhuriyet Caddesi in the centre). Antalya has many travel agencies, such as Camel Tours, who will organize trips by coach, minibus or car to the various sites at quite reasonable rates.

Antalya   ***Tourist Information***

Cumhuriyet Caddesi, THY Yanı, ✆ 0242 241 1747.

The Regional Directorate is inconveniently located on Tonguç Caddesi, next to the Turkish Radio and Television (TRT) office, ✆ 0242 343 2760.

The Old Town

Most of old Antalya's walls were removed long ago, but their course is followed by two modern boulevards, Atatürk Caddesi and Cumhuriyet Caddesi, separating the old and new towns. Where these streets meet, a surviving bastion of the Selcuk wall has been converted into an odd **clock tower**. To enter the old town in style, walk a few squares along Atatürk Caddesi to the restored **Hadrian's Gate**. Its three arches are decorative, but hardly a solid link in a fortification; in Hadrian's time, the pax Romana was so secure that it seemed cities would never again need real walls. In many places in Asia Minor there are purely ceremonial gates like these, or their ruins. This one was constructed in honour of Hadrian's visit in AD 130, and there would originally have been a statue of the emperor on top.

Antalya's old town was completely left behind in the growth boom that started in the 1970s. Today, though still a rather poor quarter, its streets of pretty Ottoman houses have survived; in parts it seems that almost half of the houses have been restored as *pansiyonlar* or restaurants, much as in İstanbul's Sultanahmet. Towards the southern end is the **Kesik Minare**, the 'broken minaret' struck by lightning long ago. The mosque it serves was originally a Byzantine church built in the 5th century, rebuilt and restored many times since. Continuing further, towards the sea, you come across a squat stone cylinder, the **Hıdırlık Tower**, believed to be the tomb of a 2nd-century Roman consul; traces of a carved fascia, symbol of the consuls' authority, can still be made out.

Surprisingly few Selcuk buildings remain in Antalya. The most important is the city's landmark, the **Yivli Minare** or 'grooved minaret', typically Selcuk in its heaviness of form but unerring sense of proportion. Its lobed shaft and stalactite balcony are unique—one of the few of Turkey's fine minarets that the visitor will remember. There are some surviving sections of the **walls** nearby, along with more lovely Ottoman houses. It's impossible to date the houses: the same style, with low tiled roofs, stucco or half-timber walls and second-floor balconies, continued for three centuries; some of them were actually built in the 1920s. An Ottoman mosque, the 16th-century **Paşa Camii**, is nearby, just behind the clock tower. At the eastern end of the old town, overlooking the sea, **Karaalioğlu Park** witnesses the nightly promenade of the Antalyalılar; it's quite an elegant park, full of big trees and tea gardens where you can watch goldfish splash in the fountains.

Another job of restoration—on a grand scale—has been performed on old Antalya's **harbour**, at the opposite side of the old town from the park. Only a few years ago this entire area (called **Kaleiçi**) was falling into ruins; the city's ambitious plan for saving it has won an international architectural award. Around the newly constructed basin for yachts and other pleasure craft, new roads, fountains, hotels, parks and terraced cafés have grown up; there are also new streets of shops crawling with carpet salesmen, whose soft entreaties are drowned out each evening by the cacophony of hundreds of birds preparing to roost. At the top of the cliffs, on Cumhuriyet Caddesi, take a moment to admire the glory and grandeur of the most audacious, indescribable **Atatürk Monument** in all Turkey. May it stand forever.

Antalya Regional Museum

West of the old town, Konyaaltı Caddesi (called *Sarampol* by many locals, and on some minibus signs) heads towards the mountains, the long beach on one side, an equally long row of modern apartments on the other. About a mile out, it passes the **Antalya Regional Museum** (*open daily exc Mon 9–6; adm*). Of all Turkey's museums, this is the most attractive in its arrangement of exhibits, and the simplest for the visitor, with clear, multilingual explanations. It contains one of the largest and best collections in the country, with exhibits ranging from the Stone Age remains from nearby Karain Cave, the earliest habitation yet discovered in Turkey, to a beautiful 6th-century relief of the archangel Gabriel. Greek and

Roman sculptures fill several large halls. One great sarcophagus, carved in the form of a temple, portrays the labours of Hercules. Another supposedly held the remains of St Nicholas of Myra (don't tell the kids it's Santa Claus's grave). Merchants from Bari in southern Italy stole the body in 1087; it remains in Bari to this day, performing miracles for the faithful and oozing a mysterious holy goo that worshippers take home in tiny phials—just as it did back in Myra in Byzantine times. The sarcophagus was a bit too heavy to take along. Antique statuary in the collection includes a group of huge Olympian gods, and some equally large emperors (Hadrian, Septimus Severus and Trajan); a relief of the twelve Lycian gods; and a famous icon of the Artemis of Perge. Best of all, perhaps, is a remarkable, almost impressionistic scene of the underworld from a grave stele, hung inconspicuously behind the Hercules sarcophagus. The Byzantines are well represented in all periods. The final rooms have a very good ethnographic collection, with a special section on the Yürük nomads of Anatolia.

Beaches

Konyaaltı Beach, extending for miles, is an extremely popular spot, barely visible from the street for all the restaurants, cafés and cabins. Still, there's room for all; you just need to go a little further out to be alone. Many visitors prefer the fine sand at **Lara Beach** about seven miles (11km) southeast of town; here also are the **Düden Waterfalls**, plunging dramatically into the sea—when there's enough water around. Don't expect much of a show in summer.

Around Antalya

The northern road leads high up into the mountains from Antalya towards Burdur and Isparta. After six miles (10km), at a crossroads, there is a choice of excursions. The right-hand route leads past a lovely forested picnic spot, the **Düzler Park**, towards **Karain Cave**, where human remains some 50,000 years old were found. Beside the cave, which is a long climb up the mountain, there's a small **museum**, probably only of interest to the most fervent aficionados of the Palaeolithic.

Termessos

Up here in the mountains, we have left classical Pamphylia completely behind. Until Roman times, the influence of the Hellenized Greek cities never extended much beyond the coast; this mountainous region was known as Pisidia, the region of a fierce confederation of native Anatolian tribes who were better left alone. One of their greatest cities was **Termessos**, its ruins accessible on a motor road 16 miles (26km) down the left-hand fork from the crossroads. The people of Termessos called themselves Solymians, giving the name to Mount Solymos, the formidable crag under whose shelter they built their city. King Iobates, as mentioned in the *Iliad*, sent Bellerophon against the Solymians and he served them just as he had the Amazons, bombing them into submission by hurling great boulders from Pegasus.

Other would-be conquerors did not fare as well. The Termessians liked to say they had defeated Alexander, who abandoned a siege here on his way to Sagalassus in 334 BC. Throughout the Hellenistic era the coastal cities were constantly at odds with the Termessians, and the Romans discreetly signed a treaty declaring the city 'friend and ally of the Roman people'. Termessos remained autonomous throughout the Roman period, and showed it by not even bothering to put the emperor's picture on its coins.

The ruins, tricky to reach without a car, are well preserved but not excavated; the difficult mountainous site is an attraction in itself, altogether different from the coastal towns. Most of the ruins are from Roman times, and in no way unusual. There is a **theatre** in good condition, an **odeon** nearby, and a small indoor theatre that also served as a **bouleuterion**. Like Athens, Termessos has its **Stoa of Attalus**, in the agora just behind the odeon, built by the Pergamene king. The main thoroughfare, called King Street by the Termessians, touches the western edge of the agora on its way north, where it turned into a **colonnaded street** of shops, once lined with statues of prominent citizens. All these are gone, but the inscriptions tell us that many were champion wrestlers; this sport was a speciality of the city, and of Pisidia, as it is among the Turks today.

An outstanding feature of Termessos' remains, if you have the time to search them out among the bushes, is the large number of **tombs**, all around the slopes to the east, west and south. Some are mere sarcophagi, others are elaborately built in the form of temples (the best are to the south) and yet others, on the northwest slopes, are façades carved out of the rocks in the manner of the Lycians. Most have inscriptions, not all tributes to the dead: many warn of the fines grave robbers or anyone attempting to reuse the tombs would incur, all mentioning specific amounts, payable to, for example, the Temple of Solymian Zeus. There are references also to the amounts payable to informers for catching evildoers in the act.

Antalya **Where to Stay**

Antalya has some of the best hotels and *pansiyonlar* in Turkey. If you're not too fussed about being near a beach, the old town is perhaps the most pleasing area: the atmosphere is convivial, there are plenty of restaurants nearby, and many places have lovely views of the harbour.

luxury

Antalya's oldest luxury hotel is the ★★★★★**Talya** at Fevzi Çakmak Caddesi 30, ✆ 0242 248 6800, ✉ 0242 241 5400. Unlike many of its competitors, it feels no need to show off: instead it has a restrained elegance and wonderful ambience. It is set dramatically on a cliff top overlooking the sea just outside the old quarter of Antalya, with a pool as well as its own private beach at the base of the cliffs.

Konyaaltı and the more distant beaches have more than their share of five-star behemoths. At the top of the list is the ★★★★★**Falez Antalya** on Konyaaltı, ✆ 0242 248 5000, ✉ 0242 248 5025, in a beautiful park-like compound with a huge three-level pool, tennis courts, and rooms with sea views. Next door, the streamlined, futuristic ★★★★★**Sheraton Voyager Antalya**, 100 Yıl Bulvarı near Konyaaltı, ✆ 0242 243 2432, ✉ 0242 243 2462, offers the best of American chain-style comforts and lots of sports and entertainments. Neither is on the beach, though they own stretches of it and provide transport.

The best golf course in Turkey awaits you duffers 20 miles east of Antalya at Belek, part of the ★★★★★**Adora Golf Hotel**, ✆ 0242 725 4051, ✉ 0242 725 4071, a truly impressive complex on a big beach. There's every imaginable amenity in the rooms, many with sea view and balcony; besides golf, all sports from tennis to windsurfing are available.

The **(S)Marina** in the old quarter of Kaleiçi at Mermerli Sokak 15, ℂ 0242 247 5490, ℮ 0242 241 1765, has gone to town on style. The reception area is an expanse of marble, covered with French-style furniture. There's a courtyard, with its swimming pool illuminated at night. Tastefully decorated rooms from $80.

Not so elegant, but all the cosier, is the nearby **Türk Evi Otelleri**, converted into a hotel from a 200-year-old row of houses backing onto the old city wall. Outlandish Ottoman and French furniture competes for your attention in the reception. More harmonious is the traditional garden, onto which the quietest rooms look out; $65.

The **Ninova** is perhaps the best of the many excellent pensions in Antalya, located in a quiet back street of Kaleiçi at Hamit Efendi Sokak 9, ℂ 0242 248 6114, ℮ 0242 248 9684. The entrance hall of this old Ottoman house is very airy, opening onto a garden filled with free-range tortoises and trees laden with oranges, which you are welcome to pick when they ripen, in October and November. Rooms vary in size, but all have air-conditioning: $50; less outside high season.

More modern places in this category are out east at Lara beach, a bit far from town but quieter. With a small private beach under the cliffs, reached by stairs, the ★★★★**Antalya Prince**, ℂ 0242 349 3968, ℮ 0242 349 3873, has air-conditioned rooms and full facilities. Also at Lara beach, the startling modern ★★★**Turist**, ℂ 0242 349 1414, ℮ 0242 349 3387, has a glass-fronted elevator, a hamam and a pool; all rooms with satellite TV and air conditioning.

The nicest in this category is in the old town. The **(S)Turban Adalya Oteli**, Antalya Kaleiçi, ℂ 0242 243 4756, was built in 1869 as the branch office of a bank. It is well worth visiting, even if only to see the magnificent lobby with its marble fountain; it's near the old harbour, and has a swimming pool. Another fine restoration job around the harbour has created the **(S)Argos**, Atatürk Ortaokulu Karşısı, ℂ 0242 247 2012, all rooms with satellite TV and air conditioning; here too there is a small pool. A more modern building in the Kaleiçi, the ★★**Aspen**, ℂ 0242 247 0590, ℮ 0242 241 3364, on Kaledibi Sokak, offers the same amenities.

The **(S)Villa Perla**, ℂ 0242 248 9793, ℮ 0242 241 2917, is an old house on Hesapçı Sokak built around a pretty courtyard; it has a good restaurant. The **Doğan**, Mermerli Banyo Sokak, ℂ 0242 247 4654, ℮ 0242 247 4006, *doganhotel@ superonline.com*, has spacious rooms set around an extensive patio and pool area— the perfect refuge from the noisy streets of the old quarter; $55.

The **Antique Pansiyon**, Paşa Camii Sokak 28, ℂ 0242 242 4615 ℮ 0242 241 5890, *fatih.sertel@garanti.net.tr*, is a 300-year-old Anatolian house carefully restored by a Dutch-Turkish couple. Its lofty reception area is separated from the small rear garden by a huge wall of glass. The en suite rooms are wood-panelled and have fans, which are not always up to the job of fighting off the summer heat. Unusually for Turkey, prices are fixed, at $20–25 depending on the size of the room.

There'll be no problem finding a reasonably-priced hotel in the newer quarters or at Lara beach; the problem is telling one from the others.

cheap

Nearly all of these are in the old town, and they fall into two categories: those in restored Ottoman-era houses, or more modern *pansiyonlar* like those in Kaş or the other resorts, usually closer to the harbour. Among the former, readers have written in praise of the **Anı Pansiyon**, Tabakhane Sokak just off Hesapçı Sokak, the main drag of the old town, ✆ 0242 247 0056; spotless rooms and filling breakfasts. For a very inexpensive room with private shower and toilet, try the **Ertan Pansiyon**, Üzun Çarşı Sokak 9, ✆ 0242 241 5535. Of the latter, modern sort, one of the best is the **Özmen**, close to the harbour at Zeytin Çıkmazı 5, ✆ 0242 241 6505, run by friendly, helpful people: nice rooms with bath, and a roof terrace with a view.

camping

The place to look for campsites is on the main road, between Antalya and Kemer. **Denizer Camping**, ✆ 0242 259 0874, at Sarısu, is fully equipped and set by the sea. Some 9½ miles (15km) west of the city, **Kindilçeşme Camping**, ✆ 0242 814 1065, offers shady spots under the pines; it too is on the shore.

Antalya   **Eating Out**

Down by the old harbour is the **Kral Sofrası**, where Antalya's best seafood is served up at touristic prices ($14 or so). Despite grumpy service, locals aren't put off dining here, due to the quality of the food. For a place where you pay for the quality of the food and service, not the location, head for **Stella's Bistro**, at Fevzi Çakmak Caddesi 3c, near Ataürk Caddesi. The menu has select dishes from around the world but Italian cuisine dominates; $14. For those on a tighter budget, the **Villa Perla**, on Hesapçı Sokak, also offers excellent food in a pretty, enclosed garden; $6.

Near Hadrian's Gate at Kocatepe Sokak 3, the **Cumba** serves good Turkish fare including *İnegöl köfte* for about $7. Tables are set in a large and leafy garden, where oversized ducks reside in undersized ponds. For a similar price, the **Hasanağa Restaurant**, next to the İmaret Camii at Mescit Sokak 15, has a huge display of over 50 mezes as you go in. There's live Turkish music on weekends in summer. If you happen to be in the vicinity of the Broken Minaret (Kesik Minare) at lunchtime, **Enişte** on Kesik Minare Sokak is a very basic place, serving fresh and delicious *mantı* for $2 per portion.

There are pleasant tea gardens in Karaalioğlu Park where you can have a whole samovar brought to your table if you mean to stay a while. At the end of Kazım Özalp Caddesi by the clock tower, **Parlak** has been famous for its barbecued chicken and cacophonous ambience for decades; $6.

A number of kebab restaurants haunt Eski Şerbetçilar Sokak, a pedestrian street at the junction of Atatürk and Cumhuriyet. Don't miss a dinner at an unpretentious-looking kebab house nearby called the **Şanlıurfalar** (because everyone there comes from out east in Şanlıurfa), set in a garden on an unnamed side street just to the left as you enter the old town by the clock tower. Ask for the *Sultan'yar*, an incredible mixed grill that entirely fills the plastic bar tray they serve it on; roughly two square feet of kebab and *pide* for less than $6, with salad and beer. Yet another good and cheap kebab house, extremely popular with the locals, is the **Antalya İşkembe Kebap Salonu no.2**, on the little pedestrian street of restaurants and cafés just across Atatürk Caddesi from the old town (Hesapçı Sokak entrance); on this street you can also find hamburgers and other heretical snacks.

Entertainment and Nightlife

Antalya can't show you a lot of nightlife, surprisingly—perhaps because the resort area and beaches are so far from the centre, and partly because so many of the fancier hotels have chosen to be enclosed compounds, with their own clubs and discos. Visitors in town stroll around Kaleiçi and the back streets of the old town, where there are plenty of places for a quiet drink.

East from Antalya

The road east from Antalya does not follow the coast. It doesn't need to; the land is flat and there are farms, citrus groves and banana plantations on either side as far as Side. Much of this land is haunted with ruins, and it is no surprise to see an ancient column sticking up in a field or along a side road, not always easy to distinguish from the concrete aeration stacks of the irrigation system. Except for Antalya and Side, all the ancient cities of this region were built inland, their ports being nothing more than a landing stage at the highest navigable point of the closest river. Consequently, all the yellow signs marking the turn-offs to sites are on the north side of the road.

Getting Around

All the sites can be reached via the busy **coastal road**. If you don't have a car, **buses** and **minibuses** ply the Antalya–Side route with great frequency, so you'll never have long to wait. Side is the base for seeing the other **ancient sites**; its **taxi** companies make a business of such excursions, and post their rates on blackboards in town ($24 for a trip to Aspendos, for example). All the turn-offs from the main road are marked with yellow signs; at some of these, such as Aspendos, taxis wait by the roadside to take in passengers descending from the minibuses. Prepare for some rough roads if you're heading for Sillyon, but there's no other way to see it than by **car** (a jeep would be better; currently there are not even any tours organized here on a regular basis).

Side's **otogar** is 300m from the tourist office, on the coastal highway towards the old town. The town has a unique service to get tourists in and out of town from it in summer—they load them in a wagon, pulled by a tractor; watching the bewildered, sunburned masses trundle by will make your day.

Tourist Information

Side: On the coastal highway at the turn-off for the town, © 0242 753 1265.

Perge

Perge is only a mile from the highway. Claiming Mopsus and Calchas as its founders, Perge prospered throughout the Classical period and into Byzantine times. Although its ruins do not show a city of great size, its theatre could seat 15,000, as many as Side or Aspendos. Perge's most famous citizen, the mathematician Apollonius (3rd century BC), was a follower of Euclid who did important work with ellipses and conic sections, contributing much of the background of Ptolemy's epicyclic theory of the universe.

The modern road to Perge passes between the **stadium**, one of the best preserved in Turkey, and the **theatre** before it reaches the parking lot at the main gate. Although as yet unexcavated, the theatre shows promise of having been even more impressive than those of Side or Aspendos. Its stage building is still present in part, along with some of its sculpted friezes; among the recognizable tableaux are scenes of Eros and Psyche, and Dionysus and Ariadne. In the stadium, the space facing the outside under the seats was rented out for shops, just as they are now in some modern Turkish stadia. Some of the runners' names and trades can still be read on the walls. Interestingly, the stadium seated fewer spectators than the theatre.

Perge's **main gate**, at the centre of the southern walls, is its outstanding feature—the Hellenistic inner gate, that is, which the Pergeans made into a grand ceremonial entrance. The outer gate, added in the 3rd century AD, is strictly utilitarian. Between the two, a large courtyard full of monuments and statues was flanked on one side by a colonnade and on the other by the **propyla**, a formal entrance to the baths, and the fountain or **nymphaion** that looked like the façade of a theatre. Many statues found here are now in Antalya's museum.

To the two round towers of the gate still partly standing, the Pergeans of the 2nd century AD added another courtyard in the shape of a horseshoe, lined with statues of the city's founders. At that time, 'founder' did not necessarily mean one who had 'founded', but could be anyone who financed any great public improvement. And so, next to Mopsus and Calchas (the statues are gone but the inscriptions remain), there are such men as M. Plancius Varus and C. Plancius Varus, both identified here by their relationship to a woman—father and brother. This becomes less surprising when we get to know the lady. Plancia Magna, whose statue can also be seen in the Antalya museum, was a member of a talented family that had migrated from Italy to Perge and become wealthy through land-holdings. One of the men attained the office of Roman consul and Plancia, as well as being a great civic benefactress, was also chief priestess of Artemis, the major cult of the city, and, for a time, even held the highest civic office in Perge, that of demiurge. Great ladies in public life were not unknown in the ancient world, but for one so completely to dominate a town—inscriptions bearing her name are found everywhere—is exceptional.

In Perge, as at Ephesus and so many other cities, the worship of Artemis, a Hellenized abstraction of the old Anatolian goddess Cybele, was far more important than that of any of the male gods. One of the archaeological puzzles here is where the Temple of Artemis, a building mentioned by many ancient writers, is located.

Compact and rectangular, Perge was cut into quadrants by two colonnaded streets and enclosed on three sides by walls, and on the north by a low hill that served as an **acropolis**, probably the original settlement of Perge. Little remains there now. The main streets had to be very wide as the depressions in the centre of them between the columns were water channels, not for sewage, but probably just a unique civic embellishment, the inspiration for the similar canal that ran down Atatürk Caddesi in Antalya before it was filled in to accommodate more traffic.

Inside the walls most of the remains are early Byzantine, a time when Perge was still prosperous: there is the small **Byzantine basilica** next to the **agora**, adjoining the inner gateway on the eastern side, and further up the main street, on the left, the foundations of the **cathedral** remain; this may mark the spot where St Paul made his first converts. At the end, under the walls of the acropolis, was another **nymphaion**. Towards the west gate, the **palaestra** built during the reign of Claudius is one of the better-preserved structures.

Sillyon

Like Perge, **Sillyon** was first built on a low, defensible hill; you must climb a bit to see what's left there. To reach it, take the signposted road to the north, nine miles (14km) past Perge on the coastal road. It was never a very important town, managing to avoid most of the quarrels of its contentious neighbours, and appears in history only when Alexander passed through.

The remains consist of foundations and streets and steps cut out of the rock of the hill. Some of the fortifications remain, including one complete square tower and a few well-preserved Byzantine buildings. A recent landslide swept away most of the theatre and all of the odeon.

Aspendos

The next ancient town, **Aspendos**, also lies north of the coast road on the banks of the Köprü Çayı, the ancient River Eurymedon, then a much larger river than now. To get to the site, take a side road for 2½ miles (4km) from the main road, passing a beautiful arched **Ottoman bridge** over the Eurymedon.

In 468 BC the final battles in the long wars between the Persians and Greeks were fought here, resulting in such crushing defeat for the Great King that Persia finally abandoned its attempt to subdue the Greek world. In a single day, the boldness of the Athenian Admiral Cimon won two victories at once, on land and on sea. Both the Persian fleet and their army were concentrated at Aspendos for another assault on the Aegean. Cimon successfully drew the fleet from its harbour in the Eurymedon, and defeated it in a day-long battle, capturing many of the Persian ships; not content with this, he dressed some of his small force of marines in Persian uniforms and sent them up the Eurymedon, where they created a diversion so that Cimon and the rest of his men, secretly landed up the coast, were able to disperse or capture the entire bewildered Persian army.

Aspendos and Side were usually the two leading cities of Pamphylia, which is perhaps why they never got on well with each other. After the Romans finally made them agree, Aspendos thrived until well into the Byzantine era; little is known of its eventual abandonment, although the wars and disruptions caused by the 7th-century Arabs certainly had much to do with it.

The Theatre of Aspendos

Aspendos has the best-preserved **Roman theatre** anywhere in the Mediterranean. This is no exaggeration; not only is the whole cavea intact, along with the arcade at the top, but the entire stage building has survived. Credit is given to the Selcuks for some preservation work, but no one yet knows what use they made of the building.

At the present entrance, a door in the centre of the stage building, is a small plaque with a message from Atatürk; his government made restoration of this theatre its first major archaeological project, and the inscription records Atatürk's wish that the Turks should not 'lock it up like a museum piece', but use it for performances of classical drama—and wrestling. This is not so strange; throughout this part of Asia Minor, wrestling matches were commonly staged in the theatres. Currently, plays are produced during the September festival, but wrestling, as elsewhere outside Thrace, is becoming increasingly rare.

Whichever you would prefer to imagine on the cards, stepping inside the theatre magically transports you into the past, evoking the lost Graeco-Roman world in a way few ruins ever can. Not that it is a building of any great architectural distinction—no offence to Zeno, its architect (2nd century AD)—it is simply that it has survived. Even without its marble veneer or the statues that once graced the interior of the stage building, it is easy to imagine what a night at the theatre in old Aspendos might have been like.

All the theatres of the Pamphylian cities had stage buildings, as all of them were built in Roman times, after this innovation had come into vogue. Earlier Greek and Hellenistic theatres had been open, as at Epidauros in Greece, sited with a striking natural backdrop for the action in the *skene* and orchestra. Later, the plays moved up to a raised stage, or proscenium, and stage buildings were used both for manipulating the sets and props, and to shut out the outside world.

Of the sculptural scheme, all that survives is a frieze of Dionysus, but on the right-hand side it's possible to make out some plaster with a red and white zigzag design. This has been identified as Byzantine work; there are similar designs in the castle towers of Alanya. Climbing to the arcades on top for the view, or to find a short cut into the city, is disappointing as the hill on which the theatre hangs is separated from Aspendos proper by a ravine. To see the rest of the town you must go around it; both sides lead to gates from which paths lead up to the city.

Aspendos has not been fully excavated, apart from the theatre, though there are remains of a few public buildings—a stoa, bouleuterion and basilica—around the agora; all the more substantial ruins are Byzantine. The reason for making the climb is to see the **aqueduct**, one of the best-preserved examples anywhere, stretching from the hill of Aspendos across the plain to the distant mountains. Four long sections still stand. The two towers may seem puzzling, but it was no problem for Roman engineers to make water flow uphill, using the principles of gravity and capillary action; the towers served to regulate the pressure and allow air to escape.

Back at the bottom of the hill, you may wish to visit the two **baths**, to the left of the theatre along the access road, and the half-buried **stadium**, to its right.

Selge

Another Pisidian city that can be reached from the coast, **Selge**, was originally called by the very un-Greek name of Estlegiys; as it became Hellenized, it grew and prospered from the manufacture of storax gum, used as incense. Selge, like Termessos in a difficult but beautiful mountain setting, has a ruined **theatre** and **stadium**, and a well-preserved Roman **bridge** over the Eurymedon. It's out of the way, 21 miles (34km) north of the coast road to the village of Beşkonak; from there a track leads the last few miles up into the mountains, to the village of Altınkaya (locals call it Zerk). Nearby, a few miles north of Beşkonak, is the recently opened **Köprülü Kanyon National Park**, a natural wonderland of forests and waterfalls.

Side

All these cities, interesting as they are, must be taken only as a prelude to **Side**. First among the Pamphylian cities of antiquity, or so it boasted, Side now must be considered the first among Pamphylia's ruins; it was the first to be substantially excavated, and so a visit here will prove much more rewarding to the non-specialist. It also has a number of beaches offering every distraction, from windsurfing to paragliding.

In the 1890s, when Crete was freed from Ottoman rule, a community of Muslim fishermen came from the island to settle here. They built a village among Side's ruins, and resisted all attempts by archaeologists and the government to relocate them. The latter are still trying, but in the meantime the villagers have made the most of their opportunity, turning their town into one of Turkey's most improbable tourist traps. Its main street, full of ice cream parlours, bars and trinket-stands, follows the route of old Side's colonnaded street, and the ancient residential quarters are filling up with hotels and pensions. It's pleasanter than it sounds. The beaches around Side's peninsula mainly attract Turkish and German families, the restaurants are good and the atmosphere relaxed (note that the beaches near the centre can be crowded and awful, and there's no public transport out to the good ones, which are largely divvied up among hotels anyhow). There is a noisy disco, but it's out in the ancient suburbs near the Byzantine basilica.

1. Nymphaion
2. Main gate
3. Byzantine basilica
4. State agora
5. Inner gate & fountain
6. Temple of Apollo
7. Temple of Athena
8. Temple of Men

History

Cyme, the Ionian city near Smyrna, founded Side as a colony in the 7th century BC; it is thought that, despite the Greek colonists, Side remained very much the native Anatolians' city, using their own language which had been replaced everywhere else by Greek.

'*Side*' means pomegranate, and the fruit was often depicted on the city's coins, so many of which survive as to suggest great prosperity, lasting well into the 6th century AD. How they made their money is another matter. Sideans, even more than the rest of the Pamphylians, had a well-earned reputation for being scoundrels, both in business dealings and in relations with other towns. In the 2nd century BC the city had an arrangement with the Cilician pirates and acted as their fence, circulating stolen goods and the pirates' captives. Until Pompey put the pirates out of business, Side ran a slave market that, if ancient writers are to be believed, handled thousands of poor souls every day.

Despite this, the Sideans never fell foul of Rome. Most of the slaves ended up in Rome, and Sidean prosperity was not affected by the Roman takeover. By the 4th century AD, however, Side had so dwindled that it built a new wall near the theatre, reducing itself by half. After a revival in the 5th and 6th centuries, the depredations of the Arabs put an end to Side after a thousand years of urban life. Most of the inhabitants gradually resettled in Antalya.

Remains of the City

There is no difficulty in finding Side; even before the turn-off is reached, the forest of signs for restaurants and pensions springs up, growing thicker as you approach the town. The modern road enters very near the ancient **main gate**, with a small semi-circular court just inside— not for decoration, as at Perge, but for defence. The ruins just outside the gate belong to the **nymphaion** or fountain. Greek cities commonly had embellishments like this outside the gates, to water animals and/or to allow travellers to refresh themselves before entering the city. The long **aqueduct**, which passes through the wall's three towers to the right of the gate, carried the water to the nymphaion and from there into the city. Sections of the aqueduct in good repair can be seen for some distance north of the city, and its path inside the walls can be traced through the 'Quarter of the Great Gate', as the northernmost district by the baths and theatre is described in inscriptions.

Inside the gate, two **colonnaded streets** begin. That on the right, leading towards the theatre, was the main thoroughfare of Side, while the street on the left goes through the Quarter of the Great Guild, heading due south. Colonnaded streets like this were the status embellishment of Roman cities, shady arcades for business and shopping that gradually replaced the old Greek agoras as the places to see and be seen in. The two in Side, totalling over a mile in length, testify to the great wealth of the city in Roman times; no other city in Asia Minor, not even Ephesus, had as much. Most of the surviving structures in the Quarter of the Great Guild date from the Byzantine afterglow, including a huge **basilica**, on the left side of the colonnaded street, a church, and an unidentified building off to the right.

Just before reaching the inner gate, the other street passes the Roman **baths** to the right and the large **agora** to the left. This was used in the 2nd century as the slave market, and it isn't difficult to imagine the crowds of woebegone captives chained to the columns. In the centre of the agora, the circular foundation and ruins belonged, quite fittingly, to the Temple of

Fortuna. Another open square, the **state agora**, stands a few hundred feet to the east, near the old sea wall. As its name implies, it was the governmental centre of Side. Most of this part of the city is partially buried under sand dunes that have accumulated over the centuries, and has not yet been excavated.

The baths, going back across the narrow neck of the peninsula, have been incorporated into the **Side Museum** (*open daily except Mon, 8–12 and 1–5; adm*), with an excellent collection based solely on the strength of what the archaeologists found here. There are lots of Roman statues, including some fine copies of earlier Greek works; reliefs of uniforms and weapons, found near one of the city gates, probably commemorate the spoils won in a victory over Pergamon, when King Attalus tried to conquer the Pamphylian coast. Some wonderful sarcophagi show the sentimental side of the ancient world's attitude to death, portraying death's door, one with the deceased's faithful dog peering out; another, a child's, is carved with birds and butterflies.

The great arch of the **inner gate** still stands, simply because, at some later time, the citizens were compelled to wall it up, leaving a smaller entrance in the centre. It is thought that a statue of an emperor in his four-horsed chariot crowned the gate, hence the name of the neighbourhood, 'Quarter of the Quadriga'. In every Pamphylian city there is evidence of gradual impoverishment; marble façades on concrete, or sarcophagi reused and statue bases with the old inscriptions blotted out and new ones added. Here, the grand **fountain** to the left of the gate was originally a monument in honour of the Emperor Vespasian, moved here from somewhere else in the city.

Here the modern village begins, built around the ruins of the old, down the colonnaded street to the end of the peninsula. The town is closed to traffic, but you may take your car if you're staying at one of the hotels or pensions. Side's well-preserved **theatre** (*open daily 8–5; adm*), adjoining the inner gate and facing the agora, dominates the centre of the city. On this flat peninsula, with no natural hillside out of which to carve one, the Sideans had to build a theatre themselves. The cavea, the largest in Pamphylia with room for some 25,000 spectators, is supported by an impressive system of vaults and arches.

A four-foot wall was built around the bottom row of seats to seal off the orchestra when combats and wild beast shows began to shove drama off the stage. The remains of two chapels, on either side of the stage building, and some inscriptions indicating seats reserved for priests, reveal that at some time in the early Byzantine era it was used as an open-air church (note the crosses carved over some of the entrances). Most of the sculptural friezes on the stage buildings remain, but the reliefs, probably scenes from the myths of Dionysus, are so completely effaced that early Christian vandalism is suspected.

Once in the modern town, you're on your own trying to find the other homes, baths and temples of old Side. The newer buildings, in and around the ruins, exasperate the archaeologist but make a picturesque setting. Unfortunately, in the last few years so much has been built inside the inner wall that it becomes increasingly difficult to trace the ruins; many have been fenced off into gardens. Ruins of some of the more important of the city's temples have been excavated at the very tip of the peninsula overlooking the **harbour**, which is now silted up. There are no natural harbours on the Pamphylian coast and Side, the foremost port city, was forced to make one out of almost nothing and dredge it continuously. 'A harbour of Side' became a figure of speech, like the labours of Sisyphus, for any unending task. Just where the water's edge once was, the platforms of the **Temple of Apollo** and the **Temple of Athena** are visible; the surrounding ruins belonged to a huge Byzantine **basilica** built over the temples, which were presumably incorporated into it. Part of the columns and architrave of Apollo's temple have been reconstructed, carved with outlandish masks on the metopes. Behind these, in what must have been a square at the end of the colonnaded street, are more ruins, of a Byzantine **fountain** and a semicircular **temple** (3rd century AD) devoted to Men, the Anatolian moon god.

Attractions near Side

While in Side, incidentally, you should avoid all proffered excursions to the **Manavgat Falls** in the mountains above Side, unless you need more souvenirs or the prospect of a three-foot waterfall particularly excites you. Leaving the town on the way to Alanya, you pass two well-preserved **caravanserais** of the Selcuks: at **Şarapsahan**, 9½ miles (15km) west of Alanya on the coast, and **Alarahan**, on the side road 5½ miles (9km) up in the mountains. Şarapsahan is fortified, testifying to the uncertainty of the sea lanes even in the best days of the Selcuks. Near Alarahan, the **Alara Castle** is a steep climb, but gives a spectacular view over the valley.

Three miles (5km) before Alanya, the highway department has constructed one of its **road-side beaches**. This is cleverly designed; a steep embankment had to be built for the road, 100 feet above the sea, so they simply added steps and built dressing rooms into the side. The effect is one of perfect isolation.

Side   ***Where to Stay***

Side has over 25,000 beds to let but the trick is to get one that is convenient for the beach, the town and the ruins while being quiet enough to allow you a peaceful night's sleep. With this in mind, follow the main street down to the harbour and bear left at the 'mosque' sign. Walk on into a bewildering array of side streets and several good, moderately priced hotels and pensions will present themselves. Some of these are noted below.

expensive

Everything fancy will be found not in Side proper, but in the beaches to either side. Locals claim the ★★★★★**Asteria Oteli**, ✆ 0242 753 1830, ✆ 0242 753 1830, to be the best in the town and they're probably right. Two miles (3km) out of town on the western beach, it has cavernous air-conditioned rooms with satellite TV, swimming pools, including a heated one indoors, and plenty of recreational facilities. If you need something directly on the beach, though, try the ★★★★★**Turquoise**, at Sorgun Mevkii, ✆ 0242 756 9330, ✆ 0242 756 9345, a palatial complex built around a garden courtyard, surrounded by forests, with every imaginable luxury and every sport on offer—including a polo ground. Like the other luxury establishments, a double room at these goes for about $100. You can enjoy much the same amenities at the ★★★★★**Sol Selin**, ✆ 0242 763 6685, ✆ 0242 763 6214, on the beach at Çolaklı Köyü.

The beaches to either side of Side are graced with a number of gleaming complexes less pretentious than the above. The ★★★**Hane**, ℗ 0242 753 2445, 6km west of town, has a good stretch of beach and a pretty park, and comfortable air-conditioned rooms; a little distant, but it has everything you'll need. A bit expensive for a *pansiyon*, but worth it, is the **Hanımeli** on Turgut Reis Sokak, ℗ 0242 753 1789, a beautifully-kept old house in a garden; $25 including breakfast.

A fair number of *pansiyonlar* are sprinkled around the village, almost all family-run places where the owners take some pride in keeping the place up (they're a bit more expensive than other towns, though, averaging about $16); those on the eastern shore boast of a view of Side's Famous Sunrises, while the westerners tell you about the view of Side's Famous Sunsets. Next to the Hanımeli, the friendly owners of the **Şen**, ℗ 0242 753 2989, offer clean, simple rooms with bath, and a roof terrace to relax with a view over the town. On the opposite side, you can settle for the sunrises at the **Çiçek**, ℗ 0242 753 1958, which is just as good in every way. Yet another similar *pansiyon* with a view is the nearby **Yıldız**, ℗ 0242 753 1157. Near the bus station there are several *pansiyonlar* if you don't mind the tractor ride or the 15-minute walk into town.

There are campsites either side of the road into the town.

Side **Eating Out**

Side has its share of tourist seafood palaces, and places where Germans would feel at home. For a seafood dinner without breaking the bank, head for **Köşeoğlu**, and its outdoor terrace on the east side waterfront: the menu includes things not often seen in Turkish restaurants, such as shrimp and octopus, and a full dinner can be had for $12. The sea laps against the walls of the **Agora Restaurant**, Turgut Reis Caddesi, which has been serving seasonal fish dishes for almost 30 years; $12. At the tip of the peninsula, **The End** on Liman Caddesi offers whatever seafood has been netted that day—from red mullet to lobster. Their speciality, however, is the *Osmanlı kebap*— ox meat with mushroom, tomato, onion, garlic and cream sauce, covered in cheese; $10 and up.

After doing the ruins of Aspendos, you can have lunch at the **Belkis**, on the road to the site in the village of the same name; outside tables in a nice setting, and simple but good food for about $6.

Entertainment and Nightlife

Next door to The End on Liman Caddesi is the **Lighthouse Disco**, a relaxed place opening onto the sea, with a diet of Turkish and western pop, hip-hop and underground music.

Cilicia

This coastal province is ready-made for tourist brochures; the historical background is as good as even the wildest imaginings of a copywriter. Mark Antony did present Cilicia to Cleopatra as a love gift—though not just for the sensuous coastal scenery or the forests and peaks of the beautiful Taurus mountains. Cleopatra, always a sharp girl, chose in this case not to see the forest for the trees. Cilicia's timber happened to be Egypt's biggest import, and the queen simply wanted to get it wholesale. Besides, these two lovers had a navy to build.

Half of Cilicia, like Lycia, is difficult country; the ancients commonly referred to the western portion as '**rough Cilicia**' and the eastern as '**smooth Cilicia**', the latter a plain created by deltas of several rivers around the present-day metropolis of Adana. Both sections have always lacked big towns and culture; rough Cilicia because there's nothing but mountains and trees, and smooth Cilicia partly because of its location on a major medieval conqueror's highway through the Cilician Gates, and partly because of the mosquito. Malaria was a problem until recent times. Few of the armies that have passed through ever felt inclined to stop, and history has mostly avoided both the Cilicias.

Rough Cilicia, impenetrable and indeed almost unknown to the Greeks and Romans, enjoyed its best hour just a century before Antony and Cleopatra had their fling, as the most notorious pirate's nest in the entire Mediterranean. Following the example of Tryphon the Voluptuary, a Governor of Kalonoros who turned to piracy after an unsuccessful revolt against the Seleucid King Antiochus, the Cilician pirates ruled the waves for a hundred years until the Romans decided to wipe them out; in 67 BC, they sent Pompey in with more ships and money than he asked for, and within six weeks the great Roman general had killed, coerced or bought off the lot of them.

Piracy made a comeback with the Arab invasions of the 7th century and Cilicia, never really prosperous at the best of times, degenerated into a beautiful wasteland. Ottoman rule did nothing to help, and until the Turkish republic, Cilicia remained the poorest, most backward and disease-ridden corner of western Anatolia. In the last 30 years, the change has been dramatic. Modern Turkey's extensive water projects have turned the once-useless coast into a garden of citrus and banana groves, with cotton the major crop on the plains of Adana.

Alanya

In Alanya, the 'pearl of the Turkish Mediterranean', not agriculture but tourism has accomplished the work of transformation. In ancient times writers sometimes included this city in Pamphylia, sometimes in Cilicia. Its great rock of a peninsula that the Greeks called *Kalonoros* or the 'beautiful mountain' makes a natural boundary stone between the two provinces; it protrudes from the sea like a great turtle's head, the beaches to either side curving away like huge flippers and the mountains rising behind forming its carapace. Today, with some 50,000 people, Alanya is by far the most important town between Antalya and Mersin. It also has some of the best beaches along the southern coast, but Alanya is a town worth visiting in its own right; no brash upstart of a resort, it has memories going back to antiquity, and some fine monuments left by the cultured Selcuk sultans.

History

Like the rest of Cilicia, ancient *Coracesium* only got in the news when pirates were using it as a base, as in the time of Tryphon the Voluptuary. But even in the worst times, the rock of Kalonoros continued to be inhabited. An almost impregnable position, it was a good place to hold. Alâeddin Keykubad discovered this when he tried to take the citadel in 1220. There are various stories of how he finally got in; one has him marrying the commander's daughter and taking the whole family back to Konya, while another says that, in a final desperate move, he had his men tie torches to the horns of thousands of goats and drive them up the hill at night, tricking the defenders into thinking a great army was coming after them; one imagines they would have found the battle cry somewhat suspicious. The most plausible version has Alâeddin making a deal with the Armenian prince who held Kalonoros—offering him another piece of land instead, and saving them both the trouble of a siege.

Alâeddin renamed the city after himself, 'Ala'iyeh', and Atatürk, on a visit during his Westernizing campaign, changed it to the more euphonious 'Alanya'. For a while after the Selcuk decline Alanya belonged to the French Lusignan kings of Cyprus, a relic from the Crusades. With the most beautiful setting along the southern coast and miles of beaches, Alanya has become a major resort, especially popular among the Germans but seeing more people from Britain every year. The lower town around the harbour and the coastal highway past the beaches on either side (those west of the citadel are less popular and less crowded) are all full of tourist clutter in the manner of Marmaris, or a Greek island. The Alanyalılar take refuge, as they have done from so many other invaders, up in the lovely old neighbourhoods above the citadel.

Getting Around

Although Alanya has no air or rail connection, regular **buses** travel to points along the coast and inland to Konya. **Cruise ships** call often in the summer, and there is also a **ferry** service to Girne (Kyrenia) in the Turkish Republic of Northern Cyprus, only a 3½ hour trip (no cars; the car ferry goes from Taşucu further along the coast to the east). In summer it usually runs daily, Wed–Sat, off season only erratically, and it's becoming an increasingly popular trip for Alanya vacationers. (The Northern Cypriots will not stamp your passport, so don't worry about harassment if you pass through Greece later.) Around the harbour you'll see plenty of **tours** on offer, to the caves and other sights around the mountain that are inaccessible by land; the average rate is about $15 a boatload, so you might look around for companions to share one.

As in Antalya, the coastal road is also the main thoroughfare of the town (called Atatürk Caddesi following the western beach and Keykubat Caddesi along the eastern beach); the **dolmuşes** can take you to any point along the beaches. There's a city bus service from the harbour up to the citadel, with stops all along the way. Alanya's **otogar** is a mile outside town, just off Atatürk Caddesi near the western beach; there's a dolmuş service.

Alanya   **Tourist Information**

Damlataş Caddesi, across from the museum, © 0242 513 1240.

The Red Tower (Kızılkule)

In the harbour, beside the fish restaurants, camel rides, cruises to everywhere and terraced tea gardens, you'll find the **Red Tower**, Alanya's landmark since Alâeddin built it in 1226. The government completely restored this octagonal 115ft bastion in 1955, and now it houses a small **ethnographic museum** (*open daily exc Mon, 8–12, 1.30–5.30; adm*).

The top floor, crenellated for cannons, offers a fine view of the city. Note how the floor is sloped with channels towards the middle—the centre of the building is one great cistern. This purely functional defensive work nonetheless ranks among the highlights of Selcuk architecture. It was constructed to protect the **Tersane** (naval dockyards) built at the same time; the two are joined by a short stretch of wall now surrounded by gardens.

From the start, the Selcuk aim in seizing coastal towns was to become a force at sea as well as on land, but as they never had enough time to really get under sail, the birth of Turkish seapower was deferred until the Ottomans, some two centuries later. The enclosed dockyards, connected by archways, are a cool, quiet and interesting place to visit. Judging from the remains of an old beak-prowed fishing boat in one yard, it seems they have been in use until recent times. The other side of the yards is protected by another tower, **Tophane**, literally the 'ball house'—an arsenal.

On Kalonoros

Besides the dockyards, the Red Tower also guarded the approaches to the citadel. From here the modern road climbs up through the **main gate** with its Selcuk inscription (in Persian, the language of Alâeddin Keykubad's court) past old Ottoman-style houses and gardens. The grandest of these, conspicuous on the lower slopes, was restored by a former American ambassador to Turkey. Where the road passes through the second level of the fortification, traces of the original Hellenistic-era wall may be seen underlying Alâeddin's work; just to the right is a small Byzantine chapel, with the walls carefully built around it.

Further on, the road skirts the **Ehmediye,** a section of old Alanya within the walls that has survived as perhaps the most charming and serene quarter in Turkey, all overgrown with plane trees and flowers among the stone walls and venerable cottages. At its centre are a *bedesten* and **caravanserai** built by the Selcuks (now a hotel), with an unusual **tomb**, the 1230 Aksebe Türbesi, and also the fine 16th-century **Sülemaniye Mosque**. Tourism has touched the Ehmediye only slightly. Some of the more enterprising residents have set up a souvenir stand on the road offering two local specialities: lace, and gourds painted with the faces of—we can only guess—Cleopatra and Bugs Bunny. If you clamber up these ramparts in the early evening, once the tour groups have gone for the day, you can sit on the walls with the swallows wheeling around you. The first muezzin's call drifts up faintly from the city below; another starts up from the other side of town; then another. Before long the air is filled with a medley of distant voices calling the faithful to prayer.

A few hundred yards further on and the road reaches the **İç Kale** (*open daily 8–sunset; adm*), the inner fortress. Once reached, a quick look down suffices to explain why the citadel was never taken by force. Most of the buildings around the İç Kale have gone to ruin; some are certainly part of the palace or governor's residence that existed here; another building with extremely thick walls can only have been a magazine. Best preserved, surprisingly, is a **Byzantine Church** that may be as early as 6th century. Inside, there are still remnants of the original frescoes on the walls. The four Evangelists must have been the theme on the pendentives, for on one a lone, fading Evangelist, his attributes gone, can still be seen poring over his book.

Most of the citadel walls have been restored in recent years. In one corner, called the **Adam Atacağı**, a platform has been erected for the view; condemned criminals were thrown off from here, according to a highly improbable local legend. The Adam Atacağı looks out over a narrow spit of land extending southwest from the rock of Alanya called **Cilyarda Burnu**, on which stand the ruins of a tower, a Byzantine monastery and chapel, and a building the Turks call the *Darphane*, or mint. There is no way of getting there on foot, but boats in the harbour take trippers to the rock and to other spots around it: the huge **Pirate's Cave** and a **phosphorescent cave**, among others, and of course you'll be shown the little secluded beach where Cleopatra took her dip in the ocean.

One final cave, the best of all, can be reached from near the beaches to the west of the rock. **Damlataş Cave**, with its forests of stalagmites in delicate colours, was discovered only in 1948. Most visitors come just to look, but sufferers from bronchitis and other ailments find its mixture of radioactivity and high humidity to have curative properties. Not far from the cave, the **Alanya Museum** (*open daily exc Mon 8–12, 1.30–5.30; adm*) in a new building contains local archaeological finds. **Market day** in Alanya is Friday, and it takes place on Tevfikiye Caddesi, north of Atatürk.

About 22 miles (35km) to the west, Alanya has spawned a new baby resort, around the broad sandy beach at **İncekum**. The Alanya tourist office is currently trying to promote the *yaylalar* (summer pastures), the lovely hills north of the city, as a day trip destination—if only for a picnic, as the Alanyalılar themselves are fond of doing—but there's no public transport and you'll need a car to get around. One spot that can almost be reached by dolmuş is the scenic valley of the **Dimçay**; the minibus will take you to the mouth of the stream, four miles (6km) east of town, but from there it's a trek of over six miles (10km) up to the dam, where there is swimming and restaurants. Directly north of Alanya, there are a number of lovely picnic sites in the *yaylalar*, pine forests, and some charming villages: **Mahmut Seydi**, with an interesting Selcuk mosque, and **Türktaş Köyü**, with a little waterfall nearby.

Alanya and İncekum   **Where to Stay**
                                                        luxury–expensive

As elsewhere on the southern coast, plenty of new pleasuredomes have opened in the last few years, both on the town's beaches and at İncekum. Two miles (3km) west of the city, the ★★★★★**Grand Kaptan**, Oba Göl Mevkii, ✆ 0242 514 0100,

⊕ 0242 514 0092, has everything you could ask for, including a private beach, watersports, and air-conditioned rooms with a sea view and balcony. Less expensively, there's the ★★★★**Club Alantur**, Dimçay Mevkii, ⊘ 0242 518 1740, ⊕ 0242 518 1756, a complex of low-rise buildings by the beach with bars and lots of sports facilities.

moderate

Alanya is the land of the three-star package hotel; there are over a hundred. Prices are all officially about the same (about $50 in season, but as elsewhere big discounts can often be managed) but there is a great difference in the amenities provided. No matter where you stay, you'll never be far from a beach. The only exception to these rules is the **(S)Bedesten**, ⊘ 0242 512 1234, ⊕ 0242 513 734, up on Kalonoros, a remodelled *han* that has been beautifully restored. Rooms are dark and musty but, with walls several feet thick, a good night's sleep is guaranteed. There is an outdoor pool. If you want to be right on the beach, the ★★★**Panorama Hotel**, Keykubat Caddesi 30, ⊘ 0242 513 1181, a 10-minute walk east of the Atatürk statue, is worth considering. Here you can stagger out of your room in the morning and plunge straight into the sea; pool, tennis and most watersports on offer.

inexpensive

The ★★**Yunusgücü**, on Atatürk Caddesi, ⊘ 0242 513 3002, must be the archetypal Turkish resort hotel, from the little flags flying out front to the forgettable restaurant, but it's a good bargain, with air-conditioned rooms and a pool for about $35. In a more isolated setting—Konaklı, 15km west of town—the ★★★**Saphir**, ⊘ 0242 565 2525, also on the beach, offers air-conditioned rooms with satellite TV, pool and tennis. A less expensive choice nearby is the ★★**Galaxy**, ⊘ 0242 545 3801, a simple place with nice rooms and a pool. If all you want is a quiet room with a balcony close to the beach, the ★★**İkiz**, ⊘ 0242 513 3155, off Atatürk Caddesi on the west beach, will do just fine.

cheap

The nicest of Alanya's cheapies, a long trek from the beach in the centre of town, is the **Günaydın**, ⊘ 0242 513 1943, on Damlataş Caddesi; decent rooms with bath and balcony, and the specific charm of being able to look down at the street life below and forget you're in a resort altogether. Not far away, on İskele Caddesi (the street that curves around the bottom of Kalonoros), the **Baba**, ⊘ 0242 513 1032, is right in the centre of the action, fun but a little noisy. Near the west beach, on Hacı Hamidoğlu Sokak, the **Saray**, ⊘ 0242 513 2811, is simple, acceptable and cheap. There are a few inexpensive pensions around the eastern beach, one being the **Yazıcıoğlu Pansiyon**, Güller Pınarı Mahalle, ⊘ 0242 513 2902.

İncekum

There's plenty more of the same here, such as the sleek modern ★★**Aspendos**, Avsallar Mahalle, ⊘ 0242 517 1091, with a big pool, tennis courts and private beach; or the ★★★**Yalıhan**, also at Avsallar Mahalle, ⊘ 0242 517 1010, air-conditioned rooms, some with a sea-view balcony; watersports arranged. *Both moderate.*

Just walk on down to the centre of Alanya, between Atatürk/Keykubat Caddesi and the harbour, and you'll find dozens of places to choose from, nearly all of them good, inexpensive and simple, with very few blatantly *turistik* restaurants. The **Gaziantep Köy'ın**, close to the port, grills a nice *tavuk şiş* (chicken), among a wide choice of other kebabs; about $6. Deservedly successful, they've opened up a second branch around the corner. For about the same price, you can sample the liver kebabs and other Turkish soul food at the **İnegol Köftecisi**, on İzzet Azakoğlu Caddesi (the *Kordon*). There is a whole street of even cheaper kebab stands off Kalgıdım Sokak, of which the **Hunkar Lokanta** will do for a quick lunch. İskele Caddesi, along the harbour, is crammed with the usual fish restaurants, averaging $12 for a three-course meal with a drink; the **İskele** is a good one, and often has live music. Slightly more expensive, but worth it, is the **Anatolian Restaurant**, around the corner on Rıhtım Caddesi: delicious seafood, including prawns and shellfish, in a lovely setting; average $14 if you don't get carried away.

Further out Keykubat Caddesi, the bar/restaurant **Cemalı Plaj** makes a proper pizza; $6 with a beer. For a country outing take Keykubat Caddesi out nearly four miles (6km) and take the turn-off left for the valley of the Dimçay; all the way up the road into the mountains are picnic spots and nice, informal restaurants under the trees that serve fresh trout and barbecue.

Entertainment and Nightlife

Like Side, Alanya is mostly a family resort, and nightlife is limited to a few discos, the occasional karaoke bar, and clubs that entertain Germans with belly-dancing displays —as *Türkische Bauchtanzerei* it doesn't seem quite so exotic. There are a few noisy bars around the harbour, including the **Pub 13** on İskele Caddesi; others are out on Keykubat Caddesi. For intrepid disco dancers, three miles east of the centre at Dimçay Mevkii are two stomping grounds—the open-air **Auditorium** and the **Koloni**, pumping out the rhythms until the early hours.

Alanya to Silifke

Leaving Alanya for the east, the Cilician coast road follows the beaches for some distance before the steep slopes of the Taurus, plunging directly into the sea, compel it to climb into a spectacular corniche that runs all the way to Silifke, bordered by thick pine forests that in summer exude an almost overwhelming fragrance. The Turkish forestry service takes good care of these, the most extensive forests in the country, and no knowledge of Turkish is needed to understand the signs, posted every few hundred feet, warning about forest fires: *One tree can make a million matches, and one match can kill a million trees.* In summer, the pines will be full of cicadas, yammering away all afternoon and making an unearthly racket. The Turks are very fond of them; children keep them as pets, and it isn't unusual to see a grown man pick one off a tree and put it on his shoulder for company. In this region, towns are few, but the entire coast is littered with ruins: Byzantine buildings and churches near the shore and crumbling fortifications of different ages on the heights.

If you're **driving**, avoid the coastal road at night. It twists and turns fiendishly and there are no crash barriers; one mistake and you're over the cliffs. Besides, during the day you can enjoy the scenery, among Turkey's loveliest. The one route inland, through the Taurus Mountains to Konya, is equally picturesque, following the Göksu valley from Silifke. **Buses** travel along the coast every hour or so (6½ hours from Alanya to Silifke; pack some sandwiches). Anamur is a sprawling town and it is difficult to see all the sites in the area without a **car**.

From Taşucu, the **car ferry** to Girne (Kyrenia) in northern Cyprus leaves at midnight daily in season, Monday–Friday; there are also frequent hydrofoils. British subjects may need a **visa** to get in, due to some political silliness, though local officials hope the problem will be ironed out soon—ask in advance. If your passport is stamped in Girne, you'll need to get a new one should you ever want to go to Greece. Ask for a stamp on a separate sheet of paper instead. Officials will comply.

Tourist Information

Anamur: second floor of the bus station, ✆ 0324 814 3529.

Silifke: Atatürk Caddesi, Veli Gürten Gözbey Caddesi, ✆ 0324 714 1151.

Castles along the Shore, and Anamur

All along this wonderful drive, there are ruins to distract you, either a few kilometres up in the hills or directly on the shore. Few of the sites really have much to show, as **Laertes**, seven miles (11km) east of Alanya, or **Seydra**, another 3½ miles (6km) after that. The next site, **Iotape**, is a little better; built on a small promontory, it has substantial ruins of a bathhouse, and a good beach below the cliffs. The best part of the drive begins at **Gazipaşa**, a fishermen's town with a beach near the ruins of an ancient town named Selinus. Twelve miles (20km) further, at the boundary between Antalya and İçel (Mersin) provinces, another undeveloped beach runs along the edge of a narrow enclosed plain full of banana fields. The village of **Kaladiran** nearby stands in the shadow of a ruined Hellenistic castle.

The first town of any size is **Anamur**, on a plateau of greenhouses. The town itself has little that is noteworthy, apart from two Turkish flags roughly the size of tennis courts fluttering high above the main road through town. There is a beach, devoid of watersports, three miles (5km) south at its suburb of **İskele**. Nearby, at the cape now called Anamur Burnu, the southernmost point of Cilicia, are the ruins of **Anemourion**, a town founded in the late Hellenistic era. Its ruins seem shabby compared with the towns of Pamphylia—no marble, only the dark conglomerate archaeologists call 'pudding stone'—but they are substantial: a church and the arcades of an aqueduct on the hillside, with a castle on top. Near the beach, there are towers and ruined tombs. Some of the mosaics unearthed at Anemourion can be seen in the small **museum** in İskele. A mile or so to the east, the 12th-century **Castle of Anamur** was built on the shore by the kings of Little Armenia, in a peaceful setting between two long beaches. The castle is almost completely intact, though not through any virtue in its construction; the Ottomans kept it in good repair after the British occupied Cyprus, and used it as a fortress in the First World War. The small mosque inside is still in use.

The coast road continues east, climbing ever higher up and down the edge of the Taurus. On the very clearest days, they say that the mountains of Cyprus, some 30 miles (50km) to the south, can be seen. **Softa Kalesi**, on a peak just after the holiday village of **Bozyazı**, was also built by the Armenians. 'Softa', in Turkish, means a student of theology, and the castle probably got its name from the chapel, still visible from the road below. On this stretch, there are several isolated beaches, but near Ovacık the road cuts inland for a while, up the forested Akdere (White Valley) and back.

When it returns to the sea, the road reaches its crescendo of scenery just before the plain of Silifke, at **Bogsak**, a pretty bay with beaches and the ruins of a medieval fort; this, and the crumbling chapel on the bay's islet, was built by the Knights of St John. While this order still occupied Rhodes and Bodrum, its fleet often gave it control of all the southern Turkish coast. **Taşucu**, an old village with a good harbour, has developed recently into a small and unpretentious beach resort; from here you can take a trip on the ferry to Girne in northern Cyprus.

Silifke

Like Alexander the Great, who left 'Alexandrias' all over three continents lest we forget, his generals and their successors who founded the Seleucid Kingdom of Persia and Syria bedevilled mapmakers with 'Seleucias' all over the Middle East. Most have fallen to ruins long ago. One survived, and almost kept its name. Ancient Seleucia ad Calycadnos, once a great, thriving city, has been whittled down by the years to plain **Silifke** on the Göksü, a piquant and humble Turkish town. There are no signs of Seleucia apart from a single standing Corinthian column with a stork on top, and traces of a theatre south of the Göksü, but the **Byzantine Castle** still peers down from the nearest crag, and on a slight rise near modern Silifke, in the east of the Göksü plain near the coastal highway, stand the ruins of a Byzantine religious complex the Turks call **Meryemlik**, with the once-great **church of Saint Thecla**. This saint, according to the hagiographers, was the first girl to throw over her fiancé for a life of chastity, and soon became the first female Christian martyr. Foundations of a colonnaded building that was once part of the monastery remain as well as the still-standing apse of the large basilica. Beneath it, recent excavations have uncovered a cavern, later carved into a chapel, where the early Christians hid. There are bits of mosaics and frescoes in the chapel, and the municipality has made it a small **museum** for architectural sculpture from Silifke.

The Göksü, though a poor excuse for a river until the spring floods, once changed the course of European history. The Germans like to think of their old Barbarossa, Kaiser Frederick I of the Holy Roman Empire, as asleep under his mountain, like King Arthur. By 1190 Barbarossa had made the empire a going concern, the most powerful state in Europe; he was on his way to the Holy Land to teach the Saracens a lesson when he met his match in the Göksü. According to the chroniclers, he unaccountably fell off his horse in the stream and drowned before anyone could reach him, in six inches of water. The crusade was aborted, and German unification postponed 700 years. Upstream from Silifke, a small plaque marks the spot in the lovely **Göksü gorge** along the road to Konya.

Across rough Cilicia, there have been few opportunities to strike inland to look at the Taurus Mountains; most of the roads are unpaved and the region remains as isolated and wild as in ancient times. The Byzantines called this land Isauria, and while its barbarous natives helped wreck the urban life of the coasts in the 5th and 6th centuries, in the process they them-selves were becoming Christianized. By the 8th century they were producing Byzantine emperors, like Leo III, the famous Iconoclast.

Anamur to Silifke **Where to Stay**

This area is not well travelled, and accommodation options are limited. This rudi-mentary state of affairs is evident long before you reach the towns: hotel adverts are daubed in white paint on roadside rock-faces.

Melleç

Above a small deserted beach on the coastal road between Gazipaşa and Anamur, the **Melleç** restaurant (*see* below) also rents out basic wooden bungalows for $8 per night, and should appeal to anyone who really wants to get away from it all.

Anamur

inexpensive–cheap

At the easternmost edge of the beach at İskele near Anamur is the **★★Anemonia**, © 0324 814 4000, @ 0324 814 1443. Clean, quiet, so-so rooms with balconies cost $23. In season, turtles lay their eggs on the beach in front of the Anemonia: hence the lack of umbrellas, sun-loungers and streetlamps at night. The hotel's private beach is effectively a cul-de-sac, bounded to the east by the 'Dragon River', so called by locals because in the days before bridges many unfortunates attempting a crossing were swallowed up and swept out to sea by it. The **Pansiyon Ünal**, © 0324 814 2091, is cheap and cheerful, if you don't mind using the bathroom down the hall.

The average price for a pension in İskele is $14, as at the **Eser**, © 0324 814 2322, a pleasant, family-run place right by the beach. At the quiet western edge of İskele is the **Ünlüselek Hotel**, © 0324 814 1973, @ 0324 814 3973. Each time the family has saved enough money, they add another floor to the hotel—they've just built a third. En suite doubles with air-con are airy but basic; excellent value at $16.

camping

There are two good camp sites in the vicinity of Anamur, the **Yalı Mocamp** in İskele, © 0324 814 1435, on the beach, with several basic rooms to let to non-campers, and the **Pullu**, © 0324 827 1151, four miles (6km) out of Anamur in the forests, but still near a beach. Both sites have restaurants and mosquitoes.

Bozyazı

The *expensive* **★★★★Vivianco** is on its own beach at Bozyazı, 13km east of Anamur, © 0324 851 4200, @ 0324 851 2291. Nice though austere air-conditioned rooms with satellite TV and balconies; hamam and gym; watersports are available.

Taşucu

In Taşucu, the **★★★★★Best Resort Hotel**, © 0324 741 6300, @ 0324 741 3005, is by far the most luxurious accommodation in the area, with large, comfortable rooms overlooking the harbour. It's right on the shore; there isn't a beach, but the huge pool more than makes up for this. With a little persuasion, the ludicrously-priced rooms should drop to under $90.

The *moderate* **Lades Motel**, Atatürk Caddesi 89, ✆ 0324 741 4008, 🖷 0324 741 4258, offers value for money. It has a swimming pool and rooms with fine sea views.

Silifke

Silifke has but one decent hotel, the **Hotel Çadır**, by the riverside on Atatürk Caddesi 8, ✆ 0324 714 2449. Although it seems stuck in a 1960s BOAC-like time-warp, the en suite rooms are very large and the service excellent; $22. The Çadır also wins the prize for having the most bizarre hotel reception desk in Turkey. Suspended from the ceiling is a huge stuffed dogfish, which dates back to the 1960s and has been disintegrating ever since: a fitting mascot for the hotel.

Silifke has very little in the way of *pansiyonlar* and much of what's there is grim. The **Akdeniz** on Menderes Caddesi will attract anyone nostalgic for the Turkey of two decades ago: grey-painted rooms with a toilet down the hall for $6 per double.

Melleç

Wherever the road meets the coast on the way to Silifke, there is sure to be a fish restaurant, often nothing more than a few tables under the trees. Most are pretty good; you just peer in the cooler and select your fish. Two that have grown up into proper restaurants are the **Melleç** and the **Tenzile**, both about 80km east of Gazipaşa. Both are good and quite a bit cheaper than seafood restaurants in the resorts, with fish dishes for $3. The Tenzile is up in the hills, without the sea view.

Anamur

İskele has several good fish restaurants, where the prices are dependent on how good the catch was that morning. The restaurant on the main T-junction at the **Cap Anamur Pansiyon** is one of the best; the nearby **Oba** is cheaper and more popular with locals. The restaurant at the **Yalı Mocamp** serves tasty if overpriced grub to the thunderous sounds of Deep Purple. Anamur has an **Ocakbaşı Restaurant** on the main highway next to the bus station, serving mezes and good kebabs for $5 per meal. Anamur's delicious tea, *ada çayı*, is famous. Made from sage flowers picked on the mountains, it possesses, so they say, innumerable healing properties.

Taşucu

The **Denizkızı**, near the harbour, is more than acceptable. The restaurant at the **Çadır Hotel** is the best place to dine in Silifke; $6. Otherwise, the **Baba Oğul** restaurant across from the otogar on Atatürk Caddesi is much better than the dinginess downstairs would suggest. Head upstairs and you emerge into the height of provincial sophistication—a pleasant pine-clad room with ceiling fans. As well as meaty fare, there's a good selection of salads. If you get the waiters to tell you the prices beforehand, you can eat very well for $5.

In ancient times, the furthest Greek civilization ever penetrated into the Taurus was the mountain city of Olbia, founded in the 3rd century BC, known as Diocaesarea to the Romans and **Uzuncaburç** to the Turks. This is your chance for an excursion into the mountains. Not only are the ruins worth the 20-mile (30km) drive, but the road itself passes through a charming landscape of rolling, well-tended farmland, reminiscent of some corner of Italy. On the way are three **Roman tombs**, small temples in form, and almost entirely intact; two, at **Çifte Anıt**, are visible from the road, and one of these is an unusual two-level temple with an arched vestibule and Corinthian columns.

'Uzuncaburç' means 'tall tower', referring to the two 70ft Hellenistic towers, one in the city and another on a nearby hilltop. It's believed there were others, forming a communications system with the coast; messages were sent by flashing the sun off polished shields in a kind of Morse code. The city itself is a much more pleasant site than any on the coast in Pamphylia, a bucolic ruin shaded with walnut and fruit trees, among vineyards and goats.

Enter the city through the **monumental gate**, with corbels and niches for long-vanished statues, leading to the usual **colonnaded street**. Just outside the gate is the theatre, unexcavated and overgrown. The pride of the ancient city, the **Temple of Zeus Olbios** is the oldest structure yet discovered using the Corinthian order (3rd century BC). The capitals are mainly on the ground, though several columns have been re-erected; the proto-Corinthian design shows traces of the Ionic scrolls from which it evolved. An apse still stands at the east end, reminding us that the temple was later pressed into service as a church. The sculptural friezes have been gathered in the garden. Their cartoon lions, boars, bulls and leopards show a distinct decline from the best work of the Greeks, but have their own charm, reminiscent of the carvings in many medieval cathedrals. From here, a crossroads of colonnaded streets will take you either to a rare, surviving arched **city gate**, or to the **Temple of Fortuna** (1st century BC), which, as fortune would have it, has now become a social club for goats. Outside the city, you may also visit the large **necropolis** of tombs, some separate, some cut into the rock, and simple sarcophagi—many with the bones visibly still inside.

The Caves of Heaven and Hell

Back along the coast, a few miles east of Silifke, feverish development is under way at the beaches around **Susanoğlu**, **Narlıkuyu** and **Atakent**. Narlıkuyu boasts one curiosity: Turkey's smallest national museum, consisting only of one small room with a fountain and a famous relief of the **Three Graces**, Aglaia, Thalia and Euphrosyne, looking much as they do in Botticelli's painting. In the 4th century there was a Roman spa around the spring here.

The Corycian caves, **Cennet** and **Cehennem**, can be most easily and truthfully explained as two great holes in the ground. They're interesting enough for the Turks, who coined these names 'heaven' and 'hell' for them, and they so fascinated the ancients that an important sanctuary of unfathomable antiquity was maintained in Cennet; it may have hosted mysteries such as those in Eleusis, or perhaps an oracle—Delphi also had a 'Corycian Cave'. Cennet, an enormous chasm difficult of entry, can be explored with the aid of a guide; at the bottom, the remains of the old sanctuary have been incorporated into a 5th-century church. The little church was never an important site for the Christians; apparently they hoped to keep the old pagan demons deep inside by building it there, like a stopper in a bottle. The chasm, turning into a cave, continues on with an underground stream, no one knows how far; many believe the stream flows to the spring of the Three Graces.

Cehennem cannot be entered at all, except by its multitude of birds; their chirping echoes weirdly through the chasm. Like its counterpart, it is enormous and bottomless. A team of alpinists went down recently, and found only the bones of the few unfortunates who had fallen in. To the Greeks, this was the lair of Typhon, the monster of monsters spawned by Mother Earth in revenge for Zeus' defeat of the Titans. Typhon actually defeated Zeus and dragged him here, from where he escaped only through the cunning of Hermes. Before succumbing to thunderbolts, however, Typhon managed to start a fine family; according to Hesiod, his offspring included the Hydra, the Chimaera and Cerberus; his grandchildren, the Sphinx and the Nemean Lion.

Kızkalesi

Getting Around

Kızkalesi is connected by frequent **bus** and **dolmuş** services to both Silifke and Mersin. The nearest **airport** is at Adana. Mersin has a **car ferry** service to Gazimağusa (Famagusta) in Northern Cyprus three times a week (Mon, Wed and Fri), though the Tasuçu–Girne **ferry** is cheaper and faster.

The growth of Kızkalesi has been secretive and stealthy; what was only a few years ago a tiny fishing hamlet is now the largest resort east of Alanya. Yet this is a resort with a difference. Foreigners are in the strict minority here and most visitors are families from the big cities of Anatolia, making Kızkalesi the most 'Turkish' of all the Turkish resorts. Those overseas visitors that do come have their chance to holiday in Turkish style, although it's worth remembering that certain Western holiday conventions—topless sunbathing for example, and excessive boozing—are simply not acceptable here. Kızkalesi has a nice beach, but there is more to the town than just sea and sand; it has two perfect Armenian castles and, within walking distance, some intriguing, barely touched historical sites.

History: Little Armenia

In ancient days Kızkalesi was **Korykos**, never a large town, although it's remembered as the place where Cicero spent two years of his exile from Rome. In the 11th century, however, Korykos achieved prominence along with its sister settlement **Elaiussa-Sebeste** (modern Ayas) when the Rubenid kings of Little Armenia made it their capital.

This odd state, formed by an opportunist group of refugee nobles after the Armenian homeland was overrun by the Selcuks, managed to survive for three centuries by a system of alliances, first with the Crusader states, and later, with the İlhanli Mongols, a remnant of the empire of Genghis Khan to which many states, both Christian and Muslim, paid tribute. Life as a Christian principality surrounded by Muslims became increasingly precarious in the 14th century, though ironically it was Peter I, the French-born King of Cyprus, who contributed the most to the end of Little Armenia. The last king of an independent Armenian state, King Leon VI, went into exile in Paris, where he is buried at St Denis.

Korykos

The Armenians concentrated their military forces at the **Castles of Korykos**. These two large fortifications, which also served as their port, were begun by the Byzantine Admiral Eustachius; the Armenians enlarged and improved them, using lots of stone from nearby ancient cities, including an entire Roman gate rebuilt into the new wall. The smaller castle, called locally the Kızkalesi or **Maiden's Castle**, stands romantically offshore on a small island; in the Middle Ages the Armenians joined it to the mainland with a causeway that enclosed their harbour, but today you either have to swim or hire a boat if you want to see it.

The Castle of the Sparrowhawk

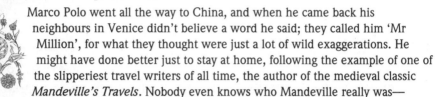

Marco Polo went all the way to China, and when he came back his neighbours in Venice didn't believe a word he said; they called him 'Mr Million', for what they thought were just a lot of wild exaggerations. He might have done better just to stay at home, following the example of one of the slipperiest travel writers of all time, the author of the medieval classic *Mandeville's Travels*. Nobody even knows who Mandeville really was— maybe an Englishman from St Albans or a Frenchman from Liège—and from all evidence he never set foot outside Europe, but merely drew on the works of real travellers and classical authors. But his book, written around 1375, was popular all over Europe and translated into many languages. When the first printing presses started up a half-century later it became one of the first best-sellers. From it, many Europeans first learned about India and the Great Khan of Cathay, and that the world was round.

As a storyteller, Mandeville is hard to beat. One of the most elegant fairy-tales in his *Travels* comes from one of these castles, concerning the demise of the Kingdom of Little Armenia. In that country, he relates, there is 'an old castle that standeth upon a rock, the which is cleped the Castle of the Sparrowhawk'. He locates it near the city of Ayas, and undoubtedly means one of the Corycian castles. In the castle was a sparrowhawk on a perch, and 'a fair lady of faerie that keepith it'. To anyone who stayed there seven days alone without sleep, the lady would appear and grant a wish. A King of Armenia stood the trial, and when the lady appeared he announced he'd had enough of power and wealth, and demanded the lady herself. For such impudence she cursed him and his nation to unending strife and impoverishment, and Little Armenia withered ever after. Another knight, a Templar, stood watch with the sparrowhawk, and asked for a purse of gold that should never empty. The lady granted it, but told the knight it would mean the end of his Order, 'for the trust and the affiance of that purse, and the great pride that they should have. And so it was.' Other men fared better in the Castle of the Sparrowhawk, though Mandeville warns that any who fail and fall asleep will be forever lost.

Is the lady of this story the 'maiden' of Kızkalesi? Perhaps—though the Turks tell visitors a different, Sleeping Beauty-type story about a princess who, it was prophesied at her birth, would die of a snakebite. Her father locked her up here, but the snake came out of a basket of fruit and got her anyhow.

The **ruins of Korykos** begin from across the main road behind the land castle and continue for several miles along the coast, merging with the remains of Elaiussa-Sebeste before coming to an end in Ayas, where the apses of two large **basilicas** are clearly visible from the road. In some areas farmers have cultivated the land around the old stones; in other parts the landscape is wild and undeveloped and there is a ghostly pleasure in exploring the ruins, identifying a house here, a cemetery there, pretending to be Heinrich Schliemann. Part of the site is given over to a huge **necropolis** dating from the 4th century AD, where there are rock tombs and ornate sarcophagi, some still with their lids, decorated with crosses, garlands and animals. In one area, some four miles (6km) north of the castles, a series of Roman-era **reliefs** is carved into the cliff—men, women, children and animals; probably this too is a funeral monument. You may chance upon these, and the necropolis, within 20 minutes of wandering, or you may search fruitlessly all day—it's that hard to find. If you're lucky, you'll meet a local who knows exactly where it is.

From Ayas, the road passes more ruins, here of the ancient towns of **Kanlıdivane** and **Soli**, as the coastal plain opens outwards into the flatlands of Smooth Cilicia. Kanlıdivane (*open daily 8am–sunset; adm*), which means 'court of blood', is a fascinating place, built around a natural chasm that was used as a necropolis; stairs lead down, and there are fragments of tombs and reliefs at the bottom. Nearby is a well-preserved Hellenistic tower and an expanse of Byzantine-era ruins. Soli, originally a Greek colony, was probably happy to be re-founded by the Romans and renamed Pompeiopolis, in honour of the conqueror of the pirates. Soli had long been the butt of jokes for the clumsy way the inhabitants had of speaking Greek; the town gives us the word *soloikos*, or solecism. The Turks call the site Viranşehir, or 'ruined city'—a common enough place name in this country. There is a good beach where people from Mersin come on weekends, and plenty of ruins; as at Side, you can trace the course of a once-impressive colonnaded street down to the harbour.

Kızkalesi

Where to Stay

expensive

The only top-class resort in the area is the ★★★★**Altınorfoz Banana** at Atakent beach 17km from Silifke, © 0324 722 4211, ✆ 0324 722 4215. Don't worry about the name; Banana is another chain, represented in other establishments such as the Banana Queen in Alanya. In a peaceful setting on the beach, this one has air-conditioned rooms, a hamam and all watersports facilities.

moderate–inexpensive

Kızkalesi must have the highest density of hotels in all of Turkey. There is, however, nothing at the top end of the accommodation market. The town is very centralized, to the point that no one seems to bother with addresses.

The ★★★**Kilikya**, © 0324 523 2116, boasts air-conditioned rooms with a view of the Maiden's Castle, a friendly and helpful staff, and a broad stretch of beach. If it's full, try either the **Hotel Hantur**, © 0324 523 2367, or the **Best Motel**, © 0324 523 2074, both good, both with en suite doubles for $22. It may sway your decision to know that the Hantur has what may well be the world's only stained-glass window of a snorkelling parrot.

The **Nobel Motel**, ✆ 0324 523 2075, is attractively priced, with bed and breakfast for two costing $14. In Kızkalesi, *pansiyonlar* are everywhere, ranging from the acceptable to the utterly vile. Be sure to see the room before agreeing to stay and remember that a better deal and better rooms can often be obtained in some of the motels listed above. The **Lüx Paşa Pansiyon**, ✆ 0324 523 2080, is plain but quiet and clean; doubles $12.

Kızkalesi   ***Eating Out***

Kızkalesi is swamped with restaurants, of which the best is the restaurant of the hotel **Kilikya**. The house speciality is *tava*, a mix of meat, aubergines, spices, tomatoes and so on. A plate of *tava*, a salad and a drink costs $6. You can eat for less at the **Güven Café** behind the Kilikya without the sea view.

Entertainment and Nightlife

On the beach is the **Disco OxyD**, a kind of futuristic Flintstones hybrid which can be fun when it gets busy. On the main road through town is **Disco Paradise**, a more conventional thunder chamber in which to lose yourself until the small hours.

The Plains: Mersin to Karatepe

In the last 50 years, much to the surprise of its inhabitants, this region has made the remarkable transformation from being one of Turkey's very poorest areas to one of its richest. With the natural fertility of the soil, some intelligent planning and a double dose of DDT, the people of **Çukurova**, as the Turks call this plain, began with cotton fields and turned them into an enormous textile industry. Adana and its port Mersin, the two largest cities of the Çukurova, have grown from almost nothing to sophisticated, up-to-date cities full of palm-lined boulevards and modern office blocks.

Getting Around

Coming from inland, take the E5 **highway** from Cappadocia across the formidable Taurus mountains. Adana and Mersin can be reached by **bus** from any major city in Turkey. Tarsus is connected by regular services to both cities.

Turkish Maritime Lines' summer **cruises** stop at Mersin, and sometimes at İskenderun. There are daily **flights** to Adana from İstanbul and Ankara, and the city is also connected by **rail** with those cities. The railway station is half a mile north of the city centre on Ziya Paşa Bulvarı. Adana's and Mersin's bus stations are both some way out of town and you'll need to take a taxi in. Within the cities there should be no need for transport; all are small and centralized.

In Adana, you can buy intercity bus tickets in offices on the Turhan Cemal Beriker Bulvarı near the tourist office, which then entitles you to a free ride to the otogar on the outskirts of town.

Mersin: İnönü Bulvarı, near the harbour, ✆ 0324 238 3271.

Adana: Atatürk Caddesi 13, ✆ 0322 363 1448.

At the airport, ✆ 0322 436 9214.

Mersin (İcel)

Nothing in Mersin is very old or of particular interest, but the city is well built and attractive, with a lovely park running almost the entire length of its shore. Mersin has grown from nothing into a city of 400,000 over the last three decades, as the port for the busy textile industries of Adana and Tarsus. Ironically, it is one of the oldest towns in the world; remains of a 6,000-year-old culture, related to that of Çatal Höyük, have been dug from a mound called Yumuk Tepe, but from then to now, there have only been small settlements. Excavations at these have unearthed a few finds, from the Hittite to Byzantine eras, that can be seen in the town **museum**. The most astounding sight in Mersin, though, is a new 650ft luxury hotel; inexplicably thrown up in the centre of town, it stands like a visitation from outer space. Who goes there, and what do they do?

Tarsus

Tarsus lies 17 miles (27km) inland to the east of Mersin. St Paul would be surprised to see his native town, an almost-abandoned ruin two centuries ago, grown into a manufacturing city of 160,000. All that survives of the ancient city is a stretch of wall and a simple, unembellished gate along the Mersin road. Antony met Cleopatra in Tarsus, so naturally the only ruin left has become **Cleopatra's Gate**. Archaeologists are up in arms about the gates' recent 'restoration', with so much new masonry added that the old structure is hardly discernible. If you stay long, they'll show you the well from 'St Paul's house', too, although as it's just a hole in the ground it's hardly worth the effort. While levelling a site in central Tarsus recently to make way for a multi-storey car park, bulldozers hit upon an old Roman road several metres below the surface. It is very well preserved, covered in huge basalt slabs still negotiable by chariot. Spaced at even intervals along the centre of the road are square drains, opening onto a deep channel below. Archaeological excavations are ongoing, but a complex of Roman shops and houses from the first century BC has already been uncovered.

There's more to see in Ottoman Tarsus, with the **Kırkkaşık Çarşısı**, the 'Market of the Forty Spoons', a dark, tunnel-like structure filled not with spoons but with tailors furiously operating foot-powered Singer sewing machines. Nearby, in a 15th-century medrese, is the town **museum** whose half-dozen rooms contain a haphazard collection of relics, including a mummified arm, lying for no apparent reason across an Urartian gold diadem. More ruins can be seen at the old port of **Gözlükule**, dating from the Hittites up to Roman times.

None of the above, of course, is exactly sufficient to turn Tarsus into a prime Anatolian tourist mecca, yet nevertheless the town is worth an hour or so—but not at night; the accommodation situation is dire. Tarsus offers the first glimpse of the Turkey you'll see further east: more women shrouded in *chador*, more baggy trousers and cloth caps, fewer cars, more donkeys, lower standards of hygiene, more beggars and a positive dearth of English speakers.

Adana

Like Mersin, **Adana** has been here for a long time but only blossomed recently. As the centre of the textile industry, the town has become Turkey's fourth largest. Unfortunately, with so much expansion and prosperity, the old town is looking increasingly shabby and neglected; even in the new districts in the north, apart from a few truly sumptuous boulevards, the city has had trouble managing its good fortune. Old Adana grew up around the **Taşköprü**, the long Roman bridge across the Ceyhan. Built under Hadrian and restored under Justinian and many other rulers since, the bridge has acquired an oddly lopsided appearance; all its arches are different sizes.

In the bazaar area, just around the corner from the 19th-century **clock tower**, is the **Ulu Cami**, a very unusual 16th-century work with towers and recesses in stalactite patterns and a unique squat minaret that resembles a lighthouse. Rising on the banks of the Seyhan next to the busy Girne bridge is the **Merkez Cami**, a grandiose affirmation in marble and glass of Adana's piety. Armed with six minarets and a dome as large as any in Turkey, it's also a wake-up call for distant Ankara to sit up and take note of this traditionally impoverished region's economic resurgence. Not that financing the project has been without problems: work began in 1988 using local money, but when funds ran out in 1997 the building was only half-finished. Enter Adana's most famous son, H. Ömer Sabancı, the Turkish Richard Branson, whose distinctive SA logo appears across the country on everything from bottles of mineral water to tyre-fitting centres. He agreed to bail out the project in return for the mosque being renamed Sabancı Merkez Camii. Thanks to this act of shrewd devotional sponsorship, work on the mosque is now almost complete. Although designed along traditional lines, the building looks heavier and squatter on the outside than İstanbul's imperial mosques. Once you cross the vast courtyard and go inside, however, the whole structure suddenly loses its ungainliness: three tiers of intricately painted domes hover high overhead; walls of hand-made İznik tiles are bathed in the light that floods through an impressive acreage of coloured glass windows. A plush fitted carpet, woven a thousand times over with a prayer rug motif, stretches across a floor with kneeling space for over 13,000 worshippers. There's room for another 15,000 more in the courtyard outside. Sabancı has invested well: by stepping in at the crucial hour, he has ensured his name will live on long after he has gone. Just to be on the safe side, however, work is underway on the luxurious Sabancı hotel just opposite. Then there's always the Sabancı Cultural Centre just up the road...

Near the bus station, Adana's **archaeological museum** has mainly Roman statues and a few Hittite reliefs. The **ethnography museum** on İnönü Caddesi is livelier, with its collection of Ottoman memorabilia. Just outside the north edge of the city, **Seyhan Dam** backs up a lake that has become a popular recreation area for local people.

East of Adana

With all the armies that have marched through this historical crossroads, down from Anatolia by way of the Cilician Gates, or along the coast, it's not surprising that so much has been built on this plain, or that so little has endured. Castles sprang up here like ice-cream stands around a carnival, over 40 of them in Adana province alone, as well as remains of civilizations from the Hittites to modern times.

There is another Roman bridge at **Misis**, just east of Adana. This town's ancient name, Mopsuestia, recalls the Homeric seer Mopsus, who was associated with so many other Cilician towns. (Mopsus' name has recently turned up in a Hittite inscription, making him the only Homeric figure so far to be a proven historical personage.) In Islamic folklore, this was the home of the great Doctor Luqman, a prototype of the physician-sorcerer of long ago. Just before the town of Ceyhan, the road from Adana passes under one of the mightiest of the medieval castles, **Yılanlıkale**. The Armenians probably built it, and the emblem between two rampant lions over the gate is thought to be the arms of the Rubenid house. During the Crusades, the Knights of St John occupied and extended Yılanlıkale. Its popular name, 'Castle of the Snake', may refer to the long silhouette of the walls as much as anything in its admittedly sinister aspect; the castle consists of three successive courts, each one higher and stronger than the last.

North of Ceyhan, the assiduous Armenians built two other formidable castles. **Tumlu**, from the 12th century, fell in 1375 to the Mamelukes of Egypt, traditional enemies of the Armenians as they would later be of the Turks. **Şiş**, overlooking the village of Kozan, was the last stronghold of the Armenians, and when a spy betrayed it to the Mamelukes in that same year the story of Little Armenia came to its unhappy end.

Few spots in Turkey are planted as thickly with relics of the past as the environs of **Kadirli**, a little town on the Ceyhan River. The ruins of no fewer than eight castles can be seen in the vicinity, as well as neolithic village mounds, Hittite rock reliefs, an aqueduct that served the Roman town of Flaviopolis, and at least two ruined cities. Few of these are impressive and few of the roads paved; the best bet for a detour from Ceyhan into the area would be to avoid Kadirli and head north to **Karatepe**, a Hittite city second only to Boğazkale in its wealth of reliefs and artefacts. On the way, you'll pass the ruins of **Kastabala**, once known as Hierapolis, a small Roman town where there are still some temple columns and buildings, under a rambling Ottoman castle on a low crag.

Karatepe

From Kastabala the countryside is lovely, with well-tended farms and fragrant pine forests reaching their peak at **Lake Aslantaş**, as fair as any spot along the Turkish coasts. King Asitiwanda, who built **Karatepe** as his summer palace, could not have enjoyed the view as much; the lake is brand new, formed by the Aslantaş Dam downstream. Here, on the 30 or so reliefs arranged under two pavilions in the open-air museum, you should expect none of the weighty religious or statist themes of the art of Yazılıkaya or Boğazkale. Perhaps by reflex, the Hittite artists added a few of their favourite fearsome lions and marble-eyed sphinxes, but most of the panels show domestic scenes—musicians with pan pipes and tambours, a mother giving suck, a merchant ship, even the king himself dining while a monkey under the table waits for hand-outs. Some reliefs are of gods, but they belong to an entirely different pantheon from those at Boğazkale; characters such as the chubby Phoenician god Bes, a bird-headed 'sun god', a centaur and an unusual 'good shepherd' figure (like the early Christian representations of Jesus) show the influence of other cultures on the tolerant and syncretic Hittites. Excavations are still under way at Karatepe, and archaeologists have yet to get the actual palace and fortress in shape for visitors.

One last castle you'll meet, whether your route takes you to the Hatay or to southeastern Anatolia, is **Toprakkale**. Its grim bulk guards the crossroads now, as it did in the Middle Ages when Crusaders and Saracens, Armenians and Mamelukes fought for its ownership. As often as it was besieged and taken, it was repaired; the key to the plain of Cilicia, Toprakkale remained in good condition for centuries.

Mersin to Tarsus   **Where to Stay**

Mersin

luxury–expensive

If by chance you should want to find out who stays in the monster mentioned earlier, it's the ★★★★★**Merit Mersin**, Kuvay Milliye Caddesi, ✆ 0324 336 1010, ✉ 0324 336 0722. As in other Turkish cities, this luxury hotel has become the social centre of Mersin, with its restaurants, disco, health club and so on. The ★★★★**Mersin**, Gümrük Meydanı, ✆ 0324 238 1040, ✉ 0324 231 2625, is centrally located, with sea views and satellite TV.

moderate–cheap

The ★★**Gökhan**, Soğuksu Caddesi, ✆ 0324 231 6256, is a solid, unspectacular city-centre hotel; it is air-conditioned, though, which can be the most important thing here in summer.

Mersin has Mersinli Ahmet Caddesi, a whole street full of good, reasonably priced hotels next to the bus station, useful if you're just passing through or need to make an early start in the morning. Try the fine **Akdeniz**, ✆ 0324 238 0187, where rooms are large and bright at $28. For an extra $3 guests have use of the hamam. Just along the street is a perfectly acceptable option, the **Derya**, No.2121, ✆ 0324 237 8069, a plain Jane of a place but clean enough. Rooms at the back are quieter; $18 for an en suite air-con double.

Adana

luxury–expensive

Adana has several good, expensive hotels, which is just as well as it's one of those cities where you may appreciate a little luxury after a day on the streets. The ★★★★★**Büyük Sürmeli Oteli**, Kuruköprü Özler Caddesi, ✆ 0322 352 3600, ✉ 0322 352 1945, is a blissful bolt hole with air-conditioning, bars and a fine restaurant. Official rates are very expensive at $160 for a double room but you may be able to negotiate if business is slack. The ★★★★**Zaimoğlu**, Özler Caddesi 72, ✆ 0322 363 5353, ✉ 0322 363 5363, *zaimoglu@zaimoglu.com.tr*, is also very opulent; en suite rooms with satellite TV go for a ridiculous $180 a double, discounted to around $100 including breakfast after a suitable display of incredulity.

moderate

The ★★**Hotel Koza**, Özler Caddesi 103, ✆ 0322 351 4657, is an acceptable, if slightly impersonal, establishment with doubles for $60, less when they're busy.

Adana has a very nice, cheap, flea-free hotel in the **Kristal Palas Oteli**, Özler Caddesi 19, ℰ 0322 352 2293, where the imperious entrance hall conceals the fact that en suite rooms cost only $8 a double. If you want, or need, to spend the absolute minimum, search in the streets surrounding the bazaar.

Tarsus

moderate

The ★★★★**Tarsus Mersin Hotel**, next to the waterfall (Şelale Mevkii), ℰ 0324 614 0600, ℰ 0324 614 0033, has the only really comfortable rooms in town, and is equipped with all the luxuries, including a pool, sauna and jacuzzi. Doubles are posted as $120, which is twice what they're expecting you to pay.

inexpensive–cheap

The **Cihan Palas** at Mersin Caddesi 40, ℰ 0324 624 1623, ℰ 0324 624 7334, is a mediocre establishment, but at least it's been recently refurbished and has quiet rooms at the back for $24.

Only one cheap hotel makes any concession whatsoever to modernity and cleanliness, and that's nothing special: the **Hotel Zorbaz**, Eski Belediye Karşısı, ℰ 0324 622 2166, which charges $10 for a double.

Adana to Tarsus   *Eating Out*

Adana is the home of the *Adana kebap*, hot and peppery, and every restaurant in town seems to serve it—although frankly, they cook it better in İstanbul. The **Yeni Onbaşılar** on Atatürk Caddesi near the tourist office has long been a favourite with locals ($3), while the **Rose Café and Bar**, İnönü Caddesi 145, is a quiet, relaxing place, good for a beer and a kebab ($3). Those with a sweet tooth should head for the **Gaziantep Şahinoğlu Baklava Salonu** at İnönü Caddesi 149B. Spotlessly clean, with a marble floor and air-con, this is the perfect retreat from the summer heat. $1.50 per portion of succulent baklava.

Tarsus has very few lokantas, most of them poor. The **Şelale Restaurant** next to the waterfall is the most inviting establishment, with outdoor tables and a good range of Turkish dishes; $8.

The Hatay

This little tongue of land, projecting into Syria to spoil Turkey's rectangularity, marks the only change in the nation's boundaries since the founding of the republic. Apart from the small chain of the Amanas Mountains running to the sea along the Gulf of İskenderun, Hatay province is really the ancient city of Antioch, now Antakya, and its hinterlands in the lower valley of the Orontes (Asi in Turkish).

During the First World War, General Allenby's Egyptian Expeditionary Force captured the Hatay for Britain but a League of Nations mandate gave the French the territory; they spent considerable effort and money over the next 16 years trying to win the goodwill of the inhabitants. When the date for the plebiscite ordered by the League finally arrived in 1939, the vote went overwhelmingly to join Turkey, and the French 'Hatay' became a historical curiosity remembered only by philatelists.

Whether you enter from the flat plain of Cilicia or the arid southeastern plateau, the contrast is striking. The fertile and well-tended countryside, its roads often lined with plane trees and oleanders, makes the Hatay one of the most civilized landscapes in Turkey. Along the coast, as soon as you have passed Toprakkale and have the Gulf of İskenderun in sight, you will be on the plain where one of the most significant battles of ancient history was fought.

Getting Around

The Hatay is off the major routes, and getting there by **bus** (there are no rail or air connections) may be difficult though not impossible. You may wish to check with the bus lines in advance for times, and you may be stuck on a bumpy minibus, especially if you're coming from the east. St Peter's Church is within walking distance of the centre of Antakya, but for many of the other early Christian sites you'll need a car. Harbiye is easily reached by **dolmuş** from Antakya.

Tourist Information

İskenderun: Atatürk Bulvarı 49, at the city pier, © 0326 614 1620.

Antakya: At the time of writing, this is on the fourth floor of the *vilayet* (provincial government headquarters, a must-see for fans of Kafka's *The Trial*). However, a new location may have been chosen by the time you read this. © 0326 216 0610.

From Issus to İskenderun

In 333 BC, Alexander the Great began his eastern campaign by invading Asia Minor; right across the peninsula, while reducing towns and dismantling satrapies, he was seeking a final showdown with the Persian King Darius. That November, he caught him at **Issus** (İssos), near the Turkish town of Dörtyol. Ancient historians credited the Persians with some 400,000 men; nevertheless the fighting was brief and one-sided. Darius barely escaped with his life, and Alexander informed him, in the subsequent diplomatic correspondence, that any future messages to him should be addressed to 'King of All Asia'. Two years lapsed before Alexander finally entered Persepolis—there were other distractions, such as the conquest of Egypt—but the Battle of Issus had already made his title a reality.

Payas (Yakacık), the first town after Dörtyol, lies in the shadow of a large modern steel mill; in the 16th century, it was the major port of the region, and substantial buildings from that period remain, notably the **Selimiye complex** built by Yavuz Selim in 1574, and a harbour castle thought to have been begun by the Venetians some centuries before. Payas' harbour silted up, and since then **İskenderun** has become the port of the Hatay and one of the largest in the Mediterranean; the ships waiting for dock-space often fill the horizon, as they do in İstanbul or Piraeus. As terminal of the busiest Middle East pipeline, the port handles all Iraq's oil exports. 'İskender' is the Arab and Turkish form of 'Alexander', and the city can trace its origins to the Macedonian foundation; other than that, İskenderun is wealthy and pleasant and remarkable only for being almost indistinguishable from Mersin.

From İskenderun the coast road can penetrate only as far as the fishing village and beach resort of **Arsuz**. South of here, ruins of a Crusader castle can be seen by boat, but a better and more accessible one lies near the route from İskenderun over the mountains, at **Bakras**, built by the Templars in the 12th century and captured soon after by Saladin himself. The castle is partially ruined, but the Gothic chapel and refectory remain.

Antakya (Antioch)

For most of the Roman era, **Antioch**, now **Antakya**, was the third-largest city of the Western world, surpassed only by Alexandria and Rome. One of Alexander's generals, Seleucus Nicator, who later created his own empire by defeating sufficient of his former comrades-in-arms, founded Antioch in 300 BC; as the Seleucid capital, it was the agent for introducing Hellenic culture into Syria. As trade routes across the new Greek Middle East grew, so did Antioch, at a rate that astounded contemporary chroniclers. At this time, the Mediterranean world had become rich and cohesive enough to trade on a large scale with India and China; the Seleucids, in the middle, collected all the transport charges. Antioch, the metropolis of the Hellenized Syrians, renowned throughout the ancient world for their craft and subtlety in business dealings, became the first western terminal of the Great Silk Route.

Secure under the Pax Romana, after 64 BC Antioch's population at one time exceeded half a million. Roman client kings of the Middle East, like Herod of Judea and the Kallinikos dynasty of Commagene, brightened their images by endowing the city with great temples and public works. Learning and art were prized, even by the high standards of the time and place, and before long Antioch vied with Athens for intellectual leadership of the empire. One of the first Christian communities was started here by St Peter himself; it grew so rapidly it became the greatest stronghold of the new faith, with enough of a hold on the population, even the upper classes, to resist most of the emperor's intermittent persecutions—even though Diocletian burned down all the churches in 301.

For a time in the 4th century, Antioch competed with Constantinople for pre-eminence in the East, and as the city was a bastion of the Arian heresy, the two became doctrinal enemies as well. Constantinople's rise meant Antioch's decline; the capital could collect taxes and draw away all the trade, although it lacked the strength or will to defend its outpost in Syria. Before the 7th century, Antioch was sacked six times by the Persians and Arabs. After a revival as a part of the Crusader kingdoms, it was sacked again, by the Mamelukes of Egypt in 1268. That was the end; the modern city was a struggling village only a century ago.

As much of its growth took place under French rule, in the period 1920–39, Antakya has very much the aspect of a French colonial city, with a slight excess of boulevards, traffic circles and palm trees. The traffic circle on the banks of the Asi, the ancient River Orontes, was obviously planned as a kind of civic centre; but here the grandest French building is not a government headquarters or school, but an Art Deco film palace. Of the ancient city, all you see are marble blocks built into the walls and streets of the pretty old village, across the river from the new town. Kurtuluş Caddesi is its main street, generally following the route of the famous colonnaded avenue of antiquity; it passes the **Habib Neccar Camii**, an exceptionally fine 17th-century mosque. On the mountains above the city, some parts of the ancient walls are well preserved, but they are difficult of access.

The main reason for visiting Antakya is the collection of Roman mosaics in the **Archaeology Museum** (*open 8.30–12, 1.30–5, closed Mon; adm*), perhaps the finest in existence, recovered from the city and its suburb of Daphne. These mosaics, in colour and detail, and in the expressiveness of the portraiture, must be counted among the greatest works of the Roman world. A face as perfectly captured as that of the unknown lady named 'Soteria' brings that world back to life, while mythological scenes like the room-sized 'Marriage of Tethys and Oceanus', attended by all the creatures of the sea, gently reproach us for not crediting the late Roman world with enough imagination.

Around Antakya

The Hatay has been a civilized country since Neolithic times, and the plain around Antakya is littered with mounds and ruins. Just north of the city along the cliffs is what the locals claim is the oldest Christian church in the world still in use. The name **St Peter's Church** (Senpiyer Kilisesi) was natural, for St Peter himself is said to have preached here. It is a cave, with a tunnel for escape during the persecutions, a cistern and, on the floor, the remains of mosaics. The carved façade, cut out from living rock, was added by the Crusaders. Antakya has a small Catholic community. Mass is said here and in the 19th-century church on Kurtuluş Caddesi on Sundays. Along the cliffs to the left of the cave are a number of rock tombs, and a mysterious relief of a woman, carved in the 2nd century BC.

The most renowned pleasure dome of the ancient world was Daphne, now **Harbiye**, a beautiful spot overlooking the Orontes with small waterfalls cascading down a series of terraces, and groves of pine and plane trees. It isn't associated with the myth of Apollo and Daphne—that all happened in Thessaly—but the Hellenized gentry of the Seleucid Kingdom thought it would have made a fine setting nevertheless. A famous temple of Apollo was erected here, and the well-to-do of Antioch surrounded it with their villas and gardens. Antony and Cleopatra courted at Daphne, and in the Roman era the Antioch games held here surpassed the old games at Olympus in popularity and importance.

Roman emperors spent time in Antioch whenever their responsibilities permitted; Julian the Apostate, having grown up here, especially favoured it. When he returned in AD 363, on his way to campaign against the Persians, and saw the Christian population wrecking the beautiful temple of Apollo at Daphne to get stone for churches, he was furious. He had it rebuilt, but the Christians immediately burned it down. Daphne shared in Antioch's misfortunes; various earthquakes knocked down what the Christians hadn't and rearranged the topography, somewhat for the worse. Today the place is known by the incongruous name of Harbiye or 'war college', but it is still a favourite resort of local people, with restaurants and picnic grounds among the waterfalls. It can be reached along the main road to the south, four miles (6 km) from Antakya.

There was a dark side to Antioch's early Christianity, leading to odd extremes. In this sophisticated metropolis, instead of a blossoming of innocence and faith what happened was an outbreak of neuroses no one could have foreseen. One outstanding manifestation was the fashion for pillar-sitting, begun by St Simeon Stylites in the 4th century and lasting into the 5th. St Simeon spent some 25 years in the air, on a series of progressively taller columns, attracting great crowds of pilgrims and penitents and interfering in imperial politics and public morals through his pronouncements from on high. Pillar-sitting became fashionable, and at one point Church chronicles report no less than 200 copycats up in the air together.

The hill where all this took place, with the ruins of the 5th-century **St Simeon Monastery**, is off the road from Antakya to the west in the direction of Samandağı. Other old monasteries in various stages of dereliction lie on the hills around Yayladağı near the Syrian border.

The road from Yayladağı to the coast leads to **Samandağı** and from there north to **Çevlik**, near the ruins of Antioch's old port, **Seleucia ad Pieria**. Gradually abandoned as its harbour silted up, the town has little left to see except the **Tunnel of Vespasian**, a series of great halls with 50-foot ceilings carved out of the rocks near the sea, used as part of Seleucia's water supply system. Even though a smaller irrigation canal was recently built through it, you can walk through this cool and lovely spot, passing in and out of the mountain, listening to the frogs. Fine beaches line the shore all around with a beautiful backdrop of green mountains, some in Turkey, some in Syria.

Antakya to İskenderun **Where to Stay**

Antakya

Antakya doesn't get many tourists and, although the town is not exactly packed with places to stay, finding somewhere suitable should not be too difficult.

expensive

Antakya's finest is the ★★★★**Büyük Antakya Oteli**, Atatürk Caddesi 8, ✆ 0326 213 5858, ✇ 0326 213 5869, with 72 air-conditioned, en suite rooms. For what you get, it's not that expensive, at $100 for a double with breakfast, but no pool. Antakya's most atmospheric hotel is the **(S)Antik Beyazıt**, Hükümet Caddesi, ✆ 0326 216 2900, ✇ 0326 214 3089, recently converted from a Hatay mansion dating back to 1903. The reception has been sympathetically restored, unlike the bedrooms, which are full of modern pine fittings; $90 per double, though this can be reduced to as little as $60 if they are not full and you are persuasive.

moderate–inexpensive

The ★★★**Hotel Orontes**, İstiklâl Caddesi 58, ✆ 0326 214 5931, has courteous and informative staff; the rooms are very nice too, and cost $44 for a double. The ★★**Hotel Atahan**, Hürriyet Caddesi 28, ✆ 0326 214 2140, has old-fashioned but clean and spacious doubles with air-con for $30.

cheap

Just beyond the Hotel Orontes in Antakya is a cluster of cheap hotels. Coming from the bus station the first encountered is the **Divan Oteli**, İstiklâl Caddesi 62, ✆ 0326 215 1518, where clean rooms with private shower and toilet go some way towards compensating for the surly, grumpy staff and noisy road. Rates are $15 for a double. Cheaper rooms are to be had at the great rambling warren that is the **Hotel Güney**, ✆ 0326 214 9713; $10 for a double with shower, $12 if you need a TV too. The rear rooms are quieter, with fine views of the walled ruins on the hills. There are pensions near the beaches at Samandağ and Arsuz.

Harbiye

Harbiye (Daphne) is quieter than Antakya, with cleaner air. If you choose to stay here, the ***Çağlayan Otel**, Ürgun Caddesi 6, © 0326 231 4269, ✆ 0326 231 5489, is good value with doubles for $26.

İskenderun

As a busy port that sees lots of businessmen, İskenderun has plenty of nice, inexpensive hotels, such as the ****Otel Bahadırlı**, Eylül Caddesi 12, © 0326 617 2923, ✆ 0326 617 5757; $35 for a comfortable double room in a central location. At Şehit Pamir Caddesi 11, the **Otel Altındişler**, © 0326 617 1011, is cheaper at $24.

The budget choice is the **Hotel Açıkalın**, Şehit Pamir Caddesi 13, © 0326 617 3732; $19 for a basic room with private shower. There are several other cheapies dotted around the port; none look too savoury.

Antakya to İskenderun **Eating Out**

Antakya

The majority of the lokantas in Antakya are bleak and dingy with kitchens that would turn a public health inspector white with shock. Nevertheless, you can still eat well, and with due regard for your digestive system, at the good hotels and at the **Sultan Sofrası Restaurant** on İstiklâl Caddesi, where a good meal will cost around $5. Above the aquarium shop at Silahlı Kuvvetler Caddesi 3, the **Antakya Evi** has original tiled floors and a pleasant open balcony; good Turkish fare costs $5. On Hürriyet Caddesi, a fast food parlour serves up a local delicacy—liver burgers for $1.

Harbiye

Harbiye has a surprising number of places, the best of which is the long-running **Boğaziçi** on Ürgen Caddesi. Part of the nearby river is channelled through its outdoor dining area; red sole mature here until they're big enough for the table. The food is plentiful and delicious, the atmosphere convivial; highly recommended for $7. Bring a car if you have one and you'll have it washed for free while you're eating. Another enjoyable option is to head for the informal outdoor restaurants in the park—sheds or tents with picnic tables among the waterfalls and pines. At these you can get a good fish or kebab dinner at lower prices than elsewhere.

İskenderun

The **Saray Lokantası** on Atatürk Bulvarı is a popular spot in the centre (about $4), as is the **Divan**, big as a barn and with swirling overhead fans.

The Black Sea

Turkey's longest coast has always been the marine back door, less favoured by nature and less prominent in history than the lands along the Aegean and Mediterranean. Jason and his Argonauts may have sailed it, but the Greek merchants and colonists behind the myth founded only a few towns, none of which ever attained much status in the ancient world. From Jason up to the present, in fact, the only intrusion the shores of the *Pontus Euxinus* ever made into history was the rise of the Pontic Kingdom in the wake of Alexander the Great's conquest in the 4th century BC. The Pontic kings gave Rome fits for a century, but when they finally succumbed to the tenacity of the legions, it put an end to Pontus as a nation forever. Since then, with the exception of the short-lived but colourful Empire of Trebizond, these shores have managed well enough to stay out of trouble.

Recently, the Black Sea has been just as successful in avoiding tourism. Both the coast and the forest-clad mountains that rise behind it have their share of scenery, more in the western half than in the east. There are a few good beaches, but the climate lacks that Mediterranean perfection; the season is short, and rains are frequent even in the summer. Even in the west, the best part of the coast begins only at Samsun; like the area around the Marmara, the coast from İstanbul eastwards has become industrialized over the last 50 years.

All along the Black Sea, with the exception of a few local resorts, there is little accommodation and restaurants are scarce. Although this is gradually changing, as yet the package tours and the magnates of the holiday industry are nowhere to be seen, and if you're not too demanding in your stretch of seaside and wish to avoid knocking elbows with your countrymen, the Black Sea may be just the place.

İstanbul to Samsun

Getting Around

A good, two-lane **highway** runs some of the way along the coast, although at times it's steep and bendy. Samsun is easily reached by **bus** from almost anywhere in the country but services west of the town—to Sinop, Amasra and Kastamonu—are suprisingly infrequent, with only two or three buses a day. İstanbul, Zonguldak, Sinop and Samsun are all connected by TML **ferry**.

Tourist Information

Bolu: Karamanlı Mah., Konuralp Caddesi 11, ✆ 0374 212 2254.

Zonguldak: Valilik building, ✆ 0372 253 8827.

Kastamonu: Nasrullah İş Hanı, ✆ 0366 212 0162.

Sinop: Valilik building, ✆ 0368 261 5207.

Safranbolu: Arasta Çarşısı 7, ✆ 0372 712 3863.

Samsun: Talimhane Caddesi 6, ✆ 0362 431 2988.

East to Zonguldak

The nearest Black Sea beach resort to İstanbul is **Şile**, popular with the Stamboullu who come here to swim and to buy the embroidered cotton shirts for which the town is renowned. Genoese merchants built the little **castle** here to protect their interests in the Black Sea, back in the days when they were snatching the Byzantine emperor's commerce out from under his nose. Drowsy **Ağva**, 19 miles (30km) on, also has a beach. After Kandıra, a further 31 miles (50km) to the east, the road leaves the coast, bypassing the promontory of Calpe and its islet just offshore, where a vision of Apollo appeared to the Argonauts; in classical times a Temple of Harmonia was built in commemoration of the event, but not a trace of it remains. This route leads to the provincial capital, **Adapazarı** (Sakarya), which should be bypassed in favour of the lake to its south, **Sapanca Gölü**. Well-dressed Turks, families and courting couples, come here at weekends to stroll contentedly along the verdant lakeside trails.

Back on the coast, the next good beach is at **Akçakoca**, which also boasts yet another ruined Genoese castle. The town was named after a general of Sultan Orhan who captured it, the first Ottoman foothold on the coast. Akçakoca is often crowded with families from the big towns to the east: **Ereğli**, whose coastline is adorned by the Middle East's largest steel mill, and **Zonguldak**. This latter city has been around since the Hittites, but only since the coal seams around it were first mined in the 1920s has it become important. Now, besides shipping out most of Turkey's coal through its large port, Zonguldak has become the centre of the country's major industrial region.

Bolu and Lake Abant

Leave any part of this coast, and you eventually find yourself in the **Köroğlu Mountains**, a long chain that separates the plains around Ankara from the sea. Though not as steep as the mountains along the eastern Black Sea, these are heavily forested, not only with pines and poplars, but with groves of oak and other deciduous trees not often seen in Turkey. **Bolu**, south of Zonguldak, lies at the centre of the country's most popular mountain recreation area. Whenever you see 'bolu' in the name of a Turkish town, as in 'İnebolu' and 'Safranbolu', you know it's at least as old as the Romans; it's how the Turks came to pronounce 'polis', and this 'Bolu' was originally Claudiopolis. Nothing very old has survived, but there's a fine **Ulu Cami** built under Yıldırım Beyazıt. Bolu has a reputation for producing the best cooks in Turkey, but its citizens complain that they all go to İstanbul.

Beautiful **Lake Abant**, just to the southwest, is perhaps the best-known mountain resort. Nearly a mile above sea level, it's kept well stocked for trout fishermen. If one lake isn't enough, try the **Yedigöller National Park** where there are seven, among forests of oak, elm and beech; here you may stalk the rare and elusive wild tulip. There's skiing at **Kartalkaya**, southwest of Bolu on the slopes of Köroğlu Dağ, the highest peak of the chain.

Köroğlu, the Robin Hood of Turkey

'Köroğlu' means 'son of the blind man', and behind the name stands a personality you should get to know if you plan to spend much time here. For these mountains are Turkey's Sherwood Forest, and Köroğlu, a real bandit who flourished at the end of the 16th century, is his country's Robin Hood. The historical evidence is limited to letters from the governor of Ankara demanding Köroğlu's arrest; there are quite a few of them. The legends, still heard in rural corners here and in eastern Anatolia, start Köroğlu out in life in much the same way as his English counterpart, sworn to outlawry to avenge a wrong done by the authorities.

His father, a groom for the lord of Bolu, had been charged with the duty of selecting a gift horse from the herd of a neighbouring bey. He picked out a lean, crippled colt, so enraging his master that he had the groom's eyes put out. Köroğlu promised to revenge his father, and, with the aid of the colt, now grown into a magic grey horse called Kirat, spent a long career doing just that. With him at his mountain hideout somewhere near Gerede lived 500 warriors, some heroes in their own right, like Demircioğlu, 'son of the blacksmith', the very picture of a Turkish Little John.

Nallıhan, the tiny village south of Bolu, is a centre of the Köroğlu legend, and here you may see one of Kirat's horseshoes still nailed to a stone wall. Strangely, these stories were always most popular out east; another cycle of them has Köroğlu's band robbing fat merchants on the pass of Çamlibel, near Sivas.

From Amasra to İnebolu

Returning to the coast, **Amasra** is a characterful little town made striking by the Genoese fortifications that still stand above two indented harbours. Being blessed with two ports made Amasra important long before the Genoese pitched up; it was first founded by colonists from Miletus and what has been unearthed from its past is now on show at the local **archaeological museum** (*open Tues–Sun 9–5.30; adm*). There is a beach here, although the cleanliness of the sea is questionable; Amasra's ports are still very much in use. East of Amasra the coastal road begins to dip and rise and curve and occasionally cut inland. The scenery is pleasant enough but there's little to entice the visitor, aside from the quiet pebble beaches that appear every few miles or so. **İnebolu** is the largest town along this stretch, boasting attractive if dilapidated traditional Ottoman houses as well as a beach. Fifteen miles further east is **Abana**, an expanding resort with a reasonable beach.

Safranbolu and Kastamonu

In Roman times, the Köroğlu Mountains formed part of the province of Bithynia; one thing they have in common with the old Bithynian villages around Bursa (*see* p.194) is the style of the houses. These square, half-timber buildings, with their tile roofs and medieval overhanging second storeys, can best be seen in towns like **Safranbolu**, **Bartın** near the coast, and in the cosy little provincial capital of **Kastamonu**.

Safranbolu was once a rich town, deriving its wealth, importance and name from its trade in saffron, the costly spice prepared from the pistils of a variety of crocus. Today the old town is isolated, hiding behind modern Safranbolu which is itself eclipsed by nearby Karabük, a thriving modern town situated on the railway, with an economy based on iron and steel.

Old Safranbolu has been declared a UNESCO world heritage site and the TTOK is active in restoration and preservation. The town is a delight to wander round. In the centre, which is closed to traffic, the cobbled alleys are shaded by vines; saddle-makers sit working in open shopfronts; streets echo to the hammers of tin- and coppersmiths and shimmer with the sprays of sparks from their metalwork. Many handicrafts are on sale in the town, but are on the expensive side; fabrics in particular tend to have inflated prices.

The large half-timber houses for which the town is famous can be seen everywhere. Several of these houses have been restored and are open to the public, notably the **Kaymakamlar Evi** (Governor's House). The plan of the house is typical of its day and explains why Ottoman houses are so large: they are designed for extended families, with each room housing one nuclear family. The rooms are multi-purpose, with facilities for cooking and washing and built-in cupboards for clothes and bed linen. They have a minimum of furniture: padded benches round the edges act as seats during the day and beds at night. The Kaymakam had the best room, with an adjoining chamber for his wives; his parents had the second-best. The individual rooms are grouped round communal areas. The large communal kitchen was used only on special occasions. Suspended above the doorway of the house is a small room for the watchman, with a commanding view of the entrance.

Another such house is the charming **Karaüzümler Evi**, replete with quiet courtyard café, on Mescit Sokak. The owners are pleased to show you round (once your feet have been enveloped in shower caps to protect the floor); cupboards in several rooms open to reveal ingenious toilet facilities. As in many of these Ottoman mansions, the quality of light inside is extraordinary, with huge windows fitted wherever there's space. Another Ottoman building worth a glimpse is the wonderful stone **Cinci Hanı**, a 17th-century caravanserai locked up at present, possibly to be reincarnated as a plush hotel.

A good view of the town can be had from what appears from below to be a castle. This is actually nothing more than some battlement-style walls surrounding a small Ottoman *türbe* on top of a hill. The imposing Renaissance-style mansion on another hill is the burnt-out shell of the **Hükümet Konağı** (Government House).

Safranbolu has been so well preserved that it can feel like an open-air museum; by contrast **Kastamonu**, 60 miles to the east, is very much more vibrant and bustling, its dilapidated old Ottoman houses cheerfully rubbing shoulders with brand new apartment blocks. The castle from which Kastamonu derives its name is, in one respect, unique in Turkey: it wasn't wrecked by Tamerlane—he built it. In modern times, the greatest thing to hit Kastamonu was Atatürk's speech here in 1925, proclaiming the Hat Reform, and the abolition of the fez. You can learn all about it (if you understand Turkish) in the pretty old building that houses the **Kastamonu Museum** (*open Tues–Sun 8.30–4.30; adm*), with a good collection of Roman-era sculpture.

Sinop

Long ago, the sailors of the Black Sea had a saying that the only reliable opportunities for landing on the southern shore were 'June, July and Sinope'. Originally a Milesian colony like Amasra, **Sinope** grew to become the pre-eminent town of Pontus during the Hellenistic era, a free trading city that maintained its liberty until King Pharnaces I annexed it to the Pontic kingdom in 183 BC. As first city and occasional capital of this kingdom, Sinope was more than compensated by the many temples and monuments the kings bestowed upon it.

Sinope contributed two tough customers to the lore of classical antiquity. The lady after whom the town was named was an Amazon queen whose charms attracted the attentions of Zeus. When the god came courting, he promised Sinope any gift she desired; she chose ever-lasting virginity, and lived happily ever after. In 413 BC, Diogenes, the original Cynic, was born here. His belief in virtue and moral freedom (far removed from latter-day cynicism) led to his decision to live the simple life of a dog, unfettered by social convention. ('Cynic' comes from the Greek word for dog.) This is the fellow Alexander the Great found one day sitting in his usual tub; the prince, always kindly disposed to cranks and philosophers, asked if Diogenes desired anything of him, and received the famous reply, 'Yes, stand out of my light.' Alexander is said to have commented, 'If I were not Alexander, I would be Diogenes.'

As the Black Sea trade dwindled during Roman times, so did Sinop (the modern spelling), and today the only natural harbour on the coast finds itself eclipsed completely by artificial ones at Zonguldak, Samsun and even Trabzon, originally a colony of Sinope. The town still makes its living from the sea. It may be a good spot for a fish dinner along the quays, but for all its past, little is left. The **castle**, built on the foundations of Mithridates' stronghold, is a Byzantine work, but the most notable building is from the 13th century, the **Alâeddin Camii**, one of the last mosques built by the dying Selçuk Empire. Outside town, there are good beaches at **Akliman**, an isolated spot on the bay, and at the fishing village of **Gerze**.

Samsun

Samsun, the largest city on the coast, is exactly the opposite of Sinop—all present and no past. The Milesians were here, too, and Samsun is just as old, but never had anything to show for itself until this century. Wherever you walk in the city's nondescript gridiron of streets, the sweet aroma of freshly cut tobacco fills the air, rising from the enormous old Tekel factory in the middle of the town which produces most of Turkey's cigarettes. Nobody smokes like a Turk, as you will have noticed, and Samsun is doing very well. The modern, well-planned and partly pedestrianised centre of the city reflects this, with its shorefront boulevard lined with palms, and smooth, cleanly designed new buildings, notably the ski-jump cultural centre. Samsun could well afford to put up the largest **Atatürk Monument** outside Ankara, but it also had good reason: the Turkish War of Independence began here, with Atatürk's escape from İstanbul on the steamer *Bandırma*. Instead of inspecting the army, as he had fooled the sultan's government into ordering him to do, he started making speeches to it and issuing manifestos to the patriots of Anatolia. Samsun welcomed him with bands and cheering crowds, and it has been a stoutly republican town ever since; ironically, it also has a reputation for being one of the most conservative Muslim cities in Turkey.

Samsun divides its busy port from the rest of the town with its **Fair**, a big park like the one in İzmir that contains the stadium, train station, public auditorium, the Luna Park, acres of gardens and the **Atatürk Museum**, which resembles a lost pavilion from some forgotten exhibition. The whole of old Samsun, full of market stalls and questionable restaurants, is in the city's west end; here the memorable structures are not old mosques but the wonderfully overdone public buildings and banks, all in a bastard French Second Empire style.

İstanbul to Samsun   ***Where to Stay***

Note that most of the small coastal towns have only very limited accommodation, with inexpensive pensions the rule.

Şile

Şile has several large beach hotels, such as the **★★Değirmen**, Plaj Yolu 24, © 0216 711 5048, ✆ 0216 711 5248, where a double costs $60 in season.

Near Bolu

At **Ömerler Köyü**, in the mountains near Bolu, the Turkish Automobile Club has built a lovely hotel, the large, Alpine-style **★★★★Koru Hotel**, Bakırlı Mevkii, © 0374 225 2290, ✆ 0374 275 2812, *koruhotel@superonline.com*, with very comfortable rooms for $140 a double. At **Karacasu Köyü** in the same region, the **★★★Bolu Termal Otel**, © 0374 262 8472, ✆ 0374 262 8307, charges a little less.

On **Lake Abant**, the **★★★★★Taksim International Abant**, © 0374 224 5012, ✆ 0374 224 5011, is the area's plushest and most expensive hotel, with all the facilities one would expect and double rooms for over $200. For almost half that, you can stay full board at the **★★★Turban Abant Hotel**, also on the lake, © 0374 224 5033, ✆ 0374 224 5031, with a sauna and a pool; meals included.

Amasra

At the **Nur Pansiyon**, Çamlık Sokak, © 0378 315 1015, a basic but acceptable double room costs $16.

Safranbolu

Safranbolu's plushest establishment is the **Havazlu Konak**, Mescit Sokak, © 0370 725 2883, ✆ 0370 712 3824, run by the TTOK and worth a peek even if you're staying in lesser lodgings. Spacious rooms, furnished in traditional Ottoman style and attractively carpeted, have undersized private bathrooms; $60 for a double, including breakfast in the sumptuous tea room, replete with interior pool and low-lying brass tables. The restaurant, however, is nothing special.

Safranbolu boasts various mid-range hotels in converted Ottoman houses of which the **Selvili Köşk**, Çeşme Mah., Mescit Sokak, © 0370 712 8646, ✆ 0370 725 2294, is a pleasant example on a quiet street. As well as a large and attractive first-floor salon, it has airy bedrooms with cupboards revealing ingenious bathrooms within (not for those unwilling to clamber), priced at $45 for a double.

Cheaper Ottoman surroundings in Safranbolu are to be found at the **Kadıoğlu Şehzade Konakları**, opposite the Selvili Köşk, ✆ 0370 725 2762, ✉ 0370 712 5657, at $20 for a double. It's easy to confuse this hotel with four others that have similar names, owned as they are by the same family. Not so the **Çiftlik Pansiyon**, uphill along a side road near the Dağdela Camii, ✆ 0370 712 1970. This modern family house is the best pension in town, home to a family bubbling over with friendliness. Some of the bedrooms have balconies with good views over the town, and the shared toilet and shower are spotless; $7 per person.

Kastamonu

Opposite the town hall, the **★★Otel Mütevelli**, Cumhuriyet Caddesi 10, ✆ 0366 212 2020, ✉ 0366 212 2017, has comfortable if unadventurous rooms for $35. Road noise may be a problem both here and at the **★Rugancı**, further along Cumhuriyet Caddesi, ✆ 0366 214 9500, ✉ 0366 212 4343, where simple double rooms with TV and bathtubs cost $24. There are a handful of cheap hotels, the best of which is the **Selvi**, on Banka Sokak, a quiet pedestrian street off the Nasrullah Meydanı, ✆ 0366 214 1763. Some of the top-floor rooms have excellent views of the castle; doubles are good value at $14.

Sinop

The **★★Otel Melia Kasım**, Gazi Caddesi 49, ✆ 0368 261 4210, ✉ 0368 261 1625, is the best on offer, solid but uninspiring. The pastel rooms have satellite TV and balconies with good views of the sea; $32.

Of the cheapies, **Hotel Denizci**, Kurtuluş Caddesi, ✆ 0368 261 0904, is characterful with a friendly owner; clean rooms with balcony and shared bathroom are $9 a double. Next door is the similarly priced **Otel Meral**, ✆ 0368 261 3100, a friendly family-run establishment which will do for a night or two.

Samsun

Samsun's top hotel is the modern but anonymous **★★★★Büyük Samsun Oteli**, Atatürk Bulvarı, ✆ 0362 432 4999, ✉ 0362 431 0749, set within small gardens and with a swimming pool. It's not cheap, however, at $130 for a double with breakfast thrown in.

The **★★Otel Vidinli**, Cumhuriyet Meydanı 4, ✆ 0362 431 6050, ✉ 0362 431 2136, has bright and spacious bedrooms, each with a sitting area, minibar and bath; $45 for a double. The 1960s furniture has been unusually well designed and constructed, lending a certain utilitarian elegance to the place. There's also a top-floor restaurant which offers live music.

The **Otel Akça**, Pazar Mah., Hastane Sokak 4, ✆ 0362 431 7350, has bright front rooms decorated with vibrant bursts of scarlet and black (oddly refreshing in light of Turkish hoteliers' obsession with the colour beige). Rooms are $18 for a double with shower, $15 without. The **Otel Necmi**, Kale Mah., Bedesten Sokak 6, ✆ 0362 432 7164, ✉ 0362 432 2029, has minuscule but quiet rooms which are tolerable for a one-night stay; the top floor has the (one) shower. $14 per double.

Bolu's cooks have a good reputation, which you may test at the **İdris** lokanta near the town hall (about $9 for a meal with wine).

Despite **Safranbolu**'s burgeoning number of hotels, evening fare tends to be limited to standard Turkish dishes in one of the uninspiring restaurants.

The most atmospheric place for lunch in **Kastamonu** is the **Frenkşah Sultan Sofrası** in the 13th-century former Sultan Cemaleddin Hamamı off Nasrullah Meydanı. The place is crammed with Ottoman curios and is an enjoyable place to sample *mantı* or, better still, the wonderful *li* or *etli ekmek*—vegetarian or meat-stuffed crêpes. A more orthodox alternative, crammed full of locals at lunchtime and in the evening, is the **Uludağ Pide ve Kebap Salonu** on the corner of Belediye and Cumhuriyet Caddesi, serving up its namesake dishes for $3.

Fish restaurants along the coast do exist, but are not numerous except in Şile. **Lake Sapanca** is rich in trout that can be sampled in any one of the many lakeside restaurants. If you're in search of the renowned *palamut* (bonito fish), try at **Şile**, near the Fair in the centre of **Samsun**, or at **Sinop**, where a clutch of fish restaurants line the quayside, among them the **Saray**, with its tables bobbing gently on the floating jetty; $8 for excellent fish.

The **Pink Panter Lokanta** in **Abana** must surely win the prize for the best-named establishment on the Black Sea; unfortunately the food doesn't quite match up to the inspired name.

Samsun to Trabzon

Leaving Samsun, the first town to the east is **Çarşamba**, which means Wednesday in Turkish (Perşembe, meaning Thursday, is 68 miles (110km) down the coast, while Pazar, Sunday, is near the Georgian border). From Çarşamba, the road takes a short cut across the delta of the Yeşilırmak. This area, like most of the Black Sea region, is extremely good farmland. From Sinop to Çarşamba, and inland along the Yeşilırmak valley, Turkish tobacco has been the major crop. Now, along the roadside up to Trabzon, there are mostly hazelnut plantations; the little *fındık*, as the Turks call it, is a surprisingly important export crop.

After Trabzon, tea plantations cover most of the land. Throughout, however, one more local speciality keeps the Black Sea farmers prosperous—the best cherries anywhere. They're indigenous here; the Romans first brought cherry trees from the Black Sea into Europe, and from there they spread throughout the world.

Getting Around

The **bus** and **dolmuş** services along this part of the coast are excellent and it is easy to hop from town to town. The centres of all the coastal towns are just off the main coastal road. Ask to be let off the bus there and not at the bus stations, which are sometimes inconveniently located inland. Giresun can be reached by **ferry** from İstanbul, Zonguldak, Sinop, Samsun and Trabzon.

Ünye: On the main coastal road next to the Ünyespar Sosyal Tesisleri, ✆ 0452 323 4952.

Ordu: Atatürk Bulvarı 116A, Belediye Binası, ✆ 0452 223 1608.

Giresun: Gazi Caddesi 72, ✆ 0454 216 0161.

Ünye and Ordu

If any town on the Black Sea shows promise of becoming a big seaside resort, it's **Ünye**, on a pretty half-moon bay with beaches, restaurants and camping sites extending for several miles on either side of the town. Ünye itself, built around a beach and a shady promenade, retains traces of fortifications built when it was ancient Oenae. Caves along the shore near the town are one of the few Black Sea haunts of the rare, elusive monk seal. Between Ünye and Ordu the road, placid since Samsun, suddenly climbs into an exuberance of corniche turns, up and around the rugged peninsula the Greeks called the Promontory of Jason. Below the cliffs lie secluded fishing villages and untouched beaches; the best of these faces an islet, within easy swimming distance of the shore, where a ruin has become a home for great flocks of seagulls. Perhaps this is the 'Island of Ares', where the Argonauts were attacked by a flock of birds dropping feathered darts. A temple of Ares was said to have been founded on the island.

Not long before the *Argo* was launched, according to the generally accepted order of myths, Hercules had tramped these shores on his ninth labour, securing the girdle of the Amazon Queen Hippolyta. The Amazon city Thermiscyra and its River Thermodon may have been at Terme, or near Ordu, if indeed it ever existed in the form mythographers have made for it. To the Greeks, this part of the Black Sea has always been associated with the Amazons, a confusion arising perhaps from Bronze Age Achaean merchants encountering matriarchal tribes during their exploratory voyages into Pontus.

The road to Ordu shows the Black Sea coast at its best: rugged, dramatic and verdant. Along some parts of the road, the trees are so draped in creepers and vines that the effect is almost tropical. Here too are isolated hamlets such as **Mersin** and pleasant coastal villages such as **Perşembe** which have so far been spared the concretization of the towns to the east.

Ordu, a real Greek foundation named Cotyora, keeps some reminders of the days of King Mithridates: the **Caleoğlu Castle**, three miles (5km) inland, and some cliff tombs like those in Amasya. There's a large beach east of the town, but if you're looking for something a little different, try the crater lake up in the mountains at **Cambaşı**, 44 miles (70km) south of Ordu, which is completely encircled by beaches. Ordu has a small **museum** in the centre of town near the helpful tourist office.

Giresun and the Route to Trabzon

The next town, **Giresun**, surrounds a small table-top peninsula with a Byzantine castle perched on top, a striking sight that is almost a mirror image in miniature of Alanya on the Mediterranean coast. Giresun is a pleasant town, brimming with breezy charm. It is also a cherry and hazelnut centre, its streets offering glimpses into warehouses with mountains of nuts being scooped into hessian sacks and loaded onto lorries for export. As well as the castle, it has an 18th-century Greek church, now a rather uninspiring **museum**, and the **tomb** of Seyit Vakas, who won Giresun for the Ottomans in 1461. **Giresun Island**, just offshore, and another candidate for Jason's Island of Ares, is the largest of the Black Sea islands, and the only one inhabited. You sometimes hear it referred to as 'Amazon Island'; locally it's believed that the ruins belong to Ares' temple and the palace of the Amazon queens who built it.

After Giresun, the beaches never seem to end but it is the wild mountain scenery that once more commands your attention. All along the route, those Pontic mountains have lurked close to the shore; now their wooded slopes press in closer, in a shade of green you would more expect to see in England than Turkey. From Samsun to Trabzon, there are no major roads inland across the mountains; this is one of Turkey's greatest areas of wilderness, and the difficulty of the terrain ensures it will remain so.

Further along the coast, **Tirebolu** not so long ago resembled a south Devon coastal village, with steep and partly cobbled streets and houses tumbling down towards the sea. Now the lovely old higgledy-piggledy homes have been hemmed in by their ferro-concrete descendants. Midway up the slender main street the town's new mosque has colourful windows and bubbles with domes; it's in a lovely location, overlooking the sea and the castle that stands in ruins on a rocky promontory. The next castle, at **Akçakale**, past Görele, was built by the Emperors of Trebizond, serving as a reminder that you are near the borders of that lost realm. As you get closer to Trabzon, the villages begin to look suburban, first **Vakfıkebir**, with a long, semi-sandy beach, then **Akçaabat**, renowned for its folk dancers.

Samsun to Trabzon   ***Where to Stay***

Ünye

moderate

Three miles (5km) west of Ünye, the ★★**Otel Kumsal**, ℂ 0452 323 4490, is a pleasant Black Sea beach hotel with doubles for $40. A further three miles west, the **Çınarsuyu** duplex chalets, ℂ 0452 342 4623, are a good option for families or groups: for $45 per night, each trapezoid chalet sleeps up to six people. Set in pleasant gardens, the complex is very close to the sea.

cheap

There are a number of pleasant family-run pensions in Ünye, notably the **Pınar**, Devrent Mevkii 23, ℂ 0452 323 3496. Bedecked in kilims and carpets, the rooms are very light and lead onto balconies; doubles (without bathrooms) are $14. A cheap hotel option is the **Burak**, near the Belediye at Belediye Caddesi 4, ℂ 0452 312 0186, where doubles are only $12.

Ordu

moderate

The status address is the ★★★**Belde**, ℂ 0452 214 3987, ℗ 0452 214 9398, *beldeotel @hotmail.com*. Set on a secluded promontory a few miles west of town, it has a hamam, sauna and pool, but it's seen better days and is overpriced at $65 a double.

The ****Turist Otel**, Atatürk Bulvarı 134, ✆ 0452 225 3140, 📠 0452 214 1950, is nothing fancy, but OK for one night; spacious but characterless rooms with private bath go for $28 a double. The **Otel Kervansaray** (which is not, unfortunately, a restored caravanserai), Kazım Karabekir Caddesi 1, ✆ 0452 214 1330, has shabby en suite doubles for $12.

Giresun

expensive

The brand new ******Hotel Basar**, ✆ 0454 212 9920, caters ostentatiously for businessmen, all soaring lobby, glass elevators and cavernous conference rooms. Staff are friendly, however, and north-facing bedrooms look out onto the sea; doubles $100.

moderate–inexpensive

Giresun has several hotels in this category, the best being the *****Kit-tur Oteli**, Arifbey Caddesi 2, ✆ 0454 212 0245, 📠 0454 212 3034, with smart rooms costing $55 a double. The ****Hotel Çarıkçı**, Osmanağa Caddesi 6, ✆ 0454 216 1026, 📠 0454 216 4578, also has a central location and is much better value, with almost comparable doubles going for $25.

The ***Er Tur**, Çapulacılar Arastası 8, ✆ 0454 216 1757, 📠 0454 216 7762, punches above its weight with quiet, clean, comfortable en suite rooms for only $20.

Tirebolu

Your best bet is the **Huzur** at Gazi Paşa Caddesi 15, ✆ 0454 411 4093, just beyond the mosque in the old town. The toilets are communal, the beds of the tubular hospital variety and the showers designed for pygmies. However, it's cheap, at $4 per person, though you may have to wander around town looking for the proprietor.

Samsun to Trabzon **Eating Out**

In **Ünye**, set in a pine grove just off the coastal road two miles (3km) west of town, the **Çamlık Restoranı** is on a terrace overlooking the sea. Fish is the Çamlık's *raison d'être*, but it's also worth nibbling on some of their regional specialities such as *mısır ekmeği* (thin cornbread with butter) accompanied by *turşu kavurması* (pickles); $7.

Ordu is a good place to eat fish: try the **Mıdının Yeri** ($9 including a service charge, unusual for Turkey), on a small pier at the shore.

In **Giresun**, the **Deniz**, on the main square, is very large but always very full ($4). For a more exclusive and tasty experience, search out the **Tibor**, on the 4th and 5th floors of İncedayı Sokak 4, a private club with marble floors and wood-panelled walls and a wide selection of alcohol. Tourists are welcome; $5 for an excellent meal. Alternatively, the top-floor restaurant at the **Hotel Basar** is a pricier but appetising option; the staff are very friendly and may let you sample the Black Sea specialities in the kitchens, such as sargan fish or *dible*—green beans with rice and a little oil.

Getting There and Around

Trabzon can be reached by **bus** or by Turkish Maritime Lines **ferries** from İstanbul. The coastal road is good, but any of the roads over the mountains to the south can be an ordeal in the winter—especially the Zigana Pass south of Trabzon, where silk and spice caravans disappeared regularly in the old days. Trabzon has an **airport**, five miles (8km) out of town, with daily flights to Ankara and İstanbul.

Trabzon is the only city on the coast too large to get around on foot. The **dolmuşes** along Kahramanmaraş Caddesi, connecting the town square with Aya Sofya, can take you to most of the sights (look for destination signs pinned to the windscreen), but to reach the old churches and monasteries of the periphery, it's either a long hike or a taxi ride. The main **bus stops** and **taxi stand** are in the square.

To get to **Sumela** from Trabzon in summer, Ulusoy **buses** leave from the offices on Taksim Caddesi, to the south-east of the main square. **Dolmuşes** run from the south-west corner of Atatürk Alanı. Or you could try getting a few people together to share a **taxi**: the tourist office should be able to help out here.

Trabzon   ***Tourist Information***

Behind the İskender Paşa Camii, next to the Hotel Benli, ℗ 0462 321 4659.

Trabzon, Trebizond, Trapezus: whatever transitions the name has undergone since the merchants of Sinope founded it in the 8th century BC, it has always had an exotic ring to Western ears. When the Greeks first came, they returned with shocking tales of a people called Mosynoecians, practitioners of open-air fornication who lived in wooden castles (they may have been related to the Picts of Scotland). For centuries after the founding of the city, Trapezus was the easternmost limit of the Greek world.

In spite of the difficulty of crossing the steep coastal mountains, Trapezus somehow managed to become an important entrepôt for trade to the east. During the Byzantine period, after trade in the Mediterranean was disrupted by the Arab conquests, all the caravans from Persia and beyond with goods to sell to Europe found their way here. By now the name had become Trebizond, and the city had reached its balmiest days when the Crusaders sacked Constantinople in 1204. Alexis Comnenus, a member of the former dynastic family whose intrigues and corruptions had contributed much to the Byzantine decline, escaped from the fallen city; in his flight he raised an army of mercenaries in Asia from what he had left of the family's wealth, occupied Trebizond and proclaimed it capital of a new empire, headed by himself under the title of Grand Comnenus.

The Comnenes

Alexis had chosen well; his new city was impregnable and brought him a good income, and the Greek population was glad to have him. He and his successors of the Comnenus house brought all the oriental luxury and ceremony of Constantinople with them. Having once more the chance to indulge their fantasies, the Comnenes spread Trebizond's fame throughout the world; in the European geographies and chronicles of the day, it conjured up the same half-legendary aura as did Baghdad or Samarkand. Its military fortunes rose and fell; at its greatest extent it held sway over all the Black Sea coast, but near its end its domains had dwindled to just the city itself. The Comnenes kept their state afloat less by military prowess than by craft, making good use of diplomacy, and ladling out tribute money to the Selcuks, Mongols and Ottomans when words failed. Like the Habsburgs, Comnenes were always careful to marry well; contemporary accounts suggest that the dynasty's greatest resource was cute princesses, much desired by the neighbouring potentates. This allowed the Grand Comneni to keep their web of alliances intact at all times.

By the middle of the 15th century, unfortunately, the only neighbour Trebizond had left was the voracious Ottoman sultan, who already had enough wives. After Mehmet Fatih captured Constantinople, Trebizond, the last free Greek state, was obviously next on his list. Mehmet appeared in 1461, with the greatest army and fleet ever seen in the Black Sea, before or since. It made the desired impression on David Comnenus, the last emperor, who surrendered the city without a shot. The Turks treated Trabzon (as they came to call it) very well, but as Genoa, and later Venice, drew off all the Eastern trade for themselves the city inevitably declined. The Russians did considerable damage when they captured the city in 1916, but Trabzon has been recovering gradually. Today, its port is busy, its suburbs expanding, and best of all, its football team is one of the most successful in Turkey.

The Modern Town

Don't be discouraged by the entrance to the town. The neglect and squalor of the port area and coastal highway, with their vistas of rubbish and broken concrete, is unnerving enough to make visitors pass right by. You have to climb the hill to get into the city, going up İskele Caddesi to the **Meydan** (also known as **Atatürk Alanı**), the main square of the modern city; once up there, you'll be relieved to see that Trabzon is quite an agreeable town after all. The square, with its shady park, city hall and fire station, with shiny red engines out on display for all to admire, is not only the centre of the business district; almost all the hotels and restaurants congregate here as well. Next to the fire station, the 16th-century **İskender Paşa Camii** commemorates a popular Ottoman governor; its shallow dome, curved like an upside-down soup plate, shows Byzantine influence.

Along Kahramanmaraş Caddesi

Either of the two big streets leading west from the square, Kahramanmaraş Caddesi or Hükümet Caddesi (which also appears as Uzun Sokak or Uzun Yol on maps), will take you to the old Greek city, but Kahramanmaraş Caddesi is by far the more interesting. It skirts Trabzon's **bazaar**, a large and colourful district of narrow streets where many of the crafts that once brought Trabzon fame—all manner of work in copper, silver and gold—are still going strong. As is common in Muslim cities, Trabzon sees no need to separate religion and commerce. The attractive 1839 **Çarşı Camii**, right at the heart of the market district, is directly connected to the 16th-century **bedesten**. All around, the maze of blind alleys and old *hanlar* with a talent for somehow looking even older than they really are give the place an air of mystery and impenetrability rare even for a Turkish market.

Further along Kahramanmaraş Caddesi, peering out from a tiny square, stands the oldest Byzantine church left in Trabzon, **Ag. Anna** (Küçük Ayvasıl Kilisesi), built in the 7th century and restored in the 9th. There is something endearing about this plain, forlorn, padlocked little church. The basilica form is unusual in Byzantine buildings—except in Trabzon, a town strictly orthodox in doctrine (St Athanasius himself is said to be buried in Trabzon), but heretical in architecture. The basilica of Ag. Anna set the pattern early, and even when later churches began to sprout domes, Trabzon's churches eschewed the centralized pattern of their counterparts in Constantinople and elsewhere. The plan of Ag. Anna has three parallel naves, the one in the centre raised to form a clerestory with a few small windows.

Old Town and Walls

To get into the old town, find your way back to Hükümet Caddesi. You soon come to the high **Tabakhane Bridge**, and beyond it, a panorama of the walls of Trebizond, rising sheer and hard above the narrow valley. From the bridge it's easy to see how the city got its name. On the opposite side there's a valley and a bridge just like this one, and between them, the old town, which the Turks call the **Kale**, stands up high very like a table—*trapeza* in Greek. Also, you can see how the city got its reputation for impregnability; above the two ravines, picturesquely filled with orchards and market gardens and latterly with ramshackle housing, the cliffs and the walls above them rise as high as 150ft. No army ever actually took Trabzon by force of arms; when the Selcuks under Alâeddin Keykubad tried to, all their assaults failed and their army was washed away in a sudden flood through the ravines.

Long, straight İç Kale Caddesi splits the old town from north to south. Old Trabzon's centre was where the İç Kale meets the roads from the two bridges; today this spot is occupied by a little square full of chairs and sleepy Turks, between the Vilayet and the **Ortahisar Camii**. This latter is as plain and severe as a mosque as it was as the Panayia Chrysokephalos, the 'Church of the Golden-headed Virgin', built by the Comneni in the 13th century. Behind it, along the western edge of the walls, once stood the **Palace of the Comneni**, of which nothing remains except a few arches and sections of wall between the houses of the district. Nor is much left at the southern end of the İç Kale, where the offices of the Trebizond state and army had their quarters, at the highest and least vulnerable end of the 'table'.

Byzantine Monuments

If you follow İç Kale Caddesi beyond the walls to the south, you will enjoy the best view of the city and its extensions up the surrounding hillsides. From out here, you can pick out three other Byzantine monuments in the steep neighbourhoods south of Atatürk Alanı—they will thus be easier to find if you wish to visit them. Following Boztepe Caddesi south takes you to two of them. **Ag. Eugenios** was one of the first works of the Comneni after their arrival, built on the site of an older church and dedicated to Trebizond's patron saint. Mehmet Fatih converted it into a mosque on the first Friday after his conquest of the city, and it has been called **Yeni Cuma Cami** (New Friday Mosque) ever since. On the other side of the hill called Boztepe stands the **Teokephastos Monastery** of the same period. One of the last churches to be built, the 14th-century Ag. Philipi, is now the **Kudrettin Mosque**. Further out, on a dirt track on the back slope of Boztepe, the little-known **Kaymaklı Monastery** contains some fascinating Armenian frescoes. Some, like the *Last Judgement* and scenes from the *Apocalypse*, go back to the 15th century. Now in use as a barn, Kaymaklı is extremely hard to find and at present the owner does not always admit tourists; ask at the tourist office.

Leaving the Kale over the western **Zagnos Bridge**, you soon find yourself in another pleasant square, with mighty plane trees surrounding Trabzon's finest Islamic work, the **Hatuniye Camii**, built by Sultan Selim I in honour of his mother; her tomb stands just outside the entrance. A surviving stretch of the city's **outer walls** can be seen nearby, running parallel to the street that leads to the seashore.

Aya Sofya

If Trabzon's most famous building must be mentioned last, it is only because it's the furthest from the centre, a good mile's walk or dolmuş ride from the Kale. Set on a little hill planted with roses, above the awful but fortunately invisible coastal highway, stands the **Aya Sofya Church**. Even though Trabzon, before 1920, had one of the largest Greek populations in Asia Minor, this church had been neglected for centuries, and was on the verge of collapse when a team of archaeologists went to work on it in the 1950s. Many parts, including the soaring cylindrical dome, have been almost completely reconstructed, but, more importantly, the original frescoes have been recovered from beneath the plaster and restored. Today, the frescoes are Trabzon's greatest tourist attraction, the finest late Byzantine art east of İstanbul.

The Aya Sofya is a building of much architectural interest, but not in the way you might expect. Most of the elements of a Byzantine church are there—the dome, the small apses and the vestiges of a central cross plan—but it seems that after so many centuries (over a millennium of Greek Christian architecture) inspiration finally gave out. Emperor Manuel Comnenus had the church built in 1245, one of the last great buildings the Greeks made when time was running out for them in Anatolia. Between the Romanesque arches, the Western-style naves with their barrel-vaulted ceilings, and the sculptural frieze of *Adam and Eve* on the south porch, there are almost as many West European and Armenian elements in the design as Byzantine. What the builders lacked, the artists more than made up for; Aya Sofya's vivid 13th-century **frescoes**, with their perfection of line and colour, have a special place in the story of the last Byzantine renaissance, the efflorescence of painting in the Greek twilight whose influence helped make possible Western Europe's own Renaissance.

Almost half of all the original paintings survived sufficiently to be restored. The best, perhaps, are those in the narthex, various scenes of miracles from the life of Jesus. There are many other familiar themes: the Annunciation, and the four Evangelists with their attributes. The Virgin Mary in the Ascension takes her place in the central apse, while a huge, half-effaced figure of the Christ Pantocrator looms over all from the dome. Most unfortunately, another scene in the porch, which depicts the Last Judgement in the manner of Bosch or Brueghel, is almost completely lost; among the remnants a lone wolf devouring souls can be made out. In the grounds of the church, a quaint tea garden operates around a traditional Black Sea farmhouse with a raised granary.

Atatürk's villa, the **Atatürk Köşkü** (*open daily 9–5; adm*), presides over a wooded slope of pines, three miles (5km) south-west of Trabzon (take a city bus, dolmuş or taxi). This moulded white concoction was constructed between 1890 and 1903 and presented to Kemal in 1931 after he expressed an interest on one of his three visits to Trabzon. After his death in 1938, the municipality appropriated the villa and subsequently turned it into a museum, with endless Atatürk memorabilia throughout, and objects in even the smallest nook and cranny paying homage to the great man. A huge billiard table greets you upon entry, resting on tiled floors redolent of William Morris, accompanied by some wonderfully solid 1930s furniture. The gardens are a peaceful spot, with a pleasant tea garden set in the pines and a restaurant next door.

South of Trabzon

The Zigana Pass

Even if you intend to push on to the end of the coast, the temptation to turn inland will be strong here; the Trabzon–Erzurum road, the last stretch of the Silk Route in the days of the Comneni, is today one of the few good roads over the steep eastern Black Sea Mountains between Samsun and Artvin. Over Zigana Pass, climbing up to 6,300ft, the road ascends more sharply, contorts along more hairpin turns and looks down over more bottomless cliffs than any mountain road you've ever seen. For your trouble, the views will be reward enough; all around, the slopes and crags are covered with forests and banks of wild flowers, at least until the treeline is crossed, which is shortly before the eternal snows of the pass. (The rest of this route is described under Erzurum, pp.475–6.)

Sumela Monastery

From the wilderness of Judea to the cloudy heights of Mount Athos, the predilection of the Greek Orthodox church has always been for monasteries perched high and precariously, fortresses in the sky that free their inhabitants from unnecessary exposure to the world below. Nowhere in Turkey is this better exemplified than at the **Sumela Monastery**, 27 miles (43km) east of Trabzon near the pretty village of Maçka. It's a remarkable sight, 1,000ft above a deep valley kept verdant by a bubbling river, the white walls of its façade standing out sharply from the sheer grey cliff in which it is embedded. Sumela was founded in the 4th century when a monk, having received divine instruction in a dream, brought to the cliff's caves an icon of the Virgin painted by the Apostle Luke. The original structure was modest but, as increasing numbers of monks came to pray before the icon and to invoke miracles from it, the complex was extended, often with the assistance of the Byzantine Emperors. By the 14th century its power and influence was second only to that of Mount Athos. Yet this eminence collapsed within the space of a year, after the fiasco of the Greek invasion and the subsequent population exchange of 1923 resulted in its monks being expelled en masse. The holy icon was spirited away to Athens and gradually, inexorably, Sumela began to crumble.

Which is why, today, the actual complex may well prove disappointing. The steep climb up to the monastery ends in a series of gutted shells, defaced by the scrawl of graffiti. Only the cave in which Luke's icon was stored has been spared, and that merely in part; sealed off by an iron grill, some of the frescoes that once beautified its interior can still be discerned. You may even wonder why you've bothered puffing hard up the cliff side at all; the answer is to be found looking out across the valley, at one of the loveliest vistas in all Turkey.

The surrounding region was once rich in convents and monasteries but today only two are left, both in appalling condition—**Peristera**, 22 miles (35km) from Trabzon and **Vazelon**, south of Maçka. Both are very difficult to reach and of interest only to serious Byzantine monastery buffs.

East of Trabzon

Tourist Information

Rize: on the 5th floor of the Valilik, to the west of town, © 0464 213 0407.

East of Trabzon, the Empire of Tea truly begins. By now, even if you've spent only a little time in Turkey, you'll have had countless glasses of tea thrust in front of you; it all comes from these green mountain slopes. Demand is high, and this far corner of the nation has become quite prosperous in a modest way. Around Rize you will notice that the women wear a very distinctive costume consisting of the *keşan*, a vertically striped black and purple or black and tan apron worn over a skirt; and the *peştemal*, a very attractive multicoloured shawl. Both these garments can be tied up to form a pouch for harvesting hazelnuts. Many of the people are Laz, a folk of obscure Caucasian origins who have been here a long time without causing any trouble; you see the old men in the cafés and buses, with their berets, big moustaches, and long watch-chains, eternally jolly and easy-going; the Turks secretly envy them. Many others are Georgians; the Republic of Georgia is just across the border.

Rize, the capital of the tea region, barely squeezes in between the mountains and the sea. Here, behind the tea slopes, mountains comprising the **Kaçkar** chain rise as high as 12,500ft. Approximately 28 miles (45km) to the east of Rize is Ardeşen and a turning to **Çamlıhemşin** and **Ayder**. Both these villages are set in magnificent mountain scenery and are suitable starting points for walks and climbs. Near Çamlıhemşin are the **Valley of Storms** (Fırtına Vadisi), and **Zil Castle** (Kale-i Zir).

It is possible to arrange a visit to one of the many tea factories lining the main road round Rize and Hopa. But beware: the strong smell of the fermenting leaves may well turn your stomach, and if you are offered a cup of tea, ask for it *açık* ('open', i.e. weak). The tea workers favour tea so strong and stewed it can act as an emetic for those not used to it.

Once you have reached **Hopa**, there is nowhere to go apart from Artvin or back to Rize. The Georgian border some 20 miles (30km) away is not worth a visit. The road from Hopa to Artvin is very scenic, climbing to the Esenbel pass. At Borçka the road crosses the River Çoruh, rapidly making its way to Batum in Georgia.

Trabzon and Around   ***Where to Stay***

Trabzon

In Trabzon most hotels are around the main square, making them convenient but often rather noisy.

luxury

With the opening up of the former Soviet Union to trade and travel, Trabzon has metamorphosed from a neglected provincial backwater to a vital stepping stone to the east. Concrete proof of this has come with the recent building of the ★★★★★**Zorlu Grand Hotel**, Kahramanmaraş Caddesi 9, ✆ 0462 326 8400, ✉ 0462 326 8458, *zorlu@zorlugrand.com*. It's stylish and impressive, with a sweeping marble double staircase leading up to a luxurious reception area the size of a small aircraft hangar. Rooms are similarly airy and well-upholstered, costing $160 a night.

moderate

The nicest mid-range hotel is the ★★★**Usta**, İskenderpaşa Mah. 3, ✆ 0462 326 5700, ✉ 0462 322 3793, *hotelusta@escortnet.com*, which has particularly helpful and attentive staff. Good doubles with air-con and bathtubs go for $50. Almost as good is the ★★★**Horon**, just north of Atatürk Alanı at Sıramağazalar 125, ✆ 0462 326 6455, ✉ 0462 321 6628. Its tatty façade belies a pleasant lobby, with two modern oil paintings showing what the management claims was Trabzon in 1880 and 1940, although the romanticized depictions look more like Trebizond *c.* 1400. Bedrooms are similar to those at the Usta, but those facing north are probably the quietest you'll find in the city. The live music in the top-floor restaurant may not be to everyone's taste. Doubles $50.

inexpensive–cheap

Trabzon has a good selection of cheap hotels, amongst which the **Nur**, next to the İskenderpaşa Camii at Cami Sokak 4, ✆ 0462 321 2798, ✉ 0462 321 9576, is the best. The staff are very friendly, the en suite rooms compact but bright. Rooms on the top floor have good Black Sea views, but are also exactly level with the nearby minaret's loudspeakers, so much so that you can hear the muezzin swallow before commencing his call to prayer. $20 per double.

The cheapie nearest to the Kale is the **London Palas** at Kahramanmaraş Caddesi 71, ✆ 0462 326 5426, with clean, spartan rooms for $22; those at the back escape most of the traffic noise, but are on the dark side. The best deal in town is at the **Yuvan** on Güzelhisar Caddesi to the north-east of Atatürk Alanı, ✆ 0462 326 6823; pleasant en suite roms, some with views of the harbour, for only $14. Next door is the **Anıl**, ✆ 0462 326 7282, offering more of the same for $22.

Rize and Hopa

A good stopover option in Rize is the ★★**Keleş Oteli**, Palandöken Caddesi 2, ✆ 0404 217 4612, with doubles for $35, more or less. The **Otel Akarsu**, off Atatürk Meydanı near the Şehir Hamamı, ✆ 0464 217 1779, is clean and good value, at $6 per person for a room without bath.

In Hopa the ★★**Papila**, ✆ 0466 351 3641, and the **Cihan**, ✆ 0466 351 4897, are two nice hotels, both priced at around $30 for a double.

Trabzon and Around   **Eating Out**

Trabzon

The **Özgür** restaurant ($8) attracts most tour groups, but there are other good, cheap restaurants, such as the **Kibris** on the main square ($4). The décor is much nicer upstairs than downstairs and you can also enjoy the view of the square. On the south-east corner of the square, the **Çınar Restaurant** sells freshly cooked dishes made from local meat and produce; for now at least it's as busy and as cheap as the McDonald's next door. At Kahramanmaraş Caddesi 5, the never-ending climb upstairs to the rooftop **Şişman Restaurant** will be rewarded with excellent inexpensive food ($5 for a kebab, salad and a beer). The **Gelik Lokantası**, Hükümet Caddesi 84, west of the square, offers a very wide selection from steam trays, at an average price of $2.

Around Trabzon

You can eat *al fresco* overlooking Trabzon at the **Piknik** on the hill of Boztepe. Equally nice is the **Kavaklık Restaurant** on the coastal road east of town.

Rize and **Hopa** have basic lokantas.

Tao-Georgia

The far northeastern corner of Turkey is wild and inaccessible territory. These lands are the former marchlands of a great kingdom, Georgia, now an independent republic on Turkey's eastern border. The former principalities of Tao and Klarjeti in the southwest of the ancient Transcaucasian kingdom today lie in Turkey, and make up the area known as Tao-Georgia (nothing to do with Chinese philosophy).

All that remains of the Georgians is their churches, beautiful in both themselves and in their settings. Built in the 9th to 11th centuries, many of the churches are nevertheless in a quite remarkable state of preservation. The architecture is similar to Armenian, but less sombre; typical features are tall naves, usually crowned with a drum and dome, and carvings of animals inspired by the Persian bestiary.

In this little-visited area the imagination easily gets out of control. You can feel like a pioneer, believing you are the only tourist ever to have slogged to a particular site, and play the 19th-century traveller discovering antiquities. The churches lie off the beaten track, some of them in *yaylalar* (summer villages) and accessible only after a strenuous walk of an hour or so. However, take heart, you are never far from the sound of running water. You can be toiling up an inhospitable mountainside, with the sound of the river below echoing up the valley, when you round a corner and come across the church sitting in a green oasis of fruit trees with a little stream running next to the path.

The Georgians

One of the most ancient **Christian** nations, Georgia was converted to the new faith in the 4th century by St Nino, a female missionary from Cappadocia who, fleeing from the Great Persecution of Diocletian, had earlier converted the Armenians. Georgia was fought over by the Byzantines and the Persians and even came under the control of Arab caliphs before settling down to be a relatively stable feudal state, ruled over by a branch of the Armenian **Bagratid** family, who claimed descent from King David of Israel.

During the reign of King David the Great of Taik (a southern province, with its capital at Oltu), the **kingdom of Georgia** extended as far as Van. David, who died in 1001, was also a great church builder and his work was carried on by his descendants, particularly King David the Restorer, who subjugated the feudal lords and defeated the Selcuks, regaining control of Tiflis (now in the Republic of Georgia). He died in 1125, after which there was relative stability for the rest of the century. Under the leadership of Queen Tamara (who reigned from 1144 to 1212), Georgia waxed into its golden age and became influential as well as stable. Tamara was an able diplomat with an expansionist foreign policy. She captured Kars and harassed northern Persia. But the **Mongols** arrived early in the 13th century and the Tao-Georgians gradually converted to Islam; by the end of the 17th century, Christianity had almost died out in the area, leaving the churches to the elements.

Given how isolated the villages are, you might expect still to find Georgian (*Gürcü* in Turkish) speakers; but no, they are always in a village 'over there'.

Artvin can be reached by **bus** from Trabzon (via Hopa), Erzurum and Kars. A **minibus** will take you from the present bus depot beside the Çoruh River up a series of hairpin bends to the centre of town, the Hükümet Konağı (Government House), from where everything lies within walking distance. Once the huge **dam project** in the valley below Artvin is completed, the bus depot will move much further up the hill to avoid the rising waters.

Yusufeli is connected to Artvin by regular **minibuses**, although the last one from Yusufeli often leaves at lunchtime. Less regular services connect Yusufeli to Erzurum and Trabzon.

The Georgian churches are scattered over the area and it is difficult to see more than two or three in one day, even if you have your own car. A **taxi** can be hired for the day from Artvin; agree on a price before setting out. **Buses** travel regularly along all the main roads, leaving Artvin from the depot at the foot of the town, so a cheaper alternative would be to catch a bus to Yusufeli or Ardanuç and get a taxi there. Even cheaper, get off the bus at the turning to the church and walk—but you won't have time to see much.

Tourist Information

Artvin: Cami Meydanı, ✆ 0466 212 3071.

The River Çoruh

The region is dominated by river valleys which provide the key to its charm, isolation and history. The River Çoruh and its tributaries such as the Tortum, Berta and Oltu are fast-flowing mountain rivers that have sliced through the rocks, making steep-sided gorges that reveal multicoloured rock strata. The valleys are littered with castles perched high on rocky outcrops, bearing testimony that times here have not always been as peaceful as they are now. Two of the largest castles, at Artvin and Ardahan, were built by Selim the Grim in the 16th century when the Ottomans were consolidating their power in the northeast. Other castles can be seen at Ardanuç and near Şavşat.

Look out for the picturesque wooden footbridges and for 'basket'-type bridges, where people haul themselves along a rope or wire while standing on a platform. Stone bridges are few and far between; there is an attractive one across the Berta.

In the valley below Artvin, work is underway on one of six **hydro-electric dams** being constructed in the north-east. Once the project is finished, the resultant lake's fingers will stretch across much of the region, as far as Şavşat and Borçka.

Artvin and Around

Artvin is a charming little provincial capital perched high on a mountainside, with a very pleasant, relaxed atmosphere, despite the narrow streets coughing with traffic for much of the day. Many of the women of the town walk freely in European dress with heads uncovered—surprising in a town so far east and so small (just over 20,000 inhabitants). It is impossible to confuse these women with the 'natashas', heavily dolled-up Russian prostitutes who have been drawn westwards since 1991 by the honeypot of Turkey's (relatively) buoyant economy. By the mid-1990s, their presence had reached epidemic proportions, but now, though they are still evident in Artvin and nearby towns such as Rize, their numbers are on the wane.

One delightful aspect of Artvin is the **pastry shops**; there are several along the main road (İnönü Caddesi), all of excellent quality. You can join in the Turkish habit of a late afternoon stroll, admiring the views of the valley, and finish with a cup of coffee and a cake or an ice cream. Artvin is also famous for its annual **bull-fighting** festival at Kafkasor in late June. However, the main reason for visiting Artvin is to use it as a base for trips to the **Georgian churches** which have survived in the valleys of this isolated region.

The alternative base is **Yusufeli**, a village nestling next to the Barhal river, slower paced and more tranquil than Artvin but with only basic accommodation on offer. In season, streetside stalls sell the biggest cabbages you're ever likely to see, the size and weight of medicine balls. This welcoming and relaxing village is also a base for many outdoor activities: rafting down 'plus five' rapids in May–August, or hiking in the Kaçkar mountains, including four-day treks to the 3,937m summit of Mount Kaçkar itself. Experienced canoeists and rock-climbers will have no lack of rivers deep and mountains high to keep them busy. (All of these activities can be organized by the **Kaçkar Outdoor Sports Centre**, run by two brothers, Özkan and Fatih Şahin, ✆ 0466 811 2393, 🖷 0466 811 3393.)

Haho and Öşk Vank

These are the two largest churches in the area, both monastery churches of cruciform plan, with a circular drum surmounted by the typical conical roof, and both built in the late 10th century by David the Great. Both can be visited from either Artvin or Erzurum as they lie roughly equidistant from these two towns, just off the main road. Haho hides in the sprawling village of **Bağbaşı**, while Öşk Vank forms the centrepiece of the compact village of **Çamlıyamaç**. The turnings to Bağbaşı and Çamlıyamaç are signposted, respectively about six miles (10km) and 12 miles (20km) north of Tortum. Both churches are little more than three miles (5km) from the main road and can be reached by car up reasonable dirt roads.

Haho is now in use as a mosque and remains in good repair. It is possible to see the interior—ask for the *bekçi* who will unlock the door for you. Some frescoes remain, particularly a large cross and star design on the ceiling of the dome, and four apostles and an angel on the apse. The predominant colour is blue. The exterior of the church is decorated with some fine carving, including on the south front a magnificent eagle grasping a small deer in its huge talons. The columns that ornament the drum and windows are delicately fluted and twisted, and topped by interestingly carved capitals. The designs are varied: geometric, floral, of birds and animals or of fruit such as pears and mulberries—particularly appropriate as the church is now surrounded by an orchard, in which you can see some remains of the other monastery buildings.

The very grand church of **Öşk Vank** is larger than Haho and more highly decorated. It is not currently in use as a mosque, and is consequently in disrepair, with parts of the roof missing. The south façade is most impressive, with a large entrance porch flanked by blind arches with a fan design carved into the top. A small chapel is attached to the south wall to the west of the porch. The exterior is decorated with much carving, including an eagle clutching a deer, as at Haho, and two angels—both headless—on the south wall, another headless angel on the west wall of the chapel, and a bull and a lion on the north wall. Again, as at Haho, the capitals of the columns that decorate the windows and drum are worth inspecting—the drum has a charming pair of kissing rabbits. The interior is well decorated with relief carving, some of the columns being carved from head to toe. The interior also contains fragments of frescoes showing biblical scenes. You can see here what Georgian letters look like—some of the frescoes have inscriptions, and there is a long painted inscription inside the porch above the south door. The ruins of another building lie to the northeast of the church.

Barhal and Dörtkilise

Further north, in the Çoruh valley, these two churches provide an architectural contrast to Öşk Vank and Haho. Instead of a dome, they have tall, steeply roofed naves, flanked by two aisles. The exterior of both churches is decorated by blind arcades and some carving. Barhal also has some exterior terracotta decoration. Both these churches were built in the 10th century. Barhal is now used as a mosque, Dörtkilise as a barn. To get to Barhal, drive first to Yusufeli, then up into the mountains to Sarıgöl and continue along the Barhal stream to the church. Dörtkilise can be reached after a drive of about three miles (5km) along the Yusufeli–Bayburt road, followed by a two-hour walk.

İşhan

İşhan lies just off the Yusufeli–Oltu road, a little after the turning to Erzurum. A new asphalt road (stabilised for the last few miles) goes direct to İşhan, winding up a mountainside so bare you wonder how people can possibly live up here. Then, after about three miles of desert, suddenly round a corner is the green village of İşhan, full of children, shade and fruit.

İşhan is a cathedral church, very elegant and similar in type and size to Haho. It has had a chequered architectural history: it was founded in the 7th century, rebuilt at the beginning of the 9th and converted in the 11th to a domed church with a lengthened west wing. The church is in good condition; the roof has gone but the walls and drum are intact. The oldest part of the church is the apse, which has an unusual arcade concentric with the wall of the apse. The arches are horseshoe-shaped and are supported on capitals carved with rosette and floral reliefs. Some frescoes remain, including one in an alcove above a window, showing a black-faced man carrying a church that could be either Barhal or Dörtkilise. The exterior of the drum is decorated with columns and a terracotta motif. The west and east fronts have blind arches, some with a fan design at the top, as at Öşk Vank. Many of the windows and doors are surrounded with fine relief carving, one showing a lion and a snake taunting each other, and a couple with lengthy Georgian inscriptions.

Yeni Rabat

The chief charm of this little church is its setting, in a cabbage patch on a lush green alpine mountainside reminiscent of Switzerland. Yeni Rabat can be reached by taking the road to Ardanuç across the Berta Bridge. The road passes along a steep-sided gorge known locally as **Cehennem Deresi** (Hell Valley). After Ardanuç—formerly the capital of Tao-Georgia, but now a pleasant village guarded by a ruined castle—take the road to Ardahan. This is not asphalt, and when it rains (and it rains often in Artvin province), it turns to mud. Some 7½ miles (12km) from Ardanuç is a yellow sign to Yeni Rabat, pointing to a field of flowers. After a stiff climb of a quarter of an hour, you get your first glimpse of the church and the summer village of four houses. The church is in relatively good condition, with the drum and dome and much of the roof still intact. Although the exterior has lost many of its dressing stones, some very worn decorative carving remains. The windows are framed with geometric relief carvings. Some stones seem to have been placed at random, as though they have been reused from former buildings, and there are some curious carvings looking like mushrooms or bundles of corn. The church, originally part of a monastery, was built in the 9th century.

Dolişhane and Porta

Both these churches lie just off the Artvin–Şavşat road, above the valley of the River Berta. **Dolişhane** is in the village of **Hamamlı** and can be reached by car; the turning is on the right bank of the river, opposite Berta Bridge. The little church was built in the early 10th century and remains in good condition. Fragments of frescoes remain in the apse; these show figures labelled in Georgian. Outside, on the south wall is a nice sundial, a common feature of both Georgian and Armenian churches. Some of the windows are decorated with carving; one has an inscription, a star of David and two angels.

Only the fit and strong should attempt to visit **Porta**. About 28 miles (45km) along the Artvin–Şavşat road, a small yellow sign points to a pretty little waterfall. The path to Porta starts by the waterfall, then winds up the mountainside, past dwarf oaks and pomegranate trees. After a strenuous climb of about an hour, just when you feel you can go no further, you will be rewarded by the sight of the church in the middle of a charming summer village of wooden houses. The village, inhabited only in August, appears untouched since the 19th century. The electric cables visible are for the winter village, a further two-mile climb away, but which can be reached by car from Şavşat. The church itself, although more ruined than some of the others, is picturesque none the less; the drum is unusual, being connected to the dome in a zigzag pattern. To the west is a small drum and dome, now used as a store for hay. To the south of the church are the remains of a large building with several small rooms with barrel vault ceilings. There is a theory that Porta is not Georgian, but Genoese; but Porta seems to be only slightly different from the others.

Artvin and Around   **Where to Stay**

With the exception of Artvin, accommodation in the far northeastern corner is sparse and simple.

Artvin

The most comfortable hotel in Artvin is the **★★Karahan**, ✆ 0466 212 1800, ✉ 0466 212 2420, on the main road, İnönü Caddesi. Most rooms have baths and cost $32 for a double. The hotel, which occupies the top four floors of a shopping centre, has splendid views of the town and valley; it is owned by two brothers, one of whom is a keen photographer and local historian. Unfortunately, even the Karahan is not immune to the allure of the steady income provided by the natasha trade. With not enough tourists to go round, hotels in Artvin face a real dilemma: succumb to natashas or go bust.

On Hamam Sokak, just behind İnönü Caddesi, the **Kaçkar**, ✆ 0466 212 3397, has double rooms with TV and few frills for $16; ask for one of the rooms on the top floor, which have excellent views.

Yusufeli

Accommodation here is cheap, cheerful and natasha-free. The **Barhal**, ✆ 0466 811 3151, has the best location, next to the bridge over the hotel's namesake river, with many rooms overlooking it. It's also the cleanest place in town, and en suite rooms are only $8.

camping

Across Yusufeli's bridge and a short walk along the river are two basic camping sites. **Greenpeace Camping**, ✆ 0466 811 2271, has the edge over **Akın Camping**.

Artvin and Around   **Eating Out**

The restaurants in **Artvin** are few and simple, but the pastry shops are excellent. The restaurant in the **Karahan Hotel** serves good 'real' food and not just the wretched grills that most hotels think they can get away with. A meal at the Karahan will cost about $6 per person. Opposite the hotel is the **Hanedan Restaurant**, which is worth a stop if you can get one of the tables at the window with panoramic views of the mountains and valley. Meals about $5.

In **Yusufeli**, the **Mahzen Restaurant** opposite the Hotel Bahal by the suspension bridge has tables overlooking the river; basic meals for $3; alcohol is also served.

If you want a good, cheap lunch while visiting the Georgian churches, plan your trip so that you are in **Ardanuç** around lunchtime. The village, despite having a population of fewer than 3,500, has an excellent lokanta, the **Lezzet Lokantası**, located just off the village square. It is modest but clean with a good range of tasty food— '*lezzet*' means 'taste'. A light lunch will cost you $3 or less.

Northwestern Anatolia

This is the real Anatolia: a stark, rough-edged, land, where bleak and empty vastnesses change in a twinkling to little green paradises and spectacular mountain scenery. The Anatolian interior still often seems like a country for explorers. Everywhere, you will see the fine caravanserais built for merchants by the medieval Selcuk sultans— and reflect that some of them were still in use in this century. This is the Turkey of sheep and shepherds and donkey carts, carpet weavers and whirling dervishes, an ageless and endlessly fascinating place. But it is modernizing along with the rest of the country, and you won't have to travel like an explorer; getting around by bus is as fast and convenient as on the coasts, and there are good hotels and places to eat almost everywhere.

To Kastamonu

To Sinop

Samsun

Merzifon

Lake Borabay

Suluova

Çankırı

Çorum

Amasya

Niksar

Esenboğa
Airport

Sungurlu

Alacahöyük

Zile

Turhal

To Erzincan

ANKARA

Delice

Yazılıkaya

Boğazkale

Tokat

Çamlıbel
Pass

To Erzincan

Elmadağ
Park

Mt. Çiçekdağ

Hattuşaş

Yozgat

Sivas

Kızılırmak River

To Divriği

To Kayseri

To Kayseri

To Kangal

To Cappadocia

To Malatya

Ancient Phrygia: Eskişehir to Gordion

Once you get to know the Phrygians, you'll wish they were still around. They had style. Just enough of their art survives to make us wish we could see more—the way they dressed and decorated their houses. And we would love to hear some of their famous music, played on lyres, cymbals and flutes in the weird, wailing 'Phrygian mode'. Musicologists would give anything for a chance; it was the foundation of the music of the classical Greeks. The Greeks may even have learned their alphabet from these talented people. Besides music, the Phrygians were famous for their roses (Midas, like King Cyrus of Persia, was one of the legendary gardeners of antiquity), for embroidery and for woven wool carpets.

The tantalizing fragments of this lost culture are well worth a visit, but it will not necessarily be easy. The three modern cities of the region—Eskişehir, Kütahya and Afyon—are all some distance away from the main sights.

Couldn't be simpler. Eskişehir, Kütahya and Afyon are all connected by rail and bus to İstanbul and İzmir. **Train** stations in these cities are within easy walking distance of the centres. As always though, **buses** are the better deal. The otogar in Eskişehir is two miles from the town centre, in Afyon just over a mile out, and in Kütahya only half a mile.

Çavdarhisar, with the ruins of Aizanoi, is easy to reach from Kütahya. There are village **minibuses**, and most Uşak- or İzmir-bound **buses** stop in the village's otogar (make sure you ask beforehand where they stop so you don't get left on the highway, 4km from the village).

Tourist Information

Eskişehir: Vilayet Binası (provincial government office), © 0222 230 1752.

Kütahya: Fuatpaşa Caddesi, in the centre, © 0274 223 1962. There is also a booth in the central Azerbaijan Park (*open summer only*).

Afyon: 2nd floor, Hükümet Konaği, © 0272 213 5447.

Eskişehir

To make up for what nature has denied this land, the Turkish Government has spent a considerable part of its development effort here. As a result, Eskişehir, the provincial capital, has grown up to become one of Turkey's largest cities. It's a joke among people here that Yenişehir ('new town') to the northwest is a crumbling old village, while Eskişehir ('old town') has become a thoroughly modern city, grown wealthy enough from its manufacture of locomotives and meerschaum pipes to water its streets twice a day to keep down the dust—and they need it. This is one of a very few places on earth where **meerschaum** is found (*meerschaum*—German 'sea-foam'—is a direct translation from the Persian *kef-i-daryâ*; it's a hydrous silicate of magnesium), and when you see any of it in tourist shops elsewhere in Turkey, the chances are it was mined and crafted here. Finely carved pipes and walking sticks can be bought very cheaply in a number of shops around town.

In ancient times, this was the Greek-Phrygian city of Dorylaeum, whose scant remains can be seen around the Selcuk castle northwest of the town. Some quite interesting examples of grave steles and columns of Dorylaeum are on display at Eskişehir's **Archaeological Museum**. On the eastern edge of the city is the 16th-century **Kurşunlu Mosque**, a complex attributed to Mimar Sinan. Eskişehir is a pleasant and animated city; the Porsuk Çayı (Beaver Creek) and its tributaries and canals run all through it, crossed by hundreds of little bridges, but it hasn't much to show the visitor.

Kütahya

Kütahya, a prosperous and amiable city that spreads under an Ottoman castle, would be unremarkable but for its **ceramics**, one of the great craft traditions of Turkey. You'll notice it as soon as you arrive; the bus station is the prettiest in Turkey, with pillars tiled from floor to ceiling. Hotels, shops and even bars in the modern town have façades covered in Kütahya tiles, and all the main streets are lined with showrooms for the scores of workshops in and around the city. The first to practise the art here were Persians, brought as captives by Selim the Grim in 1514. While the art of ceramics declined in İznik in the 18th century, Kütahya seized the opportunity to fill the gap, and now makes fine china and faïence in classic Ottoman patterns, as well as architectural tiles, used in the restorations of all the old mosques. If you are looking for something besides carpets to take home, Kütahya is well worth a stop. You can window-shop conveniently or go in and have a cup of tea; quality is high and prices relatively low, in everything from simple vases and plates to urns the size of refrigerators for your favourite paşa's seraglio. Once you have ogled at a few *çiniler*, you will see that there is a vast range of quality and price, from low-grade souvenir shop trinkets right up to hand-painted masterpieces.

Güven Çini, along Atatürk Bulvarı, has a reasonable selection of factory-printed tiles and ceramics, as well as some handmade pieces. But the best quality and range of factory tiles are to be had at **Altın Çini**; ask at their Belediye Meydanı boutique (© 0274 212 2975, 🖷 0274 216 3731) to see their nearby workshop and warehouse, which also houses a fine collection of hand-painted ceramics. In the workshop, row upon row of young apprentices sit, absorbed in their intricate painting. Some of the painters make a strange sight, plugged into the privacy of their blaring Walkmans, delicately tracing sacred Koranic script onto vases and tiles which rest on old tabloid newspapers full of semi-clad beauties. If you are interested in seeing masterworks, visit the affable Mehmet Gürsoy at his **İznik Çini**, Atatürk Bulvarı; much of his work is covered in especially beautiful tulip motifs (his symbol, and also a stylised form of 'Allah' in traditional script.)

Kütahya was the ancient *Cotiaeum*, a town several times destroyed and rebuilt, most recently by Mehmet the Conqueror; he captured it from another, more obscure Turkish tribe called the Germaniyids, for whom Kütahya served as capital. It has a few Ottoman mosques of its own, notably the 15th-century **Ulu Cami**, in a pretty garden at the end of Cumhuriyet Caddesi, the street that leads from the centre through Kütahya's bazaar district. The medrese adjoining the mosque, built by the Germaniyids, now houses Kütahya's little **museum** (*open Tues–Sun 8–12 and 1.30–5.30; adm*), a reminder that one should never pass up a provincial museum in any Turkish town, no matter how obscure. The best ones are dusty curiosity shops, like Kütahya's, that offer some genuine treasures of ancient art: surprises here include some painted geometric pots from Hacılar (some of the oldest in the world), fine grave steles with the death's door motif common on the southern coast, a big flashy Hellenistic sarcophagus with a *Battle of the Amazons*, and some unique terracotta ex votos: a weird triple-formed Hecate with torches (she was the underworld patroness of witches who was worshipped at Colophon and in Caria), and another, unidentified, goddess fondling her flowing tresses, with a bird in her other hand, a small boy by her side, and a snake emerging from her genitals. There are several versions of her; the later ones, from Roman times, are at least decently covered.

In the older neighbourhoods, on the slopes around the Ulu Cami, are many lovely Ottoman wooden houses, some of which have been restored. One of them can be visited, the **Kossuth Evi**, where Lajos Kossuth, the romantic leader of Hungary's 1848 fight for independence, spent part of his subsequent exile (at the time the Hungarians, like the Poles, were natural friends of Ottoman Turkey, having common enemies in Austria and Russia). Today the interior has been recreated as it was at the time Kossuth lived there. From nearby a track leads up to the ruined **castle**, begun under the Byzantines.

From Kütahya, the first slopes of a broad massif called **Türkmen Dağı** rise up over the horizon, stretching off to the east. On its opposite slope, in difficult hill country, is the source of the Sakarya River. There you will also find Midas City and nearly a dozen temple façades and tombs in the heartland of ancient Phrygia. There is no way over the mountain, unfortunately, and adventurous souls desiring to explore Phrygia must start from Eskişehir or **Afyon** to the south. Paved roads from either city will carry you 50 or 60 miles into the area, but then, if you're not driving, you will be at the mercy of whatever taxi drivers you can find in the villages of Seyitgazi or İhsaniye.

Aizanoi's Temple of Zeus

Aizanoi (*Aezani* in Turkish), an important town in Greek and Roman times, stood 22 miles (36km) southwest of Kütahya, near the present-day village of Çavdarhisar (the 'rye castle'). Almost nothing remains of it—nothing except the best-preserved ancient temple in Turkey. The Temple of Zeus is also one of the largest, almost 100ft across the bottom of its podium, and one of the last to be built—in the 2nd century, during the reign of Hadrian. Despite the fashion of the day for the Corinthian order, the temple is Ionian, showing the Roman preference for tall elevations and narrow columns.

Most of these columns and half the walls of the cella still stand. Parts of the frieze connecting the tops of the columns are present as well, though the pediment and roof are long gone. This pediment had been decorated at its peaks and corners with huge *acroteria*, carved stone acanthus leaves, and bits of these lie on the ground. Hadrian's reign was one of the better times for Asia Minor and the rest of the empire, when both prosperity and building talent were still undiminished. The style of the temple may have been thought old-fashioned when it was built, and less charitable critics today may find it lacking in inspiration—it has something of the air of a 1920s bank building, erected by men to whom art no longer came easily, but who did their best to strive for a quiet tastefulness. The temple's form, which you can call *pseudodipteral* (having open corridors behind the columns instead of a second row of columns), is a copy of the Temple of Zeus Sosipolis at Magnesia (Manisa), a work much admired in that era.

One Roman innovation, made possible by the temple's great height, is the cellar, with its barrel-vaulted roof. Zeus had to share his temple with the goddess Cybele, which is not unusual in a town so near Phrygia, although in Phrygia proper Cybele's orgiastic rites were conducted in the open air; it's difficult to say what went on in her subterranean sanctuary here. Relegation to the cellar implies no disrespect for Cybele, but it does wonderfully symbolize the state of mind of the ancient world. Zeus, representing reason, order, and light, rules the upper world, while just below the surface lies mystery and the unconscious bound up in the formidable personality of the great goddess. The huge acroterion on the east front was a bust of Zeus, while that on the west depicted Cybele. Here the two co-existed in a hard-earned balance that was not lost until the coming of Christianity.

Little remains of the rest of Aizanoi; if you have time you can trace the outlines of the stadium, which has an unusual arrangement in which the town's theatre closes its open end. The Temple of Zeus faced an agora fronting on the now intermittent stream that the Greeks called Rhyndakos, where there are still remnants of bridges and quays.

Afyon: City of Opium

Afyon's official name is *Afyon Karahisar*, which means 'opium black fortress'. That little product has been the city's name and its fame perhaps for millennia. Today, the poppies have largely been replaced by sunflowers; nevertheless, you'll still see vast expanses of poppy fields all around the city—supposedly the trade is strictly controlled, but Afyon still celebrates its ancient speciality with a big poppy-head fountain in the middle of town. The black **fortress** remains, on top of an enormous black rock, thrusting 741 ft into the sky. The original castle was probably Hittite, *c.* 1500 BC; it has been rebuilt many times since then and was used as a treasury by both the Selcuks and the Ottomans. In the old town, which is clustered round the foot of the rock, is the **Ulu Cami**, a fine Selcuk mosque built in 1273. It has a flat roof supported by 40 wooden columns with stalactite-carved capitals. Near the mosque are some well-preserved Ottoman houses with typical overhanging upper storeys. Also in the area is a **Mevlevi museum**, housed in a converted mosque; Afyon is not far from Konya and the Mevlâna's teachings soon found favour here.

In the new town, one building dominates all others, the **Gedik Ahmet Paşa Külliyesi**, built by a grand vezir of Mehmet the Conqueror. The mosque, the İmaret Camii, has a minaret decorated with İznik tiles, but the adjoining medrese and hamam (*currently closed*) are squat and functional, Byzantine in design but lacking the grace of that age.

The area round Afyon is famous for its **hot springs**. Some not-so-hot springs near the **Gazlıgöl** ('Gassy Lake'), north of Afyon, supply the mineral soda water you find in little green bottles all over Turkey.

The Phrygian Heartland

Anyone seriously interested in the fascinating world of pre-Hellenic Anatolia should not be discouraged from pushing into this little-visited region. The Phrygian monuments are well preserved and quite impressive in their lonely settings, and you'll have a chance for some real exploration. No archaeological area in western Anatolia is less documented, many of the sites being known only to the locals. Though Bursa's Uludağ and Murat Dağı, west of Afyon, are both taller, **Turkmen Dağı** and its surrounding peaks between Afyon and Eskişehir make the rooftop of northwestern Anatolia; many important rivers, including the Sakarya and the Menderes, have their sources here. If this area was not the most populous part of Phrygia, it was at least the holiest place. The evidence suggests that the Phrygians' religion had much to do with water; each of the great temple façades was located near a spring.

Getting Around

You have a choice of bases for seeing Midas Şehri and nearby sites, all of them inconvenient. **Afyon** is perhaps the best, since it is closest to the ruins and there are a number of village **dolmuş** lines running at least close to the sites. The village of Seyitgazi is even closer, though there is only the most rudimentary and unreliable accommodation there, and the same chance of a dolmuş that takes you more or less near the sites, and maybe, just maybe, another one to bring you back. In other words, rent a **car** if you're serious, or initiate some serious bargaining with **taxi** drivers. This is one of the few parts of Turkey where taxis are still a relatively inexpensive option for exploration; $50 for a day trip from Afyon or Seyitgazi should do it, though of course it will help if you can find a taxi driver who actually knows where the sites are and doesn't have to stop for directions every few minutes.

It's much easier visiting Gordion. From Eskişehir or Afyon, any **bus** bound for Ankara can leave you in the village of Polatlı; **dolmuş** service from there to the village of Yassıhöyük is regular enough, and you can walk from there.

Seyitgazi

If you go through **Seyitgazi**, stop for the **Mosque and Tomb of Seyit Battal Gazi**, the semi-legendary Arab warrior who died in battle here in AD 740, when the town was much more important than it is now. The tomb at the centre of this large complex was constructed around 1200 by the mother of the Selcuk sultan Alâeddin Keykubad; Seyit Gazi lies inside a sarcophagus a full 20ft long, next to his Greek wife Eleonora. The mosque and medrese were added in the 16th century by Selim I.

Midas Şehri

If there's only time for one site, head for **Midas Şehri**, the so-called 'Midas City', 15 miles (25km) southeast of Seyitgazi. Here, bordering the modern village of Yazılıkaya, the acropolis of a 6th-century BC Phrygian city, whose true name we do not know, rises up from the surrounding plains. There's little on the top, but a wealth of detail carved into its steep sides.

It was named Midas City by Captain Leake, a British traveller who discovered it in the early 1800s. At the end of the acropolis facing Yazılıkaya (not to be confused with the Yazılıkaya at Boğazkale) stands its largest and most striking monument, a temple façade some 70ft high; at its top, Leake thought he could discern the letters 'MIDAI' in a long Phrygian inscription, and reported back to the world that he had found the grave of King Midas. In truth, the Phrygian language still remains something of a mystery. Most of the letters were adapted from the Greek, however, and more likely than not, some 'Midas' had something to do with it. This is no tomb, however; the experts think of it as a kind of stage background for the outdoor rites of Cybele. Her cult statue would be placed in the niche at the bottom of the monument during the festivities.

Around the niche, the precise, symmetrical maze-like pattern that covers most of the monument's face shows the odd degree of abstraction the Phrygians had reached in their religious art. The pediment suggests roof beams resting on a central ridge-pole, and it may be that the cliff façades are representations of wooden temples that no longer exist. A second, somewhat smaller façade was carved into the north face of the hill, roughly the same in form, with a frieze along the top decorated with Greek-style acanthus-leaf designs. All around the other hillsides, both above and below the bits of the original defence wall, a day's exploration will reveal any number of other niches and altars, inscriptions, underground chambers, and other features whose uses can only be guessed at.

Sites near Midas Şehri

A third temple façade, smaller and somewhat eroded, can be seen near Yazılıkaya at **Arezastis**. You can compare all three with the whole temples in the same area, one cut out of the **Gerdek Rock** near the village of Çukurca, and another at **Hisar Kale**, five and a half miles (9km) to the southwest at Yapıldak village. Another site near Çukurca, perhaps the most unusual of all, is the **Doğanlı Kale**, an outlandishly eroded crag of limestone, honeycombed with chambers and niches, with hollows that seem to have held wooden beams and stairways at one time. Again, whatever was the purpose of this lost little piece of Cappadocia is left to the imagination. Some of the work is said to date from Byzantine times, and like the similar oddities in Cappadocia may have been used as a monastery.

The road going west from Yazılıkaya passes a **Phrygian tumulus** on its way to the village of **Kümbetköy**, which takes its name from a Roman-era tomb guarded by two lions in low relief, a recurring symbol in Phrygian art just as it was for the Hittites. South of here, on the way to Afyon, other Phrygian lions have given the villages of **Arslantaş** and **Arslankaya** their names. The temple façade at Arslankaya is a remarkable sight, carved out of a thin, twisted pinnacle of rock; two lions keep watch from its pediment while two other huge figures as high as the façade itself, though badly eroded, flank the monument. Both this and the smaller façade at Arslantaş are done in the same angular patterns as at Midas Şehri.

Pessinus

Pessinus, 10 miles (16km) south of where the Eskişehir–Ankara highway passes Sivrihisar, was the religious and geographic centre of Phrygia. Almost nothing can be seen on the site, but archaeologists have found a 1st-century AD temple at the top of a broad ceremonial stair. A college of priests ruled the city; an inscription records that half were Phrygian and half Galatian. Even during the two centuries when Pessinus was under the sovereignty of the kings of Pergamon, these priests, or *galli*, ruled the city and its hinterlands as a theocratic state, and their influence spread far beyond Phrygia's borders.

The Romans put a stop to this in their usual ingenious fashion. In 204 BC, they instructed their Pergamene allies to send them the cult figure, a *baetyl* from Pessinus. King Attalos was glad to comply; the respected Sibylline Oracle had commanded it, and the *baetyl* (probably a meteorite, like the Kaaba in Mecca) was conveyed to Rome with all proper observances and placed in a temple specially built for it. The Romans expanded their power as much through this talent for taking over other people's religions as by triumph of arms; one wonders what happened to all the statues, relics and cult objects they collected. Does the pope have them up in his attic?

In Phrygia, the worship of Cybele had much to do with bees; Greek mythographers always associated her with Aphrodite Ericyna and her golden honeycomb, the aspect worshipped at Mount Eryx in Sicily. Today, the site of Pessinus is known to the Turks as **Ballıhisar**—the Honey Castle.

Gordion, like Pessınus, is a site only an archaeologist could really love; the early Phrygian capital contains no well-preserved buildings or fine reliefs; and only parts of it have been fully excavated, though enough has been done for specialists to have drawn up a ground plan of the major palace buildings.

Much more interesting is the **Great Tumulus** on the edge of the city, which, as you might guess, everyone calls 'Midas's Tomb'. Gordion is reached from the same Eskişehir–Ankara road, 12 miles (20km) northeast of the town of **Polatlı**, with yellow signs marking the route from there. Approaching the site, you see mounds of all sizes, gradually increasing in number. The largest, most likely, were for the kings, though even mere nobles apparently had the resources to build them. Few of the smaller tumuli have been excavated; the burials in them were cleverly placed off-centre to discourage grave robbers and archaeologists. One they did find yielded the remains of a five-year-old boy, with some charming toys that are now in the Ankara Museum.

The Great Tumulus

The **Great Tumulus**, now worn down to about 160ft in height, must originally have been close to 250ft. In Turkey the only bigger example of a mound is the one near Sardis called King Alyattes's Tomb, and it's difficult to say if a taller one could be found anywhere in the world. Whether or not the king inside was a Midas or a Gordius is unknown—they alternated these names the way Danish kings do with Christian and Frederick—but he was a small man, no more than 5ft 2in, and close to 60 years of age. The tomb at the centre of the mound has been thoroughly excavated, and you can reach it through the long, lighted tunnel, recently constructed.

To build this mound, the Phrygians started with a double-walled wooden house set into the ground, covered it with stones and clay, and then piled up the earth above it. The wood—great logs of cedar that must have come from Lebanon, still sound after 2,600 years under the earth—is mortised at the corners like a frontier cabin. Inside, interestingly enough, no gold or silver was found; there were dozens of pots, many with inscriptions in the Phrygian alphabet, some exceedingly well-crafted furniture, now in Ankara, and, inexplicably, 145 brass *fibulae*—the archaeologists' word for safety-pins.

The current excavations of the city are surrounded by a fence. Having been nearly completely covered with centuries of silt from the Sakarya's floods, the site is now exposed and you can look down into the diggings and make out, at the southeastern end, the **monumental gateway**, and behind it the palace buildings and a long row, somewhat like a modern residential terrace, that belonged to the palace household. The palaces themselves consisted of a row of megaron-style structures, with a central hearth surrounded by rooms and one large hall in front serving as the entrance; it is quite likely these had façades in wood similar to the temple façades mentioned above.

Gordius and Midas

 Arrian's life of Alexander mentions that the Gordian knot was kept in the Gordion acropolis. Since nothing like an acropolis exists here, the temple complex is probably what he had in mind. According to the myth as related by Arrian, Gordius was originally a poor farmer. One day an eagle perched on his wagon tongue, and Gordius, taking it as an omen, decided to visit an oracle at Phrygian Telmessus to ask its meaning. On the way, the eagle still riding along with him, he met a local priestess who instructed him in the proper sacrifices for the oracle. He married her, and she bore him a son named Midas. In the meantime, the Phrygian king had died and the country was drifting into factional strife. The same oracle announced that a man in an ox-cart would come to bring peace to the land, and when the unsuspecting Gordius rode into the city one day, he found himself proclaimed king.

He founded the city of Gordion, the story continues, and laid up his wagon there. Over the years, a prophecy gained currency that whoever could solve the cornel-bark knot that bound the yoke to the wagon tongue would become 'master of Asia'. Much speculation has gone into the nature of this knot, although its presence here is historical fact. When Alexander passed this way—Gordion lay directly on the Persian Royal Road, the great trade and conquest route between Greece and the east—he felt obliged to fulfil the prophecy, since becoming master of Asia was exactly what he had in mind. Most commentators claim he cut the knot with his sword, which provides the most poetic solution. Robert Graves believes the knot was an alphabetic cipher, expressing the secret name of a god (Incas and ancient Britons had such devices, so why not the Phrygians?); he sees Alexander's sword stroke as a historical turning point, at which the power of blind ambition and main force broke the last barrier to the destruction of the ancient authority of religion.

Of Midas, we learn that he planted famous rose gardens and was a great musician, taught by Orpheus himself. As well as the tale of the golden touch, Midas is said to have had a pair of ass's ears planted on him by Apollo; Midas unwisely voted against the god when the latter competed in a musical contest with Midas's countryman Marsyas. His barber was supposed to keep the secret (which Midas hid from others with a conical Phrygian cap, of the kind that was the fashion during the French Revolution) but simply couldn't bear to keep quiet. He dug a hole in the ground near a river and whispered, 'Midas has ass's ears!' into it; most unfortunately for him, the reeds on the spot immediately spread the message to everyone within earshot: 'Midas has ass's ears!'

Midas's name, like Gordius's, probably has a basis in history. He, or one of the kings with that name, appears in Assyrian records as 'Mita of Mushki'. This Mushki, most likely, was the Phrygians' own name for their nation. 'Phrygian' is a Greek word meaning 'free men'. As a pastoral people without a strong state, they probably were just that.

Despite the wealth that lay behind the legend of Midas's golden touch, his capital was not to endure. The Great Tumulus was built around 720 BC, and the Cimmerians came to sack Gordion a mere couple of decades later. Though it revived in the 6th century, by Roman times writers were already sadly remarking that the once-great city was dwindling into little more than a village.

Finds from Gordion

Whatever finds the government hasn't carried off to Ankara are on display in the small **museum**. Small bits of red, white and black architectural ceramics give some idea of how the palaces originally looked; the rockpile that is Gordion today belies the Phrygian talent and liking for extensive decoration. Other artefacts include a wildly undisciplined geometric-pattern mosaic (from one of the megaron houses) that looks more post-Impressionist than ancient Phrygian, and one perfectly serviceable pair of dice.

On your way back to Polatlı, take time to notice the **Atatürk Monument** on the crest of the most prominent hill north of town. This could well be the only really successful modern memorial anywhere in Turkey; at least it's an interesting attempt at recapturing the ancient Anatolians' talent for monumental sculpture. Consisting of two long rows of marble columns of increasing height, tracing a gracefully curved silhouette over the hilltop, it's as abstract and as memorable as any work of the Phrygians.

Eskişehir to Afyon   ***Where to Stay***

Eskişehir, Kütahya and Afyon are all towns where you will have trouble spending a lot of money on hotel rooms, with little at the upper end of the accommodation market. Surprisingly, in interior towns like this there are no pretensions—you can almost always judge a place from its façade. Most of the moderately priced hotels are clean and comfortable, even if English-speaking staff are a rarity. In any town you will find something for under $10—the basic, old reliable Turkish flophouse of a decade ago. Just don't expect much beyond a tolerably clean room looking out onto a garage, and a folkloric bog down the hall.

Eskişehir

Two modest hotels next to each other on Hamamyolu Caddesi have thermal baths. The better of the two is the **★★Has Termal Oteli** at No.7, ✆ 0222 231 9191, ▨ 0222 234 6488. If it's full, try the **★Sultan Termal Otel** at No.1, ✆ 0222 231 8371. After visiting the Phrygian sites you may well appreciate the warm baths. Rates average $25 per double.

Kütahya

The best hotel in town is the **Gül Palas**, unmistakable with its lovely tile-covered façade on the central Belediye Meydanı, ✆ 0274 216 1759, ▨ 0274 216 2135. Tiles cover much of the interior too, although the tile paintings of earth-movers and quarry trucks in the stairwell may be taking the art a little too far. Bedrooms are well furnished with good en suite bathrooms; $35 including a big buffet breakfast. The basement sauna is yours for an extra $2.

A cheap option is the well-kept **Yüksel II**, ✆ 0274 212 0111, on central Belediye Meydanı. Rooms with no frills for $12 with bath, $9 without. If it's full the **Otel Köşk** nearby, ✆ 0274 216 2024, has bigger but similarly plain double rooms for $16 with bath, $14 without, although traffic noise could be a problem.

Afyon

To take in the hot springs, or merely to enjoy a night's luxury in this little-travelled region, nine miles outside Afyon is the ★★★★**Termal Resort Oruçoğlu**, on the Kütahya road, ✆ 0272 251 5050, ✉ 0272 251 5060. It's an apparition in these empty landscapes, a weird futuristic concrete spa hotel next to a big water slide in the middle of nowhere. All rooms have satellite TV, sauna and hamam; the springs will supposedly do wonders for your rheumatism and gynaecological problems. Doubles are $70.

The town's best is the ★★**Oruçoğlu**, in the centre on Bankalar Caddesi, ✆ 0272 212 0120, ✉ 0272 213 1313, a well-appointed businessman's hotel; most rooms with balcony and satellite TV, for $35. The **Otel Mesut** on Dumlupınar Caddesi, ✆ 0272 212 0429, is a lot better than its rather sorry exterior would suggest; $16.

Afyon has a number of places that will do fine for an overnight stay, including the rudimentary **Lale**, opposite the İmaret Camii, ✆ 0272 215 1580; doubles $9.

Kütahya and Afyon **Eating Out**

Kütahya

All the restaurants are near the central Belediye Meydanı. For a gastronomic splurge, the best place to go is the brightly-decorated top-floor restaurant at the **Gül Palas** on Belediye Meydanı, where a smorgasbord buffet of salads, stews and meats costs $7. The inexpensive **Meşhur** ('Famous') **İskender Salonu**, on Azerbaycan Parkı next to Belediye Meydanı lays on a quite nice bowl of *mercimek* (red lentil) soup and *iskender kebap*. The **Bursa İskender** on Atatürk Bulvarı is a simple kebab salon that tries hard; good cooking and a bill that will come to about $5 no matter what you order. The **Cumhuriyet Lokantası** nearby on Belediye Meydanı is just as good if slightly more expensive.

If your tooth is sweeter, join Kütahya's younger crowd at **İnci Pastaneleri**, just off Belediye Meydanı, where off-duty teenage army conscripts glance longingly across at the local girls as they tuck into sticky cakes and profiteroles, washed down with a deliciously gloopy distant relative of the cappuccino.

Afyon

The place to go is the excellent **İkbal Lokantası** on Uzun Carşı, close to the Oruçoğlu Oteli. It's an old-style restaurant, so popular with the locals at lunchtime that the waiters have to run while they serve the food. A meal here costs about $5. Finish your meal with *ekmek kadayıf* (bread soaked in syrup) or *vişneli ekmek tatlısı* (bread soaked in cherry juice); both come topped with a slab of the rich cream for which Afyon is renowned.

Ankara

Most people have the impression that Ankara, the capital of the Turkish Republic since 1923, is absolutely new, a modern toadstool of a city conjured up out of bleakest Anatolia by Atatürk as a symbol of his country's pride and aspirations. Modern it is of course, and toadstool beyond question, but underneath all the clutter of ministries, highways, and apartment blocks there is a genuine old city too, as old as the Hittites, and layered with memories of all the nations that have come and gone since then. Atatürk chose his capital more cleverly than at first appears. Above all, Ankara is an entirely Turkish city, and has been for eight centuries, even though the traces of the Phrygians, Greeks and Romans are still out in the open for all to see.

History

A relief map shows why the spot has always attracted so much attention. Just to the east, a gap between the Köroğlu Mountains and the bare plateau south of them forms a natural corridor called the **Halys Gates**. The Persian Royal Road and the Via Regalis of the Romans passed through here, as did conquerors from Alexander to Tamerlane. The Hittites were the first to build on Ankara's lofty citadel, and the Phrygians after them made it one of their most important cities. Dozens of Phrygian tumuli once covered the plain, but almost all have vanished. The Celtic Galatians succeeded them—there is still plenty of red hair and freckles in this part of Turkey—and Augustus annexed their lands for Rome in 25 BC. By then, the city had assumed a variant of its modern name, **Ancyra**. Europe knew it for a long period as **Angora** and it gave its name to the soft wool produced by the region's goats.

Although continuously occupied through all the centuries since, Ankara was never a great city but, as Atatürk realized, it is a natural capital of Anatolia. Its fortunes have always risen and fallen with those of its surrounding country; with the neglect and peril that was life here until the Republic, it was never able to achieve much. Also, it's a good distance from İstanbul and the intrigue synonymous with the old capital, which enabled Atatürk to make a clean break with the past.

Ankara Today

Over three million people live in Ankara now. Those who have jobs work for the government or businesses attracted by proximity to the government; those who haven't get by as best they can while looking. Much of the city's phenomenal growth, like İstanbul's, has been due to the unplanned and unwanted migration of hundreds of thousands of villagers from every corner of Turkey. For all Turks, Ankara is just the symbol Atatürk wanted it to be, the nation's pre-eminent city of opportunity, and this is one of the side effects.

In no way can Ankara be called a pleasant city. Some quarters are almost that, but Ankara is big enough and diverse enough to accommodate a whole range of adjectives. 'Ill-planned' comes to mind first. Turkey's first town planners were more civil engineers than artists. Ankara has more gratuitous highway interchanges than the rest of the country put together, some in the centre of the town where everyone can enjoy them. The exact centre, between Gençlik Parkı and the business district, is occupied by a sprawling railway yard. The

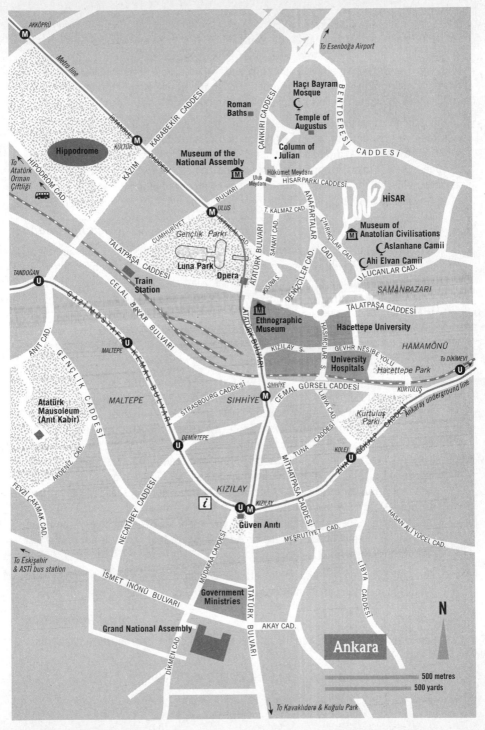

highways and the railways combine to give the city the worst air pollution in Turkey. Don't imagine for a minute that any native of Ankara minds discussing these problems. Quite the contrary; like many busy and thriving big cities, Ankara seems almost to get a perverse joy from them. The city has skyscrapers, fine parks and residential districts, trendy stores, a good university, and nothing to envy in any other Turkish town save İstanbul. And if they must sacrifice other amenities to gain these, what of it? Ankara is on top, and it knows it.

One thing the planners didn't do was to try to integrate the new Ankara with the old. As a result, the two exist uneasily side by side, with that freightyard for a border. As the newer, southern districts grow and prosper, the old town suffers. Some parts still retain the village atmosphere of old Ankara; some have deteriorated to nothing more than poor shops and junkyards, while still others have had new streets of modern buildings smashed carelessly through them. The planners seem to hope that one day the old town will just disappear.

Getting Around

Ankara is one of the cities where **taxis** not only have meters but usually use them. You'll probably need one if you arrive by **bus** or **train**. The train station is on Hipodrom Caddesi, 1½ miles (2½km) from Kızılay, the centre of the city. The huge new bus station, known variously as the AŞTİ (Ankara Şehirlerarası Terminale İşletmesi), Yeni Terminal or Yeni Otogar, is in the Soğütözü district, three miles (5km) west of the city centre. From **Esenboğa Airport**, 20 miles (33km) northeast of the city, you have a choice of a cab (about $25) or the usual THY Havaş bus to the city centre and otogar.

Ankara isn't encouraging for those who like to explore cities on foot. As well as having dirty air, it is a typical Turkish strip-city blown out of all proportion; almost any destination will be on or near the three-mile (5km) length of Atatürk Bulvarı. There's a new **underground** system with two lines: the **Ankaray** runs from the AŞTİ otogar via Kızılay to Dikimevi in the east. The second line, the **Metro**, starts at Kızılay (where it connects to the Ankaray line) and heads north-west past Ulus to the suburb of Batıkent. An **underground pass**, costing $2 for five trips, is the best value for money. **Buses** (buy tickets in the booths at the major stops, as in İstanbul) and **dolmuşes** are crowded but frequent; just look at the destination signs to see if they're going in the direction you want. If you're not ready to climb up to the Hisar, take one of the minibuses from the broad open space that serves as a terminal just east of Ulus Meydanı.

The Anıt Kabir, on its hill, and the Atatürk Orman Çifliği are best reached by taxi, but all the recreation areas in the vicinity of the city can be reached easily by bus.

Ankara   ***Tourist Information***

Gazi Mustafa Kemal Bulvarı 121, next to the Maltepe stop on the Ankaray line, ℡ 0312 231 5572.

Esenboğa Hava Limanı (at the airport), ℡ 0312 428 1700.

Museum of the National Assembly

The **Ulus Meydanı** (National Square) is where modern Ankara and modern Turkey began. Most visitors don't stop at the little grey building just off the square, but you wouldn't go to Philadelphia without seeing Independence Hall and you should take a few minutes to visit the **Museum of the National Assembly**. After the Erzurum and Sivas Congresses decided in 1919 to coordinate and extend the efforts of the local defence committees across Anatolia, elections were held wherever possible for the new Grand National Assembly; it met here for the first time on 23 April 1920. Atatürk, elected chairman on the first day, was at the time under death sentence from the İstanbul government. Greek troops were occupying the Aegean coast, and French, Italian, British and Russian forces were also present on Turkish soil, and advancing.

In this hall, with its school desks jammed together and the chairman within spitting distance of nearly every deputy, the Turks did the last thing anyone expected: they roused themselves as a nation for the first time, and prevailed against a host of enemies. Not having attended a Turkish grammar school, you will not know all the serious-looking men in the photos that cover the walls, or be familiar with the significance of the letters and declarations on display in the glass case, but you will come away with the impression that some great work was done here, and your respect for the Turks and their revolution will be increased.

Remains of Old Ankara

From here, you can walk six blocks north and 1,600 years back to the Hükümet Meydanı, and the tall, worn **Column of Julian**, currently crowned by a stork's nest. The Galatians of Ancyra, who made up most of the population in the 3rd century AD, had a reputation among their neighbours for piety to their cults of Cybele and the moon goddess Men; it's not all that surprising that they erected this monument in honour of the apostate emperor. Julian was a good general, and one of the last Roman emperors to make a serious effort to hold the eastern borders. He passed through Ancyra in AD 362 on his way to campaign against the resurgent Persians, and after a series of frustratingly indecisive encounters he fell ill and died the next year, derided by the Christians but mourned by the poets, the soldiers and all who wished the Roman cause well.

The Temple of Augustus

History has had its little joke with the Galatians. Their temple of Cybele, converted after the conquest to the worship of Augustus and of Rome, was to end its career as a Christian church; if the Christians had not maintained it for so many centuries, the **Temple of Augustus** would not have survived at all. As it is, the pediment and all the columns have fallen, but enough remains to prove that this, like the temple of Aizanoi, was, in its plan, a copy of the Zeus Sosipolis temple in Magnesia. The walls of the cella, the inner sanctuary, are inscribed with a long text in Latin and Greek, the 'Deeds of the Deified Augustus', the longest Latin inscription found anywhere. Little of it is still legible, effaced less by time than by modern Ankara's exhaust fumes; fortunately a scholarly 16th-century Spanish ambassador took the trouble to write down the full text.

Unlike some of the decadent later emperors, Augustus, a good Roman, was mildly disgusted by the idea of being worshipped. He insisted that such worship should be deferred until after his death: his advisers convinced him that the people of Syria and Asia Minor, grown accustomed to divine rulers from Persian days, would expect it. Even then, he decreed that a divine personification of Rome should take precedence in the temples. What meant more to him was effective and just government, and he took pains to ensure that his biography and political testament, including a report on the state of the empire he was leaving to his successors, would be carved into the walls of all his temples. Oddly, this is the only complete text anywhere, and the other fragments that have come to light are also in Anatolia.

Adjacent to the temple, the 15th-century **Hacı Bayram Mosque** is always full of worshippers at Friday services. Hacı Bayram was a dervish whose virtues and deeds gained for him almost the character of a saint. His memory is especially revered here in his home town, and his tomb is an object of pilgrimage.

Roman Baths

Ankara's other Roman-era attraction, the 3rd-century **Roman Baths**, stands just a little to the west on Çankırı Caddesi, the northern extension of the city's major thoroughfare, Atatürk Bulvarı. Of these baths, erected by Emperor Caracalla, enough is left to work out the *frigidarium* and *caldarium* (cold and hot rooms) and other features of this direct ancestor of the Turkish hamam, and the adjacent cloistered quadrangle that served as the *palaestra*, or exercise yard. These aren't as big as Caracalla's famous baths in Rome, but in a provincial city like Ancyra they are a remarkable monument to the perverted soul who spent whatever time he could spare from murdering his countrymen on improving the hygiene of the survivors. Noteworthy here is a good example of that useful Roman invention, central heating. Many rooms have false floors raised up on blocks; hot air circulated through these spaces from the furnace.

The Hisar

Everything else built by the Greeks, Romans, or Byzantines in Ankara still exists—but the last Byzantines, and the Turks who followed them, carried it all up the hill to the *Hisar*, the citadel. And a most remarkable citadel it is; it's common in sites in Turkey for ancient stones to be reused in fortress walls, but only here do you find a castle built of little else. Some parts of the walls are all marble and good sandstone, carved with pieces of a hundred different inscriptions and architectural trimmings. Whole courses consist of drums of ancient columns, lined up on their sides like rows of portholes on a ship. One could think of the Hisar as a huge jigsaw puzzle; if there were time and archaeologists enough, the whole of old Ancyra could be reassembled from the pieces.

It's a stiff climb up, as many would-be invaders have found. Today, the formal entrance runs from Hisarparkı Caddesi through a road lined with gardens to the top. Upon arrival you find a tranquil old Turkish town, unchanged and utterly remote from the city of skyscrapers down below. Cars can hardly get through the narrow bumpy streets, and so the neighbourhood inside the walls, though poor, is cleaner and quieter. The views from the walls are superb; to the south and west the modern city stretches to the horizon.

To the northeast, in the direction of the airport, are the plains on which Tamerlane's hordes overcame Sultan Yıldırım Beyazıt in the **Battle of Ankara** in 1402. The Turks attribute this disaster, the first serious defeat of the Ottomans, to a point of honour. Beyazıt, abandoning the first siege of Constantinople and rushing his army east to meet the advancing Tamerlane, caught him completely by surprise. To take such advantage of a noble foe seemed shameful to the young sultan, however, and he gave his enemy a day to collect itself and meet him in proper battle array. Beyazıt's exhausted troops proved no match for the nomad horsemen and Tamerlane's elephants, and in the rout that followed the sultan himself became another inmate of Tamerlane's sad menagerie of captured potentates. After this blow, it was a decade before the Ottomans recovered their strength.

Gecekondu

Looking from the east wall, you will see how Ankara's other half lives. If you imagined the shanty town districts, the *gecekondu* (*see* pp.138–9), as dreary expanses of grim hovels, you haven't given Turkey's urban migrants, raised in their village traditions of self-sufficiency, the credit they deserve. *Gecekondu*, in time, have a way of metamorphosing into decent little cottages, and the areas they create, though completely unplanned, become real neighbourhoods. The view from the walls is startling; the *gecekondu* begin at the slopes of the citadel, fill the valleys around it and climb the next hills, descending and climbing again and again, as far as the eye can see. It is a panorama of hundreds of thousands of homes, unbroken by a single landmark. Some areas have utilities and schools, others are still waiting; the worst look full of despair, while the best seem almost garden suburbs. From all of them, Ankara's poor make the long trip each day to the city centre on foot or in the tired minibuses that swarm around the Ulus district. What sustains them, as they strive to find a job or keep one, is the quietly confident hope that they, or their children, will one day do better.

Museum of Anatolian Civilisations (Anadolu Medeniyetleri Müzesi)

You have to climb halfway up the citadel hill to find the **Museum of Anatolian Civilisations** (*open Tues–Sun 8.30–5; adm*). Many visitors to Ankara come only to see this surprisingly small museum, in a beautifully restored *bedesten* of the 15th century that was once the heart of the city's bazaar. Though it's small, there are few museums anywhere in the world that can offer so many treasures from the distant past.

That is how the Turks wanted it. If you are obsessed with efficiency, consider that by spending a single day here you can spare yourself the trouble of visiting several dozen of Turkey's best-known ancient sites. Like Paris, Ankara is a cultural imperialist, and all the best Hittite reliefs, Phrygian pottery and Urartian metalwork have been brought here. It was Atatürk who first had the idea for such a collection. It was originally known as the Hittite Museum in an attempt to call the world's attention to the newly discovered works of the first great Anatolian nation, and at the same time to be an inspiration to the new nation he was trying to build. As other sites came to light in the explosion of archaeological activity here, explorations that have reshaped our knowledge of the ancient Middle East, other fine artefacts have been brought to the museum. The whole gives a solid education in this field from Paleolithic times up to the Greek colonization. Unlike so many other museums, this one does not overwhelm with endless cases of broken pots: every piece is significant, and most are works of art in their own right.

From the Neolithic Period, the prize exhibits come from Çatal Höyük, the 8,000-year-old town whose recent excavation has changed all our ideas of ancient history. One entire temple from the site has been reconstructed, with its bull's-head idols and sophisticated frescoes, and a host of figurines of the chubby mother goddess in both her forms, as fertility symbol and as mistress of wild animals. The Hittites, not surprisingly, occupy a lion's share of the exhibit space, with plenty of their curly-maned lions in attendance too. The large number of well-preserved reliefs in the museum's great hall come both from sites of the Hittite Empire, such as Boğazkale and Karatepe, and from the weaker kingdoms that rose up following its collapse. The Hittites used sculpture not only for serious religious and state subjects, but to depict scenes both from everyday life and from pure fancy; as a result, their artistic themes range from gods and kings astride their sacred mountains to sphinxes, hunting scenes and domestic tableaux—children, musicians, and a master of animals leading them in procession like a Pied Piper.

With all the attention given to the Hittites, it can be easy to overlook the works of the Hatti and other early Bronze Age peoples who preceded them. This collection remedies that. Some of their cast bronze works here must surely rank among the greatest ancient art; their style bears a striking resemblance to the celebrated bronzes of the *nuraghe* culture of Sardinia, whose ancestors may have been migrants from Anatolia. Most of these bronzes, found at Alacahöyük and other sites, seem to have been mounted on the tops of standards or sceptres. Some are stylized bulls and stags, but the most memorable are the circular or elliptical shapes, covered with various geometric lattice designs, many with stags, bulls or asses in the act of passing through the circle.

The scholars call them cosmological symbols, which they undoubtedly are, and throw up their hands in despair of ever understanding them completely. These compelling symbols fascinate the modern Turks. The government Tourist Ministry has adopted one as its motif, and on Ankara's Atatürk Bulvarı a gigantic copy of one has been erected right in the middle of the city.

Two later nations with a marvellous artistic talent, the Phrygians and Urartians, round out the museum's collection with rooms of their own. The Urartian finds come from a wide area; their empire, at its height, reached from Sivas to western Iran, from Trabzon to Aleppo. Like the Phrygians, they loved detail and geometric patterns; these can be seen adorning a bronze warrior's shield, several delicately inscribed bronze belts worn by Urartian kings and priests, and in a beautiful soapstone carving of the winged god Haldi, standing on the back of a lion under the towers and gables of a many-storeyed fortified palace. The metalwork commonly depicts gods or priests in processions, griffins or fantastical birds. The priests, if they are indeed priests, carry standards with a strange device, a square crossed by two diagonals, rare in Anatolia but a familiar symbol of the calendar in ancient Crete.

The museum has recently opened a room on a lower level, with glass cabinets full of coins, jewellery, glass, tilework and votive steles giving a whistlestop tour of Turkey since the Greeks. One cabinet is given over to works by contemporary ceramics masters from Kütahya, including Mehmet Gürsoy (*see* p.393).

Samanpazarı

Southeast of the citadel, the quarter called the **Samanpazarı** ('haymarket') contains, as well as the ramshackle bazaar, three of the oldest and most interesting mosques: the 13th-century **Aslanhane Camii** built by the Selcuks during the brief period they held Ankara, the **Yeni Cami**, and the **Ahi Elvan Camii**, built by the Ahi Brotherhood in the early 1400s.

New Ankara

A broad new highway, Talat Paşa Bulvarı, cuts off the old town abruptly, and all the land on the other side has been cleared for the huge campus of modern Turkey's educational show-piece, **Hacettepe University**. Where Talat Paşa crosses Atatürk Bulvarı stands the **Ethnographic Museum**, or Etnografya Müzesi (*closed for restoration but is due to reopen in 2000; opening times supposedly Tues–Sun 8.30–12.30 and 1.30–5.30; adm*), the first important building created by the Turkish Republic, started by Atatürk in 1925 to further the study and appreciation of native Turkish folklore and crafts. Atatürk himself lay in state here from 1938 to 1955, when his mausoleum was finished. Today the museum is the largest of its kind in the country, with rooms devoted to costumes and embroidery, metalcrafts, weapons, calligraphy, and objects collected from the dervish *tekkeler* after their dissolution. There is a 17th-century room from an Ankara home, furnished to recreate a picture of life in that era, and, best of all, some excellent wood-carving from the Selcuk period: doors and mihrabs from mosques, even the throne of the Selcuk sultans.

As well as museums, Atatürk thought his city should have formal European-style parks. The first of these lies catercorner to the Ethnographic Museum and behind the city Opera. **Gençlik Parkı** ('youth park') may not be quite as pretty as Kültür Parkı in Bursa, but its layout is much the same, with lagoons and island cafés, an open-air theatre and a **Luna Park**; this last isn't a name, but an expression that has passed into the Turkish language. Wherever the first one may have been, every amusement park in Turkey now is a Luna Park.

The Modern Districts

Like most Turkish cities, Ankara is long and thin, growing up along the main streets and the bus and dolmuş lines that traverse it. Consequently it's almost a mile from here to the centre of the modern city, the intersection called **Kızılay** ('crescent') where a curving avenue crosses Atatürk Bulvarı. The 20-storey international-style skyscraper here was Turkey's first, a big deal 20 years ago, although no one gives it a second look today because there are so many others. Across the street, the small park around the **Güven Anıtı** ('Confidence Monument') is a little oasis in the middle of the crowds and ferocious traffic of this district, which has most of Ankara's shops, offices, and hotels. The monument itself, with its glowering Atatürk and Turks gazing hopefully into the future, will make a fine exhibit in someone's archaeology museum in a millennium or two.

Another half-mile south takes you to the corner of Gülhane Caddesi and the centre of Ankara's government district. Turkey is a very centralized nation, and here the office blocks go on and on, stretching towards infinity. In the middle, in a very tired style of government architecture, stands the **Grand National Assembly**, known to the Turks as the TBMM

(Türkiye Büyük Millet Meclisi), the parliament building. Still further south, Atatürk Çaddesi becomes Embassy Row, leading to the fashionable suburbs of Kavaklıdere and Çankaya. Here is another of Atatürk's parks, **Kuğulu Park** ('swan park')—with plenty of the birds. It's a pleasant spot in which to watch the younger members of the Turkish élite disporting themselves, seeming as far from the neighbourhood of the Hisar as London is from Ouagadougou.

Tomb of Atatürk

Not far from the Kızılay, on a hilltop above the suburb of Maltepe, the Tomb of Atatürk or **Anıt Kabir**, 'monumental tomb' (*open daily 9–4.30; free*), rises like an ancient temple on an acropolis over Ankara. It means a lot to the Turks; the building is shown when Turkish television signs off every night, accompanied by the national anthem. At night the illuminated monument becomes the city's most conspicuous landmark. It took nearly ten years to build, and in it the Turks made a serious attempt to recapture some of the massive monumentality of the ancient civilizations, while establishing a new style of their own. They didn't quite bring it off although the effect is certainly impressive.

From Anıt Caddesi, you go down a long promenade lined with Hittite-style lions, leading up to a square of low stone buildings that contain a **Museum** of Atatürk and his works (*open Mon 1.30–5, Tues–Sun 9–5; free*). Exhibits range from the usual collection of gilded trinkets given by foreign leaders to the very personal: three roasted chickpeas given by Atatürk to his adopted daughter Sabiha Gökçen. Then there are the exhibits belonging firmly to the 'potato in the shape of the Virgin Mary's face' school of veneration: a whole cabinet is filled by various photographs taken long after Atatürk's death in 1938, with likenesses of the great leader's face beaming down benevolently, if a trifle indistinctly, from chance configurations of clouds.

The entire complex is packed with soldiers, an honour guard from each of the services, all enormously tall and decked out in American-style military pomp. The monument, a plain box with a decorated cornice and surrounding colonnade of square pillars, is reached by a long flight of steps. On the walls are lengthy quotes from Atatürk and İsmet İnönü, who is also buried here. Inside, the great building is empty save for Atatürk's huge sarcophagus, with glass walls affording views over the city he built.

Around Ankara

There are a number of recreation areas around the capital. Perhaps the favourite picnic-spot is the **Atatürk Orman Çiftliği**, a mile west of town. Late in his career, Atatürk started this as a model farm to introduce new agricultural methods into Turkey. Other pleasant resorts are around **Mogan Gölü** to the south, **Kızılcahamam** 50 miles (80km) to the north up in the mountains, and the skiing centre of **Elmadağ** just southeast of the city. At **Gâvurkalesi** ('infidel's castle'), 37 miles (60km) to the southwest, you can visit a religious site of the Hittites, consisting of an underground tomb and a relief depicting the weather god Teshub, his wife Hepatu and their son Sharruma, the divine family of the Hittite pantheon.

Ankara's fanciest hotels are mostly around busy Atatürk Bulvarı, between Kızılay and Kavaklıdere. The most opulent is the ★★★★★**Ankara Sheraton**, Noktalı Sokak, ✆ 0312 468 5454, @ 0312 467 1136, constructed in the shape of a giant tube. A double room costs $270, but if you've come up on the pools and intend to blow all your winnings on a luxury holiday in Ankara, do it properly and reserve the presidential suite at well over $700. Rooms at the ★★★★★**Hilton Oteli**, Tahran Caddesi, ✆ 0312 468 2888, @ 0312 468 0909, are almost as sumptuous; $255 per double. The ★★★★★**Büyuk Ankara**, 183 Atatürk Bulvarı 183, ✆ 0312 425 6655, @ 0312 425 5070, just scrapes in as a five-star place; the posted price is $220 per double but if you can bring yourself to haggle in such an establishment, do so, as the management have been known to knock up to 40% off the official rates.

In Kızılay, the **VIP Hotel** is on a pedestrian street at Karanfil Sokak 9, ✆ 0312 425 5253, @ 0312 419 9547, with cheerful multilingual staff and rooms with air-con, minibar and satellite TV; doubles $110. Also in Kızılay is the ★★★★**Ayma**, Meşrutiyet Caddesi 25, ✆ 0312 425 4600, @ 0312 419 1855, which has sizeable rooms trimmed in dark wood; pleasant but overpriced at $170. There's a nightclub in the basement if you want to let your hair down; if you want a good sleep, ask for an upper floor room at the back. On another pedestrian street nearby is the **Melodi**, Karanfil Sokak 10, ✆ 0312 417 6414, @ 0312 418 7858, where generously proportioned $80 rooms are filled with 1960s furnishings in surprisingly good condition.

The ★★★★**Best Oteli**, Atatürk Bulvarı 195, ✆ 0312 467 0880, @ 0312 467 0885, has a good restaurant and attentive staff but lacks character; doubles $105. The same company also runs the better ★★★★**Best Apart Hotel**, Uğur Mumcunun Sokağı 71, ✆ 0312 446 8080, @ 0312 446 8090, located in the quieter Gaziosmanpaşa district, with bigger rooms and a swimming pool; doubles $120.

In Maltepe, convenient for the city centre, the ★★★★**İç Kale Oteli**, Gazi Mustafa Kemal Bulvarı 89, ✆ 0312 231 7710, @ 0312 230 6133, has a novelty for Turkey: a special floor for non-smokers. Rooms are spacious but mediocre and prone to traffic noise; overpriced at $150.

moderate

The best in this category, and better than some hotels in the category above, is the **First Apart Hotel** on a quiet pedestrian street in Kızılay at İnkılap Sokak 29 ✆ 0312 425 7575, @ 0312 419 2714. The staff are courteous and knowledgeable about the area. Standard rooms costing $65 are on the small side; it's worth the extra $10 for a larger deluxe room. Bigger still are the corner rooms for $85; best value are the hotel apartments, each containing two bedrooms and a sitting room, at $145; with space for 4–6 people per apartment. A few hundred yards to the south is the ★★★**Elit**, Olgunlar Sokak 10, ✆ 0312 417 4695, @ 0312 417 4697, with a double-doored elevator you could fit a camel in. The bedrooms themselves are unexciting, albeit equipped with minibars and TV. The official price for a double is $95; the more realistic price quoted at reception is $50.

In Ulus, the ★★★**Oğultürk**, off Çankırı Caddesi at Eşdost Sokak 6, ✆ 0312 309 2900, ✉ 0312 311 8321, is a step up from the other hotels in the area, with comfortable if anonymous rooms with minibar, TV and small bathtubs for $55. Otherwise, the ★★**Spor**, Rüzgarlı Plevne Sokak 6, ✆ 0312 324 2165, ✉ 0312 312 2153, is bright, well-run and packed with businessmen; en suite rooms are on the small side and cost $40.

inexpensive–cheap

Low-budget travellers accustomed to paying next to nothing for rooms in the rest of Turkey get a nasty shock in Ankara—but that's capital cities for you. Opera Meydanı, a frantic square in the Ulus district that's within walking distance of most of the museums, is the area to find Ankara's cheaper abodes and the places listed below are either on or off that square. All offer good value for money and have rooms with en suite faciities.

Far and away the best *inexpensive* place is the **Otel Mithat**, Tavus Sokak 2, ✆ 312 311 5410, ✉ 0312 310 1054, *akman@otelmithat.com.tr*, with doubles at $20; modern and very clean rooms, some with balconies offering uninspiring views of a car park. Also good, at $24, is the ★★**Otel Akman**, Tavus Sokak 6, ✆ 0312 324 4140, ✉ 0312 324 4142.

The ★★**Klasman**, Rüzgarlı Plevne Sokak 4, ✆ 0312 310 9797, ✉ 0312 310 1030, has a brightly painted reception decked out with chat-show sofas. The large bedrooms have TV, minibar and small en suite bathtubs; doubles $26.

The **Otel Sipahi**, Kosova Sokak 1, ✆ 0312 324 0235, has big and airy rooms that are tatty but tolerable for $14 with shower, $10 without. Avoid the top floors which have water-pressure problems; there's no lift, either. If you're really strapped for cash, the **Otel Üçler**, on the eastern side of Opera Meydanı, ✆ 0312 324 4140, ✉ 0312 324 4142, has very basic doubles for $12; hot showers cost $2 a time. However, women journeying alone will find greater peace of mind elsewhere.

Ankara   **Eating Out**

If gastronomic perfection is your aim, and money is no object, patronize the superb restaurants at the five-star hotels.

The **Kınacılar Evi**, in a restored mansion in the citadel, Kalekapısı Sokak 28, has a very intimate, homely feel, with wooden ceilings and only one or two tables per room. As well as à la carte dishes, there's a $14 fixed menu of meze, salad, kebabs, two drinks and a sweet course. Bizarrely for such a beautiful old house, it has a disco bar in the cellar pumping out a mix of Turkish and western pop and rock until 4am.

Strategically located on Arjantin Caddesi, close to the big money of the five-star hotels, are a dozen or more bars and restaurants, including the **Turkish Daily News Café and Restaurant**, proving its journalistic credentials with an extensive alcohol list and a free TDN at the door. The menu casts its net widely, including a vegetarian section, albeit with a beef dish plonked in amongst the eggplant and spinach. The cherry cheesecake is particularly fine. Meals around $12. Just off Arjantin Sokak further up the hill on Kırlangıç Sokak is the **Yeşil Vadi Lokantası**, next to a small park of the same name. Packed with Ankarites, it is alive with chatter and often filled with smoke. A wide array of kebabbery is on offer, as well as a small selection of fish; $12. If it's fish you're after, the **Yakamoz Restaurant** on Koroğlu Caddesi in the fashionable suburb of Gaziosmanpaşa is well known for its fresh fish, a precious commodity in Ankara: expect to pay at least $16 for a meal.

Those looking to eat well but less expensively will have few difficulties. Behind the northeast quadrant of the Kızılay intersection, some streets have been closed off to traffic: these are a good bet for inexpensive kebab houses. As usual, the ones that look the best really are, such as the **Köşk Restaurant** at Tuna Caddesi 2 is at the sophisticated end of the kebab house scene, all plate glass and mirrors, with a pleasant terrace surrounded by small trees and bushes. It's very popular at lunchtimes, with all the traditional favourites on offer: *şiş kebap*, köfte and *pide* in the region of $2–6. Better still is the nearby **Mülkiyeliler Birliği Lokalı** at Yüksel Caddesi 12, with a café on the ground floor and a restaurant on the 1st and 2nd floors. With more Turkish traditional dishes and some world cuisine oddments, it's neither flashy nor pretentious: it just has good food and great service; $6.

Within the citadel walls are several Ottoman houses which have been converted into restaurants. Of these, the **Zenger Paşa Konağı** at Doyran Sokak 13 is the original and still the best, a charming establishment with its very own small and dusty ethnographic museum as welll as the 'Salon of the Republic', covered in ludicrously lurid murals of an inspirational nature, such as Atatürk surrounded by doves. The restaurant on the top floor has panoramic views over the city. Although you could make do with a filling *gözleme* for under $2, other Ottoman treats such as köfte or *mantı* may prove too tempting to resist; a full meal costs $8–10.

For your sweet tooth, there is an elegant patisserie, the **Tuna**, at Atatürk Bulvarı 231, with soft chairs and discreet lighting; perfect for afternoon tea and baklava.

Boğazkale and Around

Towards the east, just beyond Ankara, lies the **Kızılırmak**, the Crescent River, curving in a broad loop from its mouth near Samsun around past Ankara and through Cappadocia, back to its sources in the east near Sivas. To the Greeks this was the Halys, a name famous from the campaigns of Alexander and Xenophon, but before that its arc enclosed the home counties of the Hittite Empire, a fertile and defensible country with the Hittite capital of Hattuşaş, near modern Boğazkale, at its centre.

Getting Around

Some books recommend Ankara as a base for visiting the Hittite sites at Boğazkale. This may be the only acceptable way for travelling paşas, but it's 112 miles (180km) away and not at all necessary. A number of modest hotels exist at Çorum, or, best of all, in Sungurlu, which is the closest town to the ruins. Sungurlu can be reached by any Ankara–Samsun or Ankara–Amasya **bus**. From there, about $30 is the going rate for a complete trip by **taxi** (extra if you want to take in Alacahöyük too), taking half a day or more.

You can avoid this by taking the Sungurlu–Boğazkale village **bus** and walking to the sites, but be warned it's a good eight-mile (13km) walk if you want to see everything.

Tourist Information

Çorum: fourth floor, Valilik Binası (provincial government headquarters), Yeni Hükümet Konaği 8, ℂ 0364 2138502.

Çorum

Çorum is the major town in this region. It has little to offer the visitor—an ornate clock tower in the square and a small Selcuk castle hidden away behind the school playground— but if you're bound for Boğazkale or Amasya, you'll probably pass through it. Have a look around. It's a modern town, clean, well laid out and prosperous, with an air of happy contentment. Ankara has skyscrapers, but in places like Çorum you can see Turkey's future.

Boğazkale and Hattuşaş

Boğazkale itself is a small pretty village of prosperous farmers. All around it, in an area of roughly two square miles, lie the scattered remains of the capital of the Hittites, **Hattuşaş**. Most travellers' first great surprise on coming here is that all the excavated buildings, temples and fortifications they visit among the farms and fields of Boğazkale were in fact parts of one city, a metropolis whose four miles of walls contained nearly 200 towers. Tours of the site are organized through travel agents in Ankara, and occasionally in Çorum. If you prefer travelling on your own, the best base for the expedition is **Sungurlu**, the closest town, located on the Ankara–Samsun road.

History in the Hittite Capital

The earliest traces of habitation at Hattuşaş go back as far as 3000 BC. By about 2000 BC, there was a settlement around the citadel (Büyükkale). This would be a town of the people of Hatti, from whom Hattuşaş took its name, but it's uncertain whether it was their capital. From the many natural advantages of the site, we can guess that it might have been; besides the fertility and beauty of the area, its strategic location for trade and its suitability for defence, there are natural springs everywhere. These ensured a source of water within the walls, and may conceivably have had some importance to the religion of the place.

The first written record mentioning Hattuşaş is unsettling. Anitta, king of Kushar, a city of unknown location, is the subject of the oldest tablet in the Hittite State Archive. The inscription recalls his total destruction of the city, and the curse he put upon it, which was that it never again be inhabited. This was in about 1720 BC. We also learn from the archive, however, that by the late 17th century BC another king of Kushar had moved his capital to Hattuşaş, and styled himself 'the man from Hattuşaş' or Hattusilis. A capital it remained throughout the Hittite old kingdom and empire (c. 1600–1200 BC), with one brief interruption when King Mutawalli moved his court to the southeastern city of Dattassa for what must have been reasons of temporary political distress. Shortly after it was restored, the great palace on Büyükkale burned down, perhaps as a result of civil strife, but both the city and its fortifications reached their highest stage of development under King Tudhaliya (c. 1250 BC), shortly before the catastrophe that ended the Hittite kingdom forever.

Symptoms of the coming end do not turn up clearly from the archaeological record. Reports of wars with the frontier tribes are common enough, and according to Dr Kurt Bittel, the archaeologist who devoted much of his life to the excavations at Hattuşaş, there was a noticeable decline in building standards in the city's last period. In any case, unknown invaders annihilated both the city and empire around 1200 BC.

Afterwards, the city seems to have been abandoned until the 9th century BC, when a Phrygian or Phrygian-influenced community grew up from the ruins of the Hittite palace, a well-built, important town that unfortunately isn't mentioned in a single ancient record. Most of its works have been cleared away by archaeologists to expose the Hittite levels underneath. The famous smiling Cybele in Ankara's archaeological museum was found in the Phrygian town.

Yazılıkaya

Most visitors try to plan their trip so that they are in Hattuşaş at about noon when the reliefs carved into the rocks at **Yazılıkaya** are best seen, and most begin their visit here, at the national shrine of the deified Hittite kings. Yazılıkaya is on the heights a mile and a half (2½km) northeast of Hattuşaş.

The early Hittites seem to have conducted their rituals out of doors, not surprisingly for a people whose chief deities were gods of sun and storms. The two chambers in the natural rock formation at Yazılıkaya were thus open to the sky, even after the monumental gateway and complex of buildings (of which only the foundations remain) were constructed at the entrance to the chambers.

Bittel believes that the **small gallery** to the right served for the funeral rites of departed kings. Certainly the reliefs carved in this shadowy, narrow chamber support this. Lion-headed figures, gesturing menacingly, guard the entrance, and once inside you are confronted with the bizarre and mysterious 'sword god', about whom archaeologists do not choose to speculate. This figure has the head of a god over a body which is a composite made up of four lions symmetrically arranged, and which terminates in a tapering sword blade, pointing downwards.

Another relief in this chamber shows **King Tudhaliya**—one of the four Hittite kings of that name—in the protective embrace of the god Sharruma, both of whom are in the conventional Hittite pose: standing in profile, with the left hand pulled back and the right extended. This is a particularly fine and well-preserved work, as is the famous frieze of the '**twelve gods**' on the opposite wall. These fellows, in a row like a Bronze Age chorus line, carry curved swords or sickles and wear the conical hats allowed to Hittite deities.

Conventions of Hittite Art

Although much of the meaning of Hittite art and writing remains to be deciphered, clever and erudite scholars such as Dr Bittel have sorted out the basics, comparing the reliefs with the extensive texts found in the state archives here. You recognize a Hittite king, such as Tudhaliya, by his rounded skull cap and earring, and by his *Kalmush*, the curving Hittite sceptre that resembles a monkey's tail. Note the Turkish slippers with the upturned toes, sported by both kings and gods. Among the ideograms that accompany the king will be a winged sun-disc, almost the same as that found in the art of the Assyrians and other ancient peoples. Beneath it, there is often a pair of what look like columns topped with Ionic capitals; these are taken to mean 'great king'. The other ideograms declare the king's name.

Gods are recognized by the pointed caps, and their standing in the divine hierarchy is indicated by the number of horns on the caps. Goddesses wear long pleated skirts and tall hats like those called *polos* by the Greeks, seemingly simulating the walls and towers of a city. Both are often portrayed with animal attributes; some stand on the backs of leopards or on eagles' wings, while the greatest gods often bestride sacred mountains. The ideogram for 'god' is an ellipse, divided vertically in half.

In the small gallery, there are also niches cut into the walls that may have held burial urns of the kings. At the corner near the entrance is a statue base that once supported a figure of the god Sharruma; it's worth noting that the eyes of all the figures in the reliefs are turned towards this spot.

To the left of the small gallery, a cleft in the rocks covers what seems to have been a well or spring; oddly, archaeologists make no mention of it. The large irregularly shaped gallery to the left of this contains reliefs of 63 Hittite gods and goddesses: 42 gods marching from the left to meet 21 goddesses coming from the right. It is believed this chamber was important in the New Year celebrations that took place in the spring.

It's difficult to ascribe names or functions to most of these images. From left to right, the first twelve are the same chorus line of gods represented in the small chamber, in the same pose. The other gods on this panel are unknown. In the next section, the badly worn part that seems to be a kind of house is really, on closer inspection, two bull-headed gods supporting the sky. The four figures on the far right represent Shaushga, the local name of **Ishtar**, her two handmaidens, and the familiar Mesopotamian water-god **Ea**.

The Hittite Pantheon

The next, and largest, section portrays the chief deities of the Hittite pantheon. The first two are unnamed gods of agriculture and weather; the next, the one with the most horns, is the Weather God of Heaven, **Teshub**, facing his consort **Hepatu** depicted astride a leopard. Her son **Sharruma**, also on a leopard, is directly behind. None of the goddesses that follow have been clearly identified.

Most of the names of these deities are from the Hurrians, the people to the southeast who strongly influenced Hittite art and culture. It is interesting to speculate on the cultural sources of this complicated pantheon. If the Hittite religion followed the usual pattern of that era, it may have worked like this: the northern invaders, the Hittites from the Balkans, brought down a Zeus-like storm god and grafted him and his companions onto a matriarchial system of the indigenous Hatti folk, represented by Hepatu. Her son Sharruma is a typical Tammuz-Adonis-Osiris figure of death and rebirth; his importance as mentor and exemplar of the sacred kings betrays a strong conservative instinct in the religion. In the frieze in the large gallery, he stands among the goddesses, as one of the original deities of the country, while the imported goddess Shaushga-Ishtar keeps company with the males.

One mortal has elbowed his way into this divine congregation: **King Tudhaliya IV**, whose image is carved into the opposite wall, larger than any of the gods, with his sacred mountains and his symbols exactly as in the portrait in the small gallery. It's ironic that the last known Hittite king should be the only one to receive this treatment—apotheosis, just before *Götterdämmerung*. As in so many other cases—the Romans, the kingdom of Commagene, the Incas or Aztecs or old King Ozymandias—an excess of king-worship seems to be the sign of an overripe nation that has lost its mental balance. When Tudhaliya had himself immortalized on this rock, his civilization had not 50 more years to live; perhaps his apotheosis speaks as clearly of the coming end as anything in the state archive.

Hattuşaş: The Great Temple (Büyük Mabet)

Coming to Hattuşaş itself, most visitors begin with the ruins of the **Great Temple**, at the modern entrance to the complex. Even though this temple, with the narrow storerooms surrounding it, was built in the last century of the Hittite Empire, about 1250 BC, its site is one of the oldest parts of the city, on the slopes just below the Büyükkale fortress. Nearby, excavations have revealed older buildings that belonged to an Assyrian trading colony, or *karum*, that flourished within the city during the Hittite old kingdom.

Here, as everywhere else in Hattuşaş that has been excavated, are neatly squared stone foundations all rising to a single level, with nothing above. The Hittites used sun-baked brick, covered with plaster and probably painted, in their building; consequently, the actual walls disintegrated long ago.

Near the entrance of the temple complex are the remains of an enormous **ceremonial basin**, carved with lions. Though broken now, it was originally almost 15ft long, carved from a single piece of limestone. The entrance itself, the once-imposing gateway through which the Hittite king entered with his retinue on formal occasions, leads to a paved street where there is another basin. Here the street curves, and completely surrounds the actual temple which is recognizable by the larger and more carefully cut stones used for its foundation. In the temple, it's easy to distinguish the central courtyard and the most important chambers, which are to the northeast: two large rooms of equal size that contained statues of the weather god and sun goddess, illuminated by windows to the outside. It is most likely that the temple, as well as the surrounding storerooms, were two or three storeys high, but there is no evidence as to how the outside of the temple and its roofline looked.

The temple storerooms must have contained the treasury, although nothing of this survived the sack of the city. Many of the cuneiform tablets that have contributed so much to our knowledge of the Hittites were found here, including one that contains a list of 208 members of the temple household, including:

...18 priests, 29 women musicians, 19 scribes for clay tablets, 33 scribes for wood tablets, 35 soothsayers, 10 Hurrian singers...

The remainder is lost. Also in these storerooms are the huge jars for wine or oil, some of which bear inscriptions.

The rooms in this part of the temple were long and narrow, and opened out only onto each other at the points where there are the huge, U-shaped marble thresholds, with doorposts sunk into them. Archaeologists never mention the great green stone, found in a room at the southern end of the street leading from the gateway. It is carved into an irregular shape and polished as smooth as glass; its purpose is unknown.

To the southwest, across an ancient street, which incidentally carries the storm drains underneath it as do other streets in Hattuşaş, is another complex of rooms built around a courtyard; it is believed that this too was part of the temple complex. At its southern edge, a **subterranean fountain** was discovered in a small room with a corbelled roof.

The Fortifications

Looking out from here, two large rock formations rise up from the nearby heights to the south. The cleft parting them is partially man-made; apparently there was a well or spring inside. This area, which stretches from the limits of modern Boğazkale in an arc across to Büyükkale in the southwest, marked the southern edge of the old city wall; its foundations, as well as some of the postern gates in it, are still present.

As you follow the modern road up to Büyükkale, you pass **Ambarlıkaya** and **Büyükkaya**, other natural rock-heights to the left that the Hittites were forced to include in their defensive works. The walls that ran between these were among the most impressive achievements of the Hittite architects, with gigantic earthen dykes supporting walls that in some places climbed slopes at an angle of 45°. Castles once perched on top of both these rocks.

Büyükkale

Büyükkale, the citadel and original centre of Hattuşaş, served in late Hittite times as the capital of the state and the residence of the kings. The stairs at the entrance are near the site of the original main gate, and lead to the lowest of three ascending courtyards, this one the so-called **state agora**. The complex to the west, consisting of four long rooms, was the **State Archive**, perhaps the oldest library building in the world. Among the thousands of records found here was the famous **Treaty of Kadesh**, signed with the Egyptians in 1259 BC. We owe its preservation, ironically, to Hattuşaş's anonymous invaders. When they put Büyükkale to the torch, the clay tablets were fired as if in a kiln; otherwise they would have disintegrated long ago.

It is believed that the middle courtyard was a kind of 'buffer zone' separating the bureaucracy from the royal residences in the upper courtyard, of which little remains but two large cisterns. On the southern edge of the citadel is a line of temples and state buildings; here some of the original brick still survives.

The Southern Walls

Sometimes after a period of crisis, cities realize that their fortifications, however impressive, are not good enough; they then exert themselves to extend them farther than earlier generations had ever dreamed of doing. Thus Athens built the long walls to Piraeus, and after the Peloponnesian War Syracuse constructed the incredible series of fortifications up to Euryalos. Some episode in Hittite history caused its kings to realize that their city's Achilles' heel lay to the south, where the land slopes gradually upwards to a ridge higher than Büyükkale itself. The rulers of 14th-century Hattuşaş solved the problem by building a broad arc of walls almost three miles long across their southern suburbs, thus completing one of the most magnificent urban fortifications anywhere in the ancient world.

On its way to these walls, the modern road passes several natural heights, fortified by the Hittites, which deserve a visit. To the left of the road, the **Southern Citadel** was probably of great importance to the city, but little has yet been excavated. To the right is **Nişantepe**, the site of another castle notable for the large but unfortunately indecipherable inscription on the eastern face of the rock, referring to King Suppiluliumas. The name of the castle means 'Mark Hill' or 'Target Hill', and from here most of the other monuments of Hattuşaş can be seen, as well as the infinite hills and mountains on all sides. The name is provocative, for standing here you have the sense that the city and its environs are somehow arranged, that this is one of the centres of a vast geomantic construction. If so, the key to it was buried with the Hittites.

Nearby, across a narrow saddle of land, is another large rock and **Sarıkale**, the 'yellow castle', with rooms, courtyards and cisterns like a smaller Büyükkale. **Yenicekale**, a similar construction, crowns the mount furthest south. Foundations of four important **temples** have been discovered near the southeast corner of the walls: excavations are still under way.

Yerkapı

The **southern walls** themselves are a symmetrical configuration, with the great gateway **Yerkapı** at their centre. Even in its ruined state, Yerkapı is perhaps the most memorable sight in Hattuşaş. Only the foundations of the double wall and towers remain, but these were built on a man-made ridge some 30ft high, and here the slopes are paved to further disconcert attackers. Two long stairways, one on either side, lead down from the outer wall. The gate was decorated, or guarded, by finely carved sphinxes, one now in the museum of İstanbul, the other in Berlin.

There is a surprise directly underneath Yerkapı, a strange, sloping 200ft tunnel through the mound, built of rough Cyclopean masonry corbelled inwards, altogether unlike anything else in Hattuşaş. Archaeologists call it a sally port, a gate from which the defenders could sneak out and harry their attackers from behind, but this is a poor explanation; the tunnel is too noticeable and too carefully built and sited (lying directly north–south, on the central axis of the city). It is more likely it held some religious or ceremonial significance.

Kralkapı and Aslankapı

A third of a mile away, two other important gates, **Kralkapı** and **Aslankapı**, can be seen on either side of Yerkapı. These are well known for the reliefs that give them their names, meaning King's Gate and Lion's Gate, although like most of Hattuşaş's sculptures, they have been removed to the Ankara museum and replaced with concrete casts. The king carved on Kralkapı is probably really a god protecting the gate. Whichever he is, it is one of the Hittites' best works. The god looks remarkably placid and confident, and the axe he carries looks very serious. So do the lions of Aslankapı, although they're not nearly as well preserved. The unusual and impressive architectural feature of these gates is their well-executed parabolic arches, a form unique to the Hittites.

Many of the finds of Hattuşaş not in the Ankara museum are in the small **Boğazkale Museum** (*open daily 8–5.30; adm with the same ticket as for Hattuşaş*). These include some intricately carved seal rings, *pithoi* and other ceramics, some Byzantine steles, and an unimaginative reconstruction of the Büyük Mabet (Great Temple) of Hattuşaş.

Alacahöyük

A possible afternoon detour from Hattuşaş is to **Alacahöyük**, on a side road going back towards Sungurlu. Long before the Hittites ever entered Anatolia, as far back as 4000 BC, there was a settlement here of the indigenous Hatti people. In their best days, about 2500–2000 BC, the Hatti had one of the most advanced cultures anywhere outside Mesopotamia. Later occupations have covered up the Hatti at sites like Alacahöyük, and it's hard to tell what kind of talent they had for town-building; apart from the later Hittite reliefs, there's really little left to see. Their wonderful metal cosmological discs and figurines have already been mentioned. Most of these are in Ankara, though copies may be seen in the small **museum** here.

The Hittite reliefs, contemporary with those at Hattuşaş (and like them, concrete casts of the originals), are a puzzle. Two musicians play outlandish instruments, while two other men climb a ladder to nowhere. Archaeologists have named one figure the 'sword swallower'. There is a procession of animals, a seated female goddess, and a king and queen standing before an odd T-shaped object and what appears to be an altar with a bull on it.

Around Boğazkale   **Where to Stay**

Sungurlu

The **Hitit Moteli** (King Suppiluliumas slept here often), just outside Sungurlu, ✆ 0364 311 8042, ✉ 0364 311 3873, is the best base for seeing Boğazkale; besides beautiful landscaping, with flowers and occasional nightingales, it has a good restaurant and a swimming pool. It's located on the Ankara highway and most buses stop here. Doubles with bath $40.

Boğazkale

Boğazkale has a handful of cheap pensions, such as the **Hattuşaş Restaurant and Pansiyon** in the centre of the village, ✆ 0364 452 2013, ✉ 0364 452 2957; rooms at $6 per person. The best accommodation in the village is the **Aşıkoğlu Motel**, ✆ 0364 452 2004, ✉ 0364 452 2171, which has double rooms with private bath for $30 per person.

Çorum

The ★★★**Çorum Büyük**, 90 İnönü Caddesi, ✆ 0364 224 6092, ✉ 0364 224 6094, provides the three-star comfort in Çorum, with pleasant en suite doubles going for $45. Just along the road, at 97 İnönü Caddesi, is Çorum's old standard, the ★★**Kolağası**, ✆ 0364 213 1971, ✉ 0364 224 1556, with doubles for $26. Çorum also has several cheap pensions (about $7 per person).

Around Boğazkale   **Eating Out**

There are simple lokantas in Çorum and Sungurlu, as well as at Boğazkale itself. The restaurant at the **Hitit** motel in Sungurlu is quite good, at around $16 for a meal.

Sivas to Amasya

Getting Around

You can't get to the Amasya region by **train** from Ankara, but it is served by the slow, infrequent Samsun–Amasya–Sivas line, with good scenery through the mountains. There are no difficulties with **bus** connections anywhere, but trips through the mountains will take longer than you'd expect—although the network of paved roads is better than in most parts of Turkey. Both in Tokat and Amasya you can get a **taxi** to take you up to the high castles for about $10.

Tourist Information

Sivas: Vilayet Konağı, © 0346 221 3535.

Tokat: On the first floor of the Taş Han, © 0356 211 8252.

Amasya: Mustafa Kemal Bulvarı 27, © 0358 218 7428.

East of the turn-off for Sungurlu and Çorum, the Ankara–Sivas road follows the green and pretty valley of the River Delice before reaching **Yozgat**, an agricultural centre distinguished only by its Ottoman clock tower. After Yozgat, the road passes through one of Anatolia's emptier quarters for 130 miles (210km) before rejoining the valley of the Kızılırmak at **Sivas**, a peaceful city of 230,000 people, founded during Roman times as Sebasteia.

Sivas

Sivas first gained importance during the Middle Ages as capital of the Selcuks and other Turkish emirs. Its golden age lasted until Tamerlane sacked it in 1395. Today, Sivas is most proud of its role at the beginning of the War of Independence; during the summer of 1919, when much of the country was under foreign occupation, Mustafa Kemal (Atatürk) called together the first National Congress in this safe, remote city. On 4 September, the decision was made to ignore the İstanbul government and work for the liberation of Turkey. Today, the place where the congress met, the old boys' high school on Konak Meydanı in the centre of Sivas, is the **September Fourth Museum**, with the congress hall and Atatürk's apartments kept just as they were during that eventful hour.

Selcuk Monuments

To the south, Konak Meydanı extends into a park that contains four of medieval Sivas's finest monuments: the **Kale Cami** of 1580, the **Şifa'iye Medrese** and **Çifte Minare Camii** (twin minarets), these two facing each other across an ancient street, and the **Buruciye Medrese**. These last three structures were begun in 1271. Although by then the Selcuks had moved their capital to Konya, they still took great interest in the eastern marches. This complex, despite its ruined state, is as fine as anything they built in the west. All three have beautifully carved gateways, the Şifa'iye adorned with stern Selcuk lions, the Çifte Minare with acanthus-leaf capitals, probably borrowed from an earlier Byzantine structure. The two minarets, made from brick and blue İznik tiles, and the exterior walls are all that remain of the mosque. Already they list as much as the Tower of Pisa, so see them while you still can.

The park containing these structures was the heart of Selcuk Sivas. Above it rises the old **Kale** (citadel) on the hill: although it was occupied from the time of the Hittites, nothing remains today, and the old fort has been converted to a park. The neighbourhoods around it, to the south and west, are the oldest in Sivas, with quiet and pretty streets where the appearance of a foreigner is a rare event. Here stands the 12th-century **Ulu Cami**, and yet another Selcuk theological school, the **Gök Medrese**, also built in that great year of 1271. Although derelict, this is one of the most famous works of Selcuk architecture for its splendid gateway, with its fanciful sculptured patterns that include a melange of styles from every corner of Anatolia, with some old Byzantine carved thistles and angels thrown in.

Outside Sivas, two long and graceful **Ottoman bridges** span the Kızılırmak, lying parallel to the modern roads to Ankara and Amasya.

Divriği

To see the greatest of all medieval Turkish mosques in this corner of Anatolia, you must make the long and difficult trip to **Divriği**, 93 miles (150km) southeast of Sivas. It is easier to reach by train than by the long and roundabout routes on unpaved roads. In the 13th century, Divriği was the capital of the short-lived Mengüçeh Turkish emirate. The **Ulu Cami**, near the town citadel, is similar in form to the Selcuk mosques of Sivas or Erzurum, with its short minaret, low sloping roof, and conical *türbeler* protruding from the top. Its carved portals are judged among the best work of the age. Divriği was flourishing then, as a stop along the important trade route from Sivas down to the Euphrates valley; the sources of that legendary river are in the surrounding mountains and, consequently, a number of **caravanserais**, in various states of preservation, dot the Sivas road, most notably at **Kangal**, a village midway between the two towns.

A Dog's Life

The kangal is the Turkish sheep dog, bred in the mountains around Sivas, and if you venture out into the rocky wastes of eastern Anatolia you may see one. If you do, stay in your vehicle or, if you're on foot, keep calm and back away very, very slowly. Don't run and don't do anything daft such as hurling stones at it. You don't mess with a kangal.

As dogs go, they are hard to describe—some sort of vague cross between a St Bernard and an Alsatian. If you're in doubt as to whether the monster you've just encountered is a kangal or not, just look at its neck. If there is a viciously spiked collar about it, placed there by an Anatolian farmer to help protect his dog from predators such as bears and wolves, it's a kangal. Turks, not normally a nation of animal lovers, speak fondly of the kangal; some keep them as pets. In a way, the beast represents how they like to see themselves; loyal, tough, and hard-working yet a terrible foe when provoked. They are held in such high esteem that in the solitary sheep farms up in the mountains, where baby sitters are hard to find, parents will happily leave young children in the care of the family kangal.

A popular kangal story in Turkey is about two parents who did just that. As the mother and father were returning home, their kangal came bounding down the hill to greet them, frantic with excitement, fresh blood smeared across its muzzle and jaws. To the horrified parents, it was obvious what had happened; the kangal had gone insane and had attacked their child. In anguish, the father took up his gun; it took several shots to kill the kangal. Together, husband and wife entered the family home, preparing themselves for the sight of their mutilated infant. As they peered around the door into a room that had clearly been the site of a ferocious battle, they saw their child, distraught but otherwise unharmed. And as they drew the toddler towards them, they saw the bloodied corpse of an immense bear, its throat ripped out by the jaws of their kangal.

Besides the road to Divriği there are three other routes from Sivas: the main highway east to Erzurum, the bad road over the Tahtalı Mountains to Malatya, or a slight backtrack along the valley of the Yeşilırmak ('Green River') to the northwest. Of the three, this last is by far the most scenic, crossing the Yıldız ('star') Mountains at the pass of **Çamlıbel** and then continuing through forest and mountains that become increasingly more rugged and green the closer you come to the Black Sea.

Tokat

The farmers of the Yeşilırmak grow tobacco, among other things, and one of the Turkish monopoly's most popular brands of smokes is named after **Tokat**, a lovely town on the river that has been occupied for thousands of years. Recorded history first mentions Tokat under the name of 'Comana Pontica', the religious centre of Mithridates' Pontic Kingdom. Orestes, son of Agamemnon, is said to have visited here on his wanderings, introducing the rites of Artemis and leaving a famous image of the goddess that the Persian King Xerxes later stole.

Up on the slender peak that guards the town, the picture-book **castle** was built by the Byzantines and restored by the Turks. The Byzantines only interested themselves in holding this strategic position; under them the city dwindled, reviving under the Selcuks and other Turkish emirates who contested the town in the Middle Ages. Among Tokat's Selcuk legacy is the **Gök Medrese** of 1270, a medical college that is now the **Tokat Museum** (*open daily 8.30–12 and 1–4.30; adm*), with the usual grave steles and Turk's attic of folk arts and crafts. One tomb in the medrese belongs to Mu'in al-Din, the Selcuk vezir who built the complex. Alongside the museum is the **Taş Han**, a 17th-century caravanserai lined with artisan's cells; sitting amongst all manner of bric-à-brac within the glassed-in cloisters are numerous old men, endlessly discussing life over endless glasses of tea.

Other Ottoman contributions to Tokat include the 16th-century **Ali Paşa Camii**, centre of a group that includes a tomb and baths; the **Hatuniye Camii**, built by Beyazıt II; a fine stone bridge at the northern end of the town; and the **clock tower**, across from the Ali Paşa Camii in the town square. If all these clock towers, like the ones in Çorum and Yozgat, look alike, they should; all were built during the 19th-century reign of Abdülhamid. He may have earned his reputation as a black-hearted reactionary in a thousand ways, but he did want the Turks to know what time it was.

The great citadel of Tokat closes off one end of the valley of the Yeşilırmak, and its counter-part at **Amasya** seals the other. In between, the Yeşilırmak lives up to its name, for although the river itself is muddy brown with the soil of Anatolia, the land it waters between these two high citadels is one of the greenest and most fertile corners of the nation. Amasya itself is small, but offers some of Turkey's best travel poster shots. Squeezed into a steep valley, under cliffs carved with rock tombs of the ancient Pontic kings, and with its old Ottoman houses overhanging the winding Yeşilırmak, Amasya qualifies as one of the loveliest cities in Anatolia. Its strategic position has also gained it the attention of kings and sultans throughout the centuries, and they have endowed it with many fine buildings.

The Kingdom of Pontus

In antiquity, the Yeşilırmak was called the Iris, the messenger of the dawn, for to the Greeks this was one of the borders of the known world, beyond which lay only Amazons, Scythians and other barbarians who gave the Greeks bad dreams. As sometime capital of the various kings named Mithridates and their obstreperous Pontic kingdom, **Amaseia** gave the Romans a big headache. Rome captured the city in 70 BC, but with the revolt of Phanarces, she was forced to send Julius Caesar to finish the job. After the battle at nearby Zile in 47 BC and the destruction of the Pontic army, Caesar came up with the tag *Veni, vidi, vici*, a political slogan that was to carry him a long way.

Along the River

The centre of Amasya is a broad square on the river's edge, with one of the better equestrian Atatürks, the conqueror in his beaver hat, surrounded by resolute soldiers and anxious women, gazes fiercely at the police station across the river. From here, a pretty shaded promenade follows the river; the main street, Atatürk Caddesi, runs parallel towards the south. Between them, the shopping district surrounds a 16th-century *bedesten*, still in use. A few blocks further, past the twin domes of the **Sultan Beyazıt II Mosque** complex, the city's most impressive, is the **Amasya Museum** (*open Tues–Sun 8.30–12 and 1.30–5; adm*).

This museum contains, in its large new building, a fair collection of artefacts from the various chapters of the past. There is a good-as-new Roman bathtub and two curious cylindrical sarcophagi, as well as local arts and crafts. Some of the most beautiful objects made in the Islamic world were astronomical instruments, and there are fine examples here. The undeniable attraction of the museum, however, is the **Mongol mummies** in the adjacent Selcuk **Türbe of Sultan Mesut**. Mesut sleeps peacefully in the crypt, but the Mongols, Cumodar and Oshuga Nuyin, two governors of the 14th century who served under the renegade Khan Hülâgü and his successors, are displayed in glass cases, along with the members of an important Selcuk family and their children. The museum's sculpture garden surrounds the *türbe*: the columns with Latin inscriptions served as milestones and were found along the Roman road that traversed the valley of the Yeşilırmak.

Just around the corner from the museum is another *türbe*, that of **Halifat Gazi**, the best of the many tombs in this city. The asymmetrical decoration, with delicate geometric patterns inside small circles randomly arranged over the tomb, is a peculiarity of local architecture.

Other Sights

Two other mosques can be seen in the district above Atatürk Caddesi. Near to the old *bedesten* stands a tumbledown *han*, constructed in 1758 by order of the local paşa and used today by metalworkers and hardware sellers. On the hill behind it stands the 13th-century mosque of **Burmalı Minare**, taking its name from the spirals of its beautifully hewn 17th-century 'twisted' minaret. A few blocks further uphill, the **Fethiye Camii** was originally a Byzantine church of the 7th century.

Beyond the main square, the Yeşilırmak twists northwards. Following it along the main road, you'll find more of Amasya's medieval landmarks; first, the **Bimarhane** of 1309, an insane asylum founded during the period of Mongol rule. Despite its function, the Bimarhane has been blessed with an intricately carved gate as fine as that of any mosque. In contrast to this, the interior is starkly simple and remains unfinished, reflecting the uncertainty of the times after the collapse of the Selcuk state. A block further on lies the **Mehmet Paşa Camii** (late 15th century), and, beyond that, the early 15th-century **Beyazıt Camii**. Through much of early Ottoman history, the sons of sultans were shuffled off to Amasya as governors to keep them out of trouble until their turn on the throne. These two mosques, as well as many others in the town, are a result of the royal attention, as is the **Büyük Ağa Medrese**, just across the bridge from the Beyazıt Camii. This beautiful octagonal complex, with its interior arcade and courtyard, was founded by Beyazıt's Chief White Eunuch. The medrese is still in use today, and is home to 40 boys from all over Anatolia. Although the front door may be locked, if you knock and express an interest in looking around inside, you may well end up being shown around by a clutch of eager young students.

Maiden's Palace and Citadel

On the northern shore of the river, where the old wooden houses crowd against the banks in varying states of dilapidation, the huge rock crowned by the citadel rises straight up above them, with royal tombs burrowed out of its cliffs. According to the geographer Strabo, a native of Amasya who knew the city under both Roman and Pontic rule, the ledge above this narrow bank was the site of the Pontic royal palace, known locally as the **Maiden's Palace**, with walls that extended down to the river. Parts of these are still visible, built into the walls of the old houses of the quarter, although they're only visible once you climb the stairs of the palace proper. Here the walls have been restored in recent years, and amid the gardens you can see remains of painted arches and domes, part of the baths built by Mithridates. The strategically placed café here also offers fine views of the town.

From the rock gardens, cut stairs lead up to the **tombs** of the Pontic kings. Marvellous as these seem from down below (the city illuminates them at night), little of colour or interest has survived the centuries, and it's impossible to tell which kings were buried there. Sockets cut into the stone indicate there must have been imposing stone façades and balustrades, but nothing of these or any other artwork or grave goods exist today. Still, the effect is royal and grand enough. Visitors are usually surprised that the tombs are not merely façades themselves but entire buildings chiselled out of the dark basalt cliffs; you can walk completely around two of them, into the mountain and out again. Altogether there are four tombs here, but the surrounding region has ten more, all overlooking the Yeşilırmak and comprising the national pantheon of this forgotten kingdom.

In ancient times, Amasya's **citadel**, high above the tombs, was reputed to be impregnable, and from below it does in fact seem utterly inaccessible. However, there's a way around the back (yellow signs indicate the way from the vicinity of the Büyük Ağa Medrese) and the summit can be reached by car. Here, in a kind of museum of masonry, the building styles of the ages betray the various reworkings of the fortress, and its continuous importance over 2,000 years; first, there is ancient rough stone, then good square ashlar from the Hellenistic era, then Roman brick, and finally the characteristic Ottoman sandstone that comprises the greater part of the ruins. Flowers and some of the prettiest butterflies in Anatolia currently occupy the site, and, if the terrain is difficult, the panorama over Amasya's valley and surrounding mountains makes it all worthwhile.

At the entrance, a marble lintel with a Greek inscription has been built into walls of a later era. In the derelict lower citadel, a cistern remains that provided the fortress with its water. The upper citadel is better preserved, and here you can find the famous secret passage: look for a large surviving stretch of wall, high but not broad, with an opening in it that looks, from a distance, like a keyhole. Near its base is a spot where the wall has crumbled away to form a set of steps on its jagged edge. Climb up, and you'll see an arched brick tunnel with slippery descending steps. Supposedly it leads down to the tombs, but no one in Amasya, it seems, has ever tried it. Bring a torch and half a mile of rope.

Around Amasya

Today, as in the days of Mithridates, the area around Amasya is one of the most productive and densely populated farming regions of Turkey. The valleys of the Yeşilırmak and its tributaries, between the peaks and crags, are dotted with towns, each with its castle hovering over it and some well-built foundations of the medieval Turks at its heart. **Zile**, where Caesar conquered, is one of these, also **Merzifon**, the ancient Phazemon. **Niksar**, further east in the valley of the Kelkut Çayı, has kept its name since Roman times, or almost. The Romans called it Neocaesarea, but time has eroded the name just as it has the old fortress, one of Mithridates' strongholds. Niksar received some fine buildings from the Selcuks, notably the 12th-century **Yağıbaşan Medrese**.

It's out of the way, some 37 miles (60km) along mountainous roads from Amasya, but a trip to **Borabay Gölü**, a volcanic crater lake surrounded by forests, will reward you with some of the best scenery these mountains have to offer.

Around Amasya   **Where to Stay**

Everywhere in this region, accommodation will be clean but modest; it's a pleasant part of Turkey, but hardly overwhelmed with tourists.

Sivas

The **★★Hotel Köşk**, Atatürk Caddesi 7, © 0346 221 1150, charges $34 a double, breakfast included. The **Yavuz**, Atatürk Caddesi 86, © 0346 225 0204, is the best of the town's rather tatty selection of cheaper places; $14 per double.

Tokat

The ★★★★**Büyük Otel** is inconveniently situated in the new suburbs to the north-west of the central sights, on Demirköprü Mevkii, ✆ 0356 228 1661, ✉ 0356 228 1660. It has the standard four-star lofty glass-roofed lobby, swimming pool and rooms with mini-bar and satellite TV for a very reasonable $60.

The ★★**Burcu**, Gazi Osman Paşa Bulvarı 48, ✆ 0356 212 8494, ✉ 0356 212 2327, has good en suite rooms for $40.

Çamlıca, Gazi Osman Paşa Bulvarı 86, ✆ 0356 214 1269, ✉ 0356 212 2899, is the best of the cheapies. The carpets may be threadbare, but the rooms at the back are quiet and sunny; $14 with bathroom, $12 without. The nearby **Plevne Otel** at No.83, ✆ 0356 214 2207, has a shabby charm to it, with dilapidated but large rooms with bathroom and TV costing $12.

Amasya

This is a gem of a town, so its accommodation is correspondingly more expensive than average. Its most atmospheric offering is the **İlk Pansiyon** on Hittit Sokak 1, ✆ 0358 218 7689, a lovingly restored Ottoman mansion. Bedrooms are carpet-bedecked, with high ceilings and wooden fittings. $25–45, depending on the size of the room and whether or not it has an en suite bathroom.

Almost as good is the **Emin Efendi Pansiyon**, in a 200-year-old house overlooking the river at Hazeranlar Sokak 73, ✆ 0358 212 0852, ✉ 0358 212 1895. Double rooms for $33 are smaller and less atmospheric than the İlk, and all but one have shared bathroom facilities, but the views are the best in town. If you prefer orthodox hotel accommodation, the ★★**Büyük Amasya Oteli** has good views further along the river on the way to the Büyük Ağa Medrese, at Elmasiye Caddesi 20, ✆ 0358 218 4054, ✉ 0358 218 4056. Unremarkable en suite doubles with balcony for $45.

The **Apaydın Hotel**, Atatürk Caddesi 58, ✆ 0358 218 1184, has a brooding lobby and corridors reminiscent of an asylum, but it's cheap at $12 per double with basin.

Plain and cheap rooms can be found in indistinguishable hotels in Yozgat, Divriği, Niksar, Suluova and Merzifon.

Around Amasya   **Eating Out**

Nothing either special or unpleasant is likely to come your way. Amasya has a strip of riverside cafés from which to gaze up at the tombs, serving *pide* and kebab variations. Another people-watching platform is the creeper-festooned **Gamasuk Çay Bahçesı** in front of the Taş Han. Down a small street at Sadık Esen Sokak 3 is Amasya's best place to eat, the unprepossessing **Bahar Lokantası**, serving huge portions of *Tokat kebap* (skewered lamb, aubergine and potatoes) for $4—usually enough for two people. The **Çiçek Lokanta** in Amasya is also good and moderately priced at $3–4; the same prices prevail at the **Anadolu** in Sivas.

Southwestern Anatolia

Southwestern Anatolia

N

● Port

100km
50 miles

To Ankara

To Eskişehir

To Afyon

Cihanbeyli

Lake Akşehir

Yalvaç

Akşehir

Ilgın

Lake
Eğirdir

Şarkıkaraağaç

Eğirdir

Kızıldağ
Milli Parkı

Eflatun-
pinari

Sille

KONYA

Lake
Burdur

Lake
Beyşehir

Beyşehir

Lake
Acıgöl

Burdur

İsparta

İnsuyu Cave

Sagalassos

Kovada
Milli Parkı

Zindan Cave

Kovada Lake

Çatal Höyük

Alaca Dağı

Çumra

Bucak

Kovada

Tefenni

Cremna

Lake
Suğla

Kibyra

Çavdır

ANTALYA

T o r o s

Sertavul
Pass

Akçalı Dağları

Ermenek

Gulf
of
Antalya

The Lake District

For a change from the endless blue sky and sea, seafood and trinkets of the Mediterranean coasts, there's either the gloomy grey Marmara and the Black Sea, or this seldom-visited corner of the country, which has quite a personality. There's nothing in Europe or anywhere around the Mediterranean quite like it: sparse emerald hills and craggy mountains, enclosing enormous freshwater lakes that change colour with every mood of the weather.

Although it lies at the crossroads of routes connecting major tourist centres, the region of lakes remains relatively undiscovered; only Eğirdir has any pretensions to be a resort, and a modest one at that. The east–west road from Cappadocia and Konya to Pamukkale and Ephesus, and the north–south road from İstanbul and Bursa to Antalya and the south coast meet here. It cannot be long before the area makes better use of its position to attract tourists in greater numbers, so go now before it's too late.

Getting Around

Eğirdir, Burdur and Isparta are very accessible, being on major **bus** routes, though be warned that the roads are narrow and wind all over the map; whether you're travelling by bus or car it will always take longer than you expect (2½ hours from Eğirdir to Antalya and more than four hours to Konya). The Eğirdir tourist office will help to arrange **taxi** trips to Zindan Cave and Adada, or to Kovada; if you can find some companions, you can share the $45 that is the going rate for a carful to either—lunch included. There are regular **minibus** services to Ağlasun, Bucak and Gölhisar, but in each case you will need a **car** to reach the sites. Minibuses to Insuyu leave frequently from Burdur.

Tourist Information

Eğirdir: 2 Sahil Yolu 13 A, ✆ 0246 311 4388.

Isparta: Hükümet Konağı, ✆ 0246 218 4438.

Burdur: Cumhuriyet Meydanı 4, ✆ 0248 233 1078.

Eğirdir

This pretty lakeside town was called Acrotiri in the Byzantine era, meaning promontory; this changed into the Turkish Eğridir, with the unfortunate meaning of 'it's bent'. In the mid-1980s, the residents, tired of the jokes, changed the name to Eğirdir, which has the more satisfactory meaning of 'she is spinning'. The new name fits in with a local legend. Once there was no lake. Up in the mountains, the queen was spinning while the young prince was out hunting with bow and arrow. He shot at a deer, but the animal ran away and the arrow hit a large stone which shattered, releasing a torrent of water which drowned the prince and formed the lake. The grieving king said to his wife, '*Eğirdir! Sen eğirdir! Oğlun öldü. Sen ne yapıyorsun hâlâ?*' ('Spinning! Spinning! Your son is dead. Just what are you doing?').

Eğirdir sits on a small promontory jutting into the turquoise-blue waters of the lake, tucked under steep, enormous Mount Davras. The view from the Isparta road as you descend to the town is spectacular, especially in the evening. During Selcuk times, Eğirdir was part of the

Sultanate of Rum and capital of the lake district. When the Selcuk hegemony was broken in the mid-13th century, Eğirdir became the seat of the powerful Hamitoğulları emirs, who had control of Antalya and were able to trade with the Aegean islands, Egypt and the eastern Mediterranean. Today, Eğirdir makes its living from its excellent red apples, and increasingly from tourism. It is a humble, almost too friendly and entirely too relaxing resort where people seem absolutely delighted you've come so far to visit their town. Its nightlife consists of watching the kids play football on the lighted pitch facing the harbour. Boat tours, offered around the harbour or arranged through hotels, are nothing like as lavish as the ones on the seacoast—just a pleasant outing around the lake in a little motorboat. **Market day** is Thursday, when you may sample the apples and other specialities of the area, such as rose-water soap from Isparta; for the perfect souvenir, if you're lucky, the man who sells dried weasel skins will be around.

One of the Hamitoğulları emirs, Felekeddin Dündar, changed the name of the town to Felekabad, and built the attractive **Dündarbey Medrese**, which has been restored and converted to a shopping bazaar. The magnificent stalactite gateway formerly belonged to a ruined caravanserai three miles (5km) from Eğirdir. Other reused stones from the caravanserai can be seen in the wall which bars the entrance to the peninsula and connects the medrese to the earlier **Hızarbey Camii**. The minaret is unusual in that it is not free-standing, but sits on top of this wall. Below the minaret is an arch which allows passage between the religious complex and the inner town; on the lake side of the wall you can see doors that lead to a tunnel in the wall, for use in times of trouble. The mosque has an ornate door with a wooden porch. An unusual floral pattern is carved into the stone above the door. Inside is an İznik-tiled mihrab and a forest of wooden pillars, painted blue, which support the roof. A causeway, built in the early 1980s, joins the promontory to a small island, **Yeşilada** (Green Island). A sizeable Greek community lived here before the exchange of populations and it is possible to see old Greek buildings on the island and on the promontory, within the town's dilapidated fortress. Today the island is full of *pansiyonlar*.

The water in Eğirdir Lake is sweet and full of good fish, the hot item in the town's restaurants. It is possible to swim at the town beach, a 10min walk from the centre, though you may prefer the bigger and nicer **Altınkum** (Golden Sand) beach, less than two miles (3km) from the centre of town in the direction of Isparta, or **Bedre** beach, the best of all, nearly seven miles (11km) on the road to Barla.

Kovada National Park

About 19 miles (30km) south of Eğirdir Lake is the small **Kovada Lake**. The road from Eğirdir runs beside a canal connecting the two lakes and is lined by apple orchards which form the basis of the town's economy. In the summer, as you near Kovada, you can see the goat's-hair tents of nomads who have migrated to their *yaylalar*, summer pastures. The area round the lake is a national park, **Kovada Milli Parkı**, reputedly with 70 species each of trees and animals, including wild boar. In winter, hunting is possible.

Zindan Cave

If you get excited by bats, and the stench of bat guano, and slithering snake-like through narrow, mud-lined passages, you will enjoy a visit to **Zindan Cave**, about 17 miles (27km) southeast of Eğirdir. Old clothing, stout shoes and a torch are essential. The cave is 2.4km long and it is possible to 'walk' to the end. By the entrance is a pretty stone bridge across a little stream—very convenient for washing off the mud. On this bridge, a bit of ancient relief can be made out; it's said to be the Titan Eurymedon, father of Prometheus. Apparently the cave was a holy place in antiquity; the bridge leads to a nearby necropolis. The road passes a turning to **Adada**, where there are three almost completely preserved **Roman temples**, a nice forum and some Hellenistic buildings. After Aksu, the road passes through a magnificent gorge. Beehives dot the surrounding hills.

Another possible excursion from Eğirdir is to **Yalvaç**, 40 miles (65km) to the north. About a mile and a quarter from this village are the ruins of Pisidian Antioch, a city founded in Hellenistic times that was the capital of the province under the Romans; both St Paul and St Philip passed through. There isn't a lot to see, but Yalvaç has a small **museum** of finds from the site

Isparta and Burdur

Famous for attar of roses and carpets, **Isparta** is an attractive city of modern boulevards with lots of trees and little else; its old town was devastated by an earthquake at the end of the 19th century, leaving only the impressive **Ulu Cami**, built in 1417. The rose fields lie in the plains north of the town, but are not visible from the road. Out of them Isparta makes rose oil, rosewater soap and shampoo, rose cologne, rose-flavoured *lokum* (Turkish delight) and rose everything else. The carpets are for domestic consumption; you will find them not in tourist carpet shops, but on the floors of Turkish houses or in the town **museum** on Kenan Evren Caddesi. Another speciality of Isparta is *Isparta kebap*, made of lean roast meat—either veal or goat, but goat is tastier—wrapped in *pide* bread.

Unlike Eğirdir, **Burdur** is not directly on the lake. There is little to see in the town, apart from the **Ulu Cami**, built in the 14th century by Dündar Bey, the Hamitoğulları emir. South from the main street and across a little river is a charming residential area. Here, through the open doors of the houses, you can see carpet looms being worked. Women sit on the pavements, chatting and doing their knitting, tatting, needlework and crochet-work. The **museum** is just off the main street and houses finds from **Hacılar**, a Neolithic settlement 15 miles (24km) southwest of Burdur that was one of the successors (*c.* 6600 BC) to the more sophisticated culture of Çatal Höyük. Hacılar itself is not worth a visit; you can poke about in a field and find a few shards, but that is all.

The water of Lake Burdur is saline, containing about 21 grams of dissolved salts per litre, and it supports only very small fish. There are beaches near **Çendik**, on its south-eastern side, where it is possible to swim.

İnsuyu Cave

İnsuyu is a popular recreation spot about nine miles (14km) east of Burdur. The cave is clean and well lit, and its length of 600m can be walked in comfort. It consists of a series of grottoes with stalagmites and stalactites. Its nine lakes contain mineral water so clear it might not be there; this water is thought to be therapeutic for diabetics.

Sagalassos

The largest towns in Pisidia were Sagalassos, Termessos and Selge. Termessos was previously thought to be Pisidia's greatest city, but recent research shows that Sagalassos was both the wealthiest and the most populous. Like the other Pisidian cities, Sagalassos lies high in the mountains between Burdur and Isparta, in a spectacular setting some four miles (7km) from the village of Ağlasun. The remains are extensive and are considered by archaeologists to be well preserved; tourists will need to be imaginative.

Alexander the Great came to Sagalassos in 334 BC and captured the city. At that time there were no city walls; to the south of the main path through the city is a small flat hill, which slopes steeply to the south and from which the Sagalassians believed they could defend themselves. However, Alexander and his army managed to scale the hillside and thus took the city. Some walls were built much later, but Sagalassos was never enclosed by real city walls; the walls just connected the public areas, so that in times of trouble the population crowded into the centre. The city was abandoned in the early Byzantine period; there are three churches, one of which was never completed.

The older part of the city lies to the north of the main path. Among a few late Hellenistic buildings, the best-preserved is a 1st-century BC **Doric temple** with two standing walls but fallen columns. Southeast of the Doric temple are benches indicating a **bouleuterion**; to the northeast is a terrace supporting a heroon. The beautiful frieze from this heroon can be seen in the fire station in Ağlasun, although there are plans for a permanent museum (other carvings currently adorn a tea garden in Ağlasun). Also in the upper city is a large, well-preserved **theatre**, approximately the same size as those at Perge and Side. The **agora** lies between the theatre and the Doric temple.

The lower city dates from Roman times. **Baths** flank the lower agora, to the north of which is a large 2nd-century AD **nymphaeum**. Two temples have been identified here: the **temple of Apollo Clarius**, which was transformed into a Christian basilica, and the **temple of Antoninus Pius** (AD 138–161). To the southwest of Antoninus Pius can be seen the sarcophagi of a Hellenistic and Roman **necropolis**. At the far west is a **Christian basilica** made of the remains of two Roman monuments. The cliff face to the west of the city is full of small **rock tombs** for cremated bodies, from the 2nd and 3rd centuries AD; some are decoratively carved with animal heads and garlands. A third necropolis lies to the southeast of the theatre.

Cremna (Kremna)

If you have time for another ruined city in an isolated, picturesque setting, there's **Cremna**, an Augustan colony something over nine miles (15km) from the village of Bucak, just east of the Antalya highway. The road is stabilized rather than asphalt, and winds through scented pine forests. Cremna is situated on top of a steep hill; there is much climbing to do. The **city walls** to the west are well preserved; outside them lies a **necropolis**. As you approach the city from the southwest, you will come across the two arches of a **gate**, probably Hellenistic. Within the city, the **public agora** can be identified by the 20 steps which form its north side. A very large triple gateway, whose façade was a close copy of that of the library of Celsus at Ephesus, once stood at the top of these steps; although the steps remain, the gateway is scattered in ruins at the bottom. Behind where the archway should be are enormous **cisterns**. East of the public agora, the **Forum of Longus** contains the remains of a basilica, with some arches still standing, as well as a large inscribed pillar; this is a **dice oracle**, used in fortune-telling to interpret the throw of the dice. There's little else to see: a small **theatre** in the middle of the town, the excavated remains of a **bath** to the west, and remains of a few poorly preserved temples.

Kibyra

Kibyra is a wonderful windswept site, high on a hilltop overlooking a broad plain. The ruins are neglected save for the goatherds who bring their goats to graze on the wild thyme, producing very tasty meat ideal for *Isparta kebap*. Graves tumble down the hillside, which is littered with fluted columns and carved blocks of stone, some inscribed, including one on which the letters KIBYR can clearly be seen. The remains of several public buildings can be identified, including, on the eastern side of the hill, a well-preserved **theatre** and a less-well-preserved **stadium**. Next to the theatre is a large building with arches, now half-submerged in the soil.

Kibyra is about 60 miles (100km) from Burdur and can be reached by heading southwest via the villages of Tefenni and Çavdar ('barley') to **Gölhisar** ('lake castle'), the nearest village to Kibyra. The lake in question has, as a result of canalization, shrunk to a tiny size, leaving a broad, fertile plain between Çavdar and Gölhisar; crops grown here include sugar beet and aniseed, for the production of *rakı*.

Eğirdir to Burdur   ***Where to Stay***

Eğirdir

inexpensive

There are only a few places with any pretensions among the myriad of *pansiyonlar*, including the old reliable ★★★**Eğirdir**, Kuzey Sahil Yolu 2, ✆ 0246 311 4992, 📠 0246 311 4219, on the lake front. Simple rooms with a view for $40.

On Yeşilada, the **Atabey**, ✆ 0246 311 5006, 📠 0246 311 5592, has standard rooms for $25, with none of the charm of the nearby pensions.

cheap

Eğirdir has a wide choice of *pansiyonlar*, sweet family-run places of a very good standard that in themselves can make the trip here worthwhile. The **Lale Pansiyon**, for example, near the castle, ✆ 0246 312 2406, *lalehostel@veezy.com*: en suite rooms with a view of the lake; internet facilities; a delightful family who do everything to make you happy; and very inexpensive dinners (mom's an excellent cook). It's popular with backpackers, especially since its recent YHA affiliation. Another similar place, just as good, is the **Köşk**, ✆ 0246 311 4382, 1km out at Yazla Mahalle near the beach, with great views from most rooms.

On Yeşilada Island, **Choo Choo**, ✆ 0246 311 4926, is newer and slightly more luxurious than the other pensions, though not as cosy and welcoming. Three of the rooms are named after Utrillo, Toulouse Lautrec and Rembrandt, with appropriate prints on the walls of each room; an arty $16. One of the first pensions you see as you cross over to Yeşilada is the **ADAC**, ✆ 0246 312 3074, run by a friendly lady who indulges in good-natured back-slapping to compensate for the language barrier; bright rooms with showers and views to the east and west for $12. Other good choices are the **Akdeniz**, ✆ 0246 312 3432, at the tip of the island, and the **Halley**, ✆ 0246 312 3625; doubles $14.

Isparta

The most comfortable hotel is the modern ★★★★**Büyük Isparta Oteli**, Atatürk Caddesi 8, ✆/✆ 0246 232 4422, with doubles posted as a very *expensive* $130, but discounts are usually readily available.

The more moderate ★★**Bolat** at Demirel Bulvarı 71, ✆ 0246 223 9001, boasts a tennis court and central heating; it is very relaxing and good value at $45 for an en suite double with breakfast.

Isparta has a handful of cheap hotels and pensions, mostly around Mimar Caddesi, the main street. The **Yeni Gulistan** at No.31, ✆ 0246 218 4085, is a pleasing place to stay; a double room with phone and private shower will cost $10.

Burdur

The cheap **Hotel Özeren**, Gazi Caddesi 51, ✆ 0248 233 9607, is a good bet; doubles with showers for $18.

Eğirdir to Burdur   *Eating Out*

The star attraction here, understandably, is fish from the lake, which is inexpensive and delicious—much more delicate than most salt-water fish, and a lot like perch from the Great Lakes in America. There are also lake crayfish.

In **Eğirdir**, the **Deyra Restoran** on the waterfront, near the Eğirdir Oteli, offers a large selection of cold mezes and excellent fish in batter, served by waiters dressed in picturesque orange Adana *şalvar*. A meal costs about $6, only slightly more than the many other fish restaurants around the lake, and on Yeşilada island. At the tip of the island, the **Melodi Restoran** is good and inexpensive. Home cooking at the pensions is universally cheap and tasty, not least at the **ADAC**, where the owner jokes that if you don't like her food you don't have to pay; if you love it you should pay double.

There's nothing out of the ordinary in **Isparta** or **Burdur**—but try a goat-meat *Isparta kebap*, available almost anywhere in its town of origin.

West towards Konya

To get to Konya, it's a long and roundabout trip up the west side of Lake Eğirdir and then down the back side of the biggest of the region's lakes, **Beyşehir Gölü**, passing on the way the most unspellable, unpronounceable village in Turkey, ramshackle **Şarkıkaraağaç**. Just south of here a new national park has been established, the **Kızıldağ Milli Parkı**. To the north, **Akşehir** claims to be the home of the legendary Nasreddin Hoca; you can buy a postcard of the famous picture of him seated backwards on his donkey, and visit his tomb in a little pavilion on the town green. On the gate is a big heavy lock, though it's wide open on the other three sides.

Nasreddin Hoca

 This fellow, the clever-foolish country priest (*hoca*) who goes under the name of Goha in the Arabian Nights tales, is the classic comic figure of Turkish folklore. Outwitting himself as often as the Emperor Tamerlane, at whose court he is supposed to have lived, the Hoca's adventures are still current among all Turks; you'll see souvenir pictures of him everywhere, seated backwards on his donkey. He is very much a creation of the Sufis, the mystics of Islam who condense volumes of theology into such tales. One famous story has the Hoca walking with a friend discussing the completeness of creation. The Hoca considers that it would have been better if horses had wings; thus, they would be much more helpful to mankind. Just then some pigeon droppings fall on the Hoca's turban. He reflects, 'Allah knows best!'.

Down the eastern shore of Beyşehir Gölü, some 2½ miles (4km) off the main road at **Eflatunpınarı** is a Hittite relief, with figures of four kings and some mythological beasts, set by a small lagoon. **Beyşehir**, at the southeastern corner of the lake, is a bedraggled town that could be much nicer if it set its mind to it. It's a poor, out-of-the-way place, a reminder of what most Turkish provincial towns were like twenty years ago. Nevertheless, it's worth a stop for the **Eşrefoğlu Camii** and its *külliye*, built by the Eşrefoğlu emirs, who installed themselves here after the breakup of Selcuk power. The mosque has a beautiful interior of painted tiles and carved wood; adjacent is the *türbe* of the emirs, with more fine tiles, a medrese and a hamam.

Neither Beyşehir nor its lake get many visitors. Facilities are generally poor—this is a corner still open to exploration. In Beyşehir or any of the little fishing hamlets around the lake you may find someone with a boat to take you around the lake's many **islands**. None seems to be inhabited now, though a few have traces of Byzantine monasteries. West of Beyşehir on the lakeshore are the ruins of **Kubadabad Palace**, the summer retreat of the Selcuk sultans. There isn't much to see, but if the finds now in Konya's Karatay Medrese are any indication it must have been a marvel. (It would have been impious to build a palace to last, so in medieval times Muslim rulers always made their pleasure domes of perishable materials: mud brick covered with painted tiles, and wood. As far as we know the only medieval Muslim palace surviving anywhere is the Alhambra in Granada. Imagine what the others must have been like!)

East of Beyşehir, on the way to Konya, the bleak scenery is interrupted by a rather incredible sight, the **Atatürk 100 Yıl Ormanı** (Atatürk Centennial Forest): several million young trees, all recently planted in a wonderfully mad project to make a wasteland into a forest. In a century it will be truly impressive, even if now it looks like the world's biggest Christmas tree farm.

Some cities, such as İstanbul, are forced by their location to play a large role in the world's affairs; others may survive for millennia without contributing anything. Most fortunate of all, however, are the towns that at one time in their lives have a little empire of their own, and then move off history's stage into a long golden twilight. Bursa is one such Turkish city; Konya, the old Selcuk capital, is another.

These two have other things in common; both have wonderful patrimonies of Turkish art and architecture, and both are trying hard to manage the difficult process of becoming modern and prosperous on their own terms. Turkey often advertises itself as the 'Land of Civilizations', and with the many peoples and cultural influences that have drifted through over the centuries, it is hard to isolate anything as specifically 'Turkish', until you come to Bursa or Konya, the most Turkish of the nation's cities. Konya has a reputation for being the most conservative and devout corner of Turkey; in truth, there are plenty of other candidates for that honour. This is nothing to be alarmed about; Konya is a city where culture and tolerance have always been accounted virtues. If it has a living faith to sustain it, so much the better. The spirit of the Mevlâna still protects this city, and ensures that religion shows us only its most benign face.

History

The first we hear of Konya is as a Phrygian town called Kawania; later, under the Greeks and Romans, it became Iconium, capital of the province of Lycaonia. The Selcuks, with whom medieval Konya is usually associated, were not the first Turks in the neighbourhood; other warrior bands were around as early as the 9th century, and the Arabs of the **Abbasid Caliphate** had arrived before them, twice capturing the city from the Byzantines though they could not keep it. When the **Selcuks** came in 1076, after the Battle of Manzikert gave them control of Anatolia, Sultan Süleyman Ibn Kutulmuş made Konya his capital. Not that the city had much to commend it; its only real advantage was equal distance from all possible enemies. Perhaps the broad, treeless Plain of Konya reminded the Selcuks of their ancestral home on the Asian steppe. For a time the Selcuks, strong as they were, had a hard time holding Konya. During the first Crusade, Godfrey of Bouillon occupied the city for a short while, and Frederick Barbarossa passed through in 1190 on his way to the Holy Land. Neither of these harmed either the city or the Selcuks. Like any of the early Turkish principalities, the Selcuks' Empire of Rum was hardly a modern, centralized state; the real 'capital' was the sultan's throne, and that moved with him wherever his whims or campaigns took him. Konya, however, was the residence of the sultans, and the major beneficiary of their building work and philanthropy.

Under their intelligent and tolerant regime, Konya in the 12th and 13th centuries became a refuge for artists and men of learning, fleeing the depredations of the Mongols and Crusaders from all over the Middle East and Muslim Asia. Rulers such as **Alâeddin Keykubad**, who liked to surround himself with poets and erudite dervishes, endowed a collection of mosques and schools that has made the city the equal of İstanbul and Bursa as a showplace of Turkish architecture. They had hardly begun when the **Mongols** came in 1243 to spoil the party; they never sacked Konya, but they did put an end to the Selcuk state, which survived for a few decades afterwards only as a much-reduced, tribute-paying vassal of the Great Khan. After the fall of the Empire of Rum, the **Karamanoğulları**, the Turks from Karaman, filled the vacuum but moved the capital to their own town of Ermenek. Konya declined and did not recover until the coming of the republic.

Celâleddin Rumi, the **Mevlâna** (*see* pp.77–8), one of the great mystics of Islam and founder of the 'Whirling' Mevlevi dervishes, was the most famous of all the figures of Konya's golden age and his spirit continues to animate the city today. Throughout the Ottoman period, Mevlevi sheikhs were often close advisers to the sultan. Even in 1919, Konya elected the sheikh (the head of the order) to represent it at the first Turkish National Assembly.

Getting Around

Konya has an **airport**, with daily flights to İstanbul and İzmir. **Trains** from İstanbul pass through Akşehir, Konya and Karaman on their slow way to Adana. Here your best bet is the **bus**: as usual, there will be no problem making connections to anywhere. The **train station** is on Ferit Paşa Caddesi, about a mile southwest of the Alâeddin Hill. The **bus depot** is equally far, but towards the northwest on Ankara Caddesi; dolmuşes to the centre are infrequent, and you might as well take a cab. Konya is a compact city, and you can easily go everywhere on foot.

Mevlâna Caddesi 21, near the Mevlâna museum, © 0332 351 1074. In the **museum** there is a small bookstore with books in English about the city and the Mevlevis, as well as tapes of Mevlevi music.

The **Mevlâna festival** takes place on 10–17 December each year. Hotel rooms are hard to come by during this time and performances of the *sema*—the dervishes' whirling dances—can be sold out months in advance. The tourist office can help with making arrangements.

Alâeddin Hill

Today the dervishes may be less conspicuous, but the people of Konya like to joke that they're still going around in circles; any trip through the town is likely to lead through the **Alâeddin Bulvarı**, the circular road around the Alâeddin Hill in the centre of the city. This little mound, standing all alone in the broad plain of Konya, is a 'tell', the sort of hill that grows up wherever a small town or village occupies a site continuously for thousands of years. Later cultures, including the Selcuks, simply built over the top. The **Alâeddin Köşkü**, the palace of the Selcuk sultans, or rather the last little bit of it, still stands, lovingly preserved under a modern arched pavilion; interestingly, they built all their schools and religious buildings in stone and good brick, but, as at Kubatabad, expended only cheap mud brick and conglomerate on themselves.

Alâeddin Camii

Their **Alâeddin Camii**, begun by Sultan Rukaeddin Mesut in 1130 and finally completed by Alâeddin Keykubad in 1221, has fared somewhat better. Though well built, its position on the northern slope of the unstable mound has made almost constant restoration work a necessity. The changes and additions of various sultans over those 91 years explain the unusual form of the mosque; together with its courtyard behind the great façade, it has the shape of an open book, with a large pillared hall in one corner. The plan of this hall is that of the Selcuk 'great mosques' all over Turkey, but here the neat rows of columns are marble, reused from Greek and Byzantine buildings. There are more old columns on the façade; the Selcuks apparently found them in different sizes, and cleverly arranged them in a series of arches, slanted to match the slope of the hill. At the centre of the structure are two large *türbeler*. The largest, with a conical roof, contains the bodies of eight Selcuk sultans, including Alâeddin Keykubad, all in tiled sarcophagi; the adjacent *türbe* stands empty.

Karatay Medrese

The rest of Alâeddin Hill, once all part of the Sultan of Rum's palace grounds, has been rehabilitated and planted with pine trees and flower-beds among shady cafés. Just across Alâeddin Bulvarı from the mosque stands another Selcuk masterpiece, the **Karatay Medrese** (*open daily exc Mon, 9–12 and 1.30–5.30; adm*). Once famous for its dome of coloured tiles, this former theological school has now, fittingly, become a **museum** of Selcuk and Ottoman ceramics. Its founder, Celaleddin Karatay, was vezir to the Selcuk sultans for forty years; he is buried under the smaller dome of the medrese's mosque.

Much of this building complex, like so much else the Selcuks built, has disappeared, but fortunately the portal still stands, echoing the Alâeddin Mosque across the way, with its geometric patterns in white and blue-grey stone. Nothing symbolizes the synthesis of cultures the Selcuks tried to create better than this gate. Influences of the Arab and Persian are obvious, and the Greek declares itself in two Corinthian columns flanking the entrances; even the ancient Phrygians seem to be recalled in the geometric lattices of the lower section. This isn't too unlikely; the great Phrygian temple façades aren't very far from Konya, and they must have been known at the time.

The Dome of Stars

Few museum buildings are their own prize exhibit; nothing in the collection of this one, in fact nothing in Turkey, can compare with the Karatay's domed mosque, completely covered in miniature tiles of unsurpassed precision and intensity of colour (though unfortunately somewhat faded and damaged). These are not the large painted squares of Ottoman İznik, but a kind of mosaic, in which every colour is fired separately for perfection of colour and glaze. These geometric stars of 24 points, set in neat rows against a deep blue background, are meant to represent a firmament of stars. This is a specifically Islamic approach; in many of Turkey's museums there are carefully detailed star charts and almanacs, the legacy of the great Muslim achievement in astronomy, but hardly ever are actual stars or constellations depicted on them, as if the Islamic prohibition of images extended to the stars themselves. These geometric stars, with a hint of orange fire at the centre, shine like the real thing, and their interconnection demonstrates the divine pattern and meaning in a way that might never occur to a non-Muslim. The equally beautiful panel around the bottom of the dome is an inscription, in a flowering Kufic script, of part of the *Book of the Cow*, the first and longest *sura* of the Koran (and the most tedious stretch of inspired poetry ever written).

Of the other tiles collected for the museum, the examples of later Ottoman work look almost primitive compared to the fine Selcuk fancy; the strict avoidance of living forms was fine for theological schools, but the Selcuk princes enjoyed nothing in their art so much as the kind of birds and fantasy animals and crowned angels displayed here. One plate portrays a *simurgh*, the mythical king of the birds, the object of the mystical search in the great Persian poem *Parliament of the Birds*, which was a favourite among princes and dervishes alike in Selcuk times (and the source of Chaucer's *Parliament of the Fowles*.) Among the later work are plenty of fine ceramics from Kütahya, from 17th-century tiles to a lovely sign for a printer's shop, made in the 1920s.

Across the street, sheltered under a pavilion like the Alâeddin Köşkü, you can see the portal and sparse remains of another Selcuk school, the **Little Karatay Medrese**.

İnce Minare Medrese

If any film director ever needed a backdrop for the palace of a science-fiction Emperor of Mars, he would do well to study the portal of the **İnce Minare Medrese**, three blocks down Alâeddin Bulvarı. This is no insult either to the architect Keluk or to Fahreddin Ali, the Selcuk vezir who paid for it; the unique design and skilful carving of this gate can only be described as utterly bizarre. This complex too has suffered much during centuries of neglect; most of the outbuildings are gone, and the 'slender minaret' that gave the place its name, decorated in patterns of brick and blue tile like other Selcuk works in Sivas and Erzurum, was swatted down to stubbiness by a lightning bolt in 1901. The remains are now the **Museum of Selcuk Stone and Woodcarving**. As with the ceramics, many of the artefacts are from the Selcuk palace on Alâeddin Hill, and the same fantastical forms are represented.

Continuing your whirl around Alâeddin Bulvarı, you pass a 19th-century French church and then, one block later, come to Alâeddin Caddesi (also often called Hükümet Caddesi), the business street of the modern town and the way to the Mevlâna's tomb; there are relics of the mystic throughout the area. On Alâeddin, the many reconstructions of the 13th-century **İplikçi Camii** have left only a plain brick barn, but this is the mosque in which the Mevlâna did much of his teaching and practised his meditations. The tomb of his spiritual guide, Shems ed-Din of Tabriz, a mysterious dervish from Persia, can be seen on a side street two blocks north. The Mevlâna's own disciples murdered Shems under strange circumstances.

Further down, Hükümet Caddesi skirts the market district, passing through the large **Hükümet Meydanı** with its 16th-century **Şerafettin Mosque**, a distinguished Ottoman-style work that replaced a Selcuk original destroyed by fire; around the back is the city's best hamam. The square has been redone recently, with an underground shopping mall, the **Şaraflar Yeraltı Çarşisi**, full of glittering jewellery. Beyond that the street changes its name to Mevlâna Caddesi, and the famous green tiled dome of Rumi's tomb comes into view.

Mevlâna Museum

It is believed the site of the **Mevlâna Museum** (*open daily 9.30–5.30, Mon. 10–5.30; adm*), formerly the central *tekke* (dervish house) of the Mevlevi order and burial place of Celâleddin Rumi, was a garden belonging to the Selcuk sultans, presented as a gift to the Mevlâna's father, Bahaeddin Veled. He was buried here in 1232, and when the Mevlâna joined him in 1273, work was immediately begun on a cylindrical *türbe*. Over the years, the buildings adjacent to the *tekke* were enlarged and expanded; the whole seems to have been reconstructed in the 15th century under the patronage of the Ottoman sultans, particularly Beyazıt II. Over the nearly 700 years of the *tekke*'s existence, the *çelebiler* ('inheritors'), the descendants of the Mevlâna who assumed the hereditary leadership of the order, were men influential not only in Konya and among the dervishes but in the affairs of the empire as well.

By the 20th century, it seemed to many that such influence, and such easy living, had staled the original spiritual impulse, and the Mevlevi sheikhs were known to be among the most reactionary and self-serving upholders of the old order. Atatürk's inability to prevent them from interfering in the politics of his new republic was the main reason for his decree dissolving the dervish orders. In 1925, a year later, the Konya *tekke* became the first of Atatürk's new museums, with the title of 'Konya Museum of Ancient Works'.

Dervishes of the Mevlevi and other orders do still practise semi-openly in modern Turkey: as long as religion stays out of politics, the authorities are content. Even though this *tekke*, along with the others, has been secularized, most Turks still see it as a holy site; most of the visitors at the museum are not tourists, but Turks from all walks of life, good Muslims come to pray at the tomb of a man they regard almost as a saint. Over the last decade, large numbers of pilgrims have again started coming from the former Soviet republics of central Asia; you're sure to see many exotic faces in the crowd.

Through the entrance, incongruously embellished with a ticket window, you pass into a small courtyard. The fountain on the left is the **şadırvan**, where ablutions are performed before prayer, that on the right the **Şeb'i Arus** (wedding night pool), a gift of Yavuz Selim; the Mevlâna, in his later years, always spoke of his coming death as a 'wedding', an event to be celebrated rather than mourned, and on its anniversary every 17 December (a modern adjustment from the Muslim calendar), the dervishes perform their whirling dance, the *sema*, around this fountain in remembrance. Three small *türbeler* nearby with shallow domes were contributed by governors of the 16th century, when Konya was subject to the Karamanoğulları emirs, themselves also patrons of the Mevlevis.

The Green Dome

Inside the main building, beyond a hall containing exhibits of Islamic calligraphy, lie the Mevlâna, his father, his son Sultan Veled, and other notables of the order, all in elaborate sarcophagi covered with richly embroidered cloths, with the turbans of the deceased placed at the top; six of the sarcophagi belong to the 'men of Horosan' who accompanied the Mevlâna and his father in their flight to Konya. The famous green dome, Konya's most conspicuous landmark, rises over the Mevlâna's sarcophagus. On the outside, the blue band of tiles around the dome has the words of the *bismele*, the formula 'In the name of Allah, the compassionate, the merciful' that begins each book of the Koran; usually there will be pigeons, marching like sentries on the cornice above. Inside, the dome is covered with a pattern of geometric stars; the Mevlevis called it the 'Dome of the Pole'.

Anyone may feel sceptical seeing how much show and glitter have accumulated around the grave of a saintly and humble man. Rather than being any reflection on the Mevlâna, the vast array of sumptuous carpets, cloths and other works of art show the favour the Mevlevis always enjoyed with the powerful, for almost everything here came as gifts from sultans and princes. One of the exceptions to this is the Mevlâna's sarcophagus, a triumph of Turkish woodcarving, done by an artist named Abdulvahid solely as a labour of love. Built entirely without nails, the sarcophagus is completely covered with Mevlâna's poetry, carved in different styles and patterns of calligraphy. The introductory inscription begins: 'Here lies Mevlâna, sultan of scholars...'

His prayer carpet, said to be a wedding gift from Alâeddin Keykubad, is a work of art in its own right, but it cannot compare with another on display, a 500-year-old silk carpet from Persia, said to be the finest ever woven; it has 144 knots to the square centimetre, 2,197,000 in all—it isn't surprising it took five years to complete. Other treasures include hairs from the beard of Mohammed, in a mother-of-pearl box; huge carved rosaries that look like wooden ropes; musical instruments; books, among them the illuminated first edition of Mevlâna's great poetical work, the *Mathnawi*; and the April Cup, a huge and beautifully carved crater of gold, silver and bronze, made in Baghdad and presented to the Mevlevis by Elen Said Bahadır, the last İlhanlı Mongol ruler of Mesopotamia.

The Semahane

The **semahane**, a grand vaulted hall adjacent to the mosque and tombs, was the site of the *sema*, the whirling dance, still performed here every year in December. With its carpets and delicate chandeliers, it is as opulent as the tombs. The great chain suspended from the ceiling to balance the chandeliers was carved from a single piece of marble, link by link. Note also the separate galleries for women spectators at the *sema*; although the Mevlâna himself had little use for such foolishness, later dervishes have been notoriously afraid of women, and prefer to keep them out of sight lest they be distracted.

Other parts of the museum that may be viewed are outside the complex of tomb and *semahane*. The **dervishes' cells** line parts of the compound's walls; some have been restored to their original appearance, as has the **soup kitchen** where would-be dervishes served an apprenticeship of 1,001 days while learning the manners and precepts of the order. Next to the **sheikh's quarters**, now the museum office, stands the famous library of 5,000 old works on the Mevlevis and Islamic mysticism. The southern gate of the outer wall leads to a dervish cemetery, the **Garden of Souls**.

Other Sights

Sultan Selim I, Yavuz Selim, of all the Ottoman rulers perhaps the most devoted to the work of Mevlâna, left behind the large **Selimiye Mosque** next to the Mevlevi House. With little of the architectural sophistication Selim could get in İstanbul, where the Selimiye is one of the finest imperial mosques, this ungainly work, in elevation a simple çube, is domed and surrounded by domed arcades.

From here, a walk down Selimiye Caddesi through the **bazaar** and Konya's southern districts will reveal some of the city's other monuments. The market district, while large and colourful, is not the same sort of attraction as İstanbul's or Bursa's. Konya is not a wealthy city, and what you'll see is mostly everyday clothing and housewares. Still, there are some surprises, and some traditional craftsmen and tailors (such as Mehmet Tekelioğlu on Kunduracılar Sokak, around the corner from the Aziziye, who can make you a nice pair of traditional ladies' baggy pants, *şalvar*, in an hour).

Selim's reign also saw the construction of the **Piri Mehmet Paşa Camii**, built around the *türbe* of its founder. Another, more endearing mosque, right at the centre of the market district, is the **Aziziye Camii**, a 17th-century structure rebuilt by Sultan Abdülaziz in 1867 in the gaudiest style of Turkish rococo. In sober grey Konya this confection with its impossible minarets stands out like an uptown whore at a school board meeting. Continuing along Selimiye Caddesi, you pass another of the great Selcuk works, the 1258 **Sahip Ata Külliye**, founded by the famous vezir Fahrettin Ali. Its half-ruined state and out-of-the-way location have conspired to keep this complex obscure, but its brick and stone entrance portal is as fine as any in Konya. Konya's **archaeological museum** (*open daily exc Mon 9–12 and 1.30–5.30; adm*), two blocks further down where Selimiye changes its name to Larende Caddesi, has an unremarkable collection, except for three well-preserved Roman sarcophagi from Pamphylia. The best known, the *Hercules Sarcophagus* (*c.* AD 260), depicts the hero gliding through all twelve of his Labours.

Just outside Konya, on a side road off the main route for Beyşehir and Isparta, you can take a brief excursion (by city bus) to the pretty, bucolic village of **Sille**; here, the **Aya Eleni** church may be as old as the 5th century, but was rebuilt in the 19th. There are paintings to see inside, if the key can be found.

Konya's accommodation is mediocre: three stars is as good as you're going to get, but at least it won't cost you much. Most of the places in this category have prices listed—about $50 for a double room. Currently, this is just a joke; the bargaining starts at half or two-thirds that. An exception to this is the $80 a night ★★★**Balıkçılar Hotel**, Mevlâna Karşısı, ✆ 0332 350 9470, 📠 0332 351 3259, by a nose the poshest in town, and popular with tour groups. Rooms are air-conditioned, with satellite TV. Better value is the ★★★**Selçuk**, ✆ 0332 353 2525, 📠 0332 353 2529, on Alâeddin Caddesi. The reception has an impressive inlaid marble floor; the quiet rooms have baths, balconies and air-con. $50 a double.

Most of the others in this category are located on Mevlâna Caddesi or adjacent Hükümet Meydanı. The ★★**Hotel Konya**, ✆ 0332 351 9212, an address of some charm and a longtime favourite, is just off Mevlâna Caddesi, a block from the museum; simple rooms, quieter than the hotels on the main street, but overpriced at $35. Further down Mevlâna you can be thoroughly confused by a row of very similar hotels that all begin with S. The modern ★★**Sema**, ✆ 0332 322 1510, with TV and refrigerator in the rooms, is a good bargain at $25, or only $18 without TV or air-con. The ★★**Sifa**, ✆ 0332 350 4290, is very well run although more expensive at $50 (less if they aren't busy). The ★**Şahin**, Hükümet Alanı, ✆ 0332 351 3350, is an old-fashioned hotel with polite, old-fashioned staff; $34 (officially, at least).

cheap

Konya does have inexpensive hotels and pensions, serving the many Muslims who come to Konya on pilgrimages, but on the whole the situation is not encouraging; you might be happier splurging on a (bargained-down) $20 room in one of the places listed above. To find the cheapest places, just look in the side streets off Mevlâna Caddesi, or around the Aziziye Mosque. The ★**Başak Palas**, ✆ 0332 351 1338, is pleasant and cheap at $20 for a double with shower, $15 without; rooms with balconies have a view over the parking lot, but the quieter rooms are at the back.

On İstanbul Caddesi, the big street that crosses Mevlâna, the **Çeşme**, ✆ 0332 351 2426, is one of the better ones, with clean though dark rooms for around $20. Just beyond the Azizye Cami, the **Azizye Otel**, ✆ 0332 352 2287, is the Tardis of Konya, seemingly tiny from the outside but massive within, with dozens of relatively clean, well-maintained rooms along endless corridors illuminated by coloured light-bulbs. For what you get, it's terrific value; some $8 rooms have baths. The toilets are down the hall and are cleaned several times a day.

Konya   **Eating Out**

Don't expect anything special in the food department. Most of the tolerable restaurants (and the only ones where you can get a glass of beer) will be found along Mevlâna Caddesi around the hotels. The **Sema** on Mevlâna Caddesi is that Turkish rarity, a restaurant that advertises vegetarian food (mostly the usual aubergine stews and such; tasty though) for about $5. Konya has plenty of even cheaper lokantas, including the original **Sifa Lokanta** across the street; another one is the **Çatal** by the Mevlâna museum, good for kebabs.

Save one lunch in Konya for one of the best simple döner stands you'll find anywhere, the **Kervansaray**, on Alâeddin Caddesi.

The Plain of Konya

Tourist Information

Karaman: Yunuskent Mahalle, Ahmet Yesevi 26, third floor, ✆ 0338 213 3812.

Konya province, the largest in Turkey, is also one of its most important agricultural regions. One would hardly guess this from looking at a map: the region appears a strangely empty space, stretching over 150 miles from the lake district to Cappadocia. There's really no anomaly—it looks even emptier when you're in it. Somehow, lonesome flat country is always good for wheat, and this is one of the best. Your introduction to the breadbasket of Turkey will be any of the roads east from Konya, all of them lined with grain elevators and flour mills. Its farmers have serious faces, rosy children, and shiny new Türk Fiat tractors, and they do a lot to keep Turkey self-sufficient in food.

They were at it with much the same vigour 8,000 years ago, with enough leisure left over to create one of the world's first urban cultures, at least until archaeologists find an even older one. History used to begin with Sumer. Now with the great discoveries by James Mellaart at **Çatal Höyük**, we must say it begins here on the Plain of Konya where, long before nation-states, sky-gods or warrior castes, this town, and probably dozens like it, enjoyed what seems an easy and blessedly peaceful existence in trade and agriculture, making the beautiful works of art on display in the Ankara museum. Don't bother to visit the site—all you will get there is a lesson in the archaeologist's talent for recreating a culture from the tiniest of clues. If you are traveling this way you'll see plenty more tells; the areas west and south of Konya, as far as Karaman, have Turkey's greatest concentration of them. None have been excavated, and nobody knows what ancient treasures they might conceal.

The road that passes Çatal Höyük continues on to the Mediterranean coast at Silifke, crossing the beautiful Taurus (Toros) Mountains after **Karaman**, the Larende of ancient times and capital of the Karamanoğulları Turks after the fall of the Empire of Rum. Karaman has its castle, most noteworthy for being the only one in Turkey with its name in an electric sign on top, a 14th-century Mevlevi house called Ak Tekke, and a number of other mosques built by the Karamanoğulları. Further along through the mountains, a once-great 5th-century Byzantine monastery may be seen at **Alahan**; there are many others in various states of ruin in the area the Turks, with some exaggeration, call **Binbir Kilise** (1,001 churches). It isn't the easiest spot to reach, around the village of Madenşehir, on a dead-end dirt road some 28 miles (45km) north of Karaman. You can find someone in the village to guide you around, but from all indications little is left of what was once a substantial Cappadocian-style network of religious communities. Here also was the once-thriving city of Derbe, 18 miles (30km) north of Karaman, one of the places St Paul visited on his trip through Asia Minor; almost nothing of the city remains.

Rock Fortress
Underground City
Churches

10km
5 miles

N

Özkonak

To Hacıbektaş

Gülşehir

Kızılırmak River

Avanos

Çat

Zelve

Göreme Open-Air Museum

Çavuşin

Kızılçukor

Göreme

Üçhisar

NEVŞEHIR

Ürgüp

Ortahisar

Mustafapaşa

To Ihlara, Güzelyurt & Açıgöl

Çardak

Ayvalı

To Kayseri

Kaymaklı

Derinkuyu

Soğanlı

To Niğde & Eskigümüş

Cappadocia

North of Konya, the roads to Ankara and Kayseri pass on either side of Turkey's biggest lake, **Tuz Gölü**, the Salt Lake, a dismal corner of the republic. These roads were important in Selcuk times, and the Sultans of Rum built many elegant *hanlar*, caravanserais, along them, free to merchants and travellers. You see them on the route to Kayseri, mostly in ruins, every nine miles, the distance a caravan covered in a day. The best preserved is at **Sultanhanı**, about 60 miles (100km) northeast of Konya. Alâeddin Keykubad built it in 1229; lately it has been restored with some modern stonework as good as the Selcuks' (*open daily 9–7; adm*).

Cappadocia (Kapadokya)

Although never a distinct nation like Lydia or Phrygia, Cappadocia was known as a kingdom as early as 600 BC—it was probably really a loose confederacy of towns or tribes united to keep the Persians out, which didn't always work. Usually reduced to a tributary state of the Persian Empire, Cappadocia's rough terrain helped it survive with a modicum of independence into Roman times. Under the Romans it was still a client state, with kings named either Ariarathres or Ariobarzanes, ruling first at Nyssa (the modern Nevşehir), and later at Mazaca (today's Kayseri).

In AD 17, Emperor Tiberius' legions invited themselves in, and Cappadocia became a Roman province. Still a backwater, it never did receive its share of theatres or aqueducts; in fact its only discernible benefit from joining the Mediterranean community was a visit from St Paul, who corralled the inhabitants for Christianity with ease. St Paul never had to rebuke the Cappadocians as he did the Galatians. So fervently did they take to the new creed that Cappadocia replaced Africa as the great stronghold of Christian monasticism. St Basil, the 4th-century prelate who laid down the rules for Orthodox monks, as St Benedict was later to do for the Christians of the West, was bishop of Caesarea (Kayseri's name in Roman times); monks following his rule made the region's peculiar landscapes the biggest monastic centre of the east, a role Cappadocia was to retain for over a millennium. Generation after generation, they hollowed out the easily-worked tufa of Cappadocia's cliffs and canyons to make cave sanctuaries, and often entire churches complete with columns and domes—in all, Cappadocia has over a thousand rock-cut churches and chapels. In the 7th and 8th centuries, the monks survived the recurring attacks of Arab armies by squirrelling themselves deeper away in their mountain fastnesses. The monasteries, though much reduced, survived for over eight centuries under Turkish rule, up until the exchange of populations of 1923.

The Cappadocian Picture Show

Some 200 of Cappadocia's rock churches are decorated, though it must be said that their artistic merit is limited at best. Whether any of the works were exceptional to begin with, we will never know—many have been repainted over and over through the centuries whenever they began to fade, on up to the expulsion of the Greeks in 1923. Nevertheless, these paintings are a landmark; during the Iconoclastic troubles of the 8th century, the Cappadocian monks kept the tradition of Greek painting alive, just barely, in this inaccessible spot, scrawling red and white crosses and arabesques until the whim of Empress Irene made images permissible once again.

You'll see nothing of the sophistication of the frescoes in İstanbul's Kariye here, but Cappadocia's styles, symbols and motifs provide a useful handbook to decipher a thousand years of Greek art. For example, look out for the often-repeated image of two symmetric angels in flight, holding a crown or a cross between them. Originally these were two allegorical spirits holding a laurel crown—the seal and symbol of the Roman Empire, invented in the time of Augustus and common in all the propagandist artworks of the age; the Christians took it over later to remind people how their Church was taking the place of the dying Roman state. In works from the 6th century onward, you will see important figures, such as Jesus or Constantine, dressed in stylish tunics with a design of small rectangular plaques and white dots. These represented golden plates and jewels; such costumes were nothing but precise pictures of the Byzantine court dress in fashion since the time of Justinian—if they were good enough for the Emperor and Empress, they would do for God and the saints also.

Even as simple a symbol as the cross is worked for its historical resonance; in many scenes on the arches before the main altars, the familiar *chi-rho* monogram of Christ turns into an eight-pointed star, like an asterisk. That's another old political logo, the one adopted by Alexander the Great for his short-lived empire, and maintained by his Seleucid and Commagene successors. Keep an eye out for trivial details like the fall of draperies, the kinky folds in the clothing of figures from the 10th and 11th centuries. This very strange and stylized kind of art is unmistakable—especially to us Westerners, since it is exactly the same as in the reliefs on Romanesque churches of the early Middle Ages, heavily influenced by the Greeks.

One frequently recurring motif from that time is *Daniel in the Lions' Den*, another Byzantine obsession, as common in the churches of Cappadocia as it is in the churches of England and France (no one has a clue why it was so important). Another is *St George and the Dragon*, this one not surprisingly, since George was a native Cappadocian, supposedly a martyr under Diocletian. The saint's popularity in England is entirely a reflection of pre-Christian myth there, though in the Greek East he somehow became associated with Athanasius, the fire-breathing 4th-century orthodox Patriarch of Alexandria. George slaying the dragon allegorically meant the triumph of the Church over those who disagreed with it. In domes and apses, the common figure is *Christ Pantocrator* ('ruler of all'), sending a blessing down from heaven.

Some churches have no great pretensions, like the one near Çavuşin that shows Emperor Nicephoras Phocas on his triumphal tour through Cappadocia in the 10th century. Others are intensely spiritual, like the scene of the *Ascension* on a celestial blue background in a Göreme church. As always, it's those big, staring Byzantine eyes, eyes that look straight into your soul. No better artistic trick was ever invented for expressing the outlook of early Christianity and its transcendent God. They are eyes that ask the big questions, eyes not content with the pageantry of earthly rulers—not even with that of the Byzantine emperors.

The Cappadocian Landscape

The real history of Cappadocia begins some 30 million years ago. In the Cenozoic era Erciyes Dağı, Hasan Dağı and Melendiz Dağı, the three tall peaks that dominate the region, were still active volcanoes. Over millions of years, their eruptions covered the land between them with thick layers of volcanic tufa, a stone made of compressed volcanic ash that is soft and easily worked. A few million more years of erosion turned Cappadocia into the dream landscape that attracted the hermits and monks, and now entertains over 100,000 visitors each year.

Words fail the honest writer attempting to do justice to the Cappadocian landscape; landscape, in fact, does not even seem the right word, for no other corner of the earth can have anything like the twisted, billowing forms found in the rocks of Göreme or Ortahisar. What makes Cappadocia so exceedingly strange is the very domesticity of the place. When wandering through the valley of Göreme, you may run across a stack of tufa shaped like a banana sticking out of the ground, white as sugar, with a door and window cut at the base, hollowed out long ago by a hermit or just a local farmer. On the window is a potted geranium, and on the doormat will be a sleeping cat.

Getting Around

Wherever you're coming from, chances are you'll find a bus to Nevşehir, and then make a connection to Ürgüp, Göreme or the other villages from there. The bus station is on Gülşehir Caddesi (an extension of Lâle Caddesi) at the northern end of town; almost all buses pass through the centre first, so if you mean to stay in Nevşehir, be alert and ask them to let you off there.

Compactness is definitely one of Cappadocia's charms. The greatest part of its attractions is contained in an area about eight miles square, marked by the triangle of villages Nevşehir–Avanos–Ürgüp, with Göreme at its centre. It's not really difficult to see a lot without a car. The tourist office in Ürgüp prints a timetable of the regular Ürgüp–Nevşehir and Ürgüp–Ortahisar bus services; there's a bus every half-hour or so in season on these lines. Less frequent services take you to the underground cities, though **minibuses** (and big buses) are very frequent between Nevşehir or Ürgüp and Derinkuyu, the easiest of the underground cities to visit. But be careful planning return trips—the last ones on most lines run at 5pm, or 6 in summer.

Coming from Ürgüp, a pleasant way to enter Göreme is to take the Nevşehir bus and ask to be let off at the Kapadokya Inn Hotel. From there it is a two-mile (3km) walk downhill to Göreme; the road passes the open-air museum. You can hire a **taxi** for the day for around $50 or, less expensively, just use them to get around between the villages, if you can't wait for a bus. But no doubt about it, Cappadocia is Turkey's perfect spot for **hiking** or **biking**; the sights are suitably close together, and there are few tiring hills to climb. You'll find rental agencies in Nevşehir, Ürgüp, Üçhisar and Göreme. **Horses** are another popular way of sightseeing here. Several of the many travel agencies offer days in the saddle, or you can rent one in Göreme, Çavuşin or Avanos: travel agencies all over Cappadocia can arrange this.

Nevşehir, Niğde, and less frequently Ürgüp have regular **coach** services in all directions. If you're going on to Konya, you may have to change buses at Aksaray.

All of these see a lot of foreign visitors, and are surprisingly well-organized and helpful by the standards of interior Anatolia, especially Nevşehir's.

Nevşehir: Atatürk Bulvarı, Hastane Önü, ✆ 0384 213 3659.

Göreme: municipality office at the bus station, no phone.

Avanos: Açık Pazar Yeri (marketplace), over the bridge from the central square, ✆ 0384 511 4360.

Ürgüp: behind the pleasant tea garden in the Kültür Parkı, ✆ 0384 341 4059.

Mustafapaşa: on the central square, open irregularly in summer.

Niğde: Belediye Binası (town hall), ✆ 0388 232 3392.

Ballooning in Cappadocia

With its gentle winds and dramatic scenery, Cappadocia is a balloonists' dream. Experienced balloonists Lars-Eric Möre and Kaili Kidner of **Kapadokya Balloons** in Göreme start trips in the early morning (subject to weather conditions), spending on average ninety minutes in the air. But what a ninety minutes! After taking the balloon up to give passengers an overview of the region, they descend slowly into one of the valleys, piloting their way over tree tops and past isolated fairy chimneys. Old irrigation channels and ancient agricultural terracing suddenly become visible from the balloon's basket drifting just metres overhead. The intermittent roar of the burner startles birds in their nests just feet away from the basket and sends the odd fox scurrying for cover. A 4x4 vehicle follows the balloon throughout the trip; when it is finally time to come down, if the wind is gentle enough, the balloonists can actually land on the trailer towed by the vehicle. After a celebratory glass of sparkling wine, passengers are taken back to their hotels in time for a late breakfast. At about $240 per person, the price compares favourably to flights in the world's other great ballooning destinations such as Kenya. (Kapadokya Balloons, ✆ 0384 271 2442, ✉ 0384 271 2586, *fly@kapadokyaballoons.*)

Kırşehir and Hacıbektaş

If you are travelling from Ankara, to reach Cappadocia you pass through towns that have nothing to do with the Greek-Christian air of the cave cities, but add an Islamic angle to the ambient piety; both were the homes of mystic Muslim sects that gained great popularity in the late Middle Ages. **Kırşehir** was the headquarters of the Ahi brotherhood, a sensible, plain-living society, widespread among the artisan guilds and workmen of central Anatolia. Following the precepts of their leader, Ahi Evran, who is buried here, the Ahis became renowned less for their mystic accomplishments than for their hospitality and good fellowship. Kırşehir's medieval monuments include the **Cacabey Mosque**, built by the İlhanli Mongols, and the **Alâeddin Mosque**, of which only the richly ornamented portal remains. 'Alâeddin' stands, of course, for Alâeddin Keykubad, the indefatigable Selcuk sultan who contributed something to nearly every town in central Anatolia.

The Bektaşis

In the same century, the 13th, another dervish named Hacıbektaş Veli, preaching a message of moderation and discipline, founded the Bektaşi order. When he became spiritual leader of the newly founded Janissary corps, his order began its career as the most influential in the Ottoman state, surpassing even the Mevlevis. His tomb, and the former head Bektaşi *tekke*, are now a **museum** (*open daily 8.30–12.30, 1.30–5; adm*) in the town of **Hacıbektaş** (renamed in his honour). The tomb lies behind a gilded door; nearby is the beautiful hall where the dervishes performed their rituals, and where other notables of their order lie buried alongside three unknown women, mysteriously known only as the 'Beauties of the World'. You can also visit the soup kitchen, perhaps the most important of all the rooms of the complex for the complicated symbolism the Bektaşis and their Janissary followers built up around the eating of soup. The great cauldron hanging in the hearth is the famous *Karakazan*, the Black Kettle; the Janissaries turned it upside-down and paraded it through the streets of İstanbul to show their displeasure with the sultan whenever they felt like deposing one. A Bektaşi **festival** is still held in Hacıbektaş every year, 16–18 August.

Gülşehir, on the road south towards Nevşehir, is an attractive town with remains of early Christian settlements and churches that serve as an appetizer for the main course at Göreme. Near the Nevşehir road is a huge area of cave dwellings, necropoli and other remains, including the **Church of St John** and a complex called **Açıksaray** (the 'open palace'), a two-storey affair built into a hill, similar in many ways to the underground cities (*see* p.458). Both these sites have been heavily vandalized and their painted decoration is largely lost.

Nevşehir

From here, another 50km takes you to **Nevşehir**, Cappadocia's provincial capital and one of the convenient bases for seeing the region. Although the castle on the hill above the city dates from the Crusaders, Nevşehir is not an old city. Damad Ibrahim Paşa (born 1678), an Ottoman vezir of the Tulip Period, famous for attempts at reform and for introducing European art and culture into Turkey, was born in the tiny village of Muscara. His efforts earned him assassination in İstanbul, but not before he had refounded his home village as a city (Nevşehir means 'new town'), and built mosques, schools, libraries and an aqueduct; his statue stands in the centre of the town.

The Turks, despite their many artistic talents, have never had a clue at town design. İbrahim Paşa left Nevşehir some fine buildings, but the town itself is made of pointless streets that wander wherever they please. Nevşehir at least makes it easy to find your way around, since it's tidily chopped into quarters by Lâle Caddesi, leading north to the otogar, and east–west Atatürk Caddesi/Yeni Kayseri Caddesi, the road to Ürgüp. The benefactor's main complex of buildings stands south of the bazaar district off Lâle Caddesi, around the **Damad İbrahim Paşa Mosque**, with a lovely Turkish Baroque interior much more subtle than Konya's Aziziye. The complex includes a medrese and library, and also a hamam, still in operation and little changed since it was built. Behind the mosque, the narrow streets of old Nevşehir climb up to the ruined Selcuk **castle**. Nevşehir's **museum**, on Yeni Kayseri Caddesi (*open daily exc Mon, 8–12, 1–5; adm*), offers the typical mix of archaeological finds and old carpets and bric-à-brac.

Market day is Sunday, usually carrying on through Monday; it's a big affair. West of Nevşehir, another **underground city** (*see* p.459) has been discovered at Tatlarin (from the city turn left at Acıgöl, 13 miles/22km out; it's signposted). It isn't as impressive or as large as the ones at Derinkuyu and Kaymaklı, and has less floor space open to the public, but is less of a fixture on the tourist trail.

Üçhisar and the Fairy Chimneys

Halfway along the route between Nevşehir and Ürgüp, the triple rock of **Üçhisar** introduces you to the oddities of the region. Although the villagers of Üçhisar have long ago moved down into more modern lodgings, the peak, the largest in the area, remains laced with the tunnels and chambers they used when it served as their giant apartment house. From the top—a road leads most of the way up—there is a panoramic view of the Göreme valley, just to the east, with Mount Erciyes in the distance. Come past at night, if you can; the entire rock is illuminated, appearing like some post-impressionist skyscraper. If you mean to do any exploring in Üçhisar, *be careful*; some of the floors are weak and could collapse. Keep this caveat in mind for the rest of Cappadocia, too, though there is little danger in seeing the main attractions.

From Üçhisar to Göreme, the road passes more curiosities, including some of the famous **fairy chimneys**, tall needles of stone, often with large rocks balanced on top. Their volcanic origin is not hard to detect. As well as vast quantities of ash, Mount Erciyes would occasionally toss out some boulders of hard basalt. During the periods of erosion, these boulders protected the ash, now hardened into tufa beneath, resulting in a column that grows taller as the land around it is scoured away. Also on this road, there is a viewpoint (unmarked) to the right from which you can see one of the most remarkable corners of Göreme. By now you will certainly have been surprised at the greenness and fertility of this part of Cappadocia; if you saw pictures, you will have come expecting desert rockpiles, only to find instead rolling hills of pretty farms and vineyards (the region is famous for its wine). Beneath the good volcanic soil are the rocks, and the narrow valleys where they have been eroded away are low-set and easy to overlook. Here, masses of glistening white tufa, blown into shapes of futuristic World Fair pavilions, fill the valley, dotted here and there with doors and windows, with little gardens and citrus orchards in between. Some of the outcrops are shaped like lemons, and oddly enough the farmers use them for storing the lemons and oranges they grow here.

Göreme

Göreme is the real centre of Cappadocia, the village closest to the heart of the area. It's commercialized out of all recognition, boiling with *pansiyonlar* and carpet shops—yet somehow it's still fun. It isn't very big, thank goodness, and you can still walk a few minutes outside town and be lost among the marvels and jests of nature.

The attractions are a short walk away in the **Valley of Göreme**, which goes on and on, the scenes changing continuously; many visitors become entranced and spend days wandering along its quiet paths. If you haven't the time, at least visit the **Göreme open-air museum** (*open daily 8.30–5, until 7 in summer; adm*), where over two dozen churches, some with beautifully painted frescoes, make up the largest monastic complex in the region, all hewn out of the cliffs and crags and joined by stairs, paths, and tunnels. Two very distinct styles of Byzantine painting explain between them something of the Iconoclastic conflict of the 8th and 9th centuries, the bitter struggle over images (and church politics) that sent so many refugees into Cappadocia. Those painted just after the downfall of the Iconoclasts are awkward, almost primitive geometric patterns and symbols—the Greeks had forgotten how to draw. By the 10th century, however, in the surprisingly quick renaissance of art that followed, the monks of Cappadocia contributed some fine work: nothing really special, but a good indicator of the artistic trends of the day.

Most of the churches are called after some feature of the paintings; the **Church with the Apple** (Elmalı Kilise), for example. Many of these small churches are carved with arches, pillars, vaults and domes, distinguishable from an ordinary church only by a lack of windows. In the Church with the Apple, many of the frescoes have peeled away, revealing the simple post-Iconoclastic decoration underneath. Like many others, this one has been much defaced by graffiti, the oldest in Greek, the most recent in Turkish, as high up as an adolescent can reach. Only recently has the government, along with private foundations and UNESCO, spent money to protect and restore them (the area is a United Nations World Heritage Site).

Among the other noteworthy churches nearby are the **Church with the Buckle** (Tokalı Kilise), with painted scenes from the life of St Basil; the **Church of the Sandal** (Çarıklı Kilise), where an imprint on the floor is said to be a cast of Jesus's own footstep, brought from Jerusalem; and the **Dark Church** (Karanlık Kilise) with familiar New Testament scenes, some of the best work in Cappadocia, recently restored by UNESCO. The **Church with the Snake** (Yılanlı Kilise) shows St George with his dragon, and large figures of Helen and Constantine holding the True Cross. There's more fine work at the **Hidden Church** (Saklı Kilise), if you can find it. Further inside the complex the **Jerphanion Church** was discovered only in 1965 and named after Guillaume de Jerphanion, the French art historian who spent his life uncovering and cataloguing the Göreme paintings; it has some of the most interesting primitive frescoes, sun symbols and interlaced crosses.

Two large, self-contained monasteries can be seen near the valley, the **Firkatan** for men, and the **Girls' Monastery**, accommodating some 300 nuns, a network of tunnels, cells, and churches on three floors, carved from a large crag (the Turks call it the 'Virgins' Castle'). From here, several other attractions of the Göreme valley can be reached on foot, notably the village of **Çavuşin**, a rock-fortress similar to Üçhisar. Here though, half the original rock collapsed long ago, leaving the walls and corridors of the ancient rock town open to the sky;

in places, the crag is so thin you can see through it. A stairway off the Avanos road, just north of the village, leads up into the **Çavuşin Church**, guarded by frescoes of the angels Michael and Gabriel which were exposed by the collapse; inside are more fine paintings, scenes from the life of Christ. Up in the hills nearby is another exceptional painted church, the **Church of St John the Baptist**, with works from the 6th to 8th centuries.

Kızılçukor and Ortahisar

Kızılçukor, a village just to the east of the Nevşehir–Ürgüp road, has been a wine-making centre since antiquity, and its **Church of the Grapes** (Üzümlü Kilise) has frescoes of scenes of the harvest and wine-making, as well as the usual saints. Three miles (5km) to the south, the crumbling crag of **Ortahisar** is perhaps the only rock in the world with sash windows; there's an electric sign on top, too, and an underground tunnel (now collapsed) to a similar complex on the village's edge. Enough of Ortahisar has been repaired so that you can climb to the top for a view of further religious complexes, fairy chimneys and strange rock formations. Several churches in the area worth visiting include the **Church with the Hare** (Tavşanlı Kilise) and the **Church of the Beet** (Pancarlık Kilisesi), both with 11th-century frescoes of New Testament scenes. West of the village are the ruins of an Armenian monastic complex called **Halaşdere**, with an underground basilica.

Zelve

There is yet another canyon full of churches, 3½ miles (6km) northeast of the Göreme museum at **Zelve**—a district where, in some spots, the fairy chimneys grow as thick as trees in a forest. Two old valleys converge at the site of the complex, eroded from the warm, tan rock with an outcrop shaped like a steamship between them. It is believed that St Basil himself founded one of the first important Greek seminaries here. Among the many churches is another **Church with the Grape** (Üzümli Kilise) which has some primitive paintings. Here, too, parts of the cliffs have collapsed, exposing, in one spot, a wall lined with neatly cut compartments in rows, like pigeonholes in a post office.

At the far end of the left-hand valley, you can pick your way through a narrow natural tunnel in the rocks and come out into a beautiful isolated canyon, full of wild flowers around a running stream. Cappadocia is full of surprises like this, both natural and man-made. As times grew worse in the later days of the Byzantine Empire, when the monastic communities began to suffer from raids of marauding Turkish and Arab tribes, defence became a prime consideration. The best defence for the peaceful monks was concealment, and many of the monastic buildings are cleverly hidden in crevices in the cliff faces; undoubtedly some exist that are as yet undiscovered.

Avanos

At its northern fringes, Cappadocia touches the southernmost bend of the Kızılırmak ('red river'), the major river of central Anatolia and once (further downstream) the heartland of the Hittite Empire. The red clay along its banks has kept the potters of Avanos in business for thousands of years. Avanos is an attractive town, reached from Göreme or Nevşehir by an elaborate old bridge over the Kızılırmak. At the centre, a statue of a working potter testifies to the fame that Avanos work has always had in Anatolia. Traditionally painted red with a minimum of decoration, the pottery of the modern artisans is enjoying something of a revival, selling by the ton to Cappadocia's tourists. Just east of Avanos, on the old road to Nevşehir, stands another of the caravanserais built by the Selcuk Sultan Alâeddin Keykubad, the **Sarıhan**, with an elaborate entrance portal. Avanos and Nevşehir form the two corners of a triangle that bounds most of the sights in the region; the third point would be at Ürgüp, the most popular base for visitors to Cappadocia.

Ürgüp

Even more than Avanos, **Ürgüp** is an exceptionally lovely town, unlike any other in Turkey, with its Belgian-block paved streets and unusual designs carved into the stone of the older buildings. Like Üçhisar and Ortahisar, it has come down from the cliffs in recent decades, and today it is the main base for Cappadocian tourism. Here, however, a few of the cave houses are still occupied; one troglodyte on the edge of the town has added a cave-garage for his new car. Ürgüp has most of the region's hotels and restaurants, and also a small **museum** (*open daily exc Mon, 8–5.30; adm*) in the city park. Most of the region's vineyards are on the roads just outside Ürgüp, and you can visit the **Tursan winery** just outside town and have a few samples (and buy a crate to tide you over if you're going to Konya).

Up until the exchange of populations in the 1920s, Ürgüp and its neighbouring villages had sizeable Greek communities. If you approach Ürgüp from Nevşehir, the new one-way system takes you down into town past some fine old houses, many with wooden balconies; the exit road back up the hill passes more of the same. These are the old Greek houses, several of which have been restored and converted into hotels; one is now the main office of a firm of carpet dealers. When the Greeks left, they were replaced by Muslims from Thessalonika who spoke a Macedonian dialect. You can still hear this language spoken, especially in nearby Mustafapaşa (which had been an entirely Greek village, called Sinanos), by the original settlers and their children; grandchildren understand but are not fluent, and the language will soon die out here.

South of the town, the road to Yeşilhisar passes through other towns with cave churches: **Mustafapaşa**, with irregular dolmuş service from Ürgüp, is the first. This village wants its cut of Cappadocian tourism, and a few *pansiyonlar*, carpet shops and restaurants are starting to appear. There is little to see, though, save the restored church of **SS. Constantine and Helen** in the centre, and the 18th-century **St Basil Church** on the northern outskirts, with some of its original frescoes. South of Mustafapaşa the landscape changes completely, into a Wild West backdrop of mesas and buttes. You can swim here, at the Damsa Reservoir, created by a dam on a tributary of the Kızılırmak. There are two tiny villages in the area, **Camil**, with yet another medieval monastic complex (some good frescoes in the church of **St Stephen**), and **Taşkınpaşa**, with a much-decayed Selcuk mosque.

There is as yet no public transportation in this part of Cappadocia, and you'll need a car or a horse or some determination on your bike to push on the next 13 miles (21km) to one of the grandest and least-known sights the region has to offer: the valleys of **Soğanlı**. Here, unlike the other sites in which churches are merely cut into the rocks, is a crag that has been sculpted into a church, with even a typical Byzantine cylindrical dome; there are frescoes inside. The locals call it the **Church with the Beret** (Kubbeli Kilise). Some other rock-cut churches are nearby, including the **Church of the Snake** (Yılanlı Kilise), named for a painting of St George and the Dragon. There are more churches further up the valley, some of them painted.

Another spot you'll need transport for is **Sultan Sazlığı** (Sultan Marshes), on the southern slopes of Mount Erciyes, centre of a beautiful area of lakes, of which the largest is **Yay Gölü** (south of Yeşilhisar on the road to Niğde, turn left for Yahyalı and look for the signs). The government has recently declared the area a nature reserve; it is one of the country's major nesting areas for waterfowl, as well as a major migration stopover for flamingos, herons, cranes and dozens of other species on their way to and from Africa. The centre of the reserve is the village of **Ovaçiftlik**, a short distance from the edge of the Yay Gölü marshes; it has a small museum and observation tower, as well as the only accommodation in the area.

Underground Cities

On top of all this, the most outlandish feature of the Cappadocian fun-house has not yet even been mentioned: the **underground cities**. Thirty-six have been discovered so far, and eight have been excavated and lit for visitors, at least for a small part of their total extent. Each of them was capable of accommodating several thousand inhabitants, supplied with water by underground springs and air through elaborate ventilation systems.

None has been completely explored—they haven't even found the bottom of one yet. The best known, at Derinkuyu, goes down at least 15 floors, with air shafts as deep as 400ft. At Özkonak, the top levels cover some 3½ square miles. Strangest of all, these cities are all interconnected by a network of tunnels, some as much as six miles (9.5km) long. No one knows who built them. Medieval Christians certainly occupied them, but a Roman tomb has also been found on the seventh level of one, and a Hittite-style grain mill and Hittite seals deep in another. Except for one brief mention in Xenophon, ancient and medieval authors ignore them entirely. They must have taken centuries to create; all the tunnels and corridors are narrow, and only one man at a time could have worked at digging them. It's likely that the cities were never continuously occupied, but rather served the inhabitants of the region as refuges in times of trouble.

The history of warfare has shown that there is no such thing as an invulnerable fortress, but these may be the exception. Storming them would be quite impossible; at all the entrances, and even at many points within the cities, great round 'blocking stones' were set that could seal off the passages in a minute, with no room for the enemy to work at moving them, and with plenty of slits in the walls through which the defenders could thrust in their spears. Secret entrances and hundreds of airshaft openings are scattered over miles of difficult terrain; it would be impossible for an enemy to find them all, and wonderfully easy for the people inside to send out forces to harry the attackers, or restock their supplies.

Whoever was responsible for all this, something in it smacks of a bad case of paranoia. Even if built over a period of centuries, the effort to create such prodigies of mole-work could only come from a slave empire with a large economic surplus—of which there is no record here—or an obsession on the part of some petty rulers. There were never many big towns in this part of Anatolia, and it is highly unlikely that any enemy could have been so terrible to country people as to drive them to such extremes.

Of the underground cities that have been excavated, the most extensive are at **Özkonak**, on a dirt road 13 miles (21km) north of Avanos; and **Kaymaklı** and **Derinkuyu** (*both open daily 8–5, until 7 in summer; adm*), 12 miles (20km) and 18 miles (30km) south of Nevşehir respectively. None of the three has any special features peculiar to itself; the cities are strictly utilitarian, with no embellishment. All have 'blocking stones' and other defensive features, and churches, common dining halls and even tombs marked out in them. All three will wear you out as you climb back up from the lower levels, but the air is surprisingly fresh, and the temperature always cool.

At **Derinkuyu**, a fascinating separate underground city has been discovered. It's connected to the main one by a mile-long (1.5km) tunnel, now collapsed; at its centre is a kind of 'temple' with a grand hall supported by sixteen columns. In Derinkuyu you can also visit the unusual **Greek Church** of the 19th century, with blind arcades and lovely carvings of birds, vines and floral crosses that hint at an Armenian influence. Locked up since 1923, it has recently been restored to cash in on the boom in religious tourism occasioned by the year 2000. Inside are frescoes and carved wood details (if the guardian is not around, try asking at the village hall for the keys). Among the other underground cities that have been found are those at **Tatlarin**, west of Nevşehir (*see* above), at **Çardak**, south of Nevşehir (ask at the village hall for a tour), at **Acıgöl**, near the village of Karacören, east of Ürgüp, and at **Gülşehir**; the latter two are not open to visitors.

South and West of Göreme

Ihlara

For those not sated with the rupestrian excess of the Göreme area, little bits have spilled over into the lands west and south. On the lowest slopes of Hasan Dağı, one of the region's extinct volcanoes, the **Valley of Ihlara** has another entire complex of churches, many with excellent frescoes, in a steep and picturesque valley. No public transportation runs here (except minibuses from Aksaray, the nearest city), and it's 52km west of Derinkuyu on a back road, the most distant and hardest to reach of all the sights of Cappadocia. Nevertheless, it's worth a visit for the natural beauty of its red clay cliffs, and its relative isolation; if you're around in July or August and the churches of Göreme are full of Germans videotaping the frescoes, Ihlara is the place to go.

The sights lie in a six-mile (10km) stretch of the Melendiz river valley, in a rugged canyon between the villages of **Ihlara** and **Belisırma** (from *Peristrema*, the old Greek name for the valley); exploring them will be a day's work, but a day you won't regret. Really, you may walk in from anywhere, but the main entrance is off the road between the villages, at the centre of the old monastic community. Near this entrance are a number of churches, including the **Snake Church** (Yılanlı Kilise), where the paintings show the Last Judgement and some interesting tortures of the damned. To the north, towards Belisırma, you will find the **Church of St George** (also called Kırk Damalı Kilise, the 'church with 40 roofs'), with familiar scenes of the dragon-killer, and Greek inscriptions to the glory of the medieval Selcuk emirs; and the **Columned Church** (Direkli Kilise), one of the prettiest in the valley, with more frescoes of St George, and the Virgin and Child. South of the entrance, the

Church under the Tree (Ağaçaltı Kilise) has scenes of the Three Kings, and Daniel in the lions' den, while more well-preserved New Testament vignettes can be seen in the **Fragrant Church** (Kokar Kilise), halfway to Ihlara.

Near Ihlara, a side road leads off to the town of **Güzelyurt**, built over and below a cliff full of caves, with another 19th-century Greek church and some houses decorated in the same style as in Ürgüp. North of Belisırma, **Selime** is one of the most charming and totally unspoiled villages of Cappadocia, surrounded by fairy chimneys and other weird formations; many of its people still live in houses partially cut out of the rock, or in old monastic cells.

Eskigümüş

To the south of Göreme, the road through Derinkuyu continues on to **Eskigümüş** ('old silver'), a former troglodyte colony with yet another Byzantine monastery cut into the cliffs; especially interesting here is the large, open courtyard carved out of the rock, completely hidden from view from the outside. Cells and corridors are carved into the sides on several levels, with sockets for beams and posts that suggest the entire space was once filled with a building of several storeys completely encased in solid rock. Frescoes in the church within, from the 7th to the 11th centuries, include some particularly well-executed figures of Christ, Mary and the saints. To the left of the narthex, the 600ft escape tunnel is typical of the precautions medieval monks were forced to take.

Niğde

Niğde, a quiet provincial capital west of Hasan Dağı, marks the southern limits of the land of fairy chimneys and caves. Quiet is the word, for somehow, between Selcuks and Karamanoğulları, Mongols and Ottomans, Niğde has avoided having much history. All the same, it managed to get a good building or two from most of its medieval rulers, and while none of them is exceptional on its own, together they make a lovely, unified cityscape. Unfortunately, it doesn't seem as if anyone cares about the place; the centre is shot to hell, while folks get on in the outlying districts manufacturing cement and breeze blocks.

Sultan Alâeddin Keykubad is represented here up in the deserted citadel, in the **Alâeddin Mosque** (1223), decorated in unusual geometric flowers and wave designs; its three domes are Niğde's landmark, together with an odd minaret that looks more like a lighthouse. In the town below, the **Sungurbey Mosque** of 1335, built by and named after an İlhanlı Mongol emir, has a much more graceful, spirally fluted minaret, but the decoration of its portal and roofline, as in most works begun by the Mongols, are incomplete.

Just off Bor Caddesi, the main street, the **Akmedrese** of 1409 is the Karamanoğulları contribution, with the uncommon feature of a loggia built into its façade. Other medieval mosques, as well as schools and fountains, two lovely *türbeler* and a 16th-century *bedesten* in the bazaar under the citadel walls, combine to make Niğde one of the most architecturally distinguished cities of Anatolia. On the west side of town, the province keeps a small **museum** with a grave stele and handicrafts (but of course everyone really comes to see the Byzantine mummy).

It's hard to choose between the Cappadocian villages for a base. Although they're close together, the atmosphere in each is very different. Göreme, from where the open-air museum is but a stroll, is a vibrant, laid-back place. By contrast, Mustafapaşa is a quiet backwater, ramshackle and old-fashioned. If you have longer, Ürgüp is better, being the biggest town, refined and sophisticated with the best choice in accommodation and restaurants. Avanos has a few too, but it's a bit out of the way and is less groomed than the other villages. Nevşehir may seem the obvious choice with its good bus connections and fancy hotels, but there are no dreamy landscapes in its immediate vicinity, and staying over among the fairy chimneys is half the fun.

Nevşehir

expensive–moderate

Recent years have seen a boom in hotel building in Nevşehir, waiting for a tourist boom that so far hasn't happened. As at Konya, they take what they can get, so *always* bargain. For the time being, the best is the **★★★★★Dedeman Oteli**, 1km out of Nevşehir on the Ürgüp road, © 0384 213 9900, @ 0384 213 2158, which looks like a state mental hospital but has all the appropriate trimmings: rooms with mini-bars, satellite TV and air conditioning, hamam, disco, etc.

Much more inviting, 300 yards further along, is the **★★★★Cappadocia Lodge**, © 0384 213 9945, @ 0384 213 5092. Although the hotel's idiosyncratic design was supposedly inspired by the shape of the region's kale, it looks more like a cross between a Moroccan casbah and Breughel's tower of Babel. Comfortable, low-key rooms advertised at $140. Less expensively nearby, the **★★★Orsan**, Yeni Kayseri Yolu, © 0384 213 5329, @ 0384 213 4223, has comfortable rooms with balconies, a swimming pool and tennis courts. In the centre of Nevşehir and near the otogar, there are several overpriced three-star hotels with little to offer.

cheap

There's quite a bit of choice here, but the best bargain is probably the **Şems**, right in the centre on Atatürk Bulvarı, © 0384 213 3597. Once a hotel of some pretensions, with a star or two, it's deteriorating at a modest pace, but in the meantime you can have an acceptable room with bath for about $18. The very cheapest places in town cluster around the western end of Atatürk Bulvarı, including the **İpek Palas** at No.99, © 0384 213 1478, which is relatively clean and rock-bottom cheap at $12 for a double; the rest of the places in this area seem to be real dives.

camping

The **Dinler Camping**, © 0384 213 1428, is the serious campsite in town, with shady spots, a pool, and a restaurant/snack bar.

Üçhisar

moderate–inexpensive

The **Jardin des 1,001 Nuits**, © 0384 219 2293, @ 0384 219 2505, is as over the top as its name would suggest; rooms with panoramic views set among the fairy chimneys; some beds are on raised stone plinths. There's a restaurant. Ring ahead, since some rooms are dear, others relatively inexpensive. **Les Terrasses D'Uçhisar**, ✆ 0384 219 2792, ✉ 0384 219 2762, has somewhat dark and depressing cave rooms on the ground floor, but upstairs the rooms are bright and have splendid views; $25.

cheap

A favourite with French tourists, Üçhisar has a load of *pansiyonlar*, most of which are quite nice, and go for about $20. Some of them are built into the rock, or at least have underground breakfast rooms. Streets here are not likely to have names, but proprietors put up little signs everywhere to direct you in. One of the best is the **Anatolia**, ✆ 0384 219 2339, simple but clean and very well run. The **Kaya**, ✆ 0384 219 2441, ✉ 0384 219 2655, *kayapen@hotmail.com*, is a friendly place with views to the north. Some of the en suite rooms open out onto a terrace; doubles cost around $20.

Göreme

Competition in Göreme is fierce, so in most places prices are low and standards high. Very reasonable, and atmospheric, is the **Göreme House Hotel**, ✆ 0384 271 2668, ✉ 0384 271 2669, a recently restored stone building with large terraces and some rooms with barrel vaulting. Standard doubles are a bargain at $24, suites with jacuzzi cost twice as much. If that's full, the **Ottoman House Hotel** at Orta Mahalle 36, ✆ 0384 271 2616, ✉ 0384 271 2351, *ottoman@indigoturizm.com.tr*, is a modern, well-run establishment, grander than the Göreme House but less atmospheric. It's good value at $30 and is decorated throughout with Turkish handicrafts (it has an affiliated carpet shop which is excellent, if expensive).

Göreme is where the backpackers go and this is the place to find dozens of *pansiyonlar*, many of them with rooms cut out of the rock, so that you can live like a Byzantine ascetic, with or without bath. Almost all are modern, purpose-built and family-run, and rates are $12–18 for a double room. To choose one, go to the municipality information office at the bus station (*open 5am–11pm daily*), where you will find, pinned to the walls, photographs of all of the pensions, information on the facilities each one offers, and directions on how to get to them.

One of the best is the welcoming **Kelebek**, ✆ 0384 271 2531, ✉ 0384 271 2763, in the southwestern corner of the village. Two of its rooms are set in fairy chimneys. There are unsurpassed views of Avanos to the east and Üçhisar to the west. Another good one is the **Saksağan**, ✆ 0384 271 2164, with pyramidal chimneys, lovely rooms and friendly people, on the Nevşehir road.

The **Paradise**, near the open air museum, ✆ 0384 271 2248, has rooms carved into the rock, as does the nearby **Peri**, ✆ 0384 271 2136, with rooms right in the fairy chimneys. Both these places are very well kept, and have some rooms with baths. The **Köse Pansiyon**, ✆ 0384 271 2294, ✉ 0384 271 2577, on a back street near the PTT, is deservedly popular with backpackers, and is always a hive of activity. A pool is the latest addition to its long list of amenities.

There are plenty of campsites around: large, well-equipped ones like the **Dilek**, ✆ 0384 271 2396, and the **Kapadokya**, ✆ 0384 271 2656; both have swimming pools, and the Kapadokya also has inexpensive bungalows to rent.

Ortahisar

You may find Ortahisar a welcome alternative to Göreme or Ürgüp; it's smaller and less overloaded with tourists, although that's because there's less to do and see. A motel-style place built of native tufa, the ★★★**Burcu**, ✆ 0384 343 3200, 📠 0384 343 3500, is nothing special; its main strength is a beautiful location close to the weird rocks. There are no good *pansiyonlar.*

Avanos

At the northern end of the Cappadocian triangle, Avanos has its share of comfortable accommodation, thrown up in the recent speculative binge, although far fewer tourists stay here than was hoped. The ★★★**Büyük Avanos**, Kapadokya Caddesi, ✆ 0384 511 3577, 📠 0384 511 4863, has a pool and rooms with satellite TV, and not much else to offer. Something a little more stylish is the **(M)Sofa**, Orta Mahalle, ✆ 0384 511 4489, a charmingly furnished stone-built motel with an accommodating, English-speaking proprietor; doubles with bath $36.

Pansiyonlar are spread pretty much all over the village. The quietest ones will be found further in, up the hillside behind the town square. The **Duru** is a stiff walk up cobbled lanes at Cumhuriyet Meydanı 15, ✆ 0384 511 4005, 📠 0384 511 2402, but well worth it for the views it offers of Avanos and the Kızılırmak. The management are jovial, the en suite doubles plain but clean and the vine-covered terrace the perfect place to unwind; $20.

Just outside the town, the **Ada Camping**, ✆ 0384 511 2429, is a modern facility with everything you would ask for in a campground, including a pool; it's a bit more expensive than most.

Ürgüp

Ürgüp, like Nevşehir, has seen its share of speculative hotel building in recent years; most of them are nearly empty much of the time, and big discounts are more the rule than the exception. There are four big ones on the Nevşehir road west of the town. It's hard to distinguish between them, but the ★★★★**Perissia**, ✆ 0384 341 2930, 📠 0384 341 4524, has the best pool, plus air-conditioned rooms with balconies, minibar and satellite TV, and all the facilities you would expect in a four-star. The ★★★★**Mustafa**, down the road, ✆ 0384 341 3970, 📠 0384 341 2288, is smaller and a little more intimate, but just as well-equipped.

Ürgüp has what for our money is the finest *pansiyon* in Turkey, the **Esbelli Evi**, Esbelli Sokak 8, ✆ 0384 341 3395, 📠 0384 341 8848, *suha@esbelli.com.tr.*

Perched on a hill on the edge of town, the Esbelli is an oasis of tranquillity, due in part to the location, but also to the wonderfully warm personality of the owner, Süha Ersöz. Over more than a decade, he painstakingly converted a row of old stone houses into the Esbelli as it is today, with all but one of the eight bedrooms incorporating caves which date back to the 5th or 6th centuries. He has bought up all the ruined buildings surrounding his *pansiyon* to preserve the peaceful atmosphere, but has no plans to convert them into extra accommodation (he reasons that with any more than eight rooms he wouldn't be able to able to get to know his guests properly). Süha has gone further than anyone else to make guests feel at home: free use of the kitchen, washing machine, unlimited free beer and soft drinks in the fridge, internet, two mountain bikes, English language magazines and newspapers, a hi-fi and definitive classical CD collection in the barrel-vaulted living room, two spacious sun terraces... If you're going to spoil yourself once in Turkey, this is the place to do it: rooms are $80 and can be booked up months in advance. Ring ahead as early as possible. (*Open March–November.*)

If Esbelli's is booked up, the **Ürgüp Evi** is just a short walk further up the hill, ℰ 0384 341 3173, ℰ 0384 341 6080. Its distinct similarity to the Esbelli is not surprising, since it is owned by the stonemason who spent years working on Süha's place. All the rooms are built into the rock; one of them has a grape press cut into the wall; those furthest west are bigger and better. $70, open all winter.

moderate–inexpensive

In the middle range, a recent and unusual addition is the **(S)Alfina**, İstiklâl Caddesi, ℰ 0384 341 4822. Like so many of the old houses here, it is built into the side of a cliff; a series of terraces of tufa-built rooms with balconies. Ürgüp has a wonderful collection of moderately priced hotels, several of them being old mansions that once housed the town's well-heeled. These are intriguing places to stay at, with original features like shuttered niches in the wall and decorative carving. One such is the **Asia Minor Hotel**, İstiklâl Caddesi 38, ℰ 0384 341 464, ℰ 0384 341 2721, *cappadocia50@hotmail.com*, with vaulted stone ceilings and aromatic wooden floors; $40. Another is near the hamam and mosque, the **Elvan**, ℰ 0384 341 4191, ℰ 0384 341 3455, a few notches down on the luxury scale but cheaper at $30.

cheap

Ürgüp does not have as many budget *pansiyonlar* on offer as Göreme. Just off İstiklâl Caddesi by the central square is a pleasant, very inexpensive place in an old Greek building: the **Cappadoce**, ℰ 0384 341 4714. Opposite the hamam is the **Bahçe Hostel**, ℰ 0384 341 3314, *bahce@altavista.net*, a ramshackle but cheery backpacker sleepery, but at $15 a double you'd be better off in Göreme.

Villages South of Ürgüp

In **Mustafapaşa**, the **Old Greek House**, ℰ 0384 353 5306, ℰ 0384 353 5141, is a delight—the paint may be peeling and the wooden embellishments worn, but the faded grandeur of this 250-year-old mansion is all part of its charm. It's run by the Öztürk family who take great pride in showing guests around. There's a small marble-clad hamam from 1879, still in use, and an old kitchen: a living museum piece with a sooty fireplace the size of a small bus where bread is still made. Ask to see the cellar, virtually unchanged since it was first carved from the rock. Upstairs, the double bedrooms are very bright and airy, kitted out with orthopaedic beds and costing $35. Even the most demanding French guests sing the praises of Mrs Öztürk's cooking, which non-residents can also enjoy if they ring a few hours ahead; $7 for five dishes.

A cheaper alternative is the nearby **Manastır Pansiyon**, © 0384 353 5005, carved into the rock; a pleasant evening can be spent listening to the owner playing his *saz* in the cave bar. It's friendly; $6 per person.

Even more rustic and tranquil than Mustafapaşa is **Ayvalı**. To get there from Ürgüp, turn right down a side road just before getting to Mustafapaşa. The **Gamırasu Hotel**—though it's more retreat than hotel—is set into the rock at the beginning of a five-mile-long valley filled with caves and pigeon houses; © 0384 354 5815 @ 0384 341 5825, *gamirasu@hotmail.com*. As well as rose gardens and comfortable bedrooms with Ottoman cushions at the windows, there's also a hamam and massage room (the hotel is part-owned by a group of German therapists); doubles are $50 with balcony, $40 without. The honey, yoghurt, cheese and eggs that appear at breakfast are all produced on site, since Ibrahim is an organic farmer as well as the hotel's manager. They do excellent dinners: $6 for five dishes. Ibrahim will also pick you up from Ürgüp if you don't have your own transport.

If you want to spend time at the 'Bird Paradise' of Sultansazlığı, there is a simple but welcoming *pansiyon* campground, the **Sultan**, © 0384 658 5576, which also organizes tours and bird-watching expeditions.

Ihlara

In this last frontier of Cappadocian tourism, choices are few, but such accommodation as there is will inevitably be cheap and amiable. On the road to Aksaray is the **Akar Pansiyon**, © 0382 453 7018, @ 0382 453 7511, basic but clean en suite doubles for $18. There are other *pansiyonlar* in **Ihlara**, and also some rudimentary campgrounds.

In the neighbouring village of **Belisırma**, amongst unpaved lanes and cowpats drying in the sun, is the **Belisırma Pansiyon**, a rudimentary place with showers in wooden cupoards and basic beds for $8; ideal for those wanting to experience rural Turkish life. There are also basic camping facilities at the nearby **Aslan Restaurant**, across the bridge from the village.

Cappadocia   *Eating Out*

Nevşehir

As usual in towns like this, the place to go for a good dinner and a drink is in the town park on Atatürk Caddesi. The **Park Restoran** isn't exceptional, but you'll be glad it's there; good *börekler* and kebabs, on outside tables in the park; $8. Beyond this, the city offers simple repasts at places such as the **Hanedan**, near the hospital, with the usual mezes, *pide* and kebabs for $4. Another simple lokanta where you won't go wrong is the **Aspava**, on Atatürk Bulvarı.

Uçhisar

The cooking at **Les Terrasses D'Uçhisar** is a blend of French and Turkish styles, with predictably mouthwatering results; $6.

Göreme

The real *turistik restoran* here is the **Mehmet Paşa**, just off the main street; as in some of the restored restaurants of İstanbul, here one goes less for the cuisine than the décor—it's a tastefully-restored 18th-century mansion with some Tulip Period frescoes inside; $12. Beyond this there isn't much apart from the tourist places along the main road through the village serving so-so food at slightly inflated prices. Some of the most wholesome and best-value fare is to be had at the *pansiyonlar*.

Avanos

If you're coming through here, plan a lunch at the **Tuvanna Restaurant** on the main square, one of the best in the area: home-made *pide*, tasty kebabs, even omelettes and other breaks from the usual, for an average $6 (not to be confused with the popular *pide*-and-kebab **Tafanna**, nearby on Kenan Evren Caddesi, the main street). For something simpler, you can have a filling plate of *mantı* at the **Köşk Restaurant**, just down the street.

Ürgüp

Ürgüp has several good restaurants, notably the **Şömine** in the centre of town, where the food is always fresh. There's a large terrace for summertime eating, as well as an indoor dining room with an ornately carved fireplace open on four sides for winter. The *testi kebab* is particularly good. Lamb, or sometimes beef or turkey, is sealed in an earthenware pot and cooked for six hours, after which the pot is ceremoniously sliced open at your table; $10. Behind the Şömine is a cheaper alternative, the **Kervan Restaurant**, with an eclectic range of dishes, from kebabs to goulash and spaghetti; $6. The best of the simple lokantas is the **Kardeşler**, in the centre near the Hitit Otel, with *pide*, kebabs and just about everything else for small change. More good eating can be had at the **Kapadokya** in the centre of town. Further out is the **Hanedan**, built into the rocks on the Nevşehir road. It's a refined place, despite the stuffed foxes and pelicans glowering down from the ceiling, with perhaps the biggest choices of mezes you'll see outside İstanbul and a changing menu of surprising main courses; $15, cheaper for the lunch buffet.

South of Cappadocia

If you're coming or going to Cappadocia by way of the Niğde–Mersin road to the coast, plan a lunch stop along the way at the **Topbaşlar Restoran**, in the bus service area along the highway, just north of **Pozantı**. Surprisingly good dining in the middle of nowhere: Gaziantep-style kebabs, rich desserts and a stuffed antelope to contemplate, all for about $5.

Cappadocia's last capital, **Kayseri**, has something of a reputation. As you stroll the ancient streets around the centre of town, looking at the wealth of medieval buildings left by the Selcuks, before long a well-dressed young man will turn up, exchanging pleasantries with you in fluent English or French or German. Expressing a heartfelt interest in your wellbeing, he will offer many interesting sidelights on the city and its people to entertain you. About three minutes into the conversation, you will hear: 'You know, many (Americans, English, Germans etc.) who come to Kayseri are interested in the fine carpets and kilims made here...' You have met your first commission agent, and the further you walk, the more you'll encounter. An old Turkish proverb expresses it best: 'He can't read or write, but he's from Kayseri.' Turkish folklore abounds with tales of the Kayseri Man, the clever fellow who outwits the *kadi*, or the Jewish merchants, or the devil. He doesn't only sell carpets; Hrozny, the great Czech linguist who deciphered the Hittite hieroglyphics in 1912, found this out to his cost when the Kayseri Man sold him an inscribed tablet from the Hittite city of Kaneş and turned up again regularly over the next few months, each time with another newly 'discovered' tablet to sell; he'd bought them all for a pittance from a farmer, and dangled them before the poor scholar one at a time to get the best price.

History

Kayseri, originally called Mazaca, had existed for a long time under the Persian-influenced Kingdom of Cappadocia, but it was the Romans who first made it into a city and renamed it Caesarea, in honour of Augustus. Under the Byzantines, just as the city was growing into a religious and economic centre of some importance, the first bands of Muslim Arab raiders appeared, wrecking its prosperity, putting it to the sack on several occasions, and mangling its name into Kaisariyeh. Under that name, the city found itself playing a role in one of the stories of the Arabian Nights. The background to the long, sad *Tale of King Umar al-Numan* is the king's struggle for the city with Afridun, the 'Sultan of Constantinople'. Despite the endless treachery of the Christians, aided by the redoubtable witch 'Mother of Calamity', the soldiers of Allah prevailed. Whatever really happened, the story relates that Kaisariyeh's defenders converted to Islam to a man and invited the Arabs in for tea.

Getting to Kayseri from fairy chimney-land involves a long detour around **Erciyes Dağı**, a formidable snow-clad volcano; at 12,727ft it is Turkey's highest peak west of Ararat. The mountain was well known in classical times as Mount Argaeus, a word meaning 'bright' or 'white', and on certain days, when the sun is behind it (the mountain lies south of Kayseri), Erciyes does seem to glow, a wonderful sight wreathed in its entourage of clouds.

Getting Around

Kayseri has an **airport** with daily flights to İstanbul. It has a **railway station** too, part of the long, slow route from Ankara to Malatya or Adana. The train station is in the Devlet Yolu, half a mile north of the centre, and the **bus station** is on the state road half a mile west, both on central dolmuş routes. Any dolmuş or city bus along Talas Caddesi can take you out to the archaeological museum. Buses run hourly to Nevşehir, the capital of Cappadocia.

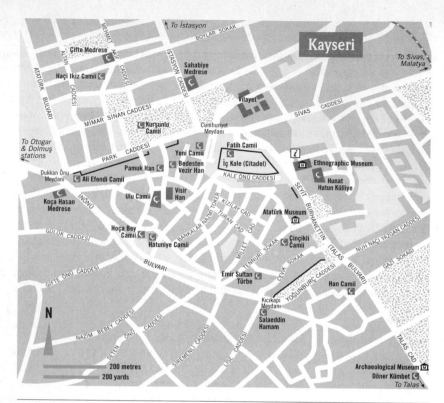

Kayseri

Tourist Information

Next to the Hunat Hatun Külliye, © 0352 222 3903.

Around the Citadel

Kayseri boasts two Atatürk monuments, one beside the other, in the chaotic **Cumhuriyet Meydanı**, where the Sivas and İstanbul roads meet at the heart of town. Most of Kayseri's fine medieval monuments are very near, but the old city around them has been bulldozed to make way for new apartment blocks and boulevards. Kayseri wants to be up to date, unlike traditional Konya, and all its old districts have suffered except the bazaar. Right on the square, the black basalt walls of the **citadel** still watch over Kayseri. Built by the Byzantines, expanded and rebuilt first by the Selcuks and again by Mehmet II, the walls explain at a glance the city's long history of unsuccessful defence. There's no height on which to build a proper fortress here, and Kayseri is the only Turkish city with a fortress on level ground. Some stretches of the city's outer walls remain, in the old quarter south of the square.

Around the square, the **Kurşunlu Camii** of 1584, sometimes attributed to Mimar Sinan, faces a grim medical school, the **Sahabiye Medrese**, and Kayseri's most important medieval structure, the **Hunat Hatun Külliye**. Across the road is the Gürgüpoğlu Konağı, an 18th-century stone mansion, now housing the city's **Ethnographic Museum** (*open Tues–Sun 8–5; adm*). Some interesting rooms contain Selcuk artefacts, ceramic tiles and coins.

Despite all the attention the Selcuk sultans lavished on Kayseri, the loveliest and best-proportioned structure in the town is not one of theirs. It is a building few tourists or even residents ever notice. The **Zeymel Abidin Türbesi** is a mausoleum built in 1886. Its elegant dome betraying influence from the city's Christian community, is very similar to that of the 1835 **Meryem Ana Church** of the Armenians; this church, near Talas Caddesi, on the east end of the old town, is worth a visit even in its present state, as a much-neglected home for a sports club. Almost all of the huge slabs of which it is built reveal strange carvings of what appear to be tools—scissors, knives, carpenter's squares, saws—and other inexplicable symbols.

Bazaar Area

In the old town just behind the citadel, a fine Ottoman house—perhaps the only one you'll see in Kayseri—has been restored as an **Atatürk Museum**. A little further to the west, if you can avoid the carpet sellers, a walk through the exotic **bazaar area** will reveal the 12th-century **Ulu Cami**; a 15th-century theological school, the **Hatuniye Medrese**; and the **Vezir Han and Bedesten**, built by the Ottomans. In the Ulu Cami you'll find most of the townspeople who aren't out selling carpets; with its recycled Corinthian columns, colourful carved mimber and wooden ceiling, it is a lovely spot, and as with many of the huge 'Great Mosques' of central Anatolia, people use it as a kind of park in which to sit and reflect.

For whatever reason, Kayseri has by far the most mausolea of any Turkish city. The classical conical-roofed *türbeler* are everywhere along the outskirts of town. The famous **Döner Kümbet** ('revolving tomb'), carved with tree-of-life motifs, was built for Shah Cihan of the Danişmend Turks, an emirate that held Kayseri through most of the 12th century, and also constructed the Ulu Cami. It stands just off Talas Caddesi south of the old town, with two other mausolea nearby; the **Emir Ali Kümbeti** and the **Sırçalı** ('crystal') **Kümbet**. To the west, the austere and dignified **Ali Cafer Kümbet** is lost among the apartment buildings of the new town; here the main street is Sivas Caddesi, broad and dismal, a perfect setting for postwar Italian cinema verité. If you follow it long enough, just as anomie sets in you'll run into the 13th-century **Çifte Kümbet**.

Near the Sırçalı Kümbet, in a large park on the southern edge of the city, the **Archaeology Museum** shows off its interesting accumulation of finds; a sympathetic-looking Neolithic goddess from nearby Sarayak, some good geometric-style pots, a Roman sphinx, baby mummies, Hittite reliefs with King Tudhalya's mark, inscribed steles of bragging potentates, cow-shaped pitchers, the best pair of Hittite lions, and the silliest pair of Roman eagles.

Around Kayseri: Hittite Ruins and Selcuk *Hanlar*

Outside Kayseri, the road to Sivas will take you to an important Hittite site: Kültepe, the 'hill of ashes', near the village of Karahöyük. Even before the Hittites, this city was a flourishing commercial centre, and it lasted well into Roman times. The inscribed tablets found here—those Dr Hrozny bought so dearly—have contributed much to our knowledge of the Hittites and their language. Kaneş was its name, and besides the city upon its mound, where the foundations of the palaces may be seen, there was a lower city just down the hill, a *karum*, or trading colony of the Assyrians. In about 1800 BC, long before the Assyrians became an empire, they were a prosperous trading people who established something like an early model of the Hanseatic league with a network of trading centres across Anatolia and

Mesopotamia. Though subject to the local rulers, they lived as closed, self-governing towns; Kaneş, itself overseen directly from Nineveh, was the head town in the system. Both the city and colony were destroyed by fire, and the wealth of objects the fleeting residents left behind constitute one of the greatest Hittite treasures; most are now in Ankara, but a few remain in the small museum on the site.

Two Selcuk caravanserais in this area are in good shape; **Sultan Hanı**, built in 1236, is some 20 miles (30km) past Kültepe on the Sivas road, and **Karatay Hanı** 30 miles (50km) outside Kayseri on the road to Malatya. Celaleddin Karatay, Alâeddin Keykubad's grand vezir who also endowed the Karatay Medrese in Konya, is responsible for both of these.

Twelve miles (20km) further on you pass the town of **Pınarbaşı**, unremarkable save that most of its inhabitants are Circassians, resettled here by the Ottomans as refugees from enforced Christianization at the hands of the Russians, who seized their home north of the Black Sea in 1829. Centuries ago, the Circassians were famous for the beauty of their women and the fierceness of their soldiers. The early Ottoman sultans, treating them as a favourite nation, made good use of both.

Kayseri   **Where to Stay**

moderate–inexpensive

Kayseri's finest is the ★★★**Hotel Almer**, Osman Kavuncu Caddesi 15, ✆ 0352 320 7970, 🖷 0352 320 7974, although you may find the cow's skull that is nailed above the entrance a trifle disconcerting. The management will assure you it's there for good luck. The hotel is bright and friendly; $65 for a double. The next best is the ★★**Hotel Turan**, Turan Caddesi 8, ✆ 0352 222 5537, 🖷 0352 231 1153, which, despite looking like a Romanian office block from the outside, actually has a quite pleasant interior, dark and soothing; the management will undoubtedly invite you to purchase carpets from their warehouse downstairs. Doubles $30.

cheap

The **Hotel Yat**, Talas Caddesi, ✆ 0352 232 7378, is typically Turkish in that its lobby promises far more than its rooms actually deliver, but it's friendly and hassle-free. Rates are $12 per person for a small room with private shower (but shared toilet) but you should be able to negotiate a reduction if it's not full. It's conveniently located near the citadel and the tourist office, as is the **Hunat Oteli**, ✆ 0352 232 4319, behind the Hunat mosque at Zengin Sokak 5, which is good value at around $8 per person. There are several other cheap hotels in this area, and a few near the bus station, although staying in the latter will require a dolmuş to get into town.

Kayseri   **Eating Out**

There are some excellent restaurants. At Millet Caddesi 5, the **İskender Kebab Salonu** has been around for years, serving the eponymous speciality for $3. Behind the Hattat Hotel, the **Otağ Et Lokantası** is popular with families; the food is good and the prices reasonable, at around $5 for a full meal with a soft drink. The **Zifayet**, located on Talas Caddesi 20, serves for $2.50 what are perhaps the best aubergine kebabs in Turkey, meaty and spicy and with an aftertaste you'll never forget.

Northeastern Anatolia

You may have seen the Dakotas or Saskatchewan, Yakutsk or the endless Gobi; you may have travelled the world over in search of the bleakest and emptiest landscapes, but you can't say you've seen it all until you've been on the lonesome Plain of Erzurum or traversed the featureless black mountains around it.

On the other hand, you might like it. There's a kind of poetry in such a landscape, so grim and still it shames its people and towns to silence. Every spot of colour—a peasant woman's bright costume, a green irrigated farm, the blue tiles of an ancient minaret—becomes meaningful. In the very stillness there is a sense of danger. Sudden, fierce blizzards rule this country's winters, and tremendous earthquakes shake its towns to dust with a regularity known in few corners of the earth. The road through Erzurum has been a route for would-be conquerors, marching in either direction, as far back as the chronicles go; at present, no foreign army has camped here for 80 years, perhaps a record in modern times.

People here respond to the precariousness of life as they do everywhere. When earthquakes wreck their hopes, they rebuild; when invaders come, they resist, and in their lives the bleakness is tranformed to dignity of bearing and a quiet friendliness that matches the landscape perfectly.

Erzurum and Around

To get there, just take the little trip east from Sivas to **Erzincan**. It's 150 miles (240km), and the road passes only four villages along the way. Erzincan, called 'Aziris' in ancient times, was once renowned as one of the most beautiful cities in Anatolia. A series of earthquakes, the worst in 1939 killing 40,000 people, and the most recent in 1991 killing 4,000, have left all the Selcuk mosques and medreses in ruins, although the town once again has been rebuilt. The Turks have invented a fancy etymology for the name, from '*Ezercan*' meaning 'life crusher'. Once known for metalwork, carpets and (according to Marco Polo, who travelled here) buckram, Erzincan today is famous only for its earthquakes. Enough of them have shattered the Urartian fortress of **Altıntepe**, 10 miles (16km) east, that little remains to be seen; the best objects, including two great lions, have been removed to Ankara.

Don't give up at Erzincan; it's only 112 more miles (180km) to **Erzurum**. Once in the town, you'll forget some of your misgivings about this trip. Erzurum, if you come from the west, may be the first Turkish city you find as exotic as you expected; it is good and grey, clean and quiet, and, apart from the modern centre, its streetscapes have not changed for centuries. In winter you can go skiing just five miles south-west of the city at **Palandöken**, Turkey's best ski resort. It also has the country's longest ski run, almost four thigh-busting miles long.

History

Erzurum guards the approaches to Anatolia, and consequently has always been an important military prize. As Theodosiopolis, it marked the eastern frontiers of the Romans and Byzantines; the waves of Turks who began battering its ramparts in the 9th century called it Arz-er-Rum, 'land of Rome', and the name stuck when the Selcuks conquered it in 1071. The Selcuks, on their westward path, never looked back, and cared little when the Saltuk Turks took it away from them. İlhanlı Mongol and Ottoman occupations were to follow; after the 1700s, control of Erzurum became a major goal of the Russian Empire. Battles took place on the plain in most of the Russo-Turkish conflicts, the last in 1916, when the Czar's troops captured it in one of their few successes in the First World War. The Turks soon reasserted themselves, however, and one of the congresses that led to Turkish independence took place here in July 1919.

Getting Around

There are two **flights** daily to Erzurum from Ankara, and two flights weekly direct to İstanbul. **Bus** connections to Erzurum are regular from Sivas, Malatya, Kars and Trabzon, the latter a spectacular route over the eastern Black Sea Mountains.

The **railway** from Ankara passes through on the way to Kars, though trains are not frequent (one a day). Erzurum's **bus station** lies a mile out of town, and the **rail station** half a mile. You probably won't require public transport for anything within the city. As in other cities where the bus station is far from the centre, it may be worthwhile to check at the bus company offices in town for times, and for the possibility of a connecting **minibus** (some companies provide this service). Minibuses regularly ply the winding route between Erzurum and Palandöken during the ski season (Nov–Apr).

Erzurum: Cemal Gürsel Caddesi 9, ✆ 0442 218 5697, 🖷 0442 218 5445.

A Tour of the Town

Over 300,000 people live in Erzurum, but it's a mystery how they support themselves. The city itself seems still to be living in an age of handicrafts and small shops. A few factories and agricultural installations lie on the outskirts, but the surrounding Plain of Erzurum, between the Çoruh Mountains to the north and the Palandöken to the south, seems utterly empty.

It's pleasant strolling around Erzurum, but don't be surprised if you find yourself tiring easily. This is Turkey's highest provincial capital, some 6,400ft above sea level. All the way from the Aegean coast, the Anatolian plateau has been gradually rising: the eastern end of it, from Erzurum to Mount Ararat, may not be as high as the Himalayas, but the peoples of the Middle East have always thought of it as the roof of the world. Many of the great rivers have their sources here: the Tigris and Euphrates, flowing down to the Persian Gulf; the Aras (ancient *Araxes*), heading for the Caspian; and the rivers of the eastern Black Sea, the Çoruh and the Yeşilırmak. Thanks to its height, Erzurum and all the lands east of it stay in the deep freeze all winter; the snow piles up and transit becomes difficult.

Cumhuriyet Caddesi, the modern main street of Erzurum, chops its way right through the old town. Huddled behind its glass and concrete banks and shops are fine narrow cobbled streets full of children and cats, lined with the city's typical grey-stone houses. Cumhuriyet Caddesi, though broad and straight, roughly follows the course of an older thoroughfare, and most of Erzurum's sights are located on or near it. Near the town hall, at the corner of Mumcu Caddesi, a small park contains the **Yakutiye Mosque and Medrese**, built by the Mongols in the 14th century. The stumpy remnant of its minaret is covered by an attractive latticework of delicate bricks and blue tiles, making the medrese an ideal location for the **Turkish and Islamic Arts and Ethnography Museum** or Türk İslam Eserleri ve Etnografya Müzesi (*open daily exc Mon 8.30–5; adm*). Wide-ranging exhibits fill the former student cells: everything from dervish wear to *oltu taşı*—black amber mined in the local mountains, which can also be found for sale in city shops.

To the east, the next mosque down is the **Ulu Cami**, built in 1179 by the Saltuk emir Abdül Muhammad. Like most of the 'Great Mosques' in Turkish cities, this one is huge and plain. Until the conquest of İstanbul, the Turkish idea of architecture was, in respect to where the artistic effort should be made, just the opposite of Christian Europe. The biggest central mosques, submitting to the puritanical streak Islam has always had, are usually little more than utilitarian prayer-halls. Islam has no cathedrals. Adornments, in stone and glazed tile, were saved for the smaller mosques and, above all, the schools, most of them endowed by a single patron anxious to be remembered.

Çifte Minare Medrese

A 13th-century Mongol princess named Huant was one of these, and her gift to Erzurum, the **Çifte Minare Medrese** (*open 8.30–5*), is one of the masterpieces of Turkish architecture. Behind the massive portal, one of the best examples of the style begun by the Selcuks, the gateway arches open to a spacious courtyard, enclosed by a two-storey gallery with a free-standing arch at its centre. From the opposite end, a vaulted hall leads to a very large and beautiful unoccupied *türbe*, with a shallow dome under the usual conical roof. The strange device on the entrance of the medrese is a symbol seen in various forms on the religious buildings of eastern Anatolia. It's a palm tree, representing the tree of life; its roots have become snakes, and an eagle perches on its topmost branch. This is an İlhanli symbol, adapted from the eagle and tree the Selcuks used before them.

Just two blocks behind the Çifte Minare, in one of the most picturesque corners of old Erzurum, a fenced garden encloses the **Üç Kümbet**, literally 'three tombs'. *Kümbet* is just another name for *türbe*—a round or octagonal mausoleum with a conical roof; these three, with the remains of Saltuk emirs of the 13th century inside them, are especially splendid examples. More than most *türbeler*, they show the Armenian influence; under Roman and Byzantine rule, Erzurum had been a predominantly Armenian town.

On the other side of Cumhuriyet Caddesi, the old lanes wander crazily upwards to the **castle**, well preserved since its last, Ottoman, rebuilding (*open 8.30–5.30*). The **clock tower**, looking out over the city from inside the castle, began life as a minaret. You can fumble your way up the precipitous spiral staircase like the muezzins of old, blinking in the sunlight as you reach the top. Directly below, nestling in the lee of the castle walls, are some of Erzurum's oldest dwellings, a surprising number of which are still covered by roofs of earth and grass. Although they look primitive, earthen roofs are ideally suited to the climate, keeping the rooms below cool in summer and cosy in winter.

Elsewhere in the castle there is little to see save Turks sneaking off the job for a snooze, and little boys pretending to be Kılıç Aslan (the legendary Selcuk emir). In the area surrounding the castle, young males coax their throbbing disco-mobiles down narrow lanes, squeezing past horse-drawn carts and old women enveloped in *ihram*. These traditional shawls are unique to the Erzurum region and are made from roughly woven, undyed sheep's wool embroidered with blue or green patterns. Vintage examples of this work can be bought in the carpet shops near the castle. New *ihram* can be found in the market district which occupies many of the streets north of here. With more donkeys and fewer plastic buckets than most, it's one of the most old-fashioned and interesting bazaars in Turkey. The old *bedesten* at its heart, the **Rüstem Paşa Çarşısı**, bristles with a host of pyramidal chimneys, creating the impression of a strange city's skyline in miniature.

West of Erzurum: the Çoruh Mountains

The black mountains that surround the Plain of Erzurum seem to close it off like a castle wall, and in fact getting out by any road except the main east–west highway can be difficult three seasons of the year. The road to Artvin and the Black Sea is decent, but a wilder and more interesting route would be to retrace your steps to Aşkale and take the route through the Çoruh Mountains to Trabzon, passing two Turkish castles that would put the imagination of a Hollywood director to shame.

Bayburt has been the main stronghold along this route since the days of the Kingdom of Trebizond; its castle, with dozens of towers, dwarfs the little village in its shadow. Stouter souls may climb up to the one at **Kale**, perched like a beret atop a needle-thin peak. From here, the road passes through **Gümüşhane**; the name, 'silver house', denotes a mint, a reminder of the ancient mines between here and Bayburt. The town is another new creation, rebuilt from the ruins of another earthquake. This is the route Xenophon and his Ten Thousand took at the end of their epic journey across eastern Anatolia. Before they could reach Trebizond and the sea, they had to cross over Turkey's highest pass, the **Zigana Geçiti**, where snow may be blowing across the road any month of the year.

East of Erzurum

If you proceed east from Erzurum, the route is equally scenic, following the boisterously rushing Aras River, through green meadows and steep canyons on its way to the Armenian border. At **Pasinler**, you see a joke of a castle, a modern restoration, of which only one side of the walls remains. It looks like a stage prop: they can't have done it up to impress tourists, and one can only wonder what the idea was. A better sight, found at Köprüköy, also known as **Çobandede** ('shepherd's valley'), is the well-preserved **Ottoman bridge**, one of the best remaining, with six graceful arches over the stream. It's attributed to Mimar Sinan, but then so is every other old bridge in Turkey.

Towards Kars

Heading east of Erzurum, the villages become rougher and poorer, the amenities fewer and the stares directed at tourists longer. **Horasan** and **Sarıkamış**, built around army bases, are two of these villages. The former is named for the great city of Turkish Central Asia, Khorasan, and probably got its start with the waves of Turkish migration that followed the Mongol destruction in that region. Near Sarıkamış, the government is constructing a ski resort, and why not? The chief distinction of Sarıkamış is its mean annual temperature of 35°F, the lowest in Turkey and equal to that of the northernmost town in Norway. At 8,600ft, the highest peak is the Cıbıtepe. At present, the resort is equipped with only two chairlifts, one T-bar and a limited number of runs. Until Sarıkamış develops further, other resorts such as Palandöken offer much more of a challenge for skiers.

Erzurum   ***Where to Stay***

If you're heading east, make the most of Erzurum's excellent choice of hotels before you're confronted by the comically bad accommodation situation in Kars. For Erzurum's priciest accommodation, you'll have to head for the hills, where the Palandöken ski resort sits in splendid isolation. In Erzurum proper, most of the mid-range and cheap lodgings (there is nothing very expensive) can be found in an area between the train station and city centre, around the busy traffic roundabout known as the Gürcü Kapı.

expensive

Five miles south-west of Erzurum at Palandöken, the ★★★★**Dedeman**, ✆ 0442 316 2414, 📧 0442 316 3607, *hotels@dedeman.com.tr*, is an overgrown chalet with all the luxuries, including satellite TV; although, as the hotel is situated at well over 7,000ft and the air is suitably chilly, its outdoor swimming pool seems just a little gratuituous; doubles $110.

The best city-centre hotel is the ★★★**Dilaver**, Aşağı Mumcu Caddesi Pelit Meydanı, ✆ 0442 235 0068, ✉ 0442 218 1148. Its big bright lobby makes a good first impression, and the well-appointed bedrooms don't disappoint either. The ambitious posted price of $100 soon comes down to a more reasonable $60 per double.

Snapping at the heels of the Dilaver in terms of comfort is the **Polat**, Kazım Karabekir Caddesi 4, ✆ 0442 218 1623, ✉ 0442 234 4598. With en suite rooms for only $22, it's the best deal in town. The Polat's one drawback is its location near the noisy Gürcü Kapı roundabout. An alternative is the nearby ★**Sefer** on İstasyon Caddesi, ✆ 0442 218 6714, ✉ 0442 212 3775, where average rooms with unusually large en suite bathrooms cost $26.

If you want to be closer to the action, head for the ★**Kral** on a side street off the main Cumhuriyet Caddesi at Erzincankapı 18, ✆ 0442 218 7783, ✉ 0442 218 6973. Once you've braved the dingy staircase, you'll be relieved to see that the beds upstairs are pleasantly clean, costing $25 for two people.

Inconveniently located on the road leading out to the bus station is the remarkably named **Oral Hotel**, Terminal Caddesi 6, ✆ 0442 218 9740, ✉ 0442 218 9749. Its grey façade is drab to an almost Soviet degree, although the décor improves once you're inside. Doubles are keenly priced at $18, with bathtubs rather than showers. Rooms at the back escape the worst of the traffic noise.

The best budget option in town is the **Yeni Çınar** on a quiet lane off the Gürcü Kapı at Ayazpaşa Caddesi 18, ✆ 0442 212 1050, ✉ 0442 233 8963. The beds are very clean indeed, with sheets so starched you can barely fold them back; prices range from $10 for a basic double to $14 for one with bathroom facilities.

A less hygienic option further along the same street is the **Arı**, Ayazpaşa Caddesi 22, ✆ 0442 218 3141, where $12 rooms are equipped with very rudimentary showers and toilets. The rooms are big and the staff friendly enough, even if they do have an aversion to changing the sheets, which you should check before agreeing to stay.

The **Hitit** at Kazım Karabekir Caddesi 27, ✆ 0442 218 7412, is cheaper still. Through the haze of cigarette smoke in the lobby you may be able to make out a TV set flickering dimly in the corner. But with its volume turned to eleven when the football's on, there'll be no mistaking the TV's presence even when you're in your room upstairs. This aside, the Hitit makes an excellent choice, setting you back only $9 for a room with shower; the embroidered bedcovers featuring exotic peacocks picked out in gold thread come as an unexpected bonus.

Erzurum   ***Eating Out***

The **Güzelyurt** at Cumhuriyet Caddesi 54 is perhaps the best restaurant in eastern Turkey. Its high-ceilinged dining room, with walls panelled in light and dark wood, has a distinct Art Deco feel to it. The solicitous waiters recite an extensive menu of

Turkish regional specialities; better still, ask to see the kitchens, where you can nose around as many pots and trays as you wish before selecting your food. Although you may be forced to eat your meal to the strains of Richard Clayderman, the restaurant serves alcohol to help you come to terms with this. About $6 for a meal, more if you turn to drink to compensate for the music.

Across the road from the Güzelyurt at Cumhuriyet Caddesi 27, the **Salon Asya** is clean and popular. They serve such standard fare as *lahmacun*, *pide* and kebabs for about $4. Another good option is the **Ziyade Salonu** on the same street to the west, where single women should feel at ease.

Out near the minibus station at Kongre Caddesi Nazik Çarşısı 8 is the **Koç Cağ Kebap Salonu**. The skewers of kebab are cooked over wood fires, turning on a horizontal axis just like the good ol' days when kebabs were in their infancy: men camping out in the desert pressed slabs of meat onto their swords, resting them over open fires until they were cooked.

Kars and Ani

Getting Around

The daily **train** from İstanbul passes through Erzincan and Erzurum on its way to Kars. At some point in the future, the town will become the jumping-off point for travellers heading into Armenia, whose border with Turkey is currently subject to the vagaries of international politics. **Bus** connections into the region from Sivas, Trabzon or the major cities of the southeast are no problem, but all routes are long and usually dreary. The new bus station is three miles outside Kars, but the bus companies all have ticket offices in the town centre; a free minibus service shuttles between these offices and the main bus station.

If you're **driving** keep in mind that distances in this area are often very great, with few services and no accommodation along the way. If you're not driving, a **taxi** is the only way to see Ani (27 miles/43km of good road, about $35 for a half-day trip). The tourist office in Kars can arrange it, as well as take care of the police formalities.

Tourist Information

Kars: Atatürk Caddesi, next to Suleiman Demirel Parkı, ℭ 0474 212 6817.

Kars

Sarıkamış may be a little colder, but **Kars** gets more snow. The word itself means 'snow' in Turkish, and here it means about 40ft in the worst winters. Most people come here only because it's the nearest town to the ruined city of Ani. Few writers have had anything good to say about it; they come by bus or train, see the shacks and mud, and bolt. It's a pity, for outside the squalid market area Kars is one of the prettier towns in the east. Its secret is that it's really a Russian town, most of it built between 1878 and 1921 when the region was part of the Russian Empire; most citizens of Kars don't know this, nor are they aware that their town was founded by the Armenians. As capital of the Bagratuni dynasty before Ani, it flourished in the 9th and 10th centuries.

The Russian Occupation

The Selcuks destroyed Kars in the 11th century, and attempts at rebuilding were foiled by the Mongols and later Tamerlane, both of whom massively damaged the town in their invasions. Just as Erzurum protects Anatolia, Kars protects Erzurum, and there has always been a garrison up in Kars castle. There's one in it now. Like Erzurum, Kars was a prize the Russians wanted badly, and they spent much of the 19th century trying to get it; in 1807, their siege failed, but in both 1828 and 1855, during the Crimean War, they wrested it from the sultan only to find the European powers forcing them to give it back. On the latter occasion, Kars was defended by a Turkish force led by British officers under General Williams. Their heroic defence against great odds was one of the famous events of the Crimean War: the English public held its breath for weeks as reports and rumours dribbled in over the telegraph line. In 1877 the Russians took Kars again and got to keep it, by the goodwill of Bismarck at the Treaty of Berlin.

Lenin and Trotsky, in a rare lapse of judgement, gave it back with the rest of the province in 1921. Atatürk and the Turkish assembly had been playing a little game with the Bolsheviks, issuing communiqués about the evils of capital and the eternal solidarity of the Russian and Turkish workers. The Soviets fell for it, and gave up their border claims to earn Turkey's friendship. They probably couldn't have held Kars in any case, with the Red Army busy elsewhere and General Kazim Karabakir's Turkish nationalist army knocking on the door.

New Town

During their 40-year occupation, however, the Russians laid out the new town south of the citadel with broad, tree-lined streets. On the business streets, Atatürk Caddesi and Karadağ Caddesi, you'll see blocks of attractive neoclassical façades. Some, like the old government buildings on Ordu Caddesi, and one semi-ruined palace that may once have served as an opera house, are wonderfully grandiose, and seem even more so in this incongruous setting. On one old Russian house, you can admire what must be the best Art Nouveau balcony in all Anatolia. Near the river, the little Kars Çayı, a few Russian cottages with nicely carved porches and window frames moulder away under the plane trees.

The Kars Çayı marks the boundary between the Russian town and the older village under the walls of the **castle**. Sultan Murat III built this fortress over the ruined Armenian foundation in the 1590s. The Turkish Army used it until recently; now the grounds inside are the town park. Murat also built the **stone bridge** over the stream.

The city's solid-fuel storage facilities are a feature at which most visitors turn up their noses. Expertly constructed 15ft beehives of dried dung are dotted all over Kars, which fights off strong local competition for the title of cowpat capital of Turkey. It's an ideal fuel for domestic use: odourless (the smell evaporates as the pats dry), slow-burning and free.

Cathedral of the Apostles

All that remains from the days when Kars was home to the kings of Armenia is its **Cathedral of the Apostles**, built by King Abbas in 937. The church has led a hard life. Only a century after its construction, Alp Arslan's Selcuks converted it into a mosque, but the Russians made it a church once again in 1878. After the recapture of the town and the dispersal of the Armenian community, the city made it a museum for a while; now it stands empty. The cathedral has managed to survive somehow in reasonably good repair; impressive in its own right, it provides a good introduction to the wealth of Armenian architecture you see at Ani.

Few builders ever piled up so much stone to cover so little space as the Armenians did. Like the Cathedral of the Apostles, most of their religious buildings are quite small, with centralized plans and a space under the dome, usually no more than 30ft in diameter, surrounded by three apses and the entrance where the fourth would be, in the form of a cross. The tip of the dome, however, may be as much as 150ft high. We don't know whether the medieval Armenians stayed at home on Sundays or squeezed themselves into their churches like sardines, but buildings like this are a kind of 'pure architecture', in which function is subordinated to form for the glory of God. The familiar outline of Armenian churches, a cylinder carved with blind arcades—pillars and arches sculpted in relief—covered with a cone-shaped dome, is a style you've probably seen in enough places already; the Selcuks and other Turkish states copied it for their mausolea.

Here, the cylinder is really a 12-sided figure, carved with mysterious figures, lions and whorls in high relief, somewhat like the decoration of the famous Armenian church on Akhtamar Island in Lake Van. Eight semidomes, the roof of the body of the church, support the central dome and drum, and inside some of the sculpture on the pendentives can still be seen, though most has fallen victim to time or the Iconoclasts. Note also the altar screen, carved from a single block of marble; here, and elsewhere in the cathedral, geometric patterns are used in a way that seems Islamic in inspiration.

The cathedral doors, with a bell and other artefacts sent as a gift from Tsar Nicholas II, can be seen at the **Kars Museum** on Cumhuriyet Caddesi, on the outskirts of the town, along with the usual ethnographic exhibits.

The protocol for visiting **Ani** is a hangover from the Soviet era. If you're planning a trip there under your own steam, you must first visit the Kars tourist office, where you will be given a permit form to take to the police station, a 10-minute walk away on the Faik Bey Caddesi. The police check your passport and ceremonially stamp your permit paper. You finally unravel yourself from the red tape at the city museum, where you must buy a ticket for Ani in advance. If you don't have your own transport, the tourist office can arrange a taxi for about $35 all in; if numbers are sufficient to fill a minibus, it will cost about $8 per head. Either way, the driver will take care of the formalities for you.

All this bureaucracy may leave you scratching your head in disbelief. If so, count yourself lucky: en route to Ani, you pass through the garrison village of **Subatan**. If the place seems to have a heavy military presence now, consider that before 1991 there were three times as many soldiers stationed in these parts. In Soviet times tourists had to trade in their passports and cameras at the garrison for a sulky conscript under orders to escort them around Ani. Strictly no dawdling, taking notes or defecting to the enemy. Ani itself lies 28 miles (45km) west of Kars, right on the Armenian border where two streams meet—the usually dry Alaca Çay and the Arpa, a tributary of the Aras. Across the Arpa, sentries will watch you through binoculars from their towers. You can wave to them, but they don't wave back. Although pointing your camera at Armenia is still forbidden, nowadays the border guards bark rather than bite and no shootings of tourists who transgress the rules have been reported.

The Armenian Kingdom

Ani's citadel, on the steep peninsula between the two streams, owes its beginnings to a 5th-century AD prince named Karisarkan, although the site had been occupied for centuries. The name came from Anahit, an ancient Persian goddess whom the Greek mythographers identified with Aphrodite; before the time of Gregory the Illuminator, she was one of the chief deities of the Armenians. Located on a major east–west caravan route, the town grew steadily through the following centuries. At the height of Armenia's golden age in the mid-10th century, King Ashot III transferred the capital here from Kars, and in the century that followed, Ashot and his successors endowed the city with the lavish array of sumptuous churches that attracts visitors today.

At that time, according to the chroniclers, Ani was a metropolis of some 100,000 people. Nothing in Europe at the time could rival it, and in the Middle East, only Constantinople, Cairo and Baghdad were as large and well built. The great wealth of the Bagratuni kings that made it all possible, unfortunately, was soon dissipated in increasing warfare against the Byzantines, their old enemies, and the Selcuk Turks, newly arrived out of Asia. The Byzantines held the independent-minded Armenians to be schismatics, and therefore thought nothing of breaking a treaty and attacking them just at the moment when their resources were concentrated against the Selcuks. Greek subversion had been undermining Armenia for a century, and Emperor Constantine IX was finally able to annex most of Armenia in 1040. By doing so, the Byzantines foolishly destroyed their own best ally, and when Ani fell to the Turks in 1064, the disaster at Manzikert that lost Anatolia to the empire forever was only seven years away.

As the Selcuks continued west, Armenian nobles were able to reassert their independence, though as isolated feudal lords, not as a united nation. Ani prospered nevertheless, until an earthquake in 1319 completely levelled the city. Now, with the eastern trade routes circumvented by the merchant adventurers of Italy, and the royal patronage gone, there was nothing to stop Ani's slide into a long decline. Today the city is a ruin, abandoned save for the tiny shepherd village outside its walls. The **walls** still stand, along with the citadel and the churches; together they make up the greatest achievement of medieval architecture to be seen anywhere in Turkey, the inspiration for Selcuk architecture and everything else in this corner of the world that is well made. Unfortunately, the Ministry of Culture, in its effort to preserve the walls, has seen fit to 'improve' upon them as well. At great expense to the state, a team of master masons has been brought in not just to strengthen the existing defences but to encase whole towers with a new stone fascia; in places, whole sections of crumbling wall have been replaced. It's like improving one of Rodin's bronzes by polishing it up with Brasso.

Walls

In spite of the best efforts of the men at the ministry, Ani still makes an overwhelming impression on the visitor. It is situated amidst rolling grassland on the very eastern edge of Turkey and when you get to the end of the long, narrow road connecting it to the present day, your imagination soon gets the better of you. If you are lucky enough to have the site to yourself, you become an honoured guest of the past: illusory buildings spring up from mossed-over foundations, paths winding through the rubble become peopled with obscure processions of old. Even before you see the churches, the attention given to even the defence walls gives an indication of the talent of the Armenian builders. The rounded, covered towers are unusual, more reminiscent of bunkers on the Maginot Line than anything from the Middle Ages. The Armenians took the time to beautify them, laying the sandstone blocks of two colours in simple designs.

Near the parking lot, the **Lion Gate** provides an entrance to the town; the sculpted lion that occasioned the name is said to have been added by Alp Arslan. Once inside, you will find two paths through the weeds that roughly follow the route of two of Ani's principal streets. The path to the left leads to the cathedral and citadel; the right-hand path to the most conspicuous monument near the gate, the Church of Our Saviour (Prkitch Kilisesi). On the way to the church you can look out for the remains of a linseed oil press, excavated at the end of the 1990s. The lower section of this large square room still survives, with a huge millstone in the centre which was powered by man or horse. Of more interest is the carefully constructed stone oil press in one corner. The milled linseed would be pounded and pressed in its square recess, producing oil which would trickle down into a container below. This was measured against a calibrated stone slab which remains in position today.

The Church of Our Saviour and Surp Gregor

Trdat, architect of the cathedral, rebuilt the **Church of Our Saviour** in the 12th century after an earthquake; it had been originally constructed in 1036 by the Pahvaluni family. The location must be bad for building, for today exactly half of the church remains, standing as if the rest had been sheared off by a monstrous axe. Don't go in: there's concern that the rest may follow.

Many visitors overlook the **Church of Surp Gregor** (Tigran Honents Kilisesi), which is a pity since it's one of the highlights of the complex. It is hidden on the cliffs above the Arpa but below the level of the city. This is only one of three churches of St Gregory in Ani, and it's easy to get confused. A prominent noble, Tigran Honents, built this one in 1215; it's the most complex of Ani's surviving churches both in design and in ornamentation. Though some 300 years younger than the church at Akhtamar, which it resembles, this one shows the same love of naturalistic detail in the finely carved animal motifs around the blind arcades. Inside, well-preserved frescoes depict some of the oddest scenes in Christendom. For those of us accustomed to the Western European or Greek tradition of religious art, these subjects are difficult to identify. The old Armenians kept a number of books from the Apocrypha in their Bible, which may explain some of them.

The twelve apostles are easy enough, and a series of pictures from the life of St Anne, mother of the Virgin Mary—a popular saint here, perhaps simply the spiritual descendant of old Anahit. Some of the others, scenes from the story of Gregory and other early Armenian saints, defy description. In two places on the walls, you see a man suspended upside down from a tree with his legs crossed—the very picture of the Hanged Man from Tarot cards. One series of paintings has an urban background of arches and gables; medieval Ani must have looked like this.

Cathedral of the Apostles

Surp Gregor Church stands at the easternmost corner of Ani, where a dry stream bed is lined with man-made caves, like those of Cappadocia. Nearby, there's another of the city gates, with a relief, crucifix and long inscription in Armenian. From here, you may either retrace your steps back along the path or cut through the jumble of mounds and ruined foundations westwards to the largest of Ani's buildings, the **Cathedral of the Apostles**, which Trdat built for Gagik I in 1010. Here, to accommodate large crowds, the centralized plan has grown into a broad rectangular nave where the dome, now collapsed, covered only the centre. Unlike European churches, with their monumental west entrances, this cathedral is oriented north–south, with the entrance at the centre of the nave; on the southern wall a tall slit of a window along the meridian was designed to flood the church with light only at high noon. Some frescoes still exist, but under Allah's whitewash, awaiting a restoration that may never come. Beyond these, the cathedral's modest decorative scheme hints at the same pious simplicity of a Turkish Ulu Cami; of all Ani's churches, it's the most austere. A single whimsical adornment is allowed in a kind of crypt entrance at the rear, built at a later date and half-hidden by weeds. In the same two-tone sandstone of the city walls, this addition is built of great stones masterfully cut into pentagons and five-pointed stars.

Menucehr Mosque (Ebul Menucehr Camii)

Back towards the palisade of the Arpa Çay, a lonely minaret protrudes from a ruined structure on the edge of the cliff. This building that the sign calls **Menucehr Mosque** is actually something of a mystery. Believed to date from the year 1072, eight years after the Selcuk conquest, it seems nevertheless to have originally been an Armenian work, not a church, but perhaps—with its colonnaded terraces and wonderful view over the Arpa—a palace. The slopes of the valley below are full of sculptural fragments obviously Armenian in style, but the small domes in the colonnades, with their inlaid stonework in geometric and stalactite patterns, suggests a Muslim hand. Whether mosque or palace, here Armenian and Islamic styles harmonize nicely, and suggest the Selcuk conquest may not have been such a disaster as historians make it out to be. The minaret has been closed since a German tourist committed suicide by leaping from its top; like many others in the Islamic world, it has 99 steps, one for each of the Names of God.

Perhaps the German suffered an attack of melancholy. This part of Ani is certainly conducive to it. Look down into the river to see the ruins of an exquisite bridge with stone towers, and another, unreachable, chapel poised gracefully on a little hill on the Armenian side. You find yourself imagining colourful royal processions, columns of victorious soldiers or caravans from Persia climbing the road from the bridge up to the city gates. Turn around, and see the city's skyline of churches still intact, with only the houses between them missing. As corpses of cities go, Ani is still warm. If it were not so beautiful, it would not be so sad.

Along the Alaca Çay

Crossing over to the Alaca Çay side of town, another bridge, more troglodyte caves and a gate and several surviving towers of the fortifications become visible. The narrow strip of land you stand on connects the city proper with the **citadel**, which is off-limits. Instead, follow the cliffs to the next St Gregory, the **Little St Gregory of Abighaurentz** (Polatoğlu Abughamrents Kilisesi), an especially tall church with an exceptionally small floor space. Built during the reign of Gagik I in 994, it features six domed apses forming a circle around the central drum and dome, all supported by columns bearing the distinctive Armenian style of capital, a variant on the Ionic form but with three scrolls instead of two. The ruin nearby, called the caravanserai, was really a church rebuilt as a mosque by the Selcuks, with the same coalescence of two styles as that seen in the Menucehr Mosque. Yet another mosque, the **Ebul Muammeran Camii** with its fallen minaret, stands as the only monument to the short-lived Ani-Shehhad Kingdom, a state formed in the confusion of the Selcuks' move westward. Hiding beneath ground level nearby are the newly excavated remains of what archaeologists think is a Zoroastrian fire temple from the 6th century BC. The four remaining columns are plain and wonderfully squat, a case if ever there was one of function over form.

The first King Gagik also gets the credit for the final **St Gregory Church** (Gagik Kilisesi), built in 1001 near the northwestern edge of the city. The church has been a victim of earthquakes, but even in its derelict state it is clear that it was one of the grandest of all, comparable in size to the cathedral. The circular form, with an interior circle of columns and four mighty piers that must have carried an enormous dome, is probably unique in Armenian architecture. The crater in the floor you almost fell into is not a baptismal font, but a well, cut right through the centre of the church and now filled with rubble. The original religion of the Armenians had much to do with sacred trees and springs, and Gregory the Illuminator made many concessions to the old order in this conversion of the nation; he kept the old hereditary caste of priests, for example, and it would be interesting to learn what else survived as well.

Returning to the Lion Gate, you pass a single wall remaining from the oldest church in Ani, a relic of the family that founded the city; the three-tiered arches of the 7th-century **Karisarkan Church** are carved with a scene of the Annunciation.

Kars has a terrible dearth of decent hotels. It's as if all the town's hotel owners met up one night and agreed to throw the hoteliers' rule book out of a top-floor window. Hotels here are less friendly and more expensive than anywhere else in eastern Turkey.

moderate

The ★★★**Karabağ** at Faik Bey Caddesi 184, ✆ 0474 212 3480, ✉ 0474 223 3089, is supposed to be the best hotel in town, and the unhelpful management make the most of it, charging $60 per double. Rooms at the front are prey to street noise; those at the sides have windows so close to the buildings next door that you're in a permanent twilight zone. Only the rooms at the back are bright and quiet. The saving grace of the hotel is its en suite toilet and shower facilities: the lashings of hot water are just what you need after a day clambering over Ani.

inexpensive–cheap

The only well-run hotel in town is the ★★**Güngören** at Halit Paşa Caddesi, Millet Sokak 4, ✆ 0474 212 5630, ✉ 0474 223 4821. Unusually for Kars, the staff are friendly and the rooms spacious and clean, with private bathtubs as well as showers. For more intense aquatherapy, head down to the hotel's sauna and hamam. The Güngören is also good value, with doubles including breakfast costing $24.

Of the other hotels in a similar price range, the only one not to smell too bad is the ★★**Temel** at Yeni Pazar Caddesi 9, ✆ 0474 223 1376, ✉ 0474 223 1323. The beds are clean and most rooms are equipped with showers and toilets. If there is any doubt in your mind as to which decade the zebra-pattern wallpaper was put up, one clue is the breakfast room's poster of the Trabzon football team, replete with long hair, walrus whiskers and outlandish sideburns.

The **Nursaray** at Faik Bey Caddesi 208, ✆ 0474 223 1364, has rudimentary doubles for $6. Rooms have basins, but the toilets and showers are communal. Next door is the **Kervansaray**, ✆ 0474 223 1990, where plain rooms cost $7 with shower or $5 without; the rather unsavoury toilets are shared.

The best dining spot in Kars is hidden away above a stationery shop on the corner of Faik Bey Caddesi and Ordu Caddesi. An inconspicuous sign by a side entrance points you up to the **Hukukçular Lokalı** or 'Lawyer's Club'. The owner, Ali Özkiran, has gone to great lengths to banish Kars' rough and ready atmosphere from his establishment: the waiters are discreet, the crockery is crested and the tablecloths and napkins are linen. Not surprisingly, the club is a fixture in the diaries of the town's tie-wearing types. A wide selection of mezes and hot dishes are on offer, with a different special each day. A full meal may cost only $4, more if you order beer or wine. Ali is working on a plan to open up a decent hotel in Kars, which can't happen soon enough.

The **Ocakbaşı** restaurant at the Güngören Hotel is the place to go for good grilled food. Near the tourist office on Atatürk Caddesi is the **Kristal Lokanta**, a colourful place with country'n'western checked tablecloths. Wholesome ready meals, including a number of simple vegetarian dishes, are on offer for $3.

Stop for a relaxing afternoon pastry at the **Sema Tatlı Pastanesi**, Faik Bey Caddesi 238. Its cheap chandeliers and white walls with gilded embellishments give it the air of a down-at-heel imperial Russian salon. It is also a good place to stock up on snacks for a trip to Ani.

Mount Ararat

If you think you've reached the end of the world at Ani, you haven't yet been to **Mount Ararat**. From Kars, or for that matter from anywhere else, there's no easy way to get there; whether you drive or take the untamed mountain buses, you will have to pick your way slowly between the peaks, sometimes on long stretches of unpaved road, before you eventually arrive. The short cut to **Kağızman** will spare you another trip to Sarıkamış, and the red, tan and green Arizona landscape between Mount Aladağ and its shorter cousin Yağlıca Dağ may or may not be worth the damage the road does to your nerves. Among the dirty and disorganized villages of this region, Kağızman stands out; the government has put a lot of money into agriculture here, and it shows.

Don't bother with the next short cut—to **Ağrı**, Turkey's most woebegone provincial capital. The east road for Iğdir follows a narrow plain and, with no little mountains crowding it, affords a view of the big ones, mostly far off across the border, their iridescent peaks catching the sun. Clouds cling to the slopes, but the winds hardly ever permit them to stay still, and the swirling mountain panorama changes by the minute. In many places along this road, the Armenian border is only a mile or so to the north, across the Aras. From this road, it looks more like Tolkien's land of Mordor, with grey cliffs wreathed in smoke, squat factories, and even a nuclear power plant belching steam.

On the Turkish side, you'll see more troglodyte caves at **Tuzluca**. At **Iğdir**, an awful place, take the right turn for **Doğubayazıt**; the entire 34 miles (55km) of this road follows the western flank of Ararat.

Doğubayazıt is definitely a frontier town of the Wild East; disconcertingly deep potholes often fill with water on the paved roads, which peter out into mud or dust without warning. The streets are full of tractors and sheep; there are few amenities and plenty of bad smells. Being on one of the main roads from Iran, it's usually full of Iranian tourists; you see them standing about on the corners, trying to get rid of some of their worthless currency.

Getting Around

Getting to Doğubayazıt on the **bus** can be difficult. Buses from Kars that claim to be going all the way may leave you stranded in Iğdır. There are direct minibuses from Van to Doğubayazıt, but some only go to Ağrı. Connecting **minibuses** do exist, but the connections sometimes aren't made. However you travel in this area, long detours around big patches of mountains will be the rule. Large sections around Ağrı are unpaved, and there's no easy route across the mountains to Van or Diyarbakır. Fortunately, the government tourist office's map is quite accurate for this region.

You can take a **taxi** to the İshak Paşa palace ($5 return trip), but the three-mile (5km) **walk**, passing nomad encampments and a military base full of gloomy soldiers, is very pleasant, albeit tough on your calf muscles.

Palace of İshak Paşa

Nothing in the town is very old. A century ago, this was all a lake bordered with marshes; travellers since ancient times have remarked on how the tremendous flow off Ararat turns all the surrounding country to a bog in the spring, though many parts have lately been drained for farming. The original settlement, **Beyazıt**, was up in the hills three miles (5km) east, near one of the most unusual attractions in eastern Turkey, the half-ruined **Palace of İshak Paşa**. The Turks like putting this pleasure dome on their travel posters. With its pointed dome and striped minaret, made in two shades of sandstone, Armenia-style, it matches its romantic setting under Ararat, and whispers to the gaping tourist of caravans laden with spices and silk, eunuchs with scimitars and dark-eyed houris in pointed slippers, with djinns and afrits and the rest of the Arabian Nights' paraphernalia just offstage.

The joke is, it's no older than the 1700s. İshak Paşa, like his father before him and his son afterwards, held the title of governor in these parts from the sultan, but the sultan was a thousand miles away; conferring the office was only a polite oriental gesture acknowledging the power these feudal lords held over the area. According to whom you ask, you will hear that İshak was an Armenian, a Kurd or a Jew, and no doubt a man of refinement, too. He built his barely fortified saray in the eclectic style, just at the time his counterparts in Europe were beginning to construct Greek or Gothic hotels and railway stations. Almost two centuries of exposure to the unforgiving climate of eastern Turkey has taken its toll on the palace; several sections of the complex have recently been re-roofed and some of the interior walls have been reinforced by ungainly steel girders.

Don't let that detract from your enjoyment of this lovely place. The sculpture of the entrance, like an old-fashioned **medrese gate**, and the tree-of-life motifs on the **fountain** in the inner courtyard are fine works, as is the mosque, built over the parapets of the castle. Inside, note the odd mimber hidden inside the wall, where the imam would have to climb up and reappear in a little window like a character in a puppet show. The upper galleries are, of course, for the ladies. İshak Paşa always had plenty on hand—the harem apartment makes up half of his palace. Each of the harem rooms is fitted with a conical stone fireplace, a reminder to fair-weather visitors that ferocious winds lash out at the beleaguered pleasure palace each winter. The ruins of the palace garden and an early 16th-century mosque can be seen on the opposite hillside. Your eyes may take a little longer to focus on the fortress, which in some weather may be difficult to distinguish from the jagged outcrops of the mountain range behind it. A fortress has guarded this mountain pass since Urartian times, although the walls have been rebuilt many times since then; the ruins lower down belong to old Beyazıt.

Noah's Ark and Ararat (Ağrı Dağı)

You may find the streets of Doğubayazıt full of lost Americans, as well as Iranians. Since the latest book about a sighting of Noah's Ark on Mount Ararat, hosts of divinity professors and evangelists have descended on the unsuspecting town. Medieval travellers like Mandeville report that the remains of the Ark were there for all to see, and we can guess that the business of peddling old planks to Christians sprang up here at an early date.

It is no disgrace if these seekers go home empty-handed. Even with aircraft and satellites to help, 600 square miles of mountain make for quite a job. Somewhere on Ararat, a holy place the Armenians called Jacob's Well has been lost for centuries. If there were any literal truth in the story of Noah, it would be a disappointment; finding the original impulse for the myth would be much more significant.

Arks and Archaeologists

Battalions of scholars have already spent careers tracking down and sorting out stories of the flood: those of Noah, of the Sumerian Utnapishtim, the Deucalion and Pyrrha myth of the Greeks and dozen of other variants from Uganda to Wales. Innumerable theories have been propounded. The school of thought that believes that myths often stem from misrepresentations of pictures in ancient religious icons, for example, sees the story of Noah deriving from a painted scene in which a ship, representing the sun in its passage through the year, carries a sacred king and animals representing the signs of the zodiac. Other scholars find in the tale a confusion of myth with real floods; tidal waves from the disaster that overtook Minoan Crete, perhaps, or a great flood in the valleys of the Tigris and Euphrates in Mesopotamia. The Utnapishtim story, from that part of the world, describes the ark as a perfect cube—intriguing, though highly unseaworthy. The Knights Templars, who knew all these old stories, used a cubic 'ark' as the altar for their secret observances.

For the moment, the last word must go to Hertha von Dechend, a renowned and remarkable scholar who has spent her life reinterpreting ancient stories as a kind of scientific shorthand for astronomical events. To her, all flood stories denote the passing of a World Age, in a vast cosmic clock measured by the procession of the equinoxes. Briefly, just as the North Pole moves around the sky every 26,000 years, so does the equinoctial colure, the point the sun occupies at the spring equinox. When it passes from one constellation of the zodiac to another (say, from Pisces to Aquarius), a new age begins and the old one, with the old constellation, is 'drowned' beneath the celestial equator. The ancients did love to water their heavens with constellations of rivers and seas, and in the astronomy of the Mesopotamians, there is not only a boat (now called *Argo*), but even a star they call Mount Ararat.

Ararat Itself

When you see Ararat (Ağrı Dağı), you won't be surprised that so many stories have grown up around it, or that so many peoples thought of it as the centre of the world. From the plain of Doğubayazıt, it rears itself startlingly heavenwards, as if out of the sea. An extinct volcano, its mass rises as neatly symmetrical as Etna or Mount Fuji. The summit, now visible, now hidden in clouds, is 3½ miles up; of its entourage of smaller peaks, those on the right are all Iranian, those to the left in Armenia. Climbing tours of Ararat can be arranged from Doğubayazıt. One reputable agency is **Mefser Tur** on Belediye Caddesi, © 0472 312 6772, @ 0472 312 7776, which charges a rather steep $800 for an all-inclusive four day climb. You will need to check carefully on the security situation prior to departure.

Doğubayazıt   ***Where to Stay***

inexpensive

The ★★★★**Ararat** on Belediye Caddesi, © 0472 312 4987, @ 0472 312 7355, benefits from a frontier star grading system. Although it has many of the amenities of a four-star hotel, such as an outdoor pool and rooms with TV, phone and chunky concrete balcony, the overall impression it gives is of a two-star with ambitions. Prices reflect this, however: $30 for a double with breakfast.

cheap

The ★★★**İsfahan** at İsa Geçit Caddesi 26, © 0472 312 5289, @ 0472 312 4479, looks good from the outside, brightly painted in blue and white and set back from the road. Inspiration ran out before they considered the interior, which is in dire need of an overhaul. Run-of-the-mill en suite rooms cost $16 for two people. Slightly more expensive, but more comfortable and welcoming, is the ★★★**Sim-er Hotel**, two miles (3km) out of town at İran Transit Yolu 3, © 0472 312 4842, @ 472 312 4843.

There are lots of cheap hotels on or off the main street offering very good value. The most welcoming is the **Tahran** at Büyük Ağrı Caddesi 124, © 0472 311 2223, @ 0472 311 2460. Downstairs the lobby is bright and the staff friendly. Upstairs the metal beds have solid mattresses for a healthy night's sleep. The sheets are spotlessly clean, the carpets filthy; $7 for a double with private toilet and shower.

The ★★**İshakpaşa**, Büyük Ağrı Caddesi Emniyet Karşısı 10, © 0472 312 7036, @ 0472 312 7644, has $10 en suite rooms with TV, phone and a balcony. It overlooks a busy traffic junction (although it's 'busy' in the same Doğubayazıt way that the Ararat Hotel is luxurious).

If you can do without a TV and balcony, the **Kenan** at Emniyet Caddesi 39, ℰ 0472 312 7869, ℮ 0472 312 7571, is at a quieter location than the İshakpaşa. Its reception is decked out in so many woven goods that you may think you've strayed into a carpet shop. Rooms of a similar quality to the İshakpaşa cost only $7. If you are counting every lira, the **Saruhan** on Büyük Ağrı Caddesi, ℰ 0472 311 3097, offers great value for money at $2 per person. Rooms are spartan but clean, with shared toilets and hot showers downstairs. Unlike in some other establishments in Doğubayazıt the chirpy staff speak English; they even have internet facilities.

camping

There are two basic camping grounds just outside town: the **İshakpaşa** just above the palace of the same name, and **Murat Camping**, just below.

Doğubayazıt   Eating Out

The only place with any pretentions in Doğubayazıt is in the **Ararat Hotel**, popular with Western travellers; dinner costs about $5. The restaurant at the **Sim-er Hotel** outside town is also very nice. Two acceptable places popular with the locals are the **Derya**, across the street from the police station on Abdullah Baydar Caddesi, and— even better—the **Doğuş Restaurant** near the bus station; both serve Turkish staple dishes for $4.

Southeastern Anatolia

This quarter of Turkey lies just outside the boundary of the known and familiar, where mere geography evaporates into myth along the banks of the Tigris and Euphrates and the mile-high shores of Lake Van, and the ghosts of numberless dead civilizations rise up to spook you from their mouldering ruins. Travellers and holiday-makers are beginning to find their way here, mostly adventurous Germans without much luggage. It isn't a part of the world that calls to mind any particular associations, unless you are a scholar familiar with names like Edessa, Harran and Carchemish, and few people ever think of it as a place in which to spend their free time. Approach it in the right frame of mind, however, and it could be a trip to remember.

This is the Middle East, make no mistake about it, with parched plains and barren hills and where sheep outnumber people. Long ago, the climate was much less dry, and the plains of the southeast marked the north edge of the Fertile Crescent, fought over by the Egyptians, Assyrians and Hittites. Biblical sites and early Christian centres abound, and the present population of Kurds, Turks and Arabs each have stories of their own about the region.

Southeastern Anatolia

Unfortunately, there has been a great deal of political unrest in this over-whelmingly Kurdish region; guerrillas of the PKK (*see* 'History', p.63–4) waged war in the mountains with Turkish security forces for much of the 1980s and '90s. After his arrest by the Turkish authorities in 1999, the PKK leader Abdullah Öcalan declared that his men would cease all military operations on Turkish soil, and many in Turkey hope that further peace initiatives from both the Kurdish and Turkish sides will allow the region to break out of its vicious circle of violence. Although you won't find many people who back the PKK (or who will admit it), you will undoubtedly encounter strong separatist feelings in many of the people you meet in this region. Atatürk is not popular here and this is no place to sing his praises; the Kurds remember all too well their revolts of the 1920s when they called for autonomy, only to be silenced by an army crackdown that cost tens of thousands of Kurds their lives. Indeed, in cities such as Diyarbakır and Mardin, the Atatürk statue is under 24-hour armed guard to protect it from desecration.

The towns with the worst reputations for political unrest over the past two decades have been the provincial capitals of Siirt, Hakkâri and

Mardin and it is wise to avoid staying overnight in any of them. Be aware, too, that there could be some danger in travelling in the rural areas of their provinces (not that you would have any reason to do so). Yet don't let these troubles put you off. It is quite safe to visit the cities and their associated tourist attractions, and thousands of people do so every year. Try to keep your finger on the pulse, however, by watching television or glancing at a newspaper before heading out east; the Turkish media always give prominent coverage to any violent incidents, and you'll need to know if there has been any recent unrest. The English language *Turkish Daily News*, available in most resorts and major cities, is a good source of pull-no-punches information.

Canvass Turks on their view on the security situation and you will soon discover the wild lack of consensus prevailing. As a nation of news junkies, most Turks have strong opinions on the safety issue, but winnowing the well-informed advice from the uninformed chaff is another matter. Similarly, consulates and embassies habitually err on the cautious side, whereas some tourist agencies tend to play down the risks.

The traveller in southeastern Anatolia needs to be aware of more than just political violence before setting out. This corner of Turkey is not geared up for tourism and there will be times when travelling here can be emotionally frazzling. Children, in particular, can be both pitiful and pestilential; some may have never seen a foreigner before and you'll find yourself enduring numerous requests for *para* (money) and *bonbon* (sweets). Adults won't thank you for doling out goodies; on the contrary, they'll be annoyed. The Kurds are a proud people who don't want their children, however poor, to grow up as beggars. They're a very conservative people, too, and those skimpy shorts that you wore so freely in Side will here induce nothing but black looks. Women should keep their legs covered at all times, preferably with a baggy skirt, and avoid sleeveless tops; such attire may also ward off sexual harassment which, unfortunately, is quite common. Don't let all this deter you from visiting the east; just act sensibly, and with not a little dignity, and all will be well.

Kahramanmaraş to Şanlıurfa

Coming from the west, from Adana or the Hatay, your first encounter in this area will be three cities whose names were changed by Atatürk. Maraş, Antep and Urfa, all as old as the Hittites, performed such service in the War of Independence, when their local defence committees beat off the invading French armies, that they now bear the titles, respectively, of *hero*, *warrior* and *glorious*: Kahramanmaraş, Gaziantep and Şanlıurfa. You may see them on maps, tourist literature and road signs in either their new or old forms. For the sake of consistency we have used the new forms throughout.

Be advised that **buses** in the region, and indeed all of eastern Anatolia, are not always up to the standard that obtains in the rest of the country—lots of cracked windscreens are the rule, and they travel at hair-raising speeds when they have a mind to. Still, there's no problem getting anywhere you want to go.

If **driving**, you need take no special precautions except to make sure that you've got plenty of extra water and a good spare—and be especially careful on the bizarre E24 speedway around Şanlıurfa. You'll have to rely on the locals for directions quite often if you're trying to find the sights in the countryside—they aren't well signposted.

Don't take your car to Soğmatar or Şuayp, especially in the summer: it won't be worth the risk, and you probably won't find the sites anyway. Instead, employ the services of **Harran Dolmuş**, behind the Şanmed hospital in Şanlıurfa, ℂ 0414 215 1575. In summer, subject to numbers, they run buses to all the sites in the area, and Harran too, with prices averaging around $20–30 per person; the more who sign up for the trip, the cheaper it becomes. If you'd prefer to see the sites alone or with your own small group, the company can organize this too, with a taxi for a long day costing around $75. **Taxi** hire can also be arranged via the local tourist information office, although they tend to be less particular about which drivers they choose. For a round trip to Harran only by taxi you should expect to pay $25.

Gaziantep and Şanlıurfa are connected by direct THY **flights** from Ankara and, less frequently, from İstanbul. Gaziantep is linked with Sivas and Malatya by **rail**.

Tourist Information

Gaziantep: 100 Yıl Kültür Parkı içi, Vilayet Konağı Arkası, ℂ 0342 230 5969.
Şanlıurfa: Göller Mah., Balıklı Göl Sokak, F-Blok No. 3–4, ℂ 0414 215 2467.

Kahramanmaraş and Gaziantep

Kahramanmaraş was once the capital of the 12th-century BC Hittite state of Gürgüm, but there's not much to the city today. If you like Hittite sculptures, the archaeological museum is good for a brief browse, and there are two 15th-century mosques; otherwise, it's a town one can bypass without guilt.

The same could be said of **Gaziantep**, but as Turkey's sixth city, bestriding the two roads into the southeast, it will probably either introduce you to the region or help you rest at the end of the trip. It's a good place for that, with nice hotels and a reputation for tasty food. Kebab houses all over Turkey proclaim 'Gaziantep style' on their signs. Despite its venerable history, Gaziantep is a thoroughly up-to-date town and its air of youthful vigour also brings with it more chewing gum on the pavements than anywhere else in Turkey.

Gaziantep owes its recent growth to a burgeoning textile industry; along with prosperity, this has brought the city an expanse of *gecekondu* neighbourhoods spreading over the surrounding hills. The city's ancient fame, the pistachio nut, is still in evidence; any sweet-shop in the town will sell you a box at astoundingly cheap prices. Like any busy, lively city, Gaziantep has its share of peculiarities: the motorcycles with sidecars like big wagons, used as informal taxis and delivery trucks in the poorer sections, and the traffic lights in the centre fitted with digital displays to count down the seconds until the lights change. From the past, the city retains an unusual fashion in minarets, some with spiral fluting and others topped with ornate wooden crow's-nests for the muezzin. In the older, eastern parts of the town, these stand side by side with asymmetrical grey stone houses whose interior stairways project over the sidewalk to form a kind of bay window, a style unique to Gaziantep.

The town's major thoroughfare begins at the central square as **Suburcu Caddesi** and changes its name several times on its way through the old town and the **bazaar**. No amount of modernity can kill off a Turkish market and Gaziantep's is as colourful as any. North of this street, the Selcuk-era **castle** is usually locked up, with the modern city around it settled in for a long siege. The castle stands on a hill formed not by nature, but by the accumulated debris of thousands of years of occupation. There are mounds like this—an archaeologist would call it a 'tell'—all over the region.

Archaeology Museum

Enough of them have been excavated for Gaziantep's **Archaeology Museum** to be worth a visit (*open 8.30–noon, 1.30–5pm, closed Mon; adm*). It lies on the north fringe of the town on İstasyon Caddesi, past the stadium and the garden cafés of the city park, where *nargile*-smoking is still very much the thing. The museum, in its modern building, claims the largest collection in the southeast, with Hittite reliefs (one depicts the god Tesup with an axe and a fork as if he were marching to dinner), some fine Roman sculpture on grave steles from as far away as Palmyra in Syria, mosaics and cylinder seals, even some recently unearthed mastodon bones to remind you that these hot plains were cool pine forests during the last Ice Age. One finely carved relief shows a smiling Hellenistic-era king shaking hands with the god Apollo. This is Antiochus I, King of Commagene, and if both the pose and subject seem somewhat presumptuous, just wait until you've seen the rest of this man's work up on Nemrut Dağı.

Carchemish

Like Gaziantep itself, most of the ancient cities in its province have little to show for their long histories. Of them, the most important was **Carchemish**, *Kargamış* in Turkish, a city straddling major trade routes between Mesopotamia and the Mediterranean that first flourished under the Hittites but only really took off when that empire was extinguished. Carchemish was sacked around the same time as Troy and Hattuşaş, *c.* 1180 BC, but it soon recovered and, as an independent Hittite kingdom surviving on trade and clever diplomacy, it lasted until the Assyrians razed it in 717 BC.

British excavations, beginning in the 1880s, contributed some of the first clues to the identity of the Hittites; the finds, now mostly in London or Ankara, attracted a lot of attention at the time, and many of the grand Edwardian dilettantes (T.E. Lawrence among them) spent time helping with the dig. Nowadays, you'll have a hard time getting here, as permission from the provincial government in Gaziantep is required. Carchemish lies right on the Syrian border, and as the Syrians are difficult neighbours the Turks keep security tight.

Birecik

Turkey doesn't have many oil deposits, but the oil isn't far away. The road from the east into Gaziantep seems a sort of pipeline in itself; more often than not, its narrow two lanes are packed solid with tank trucks going in both directions, making the ride east a thrill you'll remember, especially if you take the bus. The road crosses the Euphrates (*Fırat Nehri* in Turkish) at **Birecik**, a sorry little town on white cliffs, but well liked by the bald ibis, an almost extinct crane, now a special project of the World Wildlife Fund.

Birecik's ruined castle was built or rebuilt by the Franks of the First Crusade as a border outpost for their County of Edessa. Whatever made Count Baldwin and his merry men try to set up a state so far east—the furthest penetration into the Islamic world that the Crusaders ever made—is not clear. Founded in 1092, the County of Edessa was hardly defensible, and the Selcuks destroyed it less than 50 years later. In the First Crusade, at least, we can give the knights some credit for pious motivation; the ancient city of Edessa, now known as **Şanlıurfa**, is holy ground for Christians as well as Muslims.

Şanlıurfa (Edessa)

Abraham, according to traditions of both the Christians and the Muslims, received his summons to prophecy while living in the city. The Şanlıurfans will show you Job's cave as well, and the belief is widely current among them that Adam and Eve lived here, and that these parched hills were once the Garden of Eden. The stories must stand on their own; we cannot guess how many levels of religious meaning and historical significance lie beneath them. All the evidence we have is this city of Şanlıurfa, a holy place for millennia upon millennia. No ground could store up spiritual energy for so long without becoming at least a bit strange and otherworldly, but Şanlıurfa and its hinterlands go too far. It is the vortex of Turkey, not a Canterbury but a Salisbury Plain, full of mystery. The city, with its scholarly legacies, will seem reasonable enough, but once outside it, anything can happen.

History

The name Urfa may be a very ancient corruption of Hurri; archaeologists speculate that it was an important town of the Hurri-Mitanni confederation, the state that pushed the Hittites around until the successful reign of Hittite King Suppiluliumas I ended the Hurri ascendancy in *c.* 1400 BC. As Orhoe, or Orhai, the town continued quietly until Alexander the Great's Seleucid successors renamed it Edessa and helped it grow into its new role as clearing house of goods, gods and ideas between the Greek world and the East. Under the Byzantines, Urfa found itself attacked repeatedly by the first waves of the expanding Muslim Arabs in the 7th century, changing hands back and forth. While the soldiers were out banging their swords, Christian and Muslim scholars inside the walls and in the nearby city of Harran were beginning the great work of translation and teaching that made Greek science and philosophy available to the Muslim world. Centuries later, under the County of Edessa, the learned men of Islam were to return the favour. Books that had long been lost to the West, including important works of Aristotle, were regained by contacts made here and in the other crusader states. Along with them came the fruits of the golden era of Arabic science, works of mathematics and astronomy that were to have an incalculable influence on the West.

The Pool of Abraham

Striving to maintain something of its old distinction, Şanlıurfa is one of Anatolia's loveliest cities. Its economy is based more on pilgrimages and religious institutions than commerce, and although it seems as prosperous as Gaziantep, its air of pleasant tranquillity has not suffered. Şanlıurfa is a compact city, strung out along the 1½-mile length of Atatürk Caddesi (part of which is called Sarayönü Caddesi). Most of its sights can be seen in a day, but before you go out walking in this ferocious climate—Şanlıurfa is on the edge of the Syrian desert—take note of the best place in town for a cold drink and a spot of shade. In **Gölbaşı** (literally 'at the lakeside'), a park around the **Pool of Ayn-ı Zeliha** on the southern edge of town, are cafés, pavilions, garden paths and the biggest concentration of trees in Şanlıurfa province. Take a seat by the water and almost instantly sleek grey fish will poke their noses out expectantly. Next, a small boy will appear with a plate of seeds or chick peas to sell; you will earn a little grace for contributing to the upkeep of Şanlıurfa's sacred carp, who have inhabited this pool for thousands of years. No one knows exactly how long: local stories associate the fish with the story of Abraham. Ancient religions from Ireland to China have had the like, often carp or salmon at holy springs, but few examples have survived. The carp may not be caught or even disturbed—in Şanlıurfa they will tell you about the drunken soldier who went fishing one night and ended up with a stiff prison sentence. Some locals even maintain that the fish have abnormally high levels of phosphorus in their bodies, making them poisonous to eat. Everyone feeds them; with such a soft life, it's no wonder there are so many of them, or that they look so fat and serene as they glide through the cool waters. This pond actually serves only for the carp to make little excursions; their true abode is the nearby **Pool of Abraham**, joined by a small canal. No one knows exactly how long this has been here, or to whom it was originally sacred, although it has been associated with the goddess Astarte. The Greeks called the spring that fills the two pools 'Callirhoe', 'fair-flowing'.

In the Muslim tradition, Abraham began his career as the first prophet of monotheism in Şanlıurfa. His refusal of idolatry so outraged Nimrod, the legendary Assyrian king oddly associated with so many places in Anatolia, that he determined to have the troublesome prophet burned. An immense pyre was constructed under the walls of Şanlıurfa's citadel, but just as Abraham was being tossed onto it, God, or rather Allah, turned the fire into a flowing spring and landed him safely on his feet. On the edge of the Pool of Abraham, reflected in its waters, is an exceptionally lovely mosque, the **Halil Rahman Camii**, its three pointed domes built in the 17th century while the unusual square minaret survives from the medieval original.

Citadel

The oldest parts of Şanlıurfa's **citadel** are Roman and Byzantine, but it became the impressive castle you see today through the energy of the Frankish Crusaders, who built the towers and bastions, the donjon inside and the ditch around, cut in some places out of bare rock. The prominent landmark on top, two lone Corinthian columns, has acquired the name the **Throne of Nimrod**; no one knows who actually erected them. The spur on which the citadel rises is a part of a long cliff that bounds Şanlıurfa on its southern and eastern edges. Of the dozens of man-made and natural caves along the cliff, two are of great importance to

Muslims: the **Cave of Abraham** (İbrahim Halilullah Dergâhı) and the **Cave of Job** (Eyyüp Peygamber Makamı). Both of these are religious sites of immeasurable antiquity, and were associated with the two biblical figures before Muslims ever came here, but now they have become one of the most important places of pilgrimage in the Islamic world. Devout Turks rub shoulders with Iranian and Syrian pilgrims, who carry off holy water from the site in recycled Coke bottles. Non-Muslims may also visit, except during the month of Ramazan.

Beneath the cliffs, adjoining the gardens and two pools, a complex of mosques and schools has grown up that is worthy of this holy city. None is very old—at the very base of the cliff, one mosque with a huge dome was completed in the late 1980s—but all are in the elegant style of the Halil Rahman Camii. **Hasan Paşa Camii** and the **Mevlidi Halil Camii** make the greatest impression, but taken all together this complex, with its arches, colonnades and cloisters, gardens and fountains, is a masterpiece of urban design, eliciting praise for Allah and the city in one breath.

Old Neighbourhoods

In the old neighbourhoods, along twisting, narrow, unusually clean streets, fine old homes with stone balconies harmonize well with the design of the mosques. One motif you see everywhere, the zigzag line, always appears as if it were a symbol—on the balustrades of the Halil Rahman, on the arches above private doors, and in the metal grillwork. Like the homes in many Middle Eastern cities, Şanlıurfa's face inwards, turning their backs on the street. Beside the balconies, the doorways are the only decoration, but the citizens have made it a point of pride to beautify them; many have miniatures of the Ka'aba or other religious subjects painted over the arch. If you can find the way through this maze of streets to the east, you'll see the last remaining section of the old city wall, the **Mahmutoğlu Tower** (Mahmutoğlu Kulesi) and the gate for the Mardin road beside it.

Şanlıurfa's **bazaar** seems to have selected the very narrowest streets in which to ply its trades, just to the north of the religious complex. This is Turkey's most timeless bazaar. Carts drawn by tired donkeys push their way through the throng; knife grinders sharpen blades in a fiery shower of sparks in the musty holes in the walls that pass as workshops; women, veiled even across their eyes, glide by ethereally. You wouldn't be surprised to see Abraham himself come around the corner. **Atatürk Caddesi** skirts its edge, and continues northwards from there into the modern quarters of the town, passing several mosques with squat Persian-style minarets. One, the **Hüseyin Cami**, stands right in the middle of the avenue. Its three-domed porch gives it away as an early Ottoman work. The **Ulu Cami**, a bit further north, dates from the 12th century; the Selcuks built it immediately after their conquest of the city in commemoration of the event. Unique among the mosques of Turkey, if not the rest of the Islamic world, its minaret has a clock on top. The back streets here have some of the best of Şanlıurfa's old houses.

In the modern end of Şanlıurfa, the **Archaeological Museum** (*open 8.30–noon, 1.30–5; closed Mon; adm*) has increased its collections so much in recent years that a new section has been built; exhibits go as far back as the Assyrian colonies recently unearthed in the vicinity, and plenty of peculiar stone carvings may be seen in the sculpture garden outside. There aren't any of the customary stone lions here—just several stone pussycats.

One biblical site this area doesn't claim, surprisingly, is the Valley of Dry Bones. Don't go lightly into any trip into the empty spaces around Şanlıurfa. In winter and early spring it's almost green, but during the hot months, daytime temperatures of 110°F/43°C are common, and shade and water are rare. Without a drop of humidity, the air scorches the soil with arid blasts, and the sparse grass left over from spring crackles underfoot like broken glass. If you've always wanted to see a genuine mirage, come in July or August, though after a few hours on the plains you may not be able to distinguish them from the hallucinations.

It isn't the heat that bewilders, nor the uncanny landscape, wrinkled and ugly and covered with rocks. Both of these add much to the ambience, but the unfathomable strangeness of the place comes from the works of man. All around Şanlıurfa, the countryside is littered with caves and mounds, standing stones and cairns, ruins and inscriptions, along with such exotica as the little city, dug down several levels, around a square subterranean courtyard, visible along the road from Şanlıurfa to Gaziantep. Nobody tries to explain who built any of these; few scholars ever visit.

The Tek Tek Mountains

The best places to see lie among the awful Tek Tek Mountains east of the town. With proper directions from the Şanlıurfa tourist office, you will know where to leave the Mardin road. Along the passable dirt track south, the first sight to greet your eyes is a blue man painted on a cliff next to a small cave. It's somewhat disconcerting; it can't be too old. Every height in the Tek Tek bears some sort of marker on its summit, such as a large stone or cairn. They stand like sentinels, overlooking the valleys with their dry stream beds that once ran down to the Euphrates. The villages are hard to see, low on the ground or buried in it, with mud-walled huts and stables the same colour as the earth. Livestock grazing and even agriculture amazingly still go on; there's just enough rain in the spring to sprout a few crops. The semi-nomadic inhabitants, of uncertain nationality, are just as invisible. Not even they can stay out in the summer oven for long.

Soğmatar

Some 12 miles (20km) south of the highway, you reach the ruins of **Soğmatar**. The origin of this religious centre has evaporated in history, but a star- and planet-worshipping cult called the Sabians occupied it well into the Middle Ages. This unusual group, the origins of which are unknown, was the heir of all the astrological mysticism of the ancient Chaldeans, to which they added a good dose of Neoplatonic philosophy. Because they believed in a single God, the Muslims at first tolerated them. Sabian scholars and mathematicians played an important role at the great university at Harran, even after the sect was outlawed in the 9th century—the Muslims claimed they were performing human sacrifices.

The site has never been thoroughly examined or explained, but enough remains to suggest a little of what went on. At the centre of the modern Soğmatar village, the largest of several natural and artificial hills bears a large ruin believed to be the **Temple of the Sun**. Around it, the other heights have caves or buildings dedicated to the planetary deities, all oriented towards the sun temple; this is arranged, oddly enough, as if it were an up-to-date model of our heliocentric system. One of the hilltops, for instance, contains a cave decorated with trident shapes or pitchforks, a common symbol throughout the Mediterranean, and the hole bored through its front wall is sighted directly on the sun temple. On the cliffs above, an apparently Greek- or Roman-era relief depicts a man and a woman—the villagers claim they are Adam and Eve—and a long inscription in Syriac. Another summit has a well-preserved round tower; other remains are difficult to identify, but no doubt a complete investigation would turn up many more things of interest.

Someone from the village will be around to let you into the stable where another **shrine** can be seen. When your eyes become used to the darkness, a procession of eleven figures, badly eroded, and other Syriac inscriptions come into view, carved into the rock around which the stable is built. Around a central altar, looking down at the real bulls resting in front of them, are two relief bulls with crescent-moon horns.

Şuayp

Nine miles (15km) further on, the same road finds the once-lost city of **Şuayp**. Prosperous under the Assyrians and Romans, Şuayp was abandoned in the Middle Ages. The largest structure still standing amid its extensive ruins is a three-storey building with not arches but lintels over its windows—difficult to ascribe to any architectural period. Crosses are carved into the walls in some places. Much of Şuayp seems to have been built underground, or into the hillsides. The present village occupies many of these holes, and you may be invited in for a subterranean glass of tea. Many of these caves and warrens were carved out of the soft rock with considerable care, adorned with arches and pilasters, niches and decorative entrances.

Harran

The next stop, only nine miles (15km) from the Syrian border, is **Harran**, more easily accessible by a paved road from Şanlıurfa for those who wish to avoid the Tek Tek. Harran has been a city for perhaps 6,000 years, at times reaching prominence in trade and culture. Today, its ruins shelter a small village of semi-nomadic Arabs in beehive-shaped desert-style houses; these may be the most colourful community in Turkey, with unusually pretty children and women who wear all their jewellery all the time.

To guess at the founding of Harran is impossible—it's always been there—but only after the 9th century BC does it take its place among the big towns of the Near East. Somehow, Harran managed the neat trick of prospering under the Assyrians without being annihilated in a revolt or during the series of wars that followed the Assyrian decline. According to the *Book of Genesis*, Abraham and his family lived here for several years on their way from Ur to Canaan. In Roman times, the town had come to be known as Carrhae, and its one appearance in history was a disaster the Romans would long remember. The first Roman triumvirate consisted of Julius Caesar, Pompey and a useless fool named Crassus whom the two great generals kept around to appease the Senate. To prove his mettle while Caesar worked over the Gauls and Pompey cleared up the Cilician pirates, Crassus led an army against the Parthian (Persian) Empire. At Carrhae, in 53 BC, he walked right into a trap; his men were surrounded and cut down by the Parthians' Scythian allies—the first serious Roman defeat since Hannibal.

Later, under the Romans and Byzantines, the city became renowned as a centre of learning, and its reputation continued after the Arab conquest, as the home of the first great Islamic university. When the Mongols wrecked it in the 13th century, it stayed wrecked, though It has harboured intermittent Arab settlements ever since.

Harran's **fortress**, with unusual 10-sided towers, still remains in good condition, as do sections of the **walls**, including the **Aleppo Gate** on the southern edge. Of the rest, little survives. Most of the space within the walls serves as the Arabs' vegetable gardens and grazing lands. Of the famous **university**, barely enough remains to hint at the original opulence of the buildings.

Atatürk Dam

The ancient city of Samosata, 37 miles (60km) north of Şanlıurfa, now lies submerged under the artificial lake bordered to the south by the **Atatürk Dam**, the sixth largest in the world. At a height of over 600ft, it curves like some enormous amphitheatre for more than a mile between two hills, and holds back a lake covering hundreds of square miles. In front of the dam, a tunnel over 20ft in diameter has been drilled under 16 miles (26km) of the Şanlıurfa Yaylası (highlands) to bring this water into the south. Not surprisingly, the landscape and economy of the Şanlıurfa and Harran regions has been radically altered. Infertile plains have been supplanted by vegetable and cotton fields which spill out into the emptiness. The most diligent farmers can now squeeze three harvests a year from their lands. Such opportunity has brought unprecedented wealth to one of Turkey's poorest backwaters. The ferro-concrete houses which have sprouted up in consequence may not be as picturesque as the traditional mud homes, but as any resident will soon tell you, mud is not actually the best of building materials, it's simply the cheapest.

GAP: The Southeast Anatolia Project

The Middle East usually makes the headlines for other reasons, but its biggest story is happening right here. Turkish engineers are currently hard at work on the most ambitious development project ever attempted in the region. Atatürk Dam is only a part, though the most conspicuous one, of the Southeast Anatolia Project (*Güneydoğu Anadolu Projesi*, or GAP), designed to make this wasteland into the breadbasket of the Middle East, and at the same time produce enough electricity to make Turkey self-sufficient, and end a dangerous addiction to Russian amperage.

In its scope, GAP rivals its model, America's Tennessee Valley Authority of the 1930s. When it's finished, there will be 22 dams, 19 power plants, and irrigation schemes covering 1.7 million hectares over nine provinces. But there is much more to it than that; GAP is an attempt at nothing less than a complete transformation of the lives of all the people in Turkey's poorest region. Land reforms are turning the area from an anachronistic bastion of feudalism into a region of independent small farmers, and GAP has the goal of bringing electricity and clean water to every home in it. The sophistication of the project is impressive. GAP planners use progressive phrases like 'sustainable development', 'institution building' and 'popular participation', and unlike so many other development projects around the world, they seem to mean what they say. Other aspects include aid to local entrepreneurs for small businesses, farmers' training and extension services, health clinics and schools, locally managed irrigation co-ops, 'eco-city' and 'eco-village' pilot projects. Women, who have been kept back here more than anywhere in the country, are getting special attention, with greater access to education and 'women's community centres' to be built in every village.

But it's not all good news. There is a great deal of controversy over the planned construction of the Ilisu Dam, the reservoir of which would flood many Kurdish towns, including the ancient settlement of Hasankeyf, and necessitate the forced relocation of many inhabitants. Independent reports have been strongly critical of the negative impact the dam would have on the area and its people; at the time of writing Britain is the only country prepared to offer financial support for its construction.

At present, the physical side of GAP is about 60% complete, and the rest is planned to finish by 2010. Its total cost is estimated at $32 billion dollars, nearly all of which the Turks are supplying themselves; the World Bank at first refused assistance because of the objections Turkey's neighbours had to the project.

Whenever events in the Middle East begin to seem mysterious, think of the issue of water. Nothing is more important in this dry region, not even oil, and the water issues are usually hiding somewhere behind the turmoil of the newspaper headlines (as in the negotiations over the water-rich Golan Heights). It is no coincidence that Syria and Iraq began their heavy support for the Kurdish guerrillas of the PKK in the 1980s when the planning for the GAP was underway; both countries stand to lose some of their share of the Euphrates' water (and the water they get will be more saline after it irrigates Turkish fields). In January 1990, the Turks began filling the Atatürk Dam; they announced they would cut off the river's flow almost completely for a month, intending to send a message to the Syrians and Iraqis about their aid to the PKK. Both countries threatened war, and the Turks put the tap back on after three weeks. Turkey claims that its water policy is not political—and with neighbours like Syria and Iraq even the best intentions in the world would cause troubles. But negotiations do go on, and there is talk of a major water pipeline that could carry fresh water as far as Israel. With a little goodwill on all sides, GAP could be the first step in helping all of the ancient Fertile Crescent live up to its name once again.

Gaziantep and Şanlıurfa   ***Where to Stay***

Gaziantep

luxury

There is nothing in Gaziantep to compete with the ★★★★★**Tuğcan Hotel**, Atatürk Bulvarı 34, ℗ 0342 220 43 23, ℻ 0342 220 32 42. Strategically situated away from the bustling city centre, it is nevertheless within walking distance of all the sights. Its lofty reception area and indoor pool more than make up for the rather characterless bedrooms. Doubles $170.

moderate

On the same street as the Tuğcan but nearer the centre are two mid-range hotels. Whimsically named after the ongoing dam-building project, ★★★**GAP Hotel**, Atatürk Bulvarı 10, ✆ 0342 220 3974, ✉ 0342 234 2102, has doubles with bathtubs for $60. The hair-rinse purple carpets and five-foot bronze dog statue standing guard at reception lift this establishment out of the ordinary. Ask for rooms on the top floors so as to escape any errant vibes from the basement disco. The ★★**Velic Hotel**, Atatürk Bulvarı 23, ✆ 0342 221 2212 ✉ 0342 221 2210, has rooms of almost Japanese dimensions, with all you might need—air-con, minibar, telephone, TV— crammed into diminutive but modern bedrooms. Apart from the muezzin's early morning wake-up call, the location is surprisingly quiet. Doubles cost $40.

If you don't mind being in the thick of it, try the long-standing ★★★**Kaleli**, Hürriyet Caddesi, ✆ 0342 230 9690, ✉ 0342 230 1597, on the noisy main thoroughfare. As if to compensate for this, the staff are unusually courteous, the large rooms come with balconies and bathtubs, and the price for a double is set at a reasonable $42.

inexpensive–cheap

There are very few savoury places to sleep cheap in Gaziantep. You could plunge into the labyrinthine **Bulvar Palas**, İstasyon Caddesi 11, ✆ 0342 231 3238. Its waterless rooms are dingy, but if you can find your way through the maze of corridors to the back of the hotel, these rooms are at least quiet. Doubles are $9.

Hotel Konfor, Kamber Sokak 2, ✆ 0342 231 2223, is near the castle on a small side street off Karagöz Caddesi. Dark, well-worn doubles with shower and toilet cost $16.

Şanlıurfa

expensive

Topping the bill in Şanlıurfa is a clash between two heavyweights. Situated a stone's throw from the carp ponds is the ★★★★**Edessa**, Balıklıgöl Mevkii, ✆ 0414 215 9911, ✉ 0414 215 5589. Its reception area has a low-key elegance and the spacious rooms are decorated in subtle shades of beige. This minimalist sophistication weighs in at a hefty $140 per double. More reasonable however is the ★★★★**Harran**, Atatürk Bulvarı, ✆ 0414 313 2860, ✉ 0414 313 4918, which charges $85 per room. The big draw here is its swimming pool—the only one in Şanlıurfa, a major consideration if you're here in midsummer.

moderate

The **Gülizar Konuk Evi**, tucked away down a cobbled lane at Karameydanı Camii Yanı 22, ✆ 0414 215 0505, offers an authentic retro experience at $45 per night. You sleep as in Ottoman days of old on silk futons, which are rolled up and stored during the daytime. The wood-panelled bedrooms are part of a painstakingly restored stone house, complete with vaulted dining rooms and a secluded courtyard. Rooms have air-conditioning, which is just as well since there is only one shower (and just two toilets) to go round.

By far the best deal in town is the **Şanlıurfa Valiliği Konuk Evi** in a quiet street, the Vali Fuat Bey Caddesi, near the Selahaddin Eyyubi Mosque, ✆ 0414 215 9377, 🖷 0414 215 3045. This converted Ottoman mansion, with its improbably delicate stone staircase and heavy wooden armoires in the hallway, oozes with charm. The six en suite bedrooms filled with modern furniture jar in comparison. The courtyard outside is a postcard-writing haven and the balustraded terrace offers views of the castle. Unsurprisingly, at only $35, the rooms are often booked up far in advance.

The best of the cheaper bunch is the small and friendly **İpek Palas**, behind the Şanmed Hospital at Köprübaşı Caddesi 4, ✆ 0414 215 1546, 🖷 0414 215 1290; simple yet charming, with en suite doubles for $24. Similarly priced and more modern is the **Hotel Güven** at Sarayönü Caddesi 133, ✆ 0414 215 1700, 🖷 0414 215 1941. It may lack charm, but it has an elevator and air-con.

If money is tight you can sweat it out at the **Uğur**, Köprübaşı Caddesi 3, ✆ 0414 313 1340, an unashamedly old-style cheapie where waterless doubles cost $7. You'll be much better off at the **Doğu**, Sarayönü Caddesi 131, ✆ 0414 215 1228. The basic, clean rooms have showers, but toilets are communal. As with all hotels on the main thoroughfare, choose rooms at the back to avoid the traffic noise. Doubles cost $9,

---

Gaziantep and Şanlıurfa   ***Eating Out***

Gaziantep

There is no doubt as to the republican credentials of the **Ekim 29** café and restaurant at Çıkmaz 4, a narrow lane leading off from the pedestrianised Gaziler Caddesi. Not only is the restaurant named after the date on which the Turkish Republic was declared (October 29), but instead of the usual picture of Atatürk on the wall it has gone one better and sports a mosaic of the great man. Its walled courtyard is popular with the younger generation and is a pleasant place to relax with a drink in fine weather; you can take refuge inside if the weather gets too hot or cold. The usual array of kebabs and kindred dishes are on offer, with a meal costing about $5.

The top floor restaurant at the **Velic Hotel** is worth a visit for its panoramic views of the castle and city. The restaurant's rather clinical atmosphere may or may not be an added draw, depending on how much you are craving hygienic surroundings. $7 for a full meal of Turkish fare. Almost opposite the Velic on Atatürk Caddesi is a good place to put your feet up: the **Yeşilsu Aile Çay Bahçesi** ('Green Water Family Tea Garden'), a leafy spot where playing cards and other games is the order of the day, accompanied by never-ending rounds of tea.

Şanlıurfa

The area around the fish ponds is dotted with shady tea gardens, although the waiters there show about as much energy as the carp. The beautiful surroundings ensure that the kebabs and drinks are on the expensive side. There are no signs up to say so, but you may notice that some establishments are patronised by single men only, others by women and families.

Şanlıurfa's restaurants, though modest, are also good and inexpensive. The courtyard of the **Şanlıurfa Valiliği Konuk Evi** (*see* above) is one of the most pleasant dining spots in Şanlıurfa, particularly in the evening; a kebab, salad and drink set you back only $5. A regular fixture for the locals is the **Sofrası**, on the Atatürk Bulvarı opposite the stadium, a good 15-minute walk from the town centre. You could try the regional speciality of *içli köfte*, although the kebabs here are some of the most succulent you'll find, with a meal costing $6.

Less atmospheric but closer to the centre at Asfalt Caddesi 14 is another local favourite, the brightly lit and spotlessly clean **Tandır**. As its name suggests, the house speciality is *tandır kebab*, although there is a wide range of other dishes on offer for $3 and upwards.

Near the İpek Palas Hotel is the **Güney Lokantası**, where the food is on display as you enter, including a number of vegetarian dishes such as okra and bean stews; $4 and you should be full. For *lahmacun pide* at $2 a go, head out towards the stadium along the Atatürk Bulvarı, and after a few minutes you'll see Sümer-4 on your left, where you can watch as the dough is rolled and the *pide* baked.

You'll see things sold on the streets here that aren't found elsewhere in Turkey. Some are utterly mysterious and beyond the range of adventurousness of most travel writers, but if you come across a dangerous-looking black liquid in Şanlıurfa, it will be either *murra*, a kind of over-boiled fermented coffee, or else homebrewed Turkish root beer. Drinking either one could change your life.

Gaziantep   ***Entertainment and Nightlife***

Serving up a diet of Hollywood blockbusters, the modern **Prestige Cinema Club** is an unmistakable landmark on the city's main square. Built into its façade is the unlikely looking Old English Pub, a red-brick pastiche more akin to a Barratt's show home than an ancient ale house. For those who feel the urge to go in and slake their thirst, all the trappings of a traditional English watering hole await them inside: heavy-duty speakers, neon signs and a big-screen TV. Across the street, the rough and ready pleasures of the **Efes** beer hall beckon.

English language newspapers can be bought in Gaziantep at the Lady Bookstore, a 20-minute walk from the centre at Atatürk Bulvarı 139A.

Commagene

In the upheavals and confusions that attended the collapse of Alexander's short-lived empire, adventurers among his generals and their successors were often able to seize the main chance and carve out little tax farms to keep them in spending money. Some of the larger ones, like the Ptolemaic Kingdom in Egypt and the Seleucid Kingdom in Persia and Anatolia, were able to survive as well-organized states for a long time; others have been gathering dust in history's curiosity shop ever since.

To take the prize of most curious monarch, we offer Mithradates Kallinikos and his son Antiochus, Kings of Commagene, a small, but rich and fertile state that appeared in the 1st century BC along the Euphrates, in what is now the province of Adıyaman. For all the monuments those two left behind, you might think them rulers of a vast empire instead of the Roman puppets they really were, with a kingdom hardly more than 100 miles wide at its greatest extent. Pompey, in his campaign to bring some kind of order to Anatolia—the Senate didn't want to annex it yet—propped Antiochus on his throne in 61 BC. For almost a century, as long as the Romans found it expedient to keep them in business, the Commagene kings did their masters' bidding and spent the resources of their kingdom in self-glorification. From their subjects, they asked little more than to be treated as gods, and that their subjects should spend most of their free time carrying rocks up mountains to build them tombs.

Getting Around

Tours to Nemrut Dağı and the Commagene sites are big business in this neck of the Anatolian woods. From as far afield as Cappadocia, hotels, travel agencies and dolmuş drivers all run tours at (mostly) affordable prices. If you're entering the region from the northwest, Malatya is the most logical place to tour from, which is fine. The Malatya tourist office organizes trips to Nemrut Dağı, as do local agencies such as **Cem Tours** at Galeria İş Merkezi No.1/11, ✆ 0422 322 6666.

Independent travellers coming from the south, however, should give some thought as to where to begin their trip. Adıyaman and Kahta may seem like the most obvious bases, both being close to the mountain, but there are problems attached to going from either, not least the fact that both towns are dismal places with nothing to see and everything to avoid. The second problem is that the tour operators of both towns have the reputation of being the most rapacious, avaricious specimens of Turkish manhood to be found between Edirne and Kars. Although the touristic downturn has forced them to clean up their act in recent years, old habits die hard and you still hear horror stories about their wheeling and dealing, how they'll use every low-down trick available to squeeze a few extra lira out of the hapless tourist; the sheer worry and hassle of the experience may well spoil your enjoyment of the sites. There again, if you're dead set on seeing the summit at sunrise, these are the towns to go from. Just remember that you'll share the experience with countless others.

Booking a tour from Şanlıurfa is not a bad idea, if you can put up with a 300-mile (500km) round trip in a day, and could save you time and money. Travel agencies in Şanlıurfa charge $20 and upwards per person, not too much when you consider the cost of a bus to Kahta, two nights' accommodation there, etc. A good agency is **Harran Dolmuş**, behind the Şanmed Hospital in Şanlıurfa, ✆ 0414 215 1575.

You can visit all the Commagene sites by car, but it's a long, petrol-gobbling trip with few road signs and service stations along the backroads. You might wait until the tour buses go and follow them.

Tourist Information

Adıyaman: Atatürk Bulvarı 184, ✆ 0416 216 3840.

Nemrut Dağı

Nemrut Dağı, the mountain where Antiochus I is buried, has become one of the most popular tourist sights of Turkey, and the high seriousness of the deified Commagenes has at last got its just deserts. The tourists come in group buses to Adıyaman or the dismal village of Kahta, much closer, and at two in the morning they are dragged out of bed and tossed into minibuses for the long drive to Nemrut. Just as the first signs of dawn appear in the east, the long procession of headlights begins to snake up the mountain, and when the sun finally peeks over the horizon it finds the assemblage huddled together for warmth atop the stepped altar where Commagene hierophants once made dawn sacrifices to their defunct despot; blinking and mumbling, some trying to explain to the children what they're doing here, they gasp like people who have never seen a sunrise before, then grapple to get out their cameras and go to work.

In Kahta, they don't mention the stiff 20-minute walk from the car park and refreshment stand up to the summit. When you come to the end of the path, it joins the Processional Way, leading to the **East Terrace**, where five colossal statues face the dawn. The heads have toppled to the ground, although as Nemrut's popularity increases the Turks are considering replacing them. It would be quite a job; they weigh several tons each.

Explaining just who these five were will be difficult. The Commagene kings traced their lineage back to Alexander the Great on one side and the Persian king Darius on the other. In their little cosmopolitan state, halfway between Greece and Persia, they tried to keep up the Alexandrian principle of syncretism—combining similar gods from different cultures into a single figure, and creating out of the synthesis a new cult, with room in it for the likes of Antiochus and Mithradates. Thus the aesthetic-looking fellow on the left is not only **Apollo**, but Mithra and Helios at the same time (though everyone says he looks just like Elvis Presley). **Tyche,** the only lady present, is the 'good spirit' of the Greeks, magnified into a figure that includes all the region's myriad goddesses.

Zeus, or Ahuramazda, takes pride of place in the centre, with a pointed cap and bushy whiskers. Next comes **Antiochus,** looking completely at home in such company, and finally **Heracles,** or Artagnes or Ares. These five are flanked by pairs of equally colossal staring eagles and lions, looking perhaps for an empire to symbolize. The **altar,** a massive square of stone, is now used as a helicopter platform, with a big H painted on it. All around, and particularly on the backs of the statues, the Commagenes have left us the longest Greek inscription ever found, detailing their royal descent, their births, careers, and the rites with which they desired to be worshipped.

With all this to take in, it may escape your notice that the neat symmetrical peak of this mountain is a fake. Though the highest in the area, Nemrut isn't much of a mountain, and Antiochus found it necessary to add another 150ft of loose stones to get the desired silhouette. On the ground, it would make a fair-sized pyramid. Somewhere underneath, Antiochus lies buried, but the team of archaeologists who cleaned up Nemrut were unable to find his tomb; they feared any attempt at tunnelling would bring down the entire tumulus. Some people still hope to find it; an organization called the 'International Nemrut Foundation' is in the process of obtaining permission from the Culture Ministry to start an excavation. They think they know where to dig, and they are convinced that the treasure inside the tomb will turn out to be the 'Eighth Wonder' of the ancient world.

Another path leads around the north side of the summit to the **West Terrace**. But for the lack of an altar, this is a carbon copy of the East Terrace, where the same five gods enjoy the sunset. Here, however, the statues are in better shape, and some of the **sculptural reliefs** have survived. Three of these portray Antiochus shaking hands with gods—Apollo, Zeus and Heracles. Such scenes, with the same smiles and poses as the publicity photos in Communist newspapers, were the favourite subject for Commagene art.Another relief shows a lion with a carefully plotted backdrop of a crescent moon, stars and a planetary conjunction; from this, and the accompanying inscriptions, scholars have deduced that Antiochus's coronation took place within 10 minutes of 7.30pm on 14 July 109 BC.

A word needs to be said about all these sculptures. Not only is the work of high artistic merit, but something about these thoughtful, expressive faces seems eerily modern. The Commagenes, for all their nonsense, were sophisticated rulers living at the height of the Greek world's achievements. We give the Greeks credit for the invention of the free man, the individual, but if these reliefs of Commagene symbolize anything, it is the decay of that man, and his submission to the statist mysticisms of the East, a process that in later centuries reached its culmination in the palaces of Constantinople.

The other Commagene sites are in the valleys of the **Cendere** and **Nymphaion**, tributaries of the Euphrates, and can be seen, along with Nemrut, in a day. You may mourn for this countryside, once celebrated for its beauty and fertility; something here has gone very wrong. Although the nearby oil fields have gone some way towards eradicating the worst of the poverty, you will not see such blank, twisted faces elsewhere in Turkey. Most of the hills have eroded into slag heaps, but here and there, in a cared-for field or lonely grove of trees, you can see how the grandeur of the mountain scenery was once complemented by greenery. No doubt Commagene had more rain in ancient times, but that doesn't account for all the change. Ambitious kings have a way of making their lands waste, and perhaps what we see before us is Antiochus' true memorial. Ironically, even where nothing else grows, lovely pink oleanders line the roads.

Arsameia

Arsameia, on the Nymphaion river, served Antiochus for a capital; whatever endured of it into medieval times was incorporated into the Turkish castle called **Yeni Kale**. On the opposite hillside, the **Eski Kale**, despite its name, isn't really a castle at all, but the *hierothesion* or temple tomb Antiochus built for his father Mithradates, not quite as grand as his own. At the entrance, a large upright slab bears a relief of **Mithra**, looking towards a large cave in the side of the mountain. It may be the only image of this god you will see in Turkey, in spite of the widespread popularity of this Persian cult, which as late as the 3rd century AD could claim more followers than Christianity. It seldom penetrated the Greek upper classes deeply enough to be expressed in art.

Where Mithra directs, in the cave, is another relief which depicts King Mithradates with Helios-Apollo. There is a large cistern opening out from the cave. From here, another path leads across the mountainside to the centrepiece of the *hierothesion*, where an even larger relief has Mithradates shaking hands with a clumsily sculpted Heracles. The king, portrayed as the taller and more impressive of the two, wears a tunic decorated with eight-pointed stars, the dynastic emblem of the Commagenes, who adopted it from Alexander the Great. Next to this, a Greek inscription, similar to those on Nemrut, was carved over the entrance to a tunnel, leading over 300ft down stairs through the bare rock. What the purpose of this was, and where Mithradates may be buried, no one knows.

Karakuş

Leaving Arsameia for the third Commagene *hierothesion*, on a hill called **Karakuş**, you pass an **Ottoman bridge** over the Nymphaion; at the point where that stream, now called Kahta Çayı, empties into the Cendere stands a **Roman bridge**. Septimus Severus, who had it built, added two columns at each end, honouring himself and his family in Latin inscriptions. Almost 2,000 years after its construction, the bridge was still judged strong enough to carry the modern road. A passing petrol lorry recently proved otherwise, and the collapsed bridge is currently being reconstructed. Karakuş, a tumulus of small stones similar to Nemrut but smaller, holds the remains of Antiochus' wife. The tumulus was surrounded by tall columns surmounted by the tiresome Commagene familiars—eagles, lions and hand-shaking kings, of which only three remain erect. The eagle may have contributed the modern Turkish name: '*Karakuş*' means 'black bird'. From here it's only a short way back to Kahta.

Commagene   **Where to Stay**

Adıyaman

moderate

The ★★★**Bozdoğan** on Atatürk Bulvarı at the western edge of town, ✆ 0416 216 3999, 📠 0416 216 3630, is very much tour group territory. In keeping with this, the en suite doubles are comfortable but uninspiring, costing $45.

cheap

Amidst the hubbub of the town centre is the **Unal**, Harıkçı Caddesi 14, ✆ 0416 216 1508. It is rather basic but friendly and its staff try hard to keep customers happy; $12 for a waterless double. For just $4 more you can have an en suite double at the pleasant **Beyaz Saray Pansiyon**. This is located on the eastern side of town on the main Atatürk Bulvarı 136, ✆ 0416 216 2100, 📠 0416 216 1580. Best of all, it has a swimming pool in the garden, and one of the only passable restaurants in town.

Kahta

moderate

On Mustafa Kemal Caddesi across the way from the tourist office is the newer ★★**Hotel Bardakçı**, with anodyne en suite rooms priced at $42. South of the centre in a quieter location is the brand new ★★★**Yeni Merhaba** ('New Hello') at Çarşı Caddesi 49, ✆/📠 0416 725 7111. Though by no means a beauty, the hotel does have rooms with showers and all the gadgets you'd expect for $50 per double.

On the Mustafa Kemal Caddesi at the junction with the Nemrut Dağı road is the welcoming **Pansiyon Kommagene**, ✆ 0416 715 1092, ✆ 0416 725 5548. As well as doubles with toilet for $12, there is also a campsite. The idiosyncratic **★★Nemrut Tur** motel, also on the outskirts of town on Mustafa Kemal Caddesi, ✆ 0416 725 6881, ✆ 0416 725 6880, is overpriced at around $30 a double, depending how busy they are.

On the road to Nemrut Dağı

The road to Nemrut Dağı has a number of places to stay, of which the most pleasant budget option is the **Karadut Pansiyon**, in the tiny village of the same name, ✆ 0416 737 2169. For those who prefer a bit more comfort, the **Kervansaray**, ✆ 0416 737 2190, lies on the right-hand side of the old road to the summit, several kilometres beyond Karadut. The garden has a swimming pool, and rooms cost $20 per person, which includes dinner—not that you'd be eating anywhere else up here.

Commagene **Eating Out**

Kahta

In the centre of town are two decent eating establishments serving wholesome food, the **Yeni Yudum** at Mustafa Kemal Caddesi 123 and the **Kent Restaurant** just a few doors along. Unless your appetite is of the horse-eating variety, a meal at either should cost no more than $4. If you have your own transport and it's fish you're after, head for the nearby lake, where the **Akropolian** serves up freshwater fare on a pleasant terrace overlooking the water for under $5.

Malatya and Elazığ

Getting Around

THY **flights** connect Ankara with Malatya and Elazığ. The major east–west railroad line to Lake Van passes through Elazığ and Malatya, and the only north–south line through the eastern provinces connects Sivas with Malatya.

Harput can be reached by **bus** from Elazığ. Minibuses go to Keban and Sivrice, a village on Hazar Gölü. Sivrice is also on the **railway**, but not on the same line as Elazığ; trains branch off for Elazığ in the north, on the way to Lake Van, and Diyarbakır to the south, a dead-end line that terminates near Siirt.

Tourist Information

Malatya: Valilik Binası (in a booth behind the Vilayet, the provincial government building on the main square), ✆ 0422 323 3025.

Elazığ: Hükümet Konağı, 2nd floor, inside the Vilayet on Zübeyale Hanım Bulvarı, ✆ 0424 212 2159.

Malatya

Just north of ancient Commagene, a long chain of mountains, the **Anti-Taurus**, stretches the entire length of southeastern Anatolia from the Hatay to Lake Van. On the opposite northern slopes, the central highway from Kayseri to Van passes through difficult mountain terrain into the valley of the Murat River, climbing gradually upwards through *yaylalar* (highland pastures) crowded during the summer with nomadic herdsmen and their flocks. **Malatya**, the first and most interesting of the towns along this route, cannot stand still. Although its history has been continuous since the Hittites, it has occupied three different sites.

The modern city, founded only in the early 19th century, has already grown to a population of almost 300,000, supporting themselves by modern industry and ancient crafts; the city has had a reputation for its copper works since the Middle Ages. Today you can see these for sale in the boisterous **bazaar** area north of the PTT Caddesi. While seeking out the copperware, you'll no doubt stumble across stalls heaving with dried apricots, for which the city is renowned. The bazaar and its denizens are shielded from the sun by bleached canvas awnings and yellow sheets of corrugated plastic. As if by design, these bathe everything and everyone below in a suitably lurid shade of apricot.

Eski Malatya, the town gradually abandoned since the new foundation was begun, flourished in the 13th century as an eastern outpost of the Selcuk sultanate. Parts of the walls remain, along with some of the **Ulu Cami**, built in 1247 by the famous Selcuk architect Hüsrev: its outstanding feature, the entrance portal, is a unique work with tiny faïence tiles set into the stone almost like mosaics.

If Malatya has not stayed on one site, it does have the distinction of holding on to its name as long as any city in Turkey. Records of both the Hittites and Assyrians speak of a town kingdom of Milid, or Milidia, that made a name for itself after the Hittite collapse and lasted until the Cimmerians sacked it in the 8th century BC, only to reappear in Roman times as Melitene. The site of ancient Malatya, where ruins of the palace can be seen, are at a spot the Turks call **Aslantepe** because of the reliefs of lions that once guarded its gate and now adorn the Ankara Museum. Aslantepe lies seven miles (11km) north of modern Malatya, and Eski Malatya a further nine miles (14km) north along the same road.

Elazığ

Some 63 miles (101km) to the northeast of Malatya is another prospering modern town that tells much the same story. It, too, began in the last century; named after its founder Abdül el-Aziz, it replaced the ancient city of **Harput**, four miles (6km) to the north, after the latter was wrecked by earthquakes.

There is an enchantment in the air of Harput, high on its hilltop. This is border territory, and the people who have lived and fought here, throughout the millennia—starting with the Hurri around 2000 BC, then Hittites, Urartians, Romans, Sassanids, Byzantines, Arabs, Byzantines again, Selcuks and Ottomans—have left behind tangible evidence, and part of their spirit. The Turks feel this too; the area is full of legend and folklore.

In the centre of Harput, opposite the post office, is the 18th-century **Kurşunlu Mosque**. Walking up the main street, you pass, on your right, the **Cimşit Baths** and the **Sara Hatun**

Mosque, both 16th-century, and, on your left, the heavily restored octagonal **tomb of Mansur Baba**, built in the 12th century during the time of the Artukoğulları emirs and destroyed by the Selcuks. Opposite this tomb is the **Ulu Cami**, also dating from the 12th century. Attached to the mosque is a medrese; together they form a rectangular building with a lovely open courtyard, surrounded by brick arcades. The minaret, broken off halfway down during an earthquake, leans jauntily and is decorated with brickwork flowers. The **castle**, originally Urartian, is visible from the mosque, and was restored in 1997. Near the castle are the ruined **Hoca Hasan** baths. Back in the centre of town, the 13th-century tomb and **shrine of Arab Baba** shelters a disgusting mummy, complete with its skin. The original head has been broken off, and this is a replacement. The story goes that, in a year of drought, a woman had a dream, instructing her to take the head off Arab Baba and put it in water. This proved successful: it poured with rain and the whole town was flooded. In a second dream she was told to take the head out of the water and replace it on the body. The rain stopped, but the head didn't fit. So now Arab Baba is invested with magical qualities and people go there to pray for good fortune.

Elazığ owes its modern good fortune to the giant **Keban Dam**, built in the 1970s as the first stage of the Southeast Anatolia Project. Keban is a prohibited area, but tourists are welcome at the dam providing they produce a passport, stick with the guide and take no photographs. The approach to Keban is lovely; the road passes along a steep-sided rocky valley with the occasional waterfall. The first glimpse of the dam takes your breath away; surrounded by mountains, with the Euphrates emerging at the bottom in a beautiful mixture of blue, green and turquoise, it is a most impressive feat of engineering. Eight vast pipes, each 17ft in diameter, lead to the turbines. The dam backs up a huge lake, 250 square miles in area, nearly 560ft deep, irregularly shaped as it fills up the valleys which were once inhabited. A vast archaeological rescue operation was mounted here before the valleys were flooded; you can see the finds in the **Elazığ Museum**.

About 19 miles (30km) south of Elazığ is **Hazar Gölü**, a crater lake where camping and swimming are possible. However, as the lake is about 4,000ft above sea level, the season is very short—by late August, only the hardiest will feel like swimming. Beyond Elazığ, the country becomes steeper and less populated. **Bingöl** means 'a thousand lakes', and if 'thousand' in Turkish may really mean 'quite a few', the mountain scenery is still nice. Glaciers gouged out the lake beds two ice ages ago.

Malatya and Elazığ   **Where to Stay**

Malatya

expensive

The ★★★★**Altın Kayısı** ('Golden Apricot') on İstasyon Caddesi, ✆ 0422 238 3232, ✇ 0422 238 0083, is located away from the constant bustle of the city centre; its isolation is hardly splendid, however, with balconies commanding views of the four-lane highway out of town. Its 100 generously sized rooms have all the mod cons, including satellite TV. Doubles are posted as a high $100, but not fixed.

The best on offer is the ★★**Malatya Büyük** opposite the Yeni Cami at Zafer İşhanı 1, ✆ 0422 321 1400, 🖷 0422 321 5367. The rooms are bright and clean with small bathtubs en suite, and are keenly priced at $20 when things are quiet. Although not prey to traffic noise, the Büyük's front rooms do get the full blast of the Yeni Cami's calls to prayer; the rooms at the back, on the other hand, overlook the lively bazaar area and are the perfect place to enjoy the sound of metal shop grilles being rolled up first thing in the morning.

If street noise is of paramount concern, head for the **Huzur** on a relatively quiet back street at Nasuhi Caddesi 6, ✆ 0422 323 5928. Its rough and ready rooms are not as comfortable as the Büyük's, and those with shower and TV cost more at $25; water-less doubles cost $18. For travellers with a mental mute button they can activate before going to sleep, the traffic noise outside the ★★**Yeni Sinan** at Atatürk Caddesi 6, ✆ 0422 321 2907, should pose no problem. $25 buys you a double with TV, minibar, a large bathroom and friendly service.

cheap

If money's tight, you'll have few problems finding something, although the quality of the cheap hotels is variable. Nestling in a backstreet directly behind the Malatya Büyük at Zafer İşhanı is the best budget choice in town, the **Yeni Otel**, ✆ 0422 321 1090, where doubles with minuscule shower and toilet cubicles cost $10. With bedroom windows positioned just a few feet above the bazaar, this could make for unexpectedly early starts to the day. A cluster of cheapies lurk on PTT Caddesi, of which **Otel Merkez** is marginally less dismal than the rest.

Elazığ

moderate–inexpensive

The ★★**Beritan**, on Hürriyet Caddesi 24, ✆ 0424 218 4484, 🖷 0424 212 7970, has fine views of Harput from the top floor. The posted price for doubles is a ridiculous $100, but this soon drops by half. On the same noisy street is the more reasonably priced **Turistik Otel**, Hürriyet Caddesi 41, ✆ 0424 218 1772. Bright rooms with TV and shower cost $25. For relative peace and quiet, head for the friendly **Varran** off the busy main street at Gazi Caddesi 4A, ✆ 0424 218 5770. The large bedrooms have TV and air-con, with en suite bathrooms of equally generous proportions. Whoever decorated the place had a sense of colour coordination teetering on the anarchic. Doubles $30.

cheap

Elazığ's budget accommodation definitely falls under the category of cheap and nasty. By a whisker the least off-putting of the bunch is the **Erdem** at İstasyon Caddesi 19, ✆ 0424 218 2212. Its rooms (some with bath) have definitely seen better days; even at $12 they are overpriced.

Malatya

Opposite the Otel Merkez at PTT Caddesi 29 is the imaginatively named **Lokanta**. The lights are bright, the service attentive and the food is wholesome if unremarkable. You can select a meal for about $4 from the trays of ready food on display, which include a number of vegetarian options. A similarly dependable establishment is the **Beyaz Saray**, across the street and to the east of the Belediye on Atatürk Caddesi. Much of Malatya's city centre is given over to pleasant **tea gardens**, which can be found both in front of and behind the Vilayet.

Elazığ

The best restaurant in Elazığ is the **Altınşiş Lokantası** at Gazi Caddesi, Elliler Çarşısı 101, ✆ 0424 212 2964, where you can eat well for $5 or less. Fresh *pide* is baked on the spot, and, for parties of five people or more, the restaurant will cook special dishes, as long as they are ordered at least half a day in advance. The restaurant is difficult to find; it is on the second floor of a shopping arcade, but is open in the evening. The food in the **Beritan Hotel** also comes in for praise.

Diyarbakır and Around

From Kahramanmaraş to Bitlis and beyond, the Anti-Taurus mark the southern limits of the Anatolian plateau. To the south of it, the land descends in a broad, broken plain towards the deserts of Syria. The Tigris and the Euphrates flow here, and by the time they reach this plain they've gathered enough tributaries to rank as important rivers, sufficiently impressive in their spring floods; by June they slow down to trickles, and the assiduous Turkish farmers come down from the villages to sow whatever stretches of good land they can find among the network of streams and rocky shoals these great rivers have become. The country is fertile, and best for wheat. In spite of its cheerless sameness, these tan and treeless plains have supported large populations for millennia.

Getting Around

There are two direct **flights** per day from both Ankara and İstanbul to Diyarbakır. Otherwise, **buses** are the only way to get around this region. Local minibus services can bring you to most of the rural sights around Diyarbakır and Mardin; just check to make sure that there will be a way to get back.

Deir az-Zafaran is easily reached by **taxi** from Mardin; agree on a price that includes waiting time. For **motorists**, the same caveats mentioned previously (p.495), regarding water and difficulties in finding your way to the sights, apply here. This area may also be your introduction to **military checkpoints**, which become more common the further east you travel. Although passing through one may initially feel disconcerting, the young conscripts who check your passport and car documents are usually polite and friendly, invariably quizzing you on what country you're from, where you're heading and what your favourite football team is.

Taxis are plentiful along İnönü Caddesi, but all the sights are within walking distance in the old town. The **bus** and **train stations** are some distance out, however. If leaving the town by bus, buy the ticket in town; most companies have a free minibus service to the station.

Diyarbakır	***Tourist Information***

Dağkapı Burcu Giriş Bölümü (inside the Mountain Gate), ✆ 0412 221 2173.

Diyarbakır

The natural capital of this region is now and always has been Diyarbakır, on the banks of the Tigris (*Dicle Nehri*). Few cities in the world are older. Though its beginnings are so ancient that not even legends survive, Diyarbakır has been a town at least since the time of the Hurrians, some 5,000 years ago. A record from Assyria's archives from a later age makes the first mention of the city by its ancient name of **Amida**. Since antiquity, its citizens have brought dark, heavy basalt from the northern hills to build and rebuild its walls. Even today, these walls are the city's pride and its symbol: over the centuries they have made such an impression on the succession of travellers and conquerors who have passed beneath them that the city is renowned as 'Amid the Black'.

Whoever built here first, the town plan shows Diyarbakır in its present form to be a child of the Romans. The city, like so many from Britain to Iraq, is a classic Roman *castrum*, roughly rectangular with two broad streets connecting the four gates at the cardinal points. The Romans under Constantius II built the oldest surviving sections of Diyarbakır's walls; beneath the later façades of black basalt arches and vaults, the characteristic thin Roman brick can be seen in many places. For the Romans, the city was a crucial bastion in the defence against the Sassanid Persians. It changed hands more than once, and later Roman emperors mounted campaigns here whenever they could, among them Julian the Apostate, whose success against the Sassanids was negated by his untimely death near Amida in AD 363.

For the next 300 years, Amida was a Christian town, often brimming with refugees from the surrounding settlements that fell to the Persians. Amida's own turn came in 639, when the new **Muslim Arab** army made the city its first important conquest within the present-day borders of Turkey; from this, Diyarbakır today likes to claim Turkey's oldest mosque, the Ulu Cami, and its oldest Arabic inscriptions. Curiously, despite its formidable walls, Diyarbakır was never especially successful in keeping out conquerors. The centuries that followed the decline of the Abbasid caliphate saw dozens of them check their turbans at Diyabakır's gate. Nearly every warrior clan, great or obscure, that clutters the pages of Turkish history came to rule Amid the Black for a time: Marvanids, Selcuks, Damascus Selcuks, Nishanli, Artukid, Turkmen clans of White Sheep and Black, and more. **Ottoman** control, in the person of Selim the Grim, came in the 16th century, and Diyarbakır has been quiet ever since.

Today, besides its walls, Diyarbakır is most proud of **watermelons**. They say their farmers grow the world's biggest, weighing up to 160lb when the rains are good. The best-selling postcards in the town show hollowed-out melons with grinning children peeking out from

Diyarbakır

To Şanlıurfa

ZIYA GÖKALP BULVARI

Archaeology

CADDESİ

YUSUF AZİZOĞLU CAD.

Tigris River

KIBRIS CAD.

Nebi Camii

İç Kale

Atatürk Museum

LISE

Çifte Kapı

CADDESİ

İNÖNÜ CAD.

İZZET PAŞA CAD.

Süleymaniye Camii

Rail Station

Culture

Ulu Cami

BAZAAR

Hasan Paşa Hanı

Kurşunlu Cami

İSTASYON BULVARI

ALİ EMİRİ CADDESİ

İNÖNÜ CADDESİ

50 Yıl Parkı

Safa Camii

Ziya Gökalp Museum

BAZAAR DISTRICT

Bedesten

Surp Giragos Kilisesi

Urfa Kapı

AHMET PAŞA CADDESİ

YENİKAPI CADDESİ

Dicle Kapı

Sarı Saltık Türbesi

Behrem Paşa Camii

GAZİ CADDESİ

Dört Ayaklı Minare

YIKIKKAY SOKAK

Delliler Hanı

Evli Beden Burcu

TURISTİK CAD.

N

Mardin Kapı

Yedi Kardeş Burcu

500 metres
500 yards

inside. Diyarbakır also plays host to a commercial fair each year at the end of September, the *Ticaret ve Sanayi Fuarı*, at the end of September each year. One highlight of the festivities is a watermelon competition, in which it's the heaviest rather than the most aesthetically pleasing melon that wins the cash prize. Somewhat different criteria apply for the young women lined up at the affiliated beauty pageant. At the awards ceremony the winning girl is crowned as the *karpuz güzeli* or watermelon queen.

Like all these surprisingly large cities of southeastern Anatolia, Diyarbakır is modern, pleasant, and booming. However, although the recent political troubles seem to be on the wane, the city still has an almost tangible edge to it. Whilst its centre is colourful and lively by day and night, you should still follow your intuition and temper curiosity with caution, especially when travelling alone.

Old Diyarbakır can be entered through two gates in the northern walls. In this area, some of the walls were demolished in favour of automobile traffic, while other parts have been included in the **50 Yıl Parkı** (Fiftieth Anniversary Park), which separates the new city from the old. Near the park's centre, **Çifte Kapı**, the 'twin gates', are a more modern incision in the walls, and near them stands a small 13th-century tomb, the **Sarı Saltık Türbe**, that can serve as an introduction to the city's unique and excellent vernacular architecture. Besides basalt, the region also yields a fine pale sandstone. In all their mosques, tombs and *hanlar*, Diyarbakır's medieval architects acquired the habit of using the two together, in alternating layers, so that within its walls Amid the Black becomes, less formidably, Amid the Striped. This practice has been continued in more recent times by city planners who have surfaced Diyarbakır's pavements in alternate bands of black and white stone. The effect is very attractive, and few cities anywhere have managed the trick of evolving such a simple and lovely style to give themselves a sense of place. On many of the buildings, like the Sarı Saltık Türbe, what appear at first to be decorative plaques of the same black and white stone turn out to be Arabic inscriptions in the rectangular Kufic script, adding to the charm of the design.

The second entrance to the old town, only a few blocks east along İnönü Caddesi, is what was the Harput Gate of ancient times. This, the only gap in Diyarbakır's walls, has become the busiest corner of the modern city. Every day these streets fill up with every manner of man; peasants from the countryside, street hawkers, soldiers, porters with their packs, smug-looking businessmen in expensive suits. As a backdrop, new hotels and office blocks of seven or eight floors push their way up through the chaos of the older buildings; both new and old are hidden behind an amazing forest of signboards and placards, hanging over the pavements from the first floor to the eaves. Diyarbakır may be 5,000 years old, but this busy commercial exuberance must be very much the same as it was in new American cities of 100 years ago. You can walk down İzzet Paşa Caddesi and pretend you're on Main Street, Kansas City or Denver *c.* 1880—until you run into a mosque. In this case, it's the **Nebi** ('prophet') **Camii**, at the corner of Gazi Caddesi. This lovely and thoroughly striped mosque was built by the White Sheep clan (a Turkmen tribal federation) around 1530. Its typical minaret, striped also, like a giant ice cream parfait, is tall and square, another peculiarity of the local style.

İç Kale

From this corner, Gazi Caddesi, one of two wide cross-streets of the Roman city, leads south towards the centre, while İzzet Paşa heads towards the Tigris and the **İç Kale**, or Inner Fortress, the oldest part of Diyarbakır. The pointed arch at the entrance is said to be all that remains from the **Palace of the Artukid Turks** who once ruled here; on it can be seen their symbol, a lion attacking a bull. The bull represents worldly riches, and the lion those strong enough to seize them, an altogether fitting symbol for any Turkish warrior caste in the Gazi tradition. There's another lion on a pretty **fountain** just inside the gate.

In the citadel, under venerable trees, there's room enough only for the provincial courts, the inevitable **Atatürk Museum**, one of two in the city, and the **Süleymaniye Camii** (or İç Kale Camii) of the 16th century. Of the city's landmarks, this mosque, with its especially tall minaret, is famous for the deep underground spring that supplies the water to its *şadırvan* in the courtyard. The good-tasting water stays cold all year, which makes this a popular spot during the brutal summer days; it is probably the original spring that has supplied this citadel for 5,000 years. Outside the citadel walls, you can hire a horse-drawn carriage for a ride in the city, or else try to find your way through the narrow twisting streets of this quarter back to Gazi Caddesi. It won't be easy; the old sections of Diyarbakır are as exasperating a maze as any medieval town has anywhere. If you're lucky, you may find another fine mosque, the **Fatih Paşa Camii** of 1520, better known here as the **Kurşunlu Cami** ('bullet mosque'). These ancient residential quarters are charming, though given over to the city's poor, in the modern fad for concrete apartment blocks. If you poke around them you may find yourself an instant celebrity: most of the children have never seen foreigners.

Ulu Cami

Back on Gazi Caddesi, look for the **Ulu Cami**, just off the avenue behind a shady square that was the town's centre. This, arguably the oldest mosque in Turkey, was reconstructed out of a Byzantine church called the Martoma. Most of what you see, however, was constructed by the Selcuks in the late 11th century, and many other rulers have had a hand in the various reconstructions. The Artukids added parts of the **courtyard**, as evidenced by the lions and bulls over the main gate. This courtyard is the main attraction of this rather austere mosque. Almost everything in this spacious area was quarried from older buildings, with fascinating effect, as if old Roman and Byzantine Amida had been taken to pieces and whimsically reassembled. There are colonnades where each capital is different, columns stacked on larger columns, beautiful friezes of Greek designs next to Arabic Kufic script, intertwined with grapevines. Greek inscriptions look out from the walls in the most unlikely places.

While in this courtyard, you may hear a banging and clattering in the distance, as if a whole army of tinkers were nearby. They are—in their street in the crowded and colourful **market district** just outside these walls. As usual, every trade has its own part of the market; the ancient *bedesten* may be full of butchers now, but the street called 'Gold Alley' still glitters with scores of shops, and deals are still made in the **Hasan Paşa Hanı** of 1572, an excellent striped building that once was a great caravanserai terminal. It stands just across Gazi Caddesi from the Ulu Cami.

There are two museums within a short distance of each other in the streets just behind Ulu Cami. The **Ziya Gökalp Museum** was the home of that very influential turn-of-the century Turkish intellectual, the man credited with inventing the idea of Turkish nationalism. The home of one of his near contemporaries, the poet Cahit Sıtkı Tarancı, has become a **Culture Museum** in his honour, with exhibits of local arts and crafts. The house itself, with a typical courtyard decorated with patterns stencilled in whitewash, is a lovely example of the local fashion, and the poet's sitting room, with its stone fountain and elegant old radio, gives an insight into the heights of gracious living in the Diyarbakır of the 1930s. In this area, too, is the **Safa Camii**, with its striped porticos and one of the most unusual minarets in Diyarbakır.

South of Melek Ahmet Paşa Caddesi, the long east–west axis of the city (its name becomes Yenikapı Caddesi as it crosses Gazi Caddesi), stand two other interesting mosques. The **Behrem Paşa Camii** (1572) is claimed by some to be the jewel of Diyarbakır's mosques, and the **Kasim Padişah Camii**, just off Yenikapı Caddesi, is best known for its minaret, the

Dört Ayaklı Minare, which is very lofty, but mysteriously separated from its mosque; indeed, the minaret is set up right in the middle of the street, hoisted in the air by four broad basalt columns. The locals claim that your wish will come true if you pass between the columns seven times. Near this mosque is one of Diyarbakır's two surviving Christian churches still in use, the Armenian **Surp Giragos Kilisesi**.

Another fine *han*, the **Deliller Hanı**, stands at the south end of Gazi Caddesi, at the Mardin Gate. An Ottoman work completed in 1527, it was built especially for travellers to Mecca. The city has recently restored this *han* from the ground up, and it has reassumed its old function in a new way—as a modern hotel, with shops under the colonnades of the courtyard.

The Walls

Mardin Gate, next to an odd, square *türbe* of uncertain origin, is a good place to begin a tour of Diyarbakır's **walls**, an undertaking that could easily swallow up a day or two. Few city walls have so much of interest chiselled into them. Inscriptions in every language, some as old as the Abbasid caliphs of the early 10th century, can be found anywhere—in decorative friezes around the towers, over the gates, in corners where no one looks. Almost every gun port has an inscription, perhaps exhorting the defenders to shoot straight. In addition, there are several examples of Selcuk stonework, with their usual fantastical animals and men carved in reliefs about the towers. You can inspect the outside of the wall, walk over the top of it, and, in many places, even walk through it; numerous corridors inside the walls connect the inner chambers of the towers, which are completely protected from enemy attack.

The most impressive section is in the southwest, at a naturally weak point in the defences, where in 1208 the Artukids constructed two mighty bastions expanding outwards from earlier works of the Selcuks. The two round towers, the **Evli Beden Burcu** and the **Yedi Kardeş Burcu**, are almost identical, and are elaborately decorated on the outside. Yedi Kardeş ('Seven Brothers') probably takes its name from the seven chambers that radiate from the central hall inside. There is a story that these two towers were built by a master architect and his former student, in a competition to see who could build the strongest and best. The master, seeing that his rival had outdone him when the Evli Beden was completed, threw himself off his Yedi Kardeş Burcu in despair. From these walls, you can see a long and graceful bridge over the Tigris, built probably by the Ottomans; '**Ten Eyes**' the locals call it, from its ten arches. According to another story, the paşa who built it caused a large sum of gold to be hidden under one of its piers; no one knows which. When the bridge falls to ruin, it is supposed the money will be found, enough to construct a new one.

Diyarbakır's **Archaeological Museum** (*open 8.30–12, 1.30–5pm, closed Mon; adm*) includes items from as far back as Hittite times. It is located to the north of the city walls, next to the unmistakable pink Dedeman Hotel.

Around Diyarbakır

Most of the countryside of this region is given over to sheep and cattle; though once heavily farmed, when the rains were more frequent and the Fertile Crescent was really fertile, today these bare hills tolerate only a little dry farming. If you look carefully, on many hillsides you can make out the traces of ancient agricultural terraces. More common, however, are the networks of faint lines winding around the lower slopes; the trails left by columns of sheep. In this dry arid climate, it takes decades for them to wear away.

The landscape may be uninviting, especially in the summer, but it contains a good number of religious and antiquarian sites that foreign visitors seldom see. At **Ergani**, for instance, on the road to Elazığ, a very ancient mosque on the mountain called **Zülkifil Dağı** is dedicated as a shrine to a local prophet; Zülkifil (Ezekiel) is honoured by Muslims and Christians alike, and people of both faiths make pilgrimages here from all over southern Anatolia. Another such site, at **Çüngüş**, is an 11th-century dervish retreat still in use. To the east, in **Hani**, pilgrims come to wash in the five-sided holy **Pool of Ayn Kebir**, reputed to have great healing powers. Ruins of the Greek city of **Dakyanos** lie near the town of **Lice**. We may be hearing more from Lice in the future; archaeologists are excitedly digging up an extremely ancient settlement, several thousand years BC, at a site 19 miles (30km) north of the town. They aren't sure yet what they've found, but it seems to be one of the most important recent discoveries in the Middle East. Finally, in this region near the village of **Birklin** are caves near which is carved a relief of that most insufferable rooster of an Assyrian, King Tiglath-Pileser II, together with the usual long cuneiform inscription boasting of his many conquests.

Mardin

South of Diyarbakır, in the baking plains near the Syrian border, the highway for Mosul and Baghdad reaches a kind of world's end at **Mardin**, perched on the edge of the Syrian desert. Due south from here, the next towns of any size are Mecca and Medina, far off in Arabia.

Mardin's reason for existence is its strong citadel; the city flows down from it along a broad hillside. Though probably as old as Diyarbakır, Mardin has never been more than a distant outpost of any state that ruled it, with the possible exception of the White Sheep clan, ruins of whose palace can be seen in the citadel; coincidentally, Mardin is often called the 'white city', in counterpoint to black Diyarbakır. The pale sandstone used, as in Şanlıurfa, for its homes and monuments gives the city a striking appearance when seen from a distance. Mardin speaks four languages, transacting its business in Turkish, Kurdish, Arabic and sometimes Aramaic (Syriac), the ancient language of the Holy Land. This is spoken by the large population of Jacobite (Syrian Orthodox) Christians who have coexisted peacefully with their Muslim neighbours ever since the Arab conquest, barring a few nasty skirmishes that followed the Greek invasion in 1920.

Of the several Islamic foundations in the city, the most important is the **İsa Bey Medrese** near the citadel, an unusual building with beautifully carved friezes and medallions on its gate. Others, towards the newer quarters of the town, are the often-restored 11th-century **Ulu Cami**, originally a Selcuk work, and the 14th-century **Latifiye Camii**.

Around Mardin, again in regions likely to be explored only by the most adventurous travellers, are inviting towns like **Viranşehir**, literally the 'ruined city', with its remains of Byzantine and Roman fortifications, and **Hasankeyf**, an ancient town on the Tigris with the ruins of a once-great bridge of the 12th century and the picturesque remains of the 15th-century **Zeyfelbey Türbesi**, with its brick onion dome and patterns in different-coloured stone. This ancient site may share the same fate as many in the southeast of being submerged if the planned **Ilısu Dam**, part of the GAP, is completed.

Kızıltepe, just south of Mardin, has the ruins of the 13th-century **Ulu Cami**, built when Kızıltepe was the major city of Dunyasir. The region of the Jacobite or Syrian Christians is east of Mardin in and around **Midyat**. Several Christian monasteries here are still occupied, most notably the ancient Syrian patriarchate at **Deir az-Zafaran**, just outside Mardin.

The Deir az-Zafaran

The **Deir az-Zafaran** is sparsely populated today, its days of massive wealth and influence as the seat of the Patriarch of the Syrian Orthodox Church long gone, never to return. Founded in 762, the monastery acquired the seat in the 12th century, retaining it for some 700 years until the anti-Christian riots that followed the Greek invasion led to the Patriarchate being shifted to Damascus. The monastery is only five miles (8km) from Mardin although it seems much further away, standing alone in the scorching, terrible Mesopotamian plain, its tawny stones barely distinguishable from the featureless desert.

One of the monks speaks English and acts as a tour guide for visitors, of whom there are few. He will point out the inscription above the doorway as you enter, inscribed in Aramaic, the language of Christ and the first tongue of this small monastic community. You will see the **underground vault**, reputedly used as a site of ritual sacrifice by sun-worshippers some 4,000 years before. The ceiling of the vault is astounding; an interlocking network of huge, flat stone slabs that magically support each other without the aid of mortar. Adjacent to the vault is a **mausoleum**, the last resting place of past patriarchs.

The chapel is unspectacular—its riches were rushed to Damascus along with the patriarch in 1922. Around the chapel and in the courtyard outside are several rooms, each one containing a curio or two—a delicate floor mosaic, a photograph of a grim, bearded patriarch. In one room is a sedan chair, used to cart the patriarch around in suitably regal fashion. You won't be shown the collection plate in the chapel, but you may like to know it's there.

Towards Lake Van

To go any further eastwards, you will have to retrace your steps to Diyarbakır. From there, the road to Lake Van passes through **Silvan**, a dusty farm town built in and around the ruins of a 6th-century Byzantine fortress. Some 15 miles (24km) further on, you cross the Batman, a tributary of the Tigris, on a modern bridge built parallel to the majestic single-arched **Malabadi Bridge**, a famous work of the Artukid Turks.

Somewhere in this region, no one is sure where, one of the peculiar historical events that followed the collapse of the Seleucid Empire took place: the founding of the now completely vanished city of **Tigranocerta**. King Tigranes, surnamed 'the Great', was an Armenian prince who, through cleverness and good luck, managed to carve out a small empire for himself, with Rome's blessing, in the troubled early years of the 1st century BC. Like his father-in-law, Mithridates of Pontus, and their other relatives ruling the Kingdom of Commagene, this Tigranes made a lot of noise, depopulated a few cities to build his capital, and managed a few temporary conquests (in his case, much of Syria). And, like those other precursors of Shelley's *Ozymandias*, he found himself looking for a new job when expedience made the Romans pull in the puppet strings in 66 BC. The result, if there was any result, was just another of the sad false starts that clutter the chronicles of the Armenians, and the stones of Tigranocerta, wherever it was, have helped construct and rebuild peasant homes and stables for 2,000 years.

Just beyond the Malabadi Bridge, the highway begins climbing into the lovely Bitlis Mountains, an eastern extension of the Taurus that serves to seal off **Lake Van** and the hidden valleys of **Siirt** and **Hakkâri** provinces from the rest of Anatolia. Siirt certainly qualifies as one of the more out-of-the-way corners of Turkey; apart from the mountain scenery, the sole reason to head this way would be to visit the **Mausoleum and Museum of İbrahim Hakkı**, a complex from Ottoman times in the town of **Aydınlar**, four miles (6km) from Siirt. İbrahim Hakkı was a famous Muslim astronomer, and his observatory and instruments are here.

On the map you'll notice that the railway line from Diyarbakır ignominiously fades out in the little village of **Kurtalan**, some 28 miles (45km) short of Siirt. This, at least, deserves an explanation. It was the work of none other than Kaiser Wilhelm II, the last of his line, one of Tigranes the Great's modern-day counterparts. It's an obscure chapter in history now, but at the turn of the century, the Germans' plan for a Berlin-to-Baghdad railway was at the heart of the Kaiser's vast geopolitical scheme; he aimed to create a single economic sphere comprising all of Central Europe and the Middle East, dominated by Germany. The First World War, of course, intervened, and Kurtalan was as far as the German engineers ever got.

Bitlis, deep in the mountains, is a town that sticks in the memory for the distinctive cool grey stone and rounded windows of the old buildings, which climb up steep streets to a well-preserved **citadel** built by the Ottomans. The **Ulu Cami** here, though restored several times, was originally a 12th-century Selcuk work. From here, it's only 14 miles (22km) to **Tatvan** on Lake Van; Tatvan is the end, or rather the interruption, of another railway line, and the terminal of the T.C. Denizyolları ferry that transfers rail passengers over the lake to Van.

Diyarbakır — *Where to Stay*

Note that although Diyarbakır has a reputation as a hotbed of Kurdish nationalism, it is quite safe to stay here. Mardin, however, is best avoided as an overnight destination (day trips are fine), as are Siirt, Bitlis and Silvan.

expensive

Outside the city walls, next to the archaeological museum, the brand new ★★★★**Dedeman** is an apparition in pink on Elazığ Caddesi, ✆ 0412 299 0000, ✉ 0412 224 7353. With its pastel décor and very own lifestyle floor full of boutiques and beauty parlours, you may be forgiven for thinking you've stumbled into the latest shopping mall in Anonymityville. It does have a full checklist of amenities though, including a small pool and secure parking for $155 per night.

moderate

Diyarbakır has only one hotel that is truly excellent, and better than those at much higher prices—the ★★★★**Otel Büyük Kervansaray**, near Mardin Gate on Gazi Caddesi, ✆ 0412 228 9606, ✉ 0412 223 7731, a converted caravanserai with elegance and peace, not to mention satellite TV, hard liquor and, best of all, a large swimming pool. Prices are remarkably low: doubles cost $60 but are even cheaper if business is slack.

There's a good selection of hotels at widely varying prices. All offer rooms with private showers and are located conveniently on or off İnönü Caddesi, making room-hunting easy. The pick of the bunch is the friendly **Kaplan**, off İnönü Caddesi at Sütçü Sokak 14, ✆ 0412 224 9606, ✆ 0412 224 0187. All the well maintained rooms have air-con and TV and some have en suites with bathtubs for $20. There is also secure parking. Under the same management, equally good and identically priced, is the **Kristal**, off Kıbrıs Caddesi at Yoğurtçu Sokak 10, ✆ 0412 224 0297, ✆ 0412 224 0187.

If these are both full, you could pay more to stay at the ***Büyük** at İnönü Caddesi 4, ✆ 0412 228 1295, ✆ 0412 221 2444, offering clean, nondescript rooms for $35. The ***Balkar** at Kıbrıs Caddesi 38, ✆ 0412 228 1233, ✆ 0412 224 6936, has similar rooms with TV and air-con for $40.

cheap

The **Aslan Palas**, Kıbrıs Caddesi 21, ✆ 0412 221 1227, offers reasonable value at $15, but may be full of cigarette-sucking businessmen.

You wouldn't house Saddam Hussein in some of Diyarbakır's bottom-range hotels. Having said that, the backpackers all seem to end up at the **Hotel Van Palas**, İnönü Caddesi 3, ✆ 0412 221 1218, and seem happy enough paying $6 for a double; if it's full, try the **Otel GAP**, ✆ 0412 223 6419, next door. The rooms, which are set around a courtyard, have shower and TV and cost $5 per person.

Diyarbakır   **Eating Out**

Diyarbakır is not blessed with an abundance of good eating places, which is why its one hidden gem shines all the more if you can find it: the **Güneydoğu Gazeteciler Cemiyeti**, or Journalists' Club of Southeast Anatolia, lies on the Ali Emiri Caddesi to the west of the Mountain Gate (Dağ Kapısı). Its inconspicuous sign points you to a large, shady garden where the great and the good of Diyarbakır congregate for the city's best food—and cheapest beer. *Tava* is a house favourite, a sizzling metal platter of spicy lamb, mushrooms and tomatoes topped with cheese. Specialities of the region on offer include *haydari*, a mild yoghurt mixed with local herbs. But beware the mighty *kibe-mumbar*, a potent ribbed sausage filled with mixed meats, before which the most cast-iron of stomachs should prostrate itself in reverence. You could finish up by ordering watermelon, which arrives at your table hollowed out with a candle inside. A blow-out meal may cost $9, but you can eat well for half that.

For a more conventional dining experience, the **Otel Büyük Kervansaray** offers meals in its relaxing courtyard for $15 including wine. Otherwise, possibilities are restricted to the unremarkable lokantas, several of which have a cavalier attitude towards health regulations. An exception to this is the **Konak Sofra Salonu** near the Ulu Cami at Gazi Caddesi 90, where you can fill yourself with döner for only $3. The **Neşem Salonu** at Kıbrıs Caddesi 7/8 charges similar prices for its ready food, including *kuzu dolma*, lamb wrapped around rice and spices. The **Ünal Pastaneleri**, near the Ulu Cami, serves tea and baklava in an atmosphere that is almost refined.

Around Lake Van

Out here in Turkey's southeastern marches, on the shores of the bottle-green sea, is quite simply another world. The superbly queer lake itself, the mighty volcanoes that add so much to the scenery along its shores and the exotic landmarks of the Armenians, Urartians and Kurds all coalesce to make this unique and fascinating country.

Take the **lake** for starters. Lake Van is old, even as geological time is measured; since the volcanic upthrusts that isolated this basin, water has been able to flow in, down from the mountains, but not out. With no circulation, the lake is left to stew in its own juice, a thick broth of sulphides and mineral salts; consequently, except in the fresher water at the mouths of the feeder streams, it has always been biologically dead. One wonders what the large gull population finds to eat; apart from the *darekh*, known as the poor man's herring, there are no fish, no molluscs, and no seaweed—but no pollution. The water, though the foulest-tasting stuff anywhere, is said to be good for your skin and you can swim in it without harm, although its high mineral content makes it sting if you have any cuts. The water is almost supernaturally luminescent, as if some as yet undiscovered light source lurks deep below. Though not unusually buoyant, it has a peculiar viscous appearance, like warm gelatine. It rises in billows and wrinkles, never in ripples or waves.

Then there are the Van **cats**. This rare and bizarre breed is supposedly fond of swimming; the cats have short legs, long white hair and one yellow and one blue eye. Their breeding and export is strictly controlled. One of the first sights to greet you as you arrive in Van from the west is a hideously cute pair of eight-foot-high concrete cats, erected in the middle of a busy traffic roundabout by the Commissariat of Kitsch.

The region has always been occupied; the mountains circling Lake Van are full of **cave paintings**, some dated as far back as 15,000 years ago. The **Hurrians**, the shadowy late Neolithic people who provided the indigenous stock of so much of Anatolia, arrived some time around the third millennium BC, and the population increased markedly in the second millennium BC, when a prolonged drought in the plains to the southwest caused many of the semi-nomadic tribes of that area to migrate into the mountains. Today that migration is echoed in the annual spring wanderings of the shepherds, sometimes covering great distances, to their *yaylalar* or summer pastures in these highlands. From late May onwards their tents blossom everywhere in the mountains of eastern Anatolia, although today, more often than not, the shepherds and sheep make the trip by truck.

History

The **Hurrian-Mitanni** state that developed *c.* 1500 BC, lasting until the Assyrians exterminated it in the 9th century, marks the beginning of recorded history in the region. The **Assyrians** provide most of the records, detailing the looting and carnage caused by their forays. To them, Lake Van was the 'Upper Sea', a strategic spot on the borders of their Hittite enemies. In their records of the 10th century BC, King Shalmaneser I claims victories over a new nation, the Uratri, or Urartu, the first mention of that name in history, at a time when the **Urartians** were probably nothing more than a feudal confederation for defence against the Assyrians (Urartu was an Assyrian name; this people called themselves *Biainili*, from which comes the name of Lake Van). The blessed two centuries of Assyrian weakness that followed gave the Urartians the chance to build a nation and a culture for themselves, with its heartland around Lake Van but extending at times as far as the Black Sea and the Caspian.

Even if the refined culture of the Urartians can be better seen in the museums of Ankara and Van than at the sites themselves, you can exercise your imagination in trying to recreate this lost culture on its own grounds. First, the accounts of the Assyrian King Sargon II describe the hills around Van as thickly forested with pines, beech and oaks; so dense, in fact, that Sargon's chronicles noted that his soldiers could only march through them two abreast (there are still some of these oak groves in the mountains near Bitlis). Rising up out of the forests on natural eminences were fortified palaces with whitewashed and, most likely, elaborately decorated walls, crowned with stepped crenellations like the gables of Dutch houses. Such scenes are portrayed on Urartian metalwork, which also shows kings in their chariots hunting wild game in the forests, and the priests in their rich costumes, trimmed with gold sashes and jewellery. Ordinary people, not surprisingly, do not appear anywhere in Urartian art; some evidence from the inscriptions has led scholars to believe the Urartians were a slave society as brutal as that of their Assyrian neighbours. Their art makes this hard to believe, or rather makes us wish to disbelieve it, but probably, in that nest of snakes that was the early Middle East, it could hardly have been otherwise.

The Armenians

You don't hear much about Turkey's Armenians these days, but they're there. They keep to themselves, quietly going about their business and maintaining their churches. Their numbers are tiny yet it was not so long ago that they lived here in their millions, in cities such as Van which, up to 1915, was almost exclusively Armenian. Yet the fact that Armenians still live in Turkey at all is surprising.

As the Urartian Kingdom crumbled in eastern Anatolia in around 600 BC, the Armenians arose in their place, the new taking its name from the old, 'Armina' being 'Urartu' in the language of the most powerful nation of the day, the Persians. The Armenians were loyal vassals of the Persians and in 331 BC, when Alexander's Macedonians met King Darius's Persians at Issus, the Armenian King Orontes II supplied 40,000 foot and 7,000 cavalry to comprise the Persian right flank. In the ensuing battle, Alexander swept the field. Orontes was killed, Darius fled to die from the knives of his courtiers, and the long Armenian tradition of backing the wrong horse was born.

The **Armenian kingdom**, after Alexander's death a Seleucid province, stumbled on for a century or so, occasionally doing battle with its overlords, always losing, except during the brief, glorious career of **Tigranes the Great** (*see* p.522). Throughout the years that followed, Armenia enjoyed an independence that depended largely on the goodwill of whoever was powerful in the area at the time, be they Byzantine, Selcuk, Georgian or Ottoman. Most of the time, the big powers left them alone, despite their stubborn Christianity in a largely Islamic region. Indeed, the Armenians were the first nation to accept Christianity as its state religion, in 301, 36 years before Constantine's deathbed conversion.

The Middle Ages saw a brief Armenian renaissance. Ani boomed, art and architecture flourished, and small Armenian provinces were established on the southern coast of Anatolia; but by the 13th century, continuous raids by Mongols from the east were exerting a heavy toll on the kingdom's wealth and strength. In 1463 the **Ottomans** stepped in with ease.

For over 400 years, Turks and Armenians enjoyed a mostly peaceful coexistence, despite their differing faiths. In many ways, the Armenians became vital to the Ottoman regime; they were literate when most of the Ottoman populace was not, they had good business sense, and they held top positions in the civil service and in finance. None of this endeared them to the Ottoman peasant, particularly towards the end of the 19th century when the empire was in terminal decline and the people getting poorer by the day. It was a time when blame for the empire's ills had to be apportioned somewhere and the infidel, prosperous Armenians fitted the bill perfectly. Anti-Armenian riots began, Armenian villages were sacked and their inhabitants murdered and the sultans, eager for a scapegoat for their own woeful shortcomings, were happy to nod approvingly.

The situation worsened when the Great War began. Turkey was fighting Christian Russia, and to the Young Turks of Enver Paşa the Armenians were nothing more than the country's fifth column. To an extent, this was true. Many Armenians did see the Tsarist army as a liberating force from Turkish oppression and offered assistance accordingly. It must also be said that the Armenians would respond in kind to the brutalities meted out on them, and the sight of burning Turkish villages within the Armenian provinces became common.

Yet no one could have foreseen the solution the Young Turks had to the 'Armenian problem'. In April 1915, orders were given for the round-up and deportation of the entire Armenian population. Whether or not the Young Turk leaders also actually planned their wholesale massacre may never be known—but that is what happened. Whole towns and cities were emptied of Armenians, who were then marched south into the Mesopotamian desert, without food or water. Those who survived these forced marches were then either shot or simply left to die. Armenians working in the civil service or serving with the Turkish army were taken from their offices or barracks and shot. The Armenians claim that over a million of their countrymen were murdered; the Turkish government estimates some 250,000. Whichever, the issue will probably go on poisoning international relations indefinitely. Not so long ago, the new Armenian government shot itself in the foot, blowing a crucial trade and communications deal with Turkey by insisting the Turks publicly agree to their side of the story. Holding the modern Turkish republic responsible for the crimes of its decadent, multinational predecessor is blatantly unfair. The Turks, for their part, continue to be incredibly touchy and defensive about such affairs—Turkish politicians, especially, don't seem to have noticed that their nation is mature enough to stand a little more openness.

Getting Around

Planes connect Van to Ankara twice daily and to İstanbul once per day. İstanbul Airlines, probably the cheapest, have flights three times a week to İstanbul.

In happier days the daily **train** from İstanbul ended at Tatvan, where the T.C. Denizyolları steamer awaited to carry its passengers and freight across to Van. In recent years this service has become less reliable. Trains now frequently terminate at Elazığ and there are no set times for the ferry. If you are planning to take it, always check in advance that you're not going to be marooned in Tatvan for days on end.

Because of the rugged mountain terrain in this district, the **road** network is sparse. To travel from Van to **Akhtamar Island**, you may be able to find a minibus which goes from the centre of Van to the boat dock five miles beyond the village of Gevaş. Most probably you will have to change at Gevaş, or pay the driver another $2 to take you the final stretch to the jetty. Another option is to get on one of the intercity buses en route to Diyarbakır and other western destinations; these can drop you off right next to the dock. The ferry goes when it fills up and costs whatever the boatman feels like asking, usually around $4 per person, round trip. It's in your interest to go when others do, to avoid a long wait. If you find anyone in Van going on a group tour, ask when they're leaving and get there first.

If you're without a car, a trip to **Hoşap** can be made by bus or minibus, leaving from Cumhuriyet Caddesi near Van's tourist information office, but the return is chancy, especially if you want to stop at Çavuştepe.

The farther you get from Van, the more difficult getting around becomes. In some areas the army stops people from travelling after 3.30pm in summer, earlier in winter. Be advised that there is a security problem in the mountain fastnesses where the paved roads don't go. In Siirt and Hakkâri provinces, and the southern fringes of Van, Kurdish separatists have been known in the past to shoot up a police outpost every few months.

Tourist Information

Van: Cumhuriyet Caddesi 19, ℂ 0432 216 2018.

Süphan Dağı and Nemrut Dağı

Two mighty volcanoes crowd the north shore of Lake Van, creating a centrepiece for the region's postcard scenery. At 13,188ft, **Süphan Dağı** is the third-highest peak in Turkey, its summit snow-covered most of the year. Like Ararat, Süphan Dağı towers alone over the low hills, and provides a landmark for the entire region. The second peak, **Nemrut Dağı**, barely pokes its head above the lofty mountains behind Tatvan. Not to be confused with the Nemrut Dağı of Commagene, this Nemrut, instead of having colossi on top, boasts a lake, Nemrut Gölü, rather like the famous Crater Lake in Oregon but without the trees. Still, its odd volcanic formations create a genuine scenic wonder. Only part of the road up is asphalted and no organized transport exists. You have to climb it yourself, or find someone in Tatvan with a jeep.

Ahlat and Adilcevaz

Ahlat, on the lake shore under Nemrut, was an Armenian principality that flourished under the Selcuks, becoming so famous for stonecarving that its artists were in demand throughout Anatolia. Over the centuries, the city was gradually abandoned, and today, in this grave of a town, only the graves remain; there are several fine *türbeler* of the 13th–15th centuries, and a famous **graveyard** of distinctive Selcuk tombstones. Strangely, these heavy, rectangular, upright stones of volcanic rock, most taller than a man, have been more painstakingly carved with more elaborate designs than any of the mausolea, each with a kind of window at its centre, surrounded by calligraphy and geometric designs so densely packed that they resemble some Mayan relief. No others exist outside the Van region. Near the town of **Adilcevaz**, some 15 miles (25km) further along the shore, are the remains of an unnamed Urartian town built by King Rusa II; the Turks call it **Kefkalesi**. As the fine stone reliefs discovered here have been removed to the Van museum, little remains to be seen except for some finely squared masonry.

Akhtamar

Along the southern edge of the lake, mountains prevent the road from hugging the shore for over half the distance to Van. When the road finally winds down from the hills, it affords a wonderful prospect of the lake, its surrounding mountains, and its several islands, the largest of which is **Akhtamar**.

During the 10th and 11th centuries, the same period when the Armenian kingdom at Ani was in full flower, a separate Armenian state called Vaspurakan flourished on the shores of Lake Van. The greatest of the Vaspurakan kings, named Gagik like his contemporary in Ani, constructed a palace for himself on this lovely island *c.* 920, and raised next to it the **Church of the Holy Cross**, a sight no one should miss if they're anywhere near Lake Van.

It is perhaps the obscurity of these Armenian kingdoms that has denied their sacred structures their rightful place in the history of art. But 200 years before anything resembling them was produced in Europe, and 300 years before the best Selcuk work, this nation, with no greater cultural influence than its tenuous link to Byzantium, created a masterpiece like Akhtamar. In those rough times, it is as if the Armenians had pulled it out of a hat.

Architecture and Reliefs

In form, Akhtamar differs very little from the churches of Ani. Its central plan supports the usual drum and conical dome; here, strangely, the drum is 14-sided and irregular. What makes the church such a jewel is the wealth of sculpture, in an unusual squarish style of high relief possibly unique to this building. Later additions have defaced the structure somewhat—a low clumsy porch and what might be either a bell tower or a minaret. No one knows who's responsible for these; the porch incorporates stone from earlier Armenian works but also some Muslim gravestones very like the ones at Ahlat. The tower has a sundial, like some of the churches at Ani, but on the other hand, it also has Islamic-style stalactite decoration.

The reliefs of the original church nearly cover it from top to bottom. So rich and varied are its subjects, it seems the artists' intention was not just to tell the whole story of the Bible, but to weave in the fabric of life itself. With infinite care for detail and who knows how much time, they succeeded, and ground the warm pink sandstone of their church into a mirror of heaven and earth. Akhtamar exhausts the eye before it exhausts the interest: one could gaze upon it for days on end and still find new scenes. A brief review of the sculptural scheme follows.

At the top of the drum, a frieze of running animals is interspersed with grave and serious human faces; similar bands line the architrave and the four gables, from which the four Evangelists with their books peer out over the points of the compass. The geometric patterns over the windows of the drum have birds perched in them, while below dozens of gargoyles, large and small, lions, rams, serpents, eagles and even a guinea fowl poke out in all directions. Most have suffered some damage; someone once had nothing better to do than use them for target practice.

Near the top of the drum, another frieze, a vineyard, surrounds the entire structure, full of farmers and labourers, monsters and builders, and hunters and women dancing with bears, all peeking out from the vines. Then, below them, come the large religious scenes, spread randomly about the church. Look long enough and you'll see Adam and Eve with the serpent, saints in circles as if suspended in bubbles, sea monsters and turkeys, David and Goliath, eagles snatching hares, roosters and angels, lions and bulls, the Virgin Mary, St George and his dragon, battling bears, Jonah tumbling into the whale's mouth (the artists did their best to guess what a whale might look like), a lion licking a man's feet, a bird with a ring in its beak, Judith and Holofernes, and finally King Gagik himself offering his church of Akhtamar to Christ.

The Island

The foundations of Gagik's palace surround the church. The only other building lies on a small islet nearby, the romantic ruin of a chapel that greets you near the pier on your arrival from the mainland. Akhtamar Island is uninhabited, but it's a beautiful spot, a bare cliff rising straight out of the lake and sloping gently down to the east. There's a beach and a picnic grove, and most visitors spend the whole morning or afternoon on the island. When you're through with the church, take time to observe the equally fascinating variety of the island's natural life; besides the many birds and flowers, some of which you'll never see on the mainland, there are innumerable secret kingdoms of insects among the ruins and rocks, droning away in a hundred different voices, displaying a hundred exotic shapes and colours, including some delicate Art Nouveau dragonflies in sky blue and Lake Van green. Separated by a mile of poison water from the rest of the world, the wildlife of Akhtamar Island has evolved into a world of its own.

Gevaş and Çatak

The quay for ferries to the island lies off the Van–Tatvan road, near **Gevaş**, 19 miles (30km) from the city of Van. In Gevaş, a 14th-century Turkish princess lies in an elegant 12-sided *türbe*, and nearby there's a graveyard with some of the same curious stones as at Ahlat. In the mountains above the town, the village of **Çatak** is located in a wooded corner of the region; near it the **waterfalls of Gahnisipi** carry a distant tributary of the Tigris.

Van

The city goes back to the 9th century BC and the Urartian King Sarduri I, its founder. His capital, originally *Tushpa*, was erected on a great rock on the lake shore that has been the heart of the city throughout its existence; or at least until the First World War, when old Van was completely destroyed in battles first with the Armenians and later with the Russians. Instead of rebuilding on the spot, the people of Van instead relocated their town to a higher and healthier spot, nearly a mile from the lake. Modern Van, not surprisingly, has little of interest, but is making a credible start toward becoming a pleasant town. Like so many of these 'frontier cities' of eastern Anatolia, Van turns its best face to the world with a thoroughly modern main street, Cumhuriyet Caddesi, and two fine new mosques; these may well be the largest new mosques in Turkey. Just a block off the main street, however, are sheds and lumberyards, sheep and empty lots—a town waiting to be built.

Citadel

Very little remains of old Van apart from the **citadel** (**Van Kalesi**) on the rock three miles from the centre. Here, above the serious, neatly cut 30-ton blocks of the Urartian master masons, a succession of Armenian and Turkish rulers built Van's castle in rubble wall and mud brick, now just eroded enough to give the whole an outlandish appearance, like an outsized sandcastle after the tide has turned. The foundations of the Urartian castle, called **Sardurburcu** today, yielded numerous inscriptions that have contributed much to our knowledge of the Urartians. Most concern relations with Assyria, and the older ones are written in Assyrian cuneiform, the first script used by the Urartians, while later writings appear in their own hieroglyphs. The best examples of cuneiform can be seen in a series of tombs cut into the south side of the rock. The path to them is sealed off by a gate but a caretaker is normally on hand to show visitors around. The car park next to the castle may well be one of the most fertile training grounds for Turkey's next generation of carpet sellers. Young boys barnacle themselves to you, taking a categorical 'no' to their entreaties to mean 'Try and persuade me.'

From the citadel, the ruins of Armenian Van can be seen, as well as the second Urartian capital of **Toprakkale**, built in the last century of the kingdom's existence. Just why, no one knows; Tushpa, though often besieged, was never taken. The foundations of a temple and palace remain, but as the site is located in a military zone, it cannot now be visited.

Van Museum

However, you can see the best of both Urartian sites and many others at the **Van Museum** (*open 8–12 and 1.30–5.30, closed Mon; adm*), one block north of Cumhuriyet Caddesi, with one of the best archaeological collections of any provincial museum. Here, the outdoor sculpture garden competes with the works inside for one's attention. The star of the collection is an exquisitely carved **relief** of the god Teshup, for whom the Urartian capital was named. Teshup stands on the back of a bull, Hittite-fashion, and near him are what appear to be two tridents with their tines shaped like leaves, an unusual attribute for a god of storms. Also from the Urartians are stones that may have been **boundary markers**, oddly with Assyrian cuneiform on one side and Armenian crosses on the other. The Karakoyunlu and Akkoyunlu, Turkmen clans of Black Sheep and White, are represented with some of their **gravestones** carved as, of course, sheep; one has a maze on it.

Inside, the museum offers the best collection of Urartian **artworks**, surpassing even Ankara's. There are many examples of the intricately carved jewellery and cylinder seals, an Urartian speciality, and the well-known bronze and gold plates and belts, engraved with lions, bulls, sphinxes, hunting scenes and religious processions. One intriguing subject is a seated god with a head that resembles the famous Hatti cosmos symbols in the Ankara museum. The Urartians were also skilled in casting bronze, shown here by brooches and bells, and standards in the form of antlers. Finally, there's an Urartian **gameboard**, for which you'll have to imagine what the rules might have been (proto-backgammon?).

To remind us that even the Urartians were really mere latecomers in this ancient land, the museum also contains some of the pictographs archaeologists have found carved on rocks on the Trişin Kaya Plateau, 75 miles south of Van. Some go as far back as 9000 BC, depicting animals such as bison and reindeer that have long since died out in this region. One theory as to why these ancient pictographs look so similar to the primitive motifs appearing on some of this region's carpets and kilims is that the local women who wove them spent their summers in tents high on the plateau, surrounded by a vast outdoor gallery of neglected Stone Age art.

North of the City

To the north of the city, the road once more leaves the lakeshore, passing through a land of bare green hills; where it rejoins the lake at **Bendimahi**, there's another waterfall, on the Muradiye Creek. **Erçek Gölü**, to the south of Bendimahi, is a midget Lake Van.

Turkey's Southeast Corner

These are not the only lakes. The topography from Ararat down to the Mesopotamian plain was formed by volcanic action, and instead of neatly folded linear mountain ranges, patches and circlets of extinct volcanoes and lava plateaus surround a series of isolated basins, some low enough to be lakes. Other large lakes are nearby in the Republic of Armenia, and Lake Orumiyeh in Iran is even bigger than Lake Van. Sheep thrive here (the Turkish government reports that there are six of them for every person); difficulty of access makes this corner of Turkey one of the quietest and least known parts of the nation.

These mountain fortresses are the heart of Kurdistan, and depending on your outlook you may see them as the last strongholds of the traditional Kurdish mountain culture, or merely as backward and poor. Either way, the setting, in the streams and woods of Hakkâri province, is one of the most scenic in all Turkey. Only one road leads into this province, following the lovely valley of the River Zap as it negotiates its way through the mountains.

Some 22 miles (36km) southeast from Van, this road passes the ruins called **Çavuştepe**, the 8th-century BC Urartian palace-city of **Sardurihinili**. Sarduri II founded it and named it after himself, and here many of the finest art works of the Urartians have been found. At first glance, the long narrow ridge at the centre of a mountain basin seems much too thin for any sort of a city to fit on it. It is—only the fortress and palace stood here—but look closely down at the surrounding fields and faint traces of ancient streets and foundations will become visible, though they've been tilled over for centuries.

Sarduri's palace must have been a work of some architectural sophistication, strung out along an arrow-straight axis from the castle at the highest point of the ridge, down through the upper and lower terraces of the palace. You can follow the long corridor along this axis, past the royal apartments and offices, the cisterns and storerooms with their huge *pithoi*. As always, only the foundations (of finely worked masonry) remain; in the lower terrace a cuneiform inscription states that Sarduri built the palace and city in honour of 'Haldi, the

War God'. Sarduri goes on to speak of 'cities and gardens where nothing was before', and if you look down at the southern flank of the ridge you'll see the famous work that made it possible. The **Semiramis canal**, associated with that legendary queen but actually a project of the Urartian King Menua, is an irrigation canal still in use after 2,700 years, watering not only this basin but the plains around Van. Altogether, the canal snakes for 32 miles, crossing a range of very high hills; even the Assyrians, who mention it in their records, were impressed with it.

During the extensive excavations of Çavuştepe, tens of thousands of arrowheads (identified as Scythian in origin) were found scattered in and around the fortress and stuck in Sardurihinili's walls, testimony to the violent and sudden end of Urartian civilization and to the inability of this troubled fulcrum of the civilized world, once so blessed in human talent and natural abundance, ever to produce anything that lasts.

Hoşap

When the great states falter, isolated regions like this naturally revert to the feudal rule of the local strongman. As evidence from another age, take in the wonderfully evocative **Castle of Hoşap**, gripping the summit of a tall crag along the main road some 14 miles (23km) beyond Çavuştepe. Hoşap appears on Turkish maps as *Güzelsu*; both names mean 'sweet waters', referring to the springs in the village below, but Hoşap is a Kurdish word and this is a Kurdish castle, built in 1643 by a local despot named Sarı Süleyman in the days when Ottoman control over these parts was slipping.

Hoşap could easily be a castle on the Rhine; certainly it's the only substantial fortification in this corner of Turkey since the days of the Urartians. However he came by it, Sarı Süleyman had the money to do the job right; his great gate with its carved lions and teardrop arabesques is both impressive and beautiful. Once behind the formidable iron doors, you can see the round council room of Sarı Süleyman, directly above the gate, and the baths, gaols and harem quarters, all more or less ruined. Beyond these rises the great three-storey keep, crowned with watch towers and ports for dispensing boiling oil. From the castle, it's easy to make out the wall that once enclosed the town of Hoşap, now a mere village. Also from the castle, you can look over to the mountains of Iran and Iraq. This is about the end of the line; beyond Hoşap, you can take the scenic route as far as Hakkâri, a dull provincial capital set among some exquisite mountains, lately swarming with troops.

Van **Where to Stay**

expensive

With a lobby adorned in Urartian Art Deco, the **★★★Büyük Urartu Hotel**, Cumhuriyet Caddesi 60, ✆ 0432 212 0660, @ 0432 212 1610, is Van's nicest, spoiled only by a location in one of the dingier parts of town. Rooms, all large and en suite, cost $100 for a double, with a possible discount of 20% if you push them.

moderate–inexpensive

A far better deal can be struck at the new **★★★Yakut** on a quiet street at Posta Caddesi 8, ✆ 0432 214 2832, @ 0432 216 6351. Posted prices for en suite doubles with TV and minibar are a notional $50, but the receptionist quotes only half that. Opposite the Yakut is the ★★★**Fuat**, Posta Caddesi 7, ✆ 0432 214 0780, ✉ 0432 216 6804, where similar rooms to the Yakut are on offer for an even more competitive $22 including breakfast.

If these are full, the ★★**Sirhan** next to the Valiliği (government house) at Hükümet Konağı Yanı, ✆ 0432 214 3463, ✉ 0432 216 2867, turns out to be better on the inside than its drab exterior would suggest. Doubles cost $40 with breakfast. Next to the tourist information office is the ★★**Büyük Asur**, Cumhuriyet Caddesi, Turizm Sokak 5, ✆ 0432 216 8792, ✉ 0432 216 9461. Its faded charms may not appeal to everyone, but it has a welcoming air; en suite rooms cost $20. If your trip to the tourist information office turns out to be a baffling experience, the Asur's English-speaking manager, Remzi Bozbay, is a good impartial source of local information.

cheap

Down the road from the Yakut on Posta Caddesi is the **Tahran Hotel**, which is tolerably clean for a cheap sleep at $10 per double. The sheets are grey and the rooms are dim, but are equipped with showers and basins. Toilets are a nocturnal stumble down the hallway. Bring your torch. Cheapest of all is the **Ada Palas**, off Cumhuriyet Caddesi, ✆ 0432 216 2234, at only $3 per person; there's no shower, and your roommates may well be grizzled Iranian truckies who'll hawk and spit in the morning with a gusto you would never believe possible.

Van and Around — Eating Out

Van has several good lokantas, all serving meals for only $3–4. One unlikely venue for excellent cuisine is the **Merkez**, on the edge of town sharing the same premises and management as a petrol station. It's at İskele Caddesi Karayolları Kavşağı, a ten-minute taxi ride from the centre. Don't be put off by the mirrored glass façade, as inside they serve excellent traditional food, including *tandır kebab* and lamb which comes off the bone with no effort at all. The biggest selection of dishes is available at lunchtime. The **Çem**, next to another petrol station on İskele Caddesi, is equally popular with the locals, and has the edge over the Merkez on its meze count.

The new **Çınar Restaurant** attached to the Bayram Hotel at Cumhuriyet Caddesi 1/A is clean, bright and conveniently central with a relaxed family atmosphere. Of the lesser establishments on Cumhuriyet Caddesi, the **Sultan Sofrası** opposite the post office is the place to go if you are craving grilled chicken, and also serves variations on the theme of meat and aubergine. The **Tadım** at Kazım Karabekir Caddesi 46 is your best bet for a cheap breakfast: bread, butter, Van honey and cheese, olives and all the tea you can drink for $1.50. You could ask to try *otlu peynir*, a tangy Kurdish cheese that looks more like bread dough. If they don't have any that day, you'll be able to find some in the shops along Cumhuriyet Caddesi.

If you're visiting **Akhtamar**, the basic **lokanta** across the road from the mainland jetty serves tasty grilled lake fish for $3. Elsewhere in the province, don't expect anything special and remember to eat early; most places are closed by early evening.

Linguists say Turkish is a member of the Ural-Altaic group, which makes it related to Finnish, Hungarian and little else. Dialects are spoken by perhaps as many as 100 million Turcomans, Kirghiz, Uzbeks and others in central Asia, as well as the 50 million Turks in Turkey; a Turk from İstanbul could make himself understood as far east as Manchuria. He couldn't get far, though, in Helsinki or Budapest. This is one of the truly grey areas in linguistics, but what strongly suggests these languages have a common origin is their use of *agglutination*. Turkish has no prepositions, and most of the difficulties of the language are caused by the subtleties of the infinite number of suffixes that are tacked onto words or replace them. In this book, for instance, words may often be disguised by their endings: *Yeşil Cami*—Green Mosque, but *Rüstem Paşa Camii*—Mosque *of* Rustem Pasha.

The Turks are very proud of their language, with its long and distinguished list of poets and writers, its melodious vowel harmony, and its wealth of expressive colloquialisms. There is even a slang dictionary for Turkish. The Turks love playing word games; there are palindromes like '*Traş niçin şart?*' or 'Why get a haircut?', and long nightmares of agglutination; the longest word yet discovered in Turkish is an entire sentence:

'Çekoslovakyalılaştıramadıklarımızdanmısınız?'

meaning 'Are you the people whose nationality we cannot change to Czechoslovakian?'.

Like the French, the Turks have a semi-official body concerned with maintaining the purity of the language. In the 1930s, this was a hot political issue; reforming the language was one of Atatürk's pet ideas, and he replaced thousands of Arabic, Persian and Greek words with 'Turkish' equivalents, either invented or found in use in obscure corners of the nation. The drive for reform slowed down when parents began to have trouble understanding their children—and Atatürk's speeches.

The 1930s was also the decade of the great Alphabet Reform. Previously, Turkish, with its eight vowels, had been shoehorned into Arabic characters, which have only three, with results such as the words for 'great' and 'dead' being written the same (*ulu, ölü*). In part for this reason, but also to make European languages accessible to the Turks, Atatürk decreed that the change must be made. Throughout the decade, he travelled to almost every large town in Turkey with chalk and a blackboard. While the people crowded around in thousands to see their nation's hero, they got their first lesson in Roman letters. Amazingly, it all

Language

worked, far better, in fact, than Atatürk ever dreamed. The changeover that was supposed to take fifteen years was accomplished in five.

Learning Turkish

If you want to learn some Turkish before you go, try either *Teach Yourself Turkish* by Asuman Celen Pollard and David Pollard (Teach Yourself, 1996)), or *Colloquial Turkish* by Sinan Bayraktaroğlus et al (Routledge, 1992), both of which are available with audio cassettes to help your pronunciation. Failing that, if you can learn the numbers and some of the words listed below, you can communicate almost all your wishes, and make your stay in Turkey infinitely more fun. Literature from the Turkish Travel Office tends to overestimate the number of people you'll find who speak English or German (which does come in handy, though). Knowing just a few words will endear you to the Turks and probably prevent you from getting ripped off.

Yok is an essential word to know. Its meaning approximates to 'There is none', but it's used much more commonly than 'no' (*hayır*). It is a sentence from which there is no appeal. If a Turk is at all inclined to help you out he will exhaust all possibilities before intoning the fatal *yok*. Its positive counterpart is *var* ('There is'), always a cheering note in Turkey, although when you do get it, it may not be what you expected.

Pronunciation

This is regular and logical, since the alphabet was designed to fit the language. The vowels are pronounced as follows, not always as they would be in English:

a	between *u* in 'fuss' and *a* in 'flat'
â	faint y sound in preceding consonant; *lâleli* is lyaah-leh-lee
ay	*i* in 'bike'
e	*e* in 'pet'
i (İ)	between *i* in 'hit' and *ee* in 'meet'
ı (I)	the half-swallowed vowel sound of *a* in 'about' or *e* in unstressed 'the'
o	*o* in 'pot'
ö	the *er* sound in the middle of 'word'
u	the *oo* in 'loo'
ü	the *u* in French 'tu' or German ü

These consonants are significantly different to English:

ç	*ch* as in 'chin'
c	pronounced like the English 'j'
g	always hard, as in 'goat'
ğ	silent, as the *gh* in 'eight'; it sometimes lengthens the preceding vowel
j	*zh* as in 'measure'
ş	*sh* as in 'ship'
v	more like the English *w*

Something that could cause confusion is vowel harmony. There are two sorts of vowel: the 'back' vowels (a, undotted i, o and u) and the 'front' vowels (e, i, ö and ü). Genuine Turkish words contain one sort of vowel only and suffixes have their vowels changed, if necessary, to comply with the rules of vowel harmony. Words of foreign origin, like *şoför* (chauffeur) often contain a mixture of the two types of vowel.

Note: Turkish syllables almost always *carry equal weight.* If there is any stress, it will usually be at the end. Besides forgetting that *c* is sounded like English 'j', the most common mistake foreigners make is to put accents where they don't belong. We do it naturally, but it makes Turkish words unintelligible to the Turks.

Turkish plural forms are -ler or -lar added to the end of the word, for example *adam* (man), *adamlar* (men), or *kalem* (pen), *kalemler* (pens).

Vocabulary

We've represented the sounds of the Turkish *ü* as *eu* and *ö* as *er*. The sound of *ı* is represented by *uh* and that of *ay* as *iy*. See the chart above for the pronunciation of these vowels.

Geography, Signs and Directions

Signs

dikkat	dee-kat	caution
dur	doohr	stop
girilmez	gee-reel-mez	no entry
şehir merkezi	sheh-heer mer-keh-zee	city centre
sigara içilmez	sih-gah-rah itch-ll-mez	no smoking
tehlike	teh-lee-keh	danger
tekistikamet	tek-ee-stee-kah-met	one way
yasak bölge,	yah-sak berl-geh	forbidden area, military area,
askeri bölge	as-ker-ee berl-geh	i.e. no photographs)
yavaş	yah-vash	slow

Places

ada	ah-dah	island
bekçi	bek-chee	caretaker (lets you into monuments)
çay	chiy	stream
cadde or *caddesi*	jah-deh, jah-deh-sih	street
cami	jah-mee	mosque
çarşı	chahr-shuh	market, bazaar
çeşme	chesh-meh	fountain
çiftlik	chihft-lihk	farm
deniz	deh-nihz	sea
dere	deh-reh	valley
geçit	geh-chit	pass
göl	gerhl	lake
hamam	hah-mahm	Turkish bath
han	hahn	inn
hisar	hih-sahr	castle
höyük	her-yeuk	mound
ırmak	uhr-mahk	river
kale	kah-leh	castle

kapı	kah-puh	gate
kilise	kih-lih-seh	church
körfez	ker-fehz	bay
köy	keuy	village
kümbet	keum-beht	mausoleum
kuyu	koo-yoo	well
mahalle	ma-hal-leh	city ward or district
mevki	mev-kee	place, site
meydan	may-dahn	square
nehir	neh-hihr	river
orman	ohr-mahn	forest
pınar	puh-nahr	spring
saray	sahr-iy	palace
şehir	sheh-hihr	city
sokak	soh-kahk	street
su	soo	stream
tepe	teh-peh	hill
türbe	teur-beh	tomb
vilayet	vil-iy-eht	provincial government house
yayla	yiy-lah	mountain pastureland
yol	yohl	road
Türkiye	Teur-kee-yeh	Turkey
Akdeniz	ahk-deh-nihz	Mediterranean ('white sea')
Karadeniz	kah-rah-deh-nihz	Black Sea
Ege Deniz	eg-eh deh-nihz	Aegean Sea
Trakya	trahk-yah	Thrace
Anadolu	ah-nah-doh-loo	Anatolia
Yunanistan	yoo-nan-ih-stan	Greece
Kıbrıs	kuh-bruhs	Cyprus

Directions

where is?	*nerede?*	neh-reh-deh
where is the police station?	*karakol nerede?*	kah-rah-kol neh-reh-deh?
where is the toilet?	*tuvalet nerede?*	too-vah-let neh-reh-deh?
north	*kuzey*	koo-zay
south	*güney*	geu-nay
west	*batı*	bah-tuh
east	*doğu*	doh-oo
left	*sol*	sohl
right	*sağ*	sah
short	*kısa*	kuh-sah
long	*uzun*	oo-zoon
near	*yakın*	yah-kuhn

far	uzak	oo-zahk
here	burada	boo-rah-dah
there	şurada	shoo-rah-dah
over there	orada	o-rah-dah
stop (noun)	durak	doo-rahk
stop (imperative)	dur!	door
airport	hava alanı	hah-vah ah-lah-nuh
bus station	otogar	oh-toh-gahr
train station	gar, istasyon	gahr, ihs-tas-yohn
petrol station	benzin istasyonu	ben-zihn ihs-tahs-yohn-oo
bank	banka	bahn-kah
post office	postane	pos-tah-neh
police station	karakol	kah-rah-kol
restaurant	lokanta	loh-kahn-tah
night club	gazino	gah-zih-noh
customs	gümrük	geum-reuk
port	liman	lih-mahn
quay	iskele	ihs-keh-leh
bridge	köprü	kœr-preu

Time

morning	sabah	sah-bah
evening	akşam	ahk-shahm
night	gece	geh-jeh
week	hafta	hahf-tah
month	ay	iy
season	mevsim	mev-sihm
year	yil	yihl
this	bu	boo
next	gelecek	gel-eh-jek
now	şimdi	shihm-dee
today	bugün	boo-geun
tomorrow	yarın	yahr-uhn
yesterday	dün	deun
What time is it?	kaç saat?	kahtch saaht?
At what time?	kaçta?	kahch-tah?
When?	ne zaman?	neh zah-mahn?
Monday	Pazartesi	pah-zahr-teh-sih
Tuesday	Salı	sah-luh
Wednesday	Çarşamba	chahr-shahm-bah
Thursday	Perşembe	pehr-shem-beh
Friday	Cuma	joo-mah
Saturday	Cumartesi	joo-mar-teh-sih
Sunday	Pazar	pah-zahr

January	*Ocak*	o-jahk
February	*Şubat*	shoo-baht
March	*Mart*	mahrt
April	*Nisan*	nih-sahn
May	*Mayıs*	miy-uhs
June	*Haziran*	hah-zih-rahn
July	*Temmuz*	tem-mooz
August	*Ağustos*	ah-oos-tohs
September	*Eylül*	ai-leul
October	*Ekim*	eh-kihm
November	*Kasım*	kah-suhm
December	*Aralık*	ah-rah-luhk

Numbers

one	*bir*	bihr
two	*iki*	ih-kih
three	*üç*	eutch
four	*dört*	deurt
five	*beş*	besh
six	*altı*	ahl-tuh
seven	*yedi*	yeh-dih
eight	*sekiz*	seh-kihz
nine	*dokuz*	doh-kooz
ten	*on*	ohn
eleven	*onbir*	ohn-bihr
twelve	*oniki*	ohn-ih-kih
twenty	*yirmi*	yihr-mih
twenty-one	*yirmibir*	yihr-mihbihr
thirty	*otuz*	oh-tooz
forty	*kırk*	kuhrk
fifty	*elli*	el-lih
sixty	*altmış*	ahlt-muhsh
seventy	*yetmiş*	yet-mish
eighty	*seksen*	sek-sehn
ninety	*doksan*	dohk-sahn
hundred	*yüz*	yeuz
two hundred	*iki yüz*	ihk-yeuz
564	*beş yüz altmış dört*	besh-yeuz-ahlt-muhsh-deurt
thousand	*bin*	bihn
a thousand and one	*bin bir*	bihn-bihr
million	*milyon*	mil-yoan
billion	*milyar*	mil-yahr
2000	*iki bin*	ih-kih bihn
2001	*iki bin bir*	ih-kih bihn bihr

Note: for a number of objects, use the word *tane* (tah-neh) (piece, bit) after the number, e.g. *iki tane biletler*, two tickets (not *iki biletler*).

half	*yarım, buçuk*	yahr-uhm, boo-chook
(*buçuk* is used after numerals)		
quarter	*çeyrek*	chay-rehk
... per cent	*yüzde* ...	yeuz-deh
first	*ilk, birinci*	ihlk, bihr-ihn-jih
tenth	*onuncu*	ohn-oon-joo
hundredth	*yüzüncü*	yeuz-eun-jeu

Conversation

welcome	*hoş geldiniz*	hohsh gehl-dihn-ihz
in reply to *welcome*	*hoş bulduk*	hohsh bool-dook
	(we have found well)	
I don't understand	*anlamadım*	ahn-LAH-mah-duhm
		(stress second syllable)
I understand	*anlıyorum*	ahn-luh-yohr-oom
do you understand?	*anlıyor musunuz?*	ahn-luh-yohr moo-soon-ooz
yes	*evet*	eh-veht
no	*hayır*	hly-uhr
there is	*var*	vahr
there's none	*yok*	yohk
perhaps	*belki*	behl-kih
I know	*biliyorum*	bihl-ih-yohr-oom
I don't know	*bilmiyorum*	BIHL-mih-yohr-oom
		(stress first syllable)
Do you speak English?	*İngilizce biliyor musunuz?*	Ihng-ih-leez-jeh bihl-ih-yohr moo-soon-ooz?
I don't speak Turkish	*Türkçe bilmiyorum*	teurk-cheh bihl-mih-yohrum
Do you speak Turkish?	*Türkçe biliyor musunuz?*	Teurk-cheh bihl-ih-yohr moo-soon-ooz?
a little	*bir as*	bihr ahs
like Tarzan	*Tarzanca*	tahr-zahn-jah
(i.e. 'broken' Turkish)		
please	*lütfen*	leut-fehn
thank you (very much)	*(Çok) teşekkür ederim*	(chohk) tesh-eh-keur eh-deh-ruhm
you're welcome	*bir şey değil*	bihr shay dayl
pardon, excuse me	*affedersiniz*	ahf-feh-dehr-sih-niz
goodbye ('Allah go with you')	*Allahaısmarladık*	ahl-ahuhs-mahr-lah-duhk
goodbye ('smiling, smiling')	*güle güle*	geu-leh geu-leh

Allahaısmarladık is said by the person leaving, *güle güle* is said by the person staying behind.

hello	*merhaba*	mehr-hah-bah
hello ('peace be with you')	*selamaleyküm*	sehl-ahm-ahl-ay-keum
hello (reply to *selamaleyküm*)	*aleykümselam*	ahl-ay-keum-seh-lahm
good day	*günaydın*	geun-ahy-duhn
good evening	*iyi akşamlar*	eey ahk-shahm-lahr
good night	*iyi geceler*	eey geh-jeh-lehr
slow, wait!	*yavaş yavaş*	yah-vahsh yah-vahsh
beautiful (all-purpose compliment)	*güzel!*	geu-zehl
very good	*çok iyi*	chohk eey
How are you?	*nasılsınız?*	nah-suhl-suhn-uhz
What is this/that?	*nu nedir? o nedir?*	boo/o neh-dihr
How much is it?	*ne kadar?*	neh kah-dahr
I want...	*... istiyorum*	ihs-tih-yohr-um
how?	*niçin?*	nih-chihn
wait a minute	*bir dakika*	bihr dah-kih-kah
good for nothing! useless	*yaramaz*	yahr-ah-mahz
cheap	*ucuz*	oo-jooz
expensive	*pahalı*	pah-hah-luh
money	*para*	pah-rah
discount	*indirim*	in-dih-rihm
I want to get off [the bus]	*inecek var*	in-eh-jek vahr
sick, ill	*hasta*	hahs-tah
hot	*sıcak*	suh-jahk
cold	*soğuk*	so-ook
old	*eski*	es-kih
new	*yeni*	yeh-nih

Food and Drink

kahvaltı	kah-vahl-tuh	breakfast
öğle yemeği	er-leh yeh-meh-ee	lunch
akşam yemeği	ahk-shahm yeh-meh-ee	dinner
garson	gar-son	waiter
hesap	he-sahp	bill
ekmek	ek-mek	bread
kızarmış ekmek	kuhz-ar-muhsh ek-mek	toast
poğacı	poh-ah-juh	bun
simit	see-meet	bread ring topped with sesame seeds
tereyağ	te-re-yay	butter
reçel	reh-chel	jam
bal	bahl	honey
yumurta	yoo-moor-tah	eggs
haşlama	hahsh-lah-mah	boiled/poached

omlet	ohm-let	omelette
menemen	meh-neh-mehn	scrambled eggs with tomatoes, cheese and peppers
yoğurt	yo-oort	yoghurt
kaymak	kahy-mak	cream
tuz	tooz	salt
şeker	shek-ehr	sugar
sirke	sihr-keh	vinegar
zeytinyağ	zay-tin-ya	olive oil
turşu	toor-shoo	pickles
salça	sahl-cha	sauce

Drinks

su	soo	water
maden suyu	ma-dehn soo-yoo	mineral water
süt	seut	milk
çay	chiy	tea
ada çayı	ah-dah chiy-uh	sage tea (literally 'island tea')
elma çayı	el-mah chiy-uh	apple tea
kahve	kah-veh	coffee
Neskafe	nes-kah-veh	instant coffee
suyu	soo-yoo	juice
meyva suyu	may-va soo-yoo	fruit juice
limonata	lihm-o-nah-ta	lemonade
oralet	or-a-let	orange-flavoured hot drink
salep	sah-lep	a hot drink for winter, made from milk, sugar and salep (powdered orchid tuber)
bira	bih-ra	beer
şarap (beyaz, kırmızı)	shar-ahp (beh-yaz, kuhr-muh-zuh)	wine (white, red)
buz	booz	ice

Yemek Listesi	**yeh-mek lihs-teh-sih**	**Menu**
Meze	**meh-zeh**	**Hors d'Oeuvres**
Arnavut ciğeri	ahr-nah-voot jee-ehr-ih	'Albanian' liver (cold, spicy, fried)
cacık	jah-juhk	minced cucumber, garlic and yoghurt
fasulye	fah-sool-yeh	green beans (in olive oil)
gözleme	gurz-leh-meh	Turkish crepes
kısır	kuh-suhr	bulgar with onions, pepper and parsley
mantı	mahn-tuh	ravioli
pastırma	pahs-tuhr-mah	very spicy pastrami, with garlic

sigara böreği	sih-gah-rah ber-ay-ee	cigarette-shaped flaky pastry, with cheese or meat
sucuk	soo-jook	Turkish sausage
yalancı dolma	yahl-ahn-juh dohl-mah	stuffed vine leaves

Corba / chor-bah / Soup

düğün çorbası	dooh-oon ...	'Wedding soup'—lamb soup with eggs and lemon
et suyu	et soo-yoo	consommé (meat water)
ezo gelin çorbası	e-zoh geh-lin ...	tomato, lentil, mint and lemon soup
işkembe çorbası	ish-kem-beh ...	tripe soup with egg sauce
mercimek çorbası	mehr-jih-mek chor-bah-suh	red lentil soup
paça çorbası	pah-chah	sheep's trotters soup
şehriye çorbası	shehr-ee-yeh ...	chicken noodle soup
yayla çorbası	yiy-lah ...	rice, yoghurt, egg yolks in broth

Salata / sah-lah-tah / Salads

beyin salatası	bey-ihn ...	sheep's brain salad
çoban salatası	cho-bahn ...	mixed vegetable salad
patlıcan salatası	paht-luh-jan ...	mashed eggplant, olive oil, lemon juice and mayonnaise
tarama salatası	tah-rah-mah sah-lah-tah-suh	roe with olive oil and lemon juice
tarator salatası	tah-rah-tohr ...	sesame syrup, walnuts and garlic

Et / et / Meat

bamya etli	bahm-yah et-lih	beef with okra
biftek	bihf-tehk	beef steak
ciğer	jee-ehr	liver
cizbiz	jiz-biz	grilled meatballs
dana	dah-nah	veal
et saç kavurma	et sahtch ka-voor-ma	thin slices of lamb, tomatoes and peppers sautéed at the table
haşlama	hahsh-lah-mah	leg of lamb with carrots and celery
hindi	hin-dih	turkey
işkembe nohutlu	ish-kehm-beh noh-hoot-lu	tripe (with chickpeas)
kıyma	kee-mah	minced meat
köfte	kerf-teh	meatballs
kadın budu köfte	kah-duhn boo-doo kerf-teh	'ladies' thighs' meatballs (minced lamb and rice)
kuzu	koo-zoo	lamb
kuzu incik patlıcanlı	koo-zoo in-jik paht-luh-jahn-luh	lamb shank with eggplant
kuzu kapaması	koo-zoo kah-pah-mah-suh	lamb stew with vegetables
papazyahnisi	pah-pahz-yah-nih-sih	mutton stew
sığır	suh-uhr	beef

tavuk	tah-vook	chicken
çerkez tavuğu	cher-kez tah-voo-oo	chicken in walnut sauce
beğendili tavuk	beh-en-dih-lih tah-vook	chicken with mashed eggplant, milk and cheese

Balık — bah-luhk — Fish

barbunya	bahr-boon-yah	red mullet
barbunya kağıtta	bahr-boon-yah kah-uht-ta	red mullet in foil
dil balığı	dihl bah-luh-uh	sole
iskorpit	ihs-kor-piht	rock fish, stone bass
istavrit	is-tahv-riht	mackerel
istiridye	ihs-tihr-ihd-yeh	oyster
kalamar	kah-lah-mahr	squid
kalkan	kahl-kahn	turbot
kamsi	hahm-sih	anchovy
karagöz	kahr-ah-gerz	sargus
karides	kah-ree-des	prawn
kefal	keh-fahl	grey mullet
kılıç balığı	kuhl-uch bah-luh-uh	swordfish
kılıç şiş	kuhl-utch shish	swordfish kebabs
lüfer	leu-fehr	blue fish
mercan	mehr-jahn	pandora
midye	mihd-yeh	mussels
palamut	pahl-ah-moot	bonito
pavurya, yengeç	pah-voor-yah, yen-getch	crab
pisi balığı	pih-sih bah-luh-uh	brill

Sebze — seh-bze — Vegetables

biber	bee-behr	green pepper
domates	doh-mah-tes	tomatoes
kabak	kah-bahk	zucchini, squash
lahana	lah-han-ah	cabbage
patlıcan	paht-luh-jan	eggplant (aubergine)
yaprak	yahp-rahk	vine leaves

(any of the above can be **dolması** (dohl-mah-suh): stuffed with rice and meat)

bamya	bahm-yah	okra
bezelye	beh-zehl-yeh	peas
enginar	en-gee-nahr	artichokes
fasulye	fah-sool-yeh	beans
fava	fah-vah	broad beans
havuç	hah-vooch	carrots
ıspanak	uhs-pahn-ahk	spinach
kuşkonmaz	koosh-kahn-mahz	asparagus
mantar	mahn-tahr	mushrooms
marul	mahr-ool	lettuce

nohut	no-hoot	chickpeas
patates	pah-tah-tes	potatoes
pilav	pihl-ahv	rice
soğan	so-ahn	onion
zeytin	zay-tihn	olives

Vegetable dishes

imam bayıldı	ih-mahm bay-yuhl-duh	'the imam fainted'—eggplant stuffed with onions and garlic in olive oil
iç pilav	itch pihl-ahv	rice with chopped liver, raisins and pine nuts
bulgur pilavı	bool-goor pihl-ah-vih	bulgar with onions and tomatoes
fırında makarna	fuh-ruhn-dah mah-kahr-nah	baked macaroni, a bit like lasagna

Meyva — may-vah — Fruit

ahududu	ah-hoo-doo-doo	raspberries
armut	ahr-moot	pear
badem	bah-dem	walnuts
çilek	chih-lek	strawberry
elma	el-mah	apple
erik	eh-rihk	plum
incir	in-jeer	figs
karpuz	kahr-pooz	watermelon
kavun	kah-voon	melon
kayısı	kiy-uh-suh	apricot
kiraz	kih-rahz	cherry
muz	mooz	banana
portakal	por-tah-kahl	orange
şam fıstığı	shahm fis-tuh-yuh	pistachios
şeftalı	shef-tah-luh	peach
vişne	vish-neh	cherry

Tatlı — taht-luh — Desserts/sweets

aşure	ah-shur-eh	pudding with beans, cereals, nuts and raisins
baklava	bah-klah-vah	layered pastry with syrup and nuts
çikolata	chik-o-lah-tah	chocolate
dondurma	don-duhr-mah	ice cream
ekmek kadayıf	ek-mek kah-dah-yuhf	bread in syrup
kabak tatlısı	kah-bak taht-luh-suh	slices of pumpkin in syrup
krem karamel	krem kah-rah-mehl	caramel custard
lokma	lohk-mah	round doughnuts in syrup
lokum	lohk-uhrm	Turkish delight
muhallebi	mu-hal-le-bih	milk pudding
pasta	pah-stah	cake

peynir	pay-nihr	cheese
sütlaç	seut-lahtch	rice pudding
tavuk göğsü	tah-vook ger-seu	milk pudding with chicken breasts
tel kadayıf	tel kah-dah-yuhf	shredded wheat in syrup
un helvası	oon hel-vah-suh	halva made of flour and butter
zerde	zehr-deh	sweet rice with saffron

Verbs

If you want to try a few sentences, here are some verbs and how to use them.

The verbs 'to be' and 'to have' don't really exist in Turkish. 'To be' appears as a suffix, as in, for example

İngilizim　　　　　　*Türkün*

English—I am　　　　　Turk—you are

Var, 'there is' and *yok* 'there is not' are used in place of to have. For example:

Su var　　　　　　　*Su yok*

there is water　　　　　there is no water

Common Verbs

anlamak	ahn-lah-mahk	to understand
bakmak	bahk-mahk	to look
beğenmek	beh-ehn-mehk	to like
beklemek	behk-leh-mehk	to wait
bilmek	bihl-mehk	to know
çalışmak	chahl-ush-mahk	to work
dinlemek	dihn-leh-mehk	to listen
dinlenmek	dihn-lehn-mehk	to rest
duymak	dooy-mahk	to hear
gelmek	gehl-mehk	to come
gezmek	gehz-mekh	to walk
gitmek	giht-mehk	to go
görmek	geur-mehk	to see
içmek	ihch-mehk	to drink
istemek	ihs-teh-mehk	to want
konuşmak	koh-noosh-mahk	to speak
öğrenmek	er-ehn-mehk	to learn
öğretmek	er-eht-mehk	to teach
okumak	oh-kool-mahk	to read
sevmek	sehv-mehk	to love
uyanmak	oo-yahn-mahk	to wake up
uyumak	oo-yoo-mahk	to sleep
yazmak	yahz-mahk	to write

yemek	yeh-mehk	to eat
yüzmek	yeuz-mehk	to swim

To form the present continuous, future and past definite tenses, a tense marker is added to the verb root, followed by the suffix indicating person. Vowel harmony is obeyed.

-yor- is the present continuous tense marker. After consonants, an *i* is inserted. Thus, using *gezmek*, we have:

geziyorum	I am walking
geziyorsun	you are walking
geziyor	he/she/it is walking
geziyoruz	we are walking
geziyorsunuz	you are walking
geziyorlar	they are walking

-ecek- is the future tense marker. Before a vowel, the *k* turns into a *ğ*:

gezeceğim	I will talk
gezeceksin	you will walk
gezecek	he/she/it will walk
gezeceğiz	we will walk
gezeceksiniz	you will walk
gezecekler	they will walk

-d- is the past definite tense marker:

gezdim	I walked
gezdin	you walked
gezdi	he/she/it walked
gezdik	we walked
gezdiniz	you walked
gezdiler	they walked

A verb is turned into the negative form by inserting *-mi-* between the root and the tense marker. For example:

geziyorum	*gezmiyorum*
I'm walking	I'm not walking

A question is formed by inserting *-mi-* after the tense marker, or in the case of the past definite tense, after the whole word:

geziyorsun	*geziyor musun?*
you are walking	are you walking?
gezdin	*gezdin mi?*
you walked	did you walk?

There is no need to use the personal pronouns, except for emphasis, or if you are worried that you have got it wrong. They are:

ben	I	*biz*	we
sen	you	*siz*	you
o	he/she/it	*onlar*	they

Architectural and Artistic Terms

acroterion	acanthus-leaf decoration on the roofline of a Greek temple
acropolis	citadel; usually the original habitation of a Greek city
agora	market-place, public forum
ashlar	masonry with squared stones laid in even courses
basilica	a rectangular building of three aisles divided by columns: originally a Roman government building, later a form for Byzantine churches
bedesten	an inner chamber of a Turkish market, built to keep safe the merchant's most valuable goods
bouleuterion	council chamber of a Greek city
cami	mosque
caravanserai	inn for caravans and merchants
çarşı	bazaar
cavea	semicircle of seats in a Greek theatre
cella	inner sanctum of a Greek temple
exedra	semi-circular recess—space contained under a semi-dome
eyvan	in early Ottoman mosques, a chamber to the side of the main prayer hall
Geometric	style of early Greek pottery, roughly 900–700 BC, so called for its abstract geometric designs
gymnasium	Greek or Roman school
hamam	Turkish bath
han	inn for merchants
heroon	shrine of a hero—demigod or mortal
heykel	statue
hisar	a Turkish citadel or castle
kale	a hisar
kapı	a gate
kilim	woven wool mat
kilise	Turkish for church
külliye	complex of pious foundations (educational or charitable) around a mosque
kümbet	a *türbe* (see below)
medrese	old school of theology
megaron	large house from Mycenaean period
mescid	a place set aside for Muslim prayer; it may be anything from a small mosque in a palace or *han* to a simple room in a bus station
mihrab	niche in a mosque indicating the direction of Mecca
mimber	mosque pulpit
naos	the inner chamber of a temple, containing the cult image
narthex	outer porch of a church
nave	central aisle of basilica form church
nymphaion	sanctuary of nymphs, or public fountain
oculus	a circular opening at the top of a dome

odeion	concert hall
orchestra	the circular space at the centre of an ancient theatre; originally the dancing ground, later the centre of the action in early Greek drama
palaestra	exercise ground of a *gymnasium*
pendentives	(also known as squinches) spherical sections that support a dome over a square space
prytaneion	committee room of a *bouleuterion* (see above), locale of a city's sacred fire
şadirvan	mosque fountain
stele	an upright stone, decorated with inscriptions or a relief, often a gravestone
stoa	large colonnaded porch attached to another building
tekke	dervish lodge
temenos	sacred enclosure of a temple
türbe	a mausoleum for a ruler, political dignitary or holy man. In Turkey they are usually free-standing structures with six or eight sides, and a round or prismatic dome

Bibliography

Ancient History

Akurgal, Ekrem, *Ancient Civilizations and Ruins of Turkey*, Türk Tarih Kurumu, Ankara, 1983. The indispensable guide for anyone interested in exploring Turkey's innumerable archaeological sites in detail (though weak on eastern Anatolia).

Apollonius of Rhodes, *The Voyage of Argo*, translated by E. V. Rieu, Penguin, 1971. Jason's journey along the Black Sea coast.

Arrian, *The Campaigns of Alexander*, translated by Aubrey de Sélincourt, Penguin, 1971.

Bean, George, *Aegean Turkey*, 1966; *Turkey's Southern Shore*, 1968; *Turkey Beyond the Maeander*, 1971; *Lycia*, 1978, Ernest Benn. Fine, anecdotal accounts and detailed guides to Turkey's Greek and Roman sites, by a scholar who discovered not a few of them himself.

Bittel, Kurt, *Guide to Boğazköy*, Ankara, 1972. A must for all Hittite fans, by the archaeologists who excavated their capital.

Erzen, Prof. Dr. Afif, *Eastern Anatolia and the Urartians*, Türk Tarih Kurumu, Ankara, 1984.

Mellaart, James, *Earliest Civilizations of the Near East*, Thames and Hudson, 1965 and *Çatal Höyük*, Thames and Hudson, 1967. Two fascinating books by the archaeologist who uncovered the most important site in the Middle East since Schliemann.

Sandars, N.K. *The Sea Peoples: Warriors of the Ancient Mediterranean*, Thames and Hudson, 1978. The true story of the dark age that brought down the curtain on Troy and the Hittites.

Sinclair, T.A., *Eastern Turkey: An Architectural and Archaeological Survey*, Pindar Press, 1987. The three volumes of this work contain all you could possibly want to know, but at £135 per volume, are beyond the means of the average pocket.

Wood, Michael, *In Search of the Trojan War*, BBC, 1985. A good compilation of current thought on Troy, from the popular TV series.

Young, Rodney S, *Gordion*, Ankara, 1975. More about the Phrygians.

Byzantines and Ottomans

Barber, Noel, *The Sultans*, Simon and Schuster, 1973. The inside story.

Billings, Malcolm, *The Cross and the Crescent*, BBC Publications, 1987. A history of the Crusades.

Goodwin, Godfrey, *A History of Ottoman Architecture*, Thames and Hudson, 1971. The best book on the subject.

Goodwin, Jason, *Lords of the Horizons*, Vintage, 1999. A very readable history of the Ottoman sultans and their culture.

Lord Kinross, *The Ottoman Centuries*, Morrow, NY/Jonathan Cape, London, 1977. A well-known popular history.

Norwich, John Julius, *Byzantium: The Early Centuries* (1990), *Byzantium: The Apogee* (1993), *Byzantium: Decline and Fall* (1996), *A Short History of Byzantium* (1998), all Penguin. A marvellously readable and entertaining history of the Byzantine empire. The *Short History* is a one-volume abridgement of the previous three.

Rodley, Lyn, *Cave Monasteries of Byzantine Cappadocia*, Cambridge, 1986.

Runciman, Steven, *Byzantine Civilization*, Edward Arnold, London, 1933, and *The Fall of Constantinople, 1453*, Cambridge University Press, 1965. Excellent accounts by the foremost scholar in the field, coloured by a dislike of both Muslims and Turks.

Shaw, Stanford and Ezel, Kual, *History of the Ottoman Empire and Modern Turkey*, 2 vols, Cambridge University Press, 1976.

Modern Turkey

Garnett, Lucy M. J., *The Turkish People: their social life, religious beliefs, institutions and domestic life*, Methuen, London AMS Press NY 1909. Hard to find but very interesting account by a turn-of-the-century traveller.

Hotham, David, *The Turks*, Murray, London, 1972. One of the best books about modern Turkey.

Kazancagil, Ali and Özbudun, Ergun, eds, *Atatürk, founder of a modern state*, Anchor Hambden, Conn, 1981.

Lewis, Bernard, *The Emergence of Modern Turkey*, Oxford Library Press, 1968.

Michaud, Roland and Sabrina, *Turkey*, Thames and Hudson, 1986. Magnificent photographs.

Stewart, Deamond, *Turkey*, Life World Library, NY, 1965.

Volkan, Vamik D, Itzkowitz, Norman, *The Immortal Atatürk, A Psychobiography*. Unintentionally hilarious ('Little Mustafa's grandiose self was his basic character trait').

Religion and Folklore

And, Metin, *Karagoz: Turkish Shadow Theatre*, Dost, İstanbul, 1979. An excellent account of a dying art, readily available in Turkey.

Nicholson, Reynold A., trans., *Rumi: Poet and Mystic*, George Allen & Unwin, 1950. An introduction to the great Sufi teacher, the Mevlâna.

Önder, Mehmed, *Mevlâna and Mevlâna Museum*, İstanbul, 1985. Story of the Mevlâna's life in Konya.

Walker, Warren S. & Uysal, Ahmet E., *Tales Alive in Turkey*, Harvard University Press, 1966. An absorbing collection of Turkish folk tales and lore.

Travel Writers

Burnaby, Frederick, *On Horseback Through Asia Minor*, Alan Sutton, 1985. A fascinating account of a journey undertaken in the winter of 1876/7.

Freely, John, *Istanbul: the Imperial City*, Penguin, 1998. A sort of travel guide through time, explaining İstanbul's history and development. Very readable.

Glazebrook, Philip, *Journey to Kars*, Penguin, 1985.

Pereira, Michael, *East of Trebizond*, Geoffrey Bles, 1971. For those interested in Tao-Georgia.

Stark, Freya, *Alexander's Path*, Century, 1984; and *Ionia*, Century, 1988. Two beautiful, evocative accounts that bring Turkey's ancient cities to life.

Novels

Cleary, Jon, *The Fall of an Eagle*, 1964. Romantic thriller set in Cappadocia.

Dunnett, Dorothy, *Pawn in Frankincense*, Cassell, 1969, also available as an Arrow paperback. An historical adventure story featuring Süleyman, Roxelana, Dragut and others mentioned in this guide.

Kemal, Yaşar, *Mehmed, My Hawk*, 1961; *The Lords of Akchasaz*, 1979; and *The Sea-Crossed Fisherman*, 1985, Collins and Harvill. Turkey's leading contemporary novelist. More of his books are available in English translation.

Macauley, Rose, *The Towers of Trebizond*, Futura 1981. A classic and very funny novel about a journey in Turkey with the wonderful eccentrics Aunt Dot and Father Chantry-Pigg.

BC

c. 50,000	Neanderthal man inhabiting southwestern Anatolia
c. 8500	Oldest known urban society flourishes at Çatal Höyük
c. 5000	Neolithic cultures in southern Anatolia
c. 2500	Hatti people reach the height of their culture in the Kızılırmak valley region
c. 2000	Arrival of Hittites in Anatolia
c. 1720	Hattuşaş becomes Hittite capital
c. 1600	*Mursilis I (Hittite)*
c. 1450–1400	Series of long wars, between Egypt (19th dynasty) and the Hurri-Mitanni kingdom of east Anatolia
c. 1400	Extension of literacy to Anatolia
1380–1346	*Suppiluliumas (Hittite)*
1259	Treaty of Kadesh between Hittites and Egyptians— earliest recorded peace treaty
1260–1240	*Tudhalyas IV (Hittite)*
c. 1200	Destruction of Hittite Empire
c. 1180	Fall of Troy
c. 1000	Greeks begin to colonize Aegean coast
c. 900	Anatolian wool and timber begin to enter main Mediterranean trade routes
c. 760	*Sarduri I (Urartian)*
c. 750	Sinope, first Greek town on Black Sea, colonized by Miletus
c. 700	*'King Midas' (Phrygia)*
717	Sack of Carchemish by Assyrians
690	Cimmerians raid throughout Anatolia
612	Medes conquer Urartians, Assyria
c. 600	Kingdom of Cappadocia begins
550–530	*King Cyrus (Persia)*
546	Persians annex Lydia, Greek cities

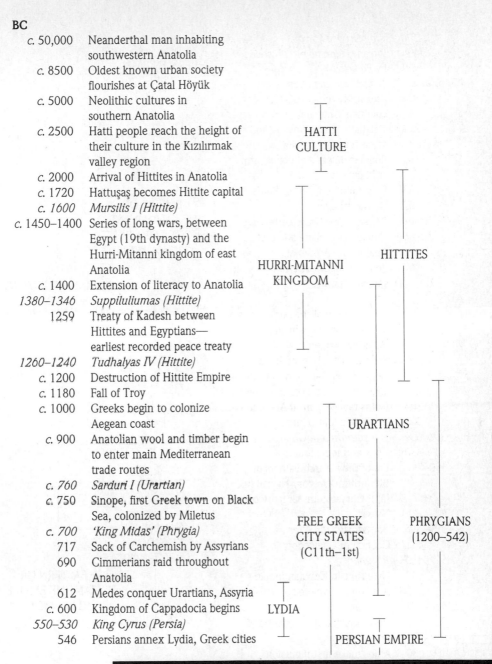

HATTI CULTURE

HURRI-MITANNI KINGDOM

HITTITES

URARTIANS

FREE GREEK CITY STATES (C11th–1st)

PHRYGIANS (1200–542)

LYDIA

PERSIAN EMPIRE

Chronology

c. 540	*King Croesus, Lydia*
494	Ionian Greek revolt, crushed by Persians
376–353	*King Mausolus (Caria)*
334	Alexander the Great conquers Anatolia
275	Galatians (Gauls) invade and settle central Anatolia
180	Romans defeat Antiochus' army at Magnesia
133	Pergamon annexed to Rome
102	Cilicia annexed
94–56	*Tigranes the Great (Armenia)*
83–66	Conquests of Syria and east Anatolia by Armenians
67	Rome clears Mediterranean shores of pirates

AD

20	Augustus establishes strict control over Anatolian client states, including Armenia
47–57	St Paul's travels in Anatolia
200–400	Continuous wars between Rome and the revived Persian empire
268	Goths ravage central Anatolia
303	Armenia adopts Christianity
306–337	*Constantine the Great*
330	Constantinople founded
350–390	Era of the Church Fathers of Byzantium: Gregory Nazianzus, John Chrysostom, Gregory of Nyssa
379–395	*Theodosius the Great*
451	Council of Chalcedon
527–565	*Justinian*
532	Nike riots in Constantinople
547	Aya Sofia completed
610–641	*Heraclius I*
627	Heraclius defeats Persians and saves the empire
630	Arabs make first incursions, capture Diyarbakır
c. 726	*Beginnings of Iconoclastic controversy*

PERSIAN EMPIRE
(549–326)

EMPIRE OF
ALEXANDER AND
SUCCESSOR STATES
(330 BC–AD 180)

ROMAN HEGEMONY
(180 BC–C4th AD

ARMENIAN
KINGDOM
(c. 300–1040)

EASTERN OR
BYZANTINE EMPIRE
(C4th–1453)

797–802	*Empress Irene*	
c. 860	*Ashot the Great (Armenia)*	
950–1050	Golden age of Armenian Kingdom	ARMENIAN
963–969	*Nicephorus Phocas*	KINGDOM
990–1020	*Gagik I (Armenia)*	
976–1025	*Basil Bulgaroctonus*	
1040	Armenia conquered by Byzantines	
1071	Battle of Manzikert; Selcuk Turks conquer most of Anatolia	
1100s	Crusaders campaign in southern Anatolia	
1200s	Revival of commerce and learning under Selcuks in Konya	SELCUK SULTANATE OF RUM
1204	Sack of Constantinople by Crusaders	
1243	Mongols invade Anatolia; defeat Selcuks at Battle of Kösedağ	
1273	First appearance of Ottomans	EASTERN OR
1300s	Various Mongol and Turkish emirates contend for Anatolia	BYZANTINE EMPIRE
1293–1324	*Osman I*	
1374–1360	*Orhan*	
1324	Ottoman capture of Bursa	
1346	Dynastic alliance between Ottomans and Byzantine Emperor	CRUSADERS
1360–1389	*Murat I*	
1389	Battle of Kossovo: Turks conquer much of Balkans	
1389–1402	*Beyazit I*	
1390–1403	Tamerlane's invasion of Anatolia	OTTOMAN
1413–1421	*Mehmet I*	EMPIRE
1421–1451	*Murat II*	
1422	First siege of Constantinople	
1420s–30s	Institution of the Janissary corps and the devşirme	
1451–1481	*Mehmet II (the Conqueror)*	
1453	Conquest of Constantinople	
1460s	Conquest of Trebizond, Konya	
1481–1512	*Beyazit II (the Mystic)*	
1480s	Civil wars of Prince Cem	
1490s	Shiite revolts in Anatolia	
1512–1520	*Selim I (the Grim)*	
1510s	Conquest of Egypt and the last surviving Turkish emirates	
1520–1566	*Süleyman I (the Magnificent)*	

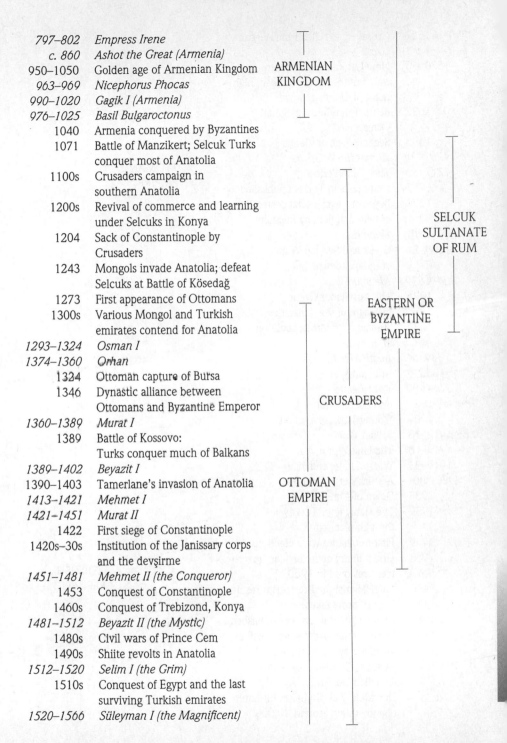

1522	Crusaders expelled from Aegean coast	
1530–50	New Ottoman Navy controls much of the Mediterranean; high point of Ottoman power	
1622	Murder of reforming Sultan Osman II	
1683	Second siege of Vienna	
1703–30	*Ahmet III*	
1717–30	The 'Tulip Period'	OTTOMAN
1727	First books in Turkish published	EMPIRE
1770	Battle of Çeşme; total destruction of Ottoman fleet by Russians	
1789–1807	*Selim II*	
1804–21	Greek and Serbian Wars of Independence	
1808–1839	*Mahmud II*	
1826	The Auspicious Event: massacre of the Janissaries	
1830	'Tanzimat' reforms; abolition of feudalism	
1839–61	*Abdül Mecit I*	
1853–6	Crimean War	
1876–1909	*Abdülhamid*	
1876	First constitution	
1909	'Young Turk' revolution	
1912–13	Balkan Wars	
1914–18	The First World War	
1919–23	Wars of Independence	
1920s–30s	Atatürk's era of reforms	
1938	Death of Atatürk	
1939	The Hatay joins Turkey through plebiscite	
1949	First free nationwide elections	
1960	First military coup; civilian government restored in 1960	TURKISH
1980	Political crisis and terrorism results in third army takeover	REPUBLIC
1983	Civilian government re-established	
1995	Islamic Refah party wins elections; dissolved by army in 1997	
1999	Arrest of Kurdish PKK leader Abdullah Öcalan Devastating earthquakes hit İzmit region, killing around 20,000	

Main page references are in **bold**. Page references to maps are in *italics*.